POPE AND THE DESTINY OF THE STUARTS

Frontispiece: Peter Angelis, 'Queen Anne and the Knights of the Garter'.
National Portrait Gallery.

POPE AND THE DESTINY OF THE STUARTS

History, Politics, and Mythology
in the Age of Queen Anne

PAT ROGERS

OXFORD
UNIVERSITY PRESS

OXFORD

UNIVERSITY PRESS

Great Clarendon Street, Oxford OX2 6DP

Oxford University Press is a department of the University of Oxford.
It furthers the University's objective of excellence in research, scholarship,
and education by publishing worldwide in

Oxford New York

Auckland Cape Town Dar es Salaam Hong Kong Karachi
Kuala Lumpur Madrid Melbourne Mexico City Nairobi
New Delhi Shanghai Taipei Toronto

With offices in

Argentina Austria Brazil Chile Czech Republic France Greece
Guatemala Hungary Italy Japan Poland Portugal Singapore
South Korea Switzerland Thailand Turkey Ukraine Vietnam

Oxford is a registered trademark of Oxford University Press
in the UK and in certain other countries

Published in the United States
by Oxford University Press Inc., New York

© Pat Rogers 2005

British Library Cataloguing in Publication Data

Data available

Library of Congress Cataloging in Publication Data

Data available

ISBN 0-19-927439-8   978-0-19-927439-0

1 3 5 7 9 10 8 6 4 2

Typeset by SNP Best-set Typesetter Ltd., Hong Kong
Printed in Great Britain
on acid-free paper by
Biddles Ltd.,
King's Lynn, Norfolk.

for Bill Speck

Acknowledgements

An undertaking of this kind, extending over many years, inevitably owes much to the collective input of colleagues, friends, and students. A more particular debt is due to Paul Baines for reading draft sections of the book and to Brian Vickers for supplying excellent advice, some of it heeded. Help in the preparation of the manuscript was provided by Elizabeth Latshaw-Foti and Michelle Lattanzio.

Sections of Chapters 4 and 6 were given in a plenary presentation to the thirteenth DeBartolo Conference in Eighteenth-Century Studies, held at Tampa in 1999.

P.R.

Contents

List of Illustrations

Frontispiece: Peter Angelis, 'Queen Anne and the Knights of the Garter'.
National Portrait Gallery.

following page 174

1 James Thornhill, 'The Exact Draught of the Fire Work'. © The British Museum.

2 Antonio Verrio, Queen's drawing room at Hampton Court, ceiling. Crown
   copyright: Historic Royal Palaces.

3 Michael Rysbrack, monument to the first Duke of Marlborough, Blenheim
   Palace. By kind permission of His Grace the Duke of Marlborough.
   Photograph: Jeremy Whitaker.

4 Arms of the South Sea Company. © National Maritime Museum.

Abbreviations

Addison	*The Works of the Right Honourable Joseph Addison*, ed. R. Hurd, 6 vols. (London, 1856).
Anecdotes	Joseph Spence, *Observations, Anecdotes, and Characters of Books and Men*, ed. J. M. Osborn, 2 vols. (Oxford: Clarendon Press, 1966).
Ashmole	Elias Ashmole, *The Institution, Laws & Ceremonies of the most worthie Order of the Garter* (London, 1693).
Ault	Norman Ault, *New Light on Pope* (London: Methuen, 1949).
Bennett	G. V. Bennett, *The Tory Crisis in Church and State 1688–1730: The Career of Francis Atterbury Bishop of Rochester* (Oxford: Clarendon Press, 1975).
Britannia	*Camden's Britannia, Newly Translated into English*, ed. E. Gibson (London, 1695).
Bucholz	R. O. Bucholz, *The Augustan Court: Queen Anne and the Decline of Court Culture* (Stanford, Calif.: Stanford University Press, 1993).
Career	George Sherburn, *The Early Career of Alexander Pope* (Oxford: Clarendon Press, 1934).
CH	John Denham, *Cooper's Hill*.
Chalmers	*The Works of the English Poets*, ed. D. P. French, 10 vols. (New York: Benjamin Blom, 1967).
CIH	Maynard Mack, *Collected in Himself: Essays Critical, Biographical, and Bibliographical on Pope and Some of his Contemporaries* (Newark, Del.: University of Delaware Press, 1982).
Churchill	Winston S. Churchill, *Marlborough: His Life and Times*, 4 vols. (London: Sphere, 1967).
Corr.	*The Correspondence of Alexander Pope*, ed. G. Sherburn, 5 vols. (Oxford: Clarendon Press, 1956).
Coxe	William Coxe, *Memoirs of the Duke of Marlborough*, ed. J. Wade, 3 vols. (London, 1848).
Drayton	*The Works of Michael Drayton*, ed. J. W. Hebel et al., 5 vols. (Oxford: Shakespeare Head Press, 1961).
Dryden	*The Works of John Dryden*, ed. E. N. Hooker et al., 20 vols. (Berkeley and Los Angeles: University of California Press, 1956–2000).
EC	*The Works of Alexander Pope*, ed. W. Elwin and W. J. Courthope, 10 vols. (London: John Murray, 1871–89).
ED	*The Diary of John Evelyn*, ed. E. S. de Beer, 6 vols. (Oxford: Clarendon Press, 1955).
Evelyn	*The Writings of John Evelyn*, ed. G. de la Bédoyère (Woodbridge, Suffolk: Boydell, 1995).
Eves	C. K. Eves, *Matthew Prior: Poet and Diplomatist* (New York, 1939; repr. New York: Octagon Books, 1973).
Ewald	W. B. Ewald, jun., *The Newsmen of Queen Anne* (Oxford: Blackwell, 1956).
Fox-Davies	A. C. Fox-Davies, *A Complete Guide to Heraldry* (1925; repr. Ware, Hertfordshire: Wordsworth, 1996).

Garden and City	Maynard Mack, *The Garden and the City: Retirement and Politics in the Later Poetry of Pope 1731–1743* (Toronto: University of Toronto Press, 1969).
Gay, *Letters*	*The Letters of John Gay*, ed. C. F. Burgess (Oxford: Clarendon Press, 1966).
Green	David Green, *Queen Anne* (London: Collins, 1970).
Gregg	Edward Gregg, *Queen Anne* (London: Routledge, 1980).
Hearne	Thomas Hearne, *The Remains*, ed. J. Bliss, rev. J. Buchanan-Brown (Carbondale, Ill.: Southern Illinois University Press, 1967).
Hunters	E. P. Thompson, *Whigs and Hunters: The Origins of the Black Act* (New York: Pantheon Books, 1975)
Jonson	*Ben Jonson*, ed. C. H. Herford, and P. and E. Simpson, 11 vols. (Oxford: Clarendon Press, 1925–32).
JTS	Swift's *Journal to Stella*, ed. H. Williams, 2 vols. (Oxford: Clarendon Press, 1948).
Legg	L. G. Wickham Legg, *Matthew Prior: A Study of his Public Career and Correspondence* (1921; repr. New York: Octagon Books, 1972).
Life	Maynard Mack, *Alexander Pope: A Life* (New Haven: Yale University Press, 1985).
Milieu	Howard Erskine-Hill, *The Social Milieu of Alexander Pope* (New Haven: Yale University Press, 1975).
Monod	Paul K. Monod, *Jacobitism and the English People 1688–1788* (Cambridge: Cambridge University Press, 1989).
New Anecs.	George Sherburn, 'New Anecdotes about Alexander Pope', *Notes & Queries*, 203 (1958), 343–9.
New Letts.	George Sherburn, 'Letters of Alexander Pope', *Review of English Studies*, NS 9 (1958), 388–406.
Parry	Graham Parry, *The Golden Age Restor'd: The Culture of the Stuart Court, 1603–1642* (New York: St Marin's, 1980).
PL	John Milton, *Paradise Lost*.
PO	*Poly-Olbion*, in Drayton, iv.
Prior	*The Literary Works of Matthew Prior*, ed. H. B. Wright and M. K. Spears, 2 vols. (Oxford: Clarendon Press, 2nd edn., 1971).
Prose	*The Prose Works of Alexander Pope*, vol. i, ed. N. Ault (Oxford: Blackwell, 1936); vol. ii, ed. R. Cowler (Hamden, Conn.: Archon Books, 1986).
Ripa	Cesare Ripa, *Baroque and Rococo Pictorial Imagery*, ed. E. A. Maser (New York: Dover, 1971).
ROL	*Rape of the Lock*
Rothery	Guy Cadogan Rothery, *Concise Encyclopedia of Heraldry* (1915; repr. London: Senate, 1994).
Sacheverell	Geoffrey Holmes, *The Trial of Doctor Sacheverell* (London: Eyre Methuen, 1973).
Schmitz	Robert M. Schmitz, *Pope's Windsor 1712: A Study of the Washington University Holograph* (St Louis: Washington University, 1952).
SDW	Pat Rogers, *The Symbolic Design of 'Windsor-Forest' Iconography, Pageant, and Prophecy in Pope's Early Work* (Newark, Del.: University of Delaware Press, 2004).
Swift, *Prose*	*The Prose Works of Jonathan Swift*, ed. H. Davis et al., 14 vols. (Oxford: Blackwell, 1939–68).
Swift, *Corr.*	*The Correspondence of Jonathan Swift*, ed. H. Williams, 5 vols. (Oxford: Clarendon Press, 1963–5).

TE	*The Twickenham Edition of the Poems of Alexander Pope*, ed. J. Butt et al., 11 vols. (London: Methuen, 1938–68).
Tour	Daniel Defoe, *A Tour thro' the Whole Island of Great Britain*, 2 vols. (London: Peter Davies, 1927).
Trevelyan	G. M. Trevelyan, *England under Queen Anne*, 3 vols. (London: Fontana, 1965).
VCH Berkshire	*The Victoria History of the Counties of England: Berkshire*, 5 vols (Folkestone: Dawson, 1972).
VCH Sussex	*The Victoria History of the Counties of England: Sussex*, 8 vols. (Folkestone: Dawson, 1973).
Wasserman	Earl R. Wasserman, *The Subtler Language* (Baltimore: Johns Hopkins University Press, 1959).
WF	*Windsor-Forest*, cited from *TE*, vol. i, ed. E. Audra and A. Williams (1961).
Wren	Christopher Wren, *Parentalia: or, Memoirs of the Family of the Wrens* (London, 1750).

Chronology 1700–1716

For the greater part of Pope's lifetime up to 1713, Britain and her allies had been at war with France, on and off—and it had been mostly on. The Nine Years War, or War of the League of Augsburg, had pitted a coalition formed by William of Orange against Louis XIV. Though this set the stage for later contests, and Marlborough took a part in some campaigns, its importance had been overtaken by the events of the greater struggle which was to follow. The Treaty of Rijswijk, concluded in 1697, forged the usual elaborate chains of compromise and concession. The French king agreed to recognize William as rightful king of England. In return the English agreed to pay James II's queen, Mary of Modena, the dowry to which she was entitled by her marriage settlement, estimated at £15,000 per annum. In fact this was never paid, either under William or under Anne. The British considered it a pension for her husband, as Matthew Prior noted (Legg, 57).

Prior, who was to figure prominently in the Utrecht negotiations, acted as secretary to the British ambassadors at the peace congress: one of his masters was Lord Jersey, a long-time patron (see p. 80, below). Pope was not really intimate with Prior by 1713, but he could have heard something of the transactions at Rijswijk for an interesting reason. Sir William Trumbull, appointed secretary of state in 1695, kept up a regular correspondence with Prior from the time that the latter went to The Hague as a junior official. In April 1697 Trumbull told Prior that he was dissatisfied with the accounts of the congress which he had received from Jersey, and asked for more detailed and informative insights into the main participants and their motives (Legg, 52). Prior's response to this letter has not been recovered, but in surviving correspondence there are some frank opinions on the delegates of other nations. When the congress opened in June 1697 Prior told his masters in London, 'You see how near we are to get into the old road of ceremony and nonsense' (Legg, 55). One of his avocations when he was whiling away his time at The Hague was the design of a medal to commemorate the death of Queen Mary in late 1694—however his contact in the office of the Secretary of State, James Vernon, told him that it was regarded as little more than 'a posey and a shred of Horace', and that he ought to represent the Queen either by the 'effigies' or else 'the motto' (Legg, 29). Prior duly wrote a long panegyrical poem on the queen. It shows how the media for encomium merged with one another.

The treaty was signed on 21 September 1697, and Prior hastened back to England with the news. So the first phase of the wars with the French came to an end.

The chronology which follows is limited to major public events. It concentrates on military, political, and diplomatic areas, and necessarily simplifies the course of the war. Matters with a direct relevance to Pope and his friends are given more prominence than would be the case in an objective survey of the period.

[*c.*1700   Pope moves to Binfield in Windsor Forest.]

1700   (1 Nov. NS) Death of Carlos II, last Habsburg ruler of Spain. Louis XIV soon accepts his will, which bequeaths the crown to Louis's grandson Philip Duke of Anjou, who succeeds as Philip V. This repudiates the Second Partition Treaty of 1700 and causes wide resentment in other European powers.

1701   (June) Act of Settlement confirms Protestant succession to the British throne of Electress of Hanover and heirs.

(6 Sept.) Death of James II; claim of the Pretender, James Francis Edward, recognized by Louis XIV.

(7 Sept.) Allied coalition, the Grand Alliance, formed.

1702   (8 Mar.) Death of William III and accession of Anne, who confirms Marlborough as captain-general.

(23 Apr.) Coronation of Queen Anne.

(4 May) England declares war with France and Spain; allied with Austria and Holland. Objects include the exclusion of the Bourbon claimant to the Spanish throne, in favour of the Habsburg claimant, Archduke Charles (later Charles VI); the recovery of trade with the Spanish Empire in the New World; the restoration of a defensive barrier for Holland; and securing the Protestant succession in England.

(Nov.) Allied success at Vigo Bay, led by Rooke and Ormonde; Spanish treasure fleet plundered.

(23 Dec.) Anne officially adopts the motto *Semper eadem.*

1704   (April) High Tories including Nottingham and Jersey purged from government, now controlled by Godolphin and Marlborough; Harley becomes secretary of state and St John secretary at war.

(24 July) Gibraltar captured by Admiral Rooke and Admiral Shovel.

(13 Aug.) After long advance into Bavaria, Marlborough confronts French army at Blenheim, together with Prince Eugène, and achieves decisive victory, preserving Austrian empire.

1705   (May) Death of Leopold I, Holy Roman Emperor, succeeded by his son Joseph I.

1706   (Feb.) Regency Act sets up machinery to bring about Hanoverian accession on death of the Queen.

(23 May) Allied forces under Marlborough defeat French at Ramillies, near Liège; thanksgiving service at St Paul's on 27 June.

(Sept.) Imperial forces under Eugène defeat French and Spanish at Turin; Papacy recognizes Charles as heir.

1707   (1 May) Official date of Union of English and Scottish parliaments, marked by thanksgiving service at St Paul's.

(25 Apr.) Victory of French and Spanish at Almanza over allies, confirming the hold of the Bourbon claimant to Spain.

1708   (10 Feb.) Godolophin and Marlborough force dismissal of Harley from government, now Whig dominated, against the wishes of the Queen.

(Mar.) Abortive attempt to land in Scotland by the Pretender and French invasion fleet, opposed by Anglo-Dutch navy; Pretender retreats to Dunkirk.

(Apr.) Whigs strengthen their position with clear victory in general election.

(11 July) Battle of Oudenard in Flanders, further victory for Marlborough.

(28 Oct.) Death of Prince George, consort of Queen Anne. Relations between the Queen and Marlboroughs now strained.

1709   (Feb.–May) Peace negotiations at The Hague fail.

(11 Sept.) Battle of Malplaquet in Flanders; partial but costly victory for the allies. At home, criticism of Marlborough increases.

(18 Oct.) Dutch Barrier treaty signed between Britain and Dutch, designed to strengthen the latter's hold on southern Netherlands.

1710   (Feb.–July) Further peace talks at Geertruidenberg (near Rotterdam) fail.

(Feb.–Mar.) Trial of High Church preacher, Dr Henry Sacheverell, before the House of Lords; Sacheverell found guilty but given light sentence. Whig ministry disintegrating.

(8 Aug.) Queen dismisses Godolphin as Lord Treasurer.

(Sept.) Tories win landslide victory in general election; Harley confirmed as head of the new ministry, with St John as his main lieutenant.

(29 Nov.) Stanhope defeated at Brihuega (near Guadalajara) in Spain, a further reverse for the Habsburg claimant.

1711   (18 Jan.) Queen dismisses Duchess of Marlborough from court offices. Secret peace negotiations between Britain and France now under way.

(6 Apr.) Death of Emperor Joseph I, to be succeeded by his brother as Charles VI.

(23 May) Harley created Earl of Oxford; made Lord Treasurer on 29 May.

(July) Matthew Prior sent to Paris to negotiate with the French minister Torcy and to arrange the separate peace deal with France.

(9 Aug.–14 Sept.) French fortress of Bouchain, near Valenciennes, besieged and taken by Marlborough, in his last major success of the war.

(7 Sept.) Official inception of the South Sea Company.

(27 Sept.) Preliminary articles for peace with France signed by both parties: a 'public' version released, other provisions kept secret from allies. Opposition to the terms from Marlborough and the Whigs mainly.

(7 Dec.) Government defeated in House of Lords, on motion by Earl of Nottingham, a Tory, to reject peace terms while Bourbon claimant left on Spanish throne.

(31 Dec.) Marlborough dismissed from all his offices; twelve new Tory peers (including Lansdowne) created to force the peace terms through parliament.

1712   (18 Jan.) Utrecht peace conference opens; Britain represented by John Robinson and Earl of Strafford.

(Jan.–Mar.) Prince Eugène visits London, unable to prevent break-up of the Grand Alliance. House of Commons repeals Barrier treaty.

(May) Duke of Ormonde (successor to Marlborough as commander-in-chief) begins summer campaign with orders to avoid confrontation and total defeat of French. In following months French drive allies out of territories in Flanders gained in 1711.

(June) St John created Viscount Bolingbroke.

(Aug.) Bolingbroke visits Paris, accompanied by Prior, to complete negotiations for treaty.

(Sept.) Marlborough retreats to the Continent, later joined by the Duchess.

(Nov.) Philip V renounces claim to French throne, improving prospects of a general peace.

1713   **(7 Mar.) Publication of *Windsor-Forest.***

(31 Mar.) Treaty of Utrecht signed by France, Britain, and Dutch republic. Austrians and Hanoverians refuse to sign. France agrees to dynastic settlement and to the splitting of the Spanish empire; Britain gains Gibraltar and Minorca, as well as Newfoundland, Nova Scotia, and Hudson Bay territories and further commercial advantages, including the *Asiento* contract to transport almost 5,000 slaves annually to Spanish America for thirty years.

(7 Apr.) Queen announces the peace in speech to parliament.

(14 Apr.) First performance of Addison's *Cato*, with prologue by Pope, excites party controversy.

(19 June) Government defeated in House of Commons on separate Anglo-French commercial treaty, sponsored by Bolingbroke.

(2 July) Peace treaty with Spain signed.

(5 July) Thanksgiving service held at St Paul's.

(Aug.–Sept.) Tories consolidate position in general election, but split between Hanoverians and Jacobites widens.

(Sept.) Breach between Queen and Oxford after his son Lord Harley married to daughter of Duke of Newcastle.

1714   (2 Mar.) Pretender decisively rejects proposals from ministry that he should renounce his Catholic faith. Any lingering hopes of restoring him to the throne now lost.

(6 Mar.) Treaty of Rastadt signed between Austria and France, brings final conclusion to the war.

(26 May) Lord Clarendon sent on mission to Hanover to mend fences (John Gay in his retinue). Relations between Oxford and Bolingbroke now soured beyond healing.

(28 May) Death of Electress Sophia of Hanover, succeeded by her son George.

(23 June) Proclamation offering reward for the arrest of the Pretender if discovered on British soil.

(27 July) Oxford dismissed as Lord Treasurer; Duke of Shrewsbury appointed as his successor on 30 July.

(1 Aug.) Death of Queen Anne, succeeded by Elector of Hanover as George I. Marlborough restored to office; Whigs dominate the new ministry.

(6 Dec.) Government proclamation orders execution of laws against papists and nonjurors.

1715   (Mar.) Whigs gain sweeping victory in general election.

(26 Mar.) Bolingbroke flees to France and becomes secretary of state to the Pretender; impeached for high treason 10 June.

(9 June) Matthew Prior arrested and questioned by Secret Committee of investigation; kept in custody until June 1716.

(16 July) Oxford committed to the Tower of London, to face trial for high treason (released July 1717, after impeachment proceedings break down).

(20 July) Riot Act passed, followed by suspension of Habeas Corpus and reactivation of laws prohibiting Catholics from living within 10 miles of London. Ormonde flees to France and is attainted (29 Aug.).

(1 Sept.) Death of Louis XIV.

(6 Sept.) Jacobite rising launched at Braemar in Scotland, led by Earl of Mar; partial success at Sheriffmuir, near Stirling (13 Nov.); subsequently defeated at Preston (14 Nov.); Pretender joins the rising at Peterhead (22 Dec.) but forced to retreat to France (4 Feb. 1716), after which he dismisses Bolingbroke.

(26 Sept.) Lansdowne sent to the Tower (released 1717).

1716   (23 Jan.) Catholics required by new law to take oaths of allegiance by this date in order to qualify for office: Pope declines to take these.

1716   (Feb.–Mar.) Trial of Jacobite lords involved in rising; Earl of Derwentwater (close companion of the Pretender) executed.

(Mar.) Pope family sell Binfield property and move to Chiswick.

Introduction

It is just over two hundred years since Queen Anne, the last Stuart monarch, came to the throne on 8 March 1702. Her reign would be marked by great achievements in literature, architecture, and science for example—this was after all the age of Newton and Halley, of Swift and Defoe, of Wren and Vanbrugh. But it was a time dominated by the long war with France, punctuated by the great victories of Marlborough as well as some less auspicious events. As Anne's reign came to an end, she was exhausted by the political and diplomatic struggles of the previous twelve years, and most of the nation greeted the Peace of Utrecht with considerable relief. But one major problem remained unresolved, the issue of the succession, and it was one which even the arrival of George I did not immediately settle, as the Jacobite rising in 1715 and subsequent events were to show. No writer reflects more of this tumultuous period than Alexander Pope, and no work of his deals with these large issues more comprehensively than *Windsor-Forest*.

This book tells the story of Pope's poem—how it came to be written, what elements went into it, how it was received, and what the aftermath was, in terms of the nation's destinies and those of the poet himself. It explores the milieu in which Pope operated, especially his audience and the support group assembled to sponsor such projects as the translation of Homer. The argument focuses on one phase of the writer's career, in which he produced his *Pastorals*, *The Rape of the Lock*, *Messiah*, and *An Essay on Criticism* among other works, as well as embarking on his Homeric enterprise. Although the main emphasis here is on *Windsor-Forest*, attention is given in Chapter 2 to some of this contemporary writing. It is obvious that *Windsor-Forest* can be fully understood only in the context of other things that were going on around Pope, and this book seeks to make the connections which will enhance its articulacy to a modern reader.

The poem is at once transparent in its texture and heavily layered in its symbolism. One is tempted to say that in the richness of its organization it comes closest to *Finnegans Wake*, except that it is not so simple. In a parallel study, *The Symbolic Design of 'Windsor-Forest'* (*SDW*), I have attempted to explore the workings of the poem, especially as they draw on classical and Renaissance modes such as the court masque, history painting, panegyric, and river poetry. Some cross-reference has been unavoidable and the argument of the present book is complemented at almost every point by the case made in its sister study. However, this is a self-contained book which devotes itself to a clear-cut task; that is, exploration of *Windsor-Forest* as it confronts the realities of its age. The fate of the Stuarts was intimately bound up with the course of war and peace, with the political battles between Whig and Tory in an intensely divided society, and with the personal situation of the monarch as she attempted to balance constitutional and dynastic forces that weighed upon her. Pope enlists a wide range of literary devices to develop his theme, some of them drawn from ancient sources such as Virgil and Ovid, others from Renaissance (Shakespeare, Spenser, Milton), and others from more recent writers such as Cowley and Denham. There are significant debts to Drayton, to William Camden, and to John Evelyn.

All these strands in the design will be examined individually. However, a principal aim of what follows is to show how Pope unites his disparate sources and models to form a single allegorical statement, which celebrates Anne and at the same time constitutes a prescient elegy for the Stuart cause. At the heart of the design lies a mythological version of national and local history. This is expressed most clearly in the central episode of 'Lodona', a river nymph named after a tributary of the Thames which runs through the forest. The passage reinvents a common Ovidian motif and makes particular use of the story of Erisichthon, from the eighth book of the *Metamorphoses*. Taking a hunt from Drayton, Pope tells the anecdote as one of purity defiled and innocence raped: but as we shall see in Chapter 7, the violator is William III (together with his henchmen and successors) and the victim is the England of the Stuarts.

To understand the nature of Pope's statement, we must reconsider some major events of the period, and look again at public events involving the Duke and Duchess of Marlborough, Oxford, Bolingbroke, and others. We need to see the relevance to the poem of many episodes—battles and sieges, diplomatic negotiations leading up to Utrecht, the formation of the South Sea Company, the visit of the four Indian kings to London, and much else. But we have also to explore Pope's personal history, since his own fortunes and those of his allies were to mirror that of the Stuart family. He too would be cast out of a patrimony (as he regarded it), in the shape of his parents' home at Binfield. Whether or not he was a committed Jacobite, a matter to be reviewed in the pages to come, he assuredly shared in the fate of many friends and colleagues who lost influence with dramatic speed between 1713 and 1715. The very man to whom *Windsor-Forest* was dedicated, Lord Lansdowne, had found himself in the Tower before the bookshops disposed of all their copies. As a result the work gains in poignancy by its calamitous timing. Where popular works of astrology needed to supply accurate predictions to justify their existence, it is the fact that events so quickly *belied* the surface optimism of *Windsor-Forest* that adds a more troubling and profound level to its vision of the fortunes of the British nation. Ultimately Pope's poem is aggrandized by the sequence of happenings which falsified its sanguine prophecy.

This book sets itself an unfashionable task. It seeks to discover in a major work of literature not unexpected fissures, but unanticipated congruence. To be specific, it argues that *Windsor-Forest* possesses more rhetorical and intellectual coherence than we generally suppose—not less. The thesis advanced is that we have missed connections in the poem's ideological structure: what might be called textual synapses. In principle, it would seem as easy to fail to discern such connective tissue as to overlook gaps, inconsistencies, and contradictions; but that is not what most contemporary criticism seems to believe. Often, the rupture we locate in literary works is a construct of our own ignorance. The more thoroughly we understand the context of a poem like *Windsor-Forest*, the less plausible becomes the hunt for loose ends and muddled purposes. While it would be an exaggeration to say that all discord resolves itself into harmony not understood, as the *Essay on Man* puts it, many putative cases of incoherence turn out to derive from a system of significance not fully understood.

Recently there have been many efforts to de-augustanize eighteenth-century literature, that is to say to destroy any notion of consensual background to writing, and to look for signs of stress, rupture, and enforced innovation.[1] This book will be an attempt to re-augustanize Pope, in the sense of tracing his deep feelings of comfort within inherited idiom. Its aim is to supply a context for re-evaluating Pope's early career in the light of his adoption and refurbishment of older models, mostly drawn from the seventeenth century. Its scope is effectively from the accession of Anne in 1702 until the putting down of the Jacobite rising in 1716, since the surface optimism of the poem was soon to be occluded. The rhetorical claims that the work makes would be overtaken, in public by a humiliation for the Stuart cause, and in private by a reluctant exile for Pope from his childhood home.

In approach, this book may be defined as historical rather than historicist. A principal aim is to discover the meaning of *Windsor-Forest* partly by locating its precise occasion, political and literary, and by tracing the artistic and intellectual genesis of its key motifs and artistic gestures. However, the argument does not assume that these meanings were in any direct way *determined* by historical circumstances, whether those of social, constitutional, religious, or economic history. It allots prime importance to the central agent, that is to the biographic figure Alexander Pope. The book is therefore ranged against readings like that of Christa Knellwolf, which look for 'ideologically irritating' features in the text, and invite us to write our own more satisfactory versions of the poem: 'Because readings which adopt interpretative closure force the illusory elements of the poem into firm definitions, it asks us to be prepared to experiment with different readings.'[2] Here we shall try to demystify these 'illusory' elements and show their internal coherence and rooted existence, partly by formal analysis of language, rhetoric, and structure.

The book aims to bring out a largely unexplored personal element in Pope's work. This relates to his own feelings of loss when his family was driven out of the forest three years after the work appeared, as an anti-Catholic backlash emerged in the wake of the 1715 rising by Anne's half-brother. The present study also seeks to review the most important scholarship bearing on the poem, and to set out our cur-

---

[1] See e.g. the interesting review of these matters in Hammond (1997: 238–90). Although Pope is the most fully discussed writer in Hammond's book, *WF* is not mentioned.

[2] Knellwolf (1998: 2, 83). See also Ch. 6, below.

rent understanding of given aspects of the poem, such as the link through *Cooper's Hill* to seventeenth-century political and moral thought.[3] All the chapters, dealing as they do with a variety of modes and areas of artistic expression, are informed by a coherent purpose: to illustrate Pope's deliberate use of poetic artifice to give topical force to inherited idioms, and to explore the crisis of the succession in 1713 in the light of earlier Stuart attempts to legitimize their rule through a variety of ornate mythological fictions.

Most important work recently on the literature of early modern England has been organized centrifugally: it starts from a set of concepts or concerns, and moves out towards a variety of texts. The method of this book might be described as centripetal: it surveys a number of social practices, ideas, and writers, and draws these into the field of *Windsor-Forest*. This proceeding is designed to show the poem as an exemplary text, as it incorporates so many of the major issues and expressive devices available to writers in this age. Pope was interested in many subjects, learned in some of them. His knowledge of history, politics, and topical events was matched by a strong awareness of the visual arts, and his deep commitment to literature ancient and modern was accompanied by a feeling for place and a sense of his own roots. Above all, his hold on language and poetic form gave him a unique ability to register the lasting import of contemporary happenings.

The book is organized on a simple plan. It consists of eight chapters setting out various aspects of the historical and literary background. Chapter 1 deals initially with matters of composition and publication, including the much-debated question of Pope's revision of his earlier draft. The second and third sections concern Pope's 'expulsion' from his own Eden in the Forest, a threat in 1713 which was to become an actuality soon after the Hanoverian accession. In the fourth and fifth sections, we shall consider Pope's main patron in his youth, Sir William Trumbull, a verderer of the Forest.

Chapter 2 is devoted to the biographic milieu in which the poem was created. The three opening sections make an assessment of the place which the work holds within Pope's developing career, including his relations with the Scriblerian group, and explore its connections with his early poetry at large. In the remaining sections we address the figure to whom *Windsor-Forest* is dedicated, Lord Lansdowne, with a view to determining those factors which may or may not have fitted him for the role.

Chapter 3 treats political issues. It first sets out Pope's version of British history, as this can be reconstructed from the poem, and considers his view of the Stuart dynasty. It then outlines the numerous elements of immediate topical reference to be found in the text, most notably echoes of the celebrations to greet the Peace of Utrecht. Next comes a matter which has been extensively discussed in recent times, that is Pope's relation to the Jacobite cause. These sections concern the onset of the rising in 1715, the identity of Pope's audience as gauged by his *Iliad* subscription list, and the possible use of Jacobite codes within the language of the poem.

---

[3] See esp. Wasserman.

Chapter 4 relates to the royal court, focusing on Anne and her closest connections. Earlier sections deal with the role of the Queen herself; her involvement in 'works of peace', celebrated in the poem; the creation of her image as monarch; and echoes of court life in *Windsor-Forest*. Following this comes an account of the ritual of blessing which the poem enacts.

The focus of Chapter 5 is on the historical associations of Windsor itself, and on the immediate surroundings of the castle. Two sections concern the cult of St George as patron saint of England, with the associated rituals of the Order of the Garter, and then the accrued symbolism of the chapel with its royal tombs. Next come attempts to weigh the importance for Pope of the funeral inscription, and to assess the wider impress of heraldry on *Windsor-Forest*. Together these issues lay the basis for a coherent symbolic design organized around the royal demesne at Windsor Castle, in its monarchical, political, historical, and chivalric dimensions.

In Chapter 6, discussion hinges on the final stages of the war and the events leading up to the peace. At the heart of this lies an exploration of the presence of the Duke and Duchess of Marlborough as part of a shadowy subtext to the poem. A famous episode to which Pope alludes, the visit to London of four Indian chiefs, forms the subject of the next section; and after this the relevance of the newly founded South Sea Company to poetic themes in *Windsor-Forest*.

The final two chapters attempt to summarize the literary contexts of Pope's work, dealing respectively with the background in classical and Renaissance writing and with more recent models. Chapter 7 begins by outlining the Virgilian, especially georgic, and Ovidian strands. Succeeding portions consider the use of Camden's *Britannia* and Drayton's *Poly-Olbion*; the influence of Spenser, Shakespeare, and Milton. In Chapter 8 aspects of the seventeenth century enter the argument, notably the relevance of Denham's *Cooper's Hill* and of various works by Cowley, as well as the debt to Evelyn's *Sylva*. Moving into Pope's own day, we encounter the presence of Addison as stimulus, foil, and rival, as well as the treatment of a standard topos, that is the four seasons. Taken together, these sections outline a connected mythological plot. In the Conclusion a number of the threads are drawn together, with the poem re-read as an intimation of Jacobite mortality.

A book constructed in this fashion could seem to rest on an overdetermined interpretive method. Again and again we shall return to the same passages, read in a different context or under a different linguistic aspect. The reason for this is simply that the poem itself works that way. A given episode may have a literal or topographic basis, but at the same time a historic or contemporary level of political meaning. Likewise, a particular image will sometimes convey a mythological allusion, but also a stock iconographic motif or an emblem in numismatics and heraldry. As we shall see, the single epithet 'golden' may call up a wide range of overlapping senses. It refers to the cornfields around the Forest, but it also evokes 'Ceres' Gifts'. Ceres herself belongs to a narrative based on myth, especially here the georgic plot inspired by Virgil; yet she has her separate iconographic identity, and her attributes (such as the wheatsheaf) have a wider life in other emblematic codes, notably heraldry. Then there are the literary associations, in Ovid for example, connected with the notion of the Golden Age. Monarchical lore had taken up some of the alchemic overtones of gold, as the noblest of metals and the proper colouring of the sun king, or queen.[4] And so on. As soon as we unravel one strand in the linguistic pattern, another makes itself apparent.

There was a long-hallowed process by which different modes of symbolic utterance were commonly interfused. In medieval times, the early writers on heraldry had actually adopted terms drawn directly from astrology and alchemy in describing blazonry: 'Even the planets, and, as abbreviations, their astronomical signs, are occasionally employed: thus, the *sun* for gold, the *moon* for silver, *Mars* for red, *Jupiter* for blue, *Venus* for green, *Saturn* for black, and *Mercury* for purple' (Fox-Davies, 77). Though this soon faded away as an armorial practice, the connections remained within people's heads. The full moon is 'unusual' in heraldry, and the most familiar deployment is some form of crescent (Rothery, 93). When pointing to the dexter side of the shield, and said to be *increscent*, the moon resembles the familiar symbol used in alchemy and astrology. Pope would have been intimately acquainted with this usage from numerous sources, not least the almanacs which penetrated so deeply into national life.[5] The 'silver Bows' of Diana's followers, mentioned at l. 169 as now to be seen transplanted to Windsor Forest, as well as the 'Crescent' of Diana and her nymph Lodona (176), call up exactly this emblem.

However, the early heralds went further and often substituted a precious stone for each of the heavenly bodies and the related tinctures: sapphire for Jupiter, emerald for Venus, and so on. The stone associated with the moon was pearl, and this was the heraldic synonym for silver in early usage. Beyond this, the moon connotes the female as against the male sun; Luna or Sirene as a goddess; Artemis or Diana as sister of Apollo. At various points in *Windsor-Forest*, each of these associations is applicable (see esp. *WF*, 159–64, 333–4). It is near the end that these alchemic suggestions are at their strongest, as Father Thames envisages a day when he will witness 'The Pearly Shell its lucid Globe infold, | And *Phœbus* warm the ripening Ore to Gold' (395–6). Douglas Brooks-Davies sees this as a conjunction of sol and luna, king and queen, with 'the lunar symbolism of the pearl, like the white background of the flag of St George', indicating Anne, the white queen, and thus cementing an alchemic design present throughout the poem.[6] But quite apart from this alchemic reading—which is filled out in Chapter 3—the mythological attributes of Diana correspond with the qualities allotted to the tincture *argent* in heraldry: chastity, innocence, wisdom.[7] Thus moon, silver, pearls, female, chastity, and much else are fused together, almost as in a pun: and Pope's allusive style opens up interpretations and indeed explanations in several branches of arcane lore.

---

[4] See Brooks-Davies (1988: 133), for the idea that the 'springing Corn' (27) of Ceres is alchemically transmuted into the gigantic gold sheaves of the 'glitt'ring Spires' (377).

[5] By this date, too, Newton's work on 'God's great Alchemy' was moving from the private to the public realm, and the chemical symbols were seen more and more in general discourse.

[6] Brooks-Davies (1988: 136).

[7] Similarly the tincture *gules* was linked with patriotism, and *purpure*, the mercurial colour, with majesty.

Necessarily this book concentrates at various stages of its running thesis on individual aspects of Pope's design. Despite that fact, it may be hoped that the cross-references and interlocking arguments will offer the reader some sense of a coherent account of the poem. Taken in isolation, the suggestion in Chapter 6 that *Windsor-Forest* keeps up a constant attack on the Duke of Marlborough may appear implausible. However, when this is linked to the demonstration in Chapter 8 that Pope rewrites Addison's *Campaign*, the assertion may seem less surprising. Again, the suggestion that Pope often reads his source in Camden's *Britannia* through *Poly-Olbion* should gain credence from the knowledge that Pope draws on Drayton's treatment of Arden in creating his own forest world.[8]

Generally speaking, Camden and Drayton are among Pope's most important predecessors, along with Denham and Dryden. However, the key texts in the background are those of Virgil and Ovid, as explored in Chapter 7. Ovid is particularly noteworthy, since he is on the surface a model only for the Lodona episode. By tracing the history of one episode in the *Metamorphoses*, that of Erisichthon, we can see how Pope identifies Windsor with the sacred groves of Thessaly. The story had been used by Drayton and also by John Evelyn in *Sylva*: in their hands the myth came to enshrine the need to preserve English woodlands in the face of political and economic pressures which might lead to their destruction. This is just one of many pointers to the relevance of Evelyn to the themes of *Windsor-Forest*.

Perhaps the best example of such density of reference in Pope's work comes at the moment when Father Thames rises up from the water. The principal literary source is Claudian's *pater Eridanus*; but Claudian was himself remembering the description of the Tiber in *Aeneid*, VIII. However, Pope may have come across this apparition in a place closer to hand: we know that he was consulting *Britannia* for antiquarian detail and for the historical ideology of his poem, and Camden's epithalamium for Thames and Isis provided a tableau of the river god with suitable attributes. Yet, because the entrance is dramatic, indeed masque-like, it seems also clearly to recall particulars in Ben Jonson's pageant for the royal 'entry' of James I to London. At the same time the language draws on various kinds of emblematic art; when Pope uses words like 'mantle' and 'azure' he is raiding the vocabulary of heraldry, as Virgil and Claudian obviously were not. Moreover, Thames presents himself in the manner of innumerable river gods in mythological painting, something which survived in art as late as Turner. As the succeeding chapters are intended to show, a single passage may lead us into a cluster of associated contexts, such is the *connectedness* of Pope's imagination.

It is easy to detect a shift in our approach within the last few decades to works such as *Windsor-Forest*. Recently Howard Erskine-Hill was able to say, with easy assurance that his observation would be unsurprising if not uncontroverted, that '*Windsor-Forest* was, of all Pope's early poems, the one with the most obvious political tendency'.[9] This is a claim which would scarcely have been made fifty or a hundred

[8] See Ch. 7, below, and *SDW*, ch. 5. [9] Erskine-Hill (1996: 85).

years ago. The reason for the change does not lie just in our greater awareness of the breadth and depth of the conflict in society which was created by disputes over the succession. It lies, too, in our greater readiness to explore the emblems, icons, and mythic touchstones by which people in the past identified their ideological loyalties, and by which they kept as it were their ideological bearings.

The point is clear if we look at Elwin's remarkable introduction to the poem for his *Works* of *Alexander Pope*, volume i, in 1871. There can be no doubt that Elwin understood much of the political context very thoroughly, and some of his comments retain a good measure of plausibility:

> Pope did not stop with applauding the Peace; he denounced the Revolution . . . The war was directed against Louis XIV, the champion of Roman Catholicism, and the Pretender. A general belief that the Protestant succession could only be secured by reducing the French king to helplessness, and that a Peace, on the other hand, which saved him and the Harley administration from ruin, would be propitious to the cause of tories, papists, and jacobites. 'They fancied,' says Bolingbroke, 'that the Peace was the period at which their millenary year would begin' . . . The ministry was torn to pieces by intestine divisions; its supporters—a heterogeneous body, who had been loosely held together by a common enmity—were rapidly throwing off their allegiance; the good will, which had been founded upon large and vague expectations, was converted into hostilitity under total disappointment; and the failing health of the Queen rendered it probable that the accession of a whig sovereign would shortly complete the discomfiture of the faction. (*EC* i. 326)

No modern historian would accept this in its entirety, but Elwin's account of the aftermath of the Peace does suggest more accurately than some narratives written later the problems for the ministry in the year following Utrecht. It was this collapse of the Harley government—originally a broad-based coalition which its leader had striven to preserve—that was on the point of surfacing as Pope wrote. In one sense, the poem is a desperate attempt to use the Peace as a last way of salvaging unity and purpose. Like everyone else on the public stage, Pope knew that it would take a major coup—a grand gesture of political imagination, some *démarche* of remarkable boldness, or a stroke of amazing luck—to ensure the future of a happy Stuart-ruled nation. *Windsor-Forest* pulls out every stop in the console of propagandist myth-making to create this hopeful prospect; but it is an act of pretence to rival that of the claimant over the water.

At the centre of this propaganda effort is a literary technique based around the traditional resources of Stuart panegyric. Indeed, Pope exploits a language of royalist celebration which goes back to the imperial triumphs of Rome, the rituals of Elizabethan England, and the orchestrated glories of the Sun King in France. Expressed at the level of textual reference, the actual words on the page, this mostly obviously takes the form of allegory and classical allusion. These were attributes of poetry to which Elwin, in common with most readers of the Victorian era, was effectively deaf.

We need make only a cursory selection of quotations to be aware of this fact:

> No writer clung more tenaciously to the lifeless phantoms of paganism, nor applied the hereditary common-places in a more servile manner . . . The poet proceeds to complete the

comparison between Diana and Queen Anne,—between the virgin huntress, and a prolific mother, who was ugly, corpulent, sluggish, a glutton and a tippler. Pope afterwards affected a disdain of royalty; he was ready enough to flatter it when he had his own ends to serve . . . Addison laughed at the whole tiresome tribe of gods and goddesses, and, with good-humoured pleasantry, warned the versifiers, who were about to celebrate the Peace, against introducing 'trifling antiquated fables unpardonable in a poet that was past sixteen' . . . [Pope] must have recognised the force of the playful satire, and thenceforward he abjured mythological trash. The passage on the death of Cowley, exemplifies, in a short compass, the unskilful use to which Pope put the worn-out rags of antiquity. (*EC* i. 330–1)

And so on at considerable length, with a routine application to Wordsworth on the business of poetry, all to show how the 'vices' of Pope's early style precluded any serious statement: 'The mind refuses to admit such jejune and monstrous fictions among the illusions of imagination.' Such an attitude towards poetic language, if carried through consistently, would impair our ability to respond to Spenser, Shakespeare, Milton, and Marvell; but this does not occur to Elwin. Moving through 'the sickly vein of counterfeit pastoral', the critic stops to deplore the tone of the dedicatory verses: 'The lines on Lord Lansdowne offend the more from the fulsomeness of the adulation.' Nothing is spared: Cowley himself is allotted a paragraph of harsh rebuke: 'His language is incessantly pitched in a high, heroic key, and then sinks in the same . . . sentence, into the tamest, meanest phrases of colloquial prose.' Later on in his diatribe, Elwin makes the familiar Victorian point about Pope's insensitivities to rural life: 'Neither in his verse, nor his letters, is there anything to indicate that he had mixed, like Thomson, Cowper, and Wordsworth, with the cottagers around him, or had divined the noble qualities which are masked by a rustic exterior' (*EC* i. 331–5).

It would be an act of supererogation to explore all the areas of prejudice which help to dictate these judgements. A Whig version of history is matched by a Whig interpretation of literary history. But it is above all one feature of Pope's writing, the use of allegory and mythological deities, which accounts for Elwin's incomprehension. Classical mythology had been pronounced dead, by Johnson and others subsequently. That the harvest becomes 'Ceres' gifts' is simply risible to Elwin; he has not the vestige of an idea as to the scale of the debt to classical civilization in Pope's world, and cannot imagine how any poet could use pagan myths for serious or playful purposes. He would have been bemused by the respect now granted to the fictions of court masque, as practised by Jones and Jonson; while he would have found the analysis of iconographic detail in the arts an escape from the Arnoldian rigour which his generation of readers brought to the classics of English literature.

There is no occasion to congratulate ourselves in turn, because we are lucky enough to be able to use the resources of modern art history, and to decode the spectacles of power with the help of recent students of popular culture. Nevertheless, it is striking that we now value in Pope exactly the qualities which Elwin picked out for ridicule. It is just those 'hereditary common-places' which animate his design in *Windsor-Forest*; without this 'mythological trash' he could never have attained his ends. Pope's is a genius of the old, a capacity to make challenging and innovatory art out of the traditional forms and language still embedded in the ideology and social practices of his own culture. He was able to sustain the comparison with Diana, so absurd to Elwin in his literal-minded and obtuse way, because the monarchy still sustained itself through rituals, ceremonial gestures, and stylized codes of behaviour, which had their origin in the ancient world and in the European baroque. This book is an attempt to unlock some of these codes, in order to show how Pope was able to articulate his vision of national destiny in terms of a coherent set of assumptions and within an intelligible system of symbolic values.

Of course to observe old conventions is not in itself any guarantee of literary success. To suppose otherwise would be as absurd as to adopt the more recent heresy, according to which mere transgressions of a code will constitute a ground of literary interest or merit. The status of *Windsor-Forest* as the last great Renaissance poem in English derives from the skill with which Pope forged connections, as he shaped different forms of emblematic language into a pattern which is not only intelligible but gracious and attractive. The rest of this book attempts to trace out the figures in the particular carpet, woven on the weft of Stuart ideology.

1

Setting

Windsor-Forest is a poem on a public theme, but it has deep roots in its author's private experience. The aim of this chapter is first to re-examine the circumstances of the work's composition, and then to detect the ways in which it dramatizes aspects of Pope's own relationships with the Forest. In his boyhood and adolescence at Binfield, a crucial influence was Sir William Trumbull, who claimed to have set the young poet to work on *Windsor-Forest*. Moreover, Trumbull was Pope's earliest important patron: the man who introduced him to the world of high politics, and the man who could imbue him with a first-hand sense of the tumultuous events of the seventeenth century. Trumbull, after all, had been born before the outbreak of the Civil War: he had lived through the reigns of Charles I, Charles II, James II, William and Mary, and Anne, not to mention the Protector.[1] In a wider sense, the poem recalls Pope's youthful days at Binfield and conveys a proleptic sense of his imminent expulsion.

COMPOSITION, MANUSCRIPT, AND PUBLISHING HISTORY

The first clear sighting we get of the poem comes in a letter from Revd Ralph Bridges, addressed to his uncle, Sir William Trumbull, on 28 October 1707. This reported that the *Pastorals* were soon to be published and that either one of these eclogues or 'the verses upon Windsor Forest' were to carry a dedication to Trumbull. In fact the opening pastoral, 'Spring', was inscribed to Trumbull (see below, pp. 39–40). Much later Trumbull told Bridges in reference to *Windsor-Forest* that he 'had long since put [Pope] on this subject, gave severall hints & at last w^n he brought it & read it, & made some little Alterations &c. not one word of putting in my Name 'till I found it in Print' (New Anecs, 346). This letter was written two months after the publication of *Windsor-Forest*, with its primary dedication to Lord Lansdowne. Most commentators agree that the work was almost certainly addressed to Trumbull in the first instance; and they further assume that, when the poem was revised

---

[1] He told Pope the story of a conversation which Charles I had with his courtiers, 'during his Troubles'; the subject was the respective merits of spaniels and greyhounds, seen as types of human behaviour at court. This Trumbull heard from 'one that was present' (*Corr.* i. 75).

to direct its thrust towards the Peace, one of the consequential changes lay in the identity of the patron addressed.

One fact complicates the position a little. George Granville, as he then was, had taken an early interest in the coming poet and, by the time that the *Pastorals* had reached a stage of being passed round in manuscript, Granville was already on Pope's mailing list. The opening eclogue had duly aligned Granville with his poetic model, by means of a reference to '*Waller*'s Strains, or *Granville*'s moving Lays' (*TE* i. 65). In a letter without date which itself may perhaps be placed around 1707, Granville mentions a friend—equally unnamed—who will bring with him to a convivial meeting 'a young Poet, newly inspir'd, in the Neighbourhood of *Cooper's-Hill*, whom he and *Walsh* have taken under their Wing; his Name is *Pope*; he is not above Seventeen or Eighteen Years of Age, and promises Miracles: If he goes on as he has begun, in the Pastoral way, as *Virgil* first try'd his Strength, we may hope to see *English* Poetry vie with the Roman, and this Swan of Windsor sing as sweetly as the *Mantuan*' (*Career*, 52). This sets out Pope's own programme for his literary career so presciently that one might suspect tampering; Lansdowne did not publish his letter until 1732, and he may have taken the chance to improve on his original handiwork. None the less, it is apparent that Granville would have been in Pope's mind as a conceivable patron from very early in his work on the poem. The fact that Granville locates him 'in the Neighbourhood of *Cooper's-Hill*' suggests not only a topographic reference—anyone who knew Pope would be aware where he lived—but a literary placement, indicating that Pope would attempt to carry on the legacy of Denham's great poem. This was not common knowledge. If Granville did indeed cast the young man for the role of swan of Windsor, at the age of 17 or 18, he was benefiting from inside information.

Pope' s own account of the poem's history exists in two forms, but neither is fully satisfactory. When he came to revise it for inclusion in the *Works* in 1737, he made a note opposite the title page of his early manuscript:

This Poem was written just after ye Pastorals as appears by ye last verse of it. That was——in ye year when ye author was—years of age. But the last hundred lines including ye Celebration of ye Peace, were added in ye year——, soon after ye Ratification of ye Treaty at Utrech- It was first printed in folio in 1 Again in folio ye same year, & afterwards in Octavo ye next. (Schmitz, 2)

Not only are the dates missing: the studied vagueness is belied by a false precision, when Pope claims that the ending was added 'soon after' the ratification of the treaty, where 'just before' would be correct.

When the poem duly made its appearance in the *Works*, a footnote was supplied at its head as follows: This poem was written at different times: the first part of it which relates to the country, in the year 1704, at the same time with the Pastorals: the latter part was not added till the year 1710. (*TE* i. 148)

At l. 290, Pope appended another note:

All the lines that follow, till within eight lines of the conclusion, were not added to the poem till the year 1710. The 425th verse, *My Humble Muse in unambitious strains*, &c. immediately followed this. (*TE* i. 175)

In Warburton's edition of 1751, the note ends differently, but the same information is relayed. Scholars have wrestled with the problems set by these statements, generally accepting 1704 as perhaps roughly accurate (though Elwin finds it 'improbable' that a start was made so early, *EC* i. 324), but substituting 1712 for the obviously inaccurate '1710'.

Independent reasons exist to suggest that Pope had embarked early in 1712 on a reconstruction of *Windsor-Forest*. These were pointed out by Norman Ault, who showed that a space was left for the poem in Lintot's *Miscellany*, published in May 1712, but this gap was left unfilled in the volume as issued. Only in 1714, when the second edition of the *Miscellany* appeared, did *Windsor-Forest* take its place, occupying the prearranged slot with the aid of a crowded typographical layout (see *TE* i. 128).[2] The surviving manuscript must have been written in 1712, as it is addressed at the start to 'the Right Honourable. *GEORGE* Ld *LANSDOWNE*', a title Granville only acquired at the start of the year. This of course does not prove that the entire revision was carried out at this time, for the manuscript is largely a fair copy with few major revisions. However, the bulk of the evidence suggests that Pope did not begin to recast his poem in earnest until the peace negotiations had reached an advanced stage.

Pope's correspondence makes no mention of the poem until late in the year 1712. On 30 October Addison wrote his famous *Spectator* paper, foretelling that a successful outcome to the peace negotiations would bring forth a bumper crop of celebratory poems. He issued a facetious edict to ban the use of pagan mythology, asserting that in an adult panegyric, 'Nothing can be more ridiculous than to have recourse to our *Jupiters* and *Junos*.' Such puerilities are inexcusable in 'a Poet that is past Sixteen'. Epic deeds should be recited plainly, without any effort to entertain the reader with 'the exploits of a River-God'. Laureates of the peace should eschew 'trifling antiquated Fables'.[3]

This paper served mainly to compliment the poem in which Addison's protégé, Thomas Tickell, had recently hailed the forthcoming treaty. *On the Prospect of Peace* had been published two days earlier, and it is no doubt largely owing to this puff in the hugely influential *Spectator* that it achieved considerable success, reaching six editions inside two years. But a subsidiary purpose on Addison's part seems to have been to cut Pope down to size, and to spoil the market for *Windsor-Forest* in advance. It is too much of a coincidence that Pope's composition should be the most mythologically dense he ever composed; that a river god should play a conspicuous role; and that it should be the work of the most famous boy poet of the age (who even claimed, as it was to turn out, that he had started his poem at the age of 16). In fact *Windsor-Forest* revives more of the 'antiquated fables' than any poem of its time:

---

[2] Ault, 27–48, argues that Pope himself edited the *Miscellany* vol., and also that a hidden contribution was a version of the story of Arethusa from Ovid (see Ch. 7 below).

[3] Bond (1965: iv. 363–4).

several of them were drawn from sources such as the *Metamorphoses* which Addison had himself used extensively. No hostilities between Addison and Pope are known prior to this juncture, and critics from Warton and Johnson onwards have tried to determine why Addison should have been upset, if he was, by the prospect of the new work from his friend.[4] By 1714 relationships had deteriorated to the point that Addison could attempt to use Tickell to oust Pope's *Iliad* with a rival translation; but at this stage there seems little obvious reason for the older man to begin a campaign against his younger colleague.

Tickell had even praised Pope in *The Prospect of Peace*, as 'the young spreading laurel' whose name was rising into fame, and had linked him with the authors of the *Spectator*, along with Congreve, Rowe, Prior, Garth, and Ambrose Philips, not to mention Oxford, Bolingbroke, and Harcourt among politicians. Pope may not have felt flattered to find himself placed next to Philips, who is described as 'a second Spenser', and as a precocious genius. Nor did it rank as a great compliment to be aligned with Swift's 'little Harrison', the short-lived poet who was helping the Earl of Strafford at the peace talks: Tickell refers to him as 'that much-lov'd youth, whom Utrecht's walls confine' (Chalmers, iii. 379). However, Pope must have seen that his rival had anticipated him in more than one regard. The *Prospect* is dedicated to John Robinson, the Lord Privy Seal, who as an active player in the Utrecht negotiations (and also a former dean of Windsor) might have suited Pope's dedicatory needs very nicely. Tickell had made his own base in Oxford a locus of historical inspiration, citing such figures as Henry V, Edward the Black prince, and his mother, Philippa of Hainault, as patrons of the university, itself dubbed 'The seat of sages, and the nurse of kings'. The links of these individuals with Oxford were slighter than those of the heroes Pope identifies with Windsor, but the hint had been provided. (See also Chapter 8 below on Addison.)

It is understandable then that Pope could see merit in Tickell's poem, and even worried that one passage in it may have forestalled his own description of the British fleet as the ships 'Tempt Icy Seas' (387–92). We know this from a letter Pope wrote to John Caryll around 29 November 1712:

Tho' you have no great opinion of Mr. Tickell's verses to the *Spectator*, I believe you'll think his poem upon the peace to have its beauties especially in the versification. There are also several most poetical images and fine pieces of painting in it, particularly the lines . . . of a child's emotion at the sight of the trophies at Blenheim, and the description of the fields after the wars . . . and the artful introduction of several noblemen by fancying coins will be struck of them in gold of Indies, are strokes of mastery. And lastly, the description of the several parts of the world in regard to our trade: which has interfered with some lines of my own in the poem called Windsor Forest, tho' written before I saw his. (*Corr.* i. 157)

Pope goes on to transcribe eight lines from Tickell, and asks his friend whether he ought not to strike out the equivalent lines in his own poem, 'either as they seem too

[4] On 11 Feb. 1713 Addison wrote to Pope, returning thanks 'for the noble entertainment you have sent me and which I have hitherto found in everything that comes from your pen' (quoted in *Life*, 865). This was presumably an advance copy of *WF*.

like his, or as they are inferior'. This looks like fishing for compliments, and six of the eight lines duly stayed where they were in *Windsor-Forest*; but plainly Pope felt some anxiety on account of the similar drift of the two poems. In addition, this concluding prophecy given to Father Thames could naturally have used the motif of coins struck 'in gold of Indies', which would have cemented the design of the poem.[5] Here Tickell had forestalled his rival.

Shortly afterwards, on 5 December, Pope reported to Caryll again, announcing that 'The poem of *Windsor Forest* has undergone many alterations, and received many additions since you saw it, but has not yet been out of my hands to any man' (*Corr.* i. 162). Later still, on 21 December, Pope updated his information to Caryll, repeating that *Windsor-Forest* would precede *The Temple of Fame* into print, but he did not yet know when. Mysteriously he refers to 'the misconstructions of some of my neighbours', over which he has unspecified apprehensions; this might refer to some aspect of *Windsor-Forest*, but if so it is not clear what is at stake. A more unambiguous reference occurs in a passage which describes Pope's efforts to write of vernal matters in bleak midwinter: 'These are the scenes the season presents to me, and what can be more ridiculous than that in the midst of this bleak prospect that sets my very imagination a shivering, I am endeavouring to raise up round about me a painted scene of woods and forests in verdure and beauty, trees springing, fields flowering, Nature laughing' (*Corr* i. 168). One interesting aspect of this remark stands out: Pope must have been working on revising the *earlier* sections of his poem—perhaps the opening glimpse of Eden, or the seasonal evocation of spring and summer, or most likely the blending of forest and river at the end of the Lodona episode. Nothing in the culminating section, added to turn the work in the direction of the Peace, would fit so well the language used in Pope's letter.

Around this time Pope must have permitted his friends and advisers to have their first glimpse of *Windsor-Forest*, now substantially ready for the press. We might assume that the mentors would be a group close to that which monitored the *Pastorals*, but in fact we have no concrete evidence as to whom Pope may have consulted. Among his earlier patrons, some can certainly be eliminated: Walsh had died in 1708, as had Sir Henry Sheeres in 1710 and, as recently as November 1712, Arthur Maynwaring. Lord Wharton had passed hopelessly out of the orbit of the Tories and government loyalists; and the Marquess of Dorchester (father of Lady Mary Wortley Montagu) seems also to have drifted away from Pope's life. That leaves loyal supporters like Garth, as well as newer friends like Caryll and Cromwell. Above all, it leaves in place Trumbull and Lansdowne, who may each have believed that he would be the addressee of the finished poem.

Early in the new year, the die was cast. Pope wrote to Lansdowne from Binfield on 10 January 1713: 'I thank you for having given my poem of Windsor Forest its greatest ornament, that of bearing your name in the front of it . . . Yet my Lord, this honour has given me no more pride than your honours have given you.'[6] The letter

---

[5] This is explored in more detail in *SDW*, ch. 6.
[6] The second sentence deliberately recalls *WF*, 289–90.

goes on to speak of a favour Pope has conferred on his patron, by sparing his modesty: in return, he begs for 'a free correction of these verses which will have few beauties, but what may be made by your blots. I am in the circumstance of an ordinary painter drawing Sir Godfrey Kneller, who by a few touches of his own could make the piece very valuable.' A neatly conventional conclusion follows: 'I might then hope, that many years hence the world might read, in conjunction with your name, that of, | Your Lordship's, &c.' (*Corr.* i. 172). The terms of the comparison are significant: Pope casts himself as blunderer-painter to Kneller, to express his relationship of blunderer-poet to Lansdowne.

Some time in February, Pope wrote again to Caryll, announcing that he had sent the poem to the press, and would dispatch copies to his friend. He went on, 'I was at the same time both glad and ashamed (when we were both at Old Windsor) that you had more lines than one of that poem by heart' (*Corr.* i. 173). Unfortunately the date of this visit by Caryll to his Berkshire friends and relatives cannot be fixed. When Pope wrote to Caryll's son John on 1 March, he confined himself to social chitchat, with no mention of his writing (*CIH*, 462–3). By that time, Pope had received his copy-money of 30 guineas (£32.5s. 0d., or now £32.25) from the bookseller Lintot on 23 February. Two weeks later, on 7 March, at the end of its long period of gestation, the poem finally came off the press.

It is time to return to the surviving manuscript, which was originally given to Jonathan Richardson, who stated that it represented 'the first copy of the author's own hand, written out beautifully, as usual, for the perusal and criticism of his friends' (*EC* i. 323–4). As today, the manuscript apparently then stopped at l. 380, lacking forty-four lines at the end of the printed version. It should be stressed that the break at this point has nothing to do with the break in composition, between early and late stages of writing, which Pope locates at l. 290. Richardson made a number of transcriptions from the manuscript into his copy of Pope's *Works* (1717), but this volume has disappeared. The holograph passed into the hands of Malone and Croker among others before surfacing in modern times; it is now in the possession of Washington University, St Louis.

The manuscript consists of a title page on a half-sheet, followed by four sheets in folio, making sixteen pages of text. Each page contains about twenty-four lines of verse. It lacks either a half-sheet or a full sheet at the end. The poem is written in Pope's formal hand, with marginal additions in an informal cursive style. Some of the added material relates to the pre-publication scan of late 1712 or early 1713, but more of it relates to the establishment of the text which appeared in the *Works* (1736)—for the latter purpose, Pope left Richardson a number of instructions to enable him to prepare the desired text. The manuscript does not appear to have been used as the printer's copy for the first edition or any subsequent printing (see Schmitz, 10–15 for all these matters).

Departures from the manuscript may be identified at several stages of the textual history: (1) The changes just mentioned which Pope made just before the poem went to press, probably in response to comments from his advisers; (2) other changes found in the 1713 printed version, which are not matched by any sign in the manuscript; (3) changes in subsequent printings of the poem, including versions in 1714, 1717, 1720, 1722, 1727, and 1732; (4) the one major overhaul Pope carried for, for the *Works* in 1736; (5) subsequent revised editions, including those of 1740 and 1743, and culminating in Warburton's edition of 1751.

The interest and importance of these categories of alteration are not uniform. Few but significant changes are made in category (1). There are many examples under category (2), but several of these are not of great moment. In general the changes between 1713 and 1735, in category (3), hold minor importance. Category (4) affords a number of illuminating changes, whilst those in category (5) are again of lesser significance. In the case of the final segment of the poem (391–434) we can obviously examine only categories (3) to (5), since these forty-four lines are not present in the manuscript.

In 1735 Pope drew attention to some of the changes when he added notes which quoted the manuscript version (more or less accurately). However, these constituted only a tiny fraction of the changes actually made, and all scholars prior to Schmitz in 1952 underestimated the extent of revision which had been carried out. Even the Twickenham edition, which appeared after Schmitz's volume was published, makes little attempt to chart the full pattern of change. In some places, even where the note indicates that a major alteration has been introduced in the printed text, the editors do not cite the manuscript verbatim. A good example occurs at l. 323, where we are given no hint of Pope's telling reference to the 'dire Morn' on which Charles I was executed (see Chapter 3, below).

As well as verbal substitutions, which comprise the bulk of the changes, Pope made a number of transpositions. In his study, Schmitz was able to identify 'twelve additions involving 167 lines, sixteen subtractions involving 33 lines, and six shifted passages of two to eight lines in length' (Schmitz, 62). These figures include one huge augmentation, the new material at ll. 291–426 (Schmitz, however, shows that the manuscript lacks ll. 291–8 as we now have them, and dubs the passage on Surrey an 'afterthought'). As regards passages which were bodily transported, the best example concerns the verses concerning Cooper's Hill (261–6), which in the manuscript occupy a paragraph of seven lines rather than six, placed *before* rather than *after* the paragraph on the Happy Man. It is this middle section which seems to have given Pope most of his architectural problems. The description of the Thames (219–34) endured much cutting and pasting: for example, ll. 223–4 originally appeared in the wind-up to the peroration, in a place corresponding to l. 363 as the poem now stands (four other lines on Venice at this point were dropped altogether). Immediately before the Thames section, at the end of the narrative of Lodona, Pope added six famous lines (211–16), which he marked in the margin of the manuscript in 1736 with a note—the printed version reads 'These six lines were added after the first writing of the poem.'

Plainly, some of the changes made to the manuscript before publication reflect Pope's continuing efforts to recast his earlier poem to fit the new needs imposed by the Peace settlement. It is impossible to know exactly how much revision was necessary, since 'we cannot reconstruct [the poem's] original form with any confidence'.[7] On the other hand, we can uncover certain traces of the archaeology of *Windsor-Forest*. The existence of the manuscript enables us to assert that Pope was rethinking the political import of the 'pastoral' sections at least as late as the end of 1712 or the start of 1713 (see p. 15).

Until about forty years ago, the prevailing view was that Pope had been forced to yoke disparate fragments together with great awkwardness, if not quite violence— a verdict with which Wasserman and the Twickenham editors (*TE* i. 125–44), amongst others, took issue. This 'new orthodoxy of the poem's integrity' has been challenged by Robert Cummings, in two of the most searching essays which have been devoted to *Windsor-Forest*.[8] The fundamental argument of both articles is that Pope failed to integrate the personal and the public, the pastoral and the political, the old material and the new. Cummings even revives some of the complaints of John Dennis, to the effect that the work is a '*Rhapsody*'. Part of the trouble lies in 'the contradiction, created by the necessity of writing a panegyric for Granville and Granville's irrelevance to the peace'. Cummings also contends that 'the assumption of some kind of identity between the motives of *Cooper's Hill* and *Windsor-Forest* is a major distraction'. Further, '*Windsor-Forest* has no business to claim the generic protection of the descriptive poem.' Other genres are excluded: 'Except incidentally, and perhaps even paradoxically, as in Thames's speech, *Windsor-Forest* is without epic pretensions.' At the same time, 'The specifically georgic model is equally suspect.' The work is reconsigned to the category of 'silvan poem' in the sense evolving from Statius, developed by Renaissance humanists, and most commonly applied to the collections of Jonson and Cowley.

Undeniably, Cummings makes a number of cogent points. In particular, he drives severe inroads into Wasserman's rather totalized view of the design. The substitution of Lansdowne for Trumbull certainly presents some difficulties, and this is an issue we shall explore in Chapter 2; at the same time, it is true that *Cooper's Hill* and *Windsor-Forest* differ in significant ways. However, Cummings seems to me to go too far the other way in seeking to demolish the 'integrity' of Pope's poem. He exaggerates the incoherence of the structure, overstates the relevance of *sylvae*, and ignores much of the evidence of the poem itself when he says that 'Compared with Denham . . . Pope is insufficiently attentive to facts of any kind.' There are two reasons for these limitations, as they seem to me, in Cummings's case. The first is that he fails to detect what might be called the symbolic logic of the work. The second is that his argument actually makes large assumptions about the early form of the poem, something he himself claims to be inappropriate.

The nature of the enterprise is conditioned, for Cummings, by the coexistence of the early, pastoral, Trumbull poem, along with the later, political, Lansdowne poem.

---

[7] Cummings (1987: 64).

[8] Cummings (1987: 63–79; 1988: 143–58). Part of Cummings's aim is to suggest a deeper debt to Politian than critics have generally been willing to grant: this is not implausible, in view of Pope's known fondness for this poet (see also *SDW*, ch. 2), but the detailed argument is not wholly convincing.

We have Pope's authority that *Windsor-Forest* did come into being in two stages, broadly corresponding with these two components. The problem stems from the fact that we do not know how much Pope revised earlier sections (i.e. the first 290 lines) prior to compiling the manuscript version. We *do* know that even after the manuscript was finished, Pope went back and made changes in the first part: moreover, right at the point where the hinge between old and new occurs, a significant addition of eight lines was made on the subject of Surrey. Cummings refers to Schmitz's edition, and he is aware of the facts; but his account largely occludes the process of revision. It is as though everything Pope had written prior to 1712 was cast in stone, and could not be touched when the later section was added on.

Part of the argument Cummings constructs is that '*Windsor-Forest* in its first and original part touches on politics only negatively and deviously—indeed hardly at all'. This is a large overstatement. It can only be defended if (1) we dismiss the relevance of the portions on the Norman kings to the reign of William III—Cummings is entitled to dispute this reading, but he does not produce any arguments either way; (2) we depoliticize all references to the reigning monarch, including those which specifically draw attention to her place in the Stuart lineage; (3) we ignore the overtones of keywords such as 'liberty'; and (4) we pay no heed to the gradual accretion of a ritualized language of concord (drawing on mythology, iconography, heraldry, and history), which prepares the way for the more overt political idiom of the conclusion. Apart from this, we can only see the poem as totally fragmentary, which is more or less what Cummings indicates, if we suppress obvious continuities—such as the Thames flowing from the Forest in the first part down to London and the ocean in the second part. This makes for a relatively simple narrative, traced more amply in *SDW*, chapter 7. Here it is enough to say that the pastoral and (loosely) georgic effects of portion A are regularly transformed into providential and prophetic elements in portion B. To give the simplest case: the 'golden Years' of l. 92 derive imaginatively from a descriptive passage on the yellow harvests as they take over the former heathland, whereas '*Albion*'s Golden Days' (425) belong to a discursive context where the Virgilian and biblical notions of a millenial dawn provide a different kind of restoration. The first process is, as it were, ecological; the second political—but the symbolic language enables the poem to straddle both forms of statement.

In any case, this book argues that there is a lot more politics running around the entire text than we may have seen. One reason that Pope shifted his attention to Lansdowne, despite some confessedly awkward effects, is that he was a newly created peer, and a likely candidate (at this juncture) for elevation to the Garter—if the latter were not plausibly imminent, Pope's reference at ll. 289–90 would be gauche beyond belief. It remains true that Lansdowne had never played a big role in the peace negotiations; but then Pope enlists him as the current treasurer of the household, rather than the erstwhile secretary at war. As we shall see in Chapter 2, Lansdowne's timely marriage linked him to the family of his wife's father, the Earl of Jersey, who had virtually full control of the initial negotiations. By 1713, only Bolingbroke would have been a realistic symbol of the peace process; even Bishop Robinson, who was Tickell's choice, or Strafford could be seen as little more than an instrument of the peace programme which Bolingbroke had, to some degree, imposed on Oxford. Lansdowne still held an important role at court, and possessed more of the Queen's confidence than his successor at the War Office (to use a term that is strictly anachronistic), who was Sir William Wyndham.

Finally, if the reading of *Windsor-Forest* which this book offers has any validity, then Pope needed a Jacobite as much as he needed a peace negotiator. Cummings maintains that Lansdowne's celebration 'as a poet and a friend, rather than as a mediator in his country's interests, is in this context impertinent'. He goes on, 'By promoting Granville to an important position in the poem Pope turns away from any issue central to the celebration of the Peace'.[9] That might be true, if the poem did not construct an elaborate machinery to make Lansdowne—celebrator of James II, heir of a tradition of royalist martyrology, grandee and lover of theatrical display, member of the court circle—into an exemplary figure of Stuart pieties. This is what Pope requires, more than a personage active at the negotiating table—Matthew Prior would have served as well for *that*. Tactfully, the Peace is celebrated as a national achievement, and as a personal triumph for the Queen. Its tutelary figure should not have involved himself too prominently in the secret negotiations with France or the controversial articles of commerce in the treaty. He ought to have been a candidate for honours such as the 'Silver *Star*' which symbolize the royal prerogative to dignify subjects and the chivalric history centred on Windsor. In this light, Pope could scarcely have made a better choice.

BINFIELD WOOD AND BAGSHOT HEATH

I can easily image to my thoughts the Solitary hours of your Eremitical Life,
in the mountains from something so parallel to it, in my own retirement at Binfield—
but Binfield, alas! is no more and the Muse is driven from those Forests of which she sung. the
Day may shortly come, when your Friend may too literally apply

> nos Patriae fines, & dulcia linquimus arva

when he may look back with regret, on the Paradise he has lost, and have only the consolation
of poor Adam

> The world lies all before him, where to chuse
> His place of rest, & providence his Guide.

(Pope to Parnell, March 1716)[10]

The opening lines of the poem expressly compare Windsor Forest to Eden. What has been largely concealed is the degree to which this section prefigures Pope's own sense of loss when he was obliged to leave his boyhood home at Binfield, only three years after the poem appeared.

A revelatory passage occurs in a letter Pope wrote from the village to his friend Henry Cromwell, dated 12 November 1711. The poet had just returned from a week

---

[9] Cummings (1988: 146).   [10] Rawson (1959: 377).

spent with his Catholic neighbour Anthony Englefield. He imagines Cromwell struggling back to London from a visit to Bath, along rough roads with a hard saddle and a bouncing horse.

What an agreeable Surprize wou'd it have been to me, to have met you by pure accident at *Bagshot*, which I was within an ace of doing, being at *Hallgrove* that very day? And to have carry'd you off triumphantly to *Binfield*, sett you on an easier Pad, & relievd the wandring Knight with a Nights Lodging, & rural Repaste, at our Castle in the Forest? (*Corr.* i. 135)

Allowing for some literary flourishes here, there is an underlying truth in Pope's belated invitation. He did indeed see his home as a rural haven for his friends and for himself. In effect, Binfield made the old proverb good—the Englishman's home stood as his 'Castle in the Forest', a symbol of retirement to match the seat of power at Windsor itself.

The parish of Binfield, with a population of some 400 people, occupied around 3,500 acres, more than half of this permanent grassland. It included 206 acres of woodland, together with 543 acres of arable land: the very mixture described in Pope's Edenic opening (11–42).[11] Its average height above sea level was some 200 feet, rising to 300 feet at one point. A few miles away near Bagshot the land at Surrey Hill reaches 427 feet. The slopes of the Chiltern Hills are visible across the Thames, and distantly to the south the Hampshire Downs—but Pope's phrase 'more humble Mountains' (35) is certainly appropriate in comparison with Mount Olympus.[12]

The Popes had their family home at Whitehill House, which lay on the southern edge of the parish of Binfield; indeed Popeswood and adjoining Priestwood are now suburbs of Bracknell, which in the eighteenth century was a village, and has now been designated as a new town. Pope's Wood, a grove of beech trees, lay half a mile north of Whitehill: it may be recalled in Pope's later line 'In Forest planted by a Father's hand' (*TE* iv. 65). As for the house itself, we have only a nineteenth-century view, taken from the back, and it seems to have been of modest dimensions. It was surrounded by rather more than fifteen acres of land. As for the manor of Binfield, this had been held by the Dancastle family since the sixteenth century; they were to retain it throughout Pope's lifetime, until it was finally sold in 1754. In the parish church lay the grave of Judith Countess of Salisbury, mother-in-law of Sir William Trumbull (*VCH* iii. 119–21).

The central symbols in this work, the forest and the river, have an equally important role in Pope's life history. Just as in the poem, the energies of his career circulated along the narrow corridor of the Thames Valley. Born in the City of London, he moved with his family upriver to Hammersmith at the age of 4. About eight years later, the Popes acquired their property, Whitehill House, at Binfield, which lay near the heart of the forest some 7 miles from the town of Windsor. It was an inter-family transaction, as the property was bought from Charles Rackett, the husband

---

[11] Sources do not reveal the precise extent of heathland, which as noted in the text was a further component of the landscape mentioned by Pope, but this was also extensive: see *SDW*, ch. 5.

[12] Pope also uses the poeticism 'Mountain' for Cooper's Hill (266), following Denham. The hill gives good views towards Windsor and the Forest, although it rises gently to a height of little more than 400 feet.

since about 1694 of Alexander's half-sister Magdalen; Rackett himself moved from Hammersmith to Bagshot. His home, Hall Grove, lay on the southern edge of the forest, where it merged into the heathland which figures explicitly in the poem.[13] But even so early, there was an ominous shadow behind the event. Within two years, Pope's father had conveyed the property to Protestant relatives of his wife, in trust for the young Alexander. This was done for one simple reason: to avert the threat of dispossession, occasioned by the fact that Catholics were technically unable to purchase real estate. There was nothing secret in the locality, however, about the family faith of the Popes. About a year after they arrived in the village, the churchwardens of the parish formally presented the couple as 'Reputed Papists' (*Career*, 36).

The young poet began his career and indeed achieved fame whilst Binfield remained his home, although he would also acquire an alternative base in the city—in 1713 this was generally the lodging of his painter-friend Charles Jervas, at Cleveland Court, St James's. It was not until after the Hanoverian succession and the first major Jacobite rising that this secure domestic setting was imperiled. In April 1716 the Popes moved to Chiswick, an act which has often been seen as little more than a measure of convenience. However, an outstandingly cogent argument has recently been mounted to show that the family were driven from their retreat as a result of mounting political pressure and the introduction by the Hanoverian regime of fresh anti-Catholic legislation.[14] First came a proclamation on 6 December 1714, which required the enforcement of existing legislation, mostly enacted in the reign of William III, that imposed restraints on Catholics and nonjurors. Then in 1715 the government introduced a fresh Act (1 Geo. I, s.2, c.13) which effectively debarred Catholics from official posts, requiring them to take oaths of allegiance by 23 January 1716: Pope apparently declined to do this. Late in the year a bill was drafted to force all Catholics to register their estates and their value: local officials were to carry out assessments, and two-thirds of each estate would be seized by the crown, or a tax imposed in lieu. This statute (1 Geo. I, s.2, c.50) was to come into effect on 26 June 1716.[15] Before that date the Catholic population had to decide whether to sell while the going was good, or hold on to their property and face crippling taxes. Most appear to have chosen to sell out, and the Popes did so on 1 March 1716, thus bringing to an end the family link with the Forest.

A more pressing day-to-day problem had arisen because of Pope's horse, a gift from Caryll: since this was worth more than £5, it was forfeit by an Act of William and Mary. As soon as the Queen died, Pope began to worry about this matter, but it was not until after the rising that the government actually reactivated the anti-Catholic legislation involved. The horse was left at Binfield with the Dancastles until 1717, when it was finally sold by Charles Rackett, the poet's brother-in-law, for 5 guineas (*Corr.* i. 404). It was in a way almost comic, but of course a serious curtailment of the invalid Pope's freedom to move from place to place.[16]

---

[13] On this aspect of the topography, see *SDW*, ch. 5.   [14] Gabriner (1990: 32–6).
[15] Edward Blount sent details of the new legislation to Pope on 23 June (*Corr.* i. 344). Pope's neighbour Henry Englefield duly registered, but refused to take the oath of loyalty (*Life*, 285).
[16] See Gabriner (1990: 46–50) for a good summary of this episode.

With some reason, Pope feared that 'innocence will be no Security to some People of my persuasion'—reprisals against Catholics were threatened in the wake of the unsuccessful rising. His friend Edward Blount wrote to him in November 1715, praising the posture of Pomponius Atticus (*Corr.* i. 321). Pope himself wrote to Trumbull of his conflicting emotions as the struggle was fought out, and commended his mentor for remaining quiet in his 'Cave in the forest' (*Corr.* i. 324). Early in 1716 he addressed Trumbull as 'some Superior Being, that has once been among Men, and now sits above at distance, not only to observe their actions . . . but sometimes charitably to influence and direct them'. Shortly afterwards, on 20 March, the poet wrote to John Caryll in the midst of a journey of valediction to his old home:

I write this from Windsor Forest, which I am come to take my last look and leave of. We here bid our papist-neighbours adieu, much as those who go to be hanged do their fellow-prisoners, who are condemned to follow them a few weeks after. I was at Whitenights [home of the Englefields], where I found the young ladies [the Blount sisters] . . . spoken of more coldly, than I could (at this time especially) have wished. I parted from honest Mr. Dancastle with tenderness; and from old Sir William Trumbull as from a venerable prophet, foretelling with lifted hands the miseries to come upon posterity, which he was just going to be removed from! (*Corr.* i. 336–7)

Trumbull was indeed to die before the end of the year, and Alexander Pope senior followed him to the grave on 23 October 1717. Pope's letter is in his plainest style, and its eloquence derives from the genuine fears of the Catholic community, so that the simile of prisoners on death row has an immediate applicability. Among friends of the poet who were currently incarcerated in the Tower was the dedicatee of *Windsor-Forest*, Lord Lansdowne.[17]

The acute sense of filial duty which marked Pope's character would have impelled him, in any circumstances, to find his parents 'some asylum for their old age', as he expressed it to Caryll (see below, p. 26). The situation was made more heavily fraught by the religious persecution they faced, and so Lord Burlington's offer of protection at Chiswick came at a most timely moment. Expulsion from the scenes of his childhood brought him even closer to the now elderly couple who had watched over him as he grew up in the forest. A few years earlier, Pope had jokingly issued a curse on his friend Mrs Marriott: 'May Providence . . . cause you to forsake your House and home; may your Possessions be alienated and put into the hands of Strangers; may your Fields bear harvests for other People . . . May you quit the Country, the Seat of Innocence and pure Delights, & live in the very Sink of all wickedness, this Towne' (*Corr.* i. 181–2). Somehow the lightly intended curse would fall on the one who pronounced it.

Another friend, who fully appreciated the scale of Pope's privation when he left his boyhood home, was Edward Blount, a relative of his favourites Martha and Teresa. Edward wrote on 24 March 1716:

[17] This seems to be the point of a bitter little joke in a letter to Caryll from Mar. 1715: 'We are invited this day to dinner at my Lord Lansdowne's; we are invited to see the lions at the Tower, gratis; by a lord who expects to have a new lodging given him by the Parliament' (*Corr.* i. 287).

Your letters give me a gleam of satisfaction, in the midst of a very dark and cloudy situation of thoughts, which it would be more than human to be exempt from at this time, when our homes must either be left, or be made too narrow for us to turn in. Poetically speaking, I should lament the loss Windsor Forest and you sustain of each other, but that methinks one can't say you are parted, because you will live by and in one another, while verse is verse. This consideration hardens me in my opinion rather to congratulate you, since you have the pleasure of the prospect whenever you take it from your shelf. (*Corr.* i. 337–8)

Blount understood, as we do not always today, that *Windsor-Forest* was the poem which spoke most clearly to Pope's 'situation', and that of fellow Catholics, after the Hanoverian regime moved in. He goes on to say that his *rura parva* are 'fasten'd' to him, and so he cannot exchange them in Pope's fashion for 'more portable means of subsistence'. Ousted from his paternal acres in Devon, Edward Blount was about to embark on a prolonged sojourn on the Continent.[18]

A more willing expatriate at this juncture was Lady Mary Wortley Montagu, who had set out on her Turkish embassy with her husband. At the end of 1716 Pope wrote her a letter which expresses his current state of mind, at least in bitter moments. He contrasts their respective situations, and concludes, ' I can never think that Place my Country, where I can't call a foot of paternal Earth my owne.' He had contemplated leaving England, perhaps to make a tour of Italy in company with the Wortley Montagus. He might even 'run into Turkey in search of Liberty; for who would not rather live a free man among a nation of Slaves, than a Slave among a nation of free men?' (*Corr.* i. 384–5). The 'paternal Earth' denied him was plainly that of the Forest, from which he had been driven out a few months earlier.

We need not press too hard on the links between 1713 and 1716. It is as though the velleities and dream-fantasies of the poem have subsequently been realized in stark actuality. Trumbull, the sage Atticus who has 'retir'd' (*WF*, 258) and sits above the fray, now becomes a hero of passive resistance. The violence associated with Williamite depredations upon the forest may now take the form of lynchings on the Papists. Civil commotion has resumed its hold on the nation, the muse has been 'driven' from the glades of Windsor, and Pope has lost his personal paradise. The worst nightmares of the poem, that is precisely those destructive aspects of life which Anne's rule has tempered, have come to pass in the wake of the Protestant succession and the rising.[19] Instead of peace and plenty, there are war and disaster— change and decay for the entire Catholic community in particular. As Pope wrote to Caryll in March 1716:

If it were generous to seek for alleviating consolations in a calamity of so much glory, one might say that to be ruined thus in the gross, with a whole people, is but like perishing in the general conflagration, where nothing we can value is left behind us. (*Corr.* i. 335)

[18] Blount's second daughter Mary would marry the ninth Duke of Norfolk in 1727, while the elder Henrietta married the Duke's brother Richard in 1739. These links with the premier Catholic family of the nation indicate less wealth or social position among the Blounts than fierce commitment to the faith, through the most difficult times.

[19] It is probably no coincidence that the first virulent attacks on Pope as a Jacobite date from the very same moment: they start to appear in the early months of 1716.

> But knottier Points we know not half so well,
> Depriv'd us soon of our Paternal Cell;
> And certain Laws, by Suff'rers thought unjust,
> Deny'd all Posts of Profit or of Trust:
> Hopes after Hopes of pious Papists fail'd,
> While mighty WILLIAM's thundring Arm prevail'd.
>
> (*TE* iv. 169)

The sale of Binfield went through on 1 March 1716, and now indeed Pope found himself deprived of his 'paternal cell'. His father had obviously meant to pass the property on to his son, but this sacred trust had been revoked by the course of events. It is clear that Pope never wholly got over this act of dispossession, although he wrote bravely later that he was no happier 'On Forest planted by a Father's hand, | Than in five acres now of rented land' (*TE* v. 65). What may have made things worse was that the poet would lease his Twickenham home from Thomas Vernon, an army contractor and MP with dubious South Sea connections. Vernon's widow later offered Pope the opportunity to buy the property, but he declined.

Instead of transferring the family home, the Popes had to face a visit from the Commission of Land Registrars, and they no doubt feared that they might be punished for their illegal purchase of Whitehill House in 1698. John Gay came down to make a farewell visit at the end of the month, and on 26 March he reported to Parnell:

Binfield alas is sold. The Trees of Windsor Forest shall no more listen to the tunefull reed of the [Popian?] swain & no more Beeches shall be wounded with the names of Teresa & Patty. Teresa & Patty are forced to leave the Groves of Mapledurham . . . as Binfield is for ever sold. (Gay, *Letters*, 29)

The Blount sisters had been obliged to leave their family home because of the marriage of their brother Michael to Mary Agnes Tichborne in the previous year. Plaintively, Gay in his letter quoted Virgil's first *Eclogue*, just as he had done to Ford on 6 July 1714.[20] The passage became a kind of family code, for Pope had used it to Parnell (above, p. 20) and to Caryll (*Corr.* i. 337): *nos Patriae fines & dulcia linquimus arva* (we leave the confines of our home and its dear fields). The next line, ominously, was *nos patria fugimus* (we are banished from home). Michael Blount had cited this line in his letter on 24 March (*Corr.* i. 338). It was a schoolroom verse which Pope would recall from his first contact with Latin poetry in his boyhood.

Troubles closed in on the Blount family as the Pretender's rising came to its wretched conclusion. Pope learnt that Lady Swinburne, the maternal aunt of Teresa and Martha, and daughter of Anthony Englefield, was in need of assistance because of her husband's implication in the rebellion. In fact Sir William Swinburne, whom she had married in 1697, had only three months to live; but his two brothers were

[20] Gay, *Letters*, 11. See below, p. 29, below.

arrested at the battle of Preston and brought to trial as rebels in May 1716. The elder, Edward, died in Newgate prison later that year; the younger, James, was ultimately pardoned.[21] In January Pope told Caryll that he had offered to visit Lady Swinburne, although this was a delicate task at present. As for her nieces, 'The Mapledurham ladies (if they be any longer called so, since their brother makes so much haste to an alienation of his affections another way) are not so unfortunate in particular, but sensible enough . . . to be very much so in partaking the afflictions of others' (*Corr.* i. 327). All around him, Pope could see the 'afflictions' that beset the Roman Catholic gentry who had formed the backdrop of his youth in Berkshire.

The move from the country took time as well as racking nerves. As Pope told Caryll on 20 April, 'My father and mother having disposed of their little estate at Binfield, I was concerned to find out some asylum for their old age; and these cares, of settling, and furnishing a house, have employed me till yesterday, when we fixed at Chiswick under the wing of my Lord Burlington' (*Corr.* i. 339). What is suppressed here is Pope's own need for an 'asylum', now that he had been ousted from the Forest. He, too, was reduced to 'settling' in a completely new environment from the one in which he had grown up.[22]

Truly this made a great watershed in Pope's life, as he wrote to John Caryll senior on 22 June: 'Tho' the change of my scene of life, from Windsor Forest to the water-side at Chiswick, be one of the grand Æra's of my days, and may be called a notable period in so inconsiderable a history' (*Corr.* i. 343). Writing to Thomas Dancastle on 7 August, he offered a not wholly convincing picture of his over-full life, then modulating into a more persuasive reflection on the scenes he had left behind:

I have not dined at home these 15 days, and perfectly regrett the quiet, indolence, silence, and sauntring, that made up my whole life in Windsor Forest. I shall therefore infallibly be better company and better pleased than ever you knew me, as soon as I can get under the shade of Priest-Wood, whose trees I have yet some Concern about. I hope, whatever licence the free-born Subjects of your Commons may take, there will yet be Groves enough left in those Forests to keep a Pastoral-Writer in countenance. Whatever belongs to the Crown is indeed as much trespas'd upon at this time in this Court as in the Country. While you are lopping off his timber, we are lopping his Prerogative. (*Corr.* i. 352)

Briefly Pope affected unconcern, boasting to Dancastle of 'how entirely I have put off the Airs of a Country Gentleman'.

Nevertheless, in the letters of the next year or two we encounter reminders of what has been lost. As to Dancastle on 18 February 1717:

The Memory of our old neighbors yet lives in me; I often give a Range to my Imagination, & goe strolling with one or other of you, up & down Binfield Wood, or over Bagshot Heath. I wish you all health, not you only, but your Horse, your Dog Lilly, &c. May your gun never fail, and your aim never miss. May your Pouch come swagging home, laden with woodcocks,

---

[21] See Erskine-Hill (1973: 207–9). According to one source, James pleaded insanity at his trial, and died as a lunatic (*EC* vi. 237).

[22] 'What new Scenes of Life I may enter into are uncertaine', one letter to the younger Caryll begins (*Corr.* i. 334).

and may those woodcocks be so fatt & good as to please Mr. Philips [the family chaplain]. (*Corr.* i. 393)

Here the rural sports of *Windsor-Forest* are revived as an emblem of friendship, solidarity, and innocent pleasure. Events in the forest during the next few years would bring this moral economy to an abrupt halt (as described more fully in *SDW*, chapter 5). Then, a few months later, Pope describes to the Blount sisters a return to his home country, with visits to Dancastle, and Sir William Compton near Wokingham. At the home of his sister and brother-in-law, Hall Grove, he had encountered Colonel Butler, a relative of Lady Arran.[23] After this he 'past the rest of the day in those Woods where I have so often enjoyd—an Author and a Book; and begot such Sons upon the Muses . . . I made a Hymn as I past thro' these Groves; it ended with a deep Sigh, which I will not tell you the meaning of' (*Corr.* i. 428).

The 'Hymn' survives with this letter in the Mapledurham papers, though it remained unpublished until the nineteenth century. It is not in the poet's strongest vein, but it does reiterate in simple language the intimate connections which had been forged in his mind between creativity, personal affection, retirement, and the Forest:

> All hail! once pleasing, once inspiring Shade,
>   Scene of my youthful Loves, and happier hours!
> Where the kind Muses met me as I stray'd,
>   And gently pressd my hand, and said, Be Ours.
> Take all thou e're shalt have, a constant Muse:
>   At Court thou may be lik'd, but nothing gain;
> Stocks thou may'st buy & sell, but always lose;
>   And love the brightest eyes, but love in vain!
>
> (*TE* vi. 194)

The constant muse would direct Pope to new subjects in the coming years, but his swerve from pastoral did not cause him to forget the 'happier hours' he had spent in the years at Binfield.

Pope had been especially concerned about the fate of the Blounts, referring to them as the 'widow and the fatherless, late of Mapledurham'. The problem here was that Michael Blount had inherited a heavily encumbered estate, and could not pay his sisters the annuities they had been left by their father. Later in life Michael had to quit Mapledurham for reasons of economy, and let it out, an indignity which the Blount girls would have registered as keenly as Anne Elliot when she felt 'sorry and ashamed' at the need to remove from Kellynch Hall. The young women were, Pope told Caryll, 'beforehand with us in being out of house and home, by their brother's marriage: and I wish they may not have some cause already to look upon Mapledurham with such sort of melancholy as we may upon our own seats when we lose

---

[23] The Butlers were a strongly Jacobite family, headed by Lord Arran's brother the Duke of Ormonde: they lived at Bagshot Park, close to Hall Grove. Pope seems to have teased Lady Arran about her hypochondria. For their involvement with Pope's own family at the time of the Berkshire Blacks episode, see *SDW*, ch. 5.

them' (*Corr.* i. 336). Pope dignifies his paternal home by calling it a 'seat', but his sense of proprietorship was more than a matter of technical possession of the 14 acres at Binfield. His solidarity with his Catholic neighbours expressed his desire to feel a part of a community of quiet virtue and sociable pleasures, such as the imagined Windsor Forest of Anne's reign had nurtured. The only way he had of regaining this sense of himself was to move back a few miles upstream to Twickenham in 1719. There he invented a new version of retirement, based on his modest villa and a garden of restricted size but immense symbolic significance, richly evoked in Maynard Mack's classic study (see *Garden and City*, 3–115).

Pope collected his *Works* in 1717, adorned with a series of commendatory poems by friends. These included lines Parnell wrote 'To Mr. Pope', which were later incorporated in the edition of his friend's works Pope was to publish in 1722. The poem touches on all the major compositions which had appeared prior to 1717, including *Windsor-Forest*. The allusion is to Lodona:

> *Ovid* himself might wish to sing the Dame,
> Whom *Windsor*-Forest sees a gliding stream:
> On silver feet, with annual Osier crown'd,
> She runs for ever thro' Poetic ground.

Thus the Thames valley is consecrated as an English Arcadia, while Pope joins Virgil in the temple of fame. However, the most heartfelt section comes with a passage of personal reminiscence near the end:

> Still, as I read, I feel my bosom beat,
> And rise in raptures by another's heat.
> Thus in the wood, when summer dress'd the days,
> When *Windsor* lent us tuneful hours of ease,
> Our ears the lark, the thrush, the turtle blest,
> And *Philomela* sweetest o'er the rest:
> The shades resound with song—O softly tread.
> While a whole season warbles round my head.[24]

Parnell seems to recall his stay at Binfield in 1714, and contrasts this idyll with his recent exile in Ireland. Christine Gerrard has convincingly linked these lines with a 'theme of exile from Arcadia' shared by Swift, Gay, and Parnell, along with Pope, in the years following the Hanoverian accession.[25] By printing Parnell's work, Pope in some measure appropriated the Irish writer's feelings of alienation. The anti-Catholic legislation has turned Pope into an exile in his own land, or an honorary Irishman. By 1717 he could reciprocate Parnell's longings: 'I have many an agreeable reverie,' he writes to his friend across the water, 'through those woods and downs, where we once rambled together' (*Corr.* i. 395). Here pastoral has become an implicit criticism of a fallen world under George I.

How far Pope's friends had mythologized the Forest, as a place consecrated to literary creation, emerges from a letter which Gay wrote to Charles Ford in the sum-

---

[24] Parnell (1989: 119–21).   [25] Gerrard (2001: 42).

mer of 1714. Pope and Parnell lay ensconced at Binfield, working on the translation of Homer, and trying to ignore the mounting political crisis: Pope spoke of 'withdrawing his thoughts as far as he can, from all the present world' (*Corr.* i. 240).[26] From his emotionally remote vantage point at The Hague, Gay cites a favourite tag from the first of Virgil's *Eclogues*, and then composes a somewhat risqué fantasy, embodying references to *The Rape of the Lock* and the *Iliad*: 'There are shades at Bingfield, Mrs Fermor is not very distant from thence; make a visit to Pope and Parnell, and while they are making a Grecian Campaign, do you as Æneas did before you meet your Venus in a Wood, he knew her by her *Locks* and so may you— but as you are a man of Honour & Modesty—think not of Hairs less in sight or any Hairs but these' (Gay, *Letters*, 11). It was indeed an idyll—the last, almost innocent fling before the convulsive events of the late summer. Such episodes of lost bliss hung around in the poet's imagination.

In the years immediately following the composition of *Windsor-Forest*, then, Pope came to see his dreams of nationhood and of personal citizenship cruelly thwarted. Paul Gabriner is surely right to maintain that the 'expulsion from Binfield' was 'a symbol of a larger disinheritance: the anti-Catholic disabilities which Pope confronted'. Equally, Gabriner makes the fair point that Whitehill House could be said to occupy a 'paradisal' situation, for 'like Milton's Eden, it was "a happy rural seat of various view", its position on Murrell's hill commanding extensive views of Ascot, Windsor, Marlow and the Thames valley in accord with the open landscape or "prospect" ideal which was coming into vogue at the time'.[27] Indeed, almost the only thing Gabriner does not do is to connect this 'lost inheritance' to *Windsor-Forest*, perhaps because it seemed anachronistic so to do. But to understand what Pope thought he had lost in 1716 enables us to reclaim what he valued about his *rura paterna*, as exemplified in *Windsor-Forest*. It can be no accident that Trumbull, the original inspiration of the poem, and the figure of virtue at its centre, is repeatedly invoked in the correspondence of 1715–16, at a juncture of national crisis which the poem had been intended to forestall. As the 'dreadful Series of Intestine Wars' (325) renewed itself in the Old Pretender's rising, all the accumulated energies of the poem came to Pope's aid in his lament over a nation torn apart, a religious community crushed, and a personal life torn to shreds.[28]

Such a reaction displays no paranoia. After all, Pope had only to think of numerous friends and acquaintances, who had suffered for their faith: sequestrations,

---

[26] It was a hollow pretence: a letter to Arbuthnot on 11 July made pretty desperate fun out of the controversial Schism Act, one of the rocks on which the Tory coalition was breaking up, and the proclamation against the Pretender issued in June (*Corr.* i. 134–5).

[27] Gabriner (1990: 57, 28). Part of the forest in this area may indeed have been planted by the hand of Pope's own father (see Brownell 1978: 120).

[28] For a convincing argument that psychological pressures helped to impel Pope towards a new genre when he wrote his *Elegy to the Memory of an Unfortunate Lady* (written c.1717), see *Life*, 318–19. Mack refers to several of the causes of stress which are mentioned in this chapter, including Pope's departure from Binfield, the uprooting of the Blounts, the death of Trumbull, and the persecution of Jacobites.

confiscations, attainders, even outlawry.[29] Several other cases are mentioned else-where in this book; but the instance closest to hand was Pope's intimate friend John Caryll, whose family estate had been seized under William III, and whose uncle had been outlawed. Eventually these disabilities were reversed: but in the mean time Caryll's own home at West Grinstead had again been sequestrated, as we shall see in the next section of this chapter. If 'the best man in England' (*Corr.* i. 512) might be so affected, what hope for others?

Perhaps Pope's most effective tribute to his mentor Trumbull comes in a sober and re-flective letter he wrote to the old man in June 1713, three months after the appearance of his poem. He addresses the patriarch at Easthampstead from his lodging in London:

But I might well be tax'd with Ingratitude if I did not assure you that the best Company in the World is no Equivalent to me for the Loss of Yours in Solitude, and that 'tis the least a Com-pliment to Windsor Forest, of all I have said, when I declare I most sincerely Envy it on your account. I shall not deny but I have made it appear very Lovely in my Poem, since I there told the World that Sir W. Trumbull was retired into it. I could not have renderd it more lovely, even tho' I had painted it as well as Mr. Jervas will the best thing in it if at his next Visit you give him leave to paint You.

   I daily meet here in my Walks with numbers of people who have all their Lives been ram-bling out of their Nature, into one Business or other, and ought to be sent into Solitude to Study themselves over again: This gives me now and then the Reflexion, how much better it might be for me, if I were in Windsor forest learning from one Man, than in London expos-ing my self perhaps to a hundred. (*CIH*, 464)

This provides more than a hyperbolic compliment to a patron. It shows how deeply Pope associated his boyhood home with quietness and self-understanding, and how he identified his urban milieu with people who were 'rambling out of their Nature'. The forest remains a place of authenticity and harmony. It was the break-up of this potential retreat which caused Pope such distress after the loss of Binfield, and the dream of an idyllic origin which fuelled his later creativity—along with its re-creation in his Twickenham estate. The seeds of almost all Pope's deepest think-ing about himself—his position in society, his poetic impulse, and his private identity—are to be found in the very public poem which is *Windsor-Forest*.

TRUMBULL, THE FOREST, AND RETIREMENT

It was while I lived in the Forest that I got so well acquainted with Sir W. Trumbull, who loved very much to read and talk of the classics in his retirement. We used to take a ride out together three or four days in the week, and at last almost every day. (*Anecdotes*, i. 31)

---

[29] e.g. Charles Wogan, a Catholic companion from earlier days at Binfield, was captured at Preston and imprisoned in Newgate: he later escaped to join the Pretender, and went on to play a distinguished role in the service of the Stuarts. He accompanied Ormonde on a mission to Russia, he was deputed to choose a bride for James Edward from the courts of Europe, and he rescued the chosen princess when she was held a prisoner on her way to meet her fiancé, in one of the great episodes in Stuart legend. It was George I who was ultimately responsible for the arrest of Princess Maria Clementina. See Miller (1965) for a vivid and not too romantic account.

Sir William Trumbull took his 'retirement' in 1697, when he resigned as secretary of state to King William—some said he was pushed into leaving, but Trumbull himself complained that he had been treated like a footman while in office. He made his home at Easthampstead Park, 2 miles south of Binfield, and was already ensconced there when the Pope family arrived. His had been a notable career: academic distinction at Oxford, a prominent position as a civil lawyer and legal bureaucrat, a succession of posts as ambassador, a lord of the treasury—when this key ministry was still held in commission—and finally secretary of state. He had twice served in the Commons (from 1695 to 1698 representing Oxford University), had been knighted in 1684, and had been admitted to the Privy Council. It was a record of public service superior to that of Atticus—indeed, rivalling that of Cicero himself. If his ostentatious withdrawal from the court into contemplative life carried a suspicion of posing, there was nothing bogus about his active existence. Shortly after he went into retirement, he was offered and refused a senior post in the Admiralty.

The family had been at Easthampstead Park since the early seventeenth century, but the manor was bought by Sir William only on his return to the district in 1696. (The seller was John Dancastle.) Numerous monarchs had visited the manor, including Henry VIII, whilst James I had frequently come to the area to hunt, and had enlarged the park at a cost of £250. The first William Trumbull (d. 1635) had been granted Easthampstead Park in 1628, along with rights to 'free chase' by an agreement with Charles I, and undertook to keep 200 head of deer for the service of the royal hunt. However, his son and successor, also William (*c*.1594–1668), had to petition Charles II after the Restoration, explaining that the herd had been destroyed during the war and could not be replaced. He was relieved of his obligations, in exchange for a higher rent. The third William, Pope's friend, took as his second wife in 1706 Judith, daughter of the fourth Earl of Stirling. Knighted in 1684, the statesman derived pleasure in his elevation; an inscription on some communion plate in the parish church of Easthampstead, dated 1707, refers to his wife's parentage and to himself as *Eq[ues]. aur[icularius]*. The coat of arms he adopted made punning use of his surname, in what is known as 'canting arms': this took the form, 'Argent, three bull's heads razed sable and breathing fire' (*VCH Berkshire*, iii. 78–9; iv. 240). It is entirely apt to Pope's purposes that Trumbull should have inherited a district of the forest which had been despoiled as a site of the 'peaceful' pursuit of game by the savage slaughters of the Civil War (see *WF*, 325, and *SDW*, chapter 5).

Easthampstead Walk included the parish and park, but extended into neighbouring parishes to a circumference of 5 miles. In 1607 the park alone occupied some 265 acres, with 200–300 fallow deer and 60 red deer. The human population of the parish in 1676 was 168, a total which had increased to 566 by the time of the census in 1801. A lawsuit brought by the Marquess of Downshire in 1813 was resolved in the Court of Exchequer; it was determined that although the parish and manor had been part of the forest since immemorial time, the park was not included in the royal holdings. In effect, the crown had forest rights within the manor and parish, but not within the park. This was Trumbull's only substantial landholding until in 1714 he bought the manor of Great Shefford, in western Berkshire, from another Catholic, Sir George Browne (see also *SDW*, chapter 5). Two years later he died at his home: in his will, proved on 18 December 1716, he left some land at Priestwood in charitable trust to the poor of the parish. In fact the manor of Easthampstead had formerly been granted to Hurley Abbey, one of several monastic foundations around Berkshire which had been destroyed in 1536 during the Henrician reformation—something no alert Catholic boy could have missed (*VCH Berkshire*, iii. 78–9).

As verderer for Easthampstead Walk, Trumbull had one official duty in his retirement. This involved overseeing the forest law in one of the sixteen administrative districts into which the royal forest was divided. Whether he felt altogether happy in performing these functions does not emerge (see also *SDW*, chapter 5). Though he had only recently returned to the district, he had been born at Easthampstead, and could see himself as a returned Odysseus, ready to find a haven on his native soil. Moreover, he was a suitable appointment both in terms of his social standing and of his unquestioned loyalty to the establishment, especially to the Church of England. In fact Trumbull was almost the only Berkshire magnate whom Pope came to know well belonging to the Anglican faith. Otherwise, the young poet's milieu consisted of the Catholic squirearchy, represented by the Englefields at Whiteknights, near Reading; the Blounts at Mapledurham, a little further upriver; and the Dancastles, who held the manor of Binfield itself. There were many intermarriages between the gentry in this group, naturally in view of the limited choice of partner which their religion allowed them. The Blount sisters were the children of Anthony Englefield's daughter Martha; while Pope's close friend Caryll was related to the Englefields, as well as to other members of the local gentry. His wife was godmother, and he was godfather, to Martha Blount. In addition Pope's half-sister Magdalen lived with her husband Charles Rackett at Hallgrove, on the south-eastern fringe of the Forest outside Bagshot.[30]

Among Pope's male Catholic friends John Caryll, a member of a family long established in Sussex and Hampshire, figures most prominently. It is through the correspondence between Pope and Caryll that we can best understand the poet's situation vis-à-vis religion and politics in the years just before and after the appearance of *Windsor-Forest*. Unfortunately no letters survive from the period prior to 1710, although it is certain that the two men were acquainted from about 1703.[31] Caryll's uncle, who was well known to Dryden, had been implicated in the assassination plot against William III and fled to the 'court' of James II in France, where he became secretary of state and was awarded a barony. As a result he was deprived of his estate at West Harting, where the new mansion of Ladyholt stood, but later his nephew managed to reclaim it. When the Jacobite peer died in France on 4 September 1711, Pope wrote an epitaph for him—lines the poet he would later adapt to form the opening of his funeral verses for Trumbull (see p. 45, below).[32] In this original

---

[30] These local connections are discussed in more detail in *SDW*, ch. 5.

[31] See *Milieu*, 58. Erskine-Hill's important section on the Carylls (*Milieu*, 42–102) remains central to any understanding of Pope's early career.

[32] *CIH*, 461–2. The exiled peer would have been in Pope's head in Nov. 1712, when we know he was at work on *WF*. John Caryll had to go to France to settle his uncle's affairs, which occasioned an unkind reference in the press. Pope mentions this in a letter to Caryll (*Corr*. i. 152).

version, the incorruptible honour and high principle which these lines attribute to the subject belong specifically to a condemned Jacobite. The Secretary of State also had a sister, Mary, who was abbess of a Benedictine convent at Dunkirk, and one of the most devoted supporters of the Stuart line. Brother and sister died in 1711 and 1712 respectively, the years in which *Windsor-Forest* assumed its final shape, leaving their nephew as the leader of a dispersed but intensely faithful family, but one still under a sentence of outlawry—an irritant which would not be removed until 1724.[33] As Pope once put it, Caryll presided over a 'little Commonwealth' embodying traditional virtues of hospitality, patronage, and charity.[34] These values crystallized around royalist politics and Catholic faith, but they also represent a fundamentally *rural* outlook familiar to many among the target audience of Pope's poem.

As the titular dedicatee of *The Rape of the Lock*, John Caryll has been recognized as a considerable presence in Pope's life at this juncture; a relative of the Petres, he made frequent visits to Ingatestone Hall, where the notorious 'rape' was supposed to have taken place. However, he is also highly relevant to the concerns of *Windsor-Forest*. We have already seen that Pope kept Caryll up to date on the poem, and that his friend had some lines by heart prior to publication. Moreover, it was with Caryll that Pope most frequently exchanged information about their common acquaintances in the Catholic community, so far as we can judge from the surviving correspondence. For example, a letter Pope wrote from Binfield on 8 January 1713, just prior to the appearance of *Windsor-Forest* before the public, discussed the affair of Mrs Elizabeth Weston, which had divided what was usually a harmonious group (*Corr.* i. 171). Like the Englefields and the Racketts, Caryll had been caught up in the dispute, which shows the extent to which as head of a major clan he had to concern himself with affairs in Berkshire.[35]

Then there was his son John Caryll junior, to whom Pope also wrote a jocose letter around this time (see p. 50); the younger Caryll was soon to find himself in conflict with the new regime in the royal forests, when the Hanoverians took over power.[36] He married Lady Mary Mackenzie, whose brother the Earl of Seaforth was involved in the 1715 rising, suffered a forfeiture of his estates and honours, and only received a pardon as late as 1726.[37] In addition Pope's friend John Caryll had three further sons and six daughters. The girls almost all entered convents in France or what is now Belgium. One of the sons became a Jesuit priest and another served the Duke of Lorraine, who had harboured the Pretender at the end of Anne's reign. The next generation remained active in the Jacobite cause, notably John Baptist Caryll (grandson of Pope's friend), who was a vigorous polemicist at the time of the 1745

[33] See Mary's letter of 1710, despairing of the peace proposals then being mooted and 'not at all disponding of our Kings restoration, and I hope not farr off' (cited in *Milieu*, 62).
[34] *Milieu*, 82. The original usage in Pope (*Corr.* i. 475) is misleadingly negative.
[35] On Mrs Weston, see Rumbold (1989: 103–6). Further disputes arose concerning Mrs Anne Cope, a cousin of Caryll's, whom Pope met in 1711 (*Corr.* i. 129).
[36] For fuller documentation, see *SDW*, ch. 5.
[37] See *Milieu*, 97. Jacobites continued to pin their hopes on the Caryll family up to the 1745 rising.

rising, and served Charles Edward and his brother Henry, the last Stuart pretender, up to his own death in 1788.[38]

Among the first, if not the very first, to see the revised *Windsor-Forest* was John Caryll—hardly an accident. This was perhaps the closest friend Pope had: a Catholic, unquestionably a Stuart supporter, and a member of the recusant nexus in which the poet moved (for a fuller account of this matter see *SDW*, chapter 5). Moreover, according to one account, the forthcoming rising would deprive Caryll of his family estate, as had happened with his uncle: 'In 1715 the manor house [of West Grinstead] was again sequestered for recusancy; as a result the elder John went to live at Ladyholt.'[39] The recusancy order was not overturned until 1736, presumably on Caryll's death in that year.[40] Here we have yet another intimation of the fate in store for Pope's friends and co-religionists in the immediate aftermath of the Hanoverian accession.[41] In fact, the circumstances forge a close link between Lansdowne, dedicatee of *Windsor-Forest*, and Caryll, dedicatee of the contemporaneous *Rape of the Lock*. When the poem suggests that Lansdowne, recently created a baron, merits further honours (289–90), there may be a strong hint that Caryll (a baron only in the Jacobite peerage) deserves to wear his own orders of merit. Instead Caryll, like Pope, would very soon be driven off his paternal estate—and for Caryll that meant a substantial number of acres. As Erskine-Hill suggests, Pope's compliments about family loyalty imply a creditable allegiance to the exiled monarch, with all the sacrifices which such an idealism brought with it (*Milieu*, 82).

This close-knit group of acquaintances gave Pope a range of opportunities for friendship, from the flirtatious to the sporty and the convivial. Trumbull was on excellent terms with the recusant community.[42] However, he himself belonged to a slightly different category, as a worldly, well-travelled, and highly educated man who stood outside the faith.

Sir William's tenure as secretary of state had not been a happy one. Even before he took office, he defined himself as a churchman, and worried that he would not be acceptable to the Whig courtiers who controlled royal business. He found himself increasingly at odds with the Junto of peers, who were not well known for their piety, and he may have been forced into resignation in 1697. The differences came to a head over the trial of Sir John Fenwick and others involved in the assassination plot against William III. (A number of Jacobite suspects were imprisoned without trial: five of these were still in Newgate as late as the accession of George II in 1727, and one spent over forty years in custody with no formal arraignment.) It appears

[38] West Grinstead was the centre for Jesuit missionary activity in Sussex: see *VCH Sussex*, VI. ii. 102.

[39] It is possible that Caryll was able to achieve some sort of composition, because he was seemingly living at West Grinstead in 1717 and 1718 (*Corr.* i. 457, 512).

[40] *VCH Sussex*, VI. ii. 90.

[41] Caryll's family had been in France from the time of the arrival of George I to the outbreak of the rising, but whether for the purposes of immunity or actually to share in its preparation is not clear (see *Corr.* i. 265, 317).

[42] He was in close contact with Anthony Englefield at the time of Pope's visit to Worcestershire in 1707 (*New Letts.*, 392–3), and seems to have been regarded as the head of the social circle in which the leading Catholic families of Berkshire moved.

that Trumbull may not have been as zealous in hunting out renegades as his masters, the Lord Justices, wished.[43] He pointedly absented himself from the vote in favour of attainting Fenwick.

Another complaint made against Trumbull, at the time he left office, was that he was hard to reach, as he spent too much time in the country. In terms of the dialectic of *Windsor-Forest*, this signallized patriotic virtue, and reflected the secretary's disdain for courtly manoeuvring. Rather foolishly he cast himself as a kind of extra in a pastoral drama: 'I find myself a very unfortunate squire, for when I am in town I have nothing to do, and yet nobody will suffer me to be idle out of it.' This pose made it easy for intriguers such as Sunderland to undermine his position. When he gave up the seals to the king, Trumbull capped his message with a Virgilian tag: *Olim haec meminisse juvabit.*[44] It was a familiar line, drawn from the speech by Aeneas to his crew during the storm in Book I of the epic; but it does not seem to be straining matters to point out that this was one of Pope's own favourite quotations in later life. In his high-minded way Trumbull devoted his retirement to pursuits such as translating Boethius. The young boy could not have found a role model whose status as guide, philosopher, and friend was more heavily imbued with the tradition of rural contemplation.

The most startling thing about Trumbull's later career has never been mentioned by any student of Pope. This concerns the active support he gave to the fanatical high-flyer Henry Sacheverell. Early in 1709 a vacancy arose for the chaplaincy of St Saviour's, Southwark. Already well known in Oxford for in his intemperate views, Sacheverell became a candidate in a highly politicized contest for the position. One of his sponsors was the High Tory Lord Weymouth, the owner of Longleat, and another former MP for Oxford University. However, no more seems to have given Sacheverell stronger support than did Trumbull, as we can gauge from his correspondence with Ralph Bridges. His nephew was naturally interested in the affair, since he was chaplain to Henry Compton, the long-serving Bishop of London, who had been tutor to the Queen when she was a girl. Both Trumbull and Bridges campaigned on behalf of Sacheverell, and when the turbulent priest was elected to the office on 24 May, he received a letter of congratulation from Trumbull, expressing the hope that he would rise still higher in the Church. What Trumbull meant by this is indicated by his efforts to secure for his protégé the opportunity to preach before the Lord Mayor of London (*Sacheverell*, 58–9; Bennett, 109).

Less than five months later, these hopes were realized in a more spectacular fashion than Trumbull may have planned. Sacheverell delivered his fateful sermon at St Paul's on 5 November, making a new fireworks day out of this anniversary. Trumbull and Bridges watched the aftermath with rapt attention, with fears on the nephew's part that anyone in a black coat (i.e. a clergyman) would be subject to a new Test Act. Week by week Bridges reported to Trumbull on the mounting campaign to punish Sacheverell. The decision to go ahead with penal sanctions was attributed to the

[43] See Garrett (1980). One of the renegades was John Caryll, uncle of Pope's friend (see p. 32, above).
[44] Somerville (1962: 145).

usual suspects: 'The fate and impeachment of the poor Doctor was some time since fully concluded upon at the Kit-Cat Club, where my Lord Marlborough, they say, was present, assented to it, and has actually enrolled himself a member of that detestable society.' In all likelihood Godolphin rather than Marlborough pressed ahead with the trial, but Trumbull may have been willing to believe what he was told.

The episode culminated in the impeachment of Sacheverell before the House of Lords in February 1710—an event watched by the whole nation, and attended by the Queen in person. Lined with the French standards captured at Blenheim, and decked out by Christopher Wren, indeed Westminster Hall served as a fittingly 'impressive theatre in which to play out with due ceremonial one of the great set-pieces of British history' (*Sacheverell*, 124). Possibly Trumbull, who had just recently backed Sacheverell so forcefully, was thankful at the light sentence which the clergyman eventually received. Among those who voted against conviction was the same Henry Compton, along with the Archbishop of York, John Sharp. The *éminence grise* behind Sacheverell's defence had been Francis Atterbury, whose machinations figured in Bridges's reports and gave Trumbull concern at times.[45]

Little by way of thick description exists in our source, the correspondence between Trumbull and Bridges. But a clear pattern does emerge: a bitter opponent of James II like Bishop Compton who was still zealous for the Protestant faith, a former supporter of William III like Weymouth who was gravitating towards the new Tory camp, and an ex-secretary of state to the king like Trumbull, who was now nailing his colours to the High Anglican mast.[46] All these men embraced Sacheverell's cause, even though he was known to possess an unstable and self-dramatizing character. The claims of the High Church had superseded all others, and these loyal adherents of the Queen had in effect abandoned the consensual politics of Marlborough, Godolphin, and Harley, as this had operated during the early years of Anne's reign. It is very hard, if not impossible, to read the evidence in any other way: Trumbull, the devoted Church of England man, was also by 1710 an adherent of the doctrine of 'the Church in danger'. Another martyr was to endure his Calvary. If Sir William voted in the election that autumn, his ballot would have done nothing to arrest the Tory landslide. Meanwhile George Granville was returned in Cornwall, profiting by his allegiances: 'Trevarion and Granville, sound as a bell, | For the Queen, the Church, and Sacheverell' (quoted in *Sacheverell*, 252).

Pope always chose his mentors with care. His almost exaggerated sense of filial piety meant that he was seeking less a substitute parent than a second father. In one of Trumbull's earliest surviving letters to Pope, he compliments Pope senior on the quality of his artichokes, and suggests that Easthampstead will be unable to rival them—thus indicating one area of shared interest between the real and the adopted

---

[45] See *Sachverell*, 57–122, and Bennett, 111–12 for the information in this paragraph. Bridges continued to keep Trumbull informed of doings in the political world throughout Anne's reign.

[46] Sir William's brother Charles (1646–1724) was a nonjuror. Formerly chaplain to Archbishop Sancroft, he resigned his cure of souls after the Revolution. One condition Sir William had tried to impose when pressed by the king to remain in office as secretary of state in 1697 had been to obtain for his brother a position as prebend of Windsor, but this had not been granted.

parent (*Corr.* i. 17). Trumbull brought with him sophistication, experience, and contacts. His first wife had been the daughter of Sir Charles Cotterell, Master of Ceremonies at the court of Charles II. (Another daughter was the mother of General
James Dormer, later a good friend of Pope, and the founder of the splendid garden
at Rousham.) Cotterell's son Charles Lodowick succeeded as Master of Ceremonies
in 1686, and he was followed by his son Clement in 1710. The latter was described
by no less than Thomas Hearne as an able antiquarian, 'well skilled in matters of
proceeding and ceremony' (Hearne, 428). Between them, the Cotterells supervised
court ceremonial from the Restoration until the end of the reign of George II. As we
shall see in Chapter 4, Pope was a good friend of Sir Clement, and possibly knew his
father too. It is another means by which an interest in state pageantry could have developed in him. Moreover, Trumbull had travelled on the Continent in the company
of Christopher Wren and Edward Browne, son of Sir Thomas. He had been on a
diplomatic mission with Samuel Pepys, who thought him unduly timorous. Among
the younger men he encouraged was Henry St John, later Bolingbroke, who described Trumbull as his 'Dear Patron, Master, and Friend'.[47] It may well have been
Trumbull who introduced Pope to St John (see Chapter 2 below).

Equally important, from Pope's point of view, Sir William had patronized Dryden, and had encouraged the elder poet's version of Virgil, just as he was to promote
the younger man's Homer. When Jacob Tonson brought out the *Works of Virgil* in
1697, it inaugurated an era of unprecedented splendour in book-making. Although
it was by no means the first subscription venture, this represented literary patronage in its most extravagant form—conspicuous artistic consumption, in fact:

One hundred first subscribers paid five guineas apiece to have their names, titles, and coats of
arms conspicuously printed beneath the elaborate 'sculptures' or 'cuts'. Among the first subscribers were Princess Anne, Prince George of Denmark, and the boy Duke of Gloucester; numerous noblemen; and such high-ranking statesmen as Lord Somers, Lord Chancellor; the
Earl of Pembroke, Lord Privy Seal; and Sir William Trumbull, Principal Secretary of State.[48]

The so-called 'second' subscribers, who paid 2 guineas each, included Congreve and
Thomas Betterton, as well as the actresses Elizabeth Barry and Anne Bracegirdle.
The list shows Dryden's depth of penetration into the political elite, but also reflects
his poetic and dramatic contacts. The artistic circles represented are precisely those
which Pope would need to conquer, through the good offices of men like Trumbull.
We may find it to the purpose that the young man's first publishing opportunities
were opened up by a letter from Tonson in April 1706, in which the bookseller mentions that he has seen a pastoral in the hands of Walsh and Congreve (*Corr.* i. 17). By
this date, too, Pope had begun to correspond with Wycherley, who enjoyed Trumbull's patronage in his turn. The nexus of patronage, whether aristocratic or commercial, which was taking shape around the young poet could never have existed
but for his neighbour at Easthampstead.[49]

[47] Dickinson (1970: 7). [48] Lynch (1971: 120).
[49] Pope's first extant letter, addressed to Wycherley in 1704, reveals that Trumbull and Congreve had
spoken to him of Dryden by this time (*Corr.* i. 2).

In company Trumbull appeared cheerful and sociable, like many self-analytical people. He early discerned the boy's promise, and set about encouraging his literary ambitions. In the first extant letter, he is already comparing his protégé with the youthful Milton (New Letts., 391). Sir William borrowed, and as often lent, books (*Corr.* i. 17; New Letts., 392): it is likely, though not susceptible of proof, that some of the historical works which went into the making of Pope's poem came from the Trumbull collection. Young Alexander was already using the woodland as an al-fresco library: 'He then frequented Windsor Forest much', Martha Blount reported after the poet's death, 'and used to read whole days there under the trees, as I have heard him often say' (*Anecdotes*, i. 20). In part this was a health regimen. Around the age of 16, Pope became so ill that he wrote a letter of farewell to his 'most particular friends'. One of these, the Benedictine Thomas Southcote, felt such anxiety that he consulted the famous physician Dr John Radcliffe and carried medical advice down to Pope in Windsor Forest. 'The chief thing the doctor ordered him, was to apply less; and to ride every day: the following his advice soon restored him to his health' (*Anecdotes*, i. 30).

Trumbull sometimes worried about his talented but physically delicate protégé, as when he saw Pope depart for 'a dreadful long Journey into Worcestershire' in the summer of 1707. Soon afterwards he felt relief when the young man returned intact, and told Bridges, 'The little Creature is my darling more and more' (New Letts., 392–3).

A SUPERIOR BEING

As we have seen, it was from his nephew, Revd Ralph Bridges, that Trumbull first heard of a new poem on the stocks in October 1707: this was *Windsor-Forest* in its earlier guise. By 1708 Trumbull was sponsoring Pope's first efforts at translating Homer, with an intermediary in the shape of Bridges, a classically trained clergy-man based at Fulham Palace, who vetted the rendering of the 'Episode of Sarpedon' from Book XII of the *Iliad*. Trumbull himself made a show of lacking the right cre-dentials for a critic, but he did so in significant terms:

There may possibly be some happy genius's, who may judge of the natural beauties of a Poem, as a man may of the proportions of a building, without having read *Vitruvius*, or knowing any thing of the rules of architecture: But this, tho' it may sometimes be in the right, must be sub-ject to many mistakes, and is certainly but a superficial knowledge; without entring into the art, the methods, and the particular excellencies of the whole composure, in all parts of it. (*Corr.* i. 45)

This exactly expresses Pope's mature view of composition, and the appeal to Vitruvian principles suggests that the two men had spent some time considering architecture as a source of aesthetic values.

In the midst of his Homeric exercise Pope found himself summarily 'Proclaimed out of Town', when the rumour of a Jacobite invasion caused the government to issue a royal proclamation, which required all adult Catholics to depart 10 miles from the cities of London and Westminster (New Letts., 394). It was a reminder to Pope, should one have been necessary, that the hostile climate of William's reign might quickly be renewed, particularly under a jittery Whig administration. He duly returned to Binfield, from which he wrote to London friends of his life as uneventful but contented: *Prandeo, poto, cano, ludo, lego, cœno, quiesco*, he cites from Martial (*Corr.* i. 42). But the truth is that Pope's rustication was not the voluntary act of a free citizen. It was demanded of him by the government, on account of his faith; and it was aroused by a panic over the Pretender. Implicitly, Pope found his loyalty was suspect, because of his religion. Some half-hearted Jacobites perhaps reflected that they might as well be hung for a sheep as for a goat; while anyone with a tincture of pro-Stuart feeling would be inclined to think of the country as a safe asylum. Undoubtedly, at some level, the Forest came to symbolize for Pope an attachment to the old values and to the old faith—and perhaps to the old cause, as well.

The episode from Homer was soon ready for Sir William's perusal, and for his approval on narrow technical grounds, since he had disclaimed knowledge of the deeper aspects of poetic art. By this time Pope was approaching his first appearance in print. This ought to have taken place in Tonson's *Miscellanies*, due to appear in late 1708 but postponed owing to the death of the Queen's consort, Prince George. In the event the volume did not appear until May 1709. Last in the contents came the most striking piece the miscellany included, Pope's *Pastorals*, written according to his own statement as early as 1704. A distinguished team of critical advisers had given careful scrutiny to the manuscript, and among them Pope names both Trumbull and Granville. The former certainly knew of the work's existence by October 1707, when Ralph Bridges reported to his uncle that he had run into Pope, who 'designs in the spring to print [his Pastorals] . . . They are to be inscribed each to some Patron, one of which you are to be' (*TE* i. 41). Another adviser was Wycherley: Pope had written to the old man of his poem, punningly styled his 'green Essays', as far back as 1705 (*Corr.* i. 5).

Trumbull's name actually appears at the head of the first poem, 'Spring'. Oddly there was no dedicatory section to 'Winter', while the twenty lines devoted to Trumbull, Garth, and Wycherley (not present in the manuscript) detract from the work's numerological symmetry by increasing its line tally from 366 to 386 lines. As for 'Spring', it opens with a bold appropriation of Windsor as the muses' elysium: 'First in these Fields I try the Sylvan Strains, | Nor blush to sport on *Windsor*'s blissful Plains: | Fair *Thames* flow gently from thy scared Spring' (1–3). Behind the conventionality of the diction lies a proud recognition of Pope's adopted home. Again, in the dedicatory lines, he returns to the theme with an allusion to Trumbull: 'Till in your Native Shades You tune the Lyre' (12). The footnote adds: 'Sir *W. Trumbal* was born in *Windsor-Forest*, to which he retreated after he resign'd the post of Secretary of State to King *William* III.' A eulogium to a local hero, but with almost all the ingredients for a damaging critique of the former monarchy set in place. 'Retreat' suggests *otium cum dignitate*, but this absolute sense is hedged with the idea that the Secretary of State has executed a principled withdrawal from a position somehow morally tainted. In the text, Pope addresses Trumbull as 'too wise for Pride, too Good for Pow'r' (7); you, claims the poet, 'To all the World Illustriously are lost' (10)—the latter plays on a famous Dryden title and recalls the knight's distinguished role as a literary patron.

In the succeeding years Trumbull continued to watch over the progress of his young friend.[50] He asked Pope 'twenty times' to give him a sight of another translation, this time from Ovid (Pope to Cromwell, 15 December 1709: *Corr.* i. 77), but the poet was reluctant to do so until it had been thoroughly revised. Eventually 'Sapho to Phaon' appeared in a collective version of Ovid's *Epistles* in March 1712. Bridges had spoken well of the poet's debut in the *Miscellanies*, and Pope acknowledged this kindness (New Letts., 395–6). Much of 1710 was spent at Binfield, and so less correspondence with Trumbull survives. We can infer that contact was maintained from good wishes passed between Pope and his London friends, notably Wycherley and Cromwell, where the poet's Berkshire friends are often mentioned.[51] By 1711 Pope's circle was widening, as he came to know some of Caryll's acquaintances such as the family of Lord Petre (of *Rape of the Lock* fame). But he still had time to consult Trumbull for the loan of a copy of John Dennis's strictures on the lately published *Essay on Criticism*, in a letter dated 10 August 1711 (New Letts., 397).

Late in 1712 Pope was back at Binfield, working on his revision of *Windsor-Forest*. Evidently he had not kept Sir William fully apprised of his new plans for the poem, to judge from a letter by Trumbull to Bridges in May 1713: the knight's objection seems to have been that Pope had introduced his name into the work (l. 258), and not as some have assumed that the dedication had been transferred to Lansdowne.[52] There is no sign that any serious breach in relations occurred as a result of this 'slippery Trick' on Pope's part, which Trumbull must have recognized as a compliment which would preserve his memory for posterity. In June 1713, as we have already seen, Pope defended his procedure by saying that he had made the Forest appear very lovely in his poem, 'since I there told the World that Sir W. Trumbull was retird into it' (*CIH*, 464).

As we should expect, the two men continued to maintain close relations during the three years which elapsed between the publication of *Windsor-Forest* and the death of Trumbull. Soon, on 21 April 1713, Bridges could report to his uncle that opinion in London had come to rank Pope, on the basis of his new poem, as 'one of the greatest genius's that this nation has bred' (New Anecs., 345: see p. 60, below). On 19 November Pope told Trumbull of his plans to organize a subscription for the *Iliad*, and added:

I can honestly say, Sir William Trumbull was not only the first that put this [the Homer trans-

[50] For further evidence of their relationship and reading, see Trumbull to Bridges, 26 Mar. 1709, cited in New Anecs., 344.
[51] In Nov. 1708 Wycherley asked Pope to send his respects to 'that most Ingenious, humane, most honourable and most learned Gentleman Sir William Trumbold' (*Corr.* i. 54). The same correspondent often mentions Anthony Englefield, whom he knew well.
[52] See p. 11, above, as well as New Anecs., 345–6.

lation] into my Thoughts, but the principal Incourager I had in it, and tho' now almost all the distinguished names of Quality or Learning in the nation have subscribed to it, there us not one of which I am so proud as of Yours.

In December 1713 Pope was making enquiries on his patron's behalf regarding the estate of Sir George Browne ('Sir Plume' in the *Rape*), which Trumbull would subsequently acquire. Implausibly the poet cast himself as a 'plain Country Fellow, who never had either Ability or Inclination to make you a Compliment', a sentiment belied as soon as the ink was on the page (New Letts., 400). A month later Pope was describing the recovery of Ralph Bridges from a dangerous illness, and hoping to meet Richard Hill, an old friend of Trumbull who lived near Jervas in Cleveland Court. Once again Pope acknowledged the repeated kindness which Sir William had shown towards him (New Letts., 401).

One month later still, and Pope was able to send the expanded version of the *Rape of the Lock* to Trumbull, and to complain about his hectic town life, which included the campaign to raise subscriptions for *Iliad* project (New Letts., 402–3). Trumbull replied on 6 March 1714, with fulsome praise of the *Rape,* and advice to Pope to 'come away and take a little time to breathe in the country' (*Corr.* i. 212). By way of response, according to the text of a letter Pope printed in 1735, came an abstract reflection on fame and friendship (*Corr.* i. 312–13); but a much more businesslike missive was sent in reality, on 17 March, to update Sir William on the subscription and other news. Pope mentioned that he had become acquainted with Sir Clement Cotterell, and as George Sherburn remarks, this was the start of an important friendship (New Letts., 403). Trumbull's first wife had been Sir Clement's sister, and hence Pope treats this acquaintance as a further obligation to his mentor. We have already noted that Cotterell as the manager of court spectacle was an apt acquaintance for the author of *Windsor-Forest.* Pope discovers another characteristic turn for complimentary address: 'So much as you pretend to be out of the world, there is a fame you give at Easthampsted, which neither [Nicholas Rowe or I] would quit for any success here.'

Soon afterwards Pope returned to Berkshire. He passed much of the anxious summer of 1714 there, entertaining his Scriblerian colleague Parnell, and awaiting the outcome of the impending constititutional crisis. After a brief trip up to London, Pope advised Trumbull that he would soon be back in the country, and gave news of a portrait by Jervas of the Trumbull family, which was to prove long in the making (New Letts., 404). He then spent July in Binfield, back in his 'old way of life again, sleep and musing' (*Corr.* i. 239). There was time for a quick visit to Swift, across the other side of the county high in the Berkshire Downs, and then a short return to London 'on the death of the Queen, moved by the common curiosity of mankind'. Pope optimistically portrayed himself to Caryll as 'below all the accidents of state-changes by my circumstances, and above them by my philosophy' (*Corr.* i. 241). It is another version of the pose of detachment which Trumbull had helped to instil in him. Meanwhile the patriarch himself remained in the country, receiving messages on the Queen's final hours from one of her physicians (Churchill, iv. 516–17).

After the arrival of the new king from Hanover, and the departure of Swift for Ireland, Pope remained at Binfield for a time with Parnell. Busy on the first book of the *Iliad*, he could imagine that for Charles Ford 'Kings and Coronations in prospect are forever before you' (*Corr*. i. 249), a foreshadowing of the exquisite lines 'To Miss Blount, on her Leaving Town after the Coronation'. There, the poet portrays a young lady imprisoned in the country, dreaming of coronations rising 'on ev'ry green', with visions 'Of Lords, and Earls, and Dukes, and garter'd Knights' (*TE* vi. 125)—a reversion to the guest list for *Windsor-Forest*. The actual ceremony took place on 20 October, and Pope made a very short trip up to town on this occasion. At this period he more than once reflected on retirement, perhaps because so many of the Tory ministers he knew had been forced to make a hasty retreat as the Hanoverian regime took control. As the time came for the publication of the first book of the *Iliad*, he was obliged to spend more time in London. Ruefully he excused himself to Trumbull for a long silence, deploring the 'Drudgery of an author in correcting Sheets'. Never missing the opportunity for a flattering turn, he added, 'I never was so much employd in my Life, tho I have often been better employd; and particularly at those times when I had nothing to do but improve my self at Easthampstead'. In his reply Trumbull thanked Pope for a copy of the poem which had been published a week or two earlier, *The Temple of Fame*—'into which you are already enter'd'—and asked Jervas to make changes to the family portrait (*Corr*. i. 281).

This was in February 1715, and by that date the first whiff of paranoia concerning the Jacobite threat could be discerned. Inspectors were appointed to ensure that Catholics held no dangerous weapons, and this kind of intervention in his private life Pope could not altogether escape even when he went down to Binfield, as he did in the early summer. He may have dined with Trumbull on 4 July, according to one interpretation of a letter from Ralph Bridges (*Corr*. i. 303). The political temperature continued to rise, as Oxford was sent to the Tower, Ormonde fled to France, Habeas Corpus was suspended, and then the Riot Act was introduced on 20 July.[53] Pope jokingly asked if he might have 'Sanctuary' at Mapledurham with the Blount sisters, according to 'the practise of good Catholiques in times of Persecution, to fly to the Protection of the Virgin Mary'. He also wondered 'whether the Meeting of two Toasts and a Poet may not be as great a Riot, as can be made by any five in the Kingdome?' (*Corr*. i. 310–11). In reality the Act prescribed twelve as the number of persons who might constitute an illegal assembly.

We should not underestimate the sense of crisis at this juncture, or the severity of the measures taken in response. 'A suspension of the *Habeas Corpus* act was decreed for the period of six months; known Jacobites were arrested and Roman Catholics suspected of disloyalty had their arms and horses impounded; the standing army

---

[53] 'The Duke of Ormond is retired & become a Rival of the Courage of that other Noble Lord, whose health is joind with the Duke's at your Table' (Pope to Blount sisters, 23 July: *Corr*. i. 308). Obviously Bolingbroke is meant. The same letter had commended Oxford's fortitude under 'the utmost Weight of Affliction from Princely Power and Popular Hatred'. Jervas reported on Ormonde's flight in a letter to Pope around 2 Aug. (*Corr*. i. 311).

was doubled and garrisons put into towns judged to be Jacobite in sympathy (Oxford and Bath were two of these).[54] Pope knew all about these things: indeed, he was planning to visit Bath and Oxford in August 1715, and even to call at the house of Sir William Wyndham, who was arrested shortly afterwards as a leader of the Rising in the West (see *Corr.* i. 310–12). As we have seen, he had been worried since 1714 that he might lose his horse and comically envisaged that he might be 'disarmed' by the government (*Corr.* i. 246). Adopting an Old Testament phraseology, Pope wrote to the Blount sisters that 'The poor distressed Roman Catholicks, now Un-hors'd and Un-charioted, cry out with the Psalmist' (*Corr.* i. 309). As the panic rose, it was enough for persons to be 'reputed Jacobites' in order to drag them into the net. Moreover, the old requirement that Catholics should retire 10 miles from the City of London was hauled out again in a proclamation on 27 July. Meanwhile Pope busied himself reading the report of the committee which had been set up to investigate the conduct of the Oxford administration: thus a Whig body now sat in judgement on the doings of Harley, Bolingbroke, Ormonde, and Strafford in the last years of the Queen. (Matthew Prior had been a witness whom the committee questioned most eagerly, though he proved far from helpful.) It seemed as though the whole ideological basis of *Windsor-Forest* was being dismantled in front of the nation.

All these government actions came in the wake of extensive rioting. Flags had waved on the dates marking Anne's accession and coronation; a crowd proclaimed James III at Manchester in May, while shortly afterwards Royal Oak Day and the Pretender's birthday provoked disturbances in almost every major town. Then a series of 'meeting-house riots' directed against Dissenters followed in June and July, ceasing abruptly at the anniversary of the Queen's death on 1 August. The old favours and emblems came out, the cry went up for Bolingbroke and Ormonde, and when the High Church mob in Oxford, drawn from town and gown, heard a rumour that their heroes (including the Queen and Sacheverell) were to be burnt in effigy, they retaliated by setting a Presbyterian chapel on fire.[55] A ministerial response appeared unavoidable, and Catholics not irrationally spoke of their fears of a backlash against them, as the prospects for a rising increased. In Stuart eyes, the worst intuitions of *Windsor-Forest* were coming horribly true. Fair Liberty had seemingly deserted Britannia, and just as Astraea withdrew to the skies after the 'golden Years' owing to the impiety of mankind, so justice had fled with the departure of Anne.

After his prolonged ramble to Bath, Pope was back 'in the Forest' by early October (*Corr.* i. 317).[56] He sent to the Blounts 'all the Fruit Mr. Dancastles Garden affords', wrapped up in pieces of paper which he wanted to have safely returned, as they were 'the Only Copies of this part of Homer'. The epic translation was in truth largely executed in the Berkshire countryside: here Pope reifies the version on which he had laboured so long as an instrument of local hospitality. Then,

---

[54] Hatton (1977: 177).

[55] Monod, 179–94 provides the most comprehensive account of these disturbances.

[56] We now know that Pope and Gay travelled down to Bath together, stopping at Mapledurham to collect a horse for Gay (*CIH*, 470, where '1717' should read 1715).

towards the end of this tumultuous year, Pope wrote to Trumbull on 29 November 1715, congratulating his friend on his resolution 'of continuing in what you call your Cave in the forest'—a pose directly modelled on Trumbull's role in the poem. In words which had to be suppressed when the letter was printed in 1735, Pope referred to his father's need for quiet, and hoped that Trumbull might be able to 'soften' the malignancies of neighbours 'by [his] mediation and good Offices'. Then came a sounding passage:

I heartily joyn with you in wishing Quiet to our native country: Quiet in the state, which like charity in religion, is too much the perfection and happiness of either, to be broken or violated on any pretence or prospect whatsoever: Fire and sword, and fire and faggot are equally my aversion.[57]

This achieves the more plangency from the fact that the poet had produced his noble apotheosis of peace only two years earlier. The rising and its aftermath destroyed a consoling dream which had been nurtured in those early years at Binfield. Symbolically, perhaps, Pope planned to spend Christmas this year 'at home in the Forest' (*Corr.* i. 322).

As Trumbull was entering the last months of his long life, on 19 January 1716, he replied to Pope, commending the Pythagorean principle of silence. Pope's letter in return, dated 16 February, is perhaps the most deeply felt of all the messages the two men exchanged. 'Most Ministers', Pope observes with a possible eye on recent delinquents, 'only retreat from the publick as Rooks do from gaming, when they are ruined themselves after having ruind thousands'. Trumbull seems to be a 'Superior Being' (see p. 23, above); if people realized just how much the retired diplomat was to be envied for the happiness he had achieved, then he would 'certainly be Impeached for such an Interested, exorbitant Philosophy'. Trumbull would join the ranks of those recently faced with impeachment—Oxford, Bolingbroke, and now others: 'The Duke of Ormond is to be impeached for High Treason,' Lintot had told Pope on 22 June 1715, 'and E: Strafford for high Crimes & Misdemeanors' (*Corr.* i. 298).[58] Lansdowne and Prior were in the Tower, condemned among the titular and actual authors of the Peace negotiations. Hearing that Trumbull has been ill, Pope concludes with the hope of his recovery: 'The Health of Body is all I can wish for you, the health of mind you give yourself' (New Letts., 405).

It was at this point that the members of Pope's family were compelled to uproot themselves and settle in Chiswick (see p. 22, above). The poet found a new aristocratic patron in Lord Burlington, and he never again resided in the countryside which had meant so much to him. It formed a decisive landmark in his life. And at almost the same moment that he was obliged to part with his family inheritance, he lost his rural monitor, when Trumbull died at the end of the year. Within twelve

---

[57] *Corr.* i. 324: see also the reconstruction of this letter in *CIH*, 467–9.

[58] The Earl of Strafford had been another to run afoul of the parliamentary inquiry into the handling of the Utrecht negotiations, and faced impeachment in Aug. 1715 on six counts of high crimes and misdemeanours. In the end parliament was unable to sustain the charges and he received a pardon.

months Pope's own father was dead. The collected *Works* of 1717 embodied a new act of self-definition: in another smaller volume a month later, Pope would include his imitation of Martial, implicitly congratulating Trumbull on his eightieth birthday (something that death forestalled by three years), as well as the juvenile 'Ode on Solitude':

> Happy the man whose wish and care
> A few paternal acres bound,
> Content to breathe his native air,
> In his own ground . . .

The *Works* also found room for Pope's epitaph on Trumbull, who had 'died in his Retirement at *Easthamsted* in *Berkshire*, 1716'. Conventional enough on the surface, these lines preserve a studied vagueness on political issues: 'An honest Courtier, yet a Patriot too,|Just to his Prince, yet to his Country true . . .' (5–6). The force of these two verses seems to be something like, 'one who served at William's court, but refused to go along with the king's policies when they were not in the interests of the nation.' Trumbull possessed, we are told, 'A scorn of wrangling, yet a zeal for truth;| A gen'rous faith, from superstition free' (8–9), which can be plausibly decoded as, 'a stout Church of England man who resisted inherited prejudices against the Catholic community'. The next verse commends 'A love to peace, and hate of tyranny', which in the aftermath of the rising may bear strong implications against the Hanoverian regime. The epitaph comes to an end with the pious statement that Trumbull 'At length enjoys that liberty he lov'd.' Why 'At length'? The only ready interpretation for this line is that Trumbull is no longer forced to conceal opinions that were repressed in late years. It is virtually impossible to make sense of this ending in a way which will identify the contested notion of 'liberty' with the status quo under George I. Moreover, we can hardly forget that the lines about patriotism had originally been applied to Lord Caryll, a proscribed Jacobite. Could Trumbull have conceivably come to sympathize in his last years with the Stuart cause? Probably not—but this is a question we ought not to dismiss out of hand.

In the memorial list which Pope drew up of his departed relative and friends, the relevant entry reads: *Anno 1716, mens, Decem. obit Gulielmus Trumbull, olim Regi Gul. a secretis, annum agens 75* [*recte 77*]. *Amicus meus humanissimus a juvenilibus annis* (*EC*, vol. i, p. ix). The key word here could be translated 'most humane', but also 'civilized' or 'considerate'. Others on the list whom we have encountered are Dryden, Betterton, Anthony Englefield, Parnell, Wycherley, and Alexander Pope senior. This is the necrology which most applies to *Windsor-Forest*. Among those recorded who died in later years are Oxford, Buckinghamshire, Edward Blount, Congreve, Fenton, Atterbury, Gay, Arbuthnot, Peterborough and Pope's mother.

From this time on, the poet would moralize his song. He would become increasingly identified as the satirical scourge of modern manners. The effusive peroration of *Windsor-Forest* would give away to the sombre ending of the *Dunciad*. The prolonged tutelage which Pope enjoyed at the hands of Trumbull had directly contributed to the creation of one great poem, but from 1716 all that lay in the past. His future dream of retirement centered on another place, Twickenham, and it had to confront the realities of a different, Hanoverian, world.

> Happy next him who to these Shades retires,
> Whom Nature charms, and whom the Muse inspires,
> Whom humbler Joys of home-felt Quiet please,
> Successive Study, Exercise and Ease.
> He gathers Health from Herbs the Forest yields,
> And of their fragrant Physick spoils the Fields.
>
> (*WF*, 237–42)

Pope's links with the Trumbull family went on after the old man's death. Inevitably, the poet's surviving connections with Lady Trumbull made his embarrassment more acute when his brother-in-law became involved in the Berkshire Blacks episode.[59] Meanwhile, his coadjutor on the *Odyssey* and the Shakespeare edition, Elijah Fenton, was employed as private tutor to Trumbull's son, William IV (1708–60).[60] According to Hearne, Fenton left the younger Trumbull as his executor when he died at Easthampstead in 1730 (Hearne 415–16; *VCH Berkshire*, iii. 80). The outcome was a monument erected by Trumbull on the north wall of the parish church, with a short epitaph by Pope. In this Fenton is characterized in terms which recall the portrait of the happy recluse in *Windsor-Forest*:

> This modest Stone what few vain Marbles can
> May truly say, here lies an honest Man.
> A poet, blest beyond a Poet's fate,
> Whom Heav'n kept sacred from the Proud and Great.
> Foe to loud Praise, and Friend to learned Ease,
> Content with Science in the Vale of Peace.
> Calmly he look'd on either Life, and here
> Saw nothing to regret, or there to fear;
> From Nature's temp'rate feast rose satisfy'd,
> Thank'd Heav'n that he had liv'd, and that he dy'd.
>
> (*TE*, vi. 318)

Once Pope had composed a mock-epitaph on Fenton in a letter to William Broome, his other assistant on the *Odyssey*: 'Fenton's body is buried on Windsor Forest; his εἴδωλον glides over those lawns' (*Corr.* ii. 296). The presence of the woodland remains with Pope all his life.[61]

---

[59] Lady Trumbull was worried by the activities of an agent provocateur who was a son of the local clergyman, Revd John Power: see *SDW*, ch. 5, for fuller information. She died in 1724.

[60] Fenton, a nonjuror, had been patronized by Bolingbroke; he included a tribute to Lansdowne in his *Epistle* to Thomas Southerne (1711), a poem which affords many interesting contrasts with *WF*.

[61] Pope had written to Broome two years earlier about Fenton's sojourn in the forest: 'I have formerly experienced how amusing, and solitary, and studious a scene that is' (*Corr.* ii. 204).

Shortly after the passage just quoted on the subject of gathering health-inducing herbs, the poem envisages its rural philosopher in the act of studying the heavens, as he 'marks the Course of rolling Orbs on high' (*WF*, 245). This is a posture sometimes congenial to Pope himself. After attending astronomical lectures by William Whiston in July 1713, as he described his mood to Caryll: 'This minute, perhaps, I am above the stars, with a thousand systems round about me, looking forward into the vast abyss of eternity, and losing my whole comprehension in the boundless spaces of the extended Creation, in dialogues with Whiston and the astronomers.' (*Corr.* i. 185). This, we again recall, proceeds from the same year that *Windsor-Forest* appeared. At some level the enlightened retirement of the hermit in this poem represents Pope's own deep aspirations, in his quest for physical and mental stability. In the end he would find the bland Addisonian pantheism of these 'boundless spaces of the extended Creation' inadequate bases for his metaphysical outlook; but at the time of writing this poem he identified to some degree with the happy recluse of the Forest.

We tend to think of Binfield as Pope's boyhood home, and thereafter as little more than an occasional retreat. Pope certainly encouraged his self-image as a man about town, and even referred to himself at the time of his family's expulsion from the Forest as 'truly a Citizen of the World' (*Corr.* i. 344). But this was in some measure a defensive posture, adopted as Pope faced the loss of his inherited plot of ground. The reality was different. Binfield was his ordinary home from the age of 12. Over the next few years he made occasional visits to London, for example when he was brought up to Will's Coffee House in 1705. Chevalier Charles Wogan, who claims to have introduced him to this society, had spent two or three summers in Binfield. He told Swift that he conducted the teenager 'from our retreat in the forest of Windsor', and had dressed him up 'à la mode'. Sherburn is right to suggest that the young Pope would have appeared 'somewhat rustic' to metropolitans (*Career*, 46).

From about 1708 the young man spent more time in the capital. Usually these stays coincided with business surrounding the publication of his works. Occasionally he strayed further afield, undertaking some early rambles—less extensive than those he conducted later in life—or visiting friends such as Walsh or Caryll. However, he still passed several months each year in Berkshire at this period. For example, he was in the country for most of 1710, and described himself to Cromwell as 'dead in a Civill Capacity, as a useless Member of the Commonwealth buryd in solitude' (*Corr.* i. 88). But the hitherto untraced reason for this self-immolation may be a proclamation requiring papists to retreat 10 miles from London, issued in March 1710 (see pp. 38–9 above). A later part of this message jokes that Cromwell may be not enough of a papist to address the dead. During the course of this same communication, Pope contrives in turn an epitaph for himself, and one for Thomas Betterton.[62] The renewal of the proclamation a year later would explain Pope's sojourn in the country, some of it spent at Caryll's home (*Corr.* i. 115), but mostly passed in Berkshire.

---

[62] Pope had known Betterton 'from a boy' (*Anecdotes*, ii. 23). They perhaps came together since the actor had retired from the stage to a farm near Reading. In 1712 Pope edited surviving literary works by his friend for inclusion in Lintot's miscellany: see *Career*, 50 and *Corr.* i. 142.

The first time that he may possibly have resided in London for the greater part of the year was 1712, and even then he came back at Binfield in November, when he wrote to Caryll about his work on *Windsor-Forest*, and also in the following January, when he wrote to Lansdowne thanking the peer for serving as dedicatee (see above, p. 15). During 1713 he made his longest sustained stay in London thus far, chiefly at the home of Charles Jervas. It is possible that he did not get away into the country until late November, despite plans to return to Berkshire in the summer. The year 1714 began in a similar way, with Pope busy in Scriblerian circles. But by April he was back in the country, working on his Homer translation, and this was his main base for the next few months. As we have seen, Parnell paid a long visit in the summer, and according to a playful letter from Pope he fell in love with Miss Blount (presumably Teresa). The two men wrote a joint letter to Gay, inviting their friend to taste the delights of country living: 'If you have design either to amend your health, or your life,' observed Pope, 'I know no better Expedient than to come hither' (*Corr.* i. 222). At one time Swift, too, was supposed to be coming down, but events ruled this out (Swift, *Corr.* ii. 74). For Pope, the death of the Queen prompted only a brief trip to the capital, prior to a stay in Bath along with Parnell. Certainly he was in Berkshire at Christmas, for he visited Whiteknights with John Caryll.

After a short time at Binfield during January 1715, the next year saw another prolonged period of residence in London, followed by a summer-long spell in the Forest. Pope's departure to work on Homer, late in May, prompted the poem 'A Farewell to London' (*TE* vi. 128-30). Ironically, this valediction to the 'dear, damn'd, distracting Town' was composed shortly before he was cast out from his rural home for good. Hoping that he might persuade Caryll to visit Mapledurham, so that they could meet, he drew attention to the salutary example set by local people as regards his own literary labours: 'The unwearied diligence I observe at this season in the country people affords one good lesson: that I ought to make hay while the sun shines' (*Corr.* i. 292). Gay came down for a brief visit in June, working on his poem *Trivia*. With a brief intermission this sojourn at Binfield probably lasted until late into the autumn.[63] By December the poet was planning to get away from London again, 'designing to pass the Christmas at home in the Forest' (*Corr.* i. 322).

At the start of 1716 Pope was in the country with Rowe; and then in March, as we have seen, he came to make a farewell visit to his home. In August, he planned on returning to Binfield shortly and on seeing the Blount sisters at Whiteknights (*Corr.* i. 350-1), but it is not clear whether this intention was realized. From that time on, his journeys to the district naturally became fewer, as he no longer had any permanent base there. 'My journy to Mr Caryl's', he tells John Dancastle in May 1717, 'is become so uncertain in point of time, that I cannot say when I could hope to call at Binfield.' He hopes rather to see Dancastle at Chiswick, 'where I shall now be pretty constantly' (*Corr.* i. 403).[64]

---

[63] A letter to Martha Blount tentatively placed at this juncture by Sherburn refers to unseasonably good weather, which increases Pope's taste for 'rural pleasures' and his reluctance to go back to the 'hurry, confusion, noise, slander, and dissension' of town life (*Corr.* i. 319).

[64] One or other of the Dancastles did visit Chiswick from time to time (see *Corr.* i. 445), which would have kept Pope abreast of local news.

Around the same date, Pope writes to the Blount sisters, 'I can't express the Desire I have of being Happy with you a few days (or nights, if you would give me leave) at Mapledurham; where I dare say, you relish the Delights of Solitude and shades, much better than I can be able to do till I see you' (*Corr.* i. 409). The compliment is uncharacteristically awkward—perhaps a sign that too much reality was pressing in on courtly platitudes. We know for certain that he passed two days at Binfield in September, en route to Oxford.[65] By December 1718 Pope was restricted to sending Christmas greetings to Thomas Dancastle, with a poignant hint of years gone by: 'I am not so totally dead to all past obligations, as not yet to remember how many woodcocks you have indulgd me in about this Season, when we drank methgelin & chatted together. I really wish myself a few frosty days in the forest' (*Corr.* i. 524). Signing off with 'Ancient fidelity and affection', the poet conjures up a picture of warmth and hospitality which would never quite be matched in his life.

Most of Pope's important early works were composed, in whole or in part, in Berkshire. Probably this category includes the first version of the *Rape of the Lock*, as well as earlier drafts, at least, of the *Essay on Criticism*. The evidence shows that Trumbull's encouragement led the young poet to embark on a full-scale translation of Homer (*Corr.* i. 45-6), and it was at Binfield that the opening sections were largely written. Pope was constantly trying to inveigle his friends down into Berkshire: 'I am very glad you continue your resolution of seeing me in my Hermitage this summer,' he tells Wycherley in April 1710 (*Corr.* i. 84). But the old poet, who had been promising to come to Binfield since 1706, remained hard to entice: 'Nothing cou'd allure Mr Wycherley to our Forests.'[66] Sometimes Pope offers hyperbolic descriptions of the advantages that would accrue. Writing after returning to his 'own Hermitage, from Mr Caryl's,' he teases Cromwell in May 1711: 'I expect much, towards the Civilizing of you in your Critical capacity from the Innocent Air and Tranquillity of our Forest, when you do me the favour to visit it.' Cromwell should prepare for his *villeggiatura* by reading a pastoral of Virgil or Theocritus every morning, and he might hope that 'Travelling and Daily Airing in an open field' might cool any tendency to critical animosity. 'In these Fields', the letter concludes, 'you will be secure of finding no Enemy, but the most faithfull and affectionate of your Friends' (*Corr.* i. 116). It is graceful badinage, of course, but with just a hint of a serious point. 'I have past part of this Christmas', Pope writes to Steele on 30 December 1711, 'with some honest Country Gentlemen, who have Wit enough to be Good-Natur'd, but no manner of Relish for criticisme or polite writing, as you may easily conclude when I tell you they never read the Spectator' (*Corr.* i. 139). The Forest could not cure all human woes, any more than pastoral could banish death and disaster; none the less, retirement from the noise and bustle of the city had evidently some power to refresh the literary imagination.

---

[65] This journey is described more fully in *SDW*, ch. 5.

[66] *Corr.* i. 52. Similarly, Pope invokes a frequent satiric formula in a verse letter to Cromwell in 1707: 'sooner shall . . . | The *Granvilles* write their Name plain *Greenfield*, | Nay, Mr. *Wycherly* see *Binfield*' (*TE* i. 26).

Apart from all this, Pope's health—never robust—suffered when he was exposed to the smoky atmosphere of London. In January 1709 he visited Wycherley, but had to retreat owing to the damage done to his 'little, tender, and crazy Carcase', as his friend termed it (*Corr.* i. 55). A year later, in May 1710, he writes to Cromwell of having recovered at Binfield from 'a dangerous Illness which was first contracted in Town' (*Corr.* i. 87). On this occasion, it is true, headaches continued to plague him in the country (*Corr.* i. 95), but more often Pope enjoyed comparatively good health in the Forest. Indeed 1711, a year much of which was spent in Berkshire, appears to have been more free from sickness than almost any period in his life, to judge from its absence in the poet's correspondence. By contrast, in the letter closest in date to the publication of the poem, he complains of headaches as he idles away his time in London: 'I am carrying on the Ceremonials of Civility, and forget the Essentials of Friendship'.[67] In the following October, he told Gay that he had been 'perpetually troubled with sickness of late', while in town, and planned to go down into the country in a month's time. There he could hope to pass his time, as he informed Swift, 'without hindrance of Busynesss'(*Corr.* i. 195, 201). Early the next year, back in London, his situation had not improved: 'I hope in a little time to get into the country, for it begins to be necessary to me', he told the elder Caryll, 'my headaches increasing daily' (*Corr.* i. 214).

Beyond question, the tribute in *Windsor-Forest* to active pleasures of the 'vig'rous Swains' whose blood 'Youth ferments' (93–6) attains a more acute poignancy from the fact that Pope, young though he still was, would never be able to engage in such sports. The most he could enjoy was a long ride in the Forest as an occasional treat. Much to the point is this passage in a letter Pope wrote at Binfield in April 1710:

I assure you I am look'd upon in the Neighborhood for a very Sober & well-disposd Person, no great Hunter indeed, but a great Esteemer of the nobler Sport, & only unhappy in my Want of Constitution for that, & Drinking. They all say 'tis pitty I am so sickly, & I think 'tis pitty Thay are so healthy. (*Corr.* i. 81)

The emphasis on rude physical health to be found in the hunting section of the poem may be part compensatory, part a kind of vicarious experience, symbolizing the good health, good nature, and uncomplicated well-being which were bound up in the Horatian idea of retirement.

An even more instructive pendant to the last passage quoted exists in another letter written at Binfield. This was from Pope to Caryll junior, in December 1712:

While you are pursuing the Sprightly Delights of the Field, springing up with activity at the Dawning Day, rowzing a whole Country with Shouts and Horns, & inspiring Animalls & Rationals with like Fury and Ardor; while your blood boils high in ev'ry Vein, your Heart bounds in your breast, & as vigorous a Confluence of Spirits rushes to it at the sight of the Fox as cou'd be stirrd up by that of an Army of Invaders; while the Zeal of the Chace devours the whole man, & moves him no less than the Love of our Country or the Defence of our Altars cou'd do. While . . . you are thus imployd, I am just in the reverse of all this Spirit & Life,

---

[67] Pope to John Caryll jr., 1 Mar. 1713, in *CIH*, 462–3.

confind to a narrow Closet, lolling on an Arm Chair, nodding away my Days over a Fire, like the picture of January in an old Salisbury Primer. (*Corr.* i. 163)

Amazingly, no editor has used this letter to gloss *Windsor-Forest*. Yet it comes as close as could be to a particular section of the text, and revelatory in regard to the poem's general aims. If we look at the passage on seasonal sports alongside the letter to Caryll, with special attention to ll. 93–100 and 147–50, we find *sprightly* (94), *field* (100), *spring*, as verb (111), *rowze* (150), *horn* (96), *blood* (93), *bounds* (99), and *spirits* (94). There are also many near-synonomous expressions: *eager* for 'Ardor', a *flood* of spirits for 'Confluence', *sylvan war* for 'Chace', *pleasing toils* of the woods and fields for 'sprightly Delights of the Field', and so on. The reference to 'an Army of Invaders' calls up the same images as the famous comparison in Pope's poem to the sons of Albion investing the enemy lines (106–10).

The congruence does not end there. In the letter, love of country and defence of 'our' altars are yoked together in a single locution. Similarly *Windsor-Forest* unites a strong vein of patriotism with an attempt to defend 'the church in danger', most obviously in the portrayal of England under Williamite control (65–72), where the 'Fanes' are ravished from gods, the temples stand naked, and all that is left are gaping tombs and empty choirs. This ruined landscape may owe something to Pope's sense of the desolation wrought when Henry VIII dissolved the monasteries, as we shall see in Chapter 3. However, other parts of the poem suggest that we are meant to think of the effects of militant seventeenth-century Protestantism on the traditional order, with the consequent need to rebuild churches, literally and figuratively.

This letter dates from the precise juncture when Pope was making his final changes to *Windsor-Forest*. At the start of this chapter we noted that he wrote to Caryll senior on this same day, 5 December 1712, with news of the progress of the poem. It makes no sense to assume that the letter to Caryll's son was unaffected by recent work on the text of the hunting episode. The extended comparison shows that Pope consciously viewed himself as a spectator, one whose health and avocations debarred him from talking part in vigorous country sports, in the way that his correspondent was able to do. Later Pope tells his young friend that he would like to make a trip to Sussex, to spend time at Findon with Caryll and a friend, 'though I believe you would run away from me as fast as your Horses cou'd carry you' (*Corr.* i. 164). The only two differences apparent in the two passages are first, the shift of season (winter in the letter, as normal for fox-hunting; summer in the poem); and second, the fox as prey rather than a stag. Caryll lived close to the Bere, Woolmer, and Alice Holt forests, where a stock of fallow deer remained; but these could be hunted only by qualified persons, and this was out of the question for the Carylls. John junior was taken up by a keeper of the forest of Bere in 1716 (*Hunters*, 137–8), and the family was in trouble again a few years later. Caryll would have had to confine himself to foxes.[68]

---

[68] These episodes are charted in *SDW*, ch. 5. One Mr Roper, whom Pope described to Caryll as keeping 'the best pack of fox-hounds in England', later rented Ladyholt and leased the stable and kennels at Findon (*Corr.* i. 156).

Two weeks later, Pope wrote to Caryll senior, and again noted the impending appearance of *Windsor-Forest*. Once more his language recalls the hunting episode in
the poem, with its mention of youthful 'Spirits' aroused in the autumn. In his letter
Pope confesses that his health has suffered during the cold of winter: 'My spirits, like
those in a thermometer, mount and fall thro' my thin delicate contexture just as the
temper of the air is more benign or inclement' (*Corr.* i. 165). Again we feel that his
evocation of 'the bold Youth' (*WF*, 155) operates as a compensatory device for his
own limited involvement in 'manly' experience.

As he approached the age of 50, around 1736, Pope undertook an imitation of one
of the most famous of Horace's lyric poems, *Odes*, IV. i. The well-known phrase *Non
sum qualis eram* . . . was rendered in a fairly literal fashion:

> I am not now, alas! the man
> As in the gentle Reign of My Queen *Anne*.
>
>   (*TE* iv. 151)

Perhaps this is little more than a middle-aged threnody for lost youth. However,
it contains a germ of truth: for all the tribulations and trials of the years of the
Oxford-Bolingbroke ministry, there had been a glimpse of existential peace when
the window of opportunity seemed to open for the Stuarts after the treaty with
France. Pope's physical health, never strong, did not improve as his life went on,
and the equanimity of spirit he hoped to preserve in the 'gentle' years of Anne
would find itself tested and sometimes fractured by tumultuous events, as soon as
the Hanoverians arrived.

2

Biography

In order to come to a full understanding of the poem, we need to locate it within Pope's career as a writer. This is because the composition of *Windsor-Forest* marks a moment of transition as he developed from a primarily descriptive poet, concerned with the matter of traditional genres such as pastoral, to a primarily satiric poet, dealing with public themes and urban issues. In the first section of the chapter, an attempt will be made to provide the context for a literary shift which parallels the swerve in Pope's private life as he left the Forest for Chiswick, on the edge of the city. This juncture follows his absorption in the Scriblerus group, with its links to the political and social elite of the metropolis. All these changes are, so to speak, immanent in the text of *Windsor-Forest*, as they were imminent in the poet's biography. The other individual who plays a central role in the genesis of the poem is its dedicatee Lord Lansdowne, a figure of more salience than most criticism has allowed. His political and literary connections help to define the governing elite, who represented a world Pope was still seeking to enter—in part by the instrument of *Windsor-Forest*, the first poem he had written on a theme of national importance and topical urgency.

A CHANGE OF LIFE

Pope celebrated his twenty-fifth birthday in 1713. The year marked a decisive shift in the direction of his writing, and in his sense of himself. Up to this time, he had practised mainly as a pastoral and descriptive poet, with one important discursive work, *An Essay on Criticism*. The only substantial work of satire he had produced was the two-canto version of *The Rape of the Lock* (1712), and even this had presented itself in a volume of miscellanies as almost an occasional piece. From this time forward Pope was to announce himself as a major satirist, with the five-canto *Rape* in 1714; as a creator of modern epic, with the translation of the *Iliad* from 1715; and as a writer of deeply felt Ovidian lament—she-tragedies in miniature—with *Eloisa to Abelard* (1717). Moreover, *vers de société*, hitherto an inconsiderable branch of his output, took on a new force with brilliant miniatures such as the epistle to Miss Blount after the coronation (1714) and *A Farewell to London* (1715). A more serious mode of Horatian verse epistle appeared with the lines to Addison (*c*.1713). Pope's last exercises in the older vein came with *The Temple of Fame* (1711), *Messiah* (1712), and *Windsor-Forest*.

We can see, too, a realignment of his friendships. The older men who had guided his early career, such as Wycherley and Garth, were no longer so important to him. His first prolonged spells in the capital brought him into the circle of Addison and Steele, but there were signs of a cooling in relations with both men by the end of 1713. Steele had quarrelled first with Swift, but as the year proceeded both Gay and Pope had been drawn into the orbit of the Tory propagandists, and battle lines were drawn up.[1] Initially Pope had been recruited to support Addison's high-minded tragedy *Cato*, and he actually wrote the prologue to this work, even though he harboured doubts about its qualities as a stage play. When the premiere arrived on 14 April, the two parties vied in their efforts to claim the work as their own. The Whigs saw the denouement as an assertion of liberty and an implicit condemnation of the peace negotiations, with a tyrannical ministry abusing its responsibilities and neglecting the nation's allies. Bolingbroke attempted to wrest the initiative by handing fifty guineas to the leading actor, Barton Booth, and congratulating him on defending liberty 'against a perpetual dictator'. In terms of the drama, this would point at Booth's character Cato, who resisted the military ambitions of Caesar. According to Tory ideology, it meant the ministry's principled opposition to Marlborough, who had besought the Queen in 1709 to appoint him captain-general for life. A pamphlet war ensued over the true meaning of *Cato*, and Pope found himself embarrassingly straddled across the political divide. The truth was that he had burned his boats with *Windsor-Forest*. His efforts to portray himself as a neutral looked increasingly strained, and his breach with Addison became almost inevitable.

Besides, Pope was now well integrated into a different circle, made up of the group who were to form the Scriblerus Club. It was late 1712 or early 1713 before Pope met Swift, but the older man had already created a web of literary associates.[2] Swift had been acquainted for some time with Dr John Arbuthnot, physician to the Queen, and Thomas Parnell, an Irish clergyman. Apart from that, Swift had moved in the circle of the ministerial leaders Robert Harley and Lord Bolingbroke: the latter had figured in the 'Society', a group of politicians and wits formed in 1711 to foster 'the improvement of friendship, and the encouragement of letters'.[3] Harley was studiously kept out of this set, but George Granville (soon to become Lord Lansdowne), Matthew Prior, and Arbuthnot were members. Indeed, the suggestion has been made that it was Lansdowne who introduced Swift to Pope. The group sometimes met when the Queen was at Windsor, as Swift regularly found occasions to attend court there.

Meanwhile, Pope had made the acquaintance of John Gay in the first half of 1711. Thus the pieces were in place for the inception of the Scriblerian scheme when Pope wrote to Gay on 23 October 1713, mentioning Swift's approval of his plans for a

[1] These two men had met by 1711, perhaps through the agency of Henry Cromwell.
[2] Sherburn states (*Career*, 71) that 'before the end of 1712 Pope was acquainted with Gay, Swift, Arbuthnot, and Parnell': this is probable but not quite certain.
[3] Bolingbroke's letter of June 1711, cited by Kerby-Miller (1950: 5).

satiric campaign against modern learning (*Corr.* i. 195). By this date Pope and Swift were dining together, and the meal in this particular week had cost Swift 5 shillings, as he carefully noted in his account book. A few days later, Swift made one of his regular visits to Windsor.[4] We shall turn to the works of the group in the next section of this chapter. Meanwhile, it bears re-emphasis that the membership of the Scriblerus Club comprised Pope, Swift, Gay, Arbuthnot, and Parnell. They were later joined by Harley, now Earl of Oxford, even if the Queen's first minister remained something of a specter at the feast, playing the role of a fifth Beatle whom no one could quite place. Yet his presence served to bring Pope closer to the centre of power. It was not *Windsor-Forest*, but the poet's next considerable work—the augmented text of *The Rape of the Lock*—which was submitted for the Lord Treasurer's advance approval (see *Corr.* i. 207).

Dr John Arbuthnot deserves more attention in this context than he has generally received. When Pope made his acquaintance around 1712, he was already the author of the most successful work of satire on behalf of the peace process, *John Bull*. Evidence of his continuing interest in the topic lies in a memorandum concerning the articles he sent to Lord Oxford on 16 April 1713.[5] In this he argues that if the 'faction', i.e. the Whigs, are not willing 'to come in to an unanimous vote of an Address of generall thanks & approbation' for the treaty, they must expect to have 'their proceedings narrowly enquir'd into'. At just about the time that he met Pope, Arbuthnot produced another widely read satire, *The Art of Political Lying*. This he sent down to Swift on 9 October 1712 from Windsor (*JTS* ii. 502), where his duties often called him—he knew the locale of the castle as well as almost anyone.

Quite apart from his literary attributes, the doctor held an important place at court. He had served as a royal physician since 1704, at first mainly in the service of Prince George, and then in 1709 he was appointed physician in ordinary to the Queen. As such, he occupied a position of delicacy as well as political relevance. He has recently been described as 'an observant and assiduous courtier', who was intimate with all the principals in struggles involving the Queen, Oxford, and Bolingbroke (Bucholz, 166). Naturally the Marlborough faction poured scorn on a court whose shining lights were 'the Scotch doctor and Abigail' (Green, 212). It was in his private lodging at Kensington Palace that the wedding of Abigail Hill and Samuel Masham took place, a true marriage of court insiders which the Queen attended. Because the doctor had the privilege of lodgings at each of the royal residences, he was certainly well apprised of the fluctuations in Anne's health—a topic of endless speculation (see *JTS* ii. 561).[6] Soon he would be one of the seven physicians present at her deathbed.

Outside his clinical skills, Arbuthnot had gained equal renown as a scientist: he

---

[4] For these details, see Thompson (1984: 161).

[5] Printed in Beattie (1967: 413–16).

[6] According to the generally well-informed Abel Boyer, in order to conceal the true state of the Queen's health, only Arbuthnot was permitted to inspect her gouty leg in the last year of her life (quoted by Green, 302).

was very friendly from Oxford days with David Gregory, the astronomer and former tutor to the Queen's ill-fated son the Duke of Gloucester.[7] Another close ally was Edmond Halley, who probably had a hand in the doctor's election to the Royal Society in 1704. When Anne visited Cambridge a year later and knighted Isaac Newton (see Chapter 4, below), Arbuthnot was in her retinue and one of many among her attendants to be rewarded with a doctorate.[8] He served with Newton, Gregory, and Christopher Wren on a committee of the Society to investigate publication of the star catalogue drawn up by John Flamsteed, and later in 1710 he was appointed to the Board of Visitors set up by the Queen to oversee the Royal Observatory. Newton and Wren were again among his colleagues, and they were joined by Halley and Dr Richard Mead.[9] He served along with Wren, Halley, and Newton on the commission to build the new churches (see Chapter 4, below). All these were valuable contacts, and some of the individuals named came into Pope's own circle shortly afterwards. There is a final connection to the events surrounding the Peace: in June 1713, the Hanoverian resident reported in a message concerning George Frideric Handel that 'The queen's physician, who is an important man, and enjoys the queen's confidence, is his [Handel's] great patron and friend, and has the composer constantly at his house.'[10] This was at the time of the national service of thanksgiving to commemorate the settlement at Utrecht, an occasion which will be described in Chapter 3.

At the climax of *Henry Esmond*, Thackeray gives a crucial role to Arbuthnot: this is to take the Pretender in his coach to meet the Queen in a garden behind the Banqueting House. In sober reality, the doctor may never have been a committed Jacobite, even though his family embraced some vehement supporters of the Stuart line. His father, most obviously, had been deprived of an episcopalian living after the departure of James II. The doctor's own brother Robert had fought at Killiecrankie for James; he later became a banker in France, served the Pretender, and was involved in financing the 1715 rising. After this the doctor was bullied by the English government into breaking off contact with his brother, but their relations were resumed by 1718. At that time, Robert Arbuthnot wrote to the Earl of Mar that his brother was 'the object of hatred of all the Marlborough faction and is forced to live amongst them with great circumspection, for they would be well pleased to find a hole in his coat'.[11] Possibly, 'Marlborough faction' here is a crude synecdoche for Whigs and Hanoverians at large.

In the same year John Arbuthnot visited France and passed time with Bolingbroke.[12] A close literary ally of Swift, he was also a colleague of men like Lansdowne

[7]   On Gregory, a Jacobite who died near Windsor in 1708, see also Ch. 6, below.

[8]   The first edition of *Tables* of ancient coins (1705) was dedicated to Anne's consort Prince George.

[9]   It was St John who pushed through the scheme for a Board of Visitors, which may have had some obscure political motivation: as soon as the Queen died, Newton lost influence at court and Flamsteed correspondingly gained in power. See Cook (1998: 380–7).

[10]   Quoted in Burrows (1994: 73). Handel received a pension from the Queen at the end of this year: it seems overwhelmingly probable that Arbuthnot had some share in recommending this grant.

[11]   Beattie (1967: 28–9).

[12]   Aitken (1968: 92). Robert Arbuthnot, who subscribed to the *Odyssey*, was known to Pope by 1724. Six years later Pope commended him to Caryll as one resembling his old acquaintance in point of 'friendship and opinions' (*Corr.* ii. 255; iii. 81).

in the Society (see below, pp. 81–2). Through Lansdowne, Swift had assisted in forwarding the military career of another brother, George Arbuthnot, who also served the Pretender in 1715.[13] In any case, as an antiquarian and student of numismatics, the doctor possessed areas of interest close to some of Pope's own.

Plainly, then, Arbuthnot was very well equipped to assist Pope; but no evidence exists to show that he made any contribution to the writing or revision of *Windsor-Forest*. Their acquaintance may have blossomed just too late. Nevertheless, in his range of concerns the doctor exemplifies the way Pope was moving at this stage of life: they became friends, we might say, as a result of their shared preoccupations—many of which showed up in the text of the poem. It is precisely from 1713 that Pope starts to display strong interest in heavenly bodies: and the first manifestation is not his attendance at Whiston's lectures,[14] but a passage of *Windsor-Forest*, where the hermit-philosopher studies the skies (245–56). Possibly it was Arbuthnot who drew to Pope's attention the catalogue of constellations which his friend Halley had edited in 1712, *Historia coelesti*. This work was based on the observations carried out by Flamsteed: its main patron was Prince George, Anne's consort, and as we have seen Arbuthnot served on the committee set up to oversee the project. Again, the adventurers who were to 'tempt Icy Seas . . . round the frozen Pole' (*WF* 389–90) would follow in the wake of Halley, who (according to Hearne) 'went as near the Southern Pole as any man yet did'.[15]

A piquant fact is that, when Swift got to know the doctor in 1711, the two men were staying at Windsor Castle. Their first joint expedition was a ride in the Forest, as Swift told Stella: 'Dr. Arbuthnott, the Queen's physician and favourite, went out with me to show me the places: we went a little after the Queen, and overtook Miss Forester [*sic*], a maid of honour, on her palfrey, taking the air . . . We met the Queen coming back' (*JTS* i. 363).[16] Not long afterwards, another riding party took place on 'the finest day in the world'. This time Swift and Arbuthnot joined in 'a noble caravan' which accompanied the Duke and Duchess of Shrewsbury, as well as Samuel and Abigail Masham. 'We rode in the great park and the forest about a dozen miles,' Stella was informed (*JTS* ii. 376). Thus the Scriblerian circle began to form, among the forest walks in the very shadow of the Castle, with the Queen regularly on the spot *in propria persona*. For much of the material in his poem, Pope did not have to cast his eyes very far afield.

The most intriguing question concerns Bolingbroke, who was never a member of the Scriblerus circle. Until recently it was assumed that Pope's first meeting with the minister took place in the winter of 1713, that is after the appearance of *Windsor-Forest*. However, the most careful student of the relations between these two men

---

[13] See *JTS* ii. 370, and Aitken (1968: 40, 84).

[14] See *SDW*, ch. 6.

[15] Quoted by Cook (1998: 329). Hearne refers to Halley's journeys to the South Atlantic in 1698–1700.

[16] In the following month Swift and Arbuthnot made a repeat foray at Windsor, visiting Cranbourne Lodge and Windsor Lodge, which was allotted to the Duchess of Marlborough. Swift called the lodge and its setting 'the finest places for nature & plantations; and the finest riding upon artificial roads made on purpose for the queen' (*JTS* i. 363).

has set out a detailed and convincing argument, to suggest that their acquaintance already went back a number of years. Brean Hammond draws on a variety of evidence to bolster this conclusion. Oddly, he does not mention one of the most direct statements Pope made to Spence, 'I was early acquainted with Lord Lansdowne, Garth, Betterton, and Wycherley—and not long after St John' (*Anecdotes*, i. 32). However, he uses the findings of Bolingbroke's biographer, H. T. Dickinson, to make clear that the young St John was a protégé of Pope's own mentor, Sir William Trumbull. As Hammond remarks, it has not been sufficiently recognized that Pope had 'a common friend, with whom they were both intimate in the first decade of the eighteenth century—a friend, moreover, who exercised considerable formative influence on both their careers'.[17] Study of the Trumbull correspondence will readily support this view.

Early on, St John declared that he had chosen Sir William for his 'pattern', whilst Trumbull gave the younger man a sermon on the strong disposition of the English towards liberty. It would be rash to interpret this as a purely Whiggish concept. When St John achieved his first ministerial office, as secretary at war in 1704, he thanked Trumbull, whose interest with Marlborough he regarded as crucial. At this time St John was seeking to detach himself from the High Tory faction, including the Earl of Jersey, who had recently been displaced from office. In the following years he continued to ask for Trumbull's advice. On one occasion he urged the retired Secretary of State to step on to the political stage in the capital again, or at least 'advise, like an old actor, those that do'. This had long been a theme of the correspondence: back in 1698 St John had regretted Trumbull's withdrawal from public life, but noted that he could not be equated with Atticus, who had been content to do no harm in his years of retirement. This collocation anticipates *Windsor-Forest* (258), as Hammond observed. For two years while out of parliament in the middle of Anne's reign, St John had posed as a rural squire at Bucklebury, which lay about 20 miles from Easthampstead in the western corner of Berkshire. Here he wrote, 'If I continue in the country, the sports of the field and the pleasures of my study will take up all my thoughts.'[18]

It was not very convincing. Predictably, by the summer of 1710 St John was back again, canvassing Trumbull's support in a bid to stand for the parliamentary constituency of Berkshire, where the old servant of the crown, if not the young Roman Catholic Pope, had a vote and some limited electoral influence. Swift was to visit St John at Bucklebury in August 1711 (*JTS* i. 326), and George Granville often stayed there; but it is not certain whether Pope ever went at this period.

Evidence of direct contact between Trumbull and St John ceases at this point. We might conclude that this was because Trumbull, the man described by Dickinson as 'the experienced, moderate Tory'[19] found St John's political conduct in office too ex-

---

[17] Hammond (1984: 24).
[18] Letter of 1 Sept. 1709, quoted in Dickinson (1970: 66). When Swift stayed at Bucklebury in 1711, he reported to Stella that St John acted like 'a perfect country gentleman', who enquired after the wheat and went to visit his hounds (*JTS* i. 326). It sounds like earnest simulation of the rural gentry.
[19] Dickinson (1970: 4).

treme. What renders this doubtful is the evidence that, as time went on, Pope continued to move in circles where Bolingbroke was admired, where high Tory measures were deemed appropriate in the effort to secure the peace and to resist the power of the Marlborough faction, and where the danger to the Church of England was regarded as one of the most acute issues facing the nation. If indeed Pope knew St John from an earlier period, there is no sign that Trumbull ever sought to urge him to discontinue the friendship.

An important piece of evidence is provided by biographical memoranda left by Pope's disciple Jonathan Richardson, seemingly dictated by the poet at Twickenham in 1730. Hammond reprints these anecdotes, but they need to be cited here. The *Pastorals*, according to Richardson, were crucial to Pope as they

Occasion'd his being known to Dr. Garth, Mr. Walsh, Mr. Gr[a]nville, with whom he both Convers'd & Corresponded, & Sir Wm Trumbal, with whom on his having then resign'd the Office of Secretary of State, he lived familiarly being his near Neighbour. By some or other of These he was soon Introduc'd into the Acquaintance of the Duke of Shrewsbury Lord Somers Mr. St. John and Ld Halifax. (New Anecs., 347)

Richardson proceeds to describe how Pope became known to Addison and was asked to write a prologue for *Cato* early in 1713. 'About the same time,' we are told, 'his Friendship began with Dr. Arbuthnot & Dr. Swift, who brought him into the Familiar Acquantance of the Lord Oxford, then Lord Treasurer.' This account presumably derives straight from Pope, and it unequivocally places the meeting with St John much earlier than the first Scriblerian contacts. In this narrative, St John belongs with the group of patrons who oversaw the writing of the *Pastorals*, and he is identified with the phase when Trumbull presided over the teenage poet's development in the Forest (see also *Anecdotes*, ii. 616–18).

A factor which has left out of account here is the association of St John with George Granville: the two men were on close terms by the turn of the century, and the younger man owed some of his first parliamentary consequence to Granville's patronage. In a volume of miscellanies published in 1701, a pindaric ode by St John hyperbolically cast his friend as 'Strephon, the glory of our British plains'. Just as the lute of Orpheus was conveyed by the muses to the heavens, so now 'One more bright Star shall in that Field appear, | And Granville's Pen adorn the glitt'ring Sphere.'[20] Here is the germ of Pope's idea that Lansdowne's verse will lift the turrets of Windsor 'nearer to the Skies', in verse which will 'add new Lustre to the Silver Star' (288–90). The tribute to Lansdowne at this point in *Windsor-Forest* indirectly celebrates Bolingbroke, who had constructed, a decade earlier, the image of Granville as an English pastoralist.

One of Pope's earliest biographers—though admittedly not the most reliable of all—was to put forward a different claim. This was that Addison had pressed his new friend Pope to show the prologue for *Cato* to Oxford and Bolingbroke, in order to make clear to them that this was not intended as a mere 'party play'. We cannot be sure if this is true: if it were, it would again put back the date of the meeting between

---

[20] Quoted from Charles Gildon's *New Miscellany of Original Poems* (1701) by Handasyde (1933: 25).

Pope and Bolingbroke. More instructive is the evidence which Hammond draws to-gether concerning the Tory clergyman Joseph Trapp. He points out that Pope men-tions Trapp in a letter written to Ralph Bridges in February 1712 (New Letts., 396). A few months later, Swift was boasting to Stella, 'I have made Trap Chapln to Ld Bullinbroke, and he is mighty happy & thankfull for it' (JTS ii. 550). As a conse-quence, Trapp dedicated his poem on the peace to Bolingbroke when the Utrecht settlement was announced. This provoked a comment from Bridges to Trumbull on 21 April 1713, which has already been quoted in part:

> I do herewith send you Dr. Sacheverels Sermon presented to You by Him and also Mr. Trapp's Poem on the Peace which . . . [is] generally reckond a good one. They both agree in crying up our Mr. Pope & say that He is one of the greatest genius's that this nation has bred. If he were but a Protestant, tho' I can't say that wou'd make him a better Poet, yet I can't forbear saying that I should like Him better. (New Anecs., 345)

It is hard to say which is the most astonishing feature of this letter. What it reveals is that Sacheverell as late as 1713 regarded Trumbull as an ally who would be flattered to receive a copy of his sermon—doubtless the one he had preached at St Luke's, Southwark, to mark the end of his three-year suspension from the pulpit. Almost as remarkable is Bridges's hearty espousal of Sacheverell and Trapp as critics on Pope, with a personal reservation only in respect of the poet's Catholic faith.

We can reasonably assume, in the words of Hammond, that 'with connections as intricate as this', it is more likely that Pope was renewing an acquaintance which went back to the earlier years with Trumbull, than that he was meeting Bolingbroke for the first time in 1713. According to Hammond again, this friendship had not ripened into anything more than 'mutual respect and a recognition of considerable community of interest', before Bolingbroke's flight to France in 1715.[21] Even this may be slightly to underestimate the case. Pope thanked Bolingbroke in the first volume of his *Iliad* translation for helping with the text and for acting as his patron (*Prose*, i. 254). This might be a routine formula; but it was presented to the world just three months after Bolingbroke had gone to join the Pretender, and in the very month that he was accused of high treason. Swift realized immediately that Pope was 'pretty bold in mentioning Lord Bolingbroke in that Preface', and Pope himself remarked that 'the Whigs say now B. is the Hero of my preface' (*Corr*. i. 301–3). It is hard to imagine a more public statement of loyalty, to the man if not also to the cause.

The later relations of the two men are complex and relatively well known. For our purposes, what has emerged is the strong possibility, to put it no higher, that Henry St John entered Pope's life as a satellite of the Trumbull circle which had presided over the beginnings of *Windsor-Forest*. In that respect, he would be in very much the same position as his good friend George Granville, another Tory whose life history was to describe a similar curve to that of St John for several years.

An inventory of the goods in Pope's villa at Twickenham was taken after his death. Among his possessions were a large number of paintings of his friends. In adjoining

---

[21] Hammond (1984: 30, 32).

rooms which looked out on to the Thames were hung portraits of individuals such as Martha Blount, Wycherley, Betterton, Lord Peterborough, Bolingbroke, Swift, Atterbury, Gay, Arbuthnot, Parnell, Prior, Burlington, Bathurst, Samuel Garth, Lady Suffolk, and Lady Mary Wortley Montagu. The last two of these, along with Atterbury and Burlington, had not yet swum fully into Pope's ken in 1713, although Lady Mary was evidently an acquaintance by July 1715 (*Corr.* i. 309). The poet may have met Burlington in early 1714, when the Earl entered a subscription for six copies of the *Iliad*; by April 1716 he was preparing to settle at Chiswick 'under the wing of my Lord Burlington' (*Corr.* ii. 339).[22] Atterbury was also a correspondent by 1716, and a year later he felt sufficiently assured of their friendship to suggest that Pope might wish to convert to the Anglican faith, following the death of Alexander Pope senior, as a means to his 'Own ease and Happiness' (*Corr.* i. 451). All the others on the list had become part of Pope's life when *Windsor-Forest* came out, in ways which render their riverside aspect truly symbolic of Pope's intellectual and political horizons at the time of the poem's appearance (see *Garden and City*, 244–58).

THE SCRIBLERIAN MOMENT

From the time of his conscription to the Scriblerian group, Pope would acquire all the stock-in-trade of a metropolitan man of letters—fame but also notoriety, friends but also enemies. His brushes with figures such as Ambrose Philips and John Dennis would set a pattern for life. The plan about which he wrote to Gay (above, p. 54) had its roots in ironical commendation of 'the high productions of *Grubstreet*', and henceforward Pope would be locked willy-nilly into the struggles of the literary marketplace. Already Swift had clashed with the notorious Edmund Curll, who issued a pirated volume of his *Miscellanies* in 1711, as the indignant author told Stella (*JTS* i. 269). Around this time Curll was busy among other tasks in sending out *Reasons which Induced Her Majesty to Create . . . Robert Harley . . . a Peer*, which appeared on 31 May 1711, as well as the preamble to the patent of John Robinson as Lord Privy Seal. He would go on to publish a secret history of the peace talks in 1712, and the next year *Observations on Cato*. Prominent on his list for 1714 is a fresh edition of Ashmole's *History of the Most Noble Order of the Garter* (see Chapter 5, below), with a portrait of the 'new' George, that is the Prince of Wales, later George II. Pope's serious squabbles with Curll did not begin until 1715, after which he spent the rest of his life in prolonged combat with the bookseller. It is a sign of his move into a buffeting urban world, after his exodus from the pastoral scenes of his youth.

Now Pope began to work regularly in a collaborative vein, especially with his Scriblerian colleagues. The work of these coadjutors was bound to influence his own writings. Swift had himself delivered his views on the peace negotiations in his famous pamphlet *The Conduct of the Allies*, published in November 1711. Here Swift

---

[22] See also *Life*, 286, for the timing of events here. Pope had already planned to spend three or four days 'in high luxury' with the Earl, probably at Burlington House in Piccadilly (*Corr.* i. 338). John Gay had become one of the Burlington circle by this date.

argues that Britain had been reduced to a pawn in the extended power play of the Austrian Empire and Holland, and had gained nothing for herself from the war. Naturally, Marlborough and the City of London were to blame, as in Swift's bitter papers for the *Examiner* in 1710: 'I have here imputed the Continuance of the War to the mutual Indulgence between our General and Allies, wherein they both so well found their accounts; to the Fears of the *Mony-changers*, lest their *Tables should be overthrown*' (Swift, *Prose*, vi. 43). From the start, the whole international struggle had been a conspiracy to weaken the landed classes: it had promoted 'the ruin of the public interest, and the Advancement of a Private', designed to 'increase the Wealth and Grandeur of a particular Family' (Swift, *Prose*, vi. 59). It was magnificent but it did not have much to do with reality. As a clincher, in a vein of bitter eloquence, Swift denounced the cost of the war: 'It will, no doubt be a mighty Comfort to our Grandchildren, when they see a few Rags hang up in *Westminster-Hall*, which cost an hundred Millions, whereof they are paying the Arrears, and boasting, as Beggars do, that their Grandfathers were rich and great' (Swift, *Prose*, vi. 55–6). The 'Rags' so contemptuously dismissed were the battle honours of Blenheim; and the scene in Westminster Hall which would have been brought back to contemporary readers was the show trial of Dr Sacheverell in 1710, a miscalculation by the Whigs which had directly led to the downfall of its ministry in favour of the Harley government (see *Sacheverell*, 251–4).

The *Conduct* was by far the most successful anti-war statement in the long pamphleteering battle; as a consequence, the work earned its author an increased authority with Harley and, especially, Bolingbroke. But nothing could reconcile the Queen to Swift. Equally quixotic was *The Windsor Prophecy*, an attack on the Duchess of Somerset, who was now occupying the place in the Queen's affections which Sarah Churchill had formerly held. This came out just before Christmas 1711, and stymied Swift's hopes of becoming dean of Wells. The prophecy, it is claimed, had been found in a small lead box under the cloisters at Windsor; it was 'written on a parchment sealed with the badge of St. George'. Swift reanimates the old story that the Duchess had connived in the murder of her second husband—who happened to be a relative by marriage of Lord Lansdowne's new bride, Mary Thynne (see p. 78, below).

Pope did not want to cause offence, as Swift happily did in these works, and he eschews all direct reference to Marlborough, a matter discussed in Chapter 6, below. All the same, the implicit politics of *Windsor-Forest* are very close to those of the *Conduct of the Allies*. The war has been destructive and inimical to the wellbeing of the country interest. It was a theme taken up in Arbuthnot's *John Bull* in 1712, where the story concerns Bull's efforts to settle a lawsuit with his rural neighbour Nicholas Frog (Holland) and his ultimate settlement with Lewis Baboon alone. Avoiding tactless detail on diplomatic issues, Pope still manages to recall the time when the United Provinces came as 'suppliant States' in order to 'bend before a *British* QUEEN' (384). And he may also have recalled Swift's devastating image of the tattered banners which would serve as a lasting reminder of national indebtedness, as financiers jacked up the burden of credit to service the war.

At just the moment *Windsor-Forest* appeared, Swift was hard at work on his *History of the Four Last Years of the Queen.* He composed this, his most ambitious foray into historiography, between September 1712 and May 1713; a draft was sent to Sir Thomas Hanmer in February. According to its printed title page, the essay was written at Windsor Castle; although the book was not published until long after Swift's death, his holograph (preserved today at the castle itself) confirms this fact. The chief aim of the *History* is to defend the conduct of the peace negotiations against Whig protests that too many concessions had been made to the French and that the allies had been betrayed. Here Swift vindicates the decision to create the twelve new peers, on the grounds that the membership of the Lords had been so composed that a countervailing force was required. This is a more ringing declaration of support than Swift had given Stella at the time: 'Our new lords patents are passed', he had written on the last day of 1711; 'I don't like the expedient, if we could have found any other' (*JTS* ii. 452). At the end of his book, Swift gives way to a certain economy in truth, when he claims that the proclamation of the peace on 5 May was greeted with 'louder Acclamations and more Extraordinary Rejoicings of the People, than had ever been Remembered' (Swift, *Prose*, vii. 167). The nation understandably heaved a sigh of relief at the end of the long hostilities, but a large part of the public remained unconvinced by the provisions of the treaty.

As indicated, the *History* did not reach print until 1758, despite the fact that the manuscript made several peregrinations between London and Dublin in quest of a publisher. Its contents were never a total secret. On 6 March 1713, the very eve of the publication of *Windsor-Forest*, Ralph Bridges wrote to Trumbull that Swift was working on an 'account of the history of the negotiations at Utrecht'.[23] Pope was only just getting to know Swift at this date, though they had both appeared in the volume of Tonson's *Miscellanies* in 1709 and already had a number of acquaintances in common. It is unlikely that Pope saw any part of the manuscript of the *History* before he completed *Windsor-Forest*, but he would have been aware of the Tory line on the Utrecht negotiations, which are elaborately set out in the *History*—Swift had access to the government's correspondence with the envoys at Utrecht. When Swift read *Windsor-Forest* immediately on publication, and commended it to Stella, he doubtless found its attitude to the peace in complete accordance with his own views.

The evidence is closely to hand. In the very month that the poem came out, Swift expressed his views on the political situation in a letter to the Archbishop of Dublin. In this he reports the continuing expectation that parliament will meet and the Queen will announce that peace has been signed. He proceeds: 'I hope, my Lord, we shall in Time unriddle you many a dark Problem, and let you see that Faction, Rage, Rebellion, Revenge, and Ambition, were deeply rooted in the Hearts of those who have been the great Obstructors of the Queen's Measures, and of the Kingdom's Happiness' (Swift, *Corr.* i. 340). Pope could hardly have put it better—but he did, in ten eloquent verses of allegory at the end of his own work (413–22).

---

[23] Quoted by Ehrenpreis (1962–83: ii. 745).

An equally direct relationship exists with Gay's poem *Rural Sports*, which actually preceded *Windsor-Forest* into print in January 1713, though here it is generally believed that Gay had seen Pope's work in advance of publication. Just before *Windsor-Forest* appeared, Pope wrote to John Caryll of 'five or 6 authors [who] have seized upon me, whose pieces of quite different natures I am obligd to consider . . . —and my own Poem to correct too' (*Corr.* i. 174). This may indicate that Pope had vetted the text of *Rural Sports*, which is addressed to him as one 'who the sweets of rural life has known' and who despises 'th'ungrateful hurry of the town'. The work proceeds:

> In Windsor groves your easy hours employ,
> And, undisturbed, yourself and muse enjoy.

(3–4)

The poem was later much revised; but the 1713 text commends Pope for his evocation of the 'soft flowing *Thames*' with its attendant river gods and nymphs.[24] Gay had evidently been impressed by *Windsor-Forest*, for he sent a copy of the poem immediately after publication to his friend Maurice Johnson, as he had done with *Rural Sports* two months earlier. Johnson, as an antiquarian, was among those best qualified to relish the 'Entertainment in Windsor Forrest' which the work afforded (Gay, *Letters*, 2).

Recently, David Nokes has drawn a persuasive contrast between the two poets. Pope, 'in offering his Arcadian vision of Windsor under a Stuart monarch . . . assumes the authoritative tones of one whose sense of belonging inspires an intuitive sympathy for the secret languages of nature and cultural history'. On the other hand, Gay 'writes as one not fostered in, but excluded from, an Arcadian paradise'.[25] Gay, long immured in the town, obtains only a brief refuge in his Devon homeland: as Nokes observes, he 'enters the countryside not to recover some lost patrimonial Eden, but as a stranger, a trespasser and a fugitive'. The contrast in perspective emerges the more clearly since both poems give detailed descriptions of pursuits such as hunting and fishing, and both celebrate a landscape renewed by the coming of peace:

> Oh happy plains! remote from war's alarms,
> And all the ravages of hostile arms;
> And happy shepherds who, secure from fear,
> On open downs preserve your fleecy care!
> Where no rude soldier, bent on cruel spoil,
> Spreads desolation on the fertile soil;
> No tramping steed lays waste to the rip'ning grain,
> Nor crackling flames devour the promis'd grain.

(357–64)

Gay generalizes a process which is tied in Pope to particular modes of destruction: the War of the Spanish Succession, and the ravages of royal tyrants, notably William II, in the Forest.

---

[24] Gay (1974: i. 41).   [25] Nokes (1995: 102–3).

On the other hand, Gay's picture of a restored paradise has much of Pope's mythopoeic and iconographic reification of stock images:

> Let Anna then adorn your rural lays,
> And ev'ry wood resound with grateful praise;
> Anna, who binds the tyrant war in chains,
> And peace diffuses o'er the cheerful plains;
> In whom again the bright Astrea reigns.
>
> (371–5)

This contrast is plain if we compare *Rural Sports*, l. 374 with *WF*, 41–2. The express political charge is less in Gay, who had no particular loyalty to the Stuarts, and celebrates Anne as just ruler rather than as a member of a particular dynasty. In terms of the wider poetic strategies, Gay may be said to be more domestic, more anecdotal, and less resplendent in diction. Both men may have looked at manuals of hunting and angling; they probably both knew Oppian's *Halieutics*, translated at this date by William Diaper (posthumously published in 1722), and they both look back to the *Georgics* as a source of primary inspiration. *Rural Sports*, overall, is a simpler work than *Windsor-Forest*, but one inhabiting the same broad generic area of poetry. It is very curious that so rarely have the two been examined in the same frame of reference, a process which is useful in isolating the complex and sophisticated design of Pope's composition, and yet serves to confirm the genuine merit of Gay's in its narrower scope.

A more gauche effort to celebrate the peace came in Gay's prologue to *The Shepherd's Week*, published in April 1714. This is addressed to Bolingbroke, although it tries to have things both ways by complimenting Oxford on his imperial achievements: the first minister 'gives to *Britain Indian* mines' (68). Gay later congratulates Oxford as founding father of the South Sea Company (see Chapter 6, below), and versifies a commonplace in referring to 'Sweet *Peace that maketh Riches*.'[26] Unluckily for Gay, the poem also gives grateful thanks to Dr Arbuthnot for saving the life of the Queen, after a false report of her death. It was a work whose optimism was falsified even more rapidly than anything Pope had written in *Windsor-Forest*.[27]

One other poem from a Scriblerian hand has very close affinities with our key text. This is a work by Thomas Parnell, whom Pope probably first met in 1712, when the Irish clergyman came over to England following the death of his wife. At this time Swift was active in seeking preferment for Parnell (see *JTS* ii. 586). As we have already noted, Parnell gave Pope great assistance in the summer of 1714 with the *Iliad* translation: he turned part of *The Rape of the Lock* into Latin (according to Goldsmith, while the poem was still incomplete), and he made a translation of a poem by Ausonius, which was not printed until after his death. This all suggests that the section of *Windsor-Forest* based on *Mosella* may possibly have received the attentions of Pope's classically adept friend.

---

[26] Gay (1974: i. 93–5).
[27] On Gay's 'anxiety' concerning his patrons and the mounting political crisis, see Wood (1988: 111–12).

The work in question, 'On Queen Anne's Peace', remained unpublished until 1758. Parnell's editors observe that it is impossible to date the poem with great accuracy, though it seems to allude vaguely to the thanksgiving service in July. They also propose that Swift may have had a hand in persuading Parnell to suppress the item, though there appears to be no real evidence of this. The close parallels with *Windsor-Forest* prompt a more likely conclusion that Parnell understandably chose not to enter into direct competition with his friend.[28]

Parnell's long poem runs to 338 lines in couplets. It opens with the familiar doublet used by Pope: 'Mother of plenty, daughter of the skies, | Sweet Peace, the troubl'd world's desire, arise' (1–2). The Queen is soon invoked: 'Great ANNA claims the song; no brighter name | Adorns the list of never-dying fame' (7–8). After a compliment to Bolingbroke, the poet goes on to describe the twelve years of costly struggle in which the nation has been engaged. Prayers for a successful conclusion to the war are sent up by a guardian angel to the heavens, described in heraldic terms ('Where orbs of gold in fields of Azure lie', 38). A litany of ministerial champions is introduced, headed by Oxford and Bolingbroke, with Bishop Robinson and the Earl of Strafford 'waft[ed]' over to the peace conference as Britain's 'Agents'. Then, more lamely, 'The Congress opens, and it will be peace' (113)—no match poetically for Pope's parody of Genesis (*WF*, 327–8). Others who earn a mention include Shrewsbury and Hamilton, whose death in his duel with Mohun requires a somewhat bathetic aside.

The poetic idiom moves into a more allegorical vein, with 'stern oppressors' likened to Miltonic devils: 'Our rebel angels for Ambition fell, | And war in Heav'n produc'd a Fiend in hell' (159–60). In Flanders during the war, Discord had held sway, attended by blind mischief, fierceness and other allegorical vices: 'High Red'ning Rage, and Various Forms of death' (177). A fiend in Gallic armour is identified as a Fury in disguise. Ultimately the guardian angel overcomes another fiend at home, representing faction and expressed as a Spenserian 'Blatant voice', disseminating hostile propaganda against the government: 'Whence Lies are utter'd, Whisper softly sounds, | Sly Doubts amaze, or Innuendo wounds' (203–4). The Whig press campaign is imaged by this beast:

> Within her arms are heaps of Pamphlets seen,
> And these blaspheme the Saviour, these the Queen.

> (205–6)

The fiends are overcome, peace returns, bidding warriors to sheath their arms, and 'Angry Trumpets cease to sound Alarms' (222; cf. *WF*, 373–4). The arts of the nation are restored along with 'chearful Plenty':

> Here wond'rous Sciences with eagles sight,
> There Liberal arts which make the world polite,
> And open Traffick joining hand in hand
> With honest Industry, approach the land.

> (237–40)

---

[28] A short poem in quatrains on the peace, *The Horse and the Olive*, which was published on 9 Apr. 1713, risked no such comparison (see Parnell 1989: 109–10).

Peace is 'long desir'd and lately found' (241), close to *WF*, 355, 'long-expected Days'.

Parnell then moves into a high panegyric gear, looking forward to the renewal of the nation under the guidance of the Queen and her principal ministers, among whom the Duke of Ormonde, Dartmouth, and Harcourt are now ranged. It is at this point that the poet imagines the Queen driving in state to the thanksgiving service ('In grand Procession to the Temple go', 288), although as we know (p. 110) the Queen was prevented by illness from attending the ceremony at St Paul's. A brief interlude characterizes the phoenix in the bright enamelled colours of *Windsor-Forest*: 'The tuft of Gold that glow'd above his head, | His spacious Train with golden feathers spread, | His gilded Bosom speck'd with purple pride, | And both his Wings in glossy purple dy'd' (305–8). Then follows the peroration: the greatest triumph is to rise to views of peace, as the victories of the war ('Fam'd BLENHEIM's field, RAMIL-LIES noble seat' not excluded) were pursued 'by wounds and deaths through plains with blood embru'd', 320). As with Pope, Parnell does not refer to Marlborough directly. Instead he ends with another evocation of the defeated powers of France and Spain, allowing a vision of Britain 'arm'd, triumphant and ador'd,' with peace restored and numerous 'Blessings all adorning ANNA's Reign' (338). It is not one of Parnell's most distinguished poems, and it illustrates the fact that even an accomplished writer could deploy a symbolic vocabulary close to Pope's without achieving a similar coherence or formal strength.

EARLY POEMS

The connections with Pope's early poetry can be set out in relatively brief terms. Following the Virgilian model, he concludes his 'georgic' *Windsor-Forest* with the very same line which had opened the first of his pastoral eclogues—the poem, significantly, dedicated to Trumbull. As well as a similarity in setting (Windsor, the Thames, 'Albion's Cliffs'), there is a common resort to the mood of Arcadian simplicity and a timeless perfection which belongs to traditional pastoral. The subject-matter of the genre, usually the idylls and complaints of lovers, is called up in *Windsor-Forest* only as a brief simile: 'As some coy Nymph her Lover's warm Address | Nor quite indulges, nor can quite address' (19–20). However, despite the public theme of the later poem, remnants of stock diction can be detected ('yellow Harvests' at l. 88, for example), transformed by their context on to a more emblematic and historicized level of signification.

Another motif first apparent in the pastoral on 'Spring' is the use of heraldic imagery. Strephon's final speech refers to 'A wondrous *Tree* that Sacred Monarchs bears' (86), which Pope glossed in his revision of 1736, 'An allusion to the Royal Oak, in which *Charles* the second had been hid from the pursuit after the battle of *Worcester*' (*TE* i. 69). This would have been even more obvious in 1709 than in 1736, but it was safer to say it when the fraught issue of the succession was less in doubt. Daphnis replies with a riddling couplet, 'Nay tell me first, in what more happy Fields | The *Thistle* springs, to which the *Lilly* yields' (89–90). This, as Pope's later note confirms, 'alludes to the Device of the *Scots* Monarchs, the *Thistle*, worn by Queen *Anne*; and

to the Arms of *France*, the *Fleur de Lys*' (*TE* i. 69). The editors point out that Anne revived the Order of the Thistle in 1703, and so 'the Thistle could henceforth be considered emblematic of the reigning monarch'. They further note that the earliest
form of the couplet read, 'Say *Daphnis*, say, what Region canst thou find, | In which
by *Thistles, Lillies* are outshin'd' and suggest that the riddle in this form 'probably alluded to the victory of the Allies over the French' at Blenheim in 1704. In the revised
version, there is an obvious pun on the word *Fields*, which 'suggests not only the
"more happy Fields" ruled by Queen Anne ... but also the heraldic fields of the
Royal Arms of England, on which, in 1707, the French lily had "yielded" pride of
place to Scotland, now united with England' (*TE* i. 40). The Union commissioners
had recommended in 1706 that the arms of England and Scotland be united, and the
Act of Union actually specified that the 'ensigns armorial of the said united kingdom be such as her Majesty shall appoint'.

A certain amount of heraldic ingenuity was required at this juncture. The
royal arms had included the French lilies since the reign of Edward III in 1340,
as *Windsor-Forest* reminds us (306). Originally the fleur-de-lis appeared in the first
and fourth quarters (azure, semé-de-lis or), with the English lions (passant
guardant in pale or) in the second and third quarters. It was the Stuarts who
changed this. James I introduced a new form of the arms, with the first and fourth
quarters divided between English and French emblems, the Scottish lion rampant
in the second, and the Irish harp in the third. This survived into Anne's reign, except
that under William and Mary the arms of Nassau had been introduced as an
inescutcheon. What happened in 1707 was that the English arms were impaled
with those of Scotland, in the first and fourth quarters, with those of France in
the second and Ireland in the third. But this arrangement was already obsolete when
Pope added his note in 1736, since George I had incorporated the arms of Hanover
(with their lordly inescutcheon of Charlemagne's crown), and there they remained
until the death of William IV (Fox-Davies, 607–8). Pope's note therefore alludes
nostalgically to the last gesture of Anglo-Scottish unity, itself a statement of Stuart
dynastic history.

These references in the *Pastorals* are much more attenuated than the elaborate pattern of armorial allusion found in *Windsor-Forest* (on this topic see below, pp.
147–51, as well as *SDW*, ch. 3). Nevertheless, they show beyond doubt that Pope was
well versed in royal heraldry by the time he started to work on the poem. They help,
too, to explain some aspects of the workings of *Windsor-Forest*. When Pope says that
the thistle was 'the Device of the *Scots* Monarchs ... worn by Queen *Anne*', he reminds us that the Queen traced her descent from a long line of Stewarts who had occupied the Scottish throne since Robert II in 1371. The thistle first appears as an
emblem on a coin of 1474, in the reign of James III; the Order was founded in 1540,
in the reign of James V. The Thistle followed the Garter in antiquity and dignity; its
gold collar matched that of the Garter, and its badge with a figure of St Andrew recalled the badge of St George (Fox-Davies, 270–1, 563). Pope naturally concentrates
on the order of knighthood local to Windsor, but he does not forget that he is

celebrating a '*British* QUEEN' (384), who united the thistle and the rose in an emblem of unity—here a family claim, as much as a stage in national evolution.

Membership of the Order of the Thistle was in the monarch's gift, and one knight in particular, the Duke of Hamilton, was showered with favours under the Harley ministry. He was elected to the Garter along with the Lord Treasurer in 1712, made a peer of Great Britain under the title of the duke of Brandon, and appointed to the Privy Council. He was poised to become ambassador to the French court, until this plan was rudely cut short by the intervention of the most famous duel in British history—in the course of which Hamilton and his opponent Lord Mohun were both killed. The affair took place at the precise moment that Pope was bringing *Windsor-Forest* to a conclusion. Actually, if the Duke had followed the Queen's wishes, he would already have been on his way to France: she wrote to Oxford urging his immediate departure, 'now the great work of Peace is in a fair way of coming to a happy conclusion' (Green, 276). On the eve of the encounter in Hyde Park, Hamilton had spent time attempting to get his official credentials as a Garter knight. The *Flying Post* reported on the duel on 18 November 1713, describing Hamilton as a 'Prince of unquestionable Bravery, [who] on all Occasions appeared for the Honour of his Country, answerable to his high Birth and Dignity, being the first Prince of the Blood Royal of Scotland, next to those of King James the VI's Line' (Ewald, 137). *Windsor-Forest*, tactfully, does not mention these circumstances, unlike Parnell's lines; but the symbolic order of the poem, prolonging the ideas sketched in 'Spring', unites thistle and rose as '*Britannia*'s Standard flies', an emblem of 'Order in Variety', with the heraldic *concordia discors* matching that of the cosmos.

This fatal duel released an immediate shock wave across London. Jacobites had convinced themselves that Hamilton's embassy to the French court was designed to produce a rapprochement with the Pretender, leading to his restoration on the death of Anne. It is true that the Duke apparently cleared the appointment with James Edward before he accepted it; but such an outcome was certainly not in Oxford's mind. Maybe the plan was rather for the Duke to lend an air of dignity to the final negotiations, while Prior did the real work.[29] Tories charged that the Whigs had set up the contest deliberately: both Mohun, a Kit-Cat partisan, and his second George Macartney were protégés of the Duke of Marlborough, and they had been closeted with him on the very day before the duel. It was further contended that Macartney had actually struck down Hamilton after the Duke dispatched Mohun. 'The Qu[een] and Ld Treasurer are in great Concern at this event', Swift informed Stella: Oxford had returned from Windsor with a message to the Duchess from Anne (*JTS* ii. 575). All the chief officers of state were summoned to an emergency meeting at Whitehall, to decide on the political measures to be taken in response to the calamity. Oxford, Bolingbroke, Harcourt, Strafford, Shrewsbury, and Buckinghamshire were in attendance—virtually Pope's home team, in terms of the ideological line-up for *Windsor-Forest*. For a time it seemed as if the government's whole strategy might be thrown off course by this desperate turn of events. Bolingbroke

---

[29] This is the suggestion of Ehrenpreis (1962–83: ii. 575).

set up a hue and cry after Macartney, who had fled to the Continent, and a royal proclamation offered a reward of £500 for his capture. In the mood of panic, plots were discovered against the life of both the Queen and her chief minister: discord was appearing truly to pervade the land, with faction roaring and furies *promoting* an orgy of bloodletting—or so Tory polemic asserted (see *WF*, 414–22).

Swift had built up a warm relationship with the Duchess, whom he called 'handsom, and airy', and he instantly went round to her house as soon as news of the duel spread through the city. He wrote to Stella that he had never witnessed 'so melancholy a Scene' as the spectacle of the weeping Elizabeth Hamilton:

For indeed all Reasons for real grief belong to her, nor is it possible for any one to be a greater loser in all regards. She has moved my very soul. The Lodging was inconvenient, & they would have removed her to anothr; but I would not suffer it; because it had no room backwards; and she must have been tortured with the noise of the Grub Street Screamers, mention her Husbands murder to her Ears. (*JTS* ii. 572)

Actually Swift may have been among these screamers: he put about in print the dubious tale that Macartney had stabbed Hamilton 'most barbarously'.[30] The general was already a *bête noire* of the Tory party, and had been dismissed from his military posts for drinking confusion to the Harley government in 1710. Privately, Swift told Stella that he loved the Duke very well, '& I think he loved me better'. Hamilton had let it be known that he wished Swift to accompany him to Paris, but he was informed that his friend 'could not be spared' by the government (*JTS* ii. 572). For the next few weeks Swift was most assiduous in his attentions to the Duchess, begging Lady Masham to get the Queen to write a letter of comfort, and trying to 'patch up' relations with Lady Orkney, who was sister-in-law to Elizabeth Hamilton. Details of the affair must almost instantly have reached Pope at Binfield: it would have been as hard for anyone in the nation to remain oblivious of the news as for a late twentieth-century American to learn nothing of the trial of O. J. Simpson. Just two weeks later, we remember, verses from the final draft of *Windsor-Forest* were on their way to Caryll.

An embarrassment to the ministry, the Duke's death was in certain respects a convenient event for Pope. The poet had managed to square the circle by complimenting both Oxford and Bolingbroke, whose growing divisions threatened to blunt the impact of the peace settlement. He had lauded both Trumbull and Lansdowne within the space of a few lines; and he had devised a poetic strategy which would please Buckinghamshire, Harcourt, and Shrewsbury. But the erratic and extreme Hamilton was another matter. A favourite of James II, he had twice landed in the Tower of London, most recently at the time of the 1708 rising. The unquestioned leader of the Scottish Jacobites, and a hero of the Edinburgh mob, he had antagonized Oxford and at times irritated even Swift. At the trial of Sacheverell, Hamilton

---

[30] In his imitation of Horace's first ode in the second book, published on 7 Jan. 1714, Swift indicated that if Steele were to toast Macartney and the ghost of Mohun, he would be well rewarded by 'her Highness and her Spouse'—that is the Duke and Duchess of Marlborough, now in exile at Antwerp. The duel was still strongly in the public mind when *WF* appeared: see Swift's reference on 8 Apr. 1713 (*JTS* ii. 656).

had defended the firebrand with passionate intensity. His long-standing quarrel with the Whig rake Lord Mohun centred on an elaborate Chancery suit over property. It was all too appropriate that the lives of these brutal and rapacious men (who had married first cousins) should have ended in such a violent fashion. Yet, as we have just seen, Hamilton was allowed to add the Garter to his Thistle, an unprecedented favour. Although she consented in 1709 to act as godmother to the Duke's third son, Lord Anne Hamilton, the Queen did not trust him, she had been forced by political exigencies to appoint him as master of the ordnance. Hamilton celebrated with an entertainment featuring drums and trumpets, and a party to fête Oxford. Then came the posting to Paris, in the attempt to tie the last knots on the peace treaty with France: the Duke bragged that the Queen had presented him with plate weighing 7,000 ounces. He was not a man to hide his light under a bushel. If Hamilton had survived, then *Windsor-Forest* would have had to include some endorsement of his conduct.[31]

There is an epilogue to this story. Pope became friendly with the Duke's widow, and in 1717 he wrote to her a slightly confusing letter (allegedly when drunk) which refers to a picture of the Duchess posed 'between a Honey-suckle and a Rose-bush'. The letter continues, 'I suppose the Painter by those Emblems intended . . . to show you are near enough related to the Thistle of Scotland to deserve the same Motto with regard to your enemies. *Nemo me impune lacessit*' (*Corr.* i. 437). This was of course the motto of the Order of the Thistle: Pope later used it in one of the illustrations to the *Dunciad Variorum*.[32]

It is especially in the area of language that we find links between *Windsor-Forest* and *Messiah* (1712)—above all in the prophetic and, precisely, Messianic idiom found at ll. 57–72 of the latter poem:

> No more shall Nation against Nation rise,
> Nor ardent Warriors meet with hateful Eyes,
> Nor Fields with gleaming Steel be cover'd o'er;
> The Brazen Trumpets kindle Rage no more;
> But useless Lances into Scythes shall bend,
> And the broad Faulchion in a Plow-share end.
> Then Palaces shall rise; the joyful Son
> Shall finish what his short-liv'd Sire begun;
> Their Vines a Shadow to their Race shall yield;
> And the Same Hand that sow'd, shall reap the Field.
> The Swain in barren Desarts with surprize
> See Lillies spring, and sudden Verdure rise;
> And Starts, amidst the thirsty Wilds, to hear

[31] For details on Hamilton's extraordinary career, see Stater (1999) and (less reliable in details) Forsythe (1928). Forsythe's assumption (1928: 141 and *passim*) that Swift wrote the *Examiner* of 20 Nov. 1712 on the episode is not based on any firm evidence.

[32] The Duchess subscribed to the *Iliad*, as did her sister-in-law Lady Orkney and her brother-in-law the Earl of Selkirk. Pope was also acquainted with Lady Mohun and her two daughters (one of whom was Lady Rich: see *Corr.* i. 345).

> New Falls of water murm'ring in his Ear:
> On rifted Rocks, the Dragon's late Abodes,
> The green Reed trembles, and the Bulrush nods . . .

(TE i. 117–19)

The common sources for these passages, in Virgil's *Eclogue* IV, addressed to the consul Pollio, and in Isaiah (especially 11, 35, and 60), are set out more fully in *SDW*, chapter 6. Both associate the coming of a new Golden Age with the birth of a child, who will reincarnate the virtues of his father. In *Messiah*, the prophecy starts with mention of a virgin conceiving (l. 8), which introduces an explicitly Astraean theme never quite brought to the surface in *Windsor-Forest*. The diction of *Messiah* is a little closer to epic, with more conscious use of periphrasis and more stock epithets; but it has the same metallic glitter as that of *Windsor-Forest*. Some passages from the sources are used in more or less an identical way in the two texts: compare *Messiah*, 60 with *WF*, 373, or the description of Salem in *Messiah* (85–94) with *WF*, 377–84 on reborn Augusta, and *Messiah*, 95–6, with *WF*, 391–6.[33] We could convey the nature of the link not too inaccurately by saying that the peroration of *Windsor-Forest* incorporates an abridged and specialized application of the Messianic vision Pope had set out in his earlier poem.

In the case of *The Rape of the Lock*, the line of continuity is subtler and harder to trace, but it is much more extensive than has been recognized. Matters kept on the margin—either deleted, or simply not treated—in *Windsor-Forest* are allowed freer play in the *Rape*. As much can be deduced from the use of traditional faery lore: the Rosicrucian implications of the 'Cross' (387) are explored in *SDW*, chapter 2; and the submerged application of the temperaments in the seasonal passages of *WF*, will be reviewed in Chapter 8, below. We can compare this with the sustained use of elements and their analogues in the *Rape*.[34] It is obvious that the references to Anne in the *Rape* are consciously flippant; but both poems make use of 'Great *Anna*' (*ROL* iii. 7) as an emblem of 'the Glory of the *British Queen*' (*ROL* iii. 13). As for the location, the satiric narrative is set 'Close to those Meads for ever crown'd with Flowr's, | Where *Thames* with Pride surveys his rising Tow'rs' (*ROL* iii. 1–2): this jokingly reinscribes the scene where Father Thames turns his gaze on the 'pompous Turrets' of Windsor (*WF*, 352). With a broad stroke of humour, Pope has Anne taking sometimes counsel and sometimes tea at Hampton Court (*ROL* iii. 8): in fact she held meetings of the Privy Council at her other riverside palace, a more serious context for events in *Windsor-Forest*. In any case we know that a Jacobite reading of the poem was possible, and was indeed foreshadowed in a deviously complicated way by Pope himself.[35] The card game which guys the imperial powers at war is played out on a 'verdant Field' (*ROL* iii. 53), which serves to parody not so much epic diction as the language of pastoral.

---

[33] For other parallels, see Weinbrot (1993: 283–5).
[34] See Fowler (1988: 154–6).
[35] Pope's sly interpretation of his poem as a Jacobite allegory, in *A Key to the Lock* (1715), also provides some insights into the workings of *WF*. See Ch. 3, below.

The Temple of Fame is relevant chiefly on two accounts: for its creation of an architectural set piece, embodying some Vitruvian principles of construction, as well as blazoning forth the great deeds of history; and for its imagination of a noble symbol of civilization, to be crushed in the bleak counter-vision of *The Dunciad*. Just so, *Windsor-Forest* and *Messiah* had envisaged a Golden Age, where *The Dunciad* foretells the coming of 'a new Saturnian age of Lead' (i. 26). It is possible, too, that Pope had some familiar concerns in his mind when he wrote at the end of the *Temple*, 'Oh! if the Muse must flatter lawless Sway, | And follow still where Fortune leads the way' (517–18). The 'lawless Sway' of *Windsor-Forest* clearly belongs to the Norman kings, to Dutch William and, it is barely suggested, to German George as he lay waiting in the wings. In Pope's later verse the suggestion is scarcely withdrawn: that is the point of his repeated protestations of independence, and his ostentatious refusals to toe the Hanoverian line. *Windsor-Forest*, one could say, make political certain attitudes in the early poetry which can elsewhere be taken as innocent or ambiguous. In that particular respect, *Windsor-Forest* is perhaps the most forward-looking of this group of poems, composed before Pope had reached the end of his twenty-sixth year.

Soon all would change, for Pope as for his friends. To his surprise John Gay found himself in the role of secretary to a special emissary, which was dispatched to Hanover as a last effort to build bridges between the Elector and the Tory administration. Gay expressed unfeigned delight at being among 'Treatys & Negotiations, Plenipotentiarys Embassadors & Envoys'(Gay, *Letters*, 11). But before the mission was properly under way Oxford had been dismissed, the Queen had died, and the golden days were over. Gay would see his hopes of establishing himself in an official position vanish into nothing; Arbuthnot would abruptly lose his post as royal physician; Swift would be left in Ireland, all prospects of an English bishopric ended for good. Oxford would be hauled off to the Tower, along with Matthew Prior and Lord Lansdowne. Bolingbroke would flee to France, and attach himself openly to the Pretender. As for Pope, he was ringed by new measures to curtail the freedom of Catholics. As he told Edward Blount a month after the new regime took over, 'I . . . am in danger of losing my horse, and stand in some fear of a country justice' (*Corr.* i. 246). Next year a planned visit to Sir William Wyndham in Somerset was aborted only just before the arrest of the politician, who joined Oxford in the Tower. Already the object of a formal rebuke by the Speaker of the Commons in April, Wyndham was arrested in his nightclothes at his house on 22 October: among the incriminating documents found in his papers were two letters by Lansdowne.[36] Briefly, Wyndham managed to escape, disguised as a clergyman, but with a reward of £1,000 on his head he got no further than the home of his father-in-law, the Duke of Somerset—Syon House, up the Thames from Chiswick. The game was up.

---

[36] Wyndham had been Chancellor of the Exchequer in the last year of the Oxford ministry. He was a fellow member with Swift of the 'Society'. His arrest came because of his role in organizing the rebellion in the west; as the son-in-law of the unreliable Duke of Somerset, he still had some friends at court. Released on bail, he never faced a trial. Through his marriage Wyndham was related to the Thynne family and thus to Lansdowne. See also Ch. 3, below.

So began a phase of psychological harassment which went on for the best part of a decade. Of course, Pope would adjust, as people do. He made new friends, such as the Earl of Burlington, the first hereditary peer with whom he established a close relationship. He would begin his strange romantic pursuit of Lady Mary Wortley Montagu. He would prosecute his scheme to get rich through the Homer translation. And he would produce his collected *Works* in 1717, an assertion of power and independence. He would, in short, succeed. But there was no longer room for another *Windsor-Forest* in this world.

LANSDOWNE

George Granville was born in 1664.[37] He was educated first in France, and then removed to Trinity College, Cambridge. At the age of 12 he composed verses of moderate precocity to the Duchess of York on her visit to the university: this was the Duke's new bride, Mary of Modena. Young Granville rolls out fluent personifications: the lady's gaze 'Strikes Envy dumb, and keeps Sedition tame' (see *WF*, 419–21). His early work, including an address to James on his accession, obtained the praise of Edmund Waller, whose poetic disciple he remained, as Pope recognized (*Anecdotes*, i. 196). Forbidden to take part in the campaign against Monmouth's rebellion, he wrote a letter to his father in October 1688 expressing his desire to fight for James against the Dutch invader; but again he was not to see action. Nevertheless he was openly identified in the circle of the king, and after the Revolution he went into retirement. In 1696 he first emerged as a dramatist with a comedy: his theatrical career culminated in an adaptation of *The Merchant of Venice* (1701), with a masque-like interlude in the second act, and an 'opera' *The British Enchanters* (1706), with an epilogue by Addison. In fact the latter is a semi-opera, with long sections of spoken dialogue. This was a form defended by Granville in his combative preface as more appropriate than French spectacles—'An English stomach requires something solid and substantial, and will rise hungry from a regale of nothing but sweet-meats'. Most of the score was provided by John Eccles, Master of the Queen's Musick. The piece enjoyed moderate success at Vanbrugh's new theatre in the Haymarket. The fullest collection of his verse was published by Tonson as *Poems on Several Occasions* (1712).

Meanwhile, Granville's political career had blossomed under Anne. He was elected MP for Fowey in 1702, 1704, and 1707, and for Cornwall in 1710. His electoral influence grew over the years, and when the Harley administration took over he moved into office.[38] His friendship with Henry St John was probably a factor here,

[37] The main source of information remains Handasyde (1933), which needs some updating but offers a reliable account of Lansdowne's political and literary career.

[38] William Walsh, in an imitation of Virgil's Pollio eclogue turned to the ends of current Whig politics, *The Golden Age Restored* (1703), envisages a takeover by the Tories in which 'Granville shall seize the long-expected chair' (Chalmers, ii. 85). Walsh, an MP and a gentleman of the horse to the Queen, was of course one of Pope's early sponsors in the poet's youth; he remained a strong supporter of the Godolphin–Marlborough alliance.

as we shall see in a moment. He was on good personal terms with the Queen, and his sister Elizabeth was by now a maid of favour to Anne. Succeeding Robert Walpole as secretary at war in 1710, he incurred the scorn of the Duchess of Marlborough, as 'one perfectly unskilled in the business, and a known Jacobite; but a flatterer of the new great man at Court [Harley] as well as an enemy to the Duke'.[39] It was not the first time Marlborough had set himself to block Lansdowne's promotion; but this time he failed. In any case, such an enmity serves of course to qualify Lansdowne further for his role in *Windsor-Forest*. Favours continued to flow, with the grant of his barony at the end of the following year. In 1712 he was made comptroller of the household and a Privy Councillor; and in 1713 advanced to the post of treasurer of the household. This was the peak of his achievement. On a visit to Barnstaple in October 1713, seven months after he had been favoured in *Windsor-Forest*, he was received like royalty and installed as high steward amidst feasting and junketing, with firing of guns and ringing of bells. Healths were drunk by worthies of the county to the Queen, Harcourt, Oxford, Bolingbroke, and Lansdowne.[40] None of them had much longer to enjoy such fulsome treatment.

Lansdowne's days in the sun were brief. Like his brother and sister, he was stripped of official appointments. Dismissed on 11 October 1714, he was arrested as a suspected leader of the rising a year later, and spent the period from 21 October 1715 to 8 February 1717 in the Tower of London, accompanied at first by his wife and daughters. Pope had remained loyal to his patron, even after the Hanoverians arrived. In the preface to the *Iliad*, published in June 1715, thanks are expressed to 'so excellent Imitator of *Homer* as the noble Author of the Tragedy of *Heroic Love*' (*Prose*, i. 255). The fate of Lansdowne after his arrest became a matter of general interest, as we can tell from an importunate enquiry which the bookseller Lintot made of Pope, when they were riding through Windsor Forest on the way to Oxford in 1716:

'Is it the opinion of your friends at Court that my Lord Lansdown will be brought to the Bar or not?' I told him I heard *not*, and I hop'd it, my Lord being one I had particular obligations to. 'That may be (reply'd Mr. *Lintott*) but by G—d if he is not, I shall lose the printing of a very good Trial.' (*Corr.* i. 374–5)

The threat of severe punishment was real: on 19 May 1716 the Grand Jury of Middlesex found a bill of indictment for high treason against Lansdowne. Potentially this could have led to a capital sentence; but the ministry delayed a full hearing before parliament, either in order to obtain fuller evidence or to hold over prosecution to intimidate others. In the end Lansdowne made a formal petition to the king for clemency, and a pardon was issued early in 1717.

On release from custody Lansdowne chose to withdraw to Longleat, but when the atmosphere again grew warm for Jacobite sympathizers, he moved to Paris in the summer of 1720. There he found himself centrally involved in the plans for a rising in 1722, all of which came to nothing when the government pounced on the alleged

---

[39] Quoted from the *Memoirs* of the Duchess by Handasyde (1933: 108).
[40] Cited from the *Post-Boy* by Handasyde (1933: 131).

Atterbury plot (see Chapter 3, below). Many suspected that his extravagant wife had
played some part in the betrayal of this plot, after her indiscreet dealings with
Colonel Charles Churchill, the spy and agent provocateur whom the ministry sent
to Paris in 1722. Ten years later the elderly peer came back to England, made his
peace with the Hanoverian regime, and published his works in two handsome volumes. He died in 1735, leaving female issue only, and thus his title expired. So, largely,
did his fame, although his verse was still present in the popular memory to the extent that he figures in Samuel Johnson's *Lives of the Poets* (1779–81). In view of the
rough treatment Johnson accords him, it might have been kinder to Lansdowne if
he had been forgotten.

   We have seen that Granville's rise to a government position in 1710 probably owes
much to his connection with Henry St John. The young St John had written a prologue to Granville's play *Heroick Love* in 1701, and during his quest of a parliamentary
seat in 1708 had sought the aid of his friend ('crony', he has been called) in gaining
nomination for one of the Cornish boroughs which lay in Granville's influence—
though on this occasion a deal could not be done. When St John came to power along
with Robert Harley, it was natural that he should remember Granville, and the post
bestowed was in fact the very one which St John had filled in his first experience of
government between 1704 and 1708.[41] All this has a relevance for *Windsor-Forest*:
Pope's commendations of a minor figure in the government reflect back on those
who had actually engineered the peace, notably Oxford and Bolingbroke.

Granville came of solidly royalist stock. The family had a history of loyalty and of
martyrship. Their most prominent member had been Sir Richard Grenville, a cousin
of Sir Walter Ralegh, who had been killed off the Azores in 1591 after a distinguished
naval career in the service of Elizabeth I. His grandson, also Sir Richard, had fought
for Charles I in the Civil War. So had George's own grandfather, Sir Bevil Grenville,
who was killed at the battle of Lansdowne on the afternoon of 5 July 1643. Sir Bevil led
a valiant charge of Cornish pikemen against the cannons of General Waller, which
were securely installed at the north end of Lansdowne Hill, on the slopes almost 800
feet above Bath. The royalist forces, climbing from a valley at the foot of Tog Hill, had
to withstand a fierce barrage from the parliamentary forces, but after a bitter struggle they obtained their objective by late evening. Sadly for them, Grenville had been
caught in the fire and was carried off to the nearby village of Cold Ashton to die. He
became one of the royalists' most esteemed heroes in the entire war; possibly with an
excess of zeal, his grandson set up three monuments to Sir Bevil, including one on
the site of his death. It is of course no accident that George Granville should have
taken the title of Lansdowne when he was elevated to the peerage.[42]

   [41] Dickinson (1970: 37).
   [42] Granville pays a tribute to his grandfather's heroic death in a note to his *Essay upon Unnatural
Flights in Poetry* (Chalmers, ii. 282). One of Sir Bevil's sons, Denis, studied at Oxford, entered the Church,
and became dean of Durham in 1684. He helped to raise money for James II, and after the Revolution he
fled to France. George was, significantly, his favourite nephew. Denis was named as archbishop of York
by the exiled James II, before his death in Paris in 1703—another of the useless honorifics which the
Granvilles managed to acquire in their loyalty to the virtual regime of the Stuarts.

George's father, Bernard Grenville, played a minor role in the restoration of the monarchy and served as groom of the bedchamber to Charles II. A much more important figure was Bernard's brother John Granville, who fought with distinction in the Civil War as a young man, aided Monk in restoring the monarchy, and was raised to the peerage in 1661. His principal title was that of first Earl of Bath, but it is his secondary title which is most noteworthy here—for he, too, commemorated his father by adopting the style of Viscount Lansdowne. The Earl was the most influential Cornish magnate of his day, and held high national office as groom of the stole and Privy Councillor. A committed royalist, it was only after prolonged soul-searching that he declared for William in 1688, and many questioned the depth of his loyalty even then.

Bernard had three sons, of whom George came in the middle. The eldest brother, Bevil Granville commanded his uncle's regiment of foot at Sedgemoor, and was rewarded by a knighthood from James II, awarded at a review of the victorious army held in Hyde Park. Subsequently, under William and Mary, Bevil served in Lord Bath's blues during Marlborough's campaign in Flanders. He became governor of Barbados in Anne's reign, but was recalled after charges of extortion were made against him. The youngest brother, Colonel Bernard Granville, became MP for Fowey, one of the Cornish boroughs under family control. His major claim to fame today is that he was father of Mary Delany, the writer and creator of flower pictures, whose second husband was Swift's friend Patrick Delany. Young Mary was brought up at court under the aegis of her uncle George and her aunt Anne, who was married to Sir John Stanley, secretary to the Lord Chamberlain. Under Queen Anne the family were at the centre of the royal household; as we have seen, George Granville himself occupied in turn the posts of comptroller and treasurer of the household. Although the latter office was something of a sinecure in the department of the Lord Steward, the Comptroller's post involved regular attendance at court and some limited political responsibility.[43] So it is not just that Granville moved in the Queen's private circle: he had a direct concern with running the business of the monarchy, a role which links him to the propagandist purposes of *Windsor-Forest.*

A succession of events early in the eighteenth century had transformed the prospects for George Granville. His father died in 1701, as did his uncle the Earl of Bath. Then his brother Bevil died on the way back from the West Indies in 1706. Granville scooped up three inheritances; his comparative penury was a thing of the past. Even more important, he acquired much more political interest. It was the Earl of Bath's legacy which made him one of the most significant figures in the electioneering battles of Queen Anne's reign.[44] We tend to skim over genealogical information in constructing our modern historical narratives, but the truth is that hard political capital was once invested in ranks and dignitaries, and families transmitted more than money from one generation to another.

The Hanoverian accession changed everything once again. Lansdowne was arrested on well-founded suspicions of inciting a West Country rising, and his brother

---

[43] Beattie (1967: 69; see also 4).   [44] See Holmes (1987); Speck (1970).

Bernard was briefly incarcerated as a possible accomplice, losing his place as a 'carver' at court. The 15-year-old Mary Granville, who had been expecting to become a maid of favour, was summarily dismissed from court. Together with her parents, she moved to rural Gloucestershire. In 1717, after Lansdowne's release from the Tower, he invited Mary to stay with him at Longleat, where he now settled. It was on this visit that Mary was introduced to her first husband, Alexander Pendarves, the middle-aged MP for yet another family borough in Cornwall, Launceston. A marriage was arranged, little to Mary's taste, no doubt in the hope of cementing the Granville political connection—a futile gesture, in view of the long proscription of the Tories under George I and George II. The marriage duly took place in 1718, and Mary was carried off to her new home in Cornwall.

At the time of the appearance of *Windsor-Forest*, Lansdowne had skilfully begun to mount his reversionary claim on the great house of Longleat. This came about as a result of his marriage to Lady Mary Thynne, née Villiers. She was the daughter of the Tory peace envoy, the Earl of Jersey. As a young girl she had been the recipient of one of the most charming poems of its kind ever written, 'To a Child of Quality', by Matthew Prior, who was a client of her father. In 1709 she married Thomas Thynne, heir to the viscountcy of Weymouth, but her new husband died of smallpox in April 1710, leaving her to bear a son only four weeks later. Just two weeks before his own ennoblement, George Granville was married to the youthful widow, on 15 December 1711. Thus Lansdowne acquired within a single month a title with historic associations and a route towards the effective control of one of the great landed estates of the nation. When Lord Weymouth, a Privy Councillor under Anne, died on 28 July 1714 (four days before his royal mistress), the gates to Longleat were open.[45] The infant Thomas Thynne was now second Viscount and heir to the family fortunes.

The Thynne motto—*J'ay bonne cause*—admits of more than one interpretation as we look at Lansdowne's life history. There is no denying that Pope's poem celebrates a careerist and a seeker after the glittering prizes of aristocracy. What Lansdowne could not gain by his immediate service to the crown, as government minister and household official, he was prepared to pick up through a judicious marriage. At the very same moment, as *Windsor-Forest* reached completion, he was attempting to scoop up the Bath title as well as the estates, but this time protracted litigation failed.[46] Pope's line about the 'Honours' Lansdowne deserved to wear *must* include the notion that his patron merited promotion to the earldom of Bath, since this cause was not lost until 1714. Moreover, this anticipated promotion carried an extra charge for the royalist programme of the poem. When Sir Bevil Grenville fell on the battlefield in 1643, he carried in his pocket a patent from Charles I creating him earl of Bath. Thus the allusion places Pope's dedicatee as the inheritor of a title bestowed by the martyr king, which had been sacrificed in loyal service to the monarch in the destructive Civil War. *Windsor-Forest* reinstates Lansdowne in a line of favour (all references are to his family name, not his baronial title). What the new

[45] Lord Weymouth was an Oxford contemporary and friend of Trumbull, and Pope had hoped that he would subscribe to the *Iliad* (New Letts., 401).

[46] Further details are supplied in *SDW*, ch. 3.

peer was able to adopt with the impunity was the Granville coat of arms: argent three clarions gules, with a garb vert as their crest (see Chapter 5, below).

Almost as crucial was the political connection forged with the Villiers family. Mary Villiers was the daughter of the first Earl of Jersey, courtier and politician; while one of her aunts was Elizabeth Villiers, later Countess of Orkney. The Countess had been in turn lady of favour to Princess (later Queen) Mary; *maîtresse en titre* (probably less in reality) to William III; and after her rejection by the King, the wife of the Earl of Orkney, a leading general in the wars. Her husband served at Blenheim, Ramillies, Oudenard, and Malplaquet; he was appointed a Knight of the Thistle in 1704 and became a lord of the bedchamber in 1714.[47] She herself was granted James II's Irish estates, a fact that rankled with Queen Anne. More importantly, she was a strenuous opponent of Marlborough from an early date. Another of Mary's aunts, Anne Villiers, married the Earl of Portland, William III's closest aide and another bitter rival of Marlborough. The Villiers girls—there were six in all—had been close companions of Princess Anne in her youth, when their mother Lady Frances Villers acted as governess to the royal children.[48]

The brother of these ladies, Edward Villiers, held numerous court offices under William and Mary, including those of master of the horse and knight marshal of the household. After various diplomatic missions, he served as one of the British negotiators at the Rijswijk conference to end the Nine Years War. As a reward he was created earl of Jersey in 1697 and afterwards became ambassador to the French court when diplomatic relations were restored. Both at Rijswijk and Paris he had the assistance of Matthew Prior, who thus became one of the few people in English public affairs who had some first-hand acquaintance with James Francis Edward Stuart as a boy. Jersey briefly held the office of secretary of state at the beginnning of the new century. According to one historian, he was 'showered with honours . . . which his very ordinary talents did not warrant' (Gregg, 75). Under Anne he retained his post as Lord Chamberlain, officiating at her coronation. However, in 1704 he was dismissed as the High Church party was purged to create the new Godolphin administration. Out of favour for the next few years, he returned to a position of influence only when Harley and St John assumed power in 1710.

At this point Jersey became the chief conduit between the ministry and the French court, represented by the shadowy Abbé Gaultier. For the first few months of the Tory government, it was by this curious agency that diplomacy with France was mainly conducted. On the one side, a secret agent of the French minister Torcy, Gaultier had lived a clandestine existence in England, serving in Jersey's own household; on the other, an unquestionably Jacobite nobleman who held no official post, and who was married to a Roman Catholic (Trevelyan, iii. 198). Jersey's wife was Barbara Chilfinch, the daughter of a minor court official under Charles II. Moreover, Gaultier was as much the Pretender's agent as the emissary of the French court.

---

[47] His brother was the Jacobite Duke of Hamilton, for whom see p. 69, above.
[48] Also in the suite was Frances Apsley, later to become mother of Pope's friend Lord Bathurst.

Jersey seems to have given his contact an assurance that on Anne's death the ministers would support the 'restoration' of the Stuart claimant to the British throne. As
a reward, Gaultier was authorized to pay Jersey the large *douceur* of £3,000 per
annum.

Initially St John had not been let in on this secret diplomacy. When Harley was
wounded by a French adventurer in March 1711, St John took over the helm, and
soon learnt what had transpired. Since he wanted to handle the peace talks himself,
he was ready enough to dispense with Jersey. Quietly, the Earl was dropped from the
negotiating process. He died suddenly the following August, having avoided any
taint of disgrace because it was in the ministry's interest to keep the earlier contacts
with France a matter of strict secrecy—the Queen had never been apprised of the
plans to set her half-brother on the throne, and she resisted Jersey's appointment to
the government on the grounds of his ill-disguised Jacobitism (Gregg, 336). A new
round of diplomacy began, with the Earl's client Matthew Prior dispatched to Paris
in July 1711.[49] This was the mission for which Swift invented a bogus rationale in *A
New Journey to Paris*. Although Jersey had not been trusted with the actual negotiations, it was still the intention of the ministry to appoint him as Lord Privy Seal and
to name him as one of the plenipotentiaries at the Utrecht congress, on the very day
when his sudden death intervened. His wife fled to Paris and made plans to educate
her younger son Henry as a Catholic, a plan which Prior managed to scotch (Legg,
194–8).

Not much of this backstairs diplomacy had come to light when *Windsor-Forest*
was published, and some of it lay hidden for decades. But Lansdowne's match with
Jersey's daughter unquestionably added to his claims as an insider—the Earl's long
connections with the royal household ensured that. Pope's dedicatee had linked
himself with a family who had held key appointments at court ever since the Revolution. If Jersey had not died in 1711, he might have served the poet's purposes almost
as well, in view of his experience in political, diplomatic, and ceremonial arenas.
Perhaps the only surprise is that Lansdowne did not choose to quarter the Villiers
arms with his own bearings. For centuries, ever since Crusading times, the family of
Villiers had used a shield combining the emblems of St George and St James—a silver field with a red cross, and on it five gold shells.[50] The family motto underlined
this message: *Fidei coticula crux* (the cross is the touchstone of faith). Lansdowne
was evidently content with blazoning his own Granville connections, in his title and
in his coat of arms. His timely marriage with a scion of the Villiers line could be left
unremarked.

Swift knew about what had been happening, though; he was in friendly touch
both with the Countess of Orkney and with her sister-in-law Lady Jersey (*JTS* ii.
615): this was apart from his acquaintance with Prior, which went back a decade. We
can be sure that Pope, too, remarked on these events in Granville's career. Otherwise

---

[49] There was a family connection once more: Matthew's beloved cousin Katharine Prior had married
Colonel George Villiers, who was himself the Earl's first cousin; and some regarded Matthew as 'an entire
Creature of my Lord *Jersey*'s' (Legg, 129).
[50] Scott-Giles (1965: 61); Foster (1902: 253).

there would be something outrageously tactless in the address he offers to his patron: writing of Surrey, he observes, 'Fair *Geraldine*, bright Object of his Vow, | Then fill'd the Groves, as heav'nly *Myra* now' (297–8). The editors gloss '*Myra*' as follows: 'The name Granville bestowed in his songs, first upon Mary of Modena, then upon Frances Brudenal, Countess of Newburgh, when the latter became his mistress' (*TE* i. 176).[51]

This body of earlier writing certainly provides the core of the allusion. Yet it would have been an extraordinary impertinence to the recently married couple for Pope to remind Lansdowne of his former mistress without any recognition of his present marital condition. The word 'now' surely indicates that there is a new 'object' of Lansdowne's vow, and this is his wife, the former Mary Villiers. The only Myra who fits the context is the dedicatee's bride. We might be tempted to think of the poet's former deity, Mary of Modena, the proud matriarch of the Stuarts, who was still doggedly maintaining the cause at Saint-Germain-en-Laye: but she could not haunt the groves of Windsor until the day that her son should be restored to the throne of England. In fact, any other assumption would convict Pope of a far lower degree of delicacy than we know him to have possessed. The compliment was not as idle as these things often are: the bride was young and beautiful, almost a quarter of a century junior to her husband. She was also, by some accounts, extravagant and wilful. According to Pope's friend, Mary Caesar, she dominated her husband: Mary Granville was 'Master Intirely of him in all things but his Mind'.[52] In later years she was openly unfaithful to her husband. Again the idyllic notions of *Windsor-Forest* were destined to wither away in the cold light of day.

REBELS AND A CAUSE

At the time of his admission to the Purple Gaiter, Granville had one recent claim to notice. He had been made one of the twenty men who earned, Garter-like, an invitation to the 'Society', popularly known as the Brothers Club. This was formed in June 1711, chiefly at the instigation of St John: however, it was Swift who was charged with the task of drafting the club rules (*JTS* i. 294). Its membership has been analysed by Charles Kerby-Miller, who divides the group into a number of categories. Four were wits without ostensible influence: Swift, Arbuthnot, Prior, and John Freind. The last-named was a physician who later became MP for Launceston (a Granville borough) and, like Prior, found himself in the Tower as a suspected Jacobite conspirator.[53] Two were also held 'some standing as men of wit' were Granville and the Earl of Orrery. Five are listed as members on account of their

---

[51] In Delarivier Manley's political satire *The New Atlantis* (1709) the poems are mentioned in a respectful account of Granville, and the keys to this work identify Myra as Jane Hyde, later Countess of Rochester, who was married to the Queen's first cousin Henry Hyde: see Manley (1991: 97, 282).

[52] Quoted by Monod in Cruickshanks and Black (1988: 32).

[53] Freind was certainly heavily involved in the Atterbury plot. He also selected the nurse to attend the infant Charles Edward Stuart. In medical matters he was an ally of Pope's friend Dr Richard Mead, who is said to have arranged for his release from the Tower.

government positions: these include St John, Sir William Wyndham, and the Duke of Ormonde. Seven are categorized as 'chosen because of their family connections'; three of these were Harley connections, two Masham family members, and one the son of Lord Keeper Harcourt. This was Simon Harcourt, whose death in 1720 prompted a characteristic epitaph from his friend Pope. Lastly there were three individuals made members for 'general or "accidental" reasons': these included Allen Bathurst, a young MP soon to join the roll of peers. Another in this category was the youthful Duke of Beaufort, who would almost certainly have sided actively with the rising but for his early death in May 1714. He had already been admitted to the Order of the Garter (see Chapter 6, below). Two names proposed but rejected included that of the Earl of Jersey. As remarked elsewhere, Robert Harley and Lord Harcourt were deliberately excluded from this grouping.[54]

Two striking facts are immediately apparent on the most cursory inspection of this list. First, all the members were avowed Tories of one description or another. Some were Hanoverians, some Jacobite in sympathy, some undeclared.[55] Most were or had been MPs. Second, the great majority of them were acquainted either with Swift (in other connections) or with Pope, or both. Disregarding Swift and Arbuthnot, at least three can be described as close friends of the poet—these were St John, Edward Harley, and Simon Harcourt. Two more, Matthew Prior and Colonel Disney, were also well known to Pope, although at this date they were closer to Swift. More astonishing than anything is the fact that *every single one* of the twenty members in question subscribed to the *Iliad* in 1715, with the lone exception of Dr Friend—and even he later subscribed to the *Odyssey*. While not all these relationships had yet fully blossomed, the list shows that Pope had already established elective affinities with a group wholly identified with the Tory cause. In that sense Granville was representative of a broader Tory grouping within the circles of power. Moreover, in a society which merged politicians with men of letters, Granville was almost alone as a genuine poet/statesman. In focusing his poem as he did, Pope hit a larger target than we might at once realize.

A few months later the famous moment arrived when the Queen suddenly pulled out a list of twelve lords from her pocket, and instructed her astonished secretary of state, Lord Dartmouth, to draw up warrants for them. Oxford had decided on this as the only way to make up a majority in order to get the peace treaty through the House of Lords, and Anne had reluctantly conceded. On 31 December 1711 the twelve new peers were officially announced in the *London Gazette*. They included two men related to the Lord Treasurer: Thomas Foley, an MP from the same Hereford/Worcester area as his cousin the Earl of Oxford, and George Hay, by courtesy Viscount Dupplin, MP for Fowey (again!) and the husband of Oxford's youngest daughter Abigail. Dupplin was almost certainly a Jacobite, at this date and later. At the time of the rising in 1715, he was arrested as a prime suspect, along with Lansdowne and the second Earl of Jersey: the latter was Edward Villiers's son, and a

[54] Kerby-Miller (1950: 5–7).
[55] Among the virtually undisguised Jacobites here were Granville himself, Dupplin, Jersey, Bathurst, Ormonde (plus his brother the Earl of Arran), Beaufort, and Freind.

crony of Pope later to be awarded Jacobite favours. In 1715 Dupplin's father and brother were also taken into custody, while his deceased sister had been the wife of the Earl of Mar, chief military leader of the rebellion.[56] Another of the new peers, Lord Bruce, was probably loyal to the Pretender (his father had been in exile for many years because of activities against William III). So quite conceivably was Bathurst, too, a more extreme figure at this stage than in his mellower years as patron of Pope. More surprising choices were Sir Thomas Trevor, Lord Chief Justice of the Common Pleas, who was an ally of Bolingbroke; and Samuel Masham, husband of the Queen's favourite Abigail. Masham had been an equerry to Prince George of Denmark; he was now cofferer of the Queen's household and MP for Windsor. They were a somewhat motley collection. Despite that, nine of the twelve subscribed to the *Iliad* three years later: anyone favoured by the Oxford ministry was likely to show up in that register of individuals wishing well to Pope.[57]

Swift carefully rehearsed the names of those on the list and commented to Stella on their introduction into the Lords on 2 January 1712. The crowd in the house was too great for him to gain entry, so he made his congratulations in the robing room. Afterwards he went to wish Lady Masham 'joy of her new honour' (*JTS* ii. 453). Some of those elevated were given a reward for previous services, some proved useful in the days to come. Many were nonentities, like political appointees in any age. The one with the most important role in the government, technically at least, was the new Lord Lansdowne.[58]

The earliest contact which can be traced between Pope and Lansdowne after the poem's appearance is a letter from the peer dated 21 October 1713. This is short but significant. The first paragraph expresses Lansdowne's pleasure that Pope has committed himself to translating Homer, and promises his friend to exert 'the utmost services . . . in promoting this work'. The second paragraph concerns John Stafford, who had received a royal pardon and a reversal of his outlawry. Stafford was a brother of the first Earl Stafford, and a member of a strongly Jacobite family (*Corr.* i. 194–5). Pope owed this man 'particular obligations', as he told John Caryll, a friend of Stafford's son (*Corr.* i. 164).[59] Lansdowne's amicable tone shows that he had been pleased with the prominence he had been accorded in *Windsor-Forest*, and that its political line had gone down well with this fervent supporter of the Stuarts.

To all appearances, Lansdowne was caught totally undecided when the relationship between his friends Oxford and Bolingbroke broke into direct conflict as the peace process went on. If anything, he seems to have sided with the Lord Treasurer.

[56] In fact his brother John Hay became the Pretender's chief secretary and adviser in 1724.

[57] Trevor, one of the three new peers who did not subscribe to the *Iliad*, is found on the *Odyssey* list.

[58] The day after his introduction to the Lords, Lansdowne attended a member of the Brothers Club, but according to Swift he was anxious to get back to his new bride (*JTS* ii. 454). At this time Swift and Lansdowne were meeting regularly, and remained on excellent terms. It is possible that Swift met Pope through this agency.

[59] Stafford's son William succeeded as second Earl, and in 1720 he was granted an elaborate 'exemplification' of badges he was entitled to use, including those of his grandfather, executed as a traitor at the time of the Popish Plot. See Fox-Davies, 461–3.

In October 1712, he made an effort to heal the breach at the christening of his eldest daughter, choosing each of them as a godfather, while the Queen allowed herself to act as a godmother. This was a striking gesture, with a child named Anne sponsored by the monarch and her two most powerful ministers. But the split between the Treasurer and the Secretary of State had now grown too wide to repair. Without a central role in government, Lansdowne remained close to the drama being played out at court. When Oxford was finally dismissed, as Anne lay on her deathbed, he was there to witness the bizarre preliminaries to the accession of George I: 'The bewildered Lansdowne saw the messengers, already booted and spurred, waiting in the anti-room for the Queen to breathe her last, before setting off post-haste for Hanover.'[60] He had indeed been a spectator at most of the key events throughout this troubled ministry; and Pope in choosing him as dedicatee had done what could be done to find an uncontroversial representative of the Tory hierarchy.

Abundant evidence has come to light which links Lansdowne with the failed rising of 1722. This attempt is now linked with the names of the conspirators rounded up by Walpole, notably Bishop Atterbury, who was deprived of his preferments and forced into exile, and Christopher Layer, who was hanged and had his skull nailed up on London Bridge. The expedition was to be led by the Duke of Ormonde, but a crucial role was allotted also to Lansdowne, who was to land in Cornwall and raise the people in his familiar West Country. How significant he had become in the exiled court is shown by the fact that the Pretender recognized him as his chief minister in Paris from the summer of 1721: oddly his rival for this post was Matthew Prior. Lansdowne was actually named as head of a government in exile, together with the Duke of Ormonde and his brother the Earl of Arran. When things began to go wrong with the plan, the Pretender turned instead to the Earl of Mar, and Lansdowne found himself reduced to a supporting role.[61] By midsummer 1722 the whole scheme was in ruins. Leaks and accusations of betrayal fired back and forth between the conspirators. Even before Atterbury was arrested in August, the proposed invasion had been abandoned, with Ormonde immured in Madrid and Goring fleeing from England in panic. Walpole's spies and informers acquired enough colourable evidence to convict the handful of conspirators who were left at home. The Jacobite court was plunged into dissension, with Mar accused of betraying the plot, and Lansdowne suspected of having used Jacobite funds to defray his notoriously profuse private expenditure (see Bennett, 282). It was a further blow to his reputation, and in fact Samuel Johnson totally obscured Lansdowne's involvement in the Atterbury affair when he compiled *The Lives of the Poets.*[62]

---

[60] Hamilton (1969: 264). The source for this is Thomas Carte, from a conversation with Lansdowne in 1724.

[61] The Pretender set up a notional Council of Regency, in case he should himself be unable to take part in the rising: all eight names on the list figured among Pope's *Iliad* subscribers, with the exception of his closest friend in the group, Atterbury.

[62] The fullest account of Lansdowne's futile efforts to negotiate a workable path of policy through the squabbles raging among groups surrounding the Old Pretender is still that of Handasyde (1933: 171–217), based on the Royal Archives at Windsor. This needs only marginal correction in the light of subsequent research.

The entire episode has its tragic dimension, and that is what emerges from the correspondence of Atterbury and his loyal friend Pope. The former bishop lived out his last days in exile, with his belief in the Pretender, always limited, now totally destroyed. When Atterbury died in 1732, his body was brought back to England, and even then his coffin was opened at Deal in the search for incriminating documents. His funeral was held in an almost empty Westminster Abbey, which of course had been Atterbury's charge as Dean, and his tomb was left without any inscription. It was almost a replay of the burial of Charles I. Once again *Windsor-Forest* points to the future, as well as the past, of Jacobite martyrdom. At the same time, the Atterbury affair has a muddled and almost farcical side too, where blundering espionage and bickering personalities enact a comic 'plot', and that is the aspect of the affair where Lansdowne mainly features. It is a grim irony that Pope's dream of a noble Stuart restoration should have fizzled out, exactly a decade later, in this absurd imbroglio. Ironic, too, that Lansdowne lost some £10,000 in the failure of the South Sea Company—a project whose inception Pope's poem sets out to vindicate, as we shall see in Chapter 6.

Windsor-Forest speaks of the 'Honours' which Landsowne deserves, and the 'new Lustre' he will add to the Garter star: actually, the only insignia he and his friend Bolingbroke would be able to flaunt in years to come were the trumpery ribbons of the Jacobite peerage. (The Pretender actually made his own meaningless award of the Garter to the flashy Duke of Wharton.) There is something pitiable about Lansdowne's protracted efforts to collect the trappings of nobility. He had begun by soliciting a peerage from Harley after the death of his brother Bevil in 1706, but the Duke of Marlborough had scotched this. When his kinsman, the young Earl of Bath, died in May 1711 and the title became extinct, he immediately reminded the Lord Treasurer that the Earl's father (Granville's uncle) had promised him the favours and estates of the family: 'it is in her Majesty's power,' he shamelessly observed, 'by owning me in some distinguishing manner to make everything easy'.[63] Despite all his efforts, this long-desired elevation was refused: and the barony he did receive at the end of this year gave him poor consolation. With an equal lack of success, Lansdowne made the ludicrous proposal that he should take the title of Earl of Corbeil, which he had somehow derived from his ancestry. Hence, in the light of these failures, his continuing eagerness to make good a claim he would advance later to the Pretender. This was to the effect that Charles II had once promised to the Granville heir, in default of male heirs in the direct line, the title of Duke of Albemarle, which had been awarded to George Monck. In fact Monck, remembered as political architect of the Restoration, was a cousin of Lansdowne's father. Nobody could confirm any such promise, but it seemed harmless in the unreal world of the Jacobites to indulge this wish. So in December 1721 a warrant was issued to create George Granville in the full dignities of his supposed ancestral line: 'Duke Marquis Earl Vicount & Baron of our Realm of England by the Style & Title of duke of Albemarle Marquis Monck & Fitzhemon Earl of Bathe Vicount Bevil & Baron Lansdowne of Bideford . . .'[64] Thus fantasy achieved what had been denied in the cold climate of reality.

---

[63] Handasyde (1933: 112).
[64] Handasyde (1933: 187). Lansdowne wrote the preamble for his own patent.

When he wrote his lines on the Garter, Pope may also have recalled Virgil's description of Priam, where Dryden's translation reads, 'His Race in after times was known to Fame, | New Honours adding to the *Latian* Name' (*Aeneid*, v. 737–8). As it turned out, Lansdowne's children would all be daughters, and so his barony expired, like the dynasty he served. There was to be no further serious attempt at a rising in the poet's lifetime, although fears of an invasion arose periodically, as in the early 1730s. Nor did Pope survive to witness Culloden, but he probably felt that the sun had set on the Jacobites' hopes as far back as 1723, by which time *Windsor-Forest* had come to seem no more than an elegy for a lost cause.

From Lansdowne's own standpoint, he was a loyal Jacobite almost in spite of himself. As part of his best-known speech to the House of Lords, on the Occasional Conformity bill in 1718, he attacked those who had aspersed the memory of Charles I, and he felt a sense of 'almost personal injury' over the misfortunes of the Stuarts— perhaps because his own ancestors had suffered so much in the cause.[65] He wrote to the Pretender in 1720, 'I was born and bred a servant of your Family: my affection for it began with my Life, and shall end with it: It is the only part of my Inheritance which Violence and Power has not been able to break into.'[66] This is a mode of loyalty based on kith and kindred which may appear absurd when we look for ideological imperatives in human conduct; but the author of *Windsor-Forest* needed no instruction in family piety.

THE CHOICE OF A PATRON

Perhaps the most mysterious and fascinating phase of George Granville's entire life is the period he spent in 'retirement' under William III.[67] Frances M. Clements has cited 'a long denunciation of courts and courtiers, of flattery and place-seeking', culminating in a section of *beatus ille* verse, which Granville wrote in 1690. It includes the following:

> Happy the man, of mortals happiest he,
> Whose quiet mind from vain desires is free . . .

The verses celebrate Wycherley, another of the young Pope's mentors, as 'Possest of little, worthy of the best' (Chalmers, ii. 269).[68] Clements quotes another poem, presumably dating from this period, which proceeds in this manner:

[65] Handasyde (1933: 167–8). The speech was immediately printed and created more of a sensation than anything else Lansdowne had written.

[66] Quoted from the Royal Archives, MS Stuart 46/66, by Monod, 269.

[67] It was probably in this phase that Granville came to know Dryden, and was prompted to write an admiring poem to his 'friend' praising 'several excellent translations of the ancient poets' (Chalmers, ii. 287). Dryden supplied commendatory verses, bequeathing his laurels to Granville, which were appended to *Heroick Love* in 1698.

[68] Granville wrote a defence of his 'personal and intimate friend' Wycherley, in a letter addressed to Henry St John (Handasyde 1933: 68). This letter, dating from around 1705–6 (by which date Pope was also acquainted with Wycherley) was reprinted in Curll's life of the dramatist (1718). In establishing the nexus of Pope's friendships during the early part of his career, we need to take account of Granville as well as Trumbull: the dedicatee of *WF* was familiar with Betterton in addition to Dryden, St John, and Wycherley.

> In quiet shades, content with rural sports,
> Give me a life remote from guilty courts,
> Where free from hopes or fears, in humble ease,
> Unheard of, I may live or die in peace.
>   Happy the man who thus retir'd from sight,
> Studies himself and seeks no other light.

(Chalmers, ii. 268)

There are assuredly striking similarities here with Pope's passage on the retired life (235–58), and Clements is right to say that Lansdowne would fit the passage more neatly insofar as the phrase 'whom the Muse inspires' is inapt for Trumbull (see *TE* i. 171). But Lansdowne in other respects is a much less suitable avatar of the retirement theme than Trumbull, and Clements's suggestion that the latter 'is merely mentioned in passing' offends against reason.[69]

First, Trumbull had made an authentic withdrawal from positions of real power—this matches ll. 235–6 of *Windsor-Forest*, whereas in Lansdowne's case he had not held any significant post at court under James II. Second, Trumbull had deliberately involved himself in the rural environment, whereas we have no evidence that Granville, as he then was, did anything comparable. Third, Trumbull made his retirement home exactly where the design of the poem requires, in the heart of Windsor Forest, near to the poet's boyhood residence. He was a forester, something no one could claim for Lansdowne at any stage. Fourth, Trumbull cultivated a vein of philosophical stoicism; Pope could look on him as an aged prophet, as we noted in Chapter 1, whereas Granville had been no more than 25 when he left court, and outside his literary effusions gave no indication that he had embraced a life of spartan austerity. On the contrary, he was known for his profuse spending, as soon as he had any money to spend; and he made a rich marriage to a wife who was also known for her lavish tastes. It would have been a tactless thing to do, putting it mildly, if Pope had celebrated Lansdowne in 1713 as an exemplar of noble living in seclusion. The man was newly married, held a major post at the centre of the monarchical structure at Whitehall, had recently held nominal oversight for the destructive war against France, and accepted favours which included a peerage. Whatever Granville may or may not have written in 1690, he had lost all plausibility as a woodland sage. There is something naive, then, about the conclusion reached by Clements: 'Lansdowne's opinion of court life changed, of course, with the accession of Queen Anne and his own return to favour, but twenty-three years before the publication of *Windsor-Forest*, he was saying things about rural retirement which Pope probably had in mind when he wrote ll. 235–58 of that work.'[70] On the contrary, Pope may have striven hard to forget Granville's former literary poses, as he attempted to dignify the munificent Baron Lansdowne in appropriate language. The role of Cincinnatus was not one which sat easily any longer on this grandee among the Tories.

As a matter of fact, some other poems by Lansdowne have a more integral

---

[69] Clements (1972: 49).   [70] Clements (1972: 51).

connection with *Windsor-Forest*. In 'The Progress of Beauty', he conducts a review of 'our gallant kings', including a section on Edward III (Chalmers, ii. 275).

The halting verse Granville produces could have taught Pope little about metrical writing, and the popular legend he mentions regarding the foundation of the Order ('Salisbury's garter') is conspicuously absent in *Windsor-Forest*. But Edward is appropriated for much the same reasons by Granville as he is by Pope (*WF*, 305). After a lament for the Revolution and banishment of Charles II, Granville contrives a compliment to his mentor: 'Then Waller in immortal verse proclaims | The shining court, and all the glittering dames', recalling Pope's claims for Surrey and Granville himself. The poem moves on to celebrate Mary of Modena, and after this a gallery of court beauties, including 'Villiers . . . of a high race', that is the Countess of Orkney. An earlier poem to Dryden describes Britain as rich in soil, yet still spreading 'her wanton sails on every shore' to import foreign wealth: 'To her own wool the silks of Asia joins, | And to her plenteous harvests, Indian mines' (Chalmers, ii. 287), an idea more deftly expressed in Pope's conclusion.

However, the most immediately relevant item in Granville's canon dates from the new century. It takes the form of a prophecy, spoken by Urganda 'by way of Epilogue, at the first representation of *The British Enchanters*' [1706]. Actually, the verses seem to correspond rather to an addition which Granville made when the play was revived in 1707, after consultations with Harley and St John: this centered on a final masque-like scene, where the Queen appeared on a throne in Woodstock Park. The cast list of the play describes Urganda as 'a good enchantress' and friend to Amadis de Gaul. Her prophecy is set against 'a scene representing the QUEEN, and the several triumphs of her majesty's reign'. Next to her, the verse tells us, stands 'victorious Marlboro', an unavoidable coupling at that date. This is the concluding passage:

> Empress and conqu'ror, hail! thee Fates ordain
> O'er all the willing world sole arbitress to reign;
> To no one people are thy laws confin'd,
> Great Britain's queen, but guardian of mankind;
> Sure hope of all who dire oppression bear,
> For all th'oppress'd become thy instant care.
> Nations of conquest proud, thou tam'st to free,
> Denouncing war, presenting liberty;
> The victor to the vanquish'd yields a prize,
> For in thy triumph their redemption lies;
> Freedom and peace, for ravish'd fame you give,
> Invade to bless, and conquer to relieve.
> So the Sun scorches, and revives by turns,
> Requiting with rich metals where he burns.
>   Taught by this great example to be just,
> Succeeding kings shall well fulfil their trust;
> Discord, and war, and tyranny shall cease,
> And jarring nations be compell'd to peace . . .

>   (Chalmers, ii. 289)

Plainly this operates at a much lower level of poetic inspiration than *Windsor-Forest*, as well as at a less sophisticated political level. All the same, the culminating section of the Utrecht poem deals in *precisely* the same verbal currency as the conclusion of *The British Enchanters*. Pope follows Granville's line of thought very closely, besides taking across some details of phrasing ('Succeeding Monarchs', *WF*, 85) and uses identical rhymes (*cease/peace*). It is part of the polite compliment that Pope should make over his patron's verse in a nobler vein; and we remember that 'Granville the polite' (*Epistle to Arbuthnot*, 135) was famous above all for that one quality.[71]

A revelatory passage on Lansdowne also figures in Tickell's *Prospect of Peace*. In this poem Tickell imagines the produce of Britain's trade, in lines immediately following those Pope had quoted in his letter to John Caryll:

> Here nearer suns prepare the ripening gem,
> To grace great Anne's imperial diadem,
> And here the ore, whose melted mass shall yield
> On faithful coins each memorable field,
> Which, mix'd with medals of immortal Rome,
> May clear disputes, and teach the times to come.
>
> (Chalmers, ii. 378)

The subjects for these medals naturally begin with the Queen ('In circling beams shall godlike Anna glow') and Marlborough ('And Churchill's sword hang o'er the prostrate foe'). They end with Bishop Robinson and Lansdowne:

> And if the Muse, O Bristol, might decree,
> Here Granville noted by the lyre should be,
> The lyre for Granville, and the cross for thee.
>
> (Chalmers, ii. 378)

This feeble antithesis creaks, but it indicates that Lansdowne, the only non-military secular figure to be modelled, was regarded by others as enough of a poet to count.[72] Pope considered the introduction of the coins one of the 'strokes of mastery' in Tickell's poem, and so it would be a passage he dare not duplicate in any obvious way.

It has been suggested that 'The medallic allusion may be a compliment to Addison, whose *Dialogues upon Medals* was first published posthumously in Tickell's

---

[71] Lansdowne's most urbane work, the *Essay upon Unnatural Flights in Poetry*, certainly left its mark on Pope's *Epistle to Augustus*: compare e.g. Granville, ll. 97–110, with Pope, ll. 209–14.

[72] Lansdowne was also the recipient of an *Epistle* from Edward Young in the same year as *WF*. As late as 1719, the Duke of Buckinghamshire could name him as a candidate for the vacant laureateship—the only peer, besides the Duke himself, who is nominated in the comic proceedings. The 'professional' writers named include Prior, Pope, Congreve, Trapp, Young, Vanbrugh, Ambrose Philips, Fenton, Gay, Southerne, Hughes, and, surprisingly, Atterbury (Chalmers, ii. 655). Lansdown figures, too, as one of the poets singled out by Gay in his verses 'On a Miscellany of Poems' (1712), accompanied this time by Buckinghamshire, Congreve, Prior, Addison, Garth, and Pope.

edition of Addison's *Works* (1721).'[73] That is entirely plausible, but it is worth adding that about 1713–15 Pope wrote his own poem 'To Mr. Addison, Occasioned by his Dialogues on Medals', although it did not reach print until 1720, and then went into the Addison edition. In this work Pope describes the way in which Ambition finds 'all her Triumphs shrink into a Coin' (24). The conquests of Caesar are reduced to thumbnail sketches, in the familiar miniaturizing mode Pope favoured: 'Beneath her palm here sad Judaea weeps . . . A small Euphrates thro' the piece is roll'd, | And little Eagles wave their wings in gold' (26, 29–30). These, of course, are the emblematic Roman eagles. In his final paragraph, Pope wonders when Britain will rival Rome in commemorating its achievements: 'In living medals see her wars enroll'd, | And vanquish'd realms supply recording gold?' Patriots, warriors, and even 'laurell'd Bards' should be preserved, 'A Virgil here, and there an Addison' (55–6, 61–2).

The wider implications of the poem have been sensitively explored by Erskine-Hill, who shows Pope to exploit the traditional iconographic vocabulary, as in his use of the figure of history.[74] A narrower point relevant here is that *Windsor-Forest* perpetuates British worthies in an alternative language to that of the Addison lines, heraldic rather than numismatic. Despite that difference, the emblems are often identical: James Craggs shall 'erect his head', etched in relief, as the Thames 'advanc'd his rev'rend Head' and as 'Grav'd on his Urn appear'd the Moon', while above 'the figur'd streams . . . *Augusta* rose in Gold' (330–6). Craggs is designated 'another Pollio', calling up recollections of Virgil's fourth *Eclogue* and of the Golden Age, which was a reference Addison had made in his own dialogues. Pope may have felt that he dare not stray into numismatics to celebrate Lansdowne—as indicated, this was immediately next to the passage in Tickell he had worried over, when writing to Caryll. However, the emblematic language he did use in *Windsor-Forest* has direct affinities with the motifs of coinage in the poem to Addison: in the latter, we hear of 'the prostrate Nile or Rhine' (28), an image of river gods lying recumbent, almost in the 'dormant' pose. Not for the only time, Tickell seems almost to have intuited the way Pope's mind was going. Poetically inferior though his engraved medals may be, they perform the same memorializing function as the coins of Pope's lines to Addison, and the shields and banners of *Windsor-Forest*.

Lansdowne was not in every way the ideal choice of patron. This is not just because, as has been pointed out, he played very little role in the Utrecht negotiations, or indeed the preliminary consultations.[75] Nor does it matter very much that his poetic career was effectively over, so that none of the 'songs' Pope requests of him were ever going to be heard, in the groves of Windsor or anywhere else. That he was doomed to lose all political influence within eighteen months, and would then spend two years in the Tower, is a positive boon for Pope's martyrology. That he was designed to take a central part in the hopelessly mismanaged rising of 1722, which ended in the disgrace and exile of Pope's great friend Atterbury, adds a further grain of retrospective pathos. What limits Lansdowne's effectiveness in the symbolic role cast for

---

[73] Cummings (1988: 147).   [74] Erskine-Hill (1965: 274–98).   [75] Cummings (1988: 146).

him is his lack of an intimate relation with the scenes of Pope's boyhood—here, Trumbull was a much more effective agent of the poem's central purposes. Lansdowne was not a forester, and his 'retirement' seems to have been political, so to speak, more than existential.[76] As a poet he descended from the line of Waller, where the Cowley/Denham inheritance would have sealed the imaginative logic more effectively.

Nevertheless, this is to apply standards of suitability which conventional decorum did not require of a poet–patron relationship. In many respects Lansdowne fills the bill admirably, and as just noted his later history served to identify his own fate with that of the doomed Stuart cause. He went down with his royal mistress, and even though he was not a Catholic he shared in the retributions meted out to Jacobites by the incoming Hanoverian regime. At the time of *Windsor-Forest*, in his public and private life, he was closely associated with Anne, as Trumbull for instance was not: we have seen that she had recently acted as godmother to his first child. This serves to connect aspects of the design of the poem, by fusing the literary and monarchical elements in the central section dealing with Windsor. After the Queen's death, it was Lansdowne whom Pope chose to visit at Longleat, when he was staying at Bath in October 1714 (*Corr.* i. 261). All in all, Pope had little reason to regret his association with the peer: 'Lord Lansdowne insisted on my publishing my *Windsor-Forest*, and the motto shows it,' he told Spence with evident satisfaction (*Anecdotes*, i. 43). We should be grateful that aristocratic patronage, a system soon on its way out, could provide this kind of support for the young Swan of Windsor.

Especially in the light of later history, some of Lansdowne's very faults equipped him for the role. As we have seen, he was assiduous in pursuit of favours (as Trumbull assuredly was not); and he had a lifelong taste for ceremonial and pomp, again unlike Pope's elderly benefactor. Nor were the grandiose dynastic plans which his vanity devised ever fulfilled: his direct family line was to become extinct, and even his Jacobite title evaporated when his nephew and heir died unmarried. His personal fortune thus stands as a metaphor for the demise of the Stuarts, and underlies the tragic subplot of *Windsor-Forest*.

One small but highly pertinent fact remains, which has never been observed. *Windsor-Forest* was published on 7 March 1713, a Saturday. On Monday 9 March, Lord Lansdowne reached his forty-seventh birthday. The poem thus constituted an anniversary gift: copies could have been transmitted in good time to the recipient at his lodgings in Whitehall, or sent down to Longleat. As often, Pope manages to implicate a personal compliment within the public celebration of '*Albion*'s Golden Days'.

[76] In fact Lansdowne did inherit from his father an enclosure in Windsor Great Park, known as Moat Park. This had been bequeathed to Bernard Granville by the Duke of Albemarle, together with the manor of Clewer on the western edge of the town of Windsor. Lansdowne always had difficulty collecting the rents on these properties, and in 1720 he sold them to Arthur Vansittart (*VCH Berkshire*, iii. 73, 82). Late in life he lived part of the time at Old Windsor, near to Moat Park, in a house belonging to his wife.

Politics

In the same breath, *Windsor-Forest* articulates a politics of the long term, one of the medium term, and one of the short term. The first concerns large historical issues, so much so that in dealing with them the poem replays some of the ideological contests of the Civil War. The second relates to the reign of Anne as it was affected by the expulsion of her father James II and the rule of her sister and brother-in-law, William and Mary. The third has to do with the immediate context of Pope's poem, as the Utrecht settlement came before the public with predictably divisive results.

Under all three aspects the nature of the Queen's personal monarchy come into question. Over the longer span, it was the hereditary claims of the Stuart kings, allied to their authoritarian procedures and dynastic pride, which had contributed to the troubles besetting the nation in the seventeenth century. All involved a notion of monarchy at odds with the views of many among their subjects. In some ways the Queen had toned down these claims, but she maintained an august sense of the royal prerogative in such matters as the disposal of honours (an issue relevant to Pope's assertion at ll. 289–90). In addition, as we shall shortly recall, she was the last to exercise sovereign powers as a thaumaturgic healer. In the medium term, Anne had broken with many of the ruling styles of William III, and her symbolic home of Windsor, as against Hampton Court or Kensington, expressed her elective affinity with traditional practices of government. To put it only a little too simply, she rejected the urban, bourgeois, and worldly ethos of her predecessor. Finally, as regards the short term, the Queen was inescapably involved in the manoeuvring which surrounded the peace process. She has been forced to create new peers to get an earlier stage of the negotiations through parliament. Now she was required to read her minister's speech to the same body, justifying as it did the tortuous diplomacy of the previous three years. Worse, the poem was published just as the troublesome firebrand Henry Sacheverell emerged from his exile as a preacher, like some dangerous terrorist leader let loose from jail to enflame the populace.

On all three counts, *Windsor-Forest* endorses the royal stance. Its sweeping historical vision exculpates the Stuarts, with some licence, from the destructive policy of the Normans and early Plantagenets, not to mention Henry VIII. Charles I is installed as a martyr-king in need of a fit memorial (see Chapter 6, below). Tactfully, the poem avoids reference to James II, but its implicit message casts William III as an agent of despoliation and repression. In the short term, Pope attributes the successful completion of the war to the merits of Anne's personal rule, abetted by the loyal service of her ministry—another polite fiction. Whether peace and plenty are likely to survive, in the far from remote prospect of the day when a Brunswick reigns, is left delicately open to question.

HISTORY

The version of English history offered in *Windsor-Forest* is conditioned by a number of factors. These include Pope's Catholic background, his predominantly literary interests, his fundamentally classical training, and the specific needs of the poem.

Several aspects of history are conspicuous by their absence. For example, there is virtually nothing of the Cambro-Britannic narrative so influential in the eighteenth century. Late in life Pope actually planned an epic on the Brut legend, describing the foundation of a new Troy on British shores,[1] but there was no room for this theme in *Windsor-Forest*. By 1718 the poet was interesting himself in the work of Aaron Thompson on Geoffrey of Monmouth. However, this Celtic world too is a side of British antiquity which leaves no trace in his early poetry, unless one counts a glancing reference to 'old *Belerium*' (316) as an ancient name for Cornwall. Druids, the ever-present recourse of barren imaginations in this period, receive no attention, except perhaps in an oblique way when the poem celebrates a rural sage (on this topic see *SDW*, chapter 5). Fifty years later it might have been difficult for a poet to be so abstemious in these respects.

More revelatory is the lack of any Arthurian element. A strained argument might be constructed, to maintain that Arthur is present, as it were, under erasure. According to some chroniclers, the Order of the Garter owed its origin to Edward III's desire to recreate the Round Table—but if so, Pope suppresses this well-known item of Windsor legend. Though he draws much on Spenser (see Chapter 7, below), his invocation of the Red Cross declines any reference to Arthur. There is no prehistory to the poem's topographic survey. The forest effectively begins with the royal afforestation by the Normans, despite the fact that the Saxon kings had hunted in the surrounding woodlands for hundreds of years, and had set up a lodge called Windlesora, something Pope learnt from Camden.[2] Likewise, the castle begins not with its earliest embodiment under the Conqueror, or even with the twelfth century, when Henry I and Henry II held court there, but with Edward III many generations later. The line, 'Whom ev'n the *Saxon* spar'd, and bloody *Dane*' (77) goes unglossed by the editors, though it holds within itself a large potential history, derived from the antiquarians Pope studied.

We may say that the effective compass of the poem lies between the Norman Conquest and the date of writing. Certain periods within this span are given special

---

[1] See Torchiana (1962), as well as *Life*, 771–4.
[2] The nature of this debt is examined in *SDW*, ch. 4.

attention; others are passed over rapidly or ignored. The key phases for Pope are these: the early Norman era; the reign of Edward III; the Tudor age, especially the time of Henry VIII (cautiously handled) and Elizabeth; the entire seventeenth century, focusing significantly on the Civil War and Commonwealth, but downplaying the reign and eviction of Anne's father James II. It has long been recognized that William III has a central role in the poem, although he is never mentioned directly. Finally, there is a steady buzz of allusion to the reign of Anne, most especially to the course of the war and the approach to a peace settlement. The last part of *Windsor-Forest* projects into an imagined future, but it contains some implied history, for example that of the Spanish empire in America.

Little firm evidence exists to show what form Pope's reading took. His library was somewhat thinly stocked in this branch of learning. It is certain that he knew the work of Camden and John Selden, and he may well have gleaned something (not necessarily at first hand) from chroniclers such as William of Malmesbury. Naturally, he had read Shakespeare, Daniel, Drayton, and other poetic exponents of historiography. But where he got his version of seventeenth-century England is even more debatable. It seems highly likely that he would have studied Clarendon's *History*, since it made such an impact on its appearance in 1702–4. Clarendon was the Queen's grandfather, too, and Pope knew others among his descendants. Which of the competing accounts of the Civil War he consulted, we can only surmise. (Lansdowne would much later enter some of these controversies.) As the poem approached Pope's own day, he would obviously require fewer jogs to his memory. It is, however, worth emphasizing that some of the sources we naturally turn to nowadays, such as Gilbert Burnet's *History of his own Times* (published 1723–34), were not yet available.

In summary fashion, we can assess Pope's view of the different monarchs (this is a monarchically organized history), even if this risks sounding like the surveys of Jane Austen or Sellar and Yeatman. William the Conqueror and his son are present as tyrannical despoilers of the forest, but importantly they both stand as an antetype of William III, a later 'invader'. The conveniently vague reference to 'Succeeding Monarchs' who 'heard the Subjects Cries' (85) and instituted a gentler regime could apply to Plantagenets or Tudors, but again the real point is to lead up to the apotheosis of Liberty under Stuart rule. Much of the material sustaining the notion of the Norman Yoke was tendentious, and the despoiling of New Forest may well have been largely fictitious; but these things were widely enough believed to sustain the use Pope makes of them.

It is here that the most famous of Pope's textual alterations occurs. The climactic couplet runs in its familiar form:

> Fair *Liberty, Britannia*'s Goddess, rears
> Her chearful Head, and leads the golden Years.

> (91–2)

From 1736, Pope printed as a footnote an earlier draft of four lines, which is indeed present in the manuscript, and identical except in small accidentals. The manuscript reads:

Oh may no more a foreign Master's Rage
With Wrongs yet Legal, curse a future Age!
Still Spread, fair Liberty! thy heav'nly Wings,
Breathe Plenty on the Fields, and Fragrance on the Springs.

(Schmitz, 23–4)

One view of the change, expressed by Schmitz, is that Pope would not have wished to 'bespatter' the Peace 'with verses open to strong partisan interpretation' (Schmitz, 9). Most critics agree with J. R. Moore that the lines were simply too dangerous to be retained.[3] There is an even stronger consideration: the editors point out, 'As a matter of fact Charles I, not William III, revived the "yet legal" forest laws, primarily to raise money independently of parliament' (*TE* i. 159). This awkward fact is enough in itself to explain Pope's alteration. E. P. Thompson calls the revised version a 'more gummy' couplet than the material it replaces; he implies that it was George I whose displeasure Pope would fear (*Hunters*, 292). The evidence seems to indicate that Pope was aiming for William, but that he discovered the facts would not quite fit his indictment of this 'foreign Master' (see also below, p. 101).

The story is resumed with the Plantagenets. Here, Pope focuses on 'Edward of Windsor', Edward III, seen as creator of the Castle as well as founder of the Order of the Garter. We have seen that this was unhistorical: Pope may not have known that, as far back as 1202, King John invested his Archbishop of Canterbury, Hugh Walter, with the dual offices of constable of the castle and warden of the forest (*VCH* ii. 343). This was to cement the very connection which the poem strives to establish. Nor does Pope seem troubled by the fact that Edward's military accomplishments were fairly limited in the end. He is present as a kind of chivalric paladin, noted for his 'long Triumphs' (304), rather than as a battlefield warrior. What he does is quarter the French arms, as much as defeat French armies. So France will 'bleed for ever under *Britain*'s Spear' (310), frozen in this heraldic pose like the dragon under George's spear in the Garter badge.

The Wars of the Roses are commemorated in eight lapidary verses, devoted to the rival claimants to the throne, Henry VI and Edward IV. The former, who was born at Windsor, is called 'the Martyr-King' and allotted the appropriate funeral honours: 'Palms Eternal flourish round his Urn' (312–13).[4] Pope's treatment of the king is dictated by the circumstances of his death, that is to say his murder in London— at the hands, perhaps, of Richard of Gloucester—and the transfer of his body from Chertsey Abbey to Windsor, some time after the remains of his conqueror Edward IV had been buried at the castle. All this could easily be seen as a parallel to the fate of Charles I. In addition, Henry VI had spent a year living in disguise in the north of England after defeats at Towton and elsewhere; this could be interpreted as equivalent to the wanderings of Charles II following the battle of Worcester. Henry became a martyr figure for the Lancastrian cause and Henry VII even proposed his canonization. A number of miracles of healing were attributed to him, and pilgrims left gifts in an alms-box alongside his tomb. Equally, however, the verses celebrate

---

[3] Moore (1951: 454).   [4] See Bossewell (1572: fos. 72–3), on heraldic palms.

Edward IV, who had after all begun the building of the Chapel. He has been united in the grave with his adversary: 'where ev'n the Great find Rest, | And blended lie th'Oppressor and th'Opprest' (317–18). Possibly Pope was confronting imaginatively the death of Anne, which seemed to be, if not imminent, an event which could not be deferred for many years; she might perhaps be buried near her brother-in-law, William III, cast as the 'oppressor' here. This was indeed to happen in 1714.

When the implicit narrative reaches the Tudors, there is another elision. Here, the most pertinent comments come from Maynard Mack, who notes the oddity that no Tudor monarch is named directly: 'The omission seems striking in view of the fact that Henry VIII is buried in a monument impossible to overlook in the same chapel with the kings already mentioned' (*Life*, 60). Mack indicates that the description of the 'levell'd Towns', 'naked Temples', 'broken Columns', and 'Heaps of Ruin', culminating in a reference to 'the sacred Quires' (67–72), may have a hidden meaning, as first proposed by the Twickenham editors (see *TE* i. 156). The suggestion is that the passage intended 'to carry our mind four centuries onward [from Norman times] to Henry's dissolution of the monasteries.' Mack goes on to argue: 'Living in Berkshire, moreover, Pope was probably witness at first hand to the sad consequences of Henry's greed in the looting of the great abbeys. No traveler to Reading . . . about as far west of Binfield as Windsor lay to the east, could fail to notice the relics of the great Benedictine abbey there, once a jewel among English religious houses . . . now in the 1700s a thirty-acre precinct of broken columns, bits of tracery, decaying vaults and spandrels, rubble.' The king's hatchet-man Thomas Cromwell had the last abbot, Hugh Faringdon, hanged, drawn, and quartered, and the buildings were pillaged for books, manuscripts, tapestries, and gold plate (*Life*, 60). This is brilliantly acute commentary. Moreover, such a line of reasoning is strengthened by the fact that in *Cooper's Hill*, Pope's most direct model, Denham had lamented the fate of a Benedictine abbey at St Anne's Hill in Chertsey, falling 'in the Common Fate' of monasteries to the 'desolation' wrought by Henry VIII (see p. 280 below).[5]

The end of Abbot Hugh has an immediate resonance. He was butchered on a platform outside the gateway of his abbey, on 15 November 1539, having been accused by Cromwell of high treason and sent down from the Tower to face a perfunctory trial at Reading. Just two years earlier, the abbot had celebrated a solemn mass for Jane Seymour, when she was buried at Windsor (*VCH Berkshire*, ii. 69–72). In that vault she had been joined by Charles I; and *Windsor-Forest* will recall the fate of the martyr-king when it reaches St George's Chapel (see Chapter 6, below). It is likely that Pope knew this story almost by heart, in view of his religion and his closeness to the locality—for Whiteknights, where he regularly stayed with the Englefield family,[6] lay less than 2 miles from the abbey ruins. In case this should seem airy specula-

---

[5] For some reason Defoe believed that 'this Abbey is now so demolished, that scarce any Remains of it are found, or the Place of it known' (*Tour*, i. 293), a large overstatement: there were plenty of surviving remnants of the fabric for Pope to contemplate, and a few survive even today. On the abbey grounds were later sited a school attended by Jane Austen and a prison, one might heartlessly say, attended by Oscar Wilde.

[6] A recent case in point was a stay of a week in Nov. 1711 (*Corr.* i. 135).

tion, we can draw on a letter to Caryll, written in the summer of 1712—the year in which Pope completed *Windsor-Forest*—which shows that he was planning to meet his friend shortly at Reading (*Corr.* i. 144). Another meeting at Whiteknights was earmarked when Pope wrote to Caryll in January 1713, just before the poem made its appearance (*Corr.* i. 170). Again, Reading was on the direct route to Mapledurham: hence a visit to the town in 1714 (*Corr.* i. 253).[7]

With his strong sense of place, and his awareness of the past, Pope was an ideal connoisseur of the ruinous. When he spent time in the rat-infested fifteenth-century manor at Stanton Harcourt in 1717 and 1718, as he told Lady Mary Wortley Montagu, he found picturesque traces of history—'about 20 broken Pikes, & a match-lock Musquet or two, which they say were used in the Civil Wars'. An arched window was 'beautifully darken'd with divers Scutcheons of painted Glass'. The 'Blazoning' on one pane, dated 1286, showed a lady of the manor; another depicts a knight, 'whose marble Nose is molderd from his monument in the church adjoining'. He ends with a reflection: 'In this Hall, in former days have dined Garterd Knights & Courtly Dames, with Ushers, Sewers and Seneschals.'[8] Here he found 'an excellent place for Retirement and Study', as he worked on his Homer (*Corr.* i. 506–7). The tone of this letter to Lady Mary is playful, even skittish: but no one could doubt that the author of *Windsor-Forest* had a profound feeling for the vestiges of chivalry, and equally for the traces of a monastic era.

As a loyal Catholic, Pope can scarcely be expected to have shown Henry VIII in a favourable light. At the same time, he was writing in *Windsor-Forest* the panegyric of a Queen who had assented to the Protestant succession, and who sought to establish a line of continuity between herself and Henry's daughter Elizabeth. The poet has recourse to a selective blindness—and it was not generally known at this time that the 'obscure' burial place of Charles I (320) was actually located in the same tomb as that of Henry VIII, in the choir between the stalls of the Garter knights.[9] Mack is surely correct to say that Pope's omission of Henry and Elizabeth 'from his blazon of British glories' and 'perhaps even the veiled allusion to the destruction of the monasteries' express 'tacitly' a view of the treatment which English Catholics had received since the Reformation (*Life*, 61).

An interesting case has been developed by Vincent Carretta, to the effect that the poem constitutes a panegyric 'celebrating the restoration of England to the limited monarchy of Elizabeth'. On this reading, the Norman Yoke is invoked in order to demonstrate the usurpation of power by the Conqueror and his successors (see ll. 73–4). The Lodona episode is seen as a metaphor for the disastrous violence of the seventeenth century; and Anne is characterized as the new Elizabeth who will restore a lost constitutional paradise, where moderate 'mixed' government supplants

[7] See also Caryll's mention of a visit to Whiteknights with Pope at the end of 1714 (*EC* vi. 221).

[8] *Corr.* i. 506–7. In fact Pope could have found the effigy of a courtly dame in the nearby church, Margaret Harcourt (d. 1461). She is one of only three women known to have been depicted in Garter robes. This was the church where two of Pope's epitaphs were placed, one (1724) on Simon Harcourt and one (1718) on two young lovers killed by lightning.

[9] The location of Charles's skeleton is often said to have been unknown until the coffin was rediscovered in 1813: but see Ch. 6, below.

the absolutism of the Stuarts, the Commonwealth under Cromwell, and William III.[10] This account contains some valid observations; but it perhaps exaggerates the 'cyclical' nature of the poem, and it fails to deal with many issues. That Elizabeth is never mentioned by name, and only once implicitly, may not be significant, since Pope does a good deal behind the back of the text; but the theory is all but sunk by the absence of all reference to the Saxon dispensation (l. 77 suggests anything but a beneficent regime), as well as the total lack of nostalgia for a medieval (or British, Celtic, Roman, or Saxon) past. It should also be observed that, unlike Denham, Pope makes no mention of Runnymede as the trajectory of the poem carries us past Cooper's Hill. A Whig constitutionalist would hardly have let this chance to celebrate Magna Carta going begging.

Carretta effaces the many indications of allegiance to a specific Stuart legacy, and the signs that in Pope's scheme of history Elizabeth is no more than a precursor to the succeeding dynasty. Most of the emblems of the poem derive from the semiology of chivalry, starting with Edward III, and the martyrology of the Stuarts, starting with James I. In all likelihood Pope saw Anne as a more conciliatory figure on the throne than her uncle and father, but it is hard to see any passage in the work where he invites her to adopt a less absolutist style of monarchy. On the contrary, the artistic idiom constantly deifies the Queen, and confers an almost divine rectitude on her doings.

THE STUARTS

The poem's coverage of Stuart history is just as patchy as that of the Tudor reigns. James I, who had few links with Windsor, is never mentioned. Instead Pope concentrates on his son Charles I, laying heavy stress on the execution of the King and his burial in a then unknown grave at Windsor without any inscription. As Mack states, the 'Fact accurst' of his execution 'is clearly implied to have been the sin from which followed the rest of England's seventeenth-century trials and disorders (plague, fire, internal divisiveness), till at last Anne brought the country's warring factions together' (*Life*, 58). This may have been 'a ridiculous hope', but it is part of the central poetic impetus of the work. We have seen that the Civil War had suspended the peaceful pursuit of the chase in Trumbull's own demesne; the missing grave of the king represented a martyrdom uncommemorated, and a blank in the record of monarchy. After all, even William the Conqueror, who had been 'himself deny'd a Grave' by an attempt to forestall his burial (*WF*, 80), eventually gained his rest.[11] It was the task of the poem to blazon the Stuart achievement afresh, and to right a historic wrong by performing posthumous rites over the martyr's tomb (see Chapter 6, below). There were, of course, those who thought that Charles too should be can

---

[10]   Carretta (1981: 425–37).

[11]   Pope refers to the account by William of Malmesbury, which alleges that a local knight interrupted the funeral ceremony at Caen, asserting that the Conqueror had 'no claim to rest in a place which he had forcibly invaded' (*TE* i. 157–8). The intended parallel with William III seems unavoidable.

onized. This was a notion with which sermons delivered on the anniversary of the martyrdom (30 January) sometimes flirted. A clergyman named Binckes, when preaching before the Lower House of Convocation in 1701, actually maintained that the execution of the king was a greater sin than the Crucifixion, since Christ had not actually been anointed, and he was simply the uncrowned King of the Jews. Binckes was appointed dean of Lichfield two years later.[12] (Amazingly, Stuart supporters on the Continent, especially those close to the devout Mary of Modena, made serious attempts to have her late husband James II canonized as a holy martyr.)

At this point there is another change in the manuscript, which is much less well known because Pope did not signalize it in any of the notes he later supplied. Where we now have the line, 'Oh Fact accurst! What Tears has *Albion* shed' (321), there was originally a more expanded statement:

> Oh Fact accurs'd! oh sacrilegious Brood
> Sworn to Rebellion, principl'd in Blood!
> Since that dire Morn what Tears has Albion shed . . .
>
> (Schmitz, 40)

A pencilled gloss in the margin is now mostly illegible, but Schmitz deciphers the words 'Too general', and concludes that 'the lines were more violent than informative and too general to distinguish the Parliamentarians' (Schmitz, 10). This seems an odd judgement. In the context, no one else can have been indicated as performing a sacrilegious act, or as committed to rebellion, or as making a principle of bloodshed. Above all, the reference to 'that dire Morn' takes us back directly to the execution at Whitehall in 1649. This expression leads more naturally into the description which follows—covering war, plague, and fire—than is the case with the printed lines as we usually read them. The most natural conclusion would be that Pope wanted to avoid controversy over the origins of the Great Fire, especially. The editors tell us, 'many persons, irrespective of political loyalties, thought the Plague and Fire to be evidence of the wrath of God' (*TE* i. 180). This is true up to a point: the potential for embarrassment in Pope's own situation was that the Monument in the City of London bore an inscription which attributed the Fire to papist influence (see *Epistle to Bathurst*, 339–40). At this stage of his career Pope may well have been reluctant to call that claim a lie, as he did later. If so, this is a pity, because the lines he took out add extra cogency to his version of seventeenth-century history.

There is one more complication. Pope refers to the Norman kings under such phrases as 'a Tyrant' (52) and 'sportive Tyrants' (59), the 'Oppressor' ruled 'Tyrannick' (74); and expressions such as 'Despotick Reign' (58) abound. 'Savage Laws' took effect (45). These locutions were all used freely by royalists after the Restoration to characterize the Interregnum. For example, John Evelyn often speaks of Cromwell as the arch-rebel, the tyrant, or the usurper, seeing him as a Satan-like

---

[12] Again the submerged rhetoric of *WF* makes fuller sense if we recall earlier Stuart polemic: works like *Eikon Basilike* presented the martyred monarch as a Christlike Man of Sorrows, suffering for his people (cf. Parry, 252–4). A favourite anagram, in a reign which saw ingenious cryptography brought to new heights, was CHAROLVS STVARTVS = CHRISTVS SALVATOR, even though this meant eliding the missing 'I'.

figure who will return God's blessed creation to a primal chaos: 'One of the bloudi-
est Tyrannies, and most prodigious oppressors that ever any age of the world pro-
duc'd.' Writing in 1659 of the need to restore the king, Evelyn refers to 'the confusion
which must of course light upon us, if we persist in our rebellion and obstinancy. We
are already impoverisht, and consumed with wars': the interlopers have 'wasted our
treasure, and destroyed the woods' (Evelyn, 95). Thus Pope was able to draw on a
body of Stuart polemic which saw England reduced to a 'waste' under the Commonwealth (*WF*, 43), and his rhetoric implies that Cromwell, as well as the Norman
kings, may serve as an antetype of William III in the role of ravisher of the nation. At
the end of the poem, Faction, Rebellion, and Persecution are ritually struck down:
in royalist idiom, these were all code words for the rule of parliament and the army
in the 1650s.

Neither Charles II nor James II is explicitly mentioned in the poem: Pope's scruples concerning the religion of Anne's father and uncle, bearing in mind her own
fierce Protestantism, may have dictated this silence. But it is equally true that William
and Mary are, on the surface anyway, left out of the narrative. Again, there would be
potential for embarrassment in dealing with the conduct of the Queen's sister. Yet, as
we have seen, the section on the Norman Yoke points unmistakably towards a criticism of William as a later 'foreign Master'. Mack has argued that 'none of Pope's lines
can be connected more than superficially with William III' and that 'the evils attributed to the Norman Williams have very little to do with the charges normally leveled
by anti-Williamites against William III' (*Life*, 853–4). Here we may be more inclined
to agree with Douglas Chambers, who contends that reference to the king 'by allusion
and symbology is . . . consonant with Pope's mode of argumentation, which implies
a coterie of those who understand'.[13] In addition, William had more connection with
his medieval forebears than we recognize today. He still claimed the title of Duke of
Normandy; in turn Anne was attended at her coronation by two extras (unemployed
Shakespearian actors, perhaps) who played the part of the Dukes of Normandy and
Aquitaine, and were solemnly called to their places by the herald.

Besides this, Mack's objection does not take account of one obvious symmetry. In
his section on the New Forest, Pope describes the death of William II, 'At once the
Chaser and at once the Prey', after he was shot by Walter Tyrrel:

> Lo *Rufus*, tugging at the deadly Dart,
> Bleeds in the Forest, like a wounded Hart.

> (83–5)

The 'anti-Williamites' had, of course, made great capital of the death of William III,
which resulted from his fall while hunting deer in Richmond Park on 21 February
1702. This event led indirectly to the inauguration of Anne's reign two weeks later. A
parallel could also be drawn with the fate of William I, who died at Rouen in 1187 after
a fall from his horse. As the editors state, 'An element of divine justice was attributed
to both accidents by opponents of William III' (*TE* i. 157). It is hard to imagine an

---

[13] Chambers (1996: 135).

educated reader of 1713, in or out of the coterie, who could forget this double narra-tive—in each case, a foreign-born king dying as a result of an accident sustained while riding in a royal park. On a more general basis, William III was blamed by the Tories for having embroiled Britain in the wars to start with, and any poem celebrat-ing the end of those wars would naturally cast him as a man of violence—as the im-plicit parallel with the Normans does.[14] Finally, it was an article of Stuart faith that the fatality to the king could be linked with the passage, just a day before he died, of the Abjuration Bill, which in effect outlawed the Pretender. William's condition was so bad that the royal assent had to be given by stamping his initials on the document as he lay on his deathbed. Jacobites had no trouble in deciphering the runes.

E. P. Thompson has pointed out that the Stuarts maintained the same forest law and sometimes operated it more stringently than their predecessors. Further, Thompson's views have been developed recently by Chambers, who contends that 'it was largely in the imaginations of such Tories as Pope that the laws of William III seemed more savage than what had preceded them'. The Williamite laws mainly strengthened provisions against deer-stealing.[15] What seems to be happening is that Pope tacitly invokes William III as an invading tyrant; his depredations are upon the nation, rather than upon the forest specifically. But above all he is remembered, be-hind the text so to speak, as the author of anti-Catholic legislation, particularly 1 Wm & M, c.9 and 2 Wm III, c.4 (see p. 114, below). The new 'Norman' was emulating his predecessors by hounding Catholics, as they had hounded the people of the New Forest. Implicitly, the poem suggests that Pope will be driven from his own refuge in the Forest, and it did not take many years of Hanoverian rule to bring this predic-tion to fulfilment.

In a powerful recent account of the poem, Howard D. Weinbrot has suggested that Nimrod represents a different tyrant, Louis XIV. He also contends that the French king reappears as Pan in the Lodona section, with the besieged nymph standing for Mary II. This is part of a sustained reading, which offers the view that Pope rejects Roman values in favour of 'modern' Christianized virtues of peace and conciliatory international politics—a shift in sympathies which Weinbrot detects more widely in eighteenth-century literature. It is certain that Pope wished to im-port a religious dimension to the ending of his poem (see Chapter 4, below), and it is equally true that Pope shared the conventional British opinion of Louis XIV as a despot and self-aggrandizing conqueror, who had been suitably put in his place by the war. However, Weinbrot's account does not deal adequately with the hatred of foreign 'usurpers' in the poem, and seems to align *Windsor-Forest* too readily with Whig panegyrics of English liberty. In addition, there is no recognition of the for-mal and stylistic features which mark Pope's work off from the Whig celebrations of the peace, which echo the procedures of earlier Stuart modes, and which form the principal subject of this book.[16]

---

[14] Pope had attacked the 'Licence of a Foreign Reign', dominated by 'Unbelieving Priests', in *An Essay on Criticism* (ll. 544–6): see *TE* i. 300–2.

[15] Chambers (1996: 128); cf. *Hunters*, 40. The whole matter is explored in *SDW*, ch. 5.

[16] Weinbrot (1993: 276–96).

Windsor-Forest handles even the reign of Anne herself in a selective fashion. The military victories of Marlborough are displaced by the triumph of a glorious peace, and everything is done to conceal the fact that the second was ultimately dependent on the first. Six lines celebrate the successful operation to raise a siege (105–10): but these famously constitute the vehicle, not the tenor, of a metaphor.[17] In general, these verses have been thought to fit most aptly the capture of Gibraltar in July 1704 (*TE* i. 161). This would suit the politics of the poem, since the siege of the city was led by Sir George Rooke, who promptly became the Tory hero of the hour, especially after an ensuing naval victory at Malaga.[18] Propagandists likened the achievement to that of Blenheim—an unreal comparison at the time, but one which three hundred years of British occupation of Gibraltar may serve to justify. The Tory admiral was sacrificed a year later when the Queen had to turn to the Whigs, but his triumph could still be used as a reminder that Marlborough had not been the lone saviour of the nation during the war. It should be noted that the manuscript version has different phrasing at l. 107: 'Pleas'd in the Gen'ral's Sight, the Host lye down . . .' (Schmitz, 24). Maybe Pope thought this would be interpreted as a favourable reference to Marlborough, for example the Duke's conduct at the siege of Bouchain in 1711.[19] Even more apposite to the passage is the fact that the Union Jack was indeed hoisted on the ramparts of Gibraltar, even though the flag of Charles III was also flown. Not until the Peace was signed was the town technically claimed in the name of the Queen.

As a matter of fact, Rooke was already a man with a popular following, before the Gibraltar expedition. In October 1702, together with his fellow Tory the Duke of Ormonde, he had commanded the raid on Vigo Bay, which turned out to be one of the great coups in the entire war. Luckily, it also effaced a botched attempt to take Cadiz just a month earlier, which involved shameful plunder by Ormonde's principal lieutenant (Trevelyan, i. 272–5) It concealed, too, a serious rift over tactics between Rooke and his colleague Ormonde. The raid led to the capture of heavily laden galleons, with immense booty, especially the ingots of silver from Spanish America—some eleven million pieces of eight in all. News of the exploit provoked huge public rejoicings, described by John Evelyn (*ED* v. 520–1). Huzzas rang out in the streets while the Queen made her way to a large service of thanksgiving at St Paul's on 12 November; as she rode in state up Ludgate Hill, she passed an inscription proclaiming, 'As threatening Spain did to Eliza bow, | So France and Spain shall do to Anna now' (Gregg, 165): the same notion is expressed in the poem (383–4). Implau-

---

[17] See Brown (1985: 30), for whom the 'real issue' is imperial war.

[18] Another admiral involved was Sir Cloudesley Shovell, who lost some of his sheen in the failed Toulon expedition of 1707. On his return Shovell met his death in the wreck of the flagship *Association* off the Scilly Islands, with the loss of almost two thousand men—an event no laureate of the British navy could bear to recall.

[19] Contemporary accounts suggest that the small Spanish garrison at Gibraltar was taken unawares and put up a rather perfunctory defence, in line with Pope's description (106–10): see *Select Documents* (1929: 83–92). It had long appeared vulnerable owing to the absence of a garrison (Trevelyan, i. 424).

sibly, Vigo had been equated with the Armada, and Rooke with Drake. The admiral was made a Privy Councillor.[20]

Windsor-Forest trades on this recollection in its culminating lines on Britain's sea power: no naval victory of any consequence had been gained in the remaining years of Anne's reign. The most lasting commemoration of this event came with the coinage of 5-guinea, 1-guinea, and half-guinea pieces inscribed with the word 'VIGO', all minted from the gold which had been looted. The 5-guinea Vigo piece is 'one of the most exotic and valuable of all British coins'.[21] In addition, all the silver crowns, shillings, and sixpences minted in 1703, together with most of the half-crowns, bore this legend.[22] To remember such episodes was to see in the mind's eye the royal effigy sculpted on the silver coins, as Britannia's goddess reared her cheerful head in numismatic glory. It was also timely in 1713 to rehabilitate Ormonde, an undisguised Jacobite who had been forced to conduct a deliberately passive campaign in the previous year (see Chapter 5, below), in order that the war could simmer down into futility. All this was intended to cast Marlborough's military success into the shade.

An even more striking omission is the Union of Scotland. The Queen had fervently supported the proposal, and it had underwritten her legitimacy as a descendant of Scottish as well as English monarchs. Some High Tories had opposed the original terms of the Union settlement, but they had been won over or outflanked. However, the Union went through a phase of marked unpopularity in Scotland, in the years following its passage; and an ugly moment occurred in 1711, when the House of Lords refused to admit one of the new peers, the Duke of Hamilton, to the seat he now claimed in his own right (Trevelyan, iii. 254). Most Episcopalians remained true to the Jacobite cause; Presbyterians were further alienated by two parliamentary measures of 1712, the Toleration Act and the Patronage Act. By the spring of 1713, at the very time of *Windsor-Forest*, yet more trouble was stoked up by the controversial Malt Tax. Scottish peers actually proposed the repeal of the six-year-old Union, and Whig members of the House of Lords joined them in an opportunistic bid to embarrass the government. Even some of the original architects of the Union, notably Somers and Argyll, were prepared to pronounce it a failure. In the end, after losing the first vote, Oxford survived by a safe margin. We can only surmise how much of this would have been apparent to Pope at the start of the year, as the latter stages of the controversy extended until the very end of May: but it did not need political antennae of exorbitant sensitivity to know at the end of 1712 that the Union was a controverted issue, which could even lead to the downfall of the ministry. Finally, there is the additional consideration that Pope would have to tread even more carefully in this area, because of the violent manner in which Hamilton had recently met his death (see Chapter 2).

---

[20] The victory could also generously be construed as a triumph for Anne's consort, Prince George, whom she had made generalissimo and Lord High Admiral at the start of her reign. The Whig campaign to cut down Rooke's achievement was led by Defoe: see his 'Hymn to the Pillory', ll. 122–49, and Backscheider (1989: 174–8).

[21] Lobel et al. (1997: 412).

[22] Seaby (1990: 132).

In any case, both the military victories and the Union had enjoyed their own tri-umphal occasions. The immediate need was to bolster the upcoming celebrations for the Peace, something which was far from attracting universal support. Pope seeks to portray the Utrecht negotiation as having ushered in a long era of peace and stability to come. By implication, the showy spectacles which had greeted Marlbor-ough's feats would be effaced, as the nation dedicated itself to a new role in the world. The language is Messianic:

> Hail Sacred *Peace*! hail long-expected Days . . .
>
> (355)

In fact the whole poem works to make good this vision of predestined inevitability, as Pope employs the rhetoric of Old Testament prophecy and the tropes of provi-dential history.[23] The ending can only succeed if the link between past and future, in what has been called 'a slippage that takes the reader from *The Georgics* to *The Aeneid*,'[24] is convincingly rooted in earlier history. That is the point of Pope's Stuart mythology, expressed in his chronicles of the British monarchy. He probably intuited that things would never play themselves out in this way. Next year the Stuart line would come to an end, and the year after that the Old Pretender would fail abjectly in his designs on the throne. Both Anne and James Francis, in their own ways, would fall into the pattern of martyrdom which Pope has established—Henry VI, Charles I, the Earl of Surrey, the victims of the Normans, the monks who were driven out by Henry VIII, and, implicitly, the Catholic preys of the new Nimrod—William III. The poem calls up a future as well as a past: just three years after its appearance, the brutal Cado-gan would be leading English and Dutch troops in a sweep through the Scottish countryside in the wake of the Jacobite rising: they were said to have left 'nothing earthly undestroyed'.[25] Unsurprisingly *Windsor-Forest* offers a lurid version of his-tory, constantly stressing the violent rape of innocence by aggressive interlopers.

Pope's history, then, is condensed and contrived. It aims to suggest a particular destiny for the nation, and underwriting Stuart mythologies. The crucial need was to endorse Anne without reopening the sores inflicted by her father's unfortunate reign and his even more unfortunate departure from the throne. This is achieved partly by rewriting the annals of British monarchy, and especially by identifying the Stuart cause with heroic martyrdom. The narrative of Anne's own reign is tailored to a related purpose. The Queen is situated at Windsor rather than Whitehall: she is the symbol of chivalric perfection, a sylvan goddess who has substituted the chase for martial exploits, and has opted for peaceful expansion of commerce instead of the aggressive reign of the conquistadores. She presides over a national restoration in which the newly built churches of the city stand for the preservation of a spiritu-ality under threat. All this involves some tendentious reasoning, as it casts Marlbor-ough as the arch-villain, more even than the junto, Godolphin, the city financiers, or war contractors. Implicitly it suggests that the Pretender, if only he were prepared to act as guardian of the Church of England, would be the natural successor to

---

[23] The case is argued at length in *SDW*, ch. 6.   [24] Chambers (1996: 85).
[25] Quoted by Sinclair-Stevenson (1973: 172). For Pope's dislike of Cadogan, see *SDW*, ch. 5.

Anne. By early 1713 this was a fragile hope, and one year later a plain impossibility. In its reconfiguration of history *Windsor-Forest* is animated by the last feeble breath of this idyllic vision.

Windsor-Forest was published on 7 March 1713. This was the eve of the anniversary of the Queen's accession: William III had died on 8 March 1702. The date marked a momentous juncture in the ritualized political calendar of early modern Britain: 'This is the day of the Qu——'s Accession to the Crown,' Swift had told Stella twelve months earlier; 'So it is a great day' (*JTS* ii. 507). On the same date fell the anniversary of an unsuccessful attempt by the French agent Guiscard to murder Harley in 1711, and on 8 March Swift noted what had become for Tories a celebration of the prime minister's safe deliverance (*JTS* ii. 634). As a result, the calendar now marked a double celebration, one honouring the Queen, the other her chief minister. Just how topical the poem was—an issue never fully explored—we should be able to recover, if we consider the immediate history of the peace negotiations and the succession crisis.[26] It is not generally realized that when *Windsor-Forest* came out, the exact terms of the treaty were still in the realms of guesswork. They were a matter of fierce debate, not just among Whigs and Tories, but among the competing factions who supported the peace process for various ends.

Anne was at Windsor, immobilized by illness, and thus providing further speculative opportunities to those who would ask, as Daniel Defoe boldly put it, 'What if the Queen should die?' On Good Friday, 2 April, Bolingbroke's half-brother George St John arrived from Utrecht with the news that the peace treaty had been signed by most of the parties, although not by the Emperor.[27] Swift went to the service at the Chapel Royal in St James's Palace, but the Queen had been too ill to attend. Later he dined at Bolingbroke's house with Addison; this was a touchy meeting and everyone needed to be 'mighty mannerly', as Swift put it, to avoid a heated political argument (*JTS* ii. 651–2).[28] In weeks to come Swift saw more of Addison when he attended rehearsals for *Cato*, the play which would attract to itself so much political controversy: he mocked 'the drab that Acts Cato's Daughter', that is Anne Oldfield, because she did not know her lines and called out at a highly emotional juncture in the drama, 'What's next?' (*JTS* ii. 654).[29]

---

[26] See Holmes (1987); as well as Green and Gregg.

[27] Only weeks before George St John had become secretary to the peace embassy in succession to Swift's protégé William Harrison, who had died suddenly on 14 Feb., an event which caused Swift great distress: 'No loss ever grieved me so much' (*JTS* ii. 619–21).

[28] Another preoccupation was the 'dull Poem of one Parson Trap', that is Joseph Trapp's *Peace: A Poem*, dedicated to Bolingbroke and published on 2 Apr. Fortunately it was not a serious rival to Pope's work. Pope had earlier commented unenthusiastically on Trapp's translations from Ovid (*Corr.* i. 106).

[29] Swift had hoped that the reward for his services would be a deanery at least, but none of the three vacancies went his way, as he learnt on 13 Apr. Another possibility, Windsor, closed on 16 Apr. All that the Queen would permit, despite lobbying by the Duke of Ormonde, was St Patrick's in Dublin (*JTS* ii. 660–2).

The Tories had been embarrassed by delays in reaching a final settlement at Utrecht and the consequent postponement of the opening of parliament, which was prorogued eleven times. They vented their impatience on the Lord Treasurer.[30] For years resentment had been building up among the rural community, where bad harvests had augmented poverty. The army had become unpopular, desertion and mutiny were beginning to appear in the forces, and opponents of the government managers were able for the first time to orchestrate a sustained campaign against the war. It was vital for the ministry to placate these critics, especially the Jacobites and Country MPs, by producing a treaty which would satisfy their pent-up desire for an end to hostilities. This would equally appease the feelings of Anne, promoted by 'her sex and Christian horror of bloodshed'.[31]

Now that the main peace negotiations had come to an end, discussion raged as to the exact form the Queen's speech at the opening of parliament should take. Swift, naturally, was one of those willing to give advice. According to his own account, he 'corrected' the Queen's speech, and drafted the vote of thanks to be offered to her in return: this was on 8 March, one day after the publication of *Windsor-Forest* (*JTS* ii. 635). In the proposed resolution of the Lords, Anne is congratulated on announcing a peace '*so honourable to Your Majesty and safe and advantageous to your Kingdoms*'. The speech goes on to express the hope that, with the blessing of God, the nation will 'in a few Years' recover from 'so long and expensive a War' (*JTS* ii. 684). This is a prose statement of the poetic drift of *Windsor-Forest*. Swift continued working on drafts up to the eve of the official ceremony, as meanwhile Anne was dragged up to Westminster to address parliament—even though she did not actually walk a step from January to August. The Queen, Swift informed Stella on 9 April, 'delivered her Speech very well, but a little weaker in her Voice' (*JTS* ii. 657).[32] In the event, the vote of thanks, signifying approval of the settlement, passed the House of Lords by a more comfortable majority than the government had feared. In her address Anne had formally announced the signing of the treaty on 31 March; and shortly afterwards, on 11 April, the full ceremony of ratification was performed. However, the Austrian Emperor and his immediate allies remained aloof and did not agree to a settlement until March 1714, after a further season of halfhearted campaigning. This has a crucial relevance, since the Elector of Hanover was among those holding out against the Utrecht agreement.

As these things went, it had been fairly tranquil on the Queen's birthday, 6 February, which was always a potential flashpoint. At court, the accustomed ceremonies took place: Swift never saw the occasion 'celebrated with so much Luxry, and fine Cloaths' (*JTS* ii. 615).[33] At the same time, out on the streets, conflicting symbols were

---

[30] Szechi (1984: 120).

[31] Oxford's comment, cited in MacLachlan (1969: 201). This remains the most informative short account of the Peace process.

[32] See also Roberts (1975: 53), on the favourable response to the Queen's speech, excepting Whig reservations concerning the claim that a 'general peace' had been achieved. For Oxford's careful drafting of the speech, with Swift's help, see Downie (1979: 176–7).

[33] A year earlier, Swift reported in addition 'an entertainment of Opera songs at night' (*JTS* ii. 481). This year Anne was ill and unable to attend a performance of Handel's new Birthday Ode, assuming it took place (see below, p. 153).

displayed in mock processions by Hanoverians and counter-demonstrations by the Jacobites. The Pretender was seen in effigy, holding out to the Pope and the devil 'proper Emblems of the Blessings we are to receive from the one, bred up in the Idolatry of Rome, and the Tyranny of France'. [34] This was the Janus face of a key date on the political calendar: birthday clothes at St James's, pope-burnings, oak-leaves, and white roses in Holborn and St Giles. Pope was demonstrably aware of both aspects of the occasion, as *Windsor-Forest* came out in this fraught atmosphere.

At the same time, the government was making every effort to suppress opposition to the peace. There was little that could be done about the Lord Chief Justice, Sir Thomas Parker, who spoke against the settlement during a meeting of the Privy Council, at which Harcourt was promoted to Lord Chancellor (*JTS* ii. 656). But next day, 8 April, the Treasurer of the Household was removed for the same offence, and other Whigs were ousted. Even the army was purged, with General Sir Richard Temple (later Pope's friend in the Patriot opposition, Lord Cobham) forced out, while Marlborough's right-hand man, General William Cadogan, who was also stripped of his offices, went with his master into exile on the Continent.

Meanwhile, at the beginning of February, the Duchess of Marlborough had left England to join her husband at Maastricht. There the couple awaited the grand showdown which had been anticipated ever since the Duke's dismissal just over twelve months earlier. Before Sarah departed, she irritated Swift by presenting to 'an insignificant woman' named Mrs Higgins an enamelled miniature of the Queen, in gold set with diamonds, which Anne had given to the Duchess. This was offered for sale 'like a piece of old fashiond plate' (*JTS* ii. 658–9). At home, the ministry of Oxford and Bolingbroke was disintegrating into faction and suspicion, and almost before the ink was dry on *Windsor-Forest* the resonant optimism of its conclusion had started to look a little hollow. The Pretender stood poised in Lorraine, and no one could be sure whether the political establishment, let alone his half-sister Anne, would support him against the Hanoverian interest if he made a bold bid for the succession. Evidence exists that both Oxford and Bolingbroke were secretly keeping open lines of communication with the claimant.

This was certainly a fraught moment at which to speak out in print. At the end of March Defoe was imprisoned for an old debt, and had to rely on the intervention of the Lord Treasurer to gain his freedom. On 11 April he was taken into custody on a warrant signed by Lord Chief Justice Parker, in connection with three pamphlets on the succession issue, including *But What if the Queen Should Die?*[35] It was said that the Queen had personally ordered his arrest, but Whig propagandists had doubtless engineered the event. Defoe was sent to the Queen's Bench prison on 22 April for two *Review* papers criticizing Parker, and only set free a week later after publishing an apology. The original charge, relating to the three pamphlets, still hung over him,

---

[34] *Flying Post*, 7–10 Feb. 1713, quoted in Rogers (1998: 2). Later in the year, on Queen Elizabeth's accession day, another pope-burning took place, as Henry Moore reported to Teresa Blount (quoted from Mapledurham papers in *Life*, 857).

[35] Parker, who had helped to manage the prosecution of Sacheverell in 1710, had been the most vigorous in efforts to secure a conviction against the printer of *The Conduct of the Allies* (*JTS* ii. 438).

and he had to go back to court facing charges of subverting the Protestant succession. Not until November did Defoe finally receive a pardon, signed by Bolingbroke, who was at Windsor with the Queen: again Harley's hand can be detected in this transaction. The episode shows how carefully writers had to steer between the cross-winds of party politics when they took up any matter of state. It also suggests one reason why Pope couched *Windsor-Forest* as allusively and impersonally as he did.

As the title of Defoe's most notorious pamphlet made clear, the precarious health of the Queen underlay this entire situation. It had long been apparent that she would be unlikely to live much longer. In the aftermath of her severe illness at Windsor in the autumn of 1712, a rumour has spread at the peace conference in Utrecht that her life was 'very precarious and in all appearance would be very short' (Green, 274).[36] On 18 April 1713 NS, the French ambassador, the duc d'Aumont, wrote to the marquis de Torcy, who was in effect the foreign minister of France, 'il y a lieu de croire, que comme on a toujours apprehendé pour la santé de la Reyne et que cette Princesse ne peut aller loin, le Conseil de France en cas ce malheur arrivivait [*sic*], a fait son plan et ses arrangements'.[37] The response of Anne's doctor, John Arbuthnot, in these circumstances was to try to manage the flow of news about her health. He sought to minimize the degree of her sickness, and even to keep others, including royal physicians, from close contact which would reveal the truth. However, he passed on information to Handel, according to the Hanoverian resident in London: 'The queen's physician, who is an important man and enjoys the queen's confidence, is [Handel's] great patron and friend, and has the composer constantly at his house . . . You must know that our Whigs rarely know anything about the queen's health.'[38] This last comment must refer to those with a strong link to Hanover. In any case, for their part, the Whigs did what they could 'to publicize and exaggerate the Queen's health problems' (Bucholz, 185–6; Swift, *Corr.* ii. 137).

PEACE TRIUMPHANT

On 5 May came the solemn proclamation of peace. Two weeks later the Queen issued an order prescribing a 'publick Thanksgiving', to celebrate the 'Just and Honourable Peace' concluded with France. The official ceremony was at first set for 16 June, and the nation was enjoined to thank God for 'such Great and Publick Blessings' as the settlement had conferred. Such an event indeed took place at Dublin on the day appointed, where the full panoply of the state was pressed into service. A musical interlude called *Peace Triumphant* followed the usual religious observances. After this came a fireworks display, replete with emblems: 'In the

---

[36] To make matters worse, there were rumours in Nov. 1712 that the Queen was to be the subject of an assassination attempt at Windsor.

[37] Quoted by Trevelyan, iii. 360. At the end of 1713, when the Queen again suffered a violent illness, Swift reported that stocks had fallen six or seven per cent (Swift, *Corr.* ii. 10).

[38] Quoted in Burrows (1994: 73).

Cypher-Work was the Sun, under which were two Angels holding a Ribbon inscribed with this Motto, *Arbitra Belli, Dictatrix Pacis*; and under this was Her Majesty's Cypher, Crown, and Scepter, plac'd on a Triumphal Arch, within which Her Majesty stood on a large Globe with this Motto over Her head, *ANNA nobis hae Otia fecit.*' The Queen's effigy was flanked on one side by the Hanoverian princes, and on the other by a mitred bishop and two clergymen. Most relevant to Pope's recent poem were some further allegorical details: 'Under Her Majesty stood *Peace*, with three Monsters on each hand, *viz. Rebellion, Sedition,* and *Faction,* under the Royal Family . . . and . . . the Clergy, *Atheism, Heresy,* and *Schism.*' The politically correct inclusion of the Hanoverian family appears to be a touch confined to the Irish celebrations. As we recall, the final tableau of *Windsor-Forest* exhibits a similar train of monsters, among which Faction and Rebellion directly echo the models at the firework display. Proceedings at Dublin ended, as ever, with 'Bonefires, Ringing of Bells, Firing of Guns, Illuminations, and other Demonstrations of Joy'.[39]

Things moved more slowly in London. Because of the Queen's illness, the celebrations were put back to 7 July, and anxious deliberations began on the correct form this occasion should take (Green, 288–9). The initial Tory desire may have been to offer something less triumphalist than the repeated outbursts of propaganda and pomp which had greeted each of Marlborough's victories during the course of the war. But by this time the peace deal was in trouble politically: the Anglo-French commercial treaty, which formed an integral element in the settlement, was defeated in the Commons on 10 June.[40] This came after loud protests from the trading community: the settlement was regarded as too favourable to France and inimical to Britain's trading partners who had been allies in the war. 'The Whigs . . . were . . . fearful lest a good trade should render an alliance with the patron of the Pretender popular in the City of London' (Trevelyan, iii. 275)—just the kind of outcome which the peroration of *Windsor-Forest* would envisage as a blessing. There was more trouble about a proposal to extend the malt tax to Scotland, causing Oxford's fragile coalition to split once more, as Ralph Bridges told Trumbull on 9 June.[41] In the light of these distractions, the occasion now seemed to call for something more resonant, after all, especially with a general election to come in August.

In order to mount its public relations campaign, the government arranged for a massive celebration. The administration achieved a coup against the Hanoverians when Handel was recruited to supply a *Jubilate* and *Te Deum*, since he was still in the employ of the Elector.[42] There was a service at St Paul's on the appointed day (7 July), attended by both houses of parliament, and guns fired at the Tower. Unfortunately

[39] See Ewald, 84–5.

[40] Unlike the main peace treaty, the commercial clauses had to be submitted for parliamentary approval. Objections were made to the removal of tariffs previously placed on French goods, notably the duties on wine.

[41] Cited by Roberts (1975: 101). Trumbull was kept well informed on all these developments and might well have discussed some of them with Pope.

[42] Handel had written a Birthday Ode for the Queen, but again it does not seem to have been performed owing to her illness. See p. 153, below.

Anne's health still did not allow her to be present, so that she held her own commemoration at St James's. Despite the absence of the Queen, London resolved not
to be outdone by Dublin, and in the evening the city mounted a large firework display on barges moored off Whitehall. The event featured some splendiferous special
effects, including thousands of rockets, cannons, balloons, 'large water-pyramids
and . . . bee-swarms . . . set with lights to swim on the water.'[43] James Thornhill
made an etching of the triumphal arch, measuring 52 feet by 64 feet, which served as
the centrepiece for these effects as the rockets fizzed and the fountains showered out
over the Thames. This was a high moment of national pageantry, designed to vindicate the entire policy of the Tory ministry and to discountenance the Marlborough
party.[44]

To look at Thornhill's etching is like consulting a visual illustration of Pope's
poem, though that had appeared four months earlier. In later editions, Pope added
a note at l. 330 which included alternative lines 'originally' written but subsequently
removed—the context is the apparition of Father Thames, advancing his 'rev'rend
Head' in one of the most starkly masque-like gestures of the poem. These additional
lines, first reported in 1736, are not in the manuscript, and may be an adroit afterthought on the author's part. The key passage runs:

> From shore to shore exulting shouts he heard,
> O'er all his banks a lambent light appear'd,
> With sparkling flames heav'ns glowing concave shone,
> Fictitious stars, and glories not her own.

The language of *Windsor-Forest* had mimicked various kinds of ceremonial display
throughout. Here the decorative surface becomes a kind of verbal pyrotechnic device; the Thames is not just a setting but a part of the display, a cooperative figure in
the national pageant ('His shining horns diffus'd a golden gleam: | With pearl and
gold his towr'ry front was drest . . .') Moreover, the key to the etching states that the
illuminations were 'Compos'd of different sorts of Fire, as Starrs, Reports, Gold &
Silver rainfire . . . &c.' If Pope had left the verses in place, he would have shown remarkable precognition of the celebrations in July—assuming that these lines were
actually written before the event.[45] Certainly the *Post-Boy* would record huge
crowds greeting the occasion with bells, bonfires, and loyal toasts which extended
until after midnight.

This commemorative display lingered in the poet's mind for some time to come.
When he wrote his ironic attack on *The Rape of the Lock* in 1715, under the title of *A*

---

[43] See Green, 289: Stephens (1982: 693).

[44] The fireworks were impressive enough to confirm William Whiston in his unlucky belief that a
chain of ships armed with rockets, moored at intervals across the sea, would be a satisfactory way of as-
certaining the longitude. This scheme, publicized in the *Guardian* a week after the peace celebrations,
was to end up on the cutting-room floor of history, but not before it had been satirized in *The Memoirs
of Martinus Scriblerus*. For Addison's own account in the *Guardian* of the display, picturing the sky as
'filled with innumerable Blazing Stars and Meteors', see Ch. 4, below.

[45] The fourth line quoted employs a formula used in the last verse of *The Rape of the Lock*, Canto I, a
work which Pope was bringing to its full form in the course of 1713. See *SDW*, ch. 1.

Key to the Lock, he made reference to the lines describing Belinda's exultant shouts at her apparent victory in the game of ombre ('a satyrical Representation of the late War', as we are told). According to the *Key,* in these verses 'the publick Rejoicings and *Thanksgivings* are ridiculed'. The italicized emphasis on the second noun inevitably calls up recollection of the *Te Deum* performed at St Paul's. The passage continues: 'Immediately upon which there follows a malicious Insinuation, in the manner of a Prophecy . . . that the Peace should continue but a short Time, and that the Day should afterwards be curst which was then celebrated with so much Joy' (*Prose,* i. 194). We can get some help in establishing the straight meanings of *Windsor-Forest* by teasing out the inversions and obliquities of this satiric pamphlet. For Pope, by 1715, the joy with which the Peace had been celebrated had indeed proved a short-lived thing. The prophetic statement of blessings conferred by the treaty, which forms so striking a conclusion to the poem, had already been falsified, and from a Stuart vantage-point a curse had replaced the benediction.

The etching by Thornhill necessarily lacks the rich baroque colouring and unctuous sensuality of his ceilings for Greenwich, executed at the same juncture. However, the 'exact draught' is precise enough to show many crucial features of the display. The triumphal arch is surmounted by the crown and royal insignia, with Anne's motto *semper eadem* prominently placed at the centre. Of course, she had deliberately borrowed this formula from Elizabeth I, a connection suggested in the poem at l. 384. Crossed swords above a shield express the cessation of hostilities. The royal cipher is surrounded by a wreath of laurel leaves. Across the cornice of the arch is inscribed *anno pacis.* The verbal message is required in order to mute some of the normal associations of a triumphal arch, part of the iconography of Victory in standard sources (e.g. Ripa, pl. 78). However, most of the other visual motifs belong to the iconographic idiom of peace. A figure obviously representing Pax stands with an olive branch aloft between the two right-hand columns of the arch; alongside her stands Conduct, according to the key, but this is unmistakably Mercury with his caduceus (itself a symbol of peace), introduced as healer, patron of merchants, and above all keeper of the divine mysteries. It is appropriate that the herald of the gods should flank the goddess of peace in such a design. On top of the arch, grouped around a pair of orbs and sceptres, stand the four cardinal virtues: Prudence with a mirror and an arrow round which an eel winds, then Temperance and Fortitude, with the most easily identifiable deity that of Justice. One of the putti alongside appears to be bearing a trumpet, often used to convey epic as it proclaims the fame of the great (see Ripa, pl. 183). The arch is flanked by tall bollards inscribed with Anne's insignia. Apart from the absence of an obvious Diana or Britannia figure, the design might have been planned to illustrate Pope's recent work.[46]

On the left-hand side of the arch, balancing Pax and Mercury, are depicted Hercules with his club, representing Courage, and a winged Victory. The presence of Hercules would point not just to the strength of the nation, but also its completion of numerous arduous campaigns over the years of war. Across the top of the

---

[46] See Stephens (1982: 693–4).

columns are suspended garlands with a badge resembling the fleur-de-lis (l. 306). At the foot of the arch, above the word LONDINI is the shield already mentioned, bearing a Greek cross and a Saltire cross superimposed. This is clearly the banner of the newly unified nation, merging the ensigns of St George and St Andrew. In other words, 'Britannia's Standard' (WF, 110), occupies the centre of the design. On either side of the shield are placed a rose and a thistle. The elaborate semiology of deities, pillars, garlands, and inscriptions matches the dense allusiveness of Pope's language.

In his etching Thornhill shows the floating stage, which extended 400 feet along the chained barges, set against a vague representation of the south bank of the river. The notional viewpoint, then, is Whitehall—the London end of the royal progress which Pope's imaginative narrative has traced, and in theory (if no longer in practice) the most overtly Stuart expression of royal architecture. The explanation which accompanies the drawing remarks that the display was 'perform'd by Coll. Hopkey and Coll. Borgard by yᵉ Direction of yᵉ Board of Ordnance'. The symbolic statement is clear: swords are being turned into ploughshares, and the armed services are practising their skills on festive manoeuvres. The 'long-expected Days' of Peace will raise the glory of the Thames to the stars (355–6), almost as the celebratory fireworks had cloven the air above the river that evening. Once more, Pope's text works like a heraldic proclamation, or an enunciation of a providential order. Windsor-Forest simply pre-empted the royal fireworks display and the Handelian Te Deum.

Provincial towns were equally keen to display their patriotic fervour. Late in May, for example, the High Church party came out in full force at Lichfield when the peace was proclaimed there. Officials of the borough led by the sheriff paraded around the streets, a great crowd of people following 'with three laurel leaves stuck in their hats with these inscriptions (A.R.) on the middle one, and Peace and Plenty on each side'. The Queen's health was drunk, and celebrations lasted into the night.[47] This incident shows that the neutral phrase 'peace and plenty' had been appropriated for Tory use, a process to which Windsor-Forest may have contributed, but which it certainly did not start.

One final convergence may be noted. The first rehearsals of Handel's Utrecht music (completed by 12 January) were held in St Paul's on 5 and 7 March 1713, with many 'persons of quality' in attendance. Another rehearsal took place in the Banqueting House at Whitehall on 19 March. In other words, the two most lasting artistic responses to the Peace both went public at the very same moment. Handel's composition has been described in terms of 'the blaze of primary colours', most specifically in the Gloria of the Jubilate.[48] There is a deliberate brightness about the scoring, a metallic and almost hierophantic brilliance: words which apply also, mutatis mutandis, to Pope's own 'orchestration' of the peace. And again we can detect an obvious debt in Handel to a seventeenth-century predecessor, this time Purcell. The Queen seems to have been pleased: by the end of the year Handel had been granted a royal pension of £200: this 'act of royal bounty' probably owed something to the influence of Dr Arbuthnot.[49] As might be expected, lesser composers also at-

---

[47] Post Boy, 4 June 1713.   [48] See Dean (1959: 20–1).
[49] See Burrows (1994: 71–4), for an up-to-date summary of these events.

tempted to seize the day. John Weldon, a former pupil of Purcell, who was now on the staff of the Chapel Royal, produced a setting of a dialogue between 'Honour, Fate and Peace'. It was performed at a concert on 20 March, with Richard Leveridge, one of the most eminent stage musicians of the day, as one of the three vocalists.[50] This, however, was competition Handel could easily ward off.

Tactfully, Pope did not attempt a personal apotheosis of Anne: all too obviously, the Queen was nearing her celestial reward. So we get nothing in *Windsor-Forest* resembling the entry of St George into heaven, a favourite subject of baroque decorative painters. Instead, we have a glorification of peace, masking a strongly partisan restatement of Stuart mythology. The forest and the river come together,[51] and in doing so they fulfil the long-held but increasingly desperate hopes of the dynasty and its supporters. Pope does more than simply tailor the old modes to fit a modern monarch. For the first time since the Revolution of 1688, the contentions surrounding the Stuart line directly involved questions of succession. For the first time since 1603, the potential monarch's own line of descent was at the heart of a constitutional struggle. It was Pope's genius to see the poetic opportunities this afforded, and to give urgent topicality to the traditional forms of courtly art.

A year after *Windsor-Forest* came the Hanoverian accession, and of course more bonfires and bells. Not too far down the road from Exeter, the town of Dorchester celebrated the coronation of the new king with a profusion of ale and a roasted ox. 'The day ended with the burning of an effigy of the Pretender; some local Jacobites riotously tried to rescue it, and moved on to attack one of the nonconformist meeting-houses. They had come a long way from the sober, restrained celebrations of 1660.'[52] It is a long way, too, from the dignified ceremonial of Pope's poem, but he may not have been all that surprised that the coming of 'a foreign master' provoked such scenes. Up and down the country, cries of 'Sacheverell for ever' were heard again. Little more than two years after the publication of *Windsor-Forest*, the Stuart arms were vaingloriously raised by the Earl of Mar at Braemar. Four months later, the Pretender arrived at Scone Palace and began serious preparations for his coronation in this historic site.[53] The fact that such an elaborate ceremony was planned so soon afterwards makes it all but certain that Jacobites were dreaming of the occasion even before the death of Anne.

JACOBITISM

In recent years a warm debate has raged over Pope's relation to Jacobitism, as a political creed and as an active movement.[54] The most careful literary assessment of

---

[50]   *London Stage* (1960–8: ii. 297).   [51]   As argued extensively in *SDW*, chs. 4 and 5.

[52]   Underdown (1992: 262); see also Monod, 176.

[53]   It would still have been part of the collective memory that Charles II had been crowned at Scone in 1651, ten years before his English coronation.

[54]   For important reconsideration of the Jacobite cause more generally, see Cruickshanks and Black (1988); Lenman (1980); Monod; and Szechi (1984). Monod in particular supplies a detailed analysis of various forms of Jacobite expression: this could serve as a cipher-key to much of the text of *WF*, as the poem is read in this book. A valuable survey of Pope's Catholic and, potentially, Jacobite background is provided by Aden (1978: esp. 3–52), although it is surprising that virtually none of this material is applied directly to *WF*.

these issues has been offered by Howard Erskine-Hill, most succinctly in an essay entitled 'Alexander Pope: The Political Poet in his Time'.[55] Here the initial focus is on a crucial passage in Pope's imitation of Horace, *Epistle* II. ii (1737), where the poet pays tribute to his father, who clung loyally to his faith in the hostile climate of William III. Pope has been describing his upbringing and education in the parental home:

> But knottier Points we knew not half so well,
> Depriv'd us soon of our Paternal Cell;
> And certain Laws, by Suff'rers thought unjust,
> Deny'd all Posts of Profit or of Trust:
> Hopes after Hopes of pious Papists fail'd,
> While mighty William's thundring Arm prevail'd.
> For Right Hereditary tax'd and fin'd,
> He stuck to Poverty with Peace of Mind;
> And me, the Muses help'd to undergo it;
> Convict a Papist he, and I a Poet.

> (58–67)

We might note the adoption of quasi-legal phraseology ('Posts of Profit or of Trust', 'Convict'), and the way in which the chiasmus of the final line binds together the Roman faith and creativity. These verses refer directly to measures enacted in William's reign, and outline the situation in which Binfield was acquired by the Popes. Moreover, Pope's filial loyalty is stressed, because legislation 'allowed, and therefore in substance encouraged' Catholics sons to repudiate their father's faith (*Life*, 40). Moreover, the previous paragraph of the epistle tells a brief anecdote of a poor soldier 'In ANNA's Wars', who fought desperately and heroically: 'He leapt the Trenches, scal'd a Castle Wall, | Tore down a Standard, took the Fort and all' (40–1). His 'great Commander' plans to besiege another city, and asks the soldier to acquire more glory in the action; but the soldier refuses: 'Let him take Castles who has ne'er a Groat' (51). As late as 1736, then, Pope was recalling the costly efforts of the war, urged on by the insatiable Marlborough—or so the Tories saw it.

Erskine-Hill makes the applications from this passage with skill and delicacy. His case rests in part on some controversial historiography, but it is mounted with a due appreciation of the uncertainties surrounding some of these issues. Most of his essay relates to the second half of Pope's career, including his defence of Bishop Atterbury when the prelate was sent to the Tower in 1722 and arraigned before the Lords the following year. At the same juncture government officials seized copies of the *Works* of the Duke of Buckingham, which Pope had edited, and the work was suppressed at the instance of the Lords. Then, during the long years of Walpole's reign Pope was engaged in an elaborate game of cat and mouse with the ministry, in part because of his renewed involvement with Bolingbroke, now back in England though with his titles unrestored. Erskine-Hill makes many good points on this

---

[55] Erskine-Hill (1982c. 123–38).

phase, and he also suggests that even *The Rape of the Lock* may contain hidden allusions to what Jacobites regarded as the 'rape' of the nation by William III. The argument here focuses on the end of Canto III, after the lock has been sliced from Belinda's hair: cold steel, we are reminded, could 'strike to Dust th'imperial Tow'rs of *Troy*' and 'hew Triumphal Arches to the Ground' (iii. 174–6). The mock-heroic level of meaning here recalls Homer and Virgil; I would add that the language is equally reminiscent of the world of Stuart pageantry, which was still standing in the precincts of the castle in *Windsor-Forest*, but had now been reduced to nothingness in the bleak Hanoverian morning.

In his recent book on oppositional poetry, Erskine-Hill has further developed his case. Again his chief emphasis lies on *The Rape of the Lock* and later poems of Pope, but he also devotes some suggestive pages to *Windsor-Forest*. For example, he points out that the trial of Dr Sacheverell reopened questions about the legitimacy of the succession. One of the managers at the trial actually cited Nimrod, as the origin of government by conquest, as against a patriarchal origin from Adam, or a contractual origin, possibly as ancient as the Romans. In addition Erskine-Hill stresses the continuing imagery of rape and conquest in Pope's poem, expressing 'the darker side of what the mythologized landscape of *Windsor-Forest* discloses'. Along with more familiar evidence, such as the dedication to Lansdowne, this material is used by Erskine-Hill to promote the verdict that *Windsor-Forest* amounts to 'a crypto-Jacobite poem'.[56]

Much has been said by now about this neo-Jacobite reading of Pope, as it has been expressed by a wide range of critics. The crucial stage for our purposes is the early part of Pope's career, up to and including the rising of 1715; and on this phase there has been less work done than on the later years. It is quite likely that the young man was not *fully* politicized until the coming of the Hanoverians brought the issues starkly home to every individual, and until he found his friends investigated, impeached, imprisoned, attainted, and exiled. But, as the whole of this book ought to show, Pope cannot have woken up on 1 August 1714 with an abrupt sense of shock: he already knew that the whole world of Stuart myth was doomed, constructed as it had been—much like the wondrous spectacles of court theatre—from tissues of unreality. Nobody underwent a sudden conversion to Jacobitism at this date. The political realities had been set before Anne ever came to the throne, when parliament passed the Act of Succession, and her father died, asking God to forgive his enemies, including his daughter. This in turn led Louis XIV to recognize James Francis Edward as king of England, with a solemn proclamation by heralds at Saint-Germain.

It is true that the hopes of the Pretender's friends had risen in the latter part of the Queen's reign, after the Sacheverell troubles and the success of the Tories in the election of 1710. The preliminary peace negotiations in 1711 had obliged France to renounce its support for the Pretender, which made advocacy of James Stuart's claims

---

[56] Erskine-Hill (1996: 71).

in some ways a less treasonable matter. Some even felt that if Anne had lived a few more months, Bolingbroke might have stepped into Oxford's shoes and renewed the prospects of a Stuart restoration. But this was whistling in the dark. Bolingbroke himself was caught unprepared: as he famously wrote to Swift, 'The Earl of Oxford was remov'd on Tuesday, the Queen dyed on Sunday . . . What a world is this, & how does fortune banter us?' (Swift, *Corr.* ii. 101). Dismissed by the new king, he made ineffective approaches to Marlborough, and then decamped to St Germain. With appropriate histrionics, he slipped away from Drury Lane theatre in between acts, disguised himself as a valet, and headed for the Continent on 27 March 1715. From Dover he wrote to Lansdowne, explaining that he had 'certain and repeated information' that the new regime intended to 'pursue [him] to the scaffold' (Churchill, iv. 525). Soon he was joined in France by one of Swift's most intimate friends, Charles Ford, the Gazetteer who had drafted the announcement of great state events, such as the death of the Queen. Ford, who had subscribed to the *Iliad*, was arrested on his return to England.[57]

There followed Bolingbroke's sojourn with the Pretender and his attainder. Unwisely he accepted a Jacobite earldom in July 1715, just as his friend Lansdowne would later do. Blamed for the failure of the rising at the end of the same year, he was removed as secretary of state to the Pretender and in effect he then abandoned the Jacobite cause. Pope kept in cautious touch with Bolingbroke while he was in France, and rallied to his side when the disillusioned exile was allowed to return to England in 1725. But by then the Stuarts had ceased to be a plausible vehicle for Bolingbroke's high-minded brand of virtuous kingship.

In sober reality, the Pretender could only have gained the throne by the power of arms, once he had declined the opportunity to renounce his faith. That was apparent to most observers long before the Queen died. Stanhope is said to have told Bolingbroke that the only two ways he could escape the gallows were to join the Whigs or to go over unambiguously to the cause of James Stuart.[58] For his part, Pope might well have accepted James III happily enough as long as the supposed monarch undertook merely to protect the papists from savage discrimination: his own support for the firmly Protestant Queen Anne, in *Windsor-Forest* and elsewhere, suggests that much. The 'liberty' he associates in the poem with the Stuart dynasty includes, though it is not confined to, active tolerance of the Catholic faith. To that extent he nailed his colours to the Stuart mast, and in effect stated his feelings of discomfort at the prospect of a Hanoverian ruler. It was a trepidation which later events were fully to justify.

Scant evidence exists to show that Pope would have gained any personal benefit from a Jacobite takeover, beyond the level of protection just mentioned. A cynical view might be that he hoped to walk into some kind of preferment or pension, which would have meant excising more than one act from the statute book. In fact

[57] It is not clear exactly when Pope got to know Ford; in the summer of 1714 Pope had sent greetings to him via Gay (*Corr.* i. 223): see also Swift, *Corr.* ii. 28.
[58] Dickinson (1970: 130).

Pope was not in the pay of the government under Anne, and is unlikely to have been so under a putative Stuart successor. True, his friend Swift had hoped that he would be granted a pension to save him from the labours on his version of Homer: 'Our Lord Oxford used to curse the Occasions that put you on Translations, and if he and the Qu——had lived you should have entirely followed your own Genius built and planted much, and writ only when you had a mind' (Swift, *Corr.* iii. 79). But once Oxford had fallen and the Queen had died, things could never have been quite the same. There were reasons good or bad why someone like Pope might follow the Pretender's banner, but expectations of rich rewards were not among these. Being a Jacobite meant paying out, not hauling in cash, and there was no certainty that things would ever be different.

At the very least the rising meant embarrassment for Pope and his family, something that is repeatedly obvious in his correspondence during 1715 and 1716. Sometimes he makes a joke of the entire imbroglio, at the cost of some strained effects—as when he writes to the Blount sisters: 'You may soon have your Wish to enjoy the Gallant Sights of Armies, Campagnes, Standards waving over your Brother's Cornfields, & the pretty windings of the Thames about *Mapledurham*, staind with the blood of Men' (*Corr.* i. 308). It is hard to know how the sisters would have reacted to this attempt to make persiflage on a contest with profound personal, as well as national, implications. For the passage constitutes a grisly undoing of all the rhetorical work of *Windsor-Forest*: in the poem, armies, campaigns, and standards had all been invoked, as part of the horrific world of slaughter brought to an end, now that there was no more 'Trace | Of War or Blood' (371–2). No longer would the sons of Father Thames 'dye with *British* Blood' the rivers of Europe (367–8). Yet that is just what was in prospect, opening up a possibility of reverting to the tumults and divisions of earlier English history, when the Darent was 'stain'd with *Danish* Blood' (348). What makes it peculiarly fearsome is that the river stained will be the Thames, not many miles upstream from Windsor, in the royal county of Berkshire, and in the vicinity of a revered Catholic mansion.[59]

There actually was a show of military strength in London when the Pretender stood poised to invade. In the same letter to the Blount sisters, on 23 July 1715, Pope refers to the camp which was being set up on Hyde Park, with the freshly raised regiments in their fine new uniforms: 'The sight of so many thousand gallant Fellows, with all the Pomp & Glare of Warr yet undeformed with battle, those Scenes which England has for many years only beheld on Stages, may possibly invite your Curiosity to this place' (*Corr.* i. 308). This preserves the comic note, but again it reminds us of what was in store for the nation. Pope moves on to describe an assembly bravely held by Lady Lansdowne, and jokingly cites a report that 'Alex. Pope, Gent.' being ready to renounce 'the Errors of the Romish Communion' would be appointed City poet—the manufacturer of laboured shows to celebrate municipal worthies at the Lord Mayor's Day show.

---

[59] For fuller argument, see *SDW*, ch. 5.

PIOUS PAPISTS AND LOYAL PATRONS

We no longer think of Jacobitism as a monolithic entity. The work of Daniel Szechi has shown just how fragmented the movement was, with marked differences opening up between the shadow court of Saint-Germain and the home-based supporters of the Stuarts. They disagreed on such matters as the need for the Pretender to convert to the Anglican faith, the prospects for a military invasion of Britain, and relations with the ministry. In many ways the Jacobite MPs were closer to Country Tories who retained a loyalty to Hanover, and these groups often cooperated. Moreover, there was a distinct phalanx of Scottish Jacobites with their own agenda.[60] Pope had dealings with all these factions, though fewest with the Scots. His links with the Pretender's court came mainly through the Caryll family, while his extensive local contacts provided the basis for his knowledge of native Jacobitism. *Windsor-Forest* appeared at a time when many of the key issues dividing the movement came to a head, and when Pope was extending his own familiarity with the world of politics. We might also recall the case of Charles Wogan, an early friend (see Chapter 1, above). Knighted by the Pretender, Wogan negotiated with princes, cardinals, and a pope—that is Clement XI, who granted James Francis a pension and supported his claim to the British throne. It was Wogan who first discovered Princess Clementina at a remote court in Silesia, and who eventually brought the Pretender his bride: she had been named after the Pope, her godfather.

Much of the evidence on Pope's relations with the Jacobites, especially during the earlier part of his career, has yet to be thoroughly sifted. It is certain that his subscription lists have something to tell us: for example, the *Iliad* clientele was recruited before the rising, and indeed before the 1715 election which consigned a large number of the poet's supporters to a permanent posture as lookers-on in the world of politics. A well-placed observer and under-secretary of state, Erasmus Lewis, told Swift just three days before the Queen's death that the new administration to be formed on Oxford's ouster would include Lord Lexington, Sir William Wyndham, Thomas Strangways, Sir John Stonhouse, and Henry Campion (Swift, *Corr.* ii. 89). All except Strangways were busy entering their subscription for the *Iliad* around this time—and he repaired the omission when the *Odyssey* list followed. Other rumours had it that the Treasury would be placed in commission, with Wyndham as First Lord and Bathurst among his colleagues. Such were the prospects for Pope's friends before the sudden 'eclipse' in 1714.

Many who had been MPs when they subscribed to the Homer edition were out of the House when the first volume appeared. Some who lost their seats were High Church Tories, often members of the October Club, who were not necessarily Stuart adherents: Sir Nicholas Morice may be such an ambiguous case. Some retired from the political affray in disgust, such as Henry Campion. But the majority were more or less openly Jacobites, and gave at least moral support to the rising when it

---

[60] See Szechi (1984).

came.[61] At least two rank-and-file Tories on Pope's list (Sir Copplestone Bampfield and Sir William Carew) were actually arrested on charges of suspected treason. With the leaders we can be more confident. Peers such as the Duke of Berwick (half-brother of the Pretender), Bolingbroke, Lansdowne, Mar, Norfolk, North and Grey, Ormonde, Powis and Strafford all entered their names on the *Iliad* list, along with Wyndham and Matthew Prior—by the time that *their* check was cashed, so to speak, most of these were either attainted or in exile.[62] Even Harcourt, who kept his nose clean at most times, was exempted from the general amnesty after the rising, along with Strafford. Lord Scarsdale ended up in the Tower, but survived to support the Pretender for another decade or more, whilst another of the twelve peers created along with Lansdowne who figures on the list, Lord Dupplin, also found himself confined on the same day as Pope's patron (see Chapter 2, above).

The most extreme case is that of the Earl of Derwentwater, whose name appeared in Pope's volume a matter of three months before he took up arms for the Stuart claimant. His mother was a natural daughter of Charles II, and so he was a first cousin once removed of the Pretender, with whom he passed his boyhood at Saint-Germain.[63] The Earl, a member of an old Catholic family from Northumberland, was beheaded at Tower Hill in February 1716. Before his trial he was given advice by two barristers, Nathaniel Pigott (1661–1737), who came to be one of Pope's most trusted counsellors and a neighbour at Twickenham; and Henry Eyre (1676–1719) of Gray's Inn, another leading Catholic lawyer who also subscribed to the *Iliad*. Derwentwater had an affectionate relationship with Mary, Lady Swinburne, a family friend and correspondent of Pope. Her husband and two of her brothers-in-law were involved in the rising: both brothers-in-law were taken prisoner at the battle of Preston, and condemned to death. Edward (1685–1716) died in jail, while James (d. 1728) pleaded insanity and escaped from custody. In addition, two Miss Swinburnes, probably sisters of Sir William, acted as couriers for the Jacobites when the Earl and his allies joined the revolt. We know that Pope was well aware of these family circumstances (see *Corr.* i. 327). Such findings swell the growing body of information which shows that the poet had many private links with

[61] Among those who had long-standing contacts with Saint-Germain was Charles Aldworth, MP for New Windsor (d. Sept. 1714): see Monod, 284.
[62] Also listed were Lady Lansdowne; Colonel Bernard Granville, Lansdowne's brother; Lady Stanley, his sister, the guardian of the future Mrs Delany (daughter of the colonel); and his sister Elizabeth, the maid of honour. We could add Lady Bolingbroke, and two of Lord Bathurst's brothers. There is the High Church Earl of Rochester: his wife Jane (one of Lansdowne's cousins, whom Pope visited at Petersham in 1717) is not listed, but her sister-in-law Lady Katherine Hyde is. Both women were among the High Church bedchamber ladies surrounding Anne at court after the Duchess of Marlborough lost favour. Naturally present are Pope's immediate allies, such as Trumbull, the Carylls senior and junior, and Edward Blount: 'Michael Blount' is assuredly the owner of Mapledurham (see *Corr.* i. 294). Another one-time Tory MP on the list whom we might forget was Sir Christopher Wren, by now superannuated as far as parliament went.
[63] The Earl's father-in-law Sir John Webb is also listed. He had offered £500 to Derwentwater as a kind of belated dowry, to bankroll the campaign in the North in 1715. It is notable that Pope remembered the Earl when, many years later at Stowe, his mount was a horse which Derwentwater had been riding before his capture at Preston (*Corr.* ii. 513).

those most centrally involved in the Jacobite movement, whatever his opinion of the Pretender may have been. Years later, Pope reflected on the mutability of things when his carriage was drawn by a horse which had allegedly been ridden by the Earl prior to his capture at Preston, during the episode which marked the end of the Jacobites' hopes (*Corr.* ii. 513).

Among those who *did* survive, it is notable that the same names are generally found for the *Odyssey* list a decade later, even though these individuals had been heavily compromised in intervening Jacobite activity. Thus, the Earl of Seaforth, brother-in-law of John Caryll junior, had fought with the Mackenzie clan at Sheriffmuir, and then been forced to take refuge in France: he was out again in 1719 and wounded at Glenshiel, but managed to escape again. His estates were seques-trated.[64] None the less, he was back on the *Odyssey* subscription, for all the world as if nothing had happened. It is beyond question that Pope was able to attract some of the most doggedly loyal adherents of the Stuart cause.

Of course, the nature of the *Iliad* campaign was such that the great names in so-ciety were on the list, regardless of their politics—Pope would altogether have failed in his objectives if that had not been the case. So we find Marlborough and Cadogan, as well as the leaders of the new Hanoverian regime: Sunderland and Stanhope, for example, not to mention their junior colleague Addison. Also present is Steele, newly knighted by the ministry for political services. The old Whig Junto is represented by Somers, but also by Pope's former patrons Wharton and Halifax. More ambiguous figures such as Somerset, Cowper, and Shrewsbury can be found as well. These men were doing little more than signalizing their existence as cultural proconsuls. What holds more significance is the solid, indeed unanimous support of Pope's friends in high politics, those implicitly endorsed in the ideological system of *Windsor-Forest*. Thus we predictably find Lansdowne, Bolingbroke, Bucking-hamshire (all entering their names for ten copies), Ormonde, Oxford, Strafford, Harcourt father and son, Abigail Masham, Dartmouth, Peterborough, and Wynd-ham represented. Some great ladies are on the list: these include Lady Orkney, the Duchess of Hamilton, and the poet Anne Finch, Countess of Winchilsea, a strong supporter of the Stuarts.[65] Among the twelve new peers created at the end of 1711, as we have seen, nine became subscribers, while all but one of the Brothers Club can be found. Naturally, the members of the Scriblerus group are present without excep-tion. Among literary colleagues and mentors are Congreve, Garth, Rowe, and Berkeley. Sir William Trumbull is of course on the roll, as is his potentially disrup-tive protégé Dr Henry Sacheverell. The gazetteer Charles Ford, whom Pope and Swift used as their intermediary, was himself 'long in confinement' after a visit to the exiled Bolingbroke in 1715.

For many among these men and women, it is easy to forget, the brief span of three years following the appearance of *Windsor-Forest* brought a total reversal of

---

[64] As noted in Ch. 1, above, his sister Lady Mary Mackenzie married the son of Pope's friend Caryll.

[65] The Duchess of Marlborough is not present, but along with her husband there are three of her daughters, including the Countess of Bridgewater, who had died as early as 24 May 1714. The Earl of Winchilsea, husband of Anne Finch, was another nonjuror on the list.

fortune. When the poem came out, they formed part of its core audience; they belonged to a ruling group who enjoyed a large parliamentary majority, and they could express their loyalty to a Stuart monarch without inhibition, provided they kept a discreet tongue on the subject of her successor. This was still the case when subscription proposals began to circulate in October 1713, and even when the proposals were reissued in May 1714 (*Career*, 125). In other words, the *Iliad* freezes the public for *Windsor-Forest*, or at least the main strand in its audience, at a final moment of dominance and self-confidence. By the time that Pope's translation began to appear in May 1715 the Tories had become a proscribed minority, and before a second instalment was published in March 1716 the Jacobite element was in complete disarray. Some of their number were in the Tower, some attainted in exile, some lying low in a quiet corner of England. Pope himself would be leaving Binfield for ever in the same month.

One more observation needs to be made about the list. It contains a small but revelatory contingent made up of the Catholic aristocracy and gentry. This recusant community seldom made much show in public life, since its members were excluded from office by reason of their refusal to take the oaths of loyalty, and the Jacobite movement spread far beyond their ranks. To students of Pope, easily recognizable names among this group are family friends such as Henry Englefield, John Dancastle, or Edward Blount. But perhaps the most intriguing cases are those of the two individuals listed under the title of the Dowager Lady Petre—Mary and Catherine, respectively mother and widow of Robert, seventh Baron Petre (the latter's Jacobite sympathies were not in doubt: see *SDW*, chapter 5). Another significant instance is that of Sir Edward Bedingfield, a Catholic baronet from Norfolk who in 1719 married Lord Burlington's sister Elizabeth. In a letter to Caryll on 7 June 1717 Pope mentioned Bedingfield along with Edward Blount and Thomas Stonor as papists with whom he was then exchanging visits (*Corr.* i. 411). The letter was written from Chiswick, near to the house where Burlington was beginning his elaborate building schemes at this very moment. There were further contacts between the three men in the 1720s, when Bedingfield was once more entered as a subscriber to the *Odyssey*.[66]

Pamphleteers hostile to Pope were quick to argue, without much show of evidence, that the entire *Iliad* translation was a covert Jacobite exercise. Even if this is not true, it must be acknowledged that it was an undertaking well supported by the community of Stuart supporters. Dr Arbuthnot was able to make a bitter pleasantry of the rumours: in a letter to Parnell written jointly with Pope, Gay, and Jervas in February 1716, he remarked with a straight face that 'Mr pope delays his Second Volume of his Homer till the Martial Spirit of the Rebells is quite quelld it being judged that his first part did some harm that way' (*Corr.* i. 332).

What is now blindingly obvious, but could not have been precisely foreseen in

---

[66] Pope was familiar with the members of Burlington's household: in Feb. 1716 he had written to the Earl's secretary, Richard Graham, member of a well-known Jacobite family. Such contacts do not indicate anything with regard to Burlington's supposed disaffection (see below, p. 126), but they do indicate a certain oddity in his familial arrangements. See Erskine-Hill (1995: 219).

1713, is the way in which events systematically negated the ideological aspirations of *Windsor-Forest*. The poem casts Trumbull as a contented figure of retirement; in the following year Swift would flee from the palace 'like a poor cast courtier', as he once said (Swift, *Corr.* ii. 90); and Pope's friends would be chased from office. By 1715 they almost all had in prospect what Pope would call 'the Scaffold, or the silent Cell.' In his verse epistle to Oxford, attached to the poems of Parnell in 1722, Pope reconfig- ured the lines celebrating Trumbull to match the fate of the Lord Treasurer, forced to retreat to 'Desarts'. The muse will trace the brave man's latest steps, 'and dignify Disgrace' (*TE* vi. 239). The implicit hero of *Windsor-Forest*, Oxford had been con- signed to a different royal castle along the river, the Tower of London, and there he was to be joined by the poem's dedicatee Lansdowne. Meanwhile, Bolingbroke and Ormonde were stripped of their honours; Swift thought that the Hanoverian regime were seeking to 'take off their heads' (see Chapter 5, below), and also feared that Prior would be hanged if he did not give evidence against his masters (Swift, *Corr.* ii. 181). In the end the impeachment of Oxford was halted, although even then he received an order from the Lord Chamberlain banning him from court—the arena where, in terms of Tory ideology, he had served the interests of the Queen and of the nation. Swift offered to follow Oxford to Herefordshire and 'be a Companion in [his] retirement' (Swift, *Corr.* ii. 276). Pope too was back in regular contact with the Earl: there was even a brief revival of the truncated Scriblerus Club in July 1718. But mostly such meetings provided an occasion for toasting absent friends, and for looking back to the years of hope under Anne.

The importance of individual names on the list is that they point to a range of con- tacts, and often to relationships, which Pope had established by 1715 at the very lat- est. In most cases, these were people who had, first, already signalized their Jacobite loyalties, and second, already had some dealings with Pope, when *Windsor-Forest* appeared.[67] It is more complex when we turn to the later subscription campaign, and again further work needs to be done. For example, scholarship has teased out many connections between Pope and the Caesar family, who were amongst the most unswerving in their devotion to the Stuart cause.[68] Mary Caesar gave the poet immense help in mounting the subscription campaign for the *Odyssey*, and he rewarded her by the unique addition of an asterisk beside her name in the list of subscribers (see also *Corr.* ii. 293). The possibility has never been properly explored that the entire campaign was indeed a cover for a fund-raising effort, in order to support the planned uprising of 1718–19. It is worth noting that some of those who subscribed to the *Odyssey* (and for that matter the *Iliad*) had apparent links with the plan to raise up to £20,000 for Swedish troops. In 1716 the Jacobites were able to offer the Swedish envoy Gyllenborg enough cash to pay for some 12,000 soldiers to support an invasion. The plan was soon uncovered by the authorities, and publicly

---

[67] Some of Pope's friends, such as Wyndham and Bathurst, later joined the Hanoverian camp. The categories used in the previous paragraph relate to their loyalties in 1713–15. Wyndham remained an oppositional figure, whom Pope lauded in his later verse (see e.g. *TE* v. 318).

[68] See Rumbold (1989: 231–50; 1992: 178–98), as well as Erskine-Hill (1982*b*).

exposed in early 1717: the project ultimately came to nothing after the death of Charles XII in the following year. Instead, the Jacobites looked to support from Spain; but the expedition mounted from Madrid in March 1719 came to an ignominious end in the Highland glens that June.

Charles Caesar, Mary's husband, had been one of the key figures in the negotiations with Sweden; and the former secretary of state under Oxford, William Bromley (another subscriber to Pope's translations) helped in the fund-raising. According to one scholar, 'Atterbury and his friends subscribed £5,000; a group connected with Charles Caesar . . . found another £5,000; while a body of Roman Catholic gentry, organized by the eccentric priest, Father Thomas Southcott, gathered in no less than £8,000' (Bennett, 209). It will surprise few who have followed the argument to this point that Atterbury should by now be one of Pope's closest friends; that the Caesar family should have established a kind of Stuart cell within British society—Mary's diary has been described as a form of royalist panegyric—or that her husband Charles should have joined his old patron Oxford in the Tower, when the plot was exposed. Equally predictable is the fact that Father Southcote should be a friend of Pope from the poet's boyhood (see also p. 38, above). From other sources we learn that Bathurst had subscribed a full £1,000. Even if Pope had no involvement in the fund-raising, he was assuredly close to those who had such a stake.

The most immediately relevant case is that of the Caesars, in view of the fact that Atterbury largely kept aloof from the practical organization of the campaign. (For his deeper implication in the planned rising of 1722, see Chapter 1, above.) Valerie Rumbold has shown in convincing detail that Mary Caesar elaborated an entire system of *virtù* around her Jacobite faith. Behind this cult lay 'a coherent vision of a group of friends formed in the golden age of Queen Anne, and the values which they embody for her'. A recurring motif is the praise of 'poets whom she is able to idealize as servants of the royal cause'. The first of these was Prior, whose own subscription volume (published in 1719) she energetically promoted. A second was Pope, although in Rumbold's view Mary 'tried to stretch the implications of his association with the wits of the age of Anne further than they would go'—a view some of the evidence assembled in this book may qualify. Directly to our point is Rumbold's demonstration that 'A key text for [Mary] was *Windsor Forest*, which she read in the light of her own emotions at the time of the Peace of Utrecht':

O the Delight I felt in hearing Her Majesty from the Thrown Deliver that Speech Which Gave Her So Much joy.

> At Length Great Anna said—Let Discord Ceace
> She Said, the World Obey'd, and all Was peace.

Further, 'She loved to recollect how "in the Happy Day's of Queen Ann" Pope had written, also in *Windsor Forest*, that "Rich Industry Sits Smiling on the Pleine | And Peace and Plenty Tell a Stuart Reigns"; and it is likely that she supported the *Odyssey* Subscription at least partly because she saw Pope's translation as asserting the centrality of her political grouping to the national culture.'[69] This is extremely shrewd; what it may underestimate is Pope's own nostalgia for the golden years, nourished by a sense of loss for which he already felt some level of foreboding in 1713. To the end of her life Mary retained her ideals, and not long before her death in 1741 she urged Pope to create a new poem for the times: 'But for Thy Windsor a New Fabrick Raise | And There Triumphant Sing Thy Soverain's Praise.'[70]

As for the Atterbury plot itself, there is little doubt where Pope's sympathies lay. He actually made a brave statement before the House of Lords at the Bishop's trial, a difficult thing for a man of his natural reticence to undertake. He remained loyal to Atterbury throughout the latter's exile in France. Others centrally involved in the plot, as remarked elsewhere, included Lansdowne, Lord Orrery, the Earl of Strafford and possibly the latter's cousin Bathurst—all well known to Pope. Among English Jacobites who assuredly had some idea of what was going on was the Duchess of Buckingham, natural daughter of James II and half-sister of the Pretender, with whom Pope kept in regular contact at this juncture.[71] But there is another clue to his position. Pope was involved at this same time in publishing the works of the Duchess's husband, John Sheffield. The licence to issue these works was held by Alderman John Barber, who was subsequently in trouble with the authorities for their seditious contents—his premises were seized and copies of the books seized (*Life*, 396). Barber's sympathies with the Stuart cause had never been a close secret. Since the time of the *Examiner*, he had been on terms of intimacy with Swift, as the Dean himself expressed it (*JTS* i. 140), and Pope had known him for some years, though on a more distant basis. At this significant juncture, when the two men were linked together for the first time as author and publisher, Barber abruptly disappeared from London, and turned up in Naples and Rome. It is generally believed that the aim of this trip was not to recoup his health, as was claimed, but to carry to the Pretender the huge sum of about £50,000 which English Jacobites had raised to support the cause. On his return he agreed to give up his printing business, perhaps in order to escape punishment for his activities on behalf of the Stuarts. Pope was embarrassed by the affair of Buckingham's *Works*, not least perhaps because he was publicly linked in an enterprise with Barber, an active promoter of the latest rising.[72]

Unlike Swift, who wrote some scathing verses on the episode, Pope did not compose anything directly on the events of 1722; but he made no effort to distance himself from the leading participants. More than a decade later, there appeared a poem called *Bounce to Fop*, which was possibly started by Swift but certainly completed by Pope. Here the poet celebrates his prominent neighbours including Bathurst and the second Earl of Oxford, who could not be described as very enthusiastic Hanove-

[69] Rumbold (1989: 241). In times of stress Mary Caesar also turned to verses by Lord Lansdowne for consolation (1989: 244).

[70] Rumbold (1989: 247).

[71] The Duchess was later involved in the Cornbury plot of the early 1730s: Rumbold (1989: 176), and Jones (1954: 180–4).

[72] For the events described here, see Rivington (1989). The true 'publishing' role for the *Works* may have been that of Jacob Tonson junior, but it was Barber who held the grant and was named on the title page (Rivington 1989: 94–9).

rians.[73] The first peer to be named is another figure from the days of the Utrecht negotiations, who was a cousin of Bathurst and undoubtedly complicit in the Atterbury plot: Pope's dog Bounce is made to say, 'My Eldest-born resides not far, | Where shines great *Strafford*'s glittering Star' (*TE* vi. 368). Strafford, incidentally, had a house in Twickenham. A pet dog, sent as a gift, had led to the arrest and conviction of Atterbury; Pope knew well enough how the gift of a puppy to Lord Strafford, Garter knight or not, could be used by unscrupulous politicians. So these later events cast their retrospective light on the figures who made up the political circle surrounding Pope at the time of *Windsor-Forest*.

Organized Jacobite propaganda made use of several channels of information. The widespread distribution of prints for political purposes has been the subject of a recent study by Richard Sharp, which documents in great detail the popularity of individual portraits of leading figures in the Stuart cause. Naturally the most common of these prints are those depicting members of the royal family, especially James II, Mary of Modena, and the two Pretenders—there are scores of items which feature James III and VIII. However, many other portraits were distributed by the same means, transmitting the image of men who frequently turn up in this book—such as Atterbury, Alderman Barber, the Duke of Beaufort, Bolingbroke, William Bromley, the Earl of Derwentwater (plus his wife and brother in separate engravings), Henry Dodwell, Thomas Hearne (who also collected these prints), Lord Lansdowne, the Earl of Mar, Lord North and Grey, the Duke of Ormonde, the Earl of Strafford, the Abbé Southcote, and Sir William Wyndham. Most of these were among Pope's subscribers. The fact that their image was aggressively circulated by the Jacobite publicity machine does nothing to contradict the assumption that the author of *Windsor-Forest* would be known by the company he kept. Sometimes these prints show insignia to which Pope had referred: thus Beaufort appears (1714) as portrayed by Dahl in Garter robes, while the same artist's picture of Ormonde (1713), advertised as the Duke's 'effigies' in 1715, is flanked by his coat of arms, itself surrounded by the Garter. This print also contains a quasi-memorial tablet which recites Ormonde's huge collection of titles and dignities: here, of course, the point is that all these honours were about to be stripped from the Duke in the autumn of 1715 (see Chapters 5 and 6, below). After the leading rebels were executed in 1716, their effigies were distributed on a composite print, together with an engraved text of their dying words.[74]

OCCULT PRACTICES

We may never know whether Pope really favoured the Jacobite cause in any active way, though the evidence provided by his dealings with Atterbury, Buckingham,

---

[73] As late as 1741 Bathurst raised a column at Cirencester, topped by a statue of Queen Anne. Pope was a principal adviser on all matters relating to the estate, and still giving 'orders' on this subject.

[74] This paragraph draws on Sharp (1996). Of course, not everyone who bought a print of these figures necessarily supported the Jacobite cause; but it seems unlikely that there were many loyal Hanoverians who responded when the *Post Man* ran advertisements in Aug. 1715 for the Ormonde print.

Southcote, and others is strongly suggestive. By 1730, however, he was certainly a member of a lodge of Freemasons, along with his close friend Arbuthnot (*Life*, 437–40), and many branches of the Masonic craft were overwhelmingly tinged with Jacobite sentiment in the period. Even after the foundation of the Grand Lodge in 1717 and a concerted effort to identify the movement with Hanoverian orthodoxy, it took time for the Jacobite element to be purged. In his exile James II had even instituted a code according to which London was the Jerusalem to be regained by his followers the Israelites.[75] Earlier, the Masonic movement had read much into the revival by James of the Knights of St Andrew (otherwise the Order of the Thistle) in 1687: for them, this represented the second birth of a society proscribed at the time of the Reformation. They hoped that the king would make this particular mark of distinction for Masons, although this does not seem to have happened in the brief period before James was forced from the throne.

Recently the work of Jane Clark on Burlington has cast light on these issues, even though it cannot be said to be conclusive, in respect to Pope's own implication especially. Clark produces a number of contemporary references to show that Burlington's architecture was widely identified with the Masonic craft. Further, she argues that Chiswick House was a symbolic temple, based on so-called Royal Arch Freemasonry. The focus of this ritual was on restoration and restitution, and at Chiswick as elsewhere it involves a Hermetic intervention designed to heal the sufferings of the exiled Jews. In Jacobite terms, Clark contends, this referred to the exiled monarch and the 'Crucifixion' of Charles I (see p. 99). The ceiling in the Red Velvet Room depicts a resurrection of the arts directed by Hermes, with a rainbow beneath an arch and zodiacal signs, common on Royal Arch banners. Moreover, in the centre of the ceiling is a star composed of eight equilateral triangles, which may be 'a composite reference to the Imperial crown (Augustus) . . . the eight-pointed Garter Star, and the sun, all-important in masonry'. Clark proceeds:

Elias Ashmole, one of the earliest known freemasons, described how this star, 'as it is usually called', was 'assumed' by Charles I. . . . Charles as sun king, with his particularly close association with the Order of the Garter, became one of the mainstays of Stuart and Jacobite symbolism. Charles's portrait, with his family, hangs in the adjacent Tribunal, where another eight-pointed star graces the floor.[76]

It should be noted too that Charles II maintained this association; one of his changes at Windsor Castle was to add the so-called Star Building, with the symbol prominently displayed on its façade. Yet again George IV was responsible for demolishing this.

Clark stresses Burlington's familiarity with the tradition of the Mercurian Monarch, and suggests that his desire to possess the designs by Inigo Jones for Stuart masques 'may have been as much for his belief in the symbolism of these great allegorical pageants as for his interest in the draughtsman himself'. At this

[75] The argument in the text follows Clark (1995: 292), as against the differing account of Jacob (1991: 23–51).
[76] Clark (1995: 295).

point Clark relates the symbolism of the Chiswick ceiling to the famous masque *Coelum Britannicum*, whose relevance to *Windsor-Forest* is set out in more detail in *SDW*, chapter 1. Finally, she cites a well known work on Freemasonry by Dr James Anderson (1721), which celebrates Burlington's role in the brotherhood. In the usual fanciful way of its kind, this book 'stresses the importance of "the glorious Augustus" who became "Grand Master of the Lodge at Rome" and of his patronage of Vitruvius, the remains of whose buildings "are the Pattern and Standard of true Masonry in all future Times"'. Equally, for Anderson 'James I and Charles I being Mason Kings, were responsible for restoring the "Augustan Stile" through "the great Palladio and the glorious Inigo Jones".'[77]

Plainly, there is much that needs careful analysis here, if only to sort out the mumbo-jumbo from the more plausible hints which may be afforded. It is important to recall, first that Burlington's Jacobite commitment remains unproved; and second that Pope probably did not meet the Earl until 1714 or 1715.[78] However, the relevance of this material is not wholly dependent on any assumptions we make about Burlington's politics. We have other well-established facts to bring under consideration. These include (1) Pope's known interest in Palladian architecture, as expressed both in its Vitruvian origins and in its revival by Jones; (2) the well-documented links between the Stuarts and modes of emblematic art which were regularly interpreted in terms of alchemy, hermeticism, Rosicrucianism, and Freemasonry—for this purpose it is not essential to show in all cases that the original creator of a masque, or any other work of art, had intended such a meaning; by Pope's day most Stuart propagandistic statements were routinely read in these ways; (3) the blending of iconographic and other evidence, as from masques, supports a view that Stuart panegyric by this date naturally draws on different expressions of a shared body of language. It might be an accident that *Windsor-Forest* refers to the zodiacal signs, or that the transformed city at the end is represented by the Roman version of the name, Augusta (336). But the 'Silver *Star*' (290) can only point in one direction, to the Garter emblem introduced by Charles I himself.

It is far more difficult to believe that Pope was oblivious to these coded messages in Stuart propaganda than that he deliberately utilized them to fill out his own vision of the *pax Romana* of Augustus, as transplanted to British soil. He would not have had to read Ashmole to be aware of the covert meanings of the emblems that suffuse *Windsor-Forest*. For that matter, he would not have needed to read Anderson's text—as Mack did, to illuminate Pope's Masonic allegiance—in order to understand the symbolism of the craft. As for the solidly grounded observation of Clark, 'The study of the stars was an important aspect of Hermetic

---

[77] Clark (1995: 295–7). It is not easy to dispute the recent finding that 'the first lodges in England, France, Spain and Italy were extended Jacobite clubs' (McLynn 1991: 532). However, the Masonic legend that either the Earl of Derwentwater (beheaded 1716) or his brother (beheaded 1746) was instrumental in establishing the earliest French lodge seems to have no foundation.

[78] Not all Clark's dates seem to fit, as is also the case with her essay, '"His Zeal is too Furious": Lord Burlington's Agents', in Corp (1998): see the review by Edward Gregg in *British Journal for Eighteenth-Century Studies*, 24 (2001), 95–6. However, the crucial point here, as argued in the text, is not the Earl's own loyalties.

philosophy and a key to secret knowledge,'[79] we may recall Pope's hermit-philosopher:

> Or looks on Heav'n with more than mortal Eyes,
> Bids his free Soul expatiate in the Skies,
> Amid her kindred Stars familiar roam,
> Survey the Region, and confess her Home!
>
> (253–6)

This might be interpreted from many perspectives, religious or pagan; but it bears one obvious mystical sense. According to this, the hermit becomes a student of the occult, who 'With Chymic Art exalts the Min'ral Powers' (243), that is practises alchemic experiments; and 'Now marks the course of rolling Orbs on high; | O'er figur'd Worlds now travels with his Eye[,] | Of ancient Writ unlocks the learned Store, | Consults the Dead, and lives past Ages over' (245–8)—that is, grows to be in touch with the 'ancient', forbidden knowledge, claimed alike by the alchemists, the hermeticists, and the 'ancient' Freemasons of the Royal Arch lodge.[80]

A related area of occult learning has been used by Douglas Brooks-Davies to enforce his account of *The Dunciad* as 'certainly susceptible of a Jacobite reading'. For this purpose Brooks-Davies treats *Windsor-Forest* as a 'prelude' to the later poem: 'Anne had restored gold in *Windsor-Forest*, *The Dunciad*'s bright Stuart counterpart.' He points to a number of passages in which Pope's text manifests 'the monarch's power to make gold' as against the alchemist's black *prima materia*, exemplified by the countryside under the Williamite tyrants. The conclusion reached is that, while Pope 'surely did not regard alchemy as a practical proposition', yet 'it still lived for him as a political metaphor'. In keeping with the thesis of the present book, Brooks-Davies contends that '*Windsor-Forest* confirms that alchemical symbolism had, by the eighteenth century, become a recognized hallmark of Stuart eulogy.'[81] Pope certainly would not have considered that the Golden Age could be restored simply through alchemical magic, but all the evidence considered here suggests that he was willing to exploit these 'outmoded' concepts in his figural design to reinvent a viable Stuart kingship (see also Chapter 7, below).

The more we learn about the poem, the more likely it seems that there *is* some tincture of alchemy in *Windsor-Forest*. As Brooks-Davies contends, Anne takes over the 'Chymic Art' of the hermit (243), and restores '*Albion*'s Golden Days' (424), after 'an apocalyptic passage in which Garter symbolism combines with Isaian prophecy and alchemy to reveal the mystical depths of Pope's commitment to Anne and the Stuart cause' (393–8).[82] Moreover, the idea of Anne as silver (or white) queen, uniting with the red king to yield pure alchemic gold, takes on more force if we see the

---

[79] Clark (1995: 295).

[80] In drawing 'Phyisck' from the herbs, he approaches the practice of the alchemist who creates 'medicine', i.e. the healing elixir.

[81] Brooks-Davies (1985: 142–3).

[82] The implications of the Garter will be discussed in Ch. 6, below, while those of the book of Isaiah are reviewed in *SDW*, ch. 6.

'unbounded *Thames*' (398) as contrasted with the iron squadrons on the banks of the Volga.[83] The ultimate cogency of these notions derives from the way they intermesh and the coherence they lend to disparate sections of the poem. Thus, if early on Ceres warms the ripening corn as a proof that 'a STUART reigns' (42), then later '*Phoebus* warms the ripening Ore to Gold' (396)—a connection that goes beyond verbal links into the deep structure of anthropological and mythological patterns of thought. Of course, hermetic studies such as alchemy and learned systems of representation such as heraldry were available to every sort of educated man or woman. But it is scarcely a matter for dispute that these branches of learning became to a disproportionate degree the province of politically disaffected groups, most obviously those who opposed the desacralizing regimes of William III and George I. Heraldry, for example, fell into a period of torpor after the ending of visitations by the heralds and effective neglect by the early Hanoverians. In that sense Stuart loyalty can sometimes be the mark of an identification with suppressed or rejected systems of meaning, as well as adherence to a given belief or to a particular ruler.

We must keep these things in perspective. There were of course adherents of the Stuarts who had no truck with hermetic lore; Jacobites who did not follow Ashmole any distance down the Rosicrucian path; admirers of the architecture of Inigo Jones who had no strong political views; Catholics who did not know or care about the heraldry of chivalric orders—and loyal supporters of the Queen who never strayed an inch from orthodoxy in thought or deed. The evidence, however, seems more and more to show that Pope was not among these easygoing Laodicean types.

---

[83] All these suggestions are made by Brooks-Davies (1985: 141–2).

4

The Queen

The main function of Queen Anne in Pope's design is almost self-evident. She appears in the role of 'Great *ANNA*' (327): she reigns, too, as 'the *British* Queen' (384), an authentic monarch, and the last of the Stuart line with an indefeasible right to the throne. For, whatever the claims of James Francis Edward were, he could not possibly have aspired to an uncontested succession. Since she was a bulwark of the Church of England and a professed supporter of the Protestant succession, the poet might enlist Anne without incurring charges of disloyalty or open Jacobitism. Her longing to pass on the crown to her own offspring had finally disappeared with the death of the young Duke of Gloucester in 1700, and by the time she came to the throne she had, however reluctantly, accepted the fact that the Hanoverians would in due course succeed her. But many contemporaries would have understood Churchill's remark that 'at heart she was a Protestant-Jacobite. While in her person and in her policy she barred the return of the rightful heir, she embodied the claims of blood and affirmed the Divine Right of Kings. She reverenced the principles the overthrow of which had brought her the crown' (Churchill, ii. 32–3). For Catholics as for Jacobites, it was these 'claims of blood' which prevailed over other considerations: Anne's own Protestantism, sincerely held, did not seriously impugn her place in the line. She could be portrayed as having undone the damage done, religiously and politically, by William III, especially in the later part of her reign as she rejected the Marlborough faction, and gave support to the High Church. Crucially, she backed the attempt to end the war, even on terms which a large part of the nation considered unduly favourable to France and Spain. 'I have this buisnes of ye Peace soe much at hart', she told the Earl of Oxford in September 1711 (Gregg, 341): it became the obsessive aim in her last years. Pointedly, too, she had resumed the practice of touching for the king's evil, which William had disparaged as foolish superstition.[1]

By using the phrase '*British* Queen', *Windsor-Forest* achieves another propagandistic goal. In the text we find *Britannia* twice, *Britain* twice, and *British* three times. The words *England* and *English* do not appear at all. As we have seen, Pope was re-

---

[1] A contemporary historian thought that she had done this to assert her hereditary claims. It was still a world where such mysterious powers authenticated monarchy: not surprisingly, the Hanoverians abandoned the practice for good. For a fuller discussion, see pp. 154–8, below.

luctant to confront the Union directly. Nevertheless, his language celebrates the full incorporation of Scotland into the joint kingdom: it was, after all, the Stuarts who had brought the crowns together, just as it was Anne who now presided over the united parliaments.[2] Today we are well aware that the forging of a nation is an elaborate and troublesome business: it was all too obvious in 1713 that the Union remained fragile, with the old animosities scarcely less apparent than they had been in the days when two independent parliaments opposed each other. Within the first three days of her reign, even before she went to be crowned, the Queen had expressed her hopes for a closer relation between the two countries, in part because the Jacobite threat hung most heavily over her Scottish realm. As long as she remained on the throne, Anne continued to support the measure, despite reservations about the Union which were expressed on both sides of the political divide. Accordingly, the imagery of concord with which *Windsor-Forest* comes to its climax must refer at some level to the fragile new entente which had been created between the two parts of the kingdom: as a matter of plain fact, few aspects of national life in the sixteenth and seventeenth centuries had been more marked by discord, ambition, persecution, vengeance and faction than Anglo-Scottish affairs (*WF*, 413–22). Events were to show very shortly afterwards that '*Rebellion*' stood ready to unleash her forces. The poem seeks to minimize these continuing dangers, and operates in an oblique way to solemnize the new British identity under Anne.

Apart from this, Pope's tribute may be construed in personal as well as political terms. The public message congratulates the Queen on the success of her servants, which means Oxford and, to a lesser extent, colleagues such as Bolingbroke. However, in the following year Pope would assemble many of Anne's private coterie among the subscribers to the *Iliad*. These included the Queen's Maid of Honour, Elizabeth Granville (sister of the dedicatee); courtiers such as Sir John Stanley (married to another of Lansdowne's sisters); the royal physicians Dr John Arbuthnot and Sir David Hamilton; and favourites such as Lady Masham. *Windsor-Forest* was meant to please many, but also to flatter the expectations of a small circle around the Queen—those who were habitués of the court and the castle, and would recognize delicate compliments inscribed in the text.

What has previously been occluded is the existence of coded references to the Queen's own personal history. Perhaps the most interesting occurs in the middle of the poem:

> O early lost! what Tears the River shed
> When the sad Pomp along his Banks was led?
> His drooping Swans on ev'ry Note expire,
> And on his Willows hung each Muse's Lyre.
>
> (273–6)

The overt reference here is to Cowley, whose body was carried down the Thames by barge from Chertsey to Westminster, prior to his funeral at the Abbey in 1667 (see

[2] The very term *British* became normal usage with the accession of the Queen's great-grandfather to the English throne in 1603 (see *OED*, 'British', 2).

Chapter 8, below). However, it would have been unbelievably tactless for Pope to have forgotten a more recent instance, involving a young man who could truly be said to have been 'early lost'. This was the heir presumptive to the throne, Prince William of Gloucester, the last child to survive from all of Anne's eighteen pregnancies. After celebrating his eleventh birthday at Windsor Castle in 1700, he fell ill and died within a few days, on 30 July, possibly from scarlet fever. His body was taken by barge from Windsor to Westminster on 1 August (the date of the Queen's own death fourteen years later). There he lay in state prior to burial at the Abbey, while Anne remained in seclusion at Windsor. She never recovered from this blow and made 30 July a day of perpetual mourning thereafter: the event precipitated a response of closing down, much like that of Victoria following the death of Albert. It was the end of hopes for unquestioned Protestant succession, an end to the Stuart dream, an end to Anne's maternal identity. From now on she would transfer her capacity for motherhood to the body politic. Mary Chudleigh had written a poem on the boy's death, deploring 'My Country's Loss' and expressing a desire to share the mother's pain, in order to help her regain 'her former Peace'.[3] As with the passage in Pope, nature droops in the face of a calamity at once public and private.

SOVEREIGN, COURT, AND COUNTRY

Happy the Man whom this bright Court approves,
His Sov'reign favours, and his Country loves.

(235–6)

Beyond the broad qualifications which have just been mentioned, the Queen fits the symbolic design of the poem in more particular ways. For example, she harboured a strong desire, especially at the outset of her reign, to enhance what R. O. Bucholz has called 'the social and symbolic life of the court'. This proceeded from her own deep respect for traditional forms, which Swift and others noted:

The most visible and popular element in this ambitious undertaking was the new Queen's revival of royal ceremony and etiquette. It is well known that Anne was, like her father and grandfather, a stickler for ceremony. Her almost obsessive interest in and extensive knowledge of courtly ritual and custom were much commented on by observers whose place it was to know, such as her groom of the stole, the Duchess of Marlborough, and her master of ceremonies, Sir Clement Cotterell.

This attempt to enlist ceremonial for political ends was expressed in her 'ostentatious attendance' at the Anglican Chapel Royal. Moreover, she attempted in Bucholz's words to 'use the big public occasions of her reign to unite a divided nation under her impartial reign'. As time went on, this effort to paper over the cracks caused by party strife proved harder and harder to sustain. But at first things went

[3] See Barash (1996: 240–2). The same writer astutely observes that in *WF* 'Anne presides over the place as well as the poet, lifting the poem's imperial ambitions to prophetic heights' (1996: 54).

well. At her first speech in parliament, less than a week after her accession, the Queen made a splendid appearance, in her crown, gold chain with the badge of St George, and 'a magnificent gown of red velvet lined with ermine and edged with gold galloon'.[4] As we shall see in the course of discussion, this deliberate self-representation in the guise of Elizabeth *rediviva* was to be maintained for several years.

Throughout the reign, events such as services of thanksgiving and royal progresses gave the monarch opportunities to portray herself as the mother of her nation: she cooperated with the aristocracy, the Church, political leaders, the armed forces, and civic dignitaries to convey this impression. Particularly useful were ceremonies with a built-in patriotic element, such as the coronation and Garter ceremonies, or those with a dynastic significance, as with the ritual of touching for the evil (all described more fully below). Twelve times a year, the Queen and leading courtiers appeared on 'collar days' wearing the badge of their order: the monarch made a special offering of gold at the altar of the Chapel Royal. In addition, a dozen thanksgiving services took place while Anne was on the throne. As her subjects tired of the war and allied victories tended to become less clear-cut and resplendent, so the ceremonies lost some of their appeal. Anne's own health began to fail, the finances of the court were growing more straitened, and political divisions undermined the intended symbolism of the occasion. In the last four years of her reign only one major service was held, that commemorating the Peace in July 1713. As we saw in Chapter 3, this was unconscionably delayed, and the Queen could not go to St Paul's because of her poor health.

Perhaps the attempt had always been doomed to failure. By the end of Anne's reign, in the view of a careful modern student, her version of 'unity and moderation ultimately had very little to offer Dissenters and Junto Whigs'. It also failed to please 'the most aggressive members of the High Church party' (Bucholz, 225). The Kit-Cat Club arranged their own unofficial ceremonies, and the Marlboroughs at one time set up what was almost an alternative court. Yet the vision had once shone brightly, and it was this which Pope sought to reanimate. The texture of *Windsor-Forest* is woven around this very 'courtly ritual and custom'. At many junctures the poem recalls pageantry of the tournament or of the theatrical masque; it harks back to chivalric entities such as the Order of the Garter, and allots a central passage to the historic nerve-centre of monarchy at Windsor. More generally, the verbal surface is coated with glittering metallic tones and sumptuous images of majesty (often couched in hieratic languages such as heraldic blazon). It is a *pièce d'occasion*, and the occasion is a national celebration of the Peace, led by the Queen in person (gout could not keep her from *this* engagement).

Pope is unlikely to have attended court before he wrote his poem. He could have learnt something about life there from Trumbull, who was in correspondence with the new Lord Steward in June 1711. Likewise the poet had already become friendly with John Gay, who was acting as secretary to the Duchess of Monmouth: this

---

[4] Bucholz, 203–5. The fascinating study by Bucholz yields new insights into court life in this reign, and offers much illumination of the world *WF* imaginatively expresses.

venerable lady had recently shown that she still had enough confidence to appear at St James's on the Queen's birthday, in sumptuous clothes and jewels worth £50,000.[5] She might have communicated to Gay what she had seen of court life since the days of Charles II. At the same time, Pope had developed close contacts with Swift and Arbuthnot, who could give him a first-hand account of daily usage, though probably just too late for this to help with *Windsor-Forest*. As observed in Chapter 2, it was with the formation of the Scriblerus Club later in 1713 that Pope came to know Oxford, even though he was most likely familiar with Bolingbroke before then. But in any case Pope was not aiming at a portrait of everyday reality. His work sets forth an idealized view of the court as an agency of the great purposes of the nation, as these were expressed in the drama of state occasions. Titbits about favourites such as Mrs Masham might feed into *The Rape of the Lock*, as they certainly permeate Swift's *Journal to Stella*. These works belong to a different literary milieu.

What does hold significance, though, is that the poem should be dedicated to Lansdowne, a politician now turned courtier. As remarked in Chapter 2, the peer had taken over as comptroller of the household in July 1712, and would move to the post of treasurer in August 1713. Equally to the point, he had married Mary Villiers, daughter of the Earl of Jersey, Lord Chamberlain at the start of Anne's reign. The post of chamberlain involved titular and sometimes actual responsibility for the major part of the royal household, with a staff of almost a thousand and a budget of over £100,000 per annum. Under his jurisdiction came numerous court offices, including that of the master of ceremonies.[6] In fact Lansdowne, responsible to the Lord Steward (Poulett), did not need to attend at court too punctiliously, but nevertheless his role made him a suitable object of dedication for a poem which embodies so much stately ritual.

A further item of evidence, which was omitted from the account of Lansdowne's career given in Chapter 2, will reveal just how well established a position he occupied in the royal hierarchy. This relates to the performance of a play he adapted from *The Merchant of Venice*: it was entitled *The Jew of Malta*, and staged on the Queen's birthday in 1711, at a time when the author was still George Granville and unmarried. The drama formed part of an impressive day of ceremonies, including 'a Dialogue in *Italian*, in Her Majesty's Praise, set to excellent Musick by the famous Mr. *Hendel*.'[7] Strikingly, *The Jew* remained the only contemporary play put on at court during the reign: a more characteristic choice had been *The Merry Wives of Windsor*, performed in 1704. In the light of this fact, it makes more sense that Pope should be willing to stress Lansdowne's powers as a writer, and to signalize his duty to 'Make *Windsor* Hills in lofty Numbers rise, | And lift her Turrets nearer to the Skies' (287–8). The play by Lansdowne had been put on by royal command, as part of the official birthday celebrations. Again, Pope must surely have been aware of the

---

[5] Luttrell (1857: vi. 688).

[6] See Bucholz, 36–63 for estimates of the scale of activity. At the end of 1713 Swift embarked on a campaign to become Historiographer Royal, enlisting the help of Arbuthnot and Lady Masham, but despite a letter of support from Bolingbroke to the Lord Chamberlain he was not to succeed.

[7] Quoted by Burrows (1994: 66).

event: there had not been 'so fine or so full a court since King Charles's time', gushed the reports.[8]

At the very end of the reign, as we know, Pope had started to collect subscribers for his *Iliad*. Among the courtiers named is Lansdowne's brother-in-law Sir John Stanley, who held the pivotal role of secretary to the Lord Chamberlain throughout the reign of Anne, and helped to control household patronage for over twenty years. (The current chamberlain, the Duke of Shrewsbury, was naturally a subscriber, too.) Separate listings cover Sir John's wife, Anne, who was Lansdowne's sister, along with another sister Elizabeth, a maid of honour. Then there is Colonel Bernard Granville, the peer's brother, who held the post of carver in ordinary. The Granvilles had rendered long service as courtiers for at least two generations, and under Anne they consolidated their family hold on court office. In a subsidiary branch of the household came Sir Clement Cotterell, who oversaw protocol as master of ceremonies: he was a neighbour of Pope after the poet moved to Twickenham, and received a mourning ring in Pope's will. While no evidence exists to show that the two men were in personal contact as early as 1713, it is likely that they knew each other by then: Cotterell was Sir William Trumbull's nephew by marriage (see Chapter 1, above). In any case, their later friendship reflects a shared interest in the symbolic accoutrements of the state. Others with a position in the royal establishment at this date who figure among the subscribers (and who nearly all appear elsewhere in this book) were the Lord Almoner, John Sharp; the Cofferer of the Household, Samuel Masham; the Captain of the Gentlemen Pensioners, the Duke of Beaufort; the Master of the Great Wardrobe, the Duke of Montagu; the Master of the Horse, the Duke of Somerset; a Lady of the Bedchamber, the Duchess of Ormonde; and many others in junior offices.[9] Lansdowne's predecessor and successor as comptroller of the household, Sir Thomas Mansell and Sir John Stonhouse, both subscribed.[10] So of course did another man who became a close friend of the poet, Sir William Wyndham, Master of the Buckhounds from 1711 to 1712—a post where the desiderata included political suitability as well as the kind of technical expertise which *Windsor-Forest* brings to bear (see Bucholz, 91–2).

If the great attempt to revitalize the court was losing impetus by 1713, then Pope may have intuited as much. On 15 March, a week after the poem came out, a period of six months' mourning began for Frederick I, King of Prussia. All persons attending court were expected to dress in sober black garments. It did not affect public life in general very much, but there were no more grand entertainments that year. Courtly dances in honour of Gloriana were put on indefinite hold. As it was to prove, the Queen lived to see only one more birthday, at Windsor in February 1714,

---

[8] See Bucholz, 218, as well as *JTS* i. 181, on the elaborate scale of this birthday ceremony.

[9] Senior office-holders at court who subscribed to the *Iliad* but had no close links to Pope include the Earl of Cardigan, the Earl of Cholmondeley, Baron Delawarr, the Duke of Northumberland, Sir William Pole, Sir William Forrester, Sir Edward Lawrence, and Thomas Coke.

[10] Other court physicians on the list along with Arbuthnot were Blackmore, Hamilton, Shadwell, and Sloane. Dr Radcliffe had lost favour at court some years earlier, and declined to attend at the Queen's deathbed, while Garth had to wait until the coming of George I. Mead attended the Queen, although not a physician in ordinary.

and even then she was confined by illness and missed the celebrations. In *Windsor-Forest*, a profoundly melancholy section in the middle recalls the 'sad Pomp' of Cowley's funeral cortege, as the poet wanders by the river and hears 'soft Musick dye along the Grove' (268). This seems almost to foretell the suspension of court odes in the last three years of the Queen's reign.

WORKS OF PEACE

We can turn to another aspect of the Queen's reign which underlies Pope's text. This concerns the support she had given to the proposal launched in 1711 to build fifty new churches for the capital, a matter which the poem recalls: 'Behold! *Augusta*'s glitt'ring Spires increase, | And Temples rise, the beauteous Works of Peace' (377–8). It is significant that the scheme is linked with peace: both had become specifically 'Tory' rallying cries, even though the party had no monopoly on pacific urges or on piety. The reason is that the measure in its current form had been dreamt up by the lower house of convocation, which was dominated by Atterbury and other High Tories. Convocation business had been close to the heart of national politics throughout Anne's reign, and some of Swift's most effective *Examiner* papers, such as no. 22 (28 December 1710), raked over these controversial matters. The clergy under Atterbury cooperated with the House of Commons under the Speaker, William Bromley, and legislation emerged much more rapidly than was usually the case. Between late February and the middle of May 1711, enough momentum was established to achieve the goal of implementing 'the great and necessary work of building more churches'.

In an address to the Queen on 9 April, the Commons disclosed some political aspects of the proposal: Neither the long expensive war, in which we are engaged, nor the pressure of heavy debts, under which we labour, shall hinder us from granting to your Majesty whatever is necessary, to accomplish so excellent a design, which, we hope, may be a means of drawing down blessings from Heaven on all your Majesty's other undertakings, as it adds to the number of those places, where the prayers of your devout and faithful subjects will be daily offered up to God, for the prosperity of your Majesty's government at home, and the success of your arms abroad.[11]

Swift used this paragraph in an *Examiner* paper on 24 May, and indeed its matter is recognizably that of Tory polemic. As will emerge shortly, Pope adopts the trope of drawing down blessings as a climactic emblem in his poem. The resulting bill promised £350,000 from Port of London duties on coal in order to construct fifty new churches in London and Westminster. The Queen, who had earlier sent a message to the Commons in support of the plan, gave her royal assent to the bill on 12 June, when it came into law as 9 Anne c.17.[12] As it turned out, only twelve buildings were ever erected, and they date from the reign of George I. None the less, the project is still known collectively as Queen Anne's churches.

    [11] Quoted by Ellis (1985: 440).   [12] Ellis (1985: 333).

This is an instructive episode in several respects. More partisan feeling was wrapped in the innocent-sounding proposal than we easily recognize today. It emerged from a deliberate coalition between the lower house of convocation and the lower house of parliament, in furtherance of a programme to defend what was provocatively described as 'the church in danger'. Like the earlier measure to introduce improved stipends for the lower clergy, it was an apparently disinterested piece of legislation which nevertheless pleased one constituency more than any other—the High Church and the Tory squires in parliament, who regarded themselves as guardians of the nation's religious establishment. Significantly, Atterbury was one of the first body of commissioners appointed to oversee the implementation of the scheme: they were 'Tories almost to a man'.[13] It is worth adding that by late 1716 Pope was asking Atterbury for comments on the preface to his *Works* before its publication. We do not know when the two men met, but it is certain that they were already 'well acquainted' before this date, and Pope 'soon became something of a son' to the older man (Bennett, 201–2). Convocation business was a subject of absorbing interest to Trumbull, too, and Ralph Bridges, who was almost a neighbour of Atterbury in Chelsea, kept his uncle apprised of developments every time the body sat in conclave.

At some level, the bill's sponsors aimed to restore not just the City churches but the fabric of London: the depredations of the Great Fire became a metaphor for the ravages of the Civil War and Commonwealth periods. Of course, the most important of the 'temples' to rise after the Fire was St Paul's Cathedral, very recently brought to completion. The half-built cathedral had been opened for a thanksgiving service to celebrate the last major peace, that of Rijswijk in 1697. The first great occasion it witnessed in its full splendour was the Utrecht commemoration in 1713 (see Chapter 3, above). On these state occasions, the cathedral became a transplanted Chapel Royal; the Lord Chamberlain decreed that the Queen's throne should be specially raised above the floor of the choir, to duplicate her position when enthroned in the House of Lords. Church and parliament, state and religion, were united. Beyond that, the designer of St Paul's, Christopher Wren, had produced the most ambitious plan of civic renewal to have emerged after the Fire, and overall Wren built or renovated some fifty churches in the capital. In addition he served as one of the commissioners for the new churches, and wrote some thoughtful comments on the way in which the scheme should be executed.[14] Wren symbolized the effort to create public monuments, rather than the private palace which had been given to Marlborough at Blenheim. It is apt to this way of viewing matters that he was dismissed from his position as surveyor-general, four years into the Hanoverian era, in favour of a semi-competent amateur architect who wrote Whiggish pamphlets (see Chapter 8, below). The subliminal message of *Windsor-Forest* is that the Queen had a personal interest in supporting the physical structure of the Church, so that its

[13] Bennett, 133. Vanbrugh was appointed a commissioner, but none of his proposed designs were accepted, and he seems to have felt himself in a beleaguered minority on the board.

[14] Wren 318–21: also available now in Soo (1998: 112–18).

spiritual life could thrive: just as she supported the fabric of the nation by implementing her peace policy.

Swift had drawn a bitter contrast in the *Examiner* of 24 May 1711 between the numerous 'Edifices' offered to the Churchills and the proposed new churches. The Romans built temples after their victories, but 'we acted all along as if we believ'd nothing of a God or his Providence'. Accordingly:

I have computed, that Fifty Churches may be built by a Medium, at Six Thousand Pound for a Church; which is somewhat *under* the Price of a *Subject's Palace*. Yet perhaps the Care of above Two Hundred Thousand Souls, with the Benefit of their Prayers for the Prosperity of their Queen and Country, may be almost put in the Balance with the Domestick Convenience, or even Magnificence of any *Subject* whatsoever.

The Queen's desire for the advancement of true religion, Swift continues, has been 'check'd by the Necessities of a long and ruinous War'.[15] Here are some of the themes of *Windsor-Forest*: the Queen's beneficence, the hope for prosperity with the end of the war, and the promise of new church-building. Under a Calvinist ruler like William III, the poem intimates, we shall be left with 'naked Temples', 'gaping Tombs', and deserted 'Quires' (68–72). These are like the 'ancient *Gothick* Structures, throughout this Kingdom, going every Year to decay', mentioned by Swift in the same paper. Repairs to such churches, he adds, 'must be left to a Time of Peace'.

Two weeks later, Swift returned to the theme in the *Examiner*. This time he linked the 'pious and noble Work' of church-building with the new scheme to establish the South Sea Company. The second of these ventures will be discussed in Chapter 6. Here we should note that both measures are attributed by Swift principally to the zeal of Robert Harley, now created Lord Treasurer and Earl of Oxford. The conclusion drawn is that most of the nation is now 'throrowly convinc'd, that the Qu—proceeded with the highest Wisdom, in changing Her Ministry and Parliament'.[16] It would have been out of the question for Pope innocently to mention the new churches as though they were unclouded by the divisive issues of the moment.

Another royal characteristic which came to the aid of the poet's design was Anne's devotion to hunting.[17] The Queen maintained this passion even when her unwieldy corpulence obliged her to follow the chase in a specially made carriage. As a famous description by Swift has it, she drove 'furiously like Jehu and is a mighty hunter like Nimrod' (*JTS* i. 324). She rode in a light one-horse chaise, 'with extraordinarily high wheels through standing corn', a feat recalling the swift huntress Diana—Anne's role model in Pope's poem.[18] One story claims that there was formerly a 'noble oak'

[15] Ellis (1985: 441–3).
[16] Ellis (1985: 466–8). After the Hanoverian accession, Gibbs lost his place as a surveyor to the new churches, in favour of a sound Whig (Little 1955: 38). Dr Arbuthnot, the friend of Swift and Pope, was removed from the Commissioners for the New Churches; and as mentioned in the text, a column designed by Gibbs which was to bear a statue of the Queen, at the west end of St Mary le Strand, was never built.
[17] This activity of the forest is explored more fully in *SDW*, ch. 5.
[18] Hill (1957: 101).

within the Forest, marked with a brass plaque, and maintains that the Queen used to mount her horse under its branches, so that she could watch the preparations for a stag-hunt (Green, 101). The need to hold council meetings at Hampton Court on occasion did not stop her: she drove back to Windsor and was able to indulge in her pleasure of 'hunting the stag' almost every day, sometimes riding up to 40 miles (*JTS* i. 328, 349).[19] All this was public knowledge: Daniel Defoe notes that Anne 'always discover'd her Delight to be at *Windsor*, where she chose the little House, as 'twas call'd, opposite the Castle, and took the Air in her Chaise in the Parks and Forest, as she saw Occasion' (*Tour*, i. 179).

Further, this meant that the Queen took special care with the forest rides, and in an attempt to avoid sharing the fate of her predecessor on the throne she commanded Henry Wise to level out the twisting rides through the park. ('Queen Anne's Ride' still cuts through the trees on the western edge.) Her employment of Wise testifies to her genuine interest in landscape gardening, reflected in the riverside garden he constructed near the castle. Thomas Durfey, with venial licence, had addressed her as 'Great Flora', on account of her love of flowers.[20] In these respects Anne can reasonably be imagined as haunting the groves in Diana's wake (165–70), and even as 'painting' the ground like Flora (38).

Strictly, the Great Park was a liminal area, between the Castle and the Forest; but in the imaginative topography of the poem Anne's demesne stretches over the entire environs of Windsor (see Chapter 5, below). Another royal sport, in addition to hunting, was just setting up home in the vicinity: Swift noted on 10 August 1711 that a horse-racing course would be instituted nearby on the following day. This was the very first meeting at Ascot, just beyond the park.[21] Anne presented cups as part of her patronage of the course, and the Queen Anne Stakes preserves this connection at Royal Ascot even today. The course replaced Datchet Mead, just across the river from Windsor, where races were held up to this time. During her reign the monarch had made at least seven visits to Newmarket, always with a full retinue; and the *London Gazette* announced shortly before Pope's poem came out that races would be held there for her majesty's gold cup and plate, early in April 1713. Of course, the 'flying Steed' in Pope's text is engaged in the hunt, but the Queen's interest in racing and in the local meeting fits Pope's evocation of her as a monarch of the open air, whose court can be held in Arden as suitably as in the city.

For Swift, as he told Stella, Windsor was a 'delicious place', and he made special mention of the long avenues in the park. In addition he described the view from his lodging, which was the apartment of one of the prebendaries of Windsor, an office that might have been open to him in April 1713. He singled out two features, Eton College and the Thames (*JTS* i. 319, 349; ii. 553). For whatever reason Pope does not mention Eton: perhaps, despite its Henrician foundation, it had become too much

---

[19] Early in her reign the Queen installed High Tories as rangers of the royal parks: Sir Edward Southwell at Windsor, and the Duke of Buckinghamshire at St James's.

[20] Strickland (1885: viii. 210).

[21] The races, originally due to be held on 6–7 Aug., actually took place on 11–13 Aug. The Duke of Somerset, as master of the horse, spent some £550 on laying out the round course (*VCH Berkshire*, ii. 305).

a seminary of Protestant and even Whiggish orthodoxy. It is the river on which the portals of the Castle gaze down, and this feature of the landscape self-evidently occupies the heart of Pope's design. Finally, in the town of Windsor itself there was a conspicuous testimony to the Queen's local presence. This was found on the façade of the new Town Hall, built by Christopher Wren, where a statue was erected in 1707, with an inscription proclaiming her identity as a goddess (*Life*, 59). Pope's deification of Anne parallels the mythical fantasy of the sculpture, with its hyperbolic verses: *Arte tua, sculptor, non est imitabilis Anna;* | *Annae vis similem sculpere, sculpe deam.*[22]

The truth is that the Queen was in many respects a natural countrywoman, although she could generally satisfy this urge in her being only when she was at Windsor. In 1695 she had lived for a time in Twickenham, right opposite the parish church where Pope's remains would ultimately be laid. There she entrusted her sickly son the Duke of Gloucester to the care of an old lady named Mrs Davies: this was a gentlewoman of the court of Charles I, who taught the boy the rudiments of Christianity, including the creed and the commandments. In spite of her advancing years, Mrs Davies 'was devout, and lived an ascetic life on herbs and fruit . . . Simple as were her habits, she enjoyed a healthy and cheerful old age'. She had planted many beautiful fruit-trees around her small estate, and allowed the members of the Queen's household to gather as many fruit as they wished so long as they did not 'break or spoil' her trees. Through the agency of Sir Benjamin Bathurst (father of Pope's friend), Anne offered Mrs Davies a sum of money in lieu of rent, but this was firmly refused.[23] It is tempting to think of this episode as the equivalent of Pope's sojourn at Binfield under the tutelage of Trumbull, and to cast Mrs Davies as a female version of the benevolent hermit of the forest in *Windsor-Forest* (235–58), withdrawn from court to cultivate the simple life.[24]

IMAGES OF MAJESTY

The Queen chose to revive a further royal tradition. This was the practice of Tudor monarchs in carrying out grand visitations, to which Maynard Mack alludes (*Garden and City*, 95). In keeping up this ritual, as in other respects, Anne followed Elizabeth. For example, during 1705 she made solemn and well-publicized progresses, first to Cambridge and Newmarket, and then to Winchester. These were full-dress occasions, with church-bells ringing, flowers strewn in her path, and the scholars of St John's on their knees as they cried out *Vivat Regina!* It was at Cambridge, too, that the Queen knighted Isaac Newton, whilst the University in

---

[22] A statue of Anne's husband Prince George was erected in the opposite niche of the Town Hall in the very year that *WF* appeared, 1713. This was at the expense of the architect's son, Christopher Wren junior.

[23] Peter Bathurst, another of Sir Benjamin's sons, played war games in St George's Hall with the young Gloucester, beneath the picture of the triumph of Edward III (Strickland 1885: viii. 51–2). Later a Tory MP and subscriber to the *Iliad*, he may have been known to Pope by 1713, when his brother Allen first became friendly with Pope.

[24] Strickland (1885: viii. 29–31).

response saw fit to 'scatter' degrees on her attendants, much as Peace scatters blessings at the end of *Windsor-Forest* (Green, 140–1). As we noted in Chapter 2, John Arbuthnot was among those to collect a doctorate. Another large retinue
accompanied the monarch to Winchester, and again elaborate ceremonial events
were held. Earlier, in 1705, Anne had entered Bath with the full Tudor panoply: she
was greeted 'about 200 Virgins richly attired, many of them like Amazons, with
Bows and Arrows, and others with gilt Scepters, and other Ensigns of the Regalia in
their Hands'.[25] So Diana in the poem is attended by 'buskin'd Virgins', who are 'arm'd
with Silver Bows' (169–70). The Hanoverians were largely to abandon this practice,
along with many of the historical appurtenances of the crown: George IV's visit to
Edinburgh in 1822 is a very rare exception.[26]

Anne's deliberate cult of Elizabeth was meant to cement her position as 'a *British
Queen*' (*WF* 384). It began with her adoption of the motto *semper eadem* and the
mimicry of Elizabethan costume on state occasions. After she had been on the
throne for only a few months, she issued an edict, requiring that whenever there was
occasion to 'embroider, depict, engrave, carve or paint her Majesty's arms', the words
semper eadem should be used (Green, 111).[27] However, something more lay behind
this decision: Anne saw a link between her own suffering at the hands of William and
Mary and the treatment which Elizabeth had received from her father, Henry VIII,
and her sister Mary. Her public relations campaign was aimed to portray her as a na-
tive-born Queen, intent on unifying her people as the energetic and shrewd Elizabeth had sought to do. In her first speech to parliament in 1702, she had referred to 'a
heart entirely English', distantly echoing Elizabeth's famous declaration at Greenwich. It was an unreal comparison in some ways, and Anne went in a different direction on many issues. As we have seen, she departed from the self-image of 'England's
Elizabeth' by stressing her determination to act as a kind of Gloriana Anglo-Scottica.
However, she knew also that Elizabeth had promoted the Order of the Garter,
though slightly toning down the cult of St George. For Pope's purposes, the most
useful aspect of this contrived link is to look forward to military and naval successes
which would bring 'suppliant States' once more 'to bend before a *British* Queen'
(384), as the Dutch had yielded in the sixteenth century. It looks as though Pope is
congratulating Anne's ministers on not giving in to the harder demands of the Dutch
in the peace negotiations, backed as these were by a broad alliance including the
Whig party and Marlborough's own connection. It scarcely matters that Pope's own
history of England would have allotted Mary I a less ignominious part to play in
events, and would have celebrated the Catholic martyrs under her sister's reign.

In reviving Tudor and Stuart modes of royalist propaganda, the Queen was perhaps responding to the extensive campaign of self-promotion which had been initi-
ated by Louis XIV.[28] Obviously, the French king had at his disposal a much more
elaborate bureaucracy of state patronage: as well as his academies and institutions,

---

[25] Boyer's *History of Queen Anne*, i. 78, cited by Bucholz, 208.
[26] For a list of the Queen's progresses (all but one carried out by 1708), see Bucholz, 212.
[27] Pope later applied the phrase to another model of female constancy, Martha Blount (*Corr.* iii. 349).
[28] See Burke (1992).

Louis had the Gobelins factory shuttling away to commemorate his achievements in tapestry. In his reign more than three hundred coins were struck to dignify the Sun King. Though William III had his own smaller medallic history published, Anne used this form of propaganda much more sparingly. Nevertheless, her motto could be seen to answer her rival's proud boast, *Nec pluribus impar,* and her revival of the cult of St George directly challenged the creation of the Order of St Louis in 1693. Usually her panegyrics were couched in less triumphalist terms, and Pope is not alone in associating Anne with olive branches rather than laurels (see also *SDW,* ch. 3).[29]

It was the task of the royal image-makers—among whom Pope can be numbered at this point—to harness the language of emblems to reinforce a sense of the Queen as a pious and charitable monarch, who cared for the prosperity of her subjects and the peace of her nation. The medallic history of Anne's reign, from its very outset, reveals some of the ways in which this was done.[30] On her accession a medal was struck which featured a bust of the Queen in her crown. The reverse showed a heart within branches of oak and either mistletoe or laurel, resting on a pedestal inscribed, *atavis regibus.* This is a quotation from the first line of Horace's first ode ('from royal ancestors'), and it applies there to Maecenas. The legend reads, 'Entirely English'. A coronation medal also issued in 1702 shows the Queen as Minerva hurling thunderbolts against a monster with legs terminating in serpents—compare the devouring snakes in *WF,* 419. On the obverse a bust of the Queen shows her hair 'bound in fillet', as the numismatists describe it. This was a style found in many designs to the end of her reign. It is, at the least, a happy accident that, in depicting Lodona's appearance, Pope should observe, 'a Fillet binds her Hair' (178).

We have already seen in Chapter 3 that the exploits at Vigo Bay had been recorded in the national coinage: equally, John Croker and others designed medals to commemorate the battle, some featuring Neptune and Victory, some quoting lines from a panegyric by Claudian, and some showing Hercules trampling on a dragon. A medal was struck in 1704 to mark the foundation of Queen Anne's Bounty (see p. 163 below): on this, the seated monarch presents a charter to her clergy, with the legend *pietas augustae.* Naturally, many medals appeared in the wake of the battle of Blenheim: some feature Marlborough alone, some depict both the Queen and her general, while others show Prince Eugène. At the same time medals were minted to celebrate the rival success which the Tories tried to set up in opposition to Marlborough's triumph, that is the capture of Gibraltar by their favourite Admiral Sir George Rooke. The same effort was made in a medal commemorating the relief of Barcelona by the Earl of Peterborough in 1706. It is doubtful how far these propaganda exercises enhanced the cause of the party, but they served to associate the Queen (who appears on the obverse) with the more fortunate military campaigns of her reign.[31]

---

[29] However, Lansdowne translated into English verse the Latin inscription on a medal presented to Louis XIV, and redirected it to Queen Anne (Chalmers, iii. 288): this is in a more bellicose vein. See also *SDW,* ch. 3.

[30] Information on medals in the two following paragraphs derives from Hawkins (1978: ii. 227–418).

[31] See the medal struck to commemorate Malplaquet.

Anne herself figures prominently in medals to mark the Union with Scotland: one bears the legend *Anna regina in quietudine turba* (Queen Anne and disturbance, or the crowd, in peace), and makes extensive use of the insignia of the Garter. Other designs link the thistle and the rose on one stalk, while some carry the motto *semper eadem*. The abortive negotiations to end the war in 1709 predictably elicited visions of Pax and Mercury, with attendant olive-branches. Campaign medals resumed their sway as the peace process came to a halt, but in 1710 the trial of Sacheverell prompted medals both for and against the priest. Even more controversial were designs which paired Anne with the Pretender, linked her with Charles I (complete with the collar and badge of the Garter), and even suggested that the Queen favoured a Stuart restoration. Numerous medals were struck at the time of the Utrecht settlement: several of these depicting Britannia are discussed in *SDW*, chapter 2. Others show Peace on the reverse, with an olive branch and sceptre, together with the legend *pax missa per orbem*. Yet another, Dutch in origin, shows Peace with a locked Temple of Janus, a globe, a cornucopia, a shipping fleet, and Mercury as protector of commerce, along with the legend *Europae pax redditur*. One set of medals at least was distributed to members of both Houses of Parliament, in the weeks following the signing of the treaty.[32]

Just how relevant these matters were to a reader in 1713 is illustrated by a *Guardian* paper which Addison wrote, when he took over the journal from Steele early in July. He devotes his essay in no. 96 to recommend that great events should be marked by the issue of coins for general circulation, and not just the award of medals to individuals. He explains that a friend of his had drawn up a scheme along these lines 'during the late Ministry', which had to be abandoned as it was 'too busie a time for Thoughts of that Nature' (a dainty euphemism). However, Addison has learnt that a paper has been presented to the Lord Treasurer, that the project is now to be put into practice, 'and that we shall have several Farthings and Half-pence charged on the Reverse with many of the glorious Particulars of her Majesty's Reign'. In the event, the death of the Queen seems to have forestalled such a plan. Addison goes on to suggest that a new coinage uniting the English and Scottish nations should be issued, with proper devices and inscriptions; and that 'there should be a Society established for the finding out of proper Subjects, Inscriptions and Devices'. This aspiration, too, for a rival to the Académie des inscriptions was to be left unrealized.[33]

We now know that the friend whom Addison mentions was none other than Swift. On 22 January 1713, he had told Stella that Oxford had 'at last fallen in with my Project . . . of coining Halfpence & Farthings, with devices like Medals, in honour of the Q, evry year changing the Device' (*JTS* ii. 606). At this very moment his friend Pope was putting the very last touches to *Windsor-Forest*, a work which creates devices like medals in honour of the Queen. Addison claimed in his paper that 'the

[32] We need to understand that contemporaries would have been able to visualize such emblems instantly when they came to Pope's work. To adapt a phrase of Leslie Hotson, our task is to find 'an apt meaning demonstrably recognizable by an [Augustan reader]' (Hotson 1977: 29).

[33] Stephens (1982: 344–5).

English have not been so careful as other polite Nations to preserve the Memory of their great Actions and Events on Medals'. Such an undertaking would be 'one of those Arts of Peace which may well deserve to be cultivated, and which may be of great use to Posterity'. Once again, Pope seems to have stolen Addison's clothes: it was *Windsor-Forest* which most lastingly struck the monarch in an apt medallic pose, intended to 'perpetuate the Glories of Her Majesty's Reign. Reward the Labours of Her greatest Subjects, keep alive in the People a Gratitude for publick Services, and excite the Emulation of Posterity'.[34]

Frequently the Queen was portrayed full face, in whatever medium she was depicted. This is true of the miniature which she presented to Colonel Daniel Parke, when the Virginian brought to Windsor news of the success at Blenheim—Marlborough had hastily scribbled a pencil note to his wife, for his aide-de-camp to carry on an epic ride across Europe. This contrasts with the habitual medallic portrayal of Louis XIV and the Pretender, who both chose often to be represented with an imperious Roman profile.[35] Sometimes this involved some straining in the composition, as when Louis was depicted in 1685 as the saviour of two million Calvinists restored to the Church: the king has turned his head at an abrupt angle to receive the laurels of the Church, and his pose resembles that on an ancient Egyptian frieze.[36] Coins, by long usage, displayed the Queen in profile, modestly draped around the shoulders. Moreover, male monarchs were commonly shown on horseback, a martial guise Anne avoided. Her elected persona was in some ways maternal, recalling the text Anne had chosen for the sermon by Archbishop Sharp at her coronation: 'Kings shall be thy nursing fathers, and their Queens thy nursing mothers' (Isaiah 49: 23)— Pope summoned up this same reference in the *Dunciad* (i. 312). Where Marlborough raised a figure of Victory on the top of his triumphal column at Blenheim, Anne had associated herself with nurturing female deities (see below, p. 156).

Equally, the Queen was seldom if ever represented in the same way that Louis posed for his statue in the Place des Victoires—as a conquering hero, with vanquished continents kneeling at her feet. Yet *Windsor-Forest* does, as we have just seen, show 'suppliant States . . . | Once more bend before a *British* Queen' (383–4). Again, Louis had witnessed the performance of an entertainment at Versailles in which the rivers of Europe all offered obeisance to the Seine. The same stock of symbolic capital is used in Pope's poem, when Father Thames predicts the future to be ushered in by the treaty:

> Hail Sacred *Peace*! hail long-expected Days,
> That *Thames*'s Glory to the Stars shall raise!
> Tho' *Tyber*'s Streams immortal Rome behold,
> Tho' foaming *Hermus* swells with Tydes of Gold,
> From Heav'n it self tho' sev'nfold *Nilus* flows,
> And Harvests on a hundred Realms bestows;

[34] Stephens (1982: 344–5). For Addison's *Dialogues upon Medals*, see *SDW*, ch. 2.
[35] See Monod, pls. 2, 3, and 4. At least once the Pretender was shown in Roman armour (Monod, 75).
[36] See Burke (1992: 58).

These now shall be no more the Muse's Themes,
Lost in my Fame, as in the Sea their Streams.

(355–62)

Pope goes on to describe the Volga, the Rhine, and the Ganges as equally eclipsed, now that their importance in war is redundant under 'a peaceful Reign' (363–6). The differences are clear. This 'Glory' is represented as remote from the *gloire* Louis had cultivated; Britain is great as an agency of pacific arts.

No more my Sons shall dye with *British* Blood
Red *Iber*'s Sands, or *Ister*'s foaming Flood . . .

(367–8)

The poem has constructed a form of panegyric to suggest that the Queen has morally outflanked the French ruler, as well as simply defeated his forces. It is one of many ways in which Pope recomposes the history of Anne's reign to write out of the record those events which on one account constituted its chief 'glories', that is the victories of the Allies. Marlborough, as usual, is relegated to the role of a butcher, of foreign troops and British soldiers alike. Equally, this passage implicitly works to rebuke the Dutch, who had struck their own medals to commemorate the victories at Blenheim, Ramillies, and Oudenarde, and had reproduced such items in a volume published at Utrecht in 1711.

Windsor-Forest is a direct intervention in the peace process, exhorting its readers to accept the deal on offer and to reject the further demands of the Allies and of Whig politicians at home. The poem reinforces a message sent out by one of the royal chaplains, Thomas Sherlock, in a sermon he delivered at St Margaret's, Westminster, on the anniversary of the Queen's accession in March 1713: 'so tender a regard has she for mankind, that notwithstanding the honours of the field she reckons it the glory of her reign that she stripped even the triumph of her arms by peace, and gave the harassed nations leave to respire'.[37] Sherlock, it may be added was a prebendary of St Paul's and a future bishop of London. Here his Anglican homily expresses the same view of Anne's gracious dispensation as does *Windsor-Forest*.

The most conspicuous effigy of the Queen in Pope's day was certainly the statue by Francis Bird, commissioned in the middle of her reign. It was completed in 1712 and placed outside the west door of St Paul's Cathedral.[38] There were four allegorical figures draped around the base, as well as a coat of arms and shield. The female figures represented Britannia with her trident, along with Hibernia, Gallia, and America with a headdress of feathers, a quiver of arrows, a severed head under one foot, and a bow in her hand. The statue was begun at the time that Anne and Sarah Churchill fell out, and partisans of the Marlboroughs fastened on to the statue a pasquinade, which was alleged by some to be the work of Samuel Garth, accusing

[37] Quoted by Carpenter (1936: 7).
[38] In 1719 Pope engaged in correspondence with Bird about the inscription for a monument to James Craggs (*Corr.* ii. 26–7). The statue of Anne now on the same site is a later replacement.

the Queen of a fatal addiction to brandy.[39] The favourable image of royalty remained, it is clear, a contested matter. In addition, James Gibbs had made plans to
erect a column no less than 250 feet tall, on which a statue of the Queen was to be
placed, in front of the church of St Mary le Strand, a scheme abandoned when the
new reign came in. This was the most recent of the 'glittering spires' of the capital:
work began in the very year of *Windsor-Forest*, 1713. The published designs for the
church show the statue positioned instead above the west porch; but this plan too
was abandoned, and an urn substituted.[40] Pope refers in *The Dunciad* to the building of St Mary's, ordered by 'Anne and Piety' (*TE* v. 99); he also mentions the removal of the maypole previously standing at this spot, a symbol of the old
pre-Commonwealth England. As an acquaintance of Gibbs (a fellow Catholic and a
client of Lord Oxford), the poet may well have known that the Queen's effigy had
been banished from this site.

   None the less, as mythological plausibilities then went, Anne could be seen as an
Astraea-like figure, bringing down peace from heaven to earth. Verrio had depicted
her in the guise of Justice on the ceiling of her own drawing room. David Green describes the picture as follows: 'Anne, balance in hand, is shown . . . enthroned
among the gods and goddesses as their equal, if not their superior [cf. *WF*, 162].
Mercury flies at her bidding. The three Graces adore her. She is attended by Time
and History, Fame and Peace. Aquarius, her birth-goddess, juggles with water, while
Envy, a three-faced fiend, is banished to a distant cell' (Green, 188; see *WF*, 419). Even
this is to omit some significant details: suspended from the Queen's neck is the
Garter badge of St George killing the dragon; she brandishes the sword of justice in
her right hand; and at her side a cornucopia spills out coronets and coins—a statement of her munificence in rewarding servants of the nation. Elevated to the clouds,
she seems to threaten a retreat to the sky, leaving Britain to the rancour and injustice
of ordinary human beings.[41]

   It has been pointed out that there is an explicit identification of Anne and Astraea
in another poem celebrating the peace.[42] *Rural Sports*, we know, was dedicated to
Pope by his friend John Gay, and published a few weeks earlier than *Windsor-Forest*.
Gay's work is closer to Pope's work in content and mood than has been generally
recognized: the Twickenham editors omit all reference to it (see also Chapter 2,
above). Pope does not invoke Astraea by name, but Brooks-Davies convincingly argues that Peace descending (ll. 429–30) performs an Astraean gesture. As the same
scholar suggests, Anne may be identified too with the lunar cult of Isis, and serve as
the 'Cynthian successor to Elizabeth'. This reading is bound to be more contentious,

---

[39] Strickland (1885: viii. 318–19). This seems to be a confusion with Garth's later poem 'On Her
Majesty's Statue', written after Anne's death and bitterly reviling her for throwing away the gains of
a reign lasting ten years when she dismissed Marlborough and betrayed the allies to France.

[40] Little (1955: 33–7). When the church was completed in 1717, the Hanoverian arms were set on the
pediment above the nave. Gibbs's main patron in 1713 was the Jacobite Earl of Mar.

[41] Kneller painted the Queen on numerous occasions, and he employed similar emblems. In her youth
he had depicted Princess Anne with a sprig of orange blossom, an anticipation of the closing scene of *WF*
which merges Anne and Pax.

[42] Brooks-Davies (1985: 35).

but the general drift of the poetic argument remains clear—the Queen embodies mystical and magical qualities of the monarch, as well as secular and political attributes, and to that extent she inherits the God-given destiny which Elizabeth's propagandists had devised for her.

Sometimes the image-makers presented a different view of Anne. In the early months of her reign, the Queen had commissioned Kneller to produce a more restrained portrait, in which she wore the mantle of the Garter knights, the star and the medallion of St George, suspended round her neck on a blue ribbon. Stripped of most the accoutrements of monarchy, she appears in this rendition as a patron of the Order which gave a particular chivalric character to Windsor as distinct from her other palaces (see Chapter 5, below). According to one source, the original of this picture 'is inserted into the panels of the gallery of St George at Windsor-castle'.[43] The portrait might serve to illustrate one of the key elements in the design of *Windsor-Forest*.

THE REGAL SHIELD

As with other aspects of the poem, heraldic and numismatic connections can be detected in the treatment of the Queen. We have seen that Anne's medal for her accession carried the legend 'Entirely English', harking back once more to the continuity she had sought to establish with her Tudor predecessor. The most apposite part of the design comes in the wreath of oak and mistletoe. The oak was generally a symbol of endurance, and according to John Bossewell's Elizabethan guide to armorial matters, 'The Oke in the old tyme was accompted chefest *inter fœlices arbore*'.[44] However, everyone knew in 1702 where the prime meaning of this signifier now lay—it recalled the deliverance of Charles II after the battle of Worcester thanks to the Boscobel oak. At one time the restored king had even planned to found an order of the Royal Oak. What had actually happened was that a medal had been cast which depicted the crown in an oak tree. In 1662 an Act of Parliament (12 Chas. II, c.14) added 29 May to 5 November and 30 January, marking the death of Charles I, as one of three 'certain solemn days', separately listed in the prayer book, with their own annual services to be commemorated in all churches. Church bells rang on this day in almost very parish, and while 30 January was celebrated as a solemn fast the corresponding holiday in May was a more festive occasion.[45] Indeed, Royal Oak Day formed over many years one of the most conspicuous items on the political calendar; it sounded a major rallying call to the Jacobites, and in the immediate aftermath of the Hanoverian accession oak-leaves became the chief badge of opposition to the new regime.[46] In their propagandistic songs, supporters of the Pretender associated

[43] Strickland (1885: viii. 144).   [44] Bossewell (1572: fo. 75ʳ).   [45] Cressy (1989: 64).

[46] e.g., on 29 May 1715 church bells rang all day in Norwich to commemorate the occasion, and most people in the street were seen to wear sprigs of oak (Hutton 1996: 290). Royal Oak Day was not generally commemorated with great fervour in Anne's reign, but moderately serious riots broke out in London and elsewhere in 1715 once her successor was on the throne (Monod, 181–2).

'the royal cause' with 'verdant boughs' (Monod, 65), which might be described as among the prime poetic materials of *Windsor-Forest*. The restoration of the monarchy was often expressed symbolically by the restorative powers of nature: as the Stuart dynasty approached its final demise, the 'green Retreats' of Windsor stand for the reviving power of the true monarch, threatened by polluting agents from Hanover.

One other connection helps to explain the importance of oaks in Pope's text: the tree was the clan badge of the Stewarts (see also Chapter 5, below). By contrast, the mistletoe, though iconographically expressive as Druidic lore, has no heraldic valency. The plant is never mentioned in *Windsor-Forest*, which confirms other indications that Pope had not yet developed an interest in Cambro-Britannic mythology (see Chapter 3, above). Nevertheless the poem's emphasis on healing does link its ideas with the Celtic cult of the oak, as the masculine principle nourished by the feminine force of water—forest and river, in this case.

A richer set of associations goes with the reference to '*Britannia*'s Standard' at l. 110. Strictly this cannot mean the royal banner, popularly known as the royal standard, since it was permitted to be flown only in the presence of the monarch. However, the phrase certainly suggests the royal arms as a national emblem; and here the Stuarts had introduced new elements. The arms had evolved over the centuries, but in Tudor times had consisted of quarterings of English lions and French lilies, surrounded by the Garter with its motto inscribed. In 1603 a major disagreement arose over the arms of the new United Kingdom, as to which charge was to occupy the first quarter of the shield, now that the Scottish emblem (a rampant lion inside a tressure fleury) had to be incorporated. In the end James and his heralds hit on a compromise, with differing forms of the arms to be used in the two parts of the nation. After the Union of the crowns in 1707, Anne adopted a new design. In the first and fourth quarters the English and Scottish emblems were placed side-by-side; in the second was the fleur-de-lis, and in the third the harp of Ireland.[47]

The amazing fact is that this British claim to France continued to be made armorially until 1801. By the start of the eighteenth century it was manifestly absurd, and when Pope apostrophizes the Queen in *The Rape of the Lock* (iii. 7), 'Here thou, great Anna! whom three realms obey', he certainly has England, Scotland, and Ireland in mind. But it did no harm playfully to invoke the old claim at a time when the nation was congratulating itself on a victory over Louis XIV's France. So Pope can permit himself a glancing mention of 'The Lillies blazing on the Regal Shield' (306) in the awareness that the fleur-de-lis was found in the royal arms of Anne, as it had been under all monarchs since Edward III adopted the title of king of France around 1340.[48] Also apropos is the condition Anne imposed on Marlborough when granting permission for Blenheim Place to be built at the nation's expense in 1705. The agree-

---

[47] This change would have been apparent to everyone, however remote from court spectacle, since it is reflected in the design of the coinage, right down to a sixpence (virtually no copper coinage was minted in Anne's reign). On the obverse of gold and silver coins, shields divided between English and Scottish arms replace undivided shields from 1707.

[48] At the same time, a tapestry of fleurs-de-lis first appeared in coinage on a florin of Edward III, minted in 1344 (Seaby 1990: 64).

ment was that on the anniversary of the battle each August, a replica of the royal standard of France which had been captured at Blenheim should be delivered to the Queen at Windsor (Coxe, 3. 423; Green, 136). The banner was made of silk, emblazoned with gilded fleurs-de-lis on a field of silver.

Anne had carried out other changes. She had banished the arms of Nassau, which William III had added as an inescutcheon to the shield, and had replaced her predecessor's Protestant boast, 'Je Maintiendray', with her own more ambiguous motto from Elizabeth. In the wake of the Union with Scotland, she revived the joint emblem of thistle and rose, springing from a single stalk. It was James I and VI who had first 'dimidiated' the Tudor rose with the Scottish thistle, when he ascended the English throne. Anne adopted the device for use on the obverse of the Great Seal (Rothery, 188). Everything that could be done heraldically to celebrate concord, and to assert historic continuity, was faithfully done. In this sense Pope's design merely picks up on the pageantry centring on Windsor as the home of British chivalry—a topic discussed more fully in Chapter 5, below at the same time, his *language* retails some of the heraldic messages of the Queen's reign.[49]

Of course, the royal arms carried huge symbolic significance. After the Restoration a statute was introduced requiring the arms to be displayed in all churches, which meant that the old boards had to be dragged out of dusty cupboards, where they had not been defaced or destroyed under the Commonwealth. Then, in due course, the accession of George I set the process in reverse: boards displaying Stuart arms were painted over with the new Hanoverian quartering. Even initial letters might be altered, for example C or J changed into G: 'but their Stuart origins may still be evident in the floreated form of the initials'.[50] Pope knew about flourishes and swash lettering, something his manuscripts often reveal—as in the exaggerated serifs he used on the title page of *Windsor-Forest*.

As far back as 1706, Matthew Prior had seen some of the poetic uses to which this material could be put. In his 'Ode, Humbly Inscrib'd to the Queen, on the Glorious Succession of Her Majesty's Arms', he had deliberately couched his verses 'in Imitation of Spenser's Stile'. The poem, celebrating Marlborough's success at Ramillies, was presented both to the Queen and to the Duke. At the outset, Prior compares Anne favourably to Elizabeth as well as to Augustus, a trope which flatters the Queen's imperial legacy without tying her closely to the Stuart dynasty. The poet adopts a style that can only loosely be described as Elizabethan, but he does seek to imbue the monarchy with a Spenserian mystery. The Whigs attacked Prior's adoption of the 'obsolete' vein of an earlier century, perhaps recognizing that this rhetorical appropriation of traditional language identified modern triumphs with ancient dynastic claims, rather than with the new men who served in Godolphin's ministry (Prior, ii. 896).

A few lines in the *Ode* may have been useful to Pope for details of his composition: as an example, Prior has 'Germania sav'd by *Britannia's* ample Shield, | And

---

[49] This issue is explored more fully in *SDW*, ch. 3.   [50] Friar (1997: 239–40).

bleeding GAUL afflicted by her Spear', which could have been in Pope's head at ll. 309–10. These lines were recalled in 1710 by the Whig *Medley*, running in opposition to Swift's *Examiner*, as an example of the compliments once paid to Marlborough, even by one of the *Examiner*'s friends in a 'most stupid Poem'.[51] More generally, Prior sensed the opportunity to create a heraldic statement on Anne's behalf, drawing on an unfulfilled plan to erect statues of the Queen and Marlborough (the latter on horseback) in Cheapside. The poem imagines the erection of such a column, on which the feats of the reign would be inscribed, and which would be decorated with the Queen's emblems, the rose and the thistle. Thus the poem sets out for Anne a plan to create a 'full Atchievement of thy great Designs', worded in precise armorial terms:

> Bright Swords, and crested Helms, and pointed Spears
> In artful Piles around the Work shall lye;
> And Shields indented deep in ancient Wars,
> Blazon'd with Signs of GALLIC Heraldry;
> And Standards with distinguish'd Honours bright
> Great Spoils, which GALLIA must to BRITAIN yield,
> From CRESSY's Battel sav'd, to grace RAMILLIA's Field.
> And as fine Art the Spaces may dispose,
>
> .   .   .   .
>
> The knowing Thought and curious Eye shall see
> Thy Emblem, Gracious QUEEN, the BRITISH Rose,
> Type of sweet Rule, and gentle Majesty:
> The NORTHERN Thistle, whom no Hostile Hand
> Unhurt too rudely may provoke, I ween;
> HIBERNIA's Harp, Device of Her Command,
> And Parent of her Mirth, shall there be seen:
> Thy vanquish'd Lillies, FRANCE, decay'd and torn,
> Shall with disorder'd Pomp the Lasting Work adorn.
>
> (Prior, i. 243–4)

Here Prior actually sets out the new form of the royal arms, which were not to be formally adopted for another year on the final passage of the Union legislation (see p. 148, above). He also alludes obliquely to the motto of the Order of the Thistle, *Nemo me impune lacessit*.

The *Ode* had set out the accomplishments of British heroes from the Black Prince onward ('Their TUDOR's hence, and STUART's Off-spring flow') as they defend the citadel of Troynovant against France. Britannia, 'sturdy as the Oak', repels all assaults, and will not be deterred by a succession of foreign invaders:

> Not the fierce SAXON, nor the cruel DANE,
> Nor deep Impression of the NORMAN Steel . . .
>
> (Prior, i. 240)

However, the poem cannot quite integrate the disparate threads of imagery, drawn

---

[51] Ellis (1985: 79).

from the Brut legend, Arthurian lore, and the myth of the Norman Yoke. Finally, it was Pope who managed to blend historic and armorial motifs to make a coherent statement of Stuart ideology. The place in which this 'achievement' came to be most effectively set up, we may perceive, was not a monument in the City of London— Pope knew that such a column might 'Like a tall bully, [lift] the head and [lye]'. It was rather in the text of *Windsor-Forest*.

Two years after the poem appeared, a royal standard was raised and a new monarch proclaimed. Not, that is, on the accession of George I in 1714, but rather with the ritual enacted at Braemar on 6 September 1715, when the Earl of Mar unfurled the Stuart banner and with it instigated the ill-fated rising.[52] '*Britannia's Standard*' had ceased to be the symbol of a newly united kingdom, now that the country had ceased to battle with a Continental enemy but was instead tearing itself into shreds—as internal divisions separated the people along lines of religious creed, national identity, political alliance, and dynastic loyalty.

VIVAT REGINA

When she came to the throne, exactly eleven years before the publication of *Windsor-Forest*, Anne was solemnly proclaimed Queen in the traditional manner:

The Kings and Heralds of arms, with such others, whose Service was requisite on that occasion, as the Knight Marshal, and his men, the Sergeant Trumpeters and Trumpets, the Sergeants at Arms, &c. being Assembled by Order, at St. James's, about Two in the Afternoon: The Proclamation it self was deliver'd (in the absence of Garter) by Sir Henry St. George Kt. Clarenceux King of Arms, together with the Order of Council for Proclaiming her Majesty, in the usual manner, which was first done before the outer Gate of the Palace of St. James's, after the Trumpets had thrice Sounded, the Privy-Council, and divers of the Nobility, and Persons of Quality, as well as Members of the House of Commons assisting thereat.[53]

In some ways this countered a rival ceremony, which had been held at Saint-Germain-en-Laye a few months earlier, when royal heralds announced James III with full pomp and parade as king of England, Scotland, and Ireland, and the court paid homage to the boy-monarch. It was one of the defining moments of politics in Pope's lifetime. The decision by Louis XIV to recognize the Pretender alienated most of the British population, and prescribed the course which the Queen would follow on dynastic issues for the remainder of her reign.

On 23 April 1702, six weeks after her accession, Anne's coronation took an equally conventional form. There was the usual elaborate procession of dignitaries, each carrying items of the regalia like iconographic attributes: 'the Earl of Huntingdon, the Scepter with the Cross; the Earls of Pembroke, Derby and Kent, the three Swords; then the Deputy Garter King of arms with his Coronet, between the Usher

---

[52] Some contemporary authorities refer to the standard as displaying simply the Pretender's monogram (J R III and VIII), while others describe a blue and gold silk banner bearing the arms of Scotland.

[53] Ewald, 21. The proclamation was repeated at the usual sites, Charing Cross, Temple Bar, and the Royal Exchange.

of the Black Rod and the Lord Mayor of London; the Lord Great Chamberlain sin-
gle . . . the Earl of Orford with the Sword of State, between the Duke of Bedford
Lord High Constable for that day, and the Earl of Carlisle Earl Marshal; the Duke of
Devonshire Lord Steward on that Occasion, with the Crown, between the Duke of
Richmond bearing the Scepter with the Dove, and the Duke of Somerset with the
Orb . . . the Bishop of Rochester Dean of Westminster with the Chalice'. The Queen
herself wore the collar of the Garter, as did all the knights of the Order present; her
train was born by the Duchess of Somerset and four other ladies, with the Earl of
Jersey in attendance.

After the recognition, when the assembled throng cried out 'Long live the Queen',
came the opening anthem, when the choir sang the words, 'Thou shalt present her
with the blessing of goodness, and shalt set a crown of pure gold on her head.' Following the declaration and oath of protestant allegiance, the Queen was given her
coronation ring, a ruby with a cross of St George engraved on it. At the designated
moment, after her anointment, Anne was dressed in velvet robes of royal purple,
which went over her dress of gold tissue. She received the orb and sceptre (the last
adorned with a dove to symbolize peace), and at length she was crowned. The ceremony proceeded with its customary gravity and slow pace. After the Queen was enthroned, the lords spiritual and temporal did homage to her, while the Treasurer of
the Household distributed—'threw about', says the *Gazette*—coronation medals.
The Archbishop gave his solemn benediction: 'May the Lord bless and keep you.'[54]
The ceremonials ended with a grand dinner held in Westminster Hall, at which the
Queen's Champion made his usual serio-comic entry, and the kings of arms and
heralds then proclaimed 'Her Majesties Stile in Latin, French and English' (Ewald,
28–9). *Windsor-Forest*, of course, renders its own version of this ceremony in its
hommage on behalf of an allegedly grateful nation. The poem too acclaims the
monarch; and, as we shall see in the next section, it ends with a benediction.

Two more weeks, and the heralds were in business again. On 4 May, Garter King
of Arms rode out from St James's to Charing Cross, Temple Bar, and the Royal Exchange, attended by 'the Pursuivants, Herauds at Arms, Horse Grenadiers, and first
Troop of Guards, with Kettle-Drums, trumpets &c.' This time the purpose was to
make a solemn announcement, which accused Louis XIV of seizing possession of
'great Part of the Spanish Dominions', of supporting the claims of the Pretender to
the British throne, and of other offences. Therefore, 'for maintaining the publick
Faith of Treaties, for vindicating the Honour of the Crown, and for preventing the
Mischiefs which all Europe is threatned with', the Queen declared war on France
(Ewald, 29). Thus the long and costly war which ended in 1713 resumed its course.
Back to the Low Countries went the Earl of Marlborough, who had already been
named as captain-general in one of the new Queen's first acts from the throne.

All this flag-waving acquired a bitter taste in the years to come. It was the aim of
Windsor-Forest to recover the lost emblematic ground, and to reinvest the pageantry

---

[54] See also p. 163, below for an extended blessing at this point in the service.

with meaning appropriate to the end of the Queen's reign. The doves and the sceptres had to be claimed for the monarch, and the warlike symbols downplayed. Trumpets were to be silenced on the battlefield, and blown in the mimic arts of chivalry. Especially, Pope wanted to draw on Windsor as a site of courtly honour, since the castle was more removed from day-to-day government and the political battles at Westminster. Anne had always loved the place, and she was in turn popular with the local populace—at least, according to newspapers such as the Tory *Post Boy* on 24 March 1702:

The Inhabitants of Windsor, the better to demonstrate their Loyalty and Affection, met the Queen, as she was going thither last Thursday in the Evening, at Slow [Slough] . . . in a Body with Flambeaux, and other Lights, from whence they attended her Majesty to the Town, with loud acclamations of, Long Live Queen ANNE.

The report tells us that fellows, masters, and scholars of Eton College also attended to proclaim their loyalty. The mayor of the borough presented the Queen with the town mace, and the constable handed her the keys of the castle: both were formally returned. The evening concluded with 'Ringing of Bells, Bonfires and Illuminations, the like never seen before in that Town' (Ewald, 25). Of course such occasions were stage-managed, and then manipulated in the press. But there was a surge of enthusiasm for the Queen on her accession, and one aim of *Windsor-Forest* is to restore this pristine state, by reconfiguring Anne first as a goddess of the woodland, whose care, like that of Diana, 'protects the Sylvan Reign' (163). Only when the monarch is established as sovereign of Windsor does the poem allow us to glimpse her as a national and imperial ruler.[55]

Every year the return of the Queen's birthday on 6 February prompted a fresh collection of celebratory tributes. An ode by the poet laureate was normally set to music and performed by the choir at the Chapel Royal in the presence of the monarch. The guns of the Tower boomed across London, a play was acted at court, and the usual bells and bonfires concluded the evening. In the later years of her reign Anne's sickness led to a scaling down of pomp.[56] However, the young Handel was commissioned to write music, unfortunately lost, for the occasion in 1711, when the glitter made a brief return; and in 1713 he composed a surviving Birthday Ode for solo singers and chorus, although there is no evidence that it was actually performed. It was the chorus which sang the refrain, 'The day that gave great Anna birth | Who fix'd a lasting peace on Earth.' Shortly afterwards, as we have seen, Handel produced a *Te Deum* for the thanksgiving service in St Paul's; and by the end of the year he had been awarded an annual pension of £200 by the grateful Queen. This was almost the last effort to keep alive a mode of court ritual which would soon wither under the Hanoverians.

---

[55] Even in the last year of her reign, the anniversary of Anne's coronation was an occasion for bonfires and illuminations, which of course also marked St George's day. Effigies of Richard Steele and a keeper of the Whig coffee house were ceremonially burnt, 'both of them having made themselves famous for affronting the best of Queens in the most odious manner possible' (newsletter of 24 Apr. 1714, quoted by Green, 308).

[56] See Bucholz, 231–4 for a full listing of concerts, balls, and plays during the reign.

'Honour your mother,' James II is supposed to have told his son as he lay on his deathbed, 'that your days may be long, and be always a kind brother to your dear sister, that you may reap the blessings of concord and unity' (Green, 87). The Pretender found it harder to maintain cordial relations with his half-sister Anne than their father might have wished. None the less, it is striking how closely these pious velleities correspond with the clamant expectations of *Windsor-Forest*. The Thames foresees 'the Blessings of a peaceful Reign', something that had eluded Anne and would never come to pass for her brother. A long future of international concord is anticipated—a prediction which, in the form Pope casts it, was already doomed. The Stuart family had lost all 'unity', and the reality of what was to come bore no relation to the old king's benign prognostications.

In the fantasy kingdom of the Pretender, some of the Stuart aspirations came to fulfilment on a virtual plane. Lansdowne and Bolingbroke attained their chimerical rank. The Earl of Mar received a dukedom in October 1715, with a patent sealed at the Pretender's retreat in Lorraine. Blue and green ribbons were scattered on titular dukes and earls. Coins showed father and son as Roman emperors festooned with honours, or portrayed them as republican patriots in the mould of Cato.[57] Medals of Prince Charles in this guise appeared, with the emblem of a withered tree shooting forth saplings. They were distributed by the Oak Society, which kept alive one branch of Stuart mythology: a leading light was John Caryll, a member of the Sussex recusant family which had included Pope's close friend, also John.[58] Absurdly, as it now seems, James Francis decided to treat his young son like the heirs of Henry V (Prince Arthur), and James I (Prince Henry). On Christmas Day 1722 he bestowed on Charles Edward, not quite 2 years old, the joint awards of the Garter and the Thistle, a gesture which in a commoner would have seemed like the act of a Bedlamite.[59]

Even more poignant is the continuing effort of the Pretenders to maintain the practice of touching for the king's evil (see the next section of this chapter). James II had continued to issue royal touch pieces and lay on hands—such were his powers believed to be that healing miracles took place at his grave in 1703.[60] His son James Francis followed the practice, even though he had never been crowned and anointed, despite the legend of a coronation at Perth during the 1715–16 rising. According to one account, which may be unreliable, James actually performed the ceremony while at Scone, during his brief stay in Scotland. Charles Edward went on touching for scrofula until late in life, long after all his hopes of succession had fluttered away; and his brother Henry carried on the custom even beyond that. As has

---

[57] See Monod, 80–91. One reason for this obsession with Rome may be the fact that 'so many important figures in early classical antiquarianism' were Jacobites (Monod, 81), although there were other factors related to the historic and geographic context of Jacobitism. One of the medals struck in connection with the abortive rising of 1708 had made pointed used of a passage in the *Aeneid*, VI, celebrating Augustus: *hic vir, hic est* . . . See Brooks-Davies (1985: 129).

[58] For several generations this was one of the most devotedly loyal families in the nation, as far as the Stuart cause went: see Monod, *passim*, as well as Ch. 1, above, and *SDW*, ch. 5.

[59] McLynn (1991: 14). James Francis had himself received the Garter from his father at the age of 4.

[60] Thomas (1973: 232).

been suggested, it is likely that 'belief in the touch quietly persisted among Jacobites in England' (Monod, 130). However, once the Hanoverians became more entrenched, this faith seems to have weakened steadily. Yet another of the sacred trappings of monarchy had been stripped off, and a poem like *Windsor-Forest* became less possible to conceive or to execute.

THE RITUAL OF BLESSING

Ritual is now a leading motif in the study of Shakespeare, as we have come to recognize the central place which traditional rites occupied in the early modern world. It is seldom that we can detect either mythical archetypes such as the scapegoat or folk customs in high Augustan poetry. However, Pope's dramatization of the peace process incorporates a number of elements of state ritual.

This can be seen in general and particular ways. The climactic act of the poem is the gesture of benediction:

> Where Peace descending bids her Olives spring,
> And scatters Blessings from her Dove-like Wing.

(429–30)

At the first level, this works as a conventional rendition of Irene or Pax. As Howard Weinbrot notes, a mode of discourse had evolved which drew on the standard attributes of the goddess: 'Irenics . . . denote orderly, benevolent pacification and, by the early to mid seventeenth century, peace within a Christian community.'[61] Yet, alongside the classical allegory, the text conveys a strong sense of the blessing delivered at the end of a religious service. To a Catholic, there might also be suggestions of the benediction as that portion of the Sanctus in the mass in which the people are blessed. Both Catholics and Anglicans would know the Benedictus as part of the daily service, and Pope himself would be familiar with the *Benedictiones diversae* found in the missal. *Windsor-Forest* had identified the Stuart dynasty with the 'Blessings' of the gods earlier on (see ll. 36 and 42), and explicitly made the connection in a single verse: 'Be mine the Blessings of a peaceful Reign' (366). That being so, the gestures of Irene can also be read as those of the historic Anne, who bestows her own benediction of peace on the nation. By contrast, the Marlborough faction were accused of having deferred the 'blessing' of peace, because of their selfish interest in prolonging the war.[62]

There is also a near-blasphemous recollection of the baptism of Christ, when the gospel tells of 'the Spirit of God descending like a dove' (Matthew 3: 16). In the Bible, the dove symbolizes not peace but innocence and promise: it regularly stands for the Holy Spirit. The rite of baptism dramatizes the process by which human beings

---

[61] Weinbrot (1997: 154).

[62] Churchill, iv. 414. Pamphleteers attacked the Whigs for trying to 'obstruct and delay the Blessing of Peace' because they relished 'War, Blood, and Confusion, as their Oliverian Progenitors formerly did' (quoted by Richards 1972: 138). This is strikingly close to the poetic reasoning of *WF*, 321–8.

enter into the kingdom of God, and are made 'regenerate and born anew of water and of the Holy Ghost'—it is quite possible that Pope intended us to see the rebirth of Britain after the war, under Stuart rule, to constitute a sacramental act.[63] This process would ultimately be completed when James III came into his kingdom, an item of religious language routinely appropriated by his supporters.

Once, in a celebrated jibe, the Earl of Peterborough likened the Peace of Utrecht to the peace of God, because it passed all understanding. His friend Pope used almost the same intuition in a more serious way. The notion of peace at the end of *Windsor-Forest* includes, but extends far beyond, the cessation of hostilities. It embraces the idea of a national restoration through unity, after the 'dreadful Series of intestine Wars' (325) in the seventeenth century. It means an end of civil harassment, which the logic of the poem has connected with the reign of William III. Under the Stuart dispensation, each 'unmolested Swain' will tend his flocks or reap his grain 'safe' on the shores of the Thames (369–70). It does not take much ingenuity to decode this as a hope that quiet country dwellers (like Pope and his Catholic neighbours in Berkshire) will be allowed to live free from persecution. Moreover, the Forest has been depicted as a haven of philosophic retirement for the Trumbull-like hermit. By these means, the concept attains a metaphysical dimension, along with its purely secular sense. Thus the Queen can bestow the ultimate blessing as a vicegerent of God, as well as a modern reincarnation of Pax.

Two particular rituals support such an interpretation. The first is the widely practised habit whereby children knelt down to receive the blessing of their parents. This act, the Tudors believed, 'doth firm and make stable the possessions and the kindred of the children'. (Likewise the opposite of this sacred gesture, a parental curse, would eradicate these things.)[64] We already know that Anne had been cast from the start of her reign as the mother of her people, a fact symbolized in the text used for the sermon at her coronation (see p. 144, above). She would be hymned in the same way at the Peace thanksgivings in 1713, as we shall see in a moment. In this way, the royal benison figures also as the act of grace which a parent performed by the 'imposition of hands'. Again, the almost sacerdotal nature of the blessing suggests laying on hands in other liturgical contexts, as in the sacrament of anointing the sick (extreme unction) or that of ordination.[65]

Secondly, there was the more specialized monarchical act of touching for the king's evil. At the start of the Stuart dynasty, James I had been reluctant to keep up this as a relic of superstition, 'the age of miracles being past'. However, the royal advisers overcame these scruples:

Touching for the king's evil gave the monarch an opportunity to display the sacredness of the

---

[63] Hovering behind the text at the end is certainly the list of beatitudes as enumerated by Christ, especially 'Beati pacifici' (Matthew 5: 9).

[64] Quoted by Thomas (1973: 604). For the way in which the parent occupied a priest-like role in this transaction, and the relevance of the entire rite to Shakespeare, see Young (1992: 169–200).

[65] It is indicative of the temper of the times that people crowded round the High Church martyr Sacheverell to kiss his hand: they touched his garments and were blessed (letter of Ann Clavering in 1710, quoted by Holmes and Speck (1967: 87)).

king and to take advantage of a centuries-old belief in the supernatural nature of kingship
. . . Popular belief provided the material for a ceremony the Crown could shape to its own
ends, giving rise . . . to an elaborate spectacle performed before an audience. Such a ceremony was highly useful for propaganda, especially when the legitimacy of a king was in question . . . For Charles I and the civil war period, the royal touch testified to the righteousness
of the principle of monarchy itself and to the sacrilege of killing the king.[66]

The ceremony flourished under Charles II and James II.[67] According to Macaulay,
the former touched almost 100,000 people, including more than eight thousand in
the year 1682.[68] James II also sought unsuccessfully to reintroduce the Catholic service attached to the rite. Touching fell into decline under William III, who regarded
it as 'a silly superstition'.[69] As is well known, Anne revived the practice and was the
last monarch to touch for the evil—except, as we have just seen, for the Stuart pretenders. Some Protestants regarded the whole business as a papist imposition. However, the ritual kept its place in the Book of Common Prayer up to 1728 in the English
version, and up to 1744 in the Latin.[70]

How seriously the Queen regarded this occasion is shown by the fact that in her
last year she was still following her usual practice of fasting for a day preceding and
abstaining (presumably from meat) several days afterwards. At the start of her reign
she had touched only forty sufferers at one time, but the numbers grew as time went
on. In 1706–7 about 1,800 gold 'pieces' were sent to her for distribution. There was
pressure to gain admission and tickets had to be issued in advance (Gregg, 148). As
late as 1711 Anne touched regularly throughout Lent, the most solemn season of the
year, and the one in which *Windsor-Forest* came before the world. She last performed the ceremony, it would appear, in April 1714.

For the ceremony, the Queen was seated on a chair of state, usually in the
Banqueting House, which was the location favoured by her uncle Charles II. A royal
chaplain knelt near her during the service, with white ribbons on his arm which
were strung with the touchpieces of 'angel gold'. By this date the reverse of the
touchpiece carried a scene of St Michael and the Dragon, from Revelation 12: 7, a
motif closely allied to that of St George. After this, the healing office began, with the
gospel taken from Mark 16: 18: 'They shall lay their hands on the sick, and they shall
recover.' This is the last act Christ performs after his return to earth, and Stuart supporters may well have been dreaming of a comparable deed of resurrection when
Anne presided at the ceremony. During the laying on of hands, the chaplain prayed
for divine blessing on the work, and after further prayers, the service came to an end.
It may be added that the order of service in Anne's Book of Common Prayer

---

[66] Willis (1992: 149): see also Thomas (1973: 227–35); Monod, 127–32.

[67] James was assisted in the ceremony by his almoner, who was also his confessor, Father Edward
Petre. This famous or notorious Jesuit was a relative of the Ingatestone family who became embroiled in
The Rape of the Lock (see *SDW*, ch. 5).

[68] For the description of one such ceremony by Evelyn, see *ED*, iii. 250.

[69] Strickland (1885: viii. 199), remarks tartly, 'William the Conqueror and William the Hollander had
equally repudiated the claim of healing the sick: they were too much occupied with killing those who
were well.'

[70] Thomas (1973: 228).

contains the lines requesting the Lord to preserve us from 'Pope and Turk', a phrase in which Pope found comic potential elsewhere.[71] All contemporaries were familiar with this sovereign remedy as an expression of royal mercy and benediction. A good indication is that the custom figures as one of the designs on a set of playing cards, dating from about 1706: the ceremony is shown on the nine of hearts. Other cards depict the proclamation of the Queen's accession, her coronation, and scenes of a royal entertainment at Windsor, along with 'the Queens Arms wth ye New Motto', that is *semper eadem*. Not for nothing has Anne been identified with the Queen of Hearts in the game of ombre played in *The Rape of the Lock*.[72]

Much has been written about this thaumaturgic practice. We are reminded by Thomas that a gold amulet on a white ribbon was hung around the neck of the scrofula patient: indeed, Samuel Johnson wore his the rest of his life, after being touched by Queen Anne. The talisman was actually a medal; we might suspect that there is an alchemic undertone to this use of gold as a transforming and rectifying agent. Conveniently enough, there is a legend according to which the touchpiece originated from gold coins made for Edward I in the Tower, which were then to be bound by the royal hands around the arm of those suffering from the evil. The gold itself was 'made' by Ramón Lully (*c*.1232–1315), a Spanish alchemist. If there had ever been any sort of truth in this story, it would have been forgotten by the time of Anne: but the association between healing power and legitimacy had certainly not been discredited. For example, a doughty Whig historian claimed that the Queen had been persuaded to resume the practice 'by way of asserting her hereditary right to the Crown'.[73] For our immediate purposes, the wider point is that the royal touch was at bottom a special form of blessing, bestowed by the monarch as God's representative. It formed part of the divinity that hedged a king, or here a Queen, in her role as guardian of her people.

To bless is defined by Webster as to hallow or consecrate by religious rite or word; secondly, to hallow with the sign of the cross; thirdly, to invoke divine care for; fourthly, to praise or glorify; and fifthly, to confer happiness or prosperity upon. An archaic sense recorded is to protect or preserve. Most of these senses would be appropriate to the climax of *Windsor-Forest*, where peace ushers in a literally blessed state for the nation. The effective agent, beneath the pagan allegory, can only be the author of the peace, that is the Queen herself.

---

[71] Strickland (1885: viii. 199–207), gives the fullest account of Anne's practice of the royal touch, but fact has to be winnowed carefully from legend.

[72] See Erskine-Hill (1984: 190; 1996: 81). When Pope was expanding the *Rape* he might have heard how popular ombre was at court: Swift mentions playing the games several times in early 1713 (e.g. 4 Mar. 1713, the week in which *WF* appeared, *JTS* ii. 632). Earlier, on 19 Sept. 1711, he had told Stella, 'The queen designs to have cards and dancing here [Windsor] next week' (*JTS* i. 363). Swift also mentions the imposition of a tax of sixpence on each deck of cards (*JTS* ii. 375): the Act which levied this tax stated that it was raised 'for carrying on the War'.

[73] John Oldmixon, *History of England* (1735), quoted by Green, 105. The persuader could have been Archbishop Sharp; but Anne may have wanted to outdo her half-brother, as well as to rebuke her predecessor for not continuing to touch.

The poem actually endows Anne with personal responsibility for the ending of hostilities. We usually read one famous couplet as a parody of the divine fiat in the first book of Genesis:

> At length great *ANNA* said—Let Discord cease!
> She said, the world obey'd, and all was *Peace*!
>
> (327–8)

Just as clearly, however, this is mimicking a royal proclamation—for example, the national fast days ordered in 1711 and 1712. On both these occasions a sermon was delivered at the Chapel Royal of St James's by George Smalridge, a chaplain to the Queen who was appointed dean of Christ Church in 1713.[74] The second sermon in particular expressed a hope that the forthcoming Peace would be 'a blessing of Divine Providence' which has been 'now for many years withheld from us'. Other addresses from pulpits up and down the land on the solemn fast day made much of God's providential intervention in the affairs of nations.[75]

In Chapter 3 we encountered an official announcement, gazetted on 19 May 1713, which ordered a public thanksgiving, and enjoined the people to express their gratitude to God for the 'Great and Publick Blessings' conferred on Britain as a result of the settlement.[76] When the ceremony took place on 7 July, a deliberate effort was made to forge a connection between the peace process and the Queen's habitual beneficence. Four thousand charity children, fitted out in new clothes, were placed in a grandstand stretching more than 600 feet in length, as the procession made its unhurried way along the Strand to the cathedral. Two hundred coaches carried Members of Parliament, bishops, and peers in full robes to the cathedral. The Lord President (Buckinghamshire), the Lord Treasurer (Oxford), and the Lord Chancellor (Harcourt) came at the end of the procession—all were friends of Pope and implicit heroes of *Windsor-Forest*. The children duly sang hymns blessing the Queen as 'A Nursing Mother to thy Fold', and celebrating the end of the war: 'Peace, His best gift, to Earth's return'd, | Long may it here remain; |As we too long its Absence mourn'd' (compare *WF*, 355).[77] Goodwill, friendship, joy, and holy love will combine to make 'all Mankind completely bless'd'. The note of a sacred task fulfilled is one shared by the closing passages of *Windsor-Forest*.

In two separate *Guardian* papers, Joseph Addison referred to the ceremonies.

[74] Smalridge had been the candidate of Archbishop Sharp and Harley when the Regius Professorship of Divinity at Oxford fell vacant in 1707, but Marlborough and Godolphin prevailed on the Queen to appoint John Potter. Sharp had also wanted Smalridge to become dean of Christ Church in 1711: this time Atterbury was preferred. In 1714 Smalridge became bishop of Bristol, and also succeeded Sharp as Lord Almoner; but in the following year he was dismissed after declining to sign a declaration against the Pretender.

[75] Marshall (1979: 83), quotes sermons by Smalridge and James Anderson, as well as the address by Bishop Hooper at the thanksgiving service on 7 July 1713.

[76] Such thanksgivings had been called for throughout the war; e.g., a proclamation was issued after the victory at Ramillies in 1706, also requiring the people to offer 'Publick and Solemn Acknowledgments' to the Almighty for the 'Blessings' which he had conferred (Ewald, 47). In Nov. 1707 a fast was proclaimed, 'for averting God's judgments, and imploring his blessing on our arms and our allies, and our forces by sea or land' (Luttrell 1857: vi. 235).

[77] Ashton (1883: 16–17); Stephens (1982: 695).

Two days after it took place, he produced a virtuoso exercise in deist rhetoric, contrasting the 'little Works of Human Invention', such as the splendid firework display mounted in the evening, with 'the great Theatre of Nature' laid out in the heavens by the divine artificer. On 11 July Addison returned to the subject, this time describing his emotions when he saw the boys and girls of the charity school, 'cloathed in the Charity of their Benefactors', as they lined the processional route between the Maypole and Exeter Exchange. In fact the maypole set up after the Restoration had fallen into disrepair and it was specially reconstructed for the Thanksgiving service. Pope's friend James Gibbs built his church of St Mary-le-Strand on the site a few years later, but the scene was to be recalled in *The Dunciad*: once a maypole had stood there,

> But now (so Anne and Piety ordain)
> A Church collects the saints of Drury-lane.
>
> (*TE* v. 99)

Anne's piety was expressed in her support for the charity school movement, which had been much bruited by her adherents. She had fostered the efforts of the Society for the Promotion of Christian Knowledge, founded by Thomas Bray in 1698: within a few years there were fifty charity schools in London alone, with more than two thousand pupils. Whereas the Williamite 'Oppressor' stretched his iron rod over the poor (74–5), the Queen's beneficent rule displayed 'that Charity and Compassion which she bears to all who stand in need of it'. It was a more affecting scene, Addison contended, than 'all the Pomps of a *Roman* Triumph'.[78] Part of his purpose may have been to distract attention from the political capital which the Tories were gaining from the end of hostilities. However, by praising the Queen for her almsgiving, he played in effect what had become a Stuart card. When he states that Anne will doubtless show her 'Royal Bounty'[79] to the children, even though they were unable to greet her in person during the ceremonies, he is echoing the language Pope had used four months earlier. The difference is that in *Windsor-Forest* the blessings are more political than philanthropic: the Queen nurtures her people not as a superior charity commissioner, but as a divinely appointed parent of her subjects.

Less than a year before this, in June 1712, Anne had announced to parliament the nature of the secret negotiations with France: her speech began, 'The Making Peace and War is the undoubted Prerogative of the Crown' (Ewald, 73). That Pope's couplet on the Queen parodies such a proclamation from the throne is a little clearer in its original draft:

> Till *ANNA* rose, and bade the Furies cease;
> *Let there be Peace*—She said; and all was *Peace*.
>
> (Schmitz, 40)

[78] Stephens (1982: 360–2, 365–7).

[79] Another recent expression of the Queen's 'bounty' was inconvenient for Pope: this was the gifts she had made to the unpopular Palatinate refugees, invited to settle by the Whig government in 1709 at a time of dearth for the English labouring population. Two thousand of the incomers turned out to be papists and were promptly sent back to Germany. See Trevelyan, iii. 60–1.

Equally, the regal gesture here suggests the bestowal of the royal assent, in the time-honoured phrase, 'La Reyne le veult.' With these words the decisive measures of Anne's reign had come to actuality: an obvious case in point is the Act for the Union of the two Kingdoms of England and Scotland. Anne went to parliament on 6 March 1707, gave the official imprimatur to the bill, and addressed both houses to express her satisfaction in lending her assent to a measure which would show that 'in My Reign so full a Provision is made for the Peace and Quiet of my People' (Ewald, 50–1). The alternative phrase to denote a veto by the sovereign was also couched in Norman French: 'La Reyne s'avisera.' It is surely interesting to find that Anne was the last monarch in history to employ this formula, when she refused to accept the Scottish Militia Bill passed by parliament, again in March 1707. She told Archbishop Sharp a few weeks earlier that she wanted his support in all matters that came before parliament 'relating to the prerogative', and insisted on maintaining her privileges in this area (Gregg, 143). Thus the lines in *Windsor-Forest* setting out the royal fiat draw attention to the Queen's rights and assert her position above parliament—or technically so, even if it was no longer in practice a position she should often maintain.

The last time Anne came to Westminster to deliver her speech at the opening of parliament was on 2 March 1714, just a year after Pope's poem had appeared. In this she again sought to bestow a beatific character to the treaty: 'I had the concurrence of the last parliament in making the Peace. Let it be the honour of this to assist me in obtaining such fruits from it, as may not only derive blessings in the present age, but even down to the latest posterity.'[80] It is touching to think that such a lasting *Pax Britannica* under Anne, the dream of both monarch and poet, was too idealized to survive in the real world. Within months the Queen was dead, soon after the parliament to which she appealed was largely disbanded, and the nation stood on the brink of civil war.

Much of the sacerdotal imagery used in these ceremonies is restated in the language of classical allegory at the end of *Windsor-Forest*. Like a herald, Father Thames proclaims the achievement of a long-sought goal of the administration: 'Hail Sacred Peace!' (355). This adjective is used advisedly: its roots lie in Latin *sacrare*, its cognates include 'sacrament', and its verbal cousins include modern French *sacre*, referring both to a coronation and to the consecration of bishops. Pope is essentially acting out the rituals of state, transmuted from a secular and political context to a prophetic and mystical mode of utterance.

That is natural, insofar as the blessing used in the Christian liturgy derives from the prayer of Zacharias in Luke 1: 68–80. This begins, 'Blessed be the Lord God of Israel,' and thanks the Lord for redeeming His people. God has raised up a horn of salvation, and spoken by the mouth of His prophets, so that the children of Israel should be saved from their enemies. This, of course, was to redeem the promise given to their forefathers. Then Zacharias turns to his son, John the Baptist, and declares that he will be called the prophet of the highest, to give knowledge of the

---

[80] Quoted by Michael (1970: i. 22).

salvation of the people, and to guide their feet 'in the way of peace'. This was one of the central texts in scripture enunciating the national destiny of the Jewish people. It did not need to be adapted very heavily to fit the liturgical context.[81]

Just now we looked at the grand thanksgiving at St Paul's in July 1713. When it was being organized a few weeks earlier, the Archbishop of York had found another apposite biblical text ready for use. This came from the Sermon on the Mount, and centred on the verse, 'Blessed are the peacemakers: for they shall be called the children of God' (Matthew 5:9). But the Queen grew anxious when she thought that the next verse might also be used: 'Blessed are they which are persecuted for righteousness' sake: for theirs is the kingdom of heaven.'[82] In the event discretion prevailed over valour, and George Hooper, the elderly bishop of Bath and Wells, preached an inoffensive sermon. As already described, this service enacted a great national ritual, with two canticles, the *Te Deum* and *Jubilate*, set in opulent fashion by Handel; and the mood of benediction would have been spoilt if a subversive notion were introduced—either side might consider themselves victims of persecution, both the Jacobites and the Marlborough faction. At the same juncture Pope had almost the same problem. His strategy was to translate his act of national celebration into the stylized and seemingly anodyne gestures of classical mythology—much as he had given Liberty a masque-like entrance earlier in the poem (91–2), partially occluding the political overtones of the word. Yet we cannot fail to be aware, by this climactic moment, that this is an allegorical statement of a historic event. As the Queen bestows her blessing of peace, it is as though she touches the nation to heal its sores and compose its divisions. The rite enacts a symbolic gesture of the royal parent.

One further ritual of state was still observed. The early Stuarts had continued to follow the almost immemorial custom by which alms were bestowed on poor people each Maundy Thursday, that is the feast of the Last Supper on the day before Good Friday. The last monarch who had personally distributed the alms and washed the feet of the recipients, 'in imitation of our Saviour's pattern of humility', had been Anne's father James II in 1685. During the reign of William and Mary, the role began to be deputed to the Lord High Almoner. Rather surprisingly, the Queen did not reinstate the practice of her ancestors, and it was not until 1932 under George V that the monarch again made the presentation in person. Nevertheless, Maundy silver continued to be struck and silver pennies distributed. The almsgiver was in fact a senior churchman who performed an act of royal bounty by proxy. Significantly, the occupant of this office under Anne was the Archbishop of York, John Sharp, often described as the Queen's favourite prelate.[83] Anne 'regarded Sharp as her "confes-

---

[81] Cf. also the canticle 'Benedicite, omnia opera', also used in the prayer book, calling on heaven and earth to bless the Lord. Among those enjoined in this way are the sun and moon, the stars, the showers and the dew, winter and summer, frost and cold, nights and days, light and darkness, mountains and hills, seas and floods, 'all ye Green Things upon the Earth', fowls of the air, beasts and cattle—a catalogue of created nature evocative of the subject matter of Pope's poetry, esp. in works such as *Messiah, An Essay on Man*—and *WF*.

[82] See also Green, 288.

[83] She had appointed Sharp early in her reign, displacing the incumbent, the Bishop of Worcester, against the wishes of many peers: see Green, 110 for the circumstances.

sor", and regularly consulted him in preparation before taking the sacrament' (Gregg, 146). Seldom, indeed, would the Queen shower her ecclesiastical blessings on expectant members of the clergy without taking advice from Sharp.

It was apt that this pillar of Anglicanism, who had preached the sermon at her coronation, should be the conduit of Anne's almsgiving: he was one of the leading figures in the establishment of Queen Anne's Bounty.[84] That fund to relieve poor clergy was paid from crown revenues, once given to the Pope, which had been annexed by Henry VIII. It amounted to a very large sum, exceeding £16,000 annually. Archbishop Sharp congratulated the Queen on outdoing all her predecessors since the Reformation: her memory, wrote the chronicler Abel Boyer, would be 'blessed in all succeeding generations' (Green, 125). The Queen's readiness to surrender the 'fruits' of an ecclesiastical benefice was admired even by political opponents of the High Church party: it confirmed her standing as a keeper of the faith and as a charitable monarch. 'This Princess, destin'd for the Safety of *Europe*, and a Blessing to her Subjects,' wrote Swift, 'began her Reign with a noble Benefaction to the Church.'[85] The Bounty was formally set up after a request to parliament by Anne on 6 February 1704—her birthday. Such acts of political symbolism carried an import which was not lost on Pope's readers.[86]

At the climax of the coronation service, mentioned a moment ago, the Archbishop of Canterbury had bestowed a blessing on the Queen, with an optimistic forecast that she would leave a numerous posterity to rule the nation after her 'by succession in all ages'—a vain hope by that time. The prayer ran as follows:

May all the blessings of heavens and earth plenteously descend upon you; the Lord give you of the dew of heaven and the fitness of the earth, a fruitful country and healthful seasons, a faithful senate and a quiet empire, wise counsellors and victorious armies, a loyal nobility and a dutiful gentry, and an honest, peaceable, and obedient commonalty.[87]

This is exactly the prescription for the nation which *Windsor-Forest* sets out, often in the most explicit terms. Consider phrases in the poem which echo the prayer: 'The shady Empire shall retain no Trace | Of War or Blood' (371–2), or the reference to the vigorous and youthful swains as the passage on seasonal lore begins (93–4). The 'fruitful country' appears in ll. 37–41, with the 'Blessings' of the gods. Most apposite of all, peace is seen 'descending' to shower her blessings at the end (430).

As it happens, the title of Lord High Almoner still exists and he continues to play a central role in the Maundy service, processing with other officers of the Royal Almonry and taking part in the liturgy. During the modern service, the celebrant refers to the alms as 'a symbol of self-giving'; which the monarch pays to God. A

---

[84] Sharp had always enjoyed far more influence at court than the Whiggish Archbishop of Canterbury, Tenison, who had been a close adviser of William III. It is a piquant thought, in the light of arguments advanced in this book, that Sharp's great hobby was coin-collecting. At his death in 1714, he left his collection to Ralph Thoresby, along with a manuscript entitled 'Observations on the Coinage of England'.

[85] Ellis (1985: 129).

[86] Swift always attributed the inception of the Bounty to Harley (see e.g. Ellis 1985: 200), but he was probably mistaken.

[87] Strickland (1885: viii. 154).

general thanksgiving, following the rite of the Book of Common Prayer, then follows; and the service concludes with a blessing. The monarchy adopted such forms to bolster their spiritual legitimacy, and throughout the year such rituals were maintained in humbler outposts of the Anglican Church. For example, the prayer book prescribed a form of service to mark the anniversary of the accession of the reigning sovereign. Originally inserted in the reign of Elizabeth, it was adapted in future reigns, including those of James II and Anne. The Queen had issued an order in council on 7 February 1704 directing that the prayers and thanksgivings on the date of her accession should follow a set pattern. Later, in 1709, a petition that the Queen might be the 'happy Mother of Children' who would faithfully succeed her was dropped after the death of her husband Prince George.[88] Apart from this, the service included a prayer for unity and concord, in the face of what the compilers of the liturgy called 'our unhappy divisions'.[89] These prayers were offered up and down the country on 8 April 1713, which happened to be a Sunday—the day after *Windsor-Forest* was published.

We shall have failed utterly to enter the contemporary mindset if we hear no overtones of religious ceremonial along these lines, when we reach Pope's concluding benediction. The more so, in view of the fact that a solemn thanksgiving service was already in the offing, to thank God for 'publick Blessings' conferred by the peace. Or, perhaps closer to the spirit of the poem, conferred by the Queen and her ministers. Then, in the following year, a more sombre service took place at Westminster Abbey, and this time it was to solemnize the interment of 'Her late most Excellent Majesty Queen ANNE, of blessed Memory'.[90]

[88] Ashton (1883: 2). Parliament petitioned the Queen to marry again after the death of Prince George, but Anne understandably rejected this insolent address.
[89] Other prayers may ultimately derive from the second collect, 'For peace', in the Anglican morning rite.
[90] *London Gazette*, 24–8 Aug. 1714, quoted by Ewald, 88.

5

Windsor

Search Windsor Castle, elves, within and out.
Strew good luck, oafs, on every sacred room,
That it may stand till the perpetual doom
In state as wholesome as in state 'tis fit,
Worthy the owner and the owner it.
The several chairs of order look you scour
With juice of balm and every precious flower.
Each fair instalment, coat, and several crest,
With loyal blazon, evermore be blest![1]

The original fortifications at Windsor date from the time of William the Conqueror, and he is appropriately the earliest English monarch mentioned in Pope's poem. As well as providing a defensive stronghold on the western side of London, the site had the advantage of lying close to a royal hunting forest which the Saxon monarchs had created. The castle itself underwent periodic refurbishment in the middle ages, but it was not until the reign of Edward III that massive construction took place to alter the character of the fortress. A century later, under Edward IV, the royal chapel of St George was erected in the Lower Ward. Both kings figure in the central section of *Windsor-Forest*, but it is the body of the martyred Charles I which will dominate Pope's sense of the castle. More generally, Windsor is the site of chivalric honour.

HONOURS AND DISHONOURS

Queen Anne died on the morning of 1 August 1714, less than eighteen months after the appearance of *Windsor-Forest*. By two o'clock that afternoon, the proclamation of her successor had been signed by all the leading officers of state, and the herald read it before a large crowd outside St James's Palace. On the very next day, the Duke of Marlborough arrived back in England: within a week he would be restored to command of the forces, in place of the Duke of Ormonde. Public mourning for the Queen was comparatively muted, and there was no lying in state. The funeral was

---

[1] The *Merry Wives of Windsor*, V. v.55–63. In the following lines Mistress Quickly, disguised as Queen of the Fairies, instructs the meadow fairies to pick out the emblem and motto of the Garter in flowers, 'Like sapphire, pearl and rich embroidery, | Buckled below fair knighthood's bended knee.'

delayed until 24 August, and then it took place 'privately', by night. Here the sense of the word 'privately' includes the fact that it was not a full-dress state funeral, even though it took place at Westminster Abbey, but of necessity there was a measure of pomp and ceremony. Six dukes bore the coffin: the Duchess of Ormonde acted as chief mourner,[2] assisted by the Dukes of Somerset and Richmond, wearing their collars of the Order of the Garter. Fourteen countesses followed, with ladies of bed-chamber and maids of honour making up the procession. The crown and cushion were carried by Norroy King of Arms: this was Peter Le Neve, who apparently stood in for the dying Garter.[3] Then came the committal service in Henry VII's chapel. This was conducted by the Dean of Westminster, also known as the Bishop of Rochester: the unruly Francis Atterbury, who would retain Pope's loyal friendship when he was sent to the Tower after the failure of a later Jacobite plot (Ewald, 88–9). Like Charles I in Pope's poem, the Queen 'of blessed Memory' went to her rest vir-tually without commemoration: 'There was to be no stone, no stylito statue . . . no royal monument, no fitting memorial, other than the churches she had sponsored' (Green, 329). In the Abbey itself, there was not one remnant of her being.[4]

At the end of the ceremony came a reading over the vault of the Queen's official style and titles. This should have been performed by Garter King of Arms, but the office was held by Sir Henry Saint-George, now in his ninetieth year.[5] The identity of his successor was in dispute. John Anstis, a Cornish MP put in by Lord Lans-downe, obtained a reversion of the patent in early 1714, only to be arrested for sup-porting the rising a year later. In the mean time the duties were carried out by another herald, no less than John Vanbrugh, who had been Clarenceux king of arms since 1704. It was therefore Vanbrugh who proclaimed the demise of the Queen and the succession of Prince George of Hanover.[6] So Anne's reign ended with a solemn enunciation of her royal credentials, followed by a declaration of those of her suc-cessor. These last were far from being universally accepted, even though no reliance is placed today on a story, widely told at the time, that Atterbury had wanted the

---

[2] Lady of the bedchamber and a close confidante of the Queen. Moreover, she was a friend of Swift; and a daughter of the Somerset family to whom Dryden had paid a fulsome verse tribute in 1700, indicating that her 'second coming' would prove a 'Millenary Year'. The poem predicts inaccurately that her son would, like her husband and her father, be admitted to the Order of the Garter. See also Ch. 6, below.

[3] Vanbrugh would shortly claim the acting office of Garter King of Arms, even though he was finally to be ousted by John Anstis, as we shall see in a moment.

[4] This was an omen of the fate of Stuart supporters in the years to come: Pope's close friend Atterbury was buried with little or no ceremony in 1732. His body was brought to the Abbey where he had long officiated, and then the coffin was stowed in a lumber room, prior to a pathetic funeral service in an empty church (see Life, 577–8). In fact Atterbury had wished to be buried without undue ceremony, but this was extreme. Pope may have intended his epitaph on Atterbury to appear on the bishop's tomb, but if so this never happened. See Erskine-Hill (1988: 216, 219).

[5] Thomas Hearne wrote contemptuously of Henry St George, reporting the view that he was a man 'of very little Learning, at least he had very little besides what qualifyd him to act as Herald'. But this was in part to set off the new Garter, who was Hearne's friend and political ally Anstis (Hearne, 164). Anstis was 'so well versed in heraldry that he is hardly excelled by any one in that profession'.

[6] In the same way Vanbrugh had acted for Sir Henry when went to invest the Prince of Hanover (later George I) with the Order of the Garter in 1706. Among the officiating party at Hanover were Lord Halifax and Joseph Addison.

Stuart claimant to be proclaimed king at Charing Cross as soon as Anne's death was known (*Anecdotes*, 1. 284).

Equally, *Windsor-Forest* had set out the Queen's title, in terms hardly less tendentious and magisterial, if less religious. Pope can be seen as writing a proleptic funeral tribute for Anne, since everyone knew in early 1713 that her days were numbered. Moreover, he embellishes her dynastic position by the very form of his poem, with its continual invocation of the devices and legends inscribed in earlier Stuart propaganda. Thus it can be said that the literary choices which Pope made, in terms of his artistic idiom, constitute a mode of proclamation of Stuart legitimacy.

There is an extraordinary sequel to the events just described. Vanbrugh and Anstis battled for several years over the succession to the post of Garter king. It was not until 1719 that the latter finally made good his claim, which derived centrally from the patent which Queen Anne had signed in March 1714.[7] Vanbrugh, we have seen, acted as 'Clarenceux named Garter' in the intervening period. Certainly, in view of his recent troubles, Anstis cannot have acted when the services of the herald were required in January 1716. The full panoply of state came into view as the seven lords implicated in the rising stood trial before their peers in Westminster Hall, with judges in their scarlet robes and Black Rod bearing his staff. An impressive cavalcade of dignitaries drove through the streets in their carriages, and finally trooped into court. At their head, attending the Lord High Steward, was Garter king in his official coat of arms. He knelt alongside Black Rod, and presented the white staff to Lord Cowper. The whole scene looks today more like a chivalric tournament than a court of law. In any event, justice was duly carried out and a unanimous vote of their fellow peers condemned all six of the accused who pleaded guilty to a sentence of death. As we have seen in Chapter 3, they included the Earl of Derwentwater, a patron of the *Iliad*, and someone close to a number of Pope's friends.

Shortly afterwards, on 12 July 1716, Vanbrugh went with the other heralds to Windsor, in order to perform an act of degradation on the Duke of Ormonde. In August 1715 the Duke had fled to France after being impeached. Later that month he had been stripped of all his dignities along with his estates by an Act of Attainder, but armorial honour was not yet fully satisfied. In the absence of a live culprit, the aim of the exercise at Windsor was to carry out a symbolic assault on his chivalric person, by means of ritualized disfigurement—a process exactly contrary to the installation of Lansdowne in his due 'Honours' which *Windsor-Forest* envisages:

The objects of the ceremony were [Ormonde's] achievements as a Knight of the Garter. After morning prayer Vanbrugh read the Sovereign's warrant at the Brazen desk. Windsor Herald

---

[7] Patent granted 2 Apr. 1714. According to one generally reliable source, Anstis obtained his patent through the interest of Oxford and Bolingbroke (Wagner 1967: 321): he certainly wrote to Oxford to ask him to get the Queen's consent. Matters were complicated by the fact that the Earl Marshal (Thomas Howard, eighth Duke of Norfolk) had been unable to act until 1704 as a minor, and after this was excluded as a Catholic. The Duke, who subscribed to the *Iliad* and was known to the Carylls, became implicated in the 1715 rising. More heavily involved was his brother, the ninth Duke, who later married the daughter of Pope's friend Edward Blount.

then ascended a ladder over the Duke's stall and first threw down the sword, then the banner rolled up, and last the helm and crest, which were severally kicked out of the choir by the officers of arms, beginning with Vanbrugh and ending with the junior pursuivant, and so out at the great west door. Finally Vanbrugh pulled down the Duke's stall plate, the soldiers standing to their arms . . . and the bells ringing.[8]

Comical as it may seem, and archaic as a ceremony of 'degradation' must appear to us, this serves as more than a tableau of political theatre. It expresses the fact that honour could be created and equally withheld, as the sovereign chose. In fact, the only time that heraldic 'abatement' ever took place was following an attainder for high treason, when the entire escutcheon might be 'reversed': the arms were torn down and erased from the records of the College of Arms. Unless the attainder itself came to be reversed—as would never happen with Ormonde—the arms along with the holder's title were void (Fox-Davies, 73).[9]

The grounds on which one convicted of treason might be duly deposed from the Order were set out by the Elizabethan writer William Harrison. Any knight found guilty of the crime would suffer 'disgrading', since he had conspired against the sovereign of the Order and broken the oath he swore on admission. It is significant that the ritual was designed not only to ensure that no disloyal member of the order should remain among 'faithful knights of renowned stomach and beautiful prowess' (a military and feudal formulation), but also to guard against any possibility that 'his arms should be mingled with those of noble chivalry'—a concept closer to the heart of *Windsor-Forest*. As described by Harrison, the ceremony envisages the presence of the knight, whose 'George and other investiture' are taken from him by his fellows 'after a solemn manner'.[10] Ormonde defeated this intention by his flight to France; but the new regime was not to be cheated of its revenge on a Jacobite leader. Obviously St George's Chapel was an apt setting for this enactment of state power veiled in pageantry, even though the motive for the occasion was more retributive than penal. Harrison describes one guilty of the 'abominable' crime of treason as having 'most traitorously conspired against our most high and mighty prince, sovereign of the order'.[11] The aim of the exercise was to brand a *political* act of opposition to the regime as a breach of faith, as a form of personal injury to the monarch, and as an offence against sanctity.

This is a characteristic battle of the day, fought out in the domain of chivalry. If we consider the identity of the rival claimants, we can see how this squabble among the heralds relates to the politics of *Windsor-Forest*. One pretender to the office of Garter king, Vanbrugh, had been backed by the Deputy Marshal, that is the Earl of Carlisle—a Kit Cat and ally of the Marlboroughs. The Earl had revived the archaic

---

[8] Wagner (1967: 330–40 at 339–40); Wagner and Rowse (1992: 43).

[9] The Duke's brother, Lord Arran, regained the estates in 1721 and technically was qualified to assume the Irish dukedom of Ormonde, but he did not ever do this. The original act extinguishing the honours of the Duke passed on 26 June 1716.

[10] Harrison (1994: 111–12).

[11] Historically, the ceremony could involve acts whereby the heralds hacked spurs from the offender's heels and broke his weapon over his head. This, as we have seen, was part of the fate Discord and her sisters were promised in *WF* (413–22).

role of Carlisle herald to qualify his protégé for the post of Clarenceux king of arms. It was he, too, who appointed Vanbrugh as comptroller of the board of works, in effect deputy to Christopher Wren. The next deputy marshal was Lord Bindon, who also gave Vanbrugh architectural work, this time at Audley End, and granted him a coat of arms, with the device of a lion issuing from a bridge (*van Brug*). The new herald had initially treated his sudden elevation in a rather offhand way, and some thought he relished most of all the chance to parade in his gold crown, silver gilt collar of SS, and velvet tabard bearing the royal arms, which made him look like 'a walking shield, in gold on crimson and blue, lined with crimson satin'.[12] He likewise incurred Swift's scorn as one who could 'by Atchievments, Arms, Device' erect a 'house' or family into instant grandeur.[13] In the case of Ormonde, by contrast, Vanbrugh was extinguishing honour at a stroke.

Ranged against the architect-herald was a more serious scholar and antiquarian, John Anstis. He was supported by the Earl Marshal—namely the Duke of Norfolk, a Catholic and suspected Jacobite.[14] As long as the Queen lived, it was possible for Anstis to obtain his reversionary patent, no doubt helped by his political patron in his home county of Cornwall, who was Lord Lansdowne. Rumour had it that Carlisle had accepted £1,000 from Sir Henry St George in return for bestowing the coveted dignity on the old man, but he then proved quite unable to advance the claims of Vanbrugh (though he did grant his client the consolation of designing Castle Howard). Four of the heralds and all the pursuivants complained about Vanbrugh's promotion over their heads: they spoke of him as a usurper, much as Stuart supporters referred to the Hanoverian line. As for Queen Anne, her personal distaste for the architect was shown when she removed him from his post at the Office of Works in April 1713, just four weeks after *Windsor-Forest* came out, as a result of a political indiscretion regarding the election at Woodstock. In fact, this was also a delayed blow at the Marlboroughs, for Vanbrugh's ill-timed intervention had referred to the 'bitter persecution' which the Duke had suffered. The reversionary patent for Anstis passed, because (as Vanbrugh himself put it), the Queen had 'now done with him'. With the forfeiture of his post as comptroller came the loss of 'all hopes of succeeding either Sir Chr: Wren, or Sir Harry St George'.[15]

Once the Hanoverians had arrived, things quickly changed. As soon as the new king set foot on English soil at Greenwich, he began to pour honours on his loyal supporters: 'The first knight that King George made is one Vanbrugh, a silly Fellow, who is the Architect at Woodstock,' reported Thomas Hearne.[16] One of Hearne's closest friends, John Anstis, was arrested on 30 September 1715 and briefly imprisoned, owing to his suspected involvement in the planned West Country rising—

[12] Downes (1987: 240).
[13] See Swift, 'Vanbrug's House' (1703), ll. 65–6: Swift (1958: i. 81).
[14] According to a later Garter, Anstis 'by gaining the Priest, had an entire influence over the young Duke' (quoted by Wagner and Rowse 1992: 23).
[15] Downes (1987: 357–63): Wagner and Rowse (1992: 45).
[16] Quoted by Downes (1987: 373).

another link with Ormonde and Lansdowne, who were due to lead this insurrection.[17] According to a later Garter, Anstis escaped punishment because he burnt all his incriminating documents just in time: for he 'made no scruple to own he was in the Intrest of the Pretender: And has told me & others, that the Pretender sent him a present of a Diamond Ring as a mark of his Esteem, which he seemed very proud of'.[18]

The government soon restored Vanbrugh to the Office of Works: as with the knighthood, he had Marlborough to thank for these marks of favour. When old Sir Henry St George finally expired in August 1715, the ministers also backed Vanbrugh in his claim to the Garter: amongst their number was Carlisle, who served as First Lord of the Treasury for a time. However, John Anstis was able to hang on with the support of the Duke of Norfolk, and even managed to retain his seat in the Commons when a new writ was issued for Launceston in 1716. He finally prevailed in his claim to the Garter, as we have seen, and went on to promote the revival of the Order of the Bath in 1725. More relevantly to our purposes, Anstis produced two sumptuous and scholarly volumes on the history of the Knights of the Garter (1724), with the declared aim of 'perpetuating the Splendour of the Order'. In that respect, at least, the chivalric ideals celebrated in *Windsor-Forest* lingered on in the new reign. A final consideration is that Anstis gave help and books from his own library to Pope's friend, the second Earl of Oxford, during the formation of the great Harleian collection.

As a result of all this, Vanbrugh would never achieve his fond desire of becoming Garter king, and he was left with the bitter reflection, 'This Anstis is a sad thief.'[19] Nevertheless he kept his grip on the equally lucrative office of Clarenceux, until he sold it for £2,500 in 1725. Thus it came about that Sir John Vanbrugh, resplendent in his 'coat of Her Majesty's arms', presided at the ritual degradation of Ormonde. For his part Anstis could scarcely have done as much in good conscience, since his patron the Earl Marshal was like Ormonde sheltering in France, while Norfolk's brother was charged with high treason for his part in the rising. The alignment of chivalric honour with the Stuart cause, which Pope had elaborately set up in *Windsor-Forest*, had now cracked apart.[20]

What of Pope's own interest in the episode? Pope did not personally dislike Vanbrugh, but as we shall see in Chapter 6 he held highly ambivalent feelings about the architect's work for the Marlboroughs. Even more to the point, Vanbrugh had risen with the Kit-Cat grandees, and in 1713 he was poised for a fall. His full restoration by 1716 shows just how completely events had dashed the hopes Pope had expressed in *Windsor-Forest*. As for the other protagonist, an unexplored link to the poet can be traced: it was Anstis who provided the grant of arms to John Shakespeare which appeared in Pope's edition of Shakespeare a few years later. Moreover, there are two references in the Horatian imitations to Anstis. One satirizes the rise of a nouveau

---

[17] See Ch. 2, above Among Anstis's manuscripts were collections relating to the Granville family.

[18] Account of Stephen Martin Leake, quoted by Wagner and Rowse (1992: 24).

[19] Vanbrugh to Newcastle, 1718, quoted in Wagner and Rowse (1992: 42) (misdated 1717).

[20] For the background to these events, see Wagner (1967: 319–46).

riche nonentity: 'A Man of Wealth is dubb'd a Man of worth, | Venus shall give him Form, and Anstis Birth' (*TE* v. 243), while the other describes how Virtue opens up the temples of eternity:

> There other *Trophies* deck the truly Brave
> Than such as *Anstis* casts into the Grave.

Pope's note reads, 'The chief Herald at arms. It is the custom, at the funeral of great peers, to cast into the grave the broken staves and ensigns of honour' (*TE* v. 326). Could the poet conceivably have been unaware of a previous occasion when a herald oversaw the ceremonial breakage of the armorial trophies of another great peer, the Duke of Ormonde?[21]

GEORGE AND GARTER

That Your Lordship receives new titles at this time is yet another national good; it is, in the midst of a war with France, to tell our enemies that the English family, their nation most dreaded formerly, is yet in its pristine glory, and it is to add honour to the Order of the Garter to have it given to such a subject of our own as may make our Sovereign's allies ambitious of it. (Matthew Prior to Duke of Shrewsbury, 5 July 1694: Legg, 23)

The fact that the funeral declaration for the monarch ought, by rights, to have been uttered by Garter King of Arms can tell us a good deal. Anne prized the Order, and rewarded her successive favourites with membership. Before she acceded to the throne, the Garter was bestowed on her consort Prince George: likewise, her ill-fated son the Duke of Gloucester had been admitted, on his seventh birthday, and was duly painted as he stood muffled in the bulky robes. Just five days after her accession, the Queen installed Marlborough, then her most trusted servant: not long afterwards, Godolphin received the honour. Then, towards the end of her reign, she created at a stroke no fewer than six new knights, all of them adherents of the Tory ministry led by Robert Harley—who was himself one of the six. The nominations were made in November 1712, when we know for a certainty that Pope was at work on revising his poem, although the installations were deferred until 1713, as we shall see presently. All these ceremonies naturally took place at Windsor, and Swift was one of the keenest observers. As we have seen, the Queen herself wore the insignia of the order at state occasions, beginning with her appearance before parliament three days into her reign; and when a service of thanksgiving for the Union with Scotland was held in May 1707, she adopted for her regalia the combined Order of the Garter and Order of the Thistle. Thus far, we may seem to be in the world of routine pageantry.

However, the Order had its home at St George's Chapel, Windsor, and its tutelary figure was the obscure East European martyr whom England had recruited after the

---

[21] For evidence that Pope was in close touch with the Duke's brother and sister-in-law just a year later, see *SDW*, ch. 5.

Crusades to remedy the lack of a national saint. It was probably Richard I who brought back the cult of the martyr, sometimes identified at this period as a Roman centurion, together with his banner, the symbol of martyrdom (Rothery, 294–5). Ronald Hutton has described the spread of George's cult following the institution of his name-day in 1222. Subsequently 'he was carefully promoted by the conqueror kings Edward III and Henry V, to rival the French St. Denis'. Celebrations were held all over the country on the saint's day, and a large body of folk customs came to be associated with his cult, notably 'ridings' through the streets. Parades and statutes in his honour were abolished alike by the Protestant reformers, only to be reinstituted under Mary. Her husband Philip, as Hutton tells us, personally led the Knights of the Garter in their traditional procession on St George's Day 1555. Under Elizabeth the cult was again discouraged, though more gently. Some of the folk rites managed to survive under the early Stuarts, until they were brusquely forbidden under the Commonwealth. A few vestiges came back with the Restoration, but essentially the cult died, compromised by its associations with Catholic hagiography. Lingering efforts have been made to revive St George's Day as a true national festival, not least the inventive placing of Shakespeare's birth on this date; but nothing has really worked.[22]

This complicated history deserves a little more analysis, especially as regards the fortunes of the saint in Tudor England. The cult of St George spread across the full span of society in the fifteenth century, and many guilds adopted his name. The largest public festivities were at Norwich, but other towns across the country witnessed processions featuring a knight bearing the red cross, with followers dressed in rich costumes of crimson and gold satin and velvet. By the early sixteenth century the date marked one of the largest national festivals in the calendar. Royal patronage sustained the cult, and shrines were set up to the saint in several places. At mid-century the Protestant reformers made George a particular target, as remarked, and statues and processions both disappeared. After a brief restoration under Mary, the feast was permitted to remain on the list of holy days under Elizabeth, but the ridings and the shrines were again banished. What is striking, however, is that the Queen retained many of the chivalric trappings of the cult while discouraging popular expressions of idolatry. For example, she preserved the annual ceremonies at Windsor, including a procession and service attended by the knights. These 'dazzling festivities' survived the attempts to impose a Protestant calendar to replace the popish cycle of saints' days. Officially, the feast of St George was abolished in 1567, but much of the pageantry was simply transferred to May Day games.[23]

A proof of these powers of survival comes in the fact that, according to most authorities, the Queen commissioned Shakespeare to produce *The Merry Wives of Windsor* in 1597, as part of the Garter festivities in that year. Aptly, there is a link with Pope's patron Lansdowne here. It was in 1702 that the poet's later adversary, John Dennis, made the earliest attempt to connect Elizabeth with the play: this came in

---

[22] See Hutton (1996: 214–17) for a full discussion.
[23] This paragraph is based chiefly on Hutton (1994: 26–7); Laroque (1991: 110–11); and Cressy (1989: 20–1).

his dedication to George Granville of *The Comical Gallants*, an adaptation of the *Merry Wives*. The story was repeated by Rowe and Pope himself in their subsequent editions of Shakespeare. In *Windsor-Forest*, Granville is introduced as the poem reaches the Castle, with the promise that he will 'crown the Forest' with immortal greens, make the neighbouring hills rise 'in lofty Numbers', and lift the 'Turrets' of Windsor to the skies (286–8). He will add lustre to the 'Silver Star' of the Order of the Garter. Thus Lansdowne will compliment Anne in her chivalric citadel as Shakespeare had celebrated Elizabeth—or so the story went. Elsewhere, it may be recalled, Shakespeare has the Duke of Bedford in *1 Henry VI* speak chillingly of the 'bonfires in France' he proposes to light, 'to keep our great Saint George's feast withal' (I. i. 154). Evidently the Queen saw some propagandistic and patriotic value in the veneration of a national hero, duly fenced within a tight chivalric code, even though her militant Protestantism forbade the worship of a saint among the populace at large. By reviving 'that ineluctably chivalric order', the Garter, it has been suggested that she 'demonstrated how ready she was to evoke the latent loyalties that clung to the chivalric tradition'.[24]

Some of the processions revived under James I and Charles I, when tournaments were held on 23 April, but all this was to meet a sudden reverse in the Civil War. In 1645 parliament in effect abolished the old calendar of saints' days: moreover, an explicit order was issued that year to clamp down on the Norwich festivities, including a ban on any 'standard with George thereon'.[25] After the Restoration of the monarchy, a number of the old folk-rites were allowed to return, but the pageantry of St George's Day never regained its earlier prominence, when the bonfires and the bells had symbolized a genuine feeling of national unity. Nor was John Aubrey successful in his attempt to hold the annual meeting of the Royal Society on the English saint's day, rather than that of St Andrew. Most likely Pope did not care particularly about the popular customs of the distant past, but he knew all about the symbolism of street-theatre, most obviously the provocative pope-burnings which survived into his lifetime and cast their shadow over the plot of the *Dunciad*. Moreover, he could hardly have failed to observe that the attack on folk pageants was generally led by those who were puritans in the narrow as well as the broader sense. What were rejected as 'pagan' remnants could often be seen as expression of popular piety; and it was in the interests of the High Church (let alone the Catholic community) to enlist these currents of feeling, however they might seem to be tainted by superstition.

It would be going too far to claim that the cult of St George operated as a major subversive force under Anne.[26] However, her promotion of the Order of the Garter represented an attempt to reclaim some of the symbolic potency of the national saint. It is significant that under the Hanoverians emphasis tended to shift to the rival Order of the Bath, which was revived with the admission of Robert Walpole in 1725. Pope gives us a clue in his disingenuous 'refutation' of the Jacobite readings of *The Rape of the Lock*, when he glosses the line, 'Of these the chief the Care of Nations

---

[24] Ferguson (1986: 76).   [25] Hutton (1994: 208).
[26] The elaborate three-day festival of St George had been abandoned in 1674.

own' (*ROL* ii. 89).[27] The commentary in the *Key to the Lock* (1715) reads, 'So St. *George* is imagined by the Papists to defend *England*; St. *Patrick, Ireland*; St. *James, Spain*, &c. Now what is the Consequence of all this? By granting that they have this Power, we must be brought back again to pray for them' (*Prose*, i. 199). The implausible-looking truth is that this is not far from what some real Jacobites may actually have hoped for in the cult of St George.

In case all this should seem remote from the day-to-day circumstances of life at court, let us recall here that Swift believed he might be created dean of Windsor in 1713, although he would have settled for the lesser dignity of a canon. As he light-heartedly reconstructed the scene in his imitation of Horace's epistle, Lord Oxford expostulated, 'A *Canon*! That's a Place too mean: | No, Doctor, you shall be a *Dean*'.[28] In fact, the clergyman actually appointed to the deanery a year later automatically became registrar of the Order of the Garter. This was the normal practice, and the outgoing dean, John Robinson, had naturally held the office. But by this time Robinson had other matters on his hands: he was in turn nominated bishop of Bristol and Lord Privy Seal, and then chief representative at the peace talks. In fact, he was the first of the British plenipotentiaries to sign the final agreement. The road from Windsor to Utrecht was a short one at times.[29]

The first meeting of the Order was held on St George's Day in 1348 or 1349. There may have been an informal Round Table created in the wake of a grand tournament held at Windsor five years earlier.[30] However, the prime function of the new society of knights was to celebrate the English victory at Crécy in 1346: Pope alludes to this at l. 305 as '*Cressi*'s glorious Field', a locution admitting of a sense that is heraldic as well as a topographic. There were twenty-five knights in addition to the king: there were also six officers, including Garter King of Arms, who was to become the Order's representative at the College of Arms and the senior figure within the armorial world.[31] Each knight had his own stall in the chapel, over which hung his banner and crest. Under the reformed regulations of Henry VIII, knights were required to wear their robes on St George's Eve and St George's Day, no matter where they found themselves.[32] On their blue mantles was embroidered the red cross on a white ground.

There were two badges. The 'greater George', 'enamelled in colours', was suspended from a collar, which was made of gold with twenty-six enamelled roses, each

---

[27] Carefully left out by Pope—because it ultimately may be read as strengthening the Jacobite interpretation—is the rest of the couplet, 'And guard with Arms Divine the British Throne.' The submerged image is that of the supporters to the royal coat of arms.

[28] Swift (1958: i. 173).

[29] It should also be remembered that the home of the order, St George's Chapel, was a 'royal peculiar', and so the Dean and Chapter were responsible not to the Archbishop of Canterbury or Bishop of Salisbury, in whose diocese the castle lay, but directly to the monarch.

[30] Friar (1997: 7).

[31] Garter King carries a silver-gilt sceptre, which bears the arms of St George impaling those of the sovereign, as well as the Garter and the motto.

[32] Holme (1688: iii. 53).

1. James Thornhill, 'The Exact Draught of the Fire Work'. © The British Museum

2. Antonio Verrio, Queen's drawing room at Hampton Court, ceiling.
Crown copyright: Historic Royal Palaces

3. Michael Rysbrack, monument to the first Duke of Marlborough, Blenheim Palace.
By kind permission of His Grace the Duke of Marlborough. Photograph: Jeremy Whitaker

4. Arms of the South Sea Company. © National Maritime Museum

surrounded by a garter, and alternated with gold knots. Holme described this badge as 'a Rich Jewel made after the form of St. *George* on Horseback slaying of the Dragon, all beset with Diamonds, and hung in a blew silk Ribbon, which is the Badge of his Knighthood of the Garter, or Order of St. *George*'.[33] In a moment of high symbolism, Charles II during his flight after the battle of Worcester had been forced to snatch off his George as he came to Boscobel and the sanctuary of the royal oak. The badge was buried by one of his followers, Colonel Blague. Soon afterwards Blague was arrested and imprisoned in the Tower of London: the George was re-trieved by Isaak Walton and brought to Blague, who managed to escape from cus-tody and take it to Charles in France. Curiously, there was a similar episode in the next great crisis of state, when the Duke of Monmouth as he fled the battle of Sedge-moor was forced to stop in a nearby village, in order to hide his Garter ribbon and badge. Elsewhere Pope recalls a moment of comparable pathos, when he imagines the Duke of Buckingham dying in poverty: 'The George and Garter dangling from that bed.'[34]

In addition there was the 'lesser George', a badge worn as a clasp on the hip to fas-ten the blue sash: an innovation made by Charles II. The distinctive feature of the re-galia came to be the 'Silver Star' which, the poem proclaims, Lansdowne himself had earned (290). It was Charles I who in 1629 had added a 'glory' of silver rays emanat-ing from the centre of the cross: this was the first star found as the device of a chival-ric order. It took the form of an eight-pointed star, with St George's cross in the middle. This emblem appeared on many coins from the time of Charles II, when milled coinage was introduced: most commonly it appears at the centre of a design with the four separate shields of England, Scotland, Ireland, France laid out in a cru-ciform plan. The quartered Stuart arms remained as a numismatic symbol for the next two hundred years.[35]

Thus Pope honours a specific Stuart embellishment of the regalia. Looking back to the same era, he would be aware that Rubens had painted Charles I in the guise of St George, rescuing his queen from a dragon representing faction (see *WF*, 421), a modern mythic reading of the Garter badge. The same emblem had appeared on coins dating from the early Stuart era, although it became a more common motif on coinage from the reign of George III, and indeed appears right up to the reign of the present monarch.

It could reasonably be asked whether Pope was likely to have any strong connec-tion with this emblem, which would cause him to enlist it and to use St George's Chapel in such a central position in his poem. The answer is yes. In the south chapel at Binfield parish church there was a fifteenth-century window on the east wall, con-sisting of three cinquefoil lights. The ancient glass showed a number of sacred fig-

---

[33] Holme (1688: iii. 39).   [34] 'Epistle to Bathurst' (303), in *TE* iii/2. 118.
[35] Friar (1997: 245–6). According to Thomas Hearne, it was the custom of knights to present family and friends with gold rings received at their installation. These usually bore the effigy of St George and came to be known as George rings. Hearne relates this as part of a long note on the saint and the order, ending with a discussion of gold coins called George's nobles, which also carried the image of St George transfixing the dragon on its reverse (his source here is probably Camden). See Hearne, 82–4. The coin was issued by Henry VIII in the 1520s (Seaby 1990: 85).

ures including St George and the dragon (*VCH Berkshire* iii. 122). Thus on his
doorstep Pope had a reminder of this powerful image. He uses the word *stain* to describe visual effects more than once, and we should remember that stained glass was
one of the main locations for armorial display: when St George's Chapel was sacked
by the parliamentary forces in 1643, the glass was one of the historic casualties. We
saw in Chapter 3 that Pope took an special interest in the 'scutcheons' on medieval
painted glass at Stanton Harcourt: all the evidence suggests that he would have had
this scene depicted at Binfield engraved on his mind.

As for the cross itself, this was heraldically described as 'argent, a cross gules'. The
red Greek cross became the most widely recognized motif of all: 'This is so generally
known in *England*,' wrote Randle Holme in 1688, 'that it is usually blazoned on St.
George's Cross, as the Cross of *England*.'[36] What had been specific to a saint and an
order became a national symbol. Pope refers to this in an appropriately patriotic
couplet: the oaks of Windsor, converted into ships, 'Bear *Britain*'s Thunder and her
Cross display, | To the bright Regions of the rising Day' (387–8). This could mean the
emblem as it was combined with the cross of St Andrew to form the Union flag.
Again this was a Stuart innovation; it had been brought in by James I in 1606, after
the union of the English and Scottish crowns. Equally familiar is the fact that the
cross of St Andrew (azure, a saltire argent) commemorates the supposed martyrdom of the Apostle. In the unified banner, the white cross was now surmounted by
a red cross, fimbriated with a thin border argent (Rothery, 295).

At first the new Union flag was ordered by proclamation to be flown by all ships;
but the royal navy objected to this universal usage. In 1634 Charles I reserved the
right to hoist the Union flag to ships of the royal navy; after the Interregnum his son
issued another proclamation, by which naval vessels were to fly the Union and all
merchant ships the flag of St George, with the latter also required to fly a Red Ensign.
The Union of parliaments demanded another change: a new Red Ensign was designed for the use of merchantmen, with the Jack again reserved for the royal fleet.
This was the situation until the assimilation of the cross of St Patrick called for a new
heraldic proclamation in 1801 (Fox-Davies, 612–13).[37]

Douglas Brooks-Davies seems to have been the first to point out, as recently as a
decade ago, that 'the red cross of St George must evoke James [the Pretender], if only
because he was most commonly known at this time as the Chevalier de St George'.[38]
This might seems almost too obvious and purely nominal a connection to be oper-
ative; but the suggestion has the direct simplicity characteristic of many overdue insights. It was precisely in this phase that the Pretender was most regularly in the
news under this very title. There was, after all, no obligation for Pope to mention St

---

[36] Holme (1688: i. 40). Compare Pope's reference in *A Key to the Lock* (1715). Slyly commenting on the
line, 'On her white Breast a sparkling Cross she bore', Pope writes: 'Alluding to the name of *Albion*, from
her *white Cliffs*, and to the *Cross*, which is the Ensign of *England*' (*Prose*, i. 185–6).

[37] This movement is the theme of *SDW*, ch. 6. It may be added that the same red cross with the addition of a bloody dagger in the first quarter formed the arms of the City of London—and of course it is
trade based on the City, circulating down the Thames to the wider world, which is celebrated in this concluding section of *Windsor-Forest*.

[38] Brooks-Davies (1988: 136).

George's Chapel explicitly, to allude to Garter ceremonial and insignia, or to refer to the cross. He avoided reference to scores of topics which defeated his purposes. It is hard to resist a simple conclusion: Pope was well aware that readers of any sophistication would make the link which Brooks-Davies proposes.

Of course, many of the symbols of the state formed a battleground for competing ideological claims. The parliamentary side had placed the red cross on their uniform during the Civil War, and the shield of St George had appeared on coins under the Commonwealth. Crosses of both St George and St Andrew featured on the great seal of the new republic—this was despite the fact that the royal arms were often defaced and destroyed in this period. Again, a Whig like Garth could use his loco-descriptive poem *Claremont* (1715), nominally at least modelled on *Windsor-Forest*, to predict a revival of the Garter under a Brunswick, who will restore new light to 'the sully'd star' (Chalmers, ii. 406). But from the time of the Restoration up to the arrival of the Hanoverians, there was little competition regarding the main colouring of Windsor, its rites and its orders: they belonged almost unquestionably to the Stuarts.

In special circumstances, individuals were who were accorded a grant of arms might be permitted to use the cross. This happened in the case of that loyal gentleman Sir Winston Churchill, father of the Duke of Marlborough. He was permitted an augmentation to his arms, with an inescutcheon of a cross gules in the form of a canton, by way of recognition of his services to the crown under both Charles I and Charles II. He placed his son, as well as his daughter, in the service of the Duke of York, later James II. It is unlikely that the Queen would have welcomed the fact that in 1713 this son, the Duke, was still entitled to bear the cross of England on his arms. As a knight of the Order, he could also display the Garter draped around the shield, with its famous motto inscribed.

Originally the cross had been borne by warriors as well as ships. According to John Speed, Edward III had 'appoynted his Souldiers to wear white Coats or Jackets, with a red Crosse before and behinde over their Armour'.[39] This applied originally to common soldiers as well as to knights, and Speed enthuses over the sight of 'the English Battles, like the rising Sunne, to glitter farre off in that oure hew'. This uniform had long been disused, but Pope alludes to a similar idea: no more will 'Groves of Lances glitter on the *Rhine*' as the 'beauteous Works of Peace' supplant combat, and '*Augusta*'s glitt'ring Spires increase' (364, 377–8).

Underlying all this symbolism lies the religious significance of the cross. John Bossewell refers to the shield of King Arthur (a cross argent, in a field vert), with its pious allusion to the Virgin in the first quarter. He adds, 'Because the Crosse is ye most triumphant signe and worthiest, the same shall first have place'.[40] As surely as for Spenser, the cross carried for Pope and his contemporaries this association with high virtues. The 'triumphant' character of the celebrations for the Peace should, ideally, have involved moral worth as well as patriotic flagwagging; but even Pope, with all the sophistication of his design, finds it hard to imbue the occasion with much religious significance.

---

[39] Scott-Giles (1965: 53).   [40] Bossewell (1572: fo. 22^r).

THE CASTLE AND THE CHAPEL

Edward III had created the Order and begun the remodelling of the Castle at almost the same moment, in the 1340s.[41] Starting with the Round Tower in 1344, the king had set about establishing a chivalric showplace for the nation. The chronicler Froissart asserted that Edward had chosen to 're-edify the Castle of Windsor, the which was begun by King Arthur, and there first began the Table Round, whereby sprang the fame of so many noble knights throughout all the world'. Ashmole, who has his moments of scepticism on other points, agreed that the king's first design was 'the restauration of King *Arthur's Round Table*' (Ashmole, 182). This was signalled in the feasts and tournaments held in January 1344, when plans were made to set up an Order of the Round Table. Before long the scheme was dropped, but not before an elaborate series of spectacles and shows designed to enhance the chivalric grandeur of Windsor (see *SDW*, ch. 1). Not for nothing was Edward surnamed 'Windsor'.

Subsequent historians have doubted whether the king had any serious interest in promulgating the Arthurian myth, vague as was the understanding of these matters, and they have suggested that the motive in establishing the new order was chiefly to underline England's claim to the French throne. This was based, rather lamely, on the fact that the king's mother Isabella was a daughter of Philip IV of France. It is certain that the symbolism of Garter regalia, centring on the cross and the image of St George, drew added significance from the adoption of the fleur-de-lis and the use of blue and gold as Garter colours—these were the tinctures of the French royal arms. (The garter itself was sky blue, matching the Stuart colours: George I changed this to the present darker shade in 1714, probably for that very reason, but the pseudo-chivalry of James Edward retained the paler blue for its meaningless order.) Almost four hundred years later, these dynastic signs still held some potency: it was the French wars of the fourteenth century which had given rise to the first great surge of royal heraldry, and now another great contest with the ancient enemy was coming to an end, with fresh opportunities for armorial display.

Edward III had signed a charter of foundation for a chapel within the castle in 1348, However, it was not until the 1470s that Edward IV undertook a full-scale restoration, expanding the scale of the building and introducing the elaborate ornamentation which we see today (*VCH Berkshire*, ii. 106–9). The king died in 1483 and left instructions for a fulsome monument, which for some reason was never completed. His tomb, like that of Charles I, bore no inscription; and a gorgeous coat of mail, studded with precious stones, which hung over it was plundered by Cromwell's soldiers.

Pope allots three full verse-paragraphs of plangent verse to the Chapel (299–328). Immediately prior to this, however, he instances a poet rather than a member of the royal family, that is the Earl of Surrey, translator of Virgil. Editors remark that Surrey had once been imprisoned in Windsor for five months in 1537, and that Pope

---

[41] Pope's most likely source for the history of Windsor is Ashmole, 127–78.

may have in mind the poem 'Prisoned in windsor' (*TE* i. 176). There are two other matters they do not observe. The first is that Surrey had spent the years 1530 to 1532 at Windsor, when he was chosen by Henry VIII as companion to his illegitimate son the Duke of Richmond (a Knight of the Garter from 1525), prior to a joint visit which the two young men made to the French court. A few years later Surrey commended his dead friend, who had married Mary Howard, Surrey's sister, in his poem 'So crewell prison'.

The second consideration is that Surrey's chivalric and military attainments are as important here as his literary accomplishments:

> *Surrey*, the *Granville* of a former Age;
> Matchless his Pen, victorious was his Lance;
> Bold in the Lists, and graceful in the Dance . . .
>
>   (292–4)

The poet had been a soldier but also a courtier; he was earl marshal at the trial of Anne Boleyn, served as steward of Cambridge University, and was awarded the Garter on St George's Day in 1541. He attended the ceremonial funeral of Jane Seymour at St George's Chapel in late 1537. Part of the trumped-up charge which permitted Henry VIII to have him executed was that Surrey had treasonably quartered the royal arms of Edward the Confessor. While Surrey's military prowess was not of outstanding renown, he did see service with his father, later third Duke of Norfolk, to put down the Pilgrimage of Grace and performed a number of exploits in the French war. The Earl acted as commander of Boulogne, which had been recently retaken, and he was named lieutenant-general of the king on sea and land. Apart from this, his own son was thought to have been a Catholic and at once time projected a marriage with Mary Queen of Scots.

Surrey, then, stands as the epitome of the Renaissance man of action and chivalry, the sort of courtier-poet now most closely identified with Philip Sidney. Pope values his local associations, but also expects us to recall his family line—that of the Howards, who acted as hereditary Earl Marshal of England for many generations. Furthermore, the verse 'Matchless his Pen, victorious was his Lance' paraphrases a Renaissance commonplace: *Tam Marti quam Mercurio*. In recalling an Elizabethan hero, skilled in both martial exploits and in poetry, Pope instinctively appeals to a habit of mind expressed in the old fondness for Latin tags and *sententiae*. Even the absurd comparison of '*Surrey*, the *Granville* of a former Age' (292) earns some thin support from the fact that Pope's dedicatee, as a young student in Paris, had won the prize 'at a Carousel or modern tournament by his skill in horseback and with foil',[42] but the stronger connection must be with Granville as secretary at war.

Finally, readers are invited to bring into their sense of the passage an unstated fact: Surrey was beheaded on Tower Hill in 1547, and thus joins a line of victims of tyranny. His fate most directly foreshadows that of Charles I, and helps to establish the chapel as a shrine to the martyrs who had been associated with Windsor Castle.

----

[42] Handasyde (1933: 10).

It is noteworthy that the lines on Surrey were a late addition (see Chapter 1, above): this suggests that Pope wanted to enhance the poetic texture at this point, and to fill out the literary and chivalric aspects of the chapel.

It is only at the start of the next paragraph that Pope turns to the monarchy, celebrating the royal founders and martyrs associated with the site. The murdered king, Henry VI, whose body was transferred to the chapel in 1484, stands as an antetype of the royal victim. Indeed, the list culminates in Charles I, recalling the fact that his remains had been taken to Windsor by night and deposited here with no funeral ceremony, no prayers, and no inscription (l. 320). A century later, workmen dug up the king's body together with his severed head, thrown into an unmarked coffin. As Pope surely knew, plans had been laid by Charles II for a mausoleum and monument to his father, designed by Christopher Wren, but these remained unexecuted (see p. 198, below).[43] There is a link here with the scheme for a restoration of Whitehall, mentioned at l. 380, which was also doomed never to be carried out. Pope shifts our mind between two key locations on the poem's symbolic itinerary. The shame of Charles I's execution at Whitehall is matched by the disgrace of his surreptitious burial at Windsor. In effect, the poem makes its own elegiac inscription at the chapel, reinstating the Stuart martyr in the dignities which had been denied him eighty years earlier.[44] Implicitly, too, the verses utter those prayers for the king which he had been refused in 1649: the burial of the dead, after all, was one of the sacraments which the Anglican Church had chosen to retain. So the final collect in the burial service hovers behind the text, with its supplication:

When we shall depart this life, we may rest in him, as our hope is this our brother doth; and that, at the general Resurrection in the last day, we may be found acceptable in thy sight, and receive that blessing, which they well-beloved Son shall then pronounce to all that love and fear thee, saying, Come, ye blessed children of my Father, receive the kingdom prepared for you from the beginning of the world.[45]

The closing formula would always be heard by royalists as pointing additionally to the kingdom on earth into which the Stuarts should come.

Even the elements seemed to conspire in the obsequies for Charles I. On the day that the king was buried, 9 February 1649, the Thames had frozen over, with an almost redundant symbolism, and a snowstorm caused a temporary whiteout in the district. Charles's coffin was covered in a black pall, which turned white in the short procession from St George's Hall to the chapel. The handful of onlookers huddled in the vault must have seen this as a dark day in the nation's memory, when an event which should have been a grand communal rite was rushed through in total obscu-

[43] Earlier, Inigo Jones had drawn up plans for what seems to have been a mausoleum for James I, but this too was unexecuted (Parry, 259).

[44] In a sense Pope is only doing what the Anglican prayer book enjoined, ever since parliament in 1662 enacted legislation requiring a service to commemorate the king's death (12 Chas II c.30): 30 January thus became one of the three 'certain solemn days' (see Ch. 4).

[45] The collect appears virtually in this form from the time of the 1549 prayer book to the 1662 version. It is a reasonably close translation of the Latin order of burial in medieval missals.

rity. For men and women in an age which put so much faith in omens from the natural world, this was a portent indeed.

A hidden sorrow lies beneath the surface of the text. Charles I had been forced to abandon Windsor Castle early in the war, when it came under parliamentary control in October 1642. Not until July 1647 did the king return, for two days, as a prisoner in his former stronghold. His last visit came on 23 December 1648, just five weeks before his death. He spent the last period of his captivity at the castle, prior to leaving for his trial on 19 January 1649 and execution on 30 January. This is another way in which the Civil War, from a royalist standpoint, had interrupted a long continuity and polluted a Stuart shrine. Then came the king's silent and surreptitious burial.[46] Aptly, Pope makes a silent and surreptitious erasure in the nation's history here: Cromwell, whose body was also subjected to posthumous indignities and whose head may have gone missing, is not accorded the grace of a mention.[47] Pope could not have guessed that a similar fate lay in store for James II, who was of course Charles's son and father of Queen Anne. His body was divided up, the heart, entrails, and brains going to a different resting place. The main part of the king's body was left in the English Benedictine chapel at Paris, awaiting the expected transfer to Westminster Abbey which never came. The sans-culottes dug it up around 1793, and that was the last that was seen of it.

The Interregnum saw the most dramatic transformations at Windsor which have ever occurred. The Dean and Chapter were expelled, and the chapel pillaged, while much of the royal picture collection was dispersed, and plate melted down to pay the wages of the parliamentary forces. Relics such as the coat of mail of Edward IV (who is mentioned at *WF*, 314) were looted, woodwork destroyed, and as we have seen the stained-glass windows broken into pieces. Royalist prisoners were confined in the castle, the Great Park became a training ground for the New Model Army, and large tracts of the park were sold off to create new farming tenancies.[48] Deer, formerly sacrosanct under forest law, had been slaughtered in droves. This last development is discussed at length in *SDW*, chapter 5, since it is part of the argument of writers such as E. P. Thompson and Douglas Chambers that this was the true 'golden age' for the foresters. What cannot be disputed is that Stuart ideology portrayed the Interregnum as a dark night in the history of Windsor, ushered in by the killing of the monarch.[49]

Pope explicitly cites Henry VI as the 'Martyr-King', an obvious jog to royalist

[46] Pope may possibly have recalled a passage in Camden's description of Reading Abbey, since this was a location with which he was undoubtedly familiar (see Ch. 3). Referring to the founder of the Abbey, King Henry II, who was buried on the site, Camden observes, 'Here Henry lies without a single stone' (*Britannia*, 144).

[47] A sign that Pope's mind was preoccupied by the events of 1649 comes in a story he told Spence in the last year of his life. It concerns the visit by a muffled stranger to see the body of Charles I, the night after the execution: the stranger turns out to be Cromwell himself (*Anecdotes*, i. 244).

[48] The Dean was Christopher Wren, father of the architect. He helped to preserve some of the ancient relics.

[49] It was only by a single vote that parliament decided in 1652 to exempt Windsor from a planned sell-off of the royal castles for ready money (*VCH Berkshire*, iii. 18). Around this time the remaining hangings which had festooned the castle were removed.

memories and republican consciences. As we have seen, the poem refers to Henry's tomb, a great site of pilgrimage, in a line which asks that 'Palms Eternal' should 'flourish round his Urn' (312–13). Here funerary art borrowed, like heraldry, from religious symbolism, which used the palm branch to represent the martyr triumphant (Rothery, 122). It is apt to the poem's setting at this juncture that the palm became a familiar attribute of the patron saint of Windsor—St George the martyr. The editors rightly note that the palms here are 'not those of victory, but of martyrdom' (*TE* i. 179). Neither Henry nor Charles, the subjects of succeeding verse paragraphs, had triumphed on earth. The lurking worry behind the poem is that Anne will not survive to enjoy the fruits of the settlement, and that the Stuart cause will be martyred to political expediency. Only in song (formally Lansdowne's, really Pope's) will the past be re-enacted, and Edward III act out the heroic role of George as dragon-slayer:

> Still in thy Song shou'd vanquish'd France appear,
> And bleed for ever under Britain's Spear.
>
> (309-10)[50]

Just as Edward III had converted the castle from its state in the days of Henry II and Henry III, so Charles II had recast it in a baroque form, with the state apartments done over by Hugh May and the decoration provided by Antonio Verrio (1675–84). In all Verrio and his assistants painted twenty ceilings, three staircases, the hall, and the chapel. This was the condition of the castle in Pope's day: a century later, when the ceilings had decayed, George IV would employ Wyatville to give it a more Gothic complexion. Only three rooms now remain in their Caroline state, but we know something about the murals which have been removed. For example, the Queen's great staircase showed scenes of mythology, principally drawn from Ovid. Likewise the king's staircase depicted on its walls the four ages of the world. All this work was ultimately supervised by Christopher Wren, as surveyor-general.[51]

As for the ceilings which do survive, their iconography parallels many details in *Windsor-Forest*. Thus the Queen's presence chamber shows Catherine of Braganza, surrounded by virtues, dispatching with her sword of justice vices including envy and sedition (cf. *WF*, 419–21). In the king's dining room, the ceiling by Verrio depicts a banquet of the gods, with carved fruit, fish, and game, whilst the wall carries a portrait of the Queen, surrounded by Grinling Gibbons's carvings of fruit and flowers, a motif explicitly borrowed in *Windsor-Forest* (37–8). The third room which has remained intact is the Queen's audience chamber, where Anne sat on a throne with a canopy of rich English velvet, 'on which are two plumes of fine feathers'—a suitably magnificent setting for a monarch whom Pope celebrates as a bright goddess, 'The Earth's fair Light, and Empress of the Main' (162, 164). In Pope's day, the walls of St

---

[50] McWhir (1981: 296), rightly notes that this image may also suggest the archangel Michael binding Satan, as well as that of St George and the dragon, but does not connect the latter to the badge of the Order which has been at the centre of this section in WF.

[51] The best account of Verrio's work in relation to contemporary practice is that of Beard (1986: 116–17).

George's Hall showed triumphs of King Edward and his son the Black Prince, in a fresco fully 118 feet in length; the ceiling displayed an apotheosis of Charles II. John Evelyn refers also to a painting of the legend of St George (*ED* iv. 317). These were taken down at the time of George IV's remodelling of the castle. Another room lost to Wyatville was the king's bedchamber, where the ceiling by Verrio depicted Charles II in his robes of state, 'with a Figure, drest in a Mantle, embroider'd with *Flower-de-luces*, representing *France*, as an humble Supplicant, kneeling at his Feet' (cited in *TE* i. 178). On the ballroom ceiling was seen '*Britannia*, with various Emblematical Figures, denoting the Liberty of Europe'. That is a fairly exact iconographic description of *Windsor-Forest*, more especially ll. 91–2.

As well as the state chambers, an important range of lodgings were provided for the main court officers. These included Garter King of Arms, who took a leading role in public ceremonies at the castle and elsewhere. He was, for instance, charged with duties at Westminster: 'When any lord shall enter the Parliament chamber, to assign him his place, according to his dignity and degree' (Fox-Davies, p. 35). This role was no sinecure towards the end of Anne's reign, especially when twelve new faces appeared at Westminster early in 1712. As it happened, the office had been held as long as most people could recall by members of one family, named with a strange aptness Saint-George. This dynasty was founded by Sir Richard Saint-George, Norroy and then Clarenceux king of arms under James I and Charles I. His son, Sir Henry the elder, became Garter at an inauspicious moment, 1644; he died the same year. After the Restoration, one of his sons, Sir Thomas, was appointed to the post in 1686, in succession to Sir William Dugdale. A brother, Henry the younger, succeeded him as Garter in 1703. The secretary of the Order was the Gentleman Usher of Black Rod, who retains important ceremonial functions at the state opening of parliament—an event which was eagerly anticipated as *Windsor-Forest* came out, and duly took place one month after the poem's appearance (see Chapter 3, above). It was Black Rod, too, who had ushered Sacheverell to the bar of the House of Lords to face his accusers in 1710; and into whose custody Lord Oxford would be consigned in July 1715, when the vicissitudes of fate saw the whole Tory edifice collapse like a stack of cards.[52]

Charles II had occasionally used his refurbished castle as a site of propagandistic ceremonies. Most notably, a mimic siege was put on in August 1674 to reenact the successful assault on Maastricht in the Dutch War, when the youthful John Churchill had conducted his first heroic exploit while serving in the French forces in the previous year. This performance was staged below the Long Terrace, as a thousand spectators witnessed a full-scale operation of mining, sapping, and gunnery, with moats and fortifications, to delight the heart of Toby Shandy. The leading actors in this virtual warfare were the Duke of York and the Duke of Monmouth, who a few months later would be drafted into the cast of Crowne's court masque.[53]

---

[52] We might also recall that Edward III created another office, that of the Windsor herald, instituted in about 1364; this was the office held by Ashmole, supreme chronicler of the castle's pageantry. One of the lesser heralds bore the title Rouge-Croix Pursuivant of Arms.

[53] See also *SDW*, ch. 1.

In the seventeenth century the castle had been at the centre of court spectacle. What we need to understand is that Anne was unique in her age in favouring Windsor so much. 'William III spent very little time there,' we are told: 'George I was very seldom at Windsor . . . George II also cared little for Windsor' (*VCH Berkshire*, iii. 21–2).[54] By contrast Anne felt happiest at the castle: 'I came yesterday from *Windsor*,' wrote Swift in October 1713, 'where I saw the Queen in very good Health, which she findeth there more than any where else' (Swift, *Corr.* i. 397). Accordingly, she kept up the tradition of her father and uncle in passing her summers regularly at Windsor, and in mounting events of state pageantry.[55] She even held meetings of the Privy Council there at times, and there were apartments set aside for the main officers of state.[56] Prior to the installation in 1713, to be described shortly, the last major ceremony had taken place on 22 December 1710, when the Dukes of Hanover (that is, the future George I), Devonshire, and Argyll were admitted to the Garter in 'the finest show that can be seen in Europe' (*VCH Berkshire*, iii. 21). These were the last Whig nominations of the reign. In charge of the ceremonial was the constable of the castle at this date, the Duke of Norfolk, another member of the family to which Surrey had belonged—yet another delicate compliment to a contemporary is enshrined in Pope's lines on the Tudor poet.[57] Anne did not alter the structural lines of the castle as her uncle had done. Her alterations were more modest, including the garden Henry Wise constructed from around 1711 between the North Terrace and the Thames—symbolically, this addition which fell into neglect under the Hanoverians. Overlooking the garden was a boudoir where the Queen received news of Marlborough's greatest triumph at Blenheim. On the other side of the castle she converted a 'neat little seat' outside the south front into her own retreat, known as the Queen's Lodge. This is where 'she would daily withdraw from the royal lodgings and the state and splendour of a victorious court to enjoy a happy retirement'.[58] Even monarchs paid lip service, at the very least, to this ubiquitous concept. But according to the Duchess of Marlborough the chief advantage of the lodge was that it enabled Abigail Masham to sneak in visitors to the Queen by the garden entrance (Green, 190).

So much for the buildings and immediate surroundings of the castle. The Windsor 'estate' also included the Little Park, stretching some 3 miles in circumference, and beyond that the Great Park, which reached about 13 miles. Both belonged to the crown. Enclosing both lay the Forest, more than 30 miles round, most of which was in private hands. Queen Anne, as we discovered in Chapter 4, enjoyed hunting deer in the well-stocked preserves. According to Defoe, the Little Park was reserved for the use of the court, while the 'other' (which may mean the Forest at large as well as the great Park) was 'open for Riding, Hunting and taking the Air for any Gentlemen

---

[54] However, public rejoicing was sometimes witnessed, as for instance the celebrations and illuminations depicted by Paul Sandby in 1768.

[55] For a time the castle held melancholy associations after her son, the Duke of Gloucester, fell ill and died at Windsor in 1700; but she continued to spend most summers there to the end of her reign.

[56] Swift used that of the Secretary of State at times (*JTS* i. 322).

[57] On the Duke, see also p. 167, above.   [58] Mackworth-Young (1982: 45).

that please' (*Tour*, i. 312). This was untrue in respect of hunting.[59] Out on the western edge of the park, 'between castle and forest', stood Cranbourne Lodge, where her mother Anne Hyde had been born: the Queen bought it from Godolphin not long before her accession (Green, 81).

There are two further points mentioned by the Twickenham editors which hold special relevance. First, the dedicatee Granville, as he then was, had paid a poetic tribute to the Garter in a work published in 1712, a matter discussed in Chapter 2. This may have been meant to advance his own claims to admission to the order, as Pope (289–90) insinuates is his desert—but the events of 1714–15 were to put such honours for ever out of reach. Second, Pope refers to Verrio's mural design in St George's Hall, already mentioned, which portrays the Black Prince's triumph over King Jean le Bon at Poitiers in 1356. In a nearby room, the Queen's Guard-Chamber, Verrio painted Britannia seated on a globe, with four continents paying tribute to her. Again we see that the idiom of *Windsor-Forest* is in close conjunction with the iconography of patriotic and commemorative art, though it could be said that Pope's highly stylized language is a little less blowsy than most baroque allegorical painting. In fact, he imagines the colours of Verrio's sumptuous scenes as fading with time, leaving only the plangent—but unwritten—songs of Granville (307–8). The idea that the colours would fade, owing to salts 'which in time and this moist climate prejudice', had occurred to John Evelyn in 1683, though he hoped that the work would preserve Verrio's name (*ED* iv. 317).[60]

As for the 'honours' which are Lansdowne's due, these are not merely abstract rewards; in context, the word suggests the trappings of office, the splendid regalia, and the battle honours which hung in the chapel (see ll. 303–5). Over each individual stall, with its enamelled plate, the knight would set up his sword, helmet, and crest with decorative mantling, while in the air above them fluttered his banner. 'The fringed banners are five feet square and the gilded and painted crests are usually carved from limewood or from pear. These remain in place during the knight's lifetime and are taken down at his death when they become a perquisite of Garter King of Arms, though they are often returned to a knight's family and displayed in a parish church or private chapel.'[61] The poem similarly displays the gilded and painted crests of historic nobility, attaching them to the home of the Garter and the home of Stuart allegiances.

CUSTOM AND CEREMONY

It is absolutely certain that Pope was au fait with much of the material which has been outlined in this chapter. He demonstrably went to the passage in *Britannia*

[59] See *SDW*, ch. 5.

[60] Perhaps Pope alluded to the fading colors as a rebuke to Verrio for transferring his services to William III (see Miller 1979: 186–7). The painter's first patrons had been the Jesuits in his native Lecce, and he had originally refused to work for the Dutch king.

[61] Friar (1997: 30).

expounding the history and rites of the Order.[62] We need not assume that he had any first-hand familiarity with Ashmole's great survey of the *Institution, Laws & Ceremonies* of the Order (1672), although the augmented edition of 1693 was the fullest recent source for anyone interested in Windsor. There was widespread popular interest in the subject, as is shown by the extraordinarily full entry provided by Daniel Defoe in his *Tour of Great Britain* just a few years later. Defoe cheerfully admits that he took his information straight from Ashmole; nevertheless, his lengthy descriptions of the castle, the chapel, St George's Hall, the park, and the history of the Garter reflect a general awareness. The entry lists both the original knights appointed by Edward III and the current roll under George I. Defoe alludes to the members of the order as 'a little *Gallaxie* of *English* Nobility, the Flower of so many Courts, and so many Ages, to whose Families the Ensigns of the Order have been an Honour'. The coats of arms above the choir-stalls provide 'a living History' of knighthood (*Tour*, i. 310–11). One of the most personal sections, not filched from Ashmole, alludes to the portrait of William III in St George's Hall, which had replaced the throne previously placed there; and the allegorical ceilings by Verrio, especially the scene of the Black Prince leading the King of France in captivity (see *WF*, 303–10).[63]

Particularly apt to the purposes of Stuart mythography is an account by Ashmole of the Garter insignia belonging to Charles I himself. Ashmole states that the garter which the king had 'worn at the Time of his Martyrdom' was a richly ornamented example, with the motto picked out in no fewer than 412 diamonds. This was sold to John Ireton, one time Lord Mayor of London and brother of the regicide Henry Ireton, for what seems today the knock-down price of £205. After the Restoration, John Ireton proved unwilling to restore this booty, and it needed an action in the King's Bench before Charles II could regain the bejewelled garter (Ashmole, 204). Out of such episodes was the Stuart legend born and sustained.[64]

Moreover, a long passage in *Cooper's Hill*—a poem which Ashmole himself cited (Ashmole, 130) in his description of Windsor—would serve to remind Pope of many historical subjects which went into his own poem. These include Edward III, the Black Prince, the founding of the Order, the quartering of the French lilies, and the selection of George as patron saint:

> When he that Patron chose, in whom are joyn'd
> Souldier and Martyr, and his arms confin'd
> Within the Azure Circle, he did seem
> But to foretell, and prophesie of him,
> Who to his Realms that Azure round hath joyn'd,
> Which Nature for their bound at first design'd.
>
> (*CH*, 101–6)

---

[62] For evidence to demonstrate the fact, see *SDW*, ch. 4.
[63] See *Tour*, i. 306–12. Like Pope (*WF*, 307–8), Defoe mentions the fact that the colors were beginning to 'fall' from Verrio's ceilings owing to salts in the lime working through the wall (*Tour*, i. 307).
[64] For a slightly different version of this story, see *VCH Berkshire*, iii. 26–7.

Ashmole likewise denominates St George as 'a most choice Champion of *Christ*, and famous *Martyr*' (Ashmole, 188). This association of sanctity with martyrdom obviously constitutes a major theme of *Windsor-Forest*.[65]

We know that 1713 was the year of Pope's endeavours as a painter, and he would assuredly recall other baroque images of Stuart kingship—most obviously Rubens's apotheosis of James I on the ceiling of the Banqueting House, described in *SDW*, chapter 2. When Anne's sister Mary died in 1695, it was there that she lay in state, with the walls lined by images of St George driving out evil spirits. This was prior to the solemn funeral to the accompaniment of dirges by Purcell, and its long cortège marshalled by heralds, with Edward Villiers, later Earl of Jersey, leading the Queen's charger. The vast sum of £50,000 was spent on the obsequies, and the event remained rooted in the national memory.[66]

There was another small way in which Pope's efforts to turn himself into a painter caught him up in the folderols surrounding admission to the Order. In the summer of 1713 Charles Jervas told Trumbull that he had been commissioned to paint the Duke of Kent in his full robes, at a Garter ceremony to be held on 4 August. On the same occasion the Earl of Oxford was installed: a promotion which Swift had foretold as early as 29 May 1711, when Harley was made Lord Treasurer (*JTS* i. 282). In the event the nomination had not been made until October 1712, when the Duke of Kent was one of the six new knights elected along with Oxford (these included Hamilton and Strafford, as we shall see presently). A solemn 'Chapter of the most Noble Order of the Garter' was held at Windsor for the investiture, attended by the Sovereign and the Knights Companions, 'habited in their mantles'. The Duke of Kent wished to ensure that Jervas was 'qualified to perform his Figure in the Garter Robes with proper Graces' (New Letts., 397). To this end Jervas seems to have taken Pope to some kind of court ceremony where full dress was worn—conceivably this was the service at St Paul's on 7 July, though neither man would normally have received an invitation to the event (unless the 'Obligation' they owe Kent includes his help in this respect). Pope was at this time deeply engaged in his studies with the painter, and had undertaken a number of copies of his master's works. Dissatisfied with the results, he wrote to Gay on 23 August of many rejected canvases, including 'three Dr. *Swift*'s', various peeresses, 'besides half a dozen Earls, and one Knight of the Garter'—presumably Kent (*Corr.* i. 187). This is a wholly flippant passage, but it is indicative of the prominence of the Garter among the semiological markers of nobility.

It was doubtless this ceremony on 4 August which the Flemish artist Peter Angelis later depicted; the new knight is shown kneeling before the Queen, his train borne by a small black page. Dignitaries of the Order surround the central figures, including robed officials who may include Garter King of Arms—but as we have seen he was the elderly Sir Henry St George, a full 89 years of age, and unlikely to

---

[65] Ashmole's *Antiquities of Berkshire* (1719) would potentially have been of use to Pope if it had appeared earlier. But this was a Curll production, and according to Thomas Hearne it displayed the bookseller's 'Impudence, Ignorance, and Carelessness' in full measure, with abundant errors in attribution and transcription (Hearne, 216–17).

[66] Hamilton (1972: 333–4).

have been present. None is identifiable as the Prelate of the Order, Jonathan Trelawney (Bishop of Winchester), or the Chancellor, Gilbert Burnet (Bishop of Salisbury). However, one of the knights in the middle of the group, immediately to the left of the kneeling figure, strongly resembles Robert Harley. It is noteworthy that Jervas's friend, Jonathan Swift, had gone down to Windsor late in July and stayed until the very day of the installation, 4 August, so he may well have witnessed the ceremony (there is no journal extant for this period: see *JTS* ii. 552).

The other knights who were elected to the Garter in 1712 included a close confidant of Oxford, Lord Poulett, as well as the Duke of Hamilton, whose history we have traced in Chapter 2, and the Earl of Strafford. Hamilton was an undoubted Jacobite, Poulett a more circumspect adherent of the Stuart cause. In some ways Strafford was the most interesting choice. He had risen fast under the Harley administration; his earldom had been conferred the previous year, and he was one of the two signatories, along with Robinson, of the Utrecht agreement. As ambassador to the Netherlands, he showed more competence and strength of mind than most of the British negotiators, even though his literacy was doubtful and Swift despised him. In later years he emerged as a crypto-Jacobite,[67] but at this stage he performed a minimally useful service for the ministry in standing up to the Dutch. On his return he was made First Lord of the Admiralty—a role of Gilbertian suitability, insofar as his role at Utrecht had been to do 'nothing in particular with becoming dignity' (Trevelyan, iii. 232). Rewards like the Garter were a natural consequence of his titular role at the peace conference.[68]

For the most part, the Order was not expressly a political institution, and over time its membership necessarily reflected changes in the ideological complexion of the age. Nevertheless, Anne's espousal of values which could be seen to imbue the Garter gave it a distinctive position during her reign. Possibly at some level she identified its patron with her well-loved husband, Prince George of Denmark, whose death in 1708 affected her almost as much as that of Prince Albert was to crush a later queen. The fact that Anne's coronation, like those of her uncle and her father, took place on St George's Day—in other respects a feast of declining significance—suggests a tribute to her husband. But the timing of this event certainly locked the Queen into a Stuart calendar of martyrology. Then, at her death a Jacobite broadside appeared, under the title of *A New Song on St. George's Day; and to the Glorious Memory of Queen Anne. With the Restauration of King Charles 2d.*

As late as 1715, in the run-up to the Rebellion, Jacobites staged a riot in London on

---

[67] Strafford was a close friend of Charles Caesar, the most uncompromising of all Jacobites, whose wife described the Earl on his death as 'Ever ready to Serve, with Head, Hand, and Heart' (quoted by Rumbold 1989: 246). See also Ch. 3, above.

[68] He was the great-nephew of the famous first Earl of Strafford, regarded by the high-flyers as the first great martyr of Stuart times. St John even wrote to the Earl at the end of 1711, comparing the situation faced by the queen with the dilemma which had confronted Charles I seventy years before (Churchill, iv. 419–20). It can be no coincidence that when Strafford was faced with a charge of treason in August 1715 a publisher reissued the articles of impeachment against his famous namesake in 1640.

23 April, commemorating the dead monarch. They brandished through the streets a portrait of Anne, together with the inscription, 'Imitate her who was so Just and Good, | Both in her Actions and her Royal Word.' (For the Queen's decisive 'word' in the poem, see *WF*, 327–8.) The crowd also shouted 'God bless the Queen' and burnt a picture of William III. Swarming past the church of St Andrew's, Holborn (where Sacheverell was now rector), they offered to sing 'the Second Part of the *Sacheverell-Tune*'. Six days later, they returned to celebrate the birthday of the Duke of Ormonde with equal fervour.[69] Plainly by now St George's Day had become a fixture in the Stuart calendar.

In *Windsor-Forest* Pope capitalized on all these circumstances when he gave so much prominence to the chapel dedicated to the saint and to the Order. At a deeper level, the mere act of celebrating the oldest order of chivalry could be interpreted as a conservative stratagem, whatever the political complexion of its current membership. Similarly, when the Queen created the six new knights, she had made a species of constitutional statement—as, for that matter, the twelve new peers, including Lansdowne, created a year earlier had represented an attempt to give a deed of short-term expediency the air of an aristocratic *acte gratuite*. For both the Queen and her poet, the image of George and his knights could be used to lend an air of historic significance to contemporary politics. The Order had become the subject of antiquarian attention, notably by Ashmole and William Dugdale, and seemed to set forth an ideal of historic continuity which raised it above the grubbier temporal concerns of the age. For those who sympathized with the Stuart cause, at this moment of impending crisis, this was just what they needed. With his learning and his sense of history, Pope sought to appropriate the language and lore of St George for the Stuarts—a dynasty whose term now looked to have all too short a date, and whose recent behaviour had often appeared both shoddy and reckless.

STORIED URNS

When we examine the passage on the chapel, it is immediately obvious that the lines on Surrey (291–9), on Edward III (299–310), on Edward IV and Henry VI (311–18), and on Charles I (319–26) all have the character of epitaphs, rather than the elegies prepared for Denham and Cowley. Each uses language and lapidary attitudes found in Pope's numerous epitaphs for friends such as Harcourt, Kneller, Digby, Fenton, Gay, and Atterbury.[70] In the fullest account of Pope's work in this area, Joshua Scodel remarks that 'commemorating the worthy is a central task of Pope's poetry, early and late'. He adds that 'Pope's epitaphs upon aristocrats and major public figures

---

[69] Monod, 180–1; Rogers (1998: 30).

[70] To take just one instance, the phrases 'weeping Vaults' and 'the Marble weeps' (*WF*, 302) are paralleled by 'weeping marble' in Pope's 'Epitaph' on Edmund, Duke of Buckinghamshire (*TE* vi. 362). We might say that this is just the sort of expression we should expect to find in a funeral inscription—but that is exactly the point.

also reveal the poet's struggles against the corruption of funerary verse.'[71] This is true, although this anxiety may be less apparent at the start of Pope's career. His first important epitaph is the one designed for Lord Caryll and subsequently adapted, as we have seen, for Sir William Trumbull. *Windsor-Forest* antedates all other significant works by Pope in this form, and gives us some indication of his attitude towards commemorating the great figures of state.

Perhaps the most characteristic item is an epitaph 'intended for' Nicholas Rowe, who was buried alongside Dryden in Westminster Abbey in 1718. In this appears the line, 'Beneath a rude and nameless stone he lies', where Pope alludes to Dryden's unmarked tomb (*TE* vi. 208): here was yet another martyr to the Stuart cause denied a proper commemoration in death. The consequence was that the Duke of Buckinghamshire erected a monument, designed by James Gibbs, for which Pope supplied an inscription:

> This *SHEFFIELD* rais'd. The sacred Dust below
> Was *DRYDEN* once: the rest who does not know?
>
> (*TE* vi. 237)

The echo of 'sacred Charles' may well be deliberate, such was Pope's reverence for Dryden. Later, however, he decided to substitute a plain epitaph in prose, and this is how the monument survives.[72] Epitaphs of this nature supply a crucial background to the portions of *Windsor-Forest* dealing with the chapel and its vaults. For Pope to stress that the tomb of the Stuart martyr was 'uninscribed' was to employ a serious form of wit, since the passage itself comes very close to the status of an inscription, in its blend of pious reflection with a chiselled precision in phrasing: 'what new Wounds, and how her old have bled?' (322). Pope uses the word 'Inscriptio' for his tribute to Swift, later incorporated into the *Dunciad*; it might be added that Swift too composed a Latin funeral inscription for the Earl of Berkeley in 1711. It may be said that generally Pope's writing shows his awareness of the traditions of epigraphy: for example, the 'Inscription' for the grotto at Stourhead clearly derives from a votive or dedicatory tablet.[73]

All around the garden which Pope created with so much love and care at Twickenham, inscriptions abounded. They appeared on the obelisk dedicated to his mother and on several other statues and urns; he also placed a motto over his gate (*Garden and City*, 31). Such verbal messages have been interpreted by Mack and others as clues to the expressive iconography of the villa and garden, in apposition to

---

[71] Scodel (1991: 277, 304). This book is excellent in relating Pope to 17th-cent. traditions of the epitaph, and offers interesting commentary on Westminster Abbey memorials (Scodel 1991: 301–11). It does not mention the passage on the St George's Chapel in *WF*.

[72] Before the epitaph went up, there were consultations with Atterbury, as dean of Westminster, about the correct form it should take: in Sept. 1720, Atterbury sent Pope a Latin inscription which was also rejected. See also Ault, 145–55; and Scodel (1991: 291–3).

[73] The immediate source may have been found in collections such as J. G. Graevius, *Thesauros antiquatum Romanorum*: see *TE* vi. 248–9. Interest in epigraphy grew rapidly with the work of Mabillon and other Maurist scholars: the Académie des Inscriptions et Belles-lettres came in Pope's lifetime to be the prime institution of classical archaeology. It must be added that, in other moods, Pope could deplore the 'sepulcral lies' which adorn holy walls: see *TE* vi. 363.

studies of Pope's cult of friendship and retirement. What we need to do beyond this is to recover the identity of these sermons in stone as *lettering* carved into physical objects. They constitute a kind of concrete poetry, whose materiality and location form part of their meaning.

An inscription in the technical sense can be anything traced, cut, scratched, or impressed on stone, metal, shell, clay, wood, or wax—but excluding coins or anything written on papyrus.[74] Pope's own epitaphs often draw attention to the mode of carving out a message in stone: for example, his lines on Simon Harcourt contain the verse, 'Oh let thy once-lov'd Friend inscribe thy Stone' (*TE* vi. 242). In this era, too, there were still public inscriptions which might excite discussion: we have already noted the anti-Catholic legend on the Monument, added in 1681, which drew Pope's attention, as well as the vainglorious *arc de triomphe* at Blenheim. As evocative as anything is the reaction of John Evelyn, when he sifted through the ruins of old St Paul's after the Great Fire. When he came on the great portico rent to pieces, he discovered intact on the architrave an inscription relating to the erection of the arch, with not a single letter defaced (*ED* iii. 58–9). At this sight Evelyn felt intense emotion, almost as a romantic archaeologist might have swooned over the vestiges of Palmyra.

Many of the founding texts of archaeology had made a special point of transcribing epigraphic materials. William Camden had produced in 1600 a short catalogue of the epitaphs on kings, queens, and nobles in Westminster Abbey, together with translations into English verse. A more significant example is John Weever's famous collection of *Ancient Funeral Monuments* (1631), limited as this is to three diocesan areas. According to Weever, 'Sepulchres should bee made according to the qualities and degree of the person deceased, that by the Tombe euery one might bee discerned of what ranke he was living.'[75] The tomb of 'sacred *Charles*' (319) thus offends against a cardinal principle of civic memory. It is the poet's task to make this inappropriate bare sepulchre 'for ever known', an act of piety made more urgent by the absence of the proper furnishings. *Windsor-Forest* sets out to make legible what the broken history of the seventeenth century has left uninscribed.[76]

In 1724 Pope wrote in a letter to Martha Blount of a visit to Sherborne, setting out his view of inscriptions as a way of memorializing virtue which would otherwise be forgotten. He describes the picturesque ruins of the old Norman castle, and then turns to the owner of the estate, who was the nonjuror Lord Digby:[77]

What should induce my Lord D. the rather to cultivate these ruins and would do honour to them, is that they do no small honour to his Family; that Castle, which was very ancient, being demolishd in the Civil wars after it was nobly defended by one of his Ancestors in the cause of the King. I would set up at the Entrance of 'em an Obelisk, with an Inscription of the Fact:

[74] Howatson and Chilvers (1993: 208). Pope would have been aware of the Monumentum Ancyranum, discovered in 1555, a Latin inscription originally engraved on bronze tablets outside the mausoleum of Augustus, recording the Emperor's deeds.   [75] Weever (1631: 10).

[76] The classic study of epigraphy as art, especially in the Italian Renaissance, is Sparrow (1969).

[77] See *Milieu*, 132–65, for a sensitive account of Lord Digby, 'Christian Nobleman', and his son Robert, whose epitaph Pope would write in 1727.

which would be a Monument erected to the very Ruins; as the adorning & beautifying them in the manner I have been imagining, would not be unlike the Ægyptian Finery of bestowing Ornament and curiosity on dead bodies. The Present Master of this Place . . . needs not to fear the Record, or shun the Remembrance of the actions of his Forefathers. (*Corr*, ii. 239)

This tribute to the head of a long-established country family incorporates some interrelated motifs we have already encountered: lament for noble buildings destroyed for selfish or partisan reasons, reverence for the distinguished dead, and a determination to preserve the 'record' of piety and loyalty. There is no tomb such as Weever described, and no individual is singled out for lamentation: the process is collective, designed to right historic wrongs in a public manner. Of course, the king in whose cause the Digby family defended their property was Charles I: again Pope forces us to confront open wounds left by the conflicts of the previous century.

Charles I, as we know, had never been granted a funeral monument. On the other hand, a large number of existing tombs and inscriptions perished during the Civil War and Commonwealth, although not as many perhaps as royalists sometimes liked to suggest. The puritans were hardest on 'superstitious' monumental brasses carrying papist legends or images. Conservative writers were able to use iconoclasm as an emblem of the destructive forces which had ruptured historical continuity.[78] The lines in the poem utter a plea to keep fresh the memory of Windsor's glorious dead in the face of the threat of annihilation, when the 'naked Wall' is left 'inanimate' (308). Poetry will animate what may otherwise crumble away.

Even if Pope had somehow overlooked the growing interest in inscriptions, he can scarcely have missed a controversy which had blown up in recent years. For one thing, several of the participants were personally known to him. The dispute was fed by competition among antiquarians to recover the traces of Roman Britain, a desire prompted most urgently by Camden's great founding text. As Joseph Levine points out, 'Next to coins, inscriptions were the most plentiful and helpful of all the Roman antiquities that were available in the British Isles.'[79] It was the belief of Hearne—anticipating the ideas of R. G. Collingwood—that coins and inscriptions were more reliable than manuscripts as aids to historical enquiry. At this juncture, late on in Anne's reign, a number of scholars became exercised by an inscription which had been discovered in 1708 at Walcot on the edge of Bath. It was on a gabled tombstone commemorating the death and funeral of a Roman legionary.[80] First to decipher and interpret it, a year later, was Thomas Hearne, who had recently been editing John Leland's *Itinerary* and was now contemplating an edition of *Britannia*. Between them Leland and Camden had done most to bring epigraphic remains to the attention of a broad public: indeed, Camden had recorded all known examples throughout the country. Promptly, Hearne's readings of the inscription were challenged by other proto-archaeologists, including Roger Gale, Henry Dodwell, and William Musgrave.

---

[78] On the 'obsessive concern' with the provision of architectural tombs for the nobility in place of monasteries, and their destruction in the Reformation and the Civil War, see Thomas (1973: 721).

[79] Levine (1977: 217).

[80] See item 156, in Collingwood and Wright (1965: i. 51).

This dispute went on sporadically from about 1708 to 1715. In the end the most accurate transcription proved to be that of Dodwell. Under William III, Dodwell had been driven by his High Church views from Oxford, where he was Camden professor of ancient history. Now he was living at Shottesbrooke in Berkshire under the patronage of the nonjuror Francis Cherry, who had also given the local boy Hearne his start in the scholarly life. Shottesbrooke has been described as 'a refuge and a home to many distinguished nonjurors' (*VCH Berkshire*, iii. 166): for example, Cherry had shielded the great nonjuring scholar George Hickes when he was compiling his major study of the Saxon language, published in 1703.[81] Hearne looked on the house as 'sometimes like a College'. The most noteworthy aspect of this situation is that Shottesbrooke lay deep within the Forest, just 4 miles north of Binfield. It is intriguing to speculate that this local 'college' might have been available to Pope, who was a member of a group even more restricted in its civil rights than the nonjuring community. Cherry was a collector of books and coins, which would make his company an education in itself. An afternoon's ride could have brought the poet to this storehouse of apposite learning, as he worked on *Windsor-Forest*. Unfortunately Pope nowhere refers to Cherry and, although this might proceed from discretion, we must assume in the absence of positive evidence that he had no contact with the Shottesbrooke circle.[82] Yet its mere existence would have confirmed his notion of the Forest as a haven for those who had been unjustly excluded on account of their religion. By a melancholy coincidence, Cherry died in the same year that the poem came out.[83]

When the debate over the Bath inscription erupted, Dodwell had also been busy writing an account of the famous shield of Dr Woodward, that is another supposedly 'Roman' antiquity.[84] In this second task Dodwell was to be joined by members of the Scriblerus Club who had enjoyed the friendship of Anne's Tory ministry: almost certainly it was Pope and Arbuthnot who drafted the sections of the *Memoirs of Martinus Scriblerus* which make robust fun of the shield, perhaps around 1714.[85]

Woodward is in his idiosyncratic way a representative man of his time, or to be more specific a representative figure of high culture in Pope's day. He had a large

[81] Evelyn, Pepys, and Atterbury were among the subscribers: see Levine (1991: 364). The work included a significant discussion of coinage, based on the work of Sir Andrew Fountaine, a friend of Swift. Hearne has been thought to be the butt of Pope's satire on the antiquarian Wormius in *The Dunciad*, but the poet's note states, apparently without irony, that he had studied many 'curious tracts' published by Hearne 'to his great contentment' (*TE* v. 171).

[82] Dr Arbuthnot, also a numismatist, had come into contact with Cherry in 1708. Whilst at Windsor, he had been called to attend his old friend, the astronomer Dr David Gregory at Maidenhead. Unfortunately, by the time the doctor arrived, his patient had died, and Cherry had helped with the burial, which took place locally (see Aitken 1968: 32). Gregory was another prominent Jacobite.

[83] According to one story, Cherry met William III while hunting, and tried to coax the king's horse down a steep bank, in the hope that its rider would break his neck (Monod, 139). This looks like a *post facto* invention, bearing in mind the manner of the king's actual death: but it accurately reflects the animosity felt by some nonjurors.

[84] See Levine (1977), for a brilliantly illuminating account of this extraordinary episode.

[85] For the background to the composition of the *Memoirs*, see Kerby-Miller (1950). The editor (p. 207) shows that the satirists were familiar with Dodwell's treatise on the shield, published by Hearne in 1713.

cabinet of antique curiosities, which included coins, tiles and bits of pavement thought to be evidence of the life lived in 'ancient heathen Rome'.[86] This area of enquiry had been given a boost by the excavations carried out during the rebuilding of London after the Fire: no less a figure than Christopher Wren had written about the earliest discoveries, such as a stone with an inscription found near Ludgate, and a vast hoard of urns which had turned up in a pit off Cheapside.[87] Other archaeologists joined in with their theories concerning the vestiges of Roman London which had been recovered: a particularly fraught issue was raised by the supposed Temple of Diana, described in *Britannia* (330–1), which had been traditionally located beneath St Paul's. Like Wren, most of the commentators were sceptical about this temple. Of course, the architect was the best qualified to form a judgement: he actually included an account of the Temple of Diana at Ephesus, taken from Pliny, in his *Tracts on Architecture* (begun in the 1670s), and made a conjectural reconstruction of the plan and elevation.[88] However, Woodward bucked the trend. In his *Account of some Roman Urns*, written in the form of a letter to Wren in November 1711 and published in 1713, he described a new find made in Bishopsgate, which included a stretch of the Roman city wall as well as a large number of funeral urns. Near the end of the *Account* he expressed his reasons for believing that the old tradition was right after all: there had after all been a Temple of Diana on the site of St Paul's.

In support of his case, Woodward adduced a small statue which had been found near St Paul's during the rebuilding of the city after the Fire. This, too, he identified as portraying Diana. In order to establish its authenticity, he surveyed a number of representations of the goddess, including items at the Farnese, Versailles, and private galleries—as well as the long tradition of effigies on coins. To make the point, Woodward compares iconographic details: the bow in the left hand, the quiver, the habit girded up to the knees, and the hair wreathed and gathered into knots. It is astonishing how widely the author ranges to make his case. In reality, Pope held a low opinion of most modern depictions of Diana, and conveyed this in a letter to Caryll in 1727. Yet the differences between the aesthetically fastidious poet and the voraciously acquisitive antiquarian should not blind us to an underlying similarity. Diana and her followers, with their silver bows, buskins, fillet binding the hair, and painted quivers (*WF* 169–70, 175–80), replicate in the poem the details Woodward used to vindicate an archaeological judgement.[89]

The Scriblerians had Woodward's *Account* in mind when they drew up one of their earliest satires on misapplied antiquarian learning, *The Origine of Sciences*,

[86] This paragraph is based on the chapter entitled 'Roman London' in Levine (1977: 133–50), and sources listed there. Woodward especially prized an urn which, on the basis of its inscription, he believed to have been one mentioned by Horace—almost certainly a delusion on his part.

[87] See Wren, 266–7, for a description of these finds. Soo (1998: 26–30), reprints this material, and supplies useful background (1998: 18–21). Information on the discoveries was reported by Robert Plot in *Britannia*.

[88] Wren, 360–1: now also available in Soo (1998: 169–73). In addition Wren described Vespasian's Temple of Peace (Wren, 362–3; Soo 1998: 173–8). Pope could not have seen these works, which remained in manuscript in his lifetime; but the subject matter chimes with that of *WF*, 378.

[89] Levine (1977: 148–50).

which was probably put together by Pope, Arbuthnot, and Parnell in the summer of 1714.[90] A more conspicuous attack on Woodward came with the character of Dr Fossile in *Three Hours after Marriage*: this explosive farce co-authored by Gay, Pope, and Arbuthnot was first performed in January 1717. What immediately concerns us here is that the 'restoration' of the capital had brought to the surface a sense of the Roman identity of London, an awareness taken to extreme lengths by a man like Woodward. On a more profound level, this process might encourage writers to envisage the city as 'Augusta', and to reinvest the stale poeticism 'temples'—for 'churches'—with an ideal of *renewal*, whereby ancient civilization and ancient virtue should be brought back to life on British soil (see *WF*, 377–8).

Almost all Scriblerian targets attain the condition of a victim because they evoke a buried interest on the part of the satirists: that is to say, they reflect some deflected or thwarted concern with the subject in Pope and his friends. This is certainly so in the case of antiquarian studies. Abundant evidence exists to show that the whole Scriblerus project revolved around the group's intense preoccupation with the study of older history. Indeed Cornelius, father of Martinus Scriblerus, was 'by Profession an Antiquary'. Arbuthnot became heavily embroiled in disputes with men like John Woodward; and Pope himself was caught up in some of these episodes. His own friends and allies included notable collectors and virtuosi such as Dr Richard Mead and Sir Hans Sloane. Mead, we might add, possessed a sixteenth-century shield depicting the presentation of the keys of Carthage to Scipio Africanus: it was images such as this, collected by the indefatigable antiquarians, which filled Pope's memory as he wrote of 'great *Scipio*' (257).[91] Moreover, a fellow-member of the Scriblerian Club was Robert Harley, Earl of Oxford, the unsung hero of the closing prophecy in *Windsor-Forest*.[92] Harley's collections included several items relating to Roman Britain; in 1716 he acquired through the palaeographer Humphry Wanley the papers of John Bagford, a prominent antiquarian who acted as an agent for Woodward and Sloane among others.[93]

So it is altogether understandable that the writer who, with his colleagues, made fun of the fantastic interpretations of Dr Woodward's shield was also the writer who compiled elaborate 'Observations on the Shield of Achilles', setting out in detail the content and compositional practices of this passage in the *Iliad*. Pope praises Homer's technique in these words: 'The shield is not only described as a piece of sculpture but of painting: the outlines may be supposed engraved, and the rest enameled, or inlaid with various-coloured metals' (*TE* viii. 361). If there is a single poem in the canon of English literature whose methods are suggested by these

[90] See Beattie (1967: 227–9); Kerby-Miller (1950: 41).

[91] The evidence to link Pope with antiquarian discourse and practices is too lengthy to list here. One immediately relevant fact is that Dr Mead, like so many of Pope's friends, was keenly interested in the history of coins (see *SDW*, ch. 2). It does not help to clarify all the issues raised by this question to find that Edmund Curll was often involved in the contests of antiquarians, and fomenting trouble, as between Woodward and Hearne in 1712. See Beattie (1967: 220–1).

[92] See *SDW*, ch. 6.

[93] Levine (1977: 139–40). Another friend of Hearne who assembled a large collection of inscriptions was the herald John Anstis (see above, p. 169).

words it is surely *Windsor-Forest.* Moreover, Pope's analysis of the separate compartments of the shields indicates the kind of ordonnance he had been seeking to achieve in his own poem: 'This quiet picture is a kind of *Repose* between the last, and the following, active pieces.' Nothing is more wonderful in Homer, Pope declares, 'than his exact observation of the *contrast,* not only between figure and figure, but between subject and subject'. Equally, we find 'all his figures differently *characterized,* in their expressions and attitudes, according to their several natures' (*TE* viii. 364–70). *Windsor-Forest* itself works in contrasting bands of subject matter, and takes great care to display allegorical figures such as Ceres, the Thames, and Peace in their most expressive poses.

Poor Woodward's 'Roman' shield was bogus, insofar as its provenance and supposed meanings were concerned: in this it was a burlesque of the shield of Achilles, whose aesthetic principles helped to govern those of *Windsor-Forest.* In a similar way the inscription from Bath, though authentic in origin, was the subject of conflicting and often erroneous interpretations. Yet there was a corpus of serious epigraphy, which Pope could draw on to give his own work a kind of Roman gravity. As Levine points out, the Bath inscription was only one of thousands to be deciphered and transcribed in this era. The curiosity which it inspired 'was simply another sign of the immense enthusiasm for ancient Rome common to the Augustans'.[94] There is thus a concealed level of political or cultural commentary in the decision to engrave a funeral tribute to the martyr-kings of England at St George's Chapel. Pope is assimilating the English monarchs to a classic mode of commemoration—especially as he inscribes his lines into the bare stone of Charles's tomb. The need is greater because the burial-place still lacks even the funeral urn around which the palms of an earlier martyr, Henry VI, are allowed to flourish (*WF,* 312).

The import of Pope's lines becomes clearer if we look at the cultural context of monuments in the Stuart era, as they express allegiance to a chivalric code. Recently, Nigel Llewellyn has described chivalry as part of a pattern of social relations in post-Reformation England. Not everyone could read the code, according to Llewellyn, but most could understand it as 'a species of social practice restricted to an elite and used in a corporate way to preserve its distinction'. The value of chivalry to the elite group lay partly in its function as a symbol of breeding and morality, and this symbolism was often maintained by artefacts. Llewellyn explores the use of funeral monuments as a component of this culture, seeking to show how tombs 'replaced the individual knight after death by displaying heraldry and registering social status against a whole series of hierarchies'. The main evidence for this proposition is drawn from the family tombs of the St Johns of Lydiard in Wiltshire. Their monuments, dating mainly from the first half of the seventeenth century, had excited the fervent admiration of John Aubrey when he visited the village of Lydiard Tregoze about 1660. He spent many hours copying out inscriptions and heraldic devices from the church.[95]

---

[94] Levine (1977: 218–19).   [95] Llewellyn (1990: 145–60).

It happens that Pope's friend Bolingbroke was a direct descendant of the Wilt-shire branch of the St Johns: indeed, he was probably born at Lydiard. His paternal grandfather was Sir Walter St John, one who trimmed during the Civil War and abandoned the strong royalist traditions on this side of the family. Yet he harboured an inordinate pride in his lineage, and always hoped that his grandson, young Henry, would carry on the family tradition with dignity.[96] Among the tombs the boy would have seen at an impressionable age was that of the Golden Cavalier—a life-size statue of Edward St John, killed at Newbury in 1642, who stands in effigy with gilded armour and a prominent armorial shield. It was said that his funeral brought out more escutcheons than the interment of a duke, and pennons 'out of all proportion'.[97]

Heraldic data to provide quarterings on the St John monuments had been sup-plied by Clarenceux King of Arms, who was none other than Sir Richard St George—he happened also to have married a daughter of the family. Blood, in Llewellyn's apt phrasing, still retained its place 'supported by chivalry and the well-documented revivals of the joust and other neo-medieval knightly pursuits'. It was also supported by heraldry itself, since heraldry was a means of 'signalling the phys-ical occupation of land and power'. More specifically, the granting of arms and their display in such places as a tomb aided a process which 'sought to impose social order on the chivalrous, upper ranks of Tudor and early Stuart society'. Family continuity was also expressed in inscriptions, for example by listing ancestors on a tablet.[98]

What we may find hard to understand today is that the funeral of an aristocrat was supervised by heralds from the College of Arms. In the late Tudor and early Stuart period, it might take a full month to organize such an occasion, which could cost many hundreds of pounds. As Lawrence Stone points out, 'Though the service took place in church, the master of ceremonies was not the parson but the heralds, and the affair was characterized more by the rituals of antiquarian feudalism than by those of Christianity.' The lavish tombs subsequently erected might cost a further £1,000, and they too were designed to express a mode of symbolic longevity. Only in the 1630s, as the impact of puritan criticism increased, did a fashion set in for less grandiose monuments.[99]

Pope did not belong to this class in society: his family bore no coat of arms. How-ever, his contacts with members of a family such as the St Johns would have shown him that, at the level of aspiration if no further, the aristocracy and gentry were still seeking in the late Stuart age to preserve their caste by devices such as those just de-scribed. Llewellyn refers to a belief in 'the immortality which honourable deeds conferred', and concludes that 'funeral monuments to chivalric men ensured that this memory was sustained by inscription of the image of the armoured chivalric knight'.[100] This observation is relevant in two ways to Pope's task. In the first place, St George's Chapel was itself the nerve-centre of chivalric knighthood in Britain.

[96] Dickinson (1970: 1–2). Sir Walter's wife Joanna came from the puritan Bletsoe branch of the St Johns, and remained loyal to the parliamentarian cause.
[97] Quoted by Llewellyn (1990: 150).
[98] Llewellyn (1990: 147–51).   [99] Stone (1967: 260–4).   [100] Llewellyn (1990: 155).

Secondly, Windsor harboured the remains of the monarchs who stood at the head of orders such as the Garter. Under both aspects, the emblematic codes of private families are made available to the poet in his desire to commemorate the virtues of one public family. Thus, Pope is able to make his own statements about the *national* memory by way of funeral inscriptions and heraldic emblems. He draws his own device for the tombs of the martyred kings who lay at Windsor.

One more extraordinary series of events provides a context for Pope's lines. On the eve of the anniversary of the death of Charles I, 29 January 1678, the House of Commons voted £70,000 to give the king a solemn funeral, and 'to erect a Monument for the said Prince of glorious Memory'. Next day Thomas Sprat preached a commemorative sermon before the house, congratulating members on their resolution and on giving 'a Resurrection' to the king's memory by 'designing magnificent Rites to his sacred Ashes'. From now on, Sprat states, the king's heroic worth will be delivered down to posterity, 'not only freed from Calumny, or Obscurity, but, in all Things, most illustrious'. Pope similarly hopes to make the 'sacred' king's tomb 'for ever known', though its location at present is 'obscure'. As surveyor-general, Wren was ordered to make plans for a mausoleum, and in response he prepared drawings of a rotunda topped by a dome and lantern, surrounded by a circular colonnade of Ionic pillars. Detailed estimates were made for the scheme, including statues and mosaic work, which would have cost £43,663. The king approved the scheme, but for some reason the plan never went into effect.[101]

An elaborate royal tomb was envisaged which could serve for the interment of other monarchs: it would have been situated at the east end of St George's Chapel, where Henry VIII had been buried and where Charles himself had begun the erection of a shrine:

This Place King *Charles* the First, of ever blessed and glorious memory, intended to enlarge and make fit and capable, not only for the interment of his own Body, but also for the Bodies of his Successor Kings of *England*, had not bad Times drawn on, and such as, with much ado, afforded him but an obscure Grave, near the first Haut-pace in the Quire of the Chapel, his Head lying over-against the eleventh Stall on the *Sovereign's Side*, and in the same Vault where the Bodies of King *Henry* the Eighth, and his Queen *Jane*, yet remain.

There is a faintly grisly sequel. Neither Charles II or James II ever carried out this sumptuous memorial to his father. However, the vault was opened in 1696 to receive a stillborn child of the then Princess Anne. It was found that, after all, a lead band round Charles's coffin carried the minimalist inscription 'KING CHARLES, 1648.' We are told that Queen Jane's coffin was intact, but that of her husband was sunk inwards, and the lead and wood consumed by the embalming fluids.[102] In addition,

---

[101]   The principal source here is the *History of England* (1707) by the Tory writer Laurence Echard, cited by Wren 331–2. For a later discussion, including mention of Anne's stillborn child, see Sir Henry Halford's *Account of what Appeared on Opening the Coffin of King Charles I* (1813).

[102]   The monument for Henry VIII, built around 'a little *Gothick Building*' originally put up by Cardinal Wolsey, was demolished in 1646, by command of the Long Parliament, and the copper gilt statues adorning it were stripped away (Echard, cited by Wren, 332).

our immediate source here, the historian Laurence Echard, attempts to bring proof against the insinuations of Lord Clarendon that the body of Charles had disappeared; witnesses are cited to testify that the coffin was opened prior to burial, and that they recognized the king (Wren, 330).

The most relevant details have still to be described. They lie in the 'general Plan, Orthography, and Section, with the Statues and Ornaments, designed for the *Tomb of King Charles the First*', set out by Wren's son in *Parentalia*, and now preserved at All Souls College, Oxford.[103] The monument designed for Charles himself, in the central niche of the tomb, was described in this way:

> Four Statues, Emblems of heroick Virtues, standing on a square Basis, or Plinth, and pressing underneath, prostrate Figures of Rebellion, Heresy, Hypocrisy, Envy &c. support a large Shield, on which is a Statue erect of the *royal* Martyr, in modern Armour; over his Head is a Group of Cherubims, bearing a Crown, Branches of Palm, and other Devices. (Wren, 332)

The statuary was designed in alternative versions, either for brass or for marble. Now it is highly unlikely that Pope ever saw these drawings. But there was no need for him to do so. His own artistic vocabulary embraced a similar range of 'Emblems' and 'Devices'. A train of virtues, led by Peace and Plenty, dignify the actions of the Diana-like heroine of his poem. The concluding tableau displays figures of Rebellion, Faction, Persecution, Envy—et cetera. The 'Palms' which flourish over the 'weeping Vaults' of earlier martyr-kings are made in the poem to stretch symbolically over Charles I. Even though Wren's mausoleum remained merely in potential, Pope was able to construct a verbal *tombeau* for the Stuart hero. A generation earlier, Stuart supporters had hoped to draw the king's resting-place out of obscurity and into the light of history: they failed, but *Windsor-Forest* succeeded in restoring collective memory.[104]

One bitter irony remained. It was the 'usurper' Cromwell who had been granted a 'fully royal' funeral, as David Starkey has recently put it, with all the escutcheons and insignia of monarchy.[105] John Evelyn had noted with distaste the spectacle of '*Oliver* lying in Effigie in royal robes, & crown'd with a Crown, scepter, & Mund, like a king' (*ED* iii. 224). This was truly to usurp what the Stuarts regarded as their own prerogative in death. Evelyn had been equally disgusted by the showy send-off awarded to the regicide Ireton in 1652, when the heralds appeared in new state regalia (*ED* iii. 57). The rule of the saints had meant a wholesale appropriation of the sigils of ancient monarchy.

---

[103] The book was compiled by the architect's son, also Christopher, and edited for publication by his grandson Stephen.

[104] A legend survives that Pope suggested to Rowe that he should write a tragedy on the subject of Charles I, or alternatively on another Stuart martyr, Mary Queen of Scots: this was during the dramatist's visit to Binfield in 1713 (*EC* vi. 367). The story is probably not reliable.

[105] Starkey (1999: 19).

THE BOAST OF HERALDRY

In recent times, genealogy and heraldry have rarely been invoked to settle anything more momentous than the ownership of a single landed property or the right to a title, usually carrying no power with it. Once it was different. John Dee had tried to settle the whole question of the origins of the British nation by an appeal to armorial evidence:

Dee tried to establish the relationship between Brutus and Arthur by a genealogical study of Arthur's coat of arms. He claims that Arthur's arms—three gold crowns in a field of azure—were appropriated to the 'enheritable Monarchy of LOEGRE' from the time of Brutus, and this coat Arthur 'quartered wᵗ the Troian coat of his Auncestors: as in the Antiquityes of Aeneas you may see'.[106]

It was the sort of thing Queen Elizabeth, who was Dee's most important patron, liked to hear; and it was a message taken seriously even by his protégés, Camden and Speed, for all their depth of knowledge in history and chorography. Dee had many other disciplines, occult and as it were secular, at his disposal; but he chose to decide this fraught issue on heraldic grounds. Many of Dee's beliefs lived on in the person of Elias Ashmole, who died four years after Pope was born. It is not all that surprising if some tincture of the ancient lore hung around in people's minds at the start of the eighteenth century, even though the occult sciences seem generally to have been on the retreat.[107] Pope has no room for Brutus or Arthur in *Windsor-Forest*, but his use of Camden alone would have forced him to consider Windsor in its role as the very nerve-centre of English chivalric history (see pp. 171–4).

For at least two centuries writers on heraldry had stressed the basis of chivalry in a code of virtuous behaviour. A work like John Bossewell's *Workes of Armrie*, published by Richard Tottel in 1572, operates almost as a conduct book in places. Bossewell gives the title 'The Concordes of Armorie' to his opening section, which is a suggestive name in respect of the themes of *Windsor-Forest*. The author sets out a review of the four cardinal virtues, and analyses the qualities of each (4ʳ–8ʳ). It might almost be a programme for *The Faerie Queene*. The larger seventeenth-century manuals indulge in less overt moralizing, and technical description of charges now occupies a larger relative space. Nevertheless, Elias Ashmole begins his monumental survey of the Garter with a section on 'Vertue and Honour', instructing the reader on the very first page that honours exist to encourage merit by reward. He soon moves on to a chapter entitled 'Of the *Dignity, Honour,* and *Renown of* Knighthood' (Ashmole, l, 43). Only after going through these elaborate preliminaries does Ashmole turn to the actual lore of the Garter. Similarly, writers such as Dugdale, Sylvanus Morgan, and Holme, leading authorities in the grammar and syntax of armorial bearings, stress the underlying morality which this language serves. The duality is expressed in words like *courtesy, chivalry, nobility,* and *honour.* Moreover, the most popular charges on a coat of arms often had a lit-

---

[106] French (1989: 193–4).   [107] Thomas (1973: 197).

eral meaning together with an emblematic, mythological, or tropological sense: the sun may be the actual sun, or alternatively Apollo. This is of some importance in considering the arms of a particular family, where for example a pun on a name such as Greenwood may be augmented by a studied mythological aptness in the emblem chosen.

It follows that references in the poem to figures in myth may have more than a strictly iconographic element: they may also possess distinct heraldic overtones. For example, Pope refers at l. 39 to the agricultural prosperity of the Windsor region: 'Here *Ceres*' Gifts in waving Prospect stand.' We are familiar with the emblematic tradition in which Ceres was represented by her attribute of a sheaf of wheat; and under the literary aspect we can discern an allusion to the festival of Ceres in the first of *Georgic* Virgil's. But consider too Bossewell's description of the charge 'Garbe, or wheatshafe': '*Ceres* wyfe of *Osiris* king of Egypte, dyd first inuente sowynge of wheate, and Barlye, which before dyd growe wilde amōg other herbes . . . Of her, *Ouide* maketh mencion, saynge, *Prima Ceres vnco glebam dimouit ratro.* | *Prima dedit fruges: alimentaque initia terris.*'[108] The legends associated with Ceres formed a stock ingredient of masques and court entertainments. As Delarivier Manley put it, with perhaps over-heavy irony, in *The New Atalantis*, young aristocrats 'sung and acted the history of the gods, the rape of Proserpine, the descent of Ceres, the chastity of Diana, and such pieces that tended to the instruction of the mind'.[109]

However, in the ancient world the cult of Ceres had been connected with the plebs, and fertility rites in early modern England remained part of the popular mentality. A traveller in 1598 reported coming on a harvest-home celebration, in which country people crowned their last load of corn with flowers, 'having besides an image richly dressed, by which perhaps they would signifiy Ceres'.[110] This took place in the vicinity of Windsor, aptly to our purpose. A new historicist reading of *Windsor-Forest* might build on this range of associations, from hieratic forms to authentic folk customs. Pope was able to enlist a rich idiom, now unavailable to us, in which the image of 'laughing Ceres' (*Epistle to Burlington*, 176) might call up a variety of social practices and ideological contexts, from the most formal to the most demotic.

As noted in Chapter 2, the family crest of the Granvilles was a garb vert: Pope may therefore be attempting to compliment his patron by alluding to a branch of his 'achievement' as a peer. The idea that the former secretary at war was the best person to beat swords into ploughshares may strike us as implausible; but the recollection of his crest, with its agricultural associations, would help to cast him in this role. The use of the wheatsheaf as a charge goes back as far as the thirteenth century. It is to the present point that 'garbs are associated with the coats of arms of families who held land under the feudal system'.[111] When Lansdowne adopted the crest of the Granville family, with its garb vert, he was seeking to establish a claim to a lineage that went back as least as far as the Barons' Wars. But he was asserting a right to landed property, acreage as well as antiquity.

---

[108] Bossewell (1572: sig. 84ʳ).   [109] Manley (1991: 32).
[110] Laroque (1991: 158).   [111] Brockhampton Press (1997: 96).

There are similar considerations in respect of such common heraldic motifs as the eagle and the dove: as well as the palm and the olive. We need only think of the closing lines of *Windsor-Forest*, which adumbrate the new dispensation to follow in the wake of Utrecht:

> Where Peace descending bids her Olives spring,
> And scatters Blessings from her Dove-like Wing.
>
> (429–30)

This looks like an orthodox iconographic usage, and so it is. But the same message, tropologically, was conveyed by the heraldic employment of these images.[112] Bossewell glosses the olive: 'This is a Royall tree . . . It is a tree of peace', and goes on to narrate the story of the dove sent forth by Noah in Genesis 8. The heraldic example is of a field argent, with 'an hande Gules, holdyng a branche of Olive proper. *Diodore* sayeth, that the tree which beareth the Olive, is a figure of peace and tranquilitie.'[113] In one way, this tells us nothing we would not have known without the heraldic information; but in a poem where armorial language has figured so strongly, there may be an additional current of meaning if we can incorporate a sense of the olives 'springing' as in a coat of arms. Certainly when the reference is explicitly to a heraldic emblem, such as the one we have already encountered, 'The Lillies blazing on the regal Shield' (306), it is helpful to rediscover the moral attributes inscribed in the heraldic portrayal of the fleur-de-lis. According to Bossewell, 'Touching the floure, *Plinye* sayeth, that the Lillye is next to the Rose in worthynes and noblenes. Nothing is more gracious than the Lillye in fayrenes of colour, of swetenes of smell, and in effecte of workynge and vertue.'[114] The fleur-de-lis also appeared on the chief of the arms of Eton College, adjoining Windsor. One odd fact is that Pope's original draft, at l. 284 in the manuscript, reads 'With Iris blazeing on the Regal Shield' (Schmitz, 39). This was incorrect as a technical description of the quartering of the French arms, although the fleur-de-lis as a heraldic device is distinct from the lily, and is thought to represent a stylized form of the iris. Pope may or may not have known this.

Beyond this, it is worth considering the armorial context of this passage. Pope is celebrating the victories of Edward III and his son the Black Prince. When the prince died in 1376, he was buried not at Windsor but at Canterbury. In the cathedral his tomb was emblazoned with a variety of chivalric signs, particularly an effigy in plate and mail armour, with a royal crest above his coronet. Preserved in the same chapel are his sword, shield, and other appurtenances, as carried at his funeral. The shield has the arms of England and France quartered, just as Pope's line suggests; these are also found on the jupon or surcoat which the prince is wearing in his effigy. Another decorative motif on the tomb is the prince's shield 'For Peace', which is in effect the emblem of the Prince of Wales, three ostrich feathers, with the motto 'Ich dien'. Thus the son of the founder of the Order of the Garter (and one of the original knights)

---

[112] Doves carried an olive branch in their beak, as a common motif in heraldry.
[113] Bossewell (1572: sig. 74ᵛ).   [114] Bossewell (1572: sig. 76ʳ).

could be endowed with a more or less plausible connection with an honourable peace, through the transcendental language of heraldic pomp. Small matter that in historic reality, the Hundred Years War still had the greater part of its span to run.

Even those with the most limited interest in heraldry would have been alerted to the process of ennoblement, which had entered everyday politics at the close of 1711 with the creation of twelve new peers to force the peace treaty through the Lords. Equally, the sudden nomination of six new Garter knights in September 1712, among them the Earl of Oxford (thus elevated only the previous year) focussed attention on the ranks of chivalry. At this point Oxford overreached himself. Curiously, his big mistake in his dealings with the Queen also involved an issue of the creation of peers. Oxford married his son Lord Harley to a rich heiress, Lady Henrietta Cavendish-Holles, daughter of the Duke of Newcastle. According to Bolingbroke, indeed, this was the 'ultimate end' of Oxford's ministry (Swift, *Corr.* ii. 415). A condition of the marriage treaty, on the part of the Holles family, was that the duchy of Newcastle, dormant since the recent death of the last Duke, should be bestowed on the young Harley. Oxford thought, or claimed to have thought, that Anne had agreed to this measure, and boldly asked for the dukedom to be granted. The Queen angrily refused, and thereafter her attitude towards her chief minister seems to have changed. From this date (September 1712) until his fall almost two years later, Oxford was always struggling unsuccessfully to regain Anne's trust.

This is an index of just how much weight was then attached to dignities and the 'gradation of titles'. Each time a new peer was created, Edmund Curll would publish the lengthy preambles to their patents. Such credentials were prepared for the Utrecht negotiators, like Robinson and the Earl of Strafford; and around the same time for men like Harcourt, Orrery, and the Duke of Hamilton, who moved in the same circle as Lansdowne. Occasionally serious writers were involved in composing the patents. For instance, the Latin preamble to the one naming Charles Montagu as Baron Halifax in 1703 was written by Matthew Prior (Prior, ii. 764–5). Soon after the earldom of Oxford was created on 23 May 1711, the preamble for this peerage appeared in Latin, composed by John Freind, and English, the latter possibly drafted by Swift. Curll's edition came out on 4 June (see also *JTS* i. 265–78). As could often happen in this period, the citation managed to incur controversy, since it was felt by the Whigs to reflect on Godolphin.[115] Another dignity was postponed for a few days: this was Oxford's appointment as Lord Treasurer, deliberately made on 29 May, which was the anniversary of the Stuart restoration in 1660. It was Oxford, too, who persuaded the Queen to create the twelve new peerages at the end of the same year, an encroachment on a personal prerogative which she jealously guarded. The crest to the new Earl's coat of arms, we might add, was a silver castle with triple towers; it hardly needs saying that the only castle he frequented while he was the Queen's first minister was the one named in the poem, 'Where *Windsor*-Domes and pompous Turrets rise' (352).

[115] Ellis (1985: 461–2).

A similar preoccupation with rank can be seen in Oxford's principal coadjutor, Henry St John. Swift's first surviving letter to St John hints at dignities to come; 'If the Queen gave you a Dukedom and the Gart^r to morrow with the Treasurers staff at the end of them,' he wrote, 'I would regard you no more than if you were not worth a groat' (Swift, *Corr.* i. 205). Similarly, Pope held out to Lansdowne the prospect of a Garter he was never to wear. As for St John, he probably counted on a peerage along with his colleague Harley in 1711, but his elevation was delayed, perhaps because he was still needed in the Commons, as Swift suggested (*JTS* ii. 451). In July 1712 St John wrote to Oxford asking whether the Queen might be persuaded to grant him the revived title of Earl Bolingbroke. A lesser peerage was all that Anne would countenance. Belatedly he tried to withdraw his request, but was told the Queen had already made known her pleasure in naming him a viscount. 'He desir'd,' reported Swift, 'I would draw the Preamble of his Patent; but I excused my self from a Work that might lose me a great deal of Reputation, and get me very little. we would fain have the Court make him an Earl, but it will not be, and therefore he will not take the title of Bullenbrook, which is lately extinct in the elder Branch of his Family' (*JTS* ii. 545). A few days later Swift informed Stella that 'Secty St. John is made Viscount Bullinbrook' (*JTS* ii. 549–50). Oxford's rival had to settle for a seat in the Lords with a peerage inferior to that of his government colleagues, and this rankled with him ever afterwards. (It was the only viscountcy created in the Queen's entire reign.) Bolingbroke wrote to Sir William Wyndham several years later that he had been 'dragged into the House of Lords in such a manner as to make my promotion a punishment, not a reward' (Trevelyan, iii. 228). When Oxford fell, Bolingbroke was expecting to succeed as Lord Treasurer: 'I was told,' Swift wrote, 'that an earldom and the Garter were intended for him in a fortnight'—but the death of the Queen just five days later blighted these hopes (Swift, *Prose*, viii. 132). In any case, Bolingbroke would forfeit all the honours which he did manage to acquire, when he suffered attainder after fleeing to the service of the Pretender in 1715.

He had chosen a modest-looking motto to accompany his armorial bearings: *Nec quaerere nec spernere honorem*. His claim was soon to be tested. In October 1712, the six new Garter knights were announced. Oxford, Strafford, and the Duke of Hamilton were on the list, along with the Duke of Beaufort, an unregenerate Jacobite and a member of the Brothers' Club. Absent, to his lasting chagrin, was Bolingbroke. As we have seen in Chapter 2, Hamilton, the leader of the Scottish Jacobites, was to have become Anne's first ambassador to the French court, but he was killed in a duel shortly after his election to the Order. In this fraught and divisive atmosphere Bolingbroke set out for Paris, as the minister overseeing the secret peace negotiations. All this happened in the months leading up to the publication of *Windsor-Forest*, as Pope worked on his new version glorifying the settlement at Utrecht. To give an account of the negotiations which would have satisfied the Queen, Oxford, and Bolingbroke, as well as lesser figures such as Strafford or the dedicatee Lansdowne, would have tested the abilities of the most consummate politician. Small wonder that Pope had recourse to the obliquities of allegory and ritualized language.

The pertinence of such heraldic issues is a matter of judgement, not undisputed fact. But the material assembled here does at the very least support the interpretation of *Windsor-Forest* which this book sets out, in that the consecrated language of armorial lore acted out the same royalist myths as Stuart court pageantry. Undeniably, the assertions of heraldry at this date laid the bearer's claim to dynastic succession, to hereditary power, and to historic continuity. St John in reviving the Bolingbroke peerage was insinuating a connection with the Lancastrian kings. However, his crest of a falcon rising alluded to the Yorkist line, for the falcon was a badge of Edward III adopted by his grandson Richard II.

As for Harley, in selecting his title, he denominated himself as a successor to the Earls of Oxford in Plantagenet times, most obviously Aubrey de Vere, tenth Earl, a follower of the Black Prince. He took as his secondary title Earl of Mortimer, added in case the disputed Oxford earldom should have to be relinquished, as 'critics conned with unusual attention the genealogies which the College of Heralds prepared' (Churchill, iv. 327). By adopting this style Harley recalled the numerous prominent members of the Mortimer family, Welsh borderers as he was. The most famous of these was Roger Mortimer, first Earl of March, lover of Queen Isabella and effective ruler of the nation during the minority of Edward III. This Mortimer came to an ignominious end when he was hanged, drawn, and quartered at Tyburn in 1330. Naturally, Harley's opponents did not fail to make *this* connection. But the new peer probably had in mind rather the second Earl of March, grandson of the first Earl, who accompanied Edward III to the French wars, and was one of the original twenty-five Garter knights in 1348. Such links were bolstered by the adoption of heraldic motifs associated with the earlier peers. Heralds were active at this juncture in establishing, or inventing, genealogies, and as recently as 1709 Arthur Collins had produced the first edition of his *Peerage*, long the bible of family honours.[116] What look to us like feudal remnants were, as late as this, the siglia expressive of active political contestations.

A vital issue here concerns the Queen's prerogative in granting peerages. It is generally agreed that 'as the fount of honour, [she] was reluctant to dilute the peerage by additional creations', and further that 'in terms of creation and promotion in the peerage, the Queen's personal prejudices were crucial' (Gregg, 142–3). Hence her reluctance to accept Harley's proposal to create the twelve new peers, with the aim of speeding the passage of the peace measures, and her absolute refusal to elevate St John to the earldom he coveted. These were matters which lay, in her view, outside and above the day-to-day activities of parliamentary government. After the rush of peerages in 1711, only one new barony was created in the rest of her reign; no dukedom was instituted after November 1711 (when Hamilton was given a British title) and no earldom after that of Strafford in September of the same year.

We cannot be sure that Pope followed all the developments we have been tracing. What is certain is that by the time of the *Pastorals* he was alive to the imagistic possibilities of the royal arms, as we have already discovered in Chapter 4.[117] Moreover,

---

[116] Wagner (1960: 318–26).

[117] Pope also used a facsimile of the royal arms at the head of the later *Dunciad*, in a mock-announcement by the Lord Chamberlain.

evidence exists that, only a few years later, he was considered to have some skill as a heraldic designer. In 1719 he was asked to 'propose a Seal with a suitable Motto to it, for the Royal Academy of Musick' (*Life*, 853). The directors of this enterprise included his close friend Arbuthnot, who would have known if this had been an absurd request. In fact Pope declined.[118]

The last indication is more speculative. As we have seen, Pope describes the landscape of the Forest in these terms: 'Here waving Groves a checquer'd Scene display' (17), with a near-echo of the technical term *checky*. Now, that very field is actually found in one coat of arms, described in non-technical language as 'a blue and white chequered fess on gold'.[119] (The technical formula is 'or, a fess chequy azure and argent'.) This was the shield of the Stuart, more properly Stewart, family. Likewise the groves of Windsor, part admitting and part excluding light, alternate the hues in a single couplet of checkered tones:

> Here in full Light the russet Plains extend;
> There wrapt in Clouds the blueish Hills ascend.
>
> (23–4)

In the background are the 'fruitful Fields', with their 'tufted Trees and springing Corn' (26–7).[120] A little later on, we hear of the 'yellow Harvests' spread across this countryside: liberty 'leads the golden Years' of prosperity (88, 92). Symbolically, the Stuart dispensation covers the earth with a tincture of gold. Thus the brightly lit plains and the 'blueish Hills', with the waving cornfields in the background, match the alternating strips of dark and light—*azure* and *argent*—on the field, *or*, of the Stuart arms.[121] It is as though Pope has placed Anne's hereditary family bearing as an *escutcheon of pretence* on the royal arms, treating her as the bride of the nation.[122] Since the object of such marshalling is to indicate 'sovereignty, dominion, alliance, descent, or pretension' (Fox-Davies, 523), this would be a coded way of asserting the right of the Stuarts to the throne. It all begins to appear less and less like a coincidence.

[118] Many others with whom Pope was in contact were jealous of their armorial dignity. For example, no less than eighteen badges belonging to 'the illustrious family' of Stafford were certified by Garter King of Arms in 1720 (Neubecker 1997: 208). Garter was John Anstis, who had just managed to clear himself from charges laid at the time of his arrest as a suspected Jacobite in 1715 (see p. 170, above). His great *Register of the Most Noble Order of the Garter* was to follow in 1724.

[119] Scott-Giles (1965: 85).

[120] The oak was the badge of the Stewart clan, as remarked in Ch. 4.

[121] The two colors blue and white were enough to identify the Pretender in a contemporary account of the ceremony planned by the Whigs to mark the accession of Queen Elizabeth: see *Protestant Post Boy*, 20 Nov. 1711, quoted by Ashton (1883: 347). They also featured in the arms of the house of Lancaster and their livery—a connection, as we have just seen, which Bolingbroke was seeking to revive.

[122] In this case this seems fanciful, we should recall that the Cromwells, William III and George III all placed such an inescutcheon (for Nassau, Hanover, etc.) on the royal arms, while the children of Queen Victoria and Prince Albert introduced those of Saxony.

6

The War and the Peace

It is impossible to make full sense of *Windsor-Forest* without understanding something of the peace process. The tortuous negotiations went on for two years, although this was by no means the first attempt to bring the long drawn-out War of the Spanish Succession toward a conclusion. Like it or not, Pope was entering a fierce public debate. His aim was primarily to endorse the settlement at Utrecht, without elaborating on its detailed provisions. He wished to celebrate the Queen, who had not disguised her wish to see an end to a conflict which had dragged on relentlessly since the opening weeks of her reign. At the same time that the poem recognized Anne as the titular architect of the peace, it implicitly endorsed the part played by Oxford and Bolingbroke, along with lesser instruments of government policy. Strafford as First Lord of the Admiralty would be flattered by Pope's tribute to naval power and as negotiator at Utrecht by lines extolling the peace. By courtesy, at least, Lansdowne could be commended for his stint as secretary at war from 1710 to 1712 (see Chapter 2, above), little as this had to do with any events now unfolding.

This chapter reviews the context in which the war ended and the treaty came to be signed, as well as some of the events during this phase which surface in the text of *Windsor-Forest*. Inevitably, the fortunes of the Duke and Duchess of Marlborough will be central to this discussion. But to set Pope's poem, especially its conclusion, in its proper worldwide frame, we need to look also at some related matters: these include the visit of the Indian kings to London in 1710, the inception of the South Sea Company in the following year, and the sudden burst of interest in Pacific voyages which occurred after the return of Woodes Rogers in 1712.

LET DISCORD CEASE

> PAX, PAX, PAX, or A PACIFICK POSTSCRIPT to the *POST-BOY*
>
> *Post-Boy*, 3 April 1713

By the time that the treaty came to be signed at Utrecht, the war had lost popularity with large sections of the public.[1] Few grand military successes on the scale of

---

[1] 'Tories had opposed the war from the beginning; as early as the 1702 election they had said that the reason for the war was Whig greed for war profits' (Richards 1972: 136).

Blenheim and Ramillies seemed to appear on the horizon. The bitter campaign waged in the press against Godolphin and Marlborough had helped to sway the voting in 1710, giving the Tories a majority of about 150. At that time, the Sacheverell affair had arrogated most attention. As the nation prepared for the election of 1713, it was the peace treaty which dominated in the prints and pamphlets. Of course, we must not imagine a modern electorate kept informed round the clock with coverage of the issues. All the same, there were about a quarter of a million voters (admittedly less than 5 per cent of the total population) and politicians enjoyed abundant means of influencing their decisions, by licit means or otherwise. If one thing is certain, it is that Pope's patron Lord Lansdowne was deeply involved in the run-up to the elections. He stood unrivalled as the principal borough-monger in Cornwall, the county most disproportionately endowed with seats—forty-four constituencies. His private interest was far more vital to the fortunes of the ministry than any moderate ability he had shown in government or than the privileges attached to his position at court.

As early as September 1712, when Pope was still hard at work on completing his poem, Lansdowne wrote to the Lord Treasurer, expressing his concern that the two seats in the borough of Truro were in danger of being lost at the next election. This was despite the fact that the peer had 'appropriated every penny of [his] own rents for service of this kind'. With some justification, Lansdowne claimed that 'the contention and expense' involved in the election had risen to an unprecedented level.[2] In fact the Tories were to do well in the election, and afterwards a gratified Lansdowne would send Oxford a list of those who had succeeded: it was 'the largest return of persons particularly devoted to the Queen's service, and the interest of their country, that ever came from hence, in which no less than twenty are of my own nomination'.[3] While other factors entered into these political calculations, it is clear that electoral managers required popular issues as well as a store of money and beer to hand out. Expenses were one thing, but contention did not go on in a vacuum: the big issues of the day surfaced even in tiny closed corporations such as Cornwall so amply possessed, and they decided the result in all the larger boroughs and counties. While it is absurd to look on *Windsor-Forest* as an electoral manifesto, we should be extraordinarily naive to suppose that Lansdowne would have happily seen his name stand at the head of a poem which offered anything less than wholehearted support to the peace treaty.

Plainly, the rights and wrongs of the Utrecht settlement formed a heavily contentious issue. Adherents of the government tried to portray the war party as a narrow circle of corrupt contractors and city brokers reaping financial gain from the continued hostilities. In reality, the opposition could draw on a number of popular issues and emotionally charged arguments. Many felt that the great Duke had been shabbily treated, after his long and successful career as a general. The restraining orders imposed on Ormonde, which caused him effectively to desert Prince Eugène in the field, contrasted sharply in the public imagination with the mighty days

---

[2] Lansdowne to Oxford, 30 Sept. 1712, cited by Speck (1970: 51). See also Handasyde (1933: 120–1).
[3] Lansdowne to Oxford, 11 Sept. 1713, cited by Speck (1970: 34).

of Marlborough's campaigns a few years earlier. Others were embarrassed by the duplicities involved in the negotiations, as well as the betrayal of Dutch allies. Even the Tories were divided among themselves on collusion with the French, and the commercial clauses which followed on the main treaty alienated some of the ministry's natural supporters.

The war of words surrounding the end of this conflict has been narrated many times. It happens that some outstanding polemical writers were ranged against one another in the debate: Swift, Pope, Manley, Maynwaring, and Steele amongst others. Above all, the contest of those mighty opposites, Marlborough and Swift, has come to appear as a classic struggle between pen and sword—although the Duke had plenty of pens busy on his behalf, in the public prints and in the private communications of his formidable Duchess. *Windsor-Forest* makes no reference by name to John or Sarah Churchill, and equally the word 'Blenheim' is studiously omitted. However, the text is pervaded by allusions to warfare, many of which can only be read in context as pertaining to the particular war which was just coming to its end. Moreover, the poem attempts in more than one place a systematic subversion of Addison's *Campaign*, the work which had done most to deify the victor at Blenheim. A careful review of the evidence will show that Pope was very well aware, too, of what was happening in the neighbouring county to his own, as the nation's grateful tribute to Marlborough slowly took shape in the quiet environs of Oxford. Indeed, if Pope had wished like so many other poets of the day to shower complimentary references on the rising palace, he need not have made the slightest alteration to his design. The little Evenlode meanders round the southern edge of the Blenheim estate, and then just 4 miles downriver it joins 'the winding *Isis*' (340). Nothing would have been easier than to add the Evenlode to the catalogue of tributaries joining the Thames, and to insert a paean to Marlborough at this point.

DUKE AND DUCHESS

English politics under Anne are inseparable from the Duke and Duchess of Marlborough, the most powerful man and woman among the Queen's subjects for most of her reign. Any work of literature which dealt with the history of this period would inescapably run head-on into these two figures. Pope had a larger problem, which meant that he had either to confront the Churchills or to devise a stratagem to evade the issues they raised. This was first because he was not dealing with abstract constitutional issues, but was allegorizing the fate of Britain in the person of the monarch herself. As everyone knows, the couple had a uniquely close relationship with the Queen. A second difficulty arose because the poem dealt with the cessation of a war which had dominated Europe for two decades, and which had seen the Duke play a decisive part throughout its course.

We need to keep a hold on both these points if we are to understand the situation in which Pope wrote his poem. The Churchills had identified themselves with Anne as early as 1683. John Churchill came to prominence under Charles II and served the

Duke of York, later James II, whose mistress was his sister Arabella. Sarah became lady of the bedchamber to Princess Anne soon after her marriage to Prince George of Denmark in 1683. As Anglicans they had limited influence during the reign of James II, even though John played a distinguished part in averting what could have been a disaster at Sedgemoor. Equally, his defection from James to the incoming William in 1688, together with Sarah's flight to Nottingham with Princess Anne, failed to ensure them an easy ride during the reign of William and Mary. The Churchills remained loyal to Anne, and this led to strained relations with both members of the royal couple. William could not afford to dispense with his most competent general, but little genuine trust evolved between the two men.

All this changed with the accession of Anne. She immediately appointed Marlborough as captain-general, bestowed the Garter on him, and gave further marks of her favour, including a dukedom in December 1702. His most spectacular victories in the resumed Continental campaigns occurred soon afterwards, at a time when Sarah still held the place of closest confidence in Anne's household. Soon after his triumph at Blenheim came a spectacular pageant through the streets of London, and then a royal grant of the manor of Woodstock, with over 15,000 acres, a site truly fit for a palace. In her announcement to parliament, Anne called it 'the Castle of Blenheim', as though to emphasize its capacity to rival Windsor. Sarah, who disliked the entire project, had thought Christopher Wren the only architect of the stature required for such a monumental undertaking, but she was overruled and the Duke's Kit-Cat friend Vanbrugh brought in to do the job. At his new playhouse in the Haymarket, Vanbrugh even managed to introduce the main prospect of Blenheim into the scenery for George Granville's play *The British Enchanters*.[4] Meanwhile Sarah had managed 'to engross the three most prestigious and lucrative court positions open to a woman: groom of the stole, mistress of the robes, and keeper of the privy purse' (Bucholz, 111).

By the middle of the reign, things were starting to go wrong. Marlborough unwisely considered an offer by the Emperor to become viceroy of the Netherlands, though in the end he was forced to refuse it. His military progress no longer made for a saga of unbroken success, and he faced rifts with some of the allies. In 1709 he petitioned the Queen to be made captain-general for life, a mistake which his enemies would bring up for the rest of his days. Meanwhile Sarah had steadily lost ground with Anne, whom she accused of lesbian urges after her royal mistress chose a new favourite in Abigail Masham. In August 1708 the Queen and her subject almost came to blows as their coach drove to St Paul's for a thanksgiving service after the battle of Oudenard. After this their relations never regained cordiality, let alone the former intimacy. Sarah now became almost as much a liability for her husband as she had previously been an asset. Money was even withheld for the building of Blenheim, to the delight of the Tory squires who had resented such costly outlay on the 'gold mine' of the palace.

---

[4] McCormick (1991: 121) (where Granville is wrongly identified as a member of the Kit-Cat Club). For the play, see Ch. 2, above.

By January 1711 Anne's patience was at an end, and Sarah was forced to hand over the gold key which symbolized her office as mistress of the robes.[5] In a last effort to gain further respite for his wife, the Duke abased himself: 'The invincible captain and statesman who for ten years had led Europe against France, now fell on his knees at the Queen's feet in personal supplication for his wife's employment . . . Let us make haste to draw the curtain upon an unnatural spectacle which reduces the stature of the soldier without raising the majesty of a queen' (Churchill, iv. 309–10). All that the Tories wished was to draw the curtain on Sarah's long period of influence. Since there were hardly any secrets at court, Pope might have remembered this scene in his poem:

> There Kings shall sue, and suppliant States be seen
> Once more to bend before a *British* QUEEN.
>
> (382–3)

Yet the Duke remained in post. Even the fall of the ministry in 1710 did not topple him; he had been allied with Godolphin and Harley in earlier years, but he was anachronistically dedicated to the service of the monarch, in an age of increasing polarity and party-strife. Not until the end of 1711 did the blow fall, in the aftermath of the Queen's speech to parliament on 7 December and the fierce debate in the Lords on a motion by the Earl of Nottingham proposing 'No peace without Spain.'[6] At the turn of the year, the Duke was dismissed, Ormonde was installed as commander with orders to conduct a campaign of negative inutility, and the negotiations for peace went ahead. Late in November 1712 the Duke began a self-imposed exile on the Continent, at the very moment Pope was busily revising *Windsor-Forest*. Sarah joined her husband at Maastricht in February, shortly before the poem appeared. Neither was to return to England until after the Queen's death.

This, then, was the hot news when *Windsor-Forest* came before the public. The peace treaty had not yet been signed, still less ratified; but the Duke and Duchess had made their well-publicized departures. On the night that reports of the peace finally broke, the Tories embarked on robust celebrations, while a Whig gathering hosted by Samuel Garth and attended by George Berkeley drank a half-hearted toast to the absent Duke, 'though they had not the heart to speak one word against the peace'.[7] To say that the poet had followed all these events closely is to assume very little, as almost everyone in the country had done so. Half-jokingly (but *only* half) Pope would explicate a passage in *The Rape of the Lock* as a reference to the Duke's dismissal. As we saw in Chapter 3, Pope suggests in *A Key to the Lock* that the game of ombre in

---

[5] Roberts (1975: 107–10). The following June, work stopped on the palace, and was not resumed until after the Queen's death. The Duke was even threatened with a government lawsuit to force him to return unauthorized expenditure on the construction (Churchill, iv. 477).

[6] The Queen's speech, drafted of course by the ministry, had virtually accused the Duke of being one of 'those who delight in war', though she afterwards claimed she meant no more than to quote from the prayer book, i.e. Psalm 68: 30 in the morning service. From a gallery in the Lords' chamber, the Queen listened as Marlborough justified his conduct in the debate, which resulted in an unexpected defeat for the ministry. The Duke seldom spoke in parliament.

[7] Berkeley (1948–57: viii. 67).

Canto III represents an allegory of the War. In the same passage, he mischievously glosses the lines on 'mighty *Pam*', who is condemned to fall 'undistinguished' in the course of the game (iii. 61–4), as a 'Description of the Disgrace under which the D. of *M.* then suffer'd' (*Prose*, i. 193). Sideswipes of this kind are characteristic of a pamphlet which appears to support many of the political readings which, on the surface, it offers to expunge.[8]

Throughout the war, John Churchill had occupied the centre of the national stage, as courtier, politician, diplomat, and soldier. Every year, until the Harley ministry pointedly abstained in 1710, parliament had offered him a vote of thanks, giving him the semi-official status of saviour of the nation. Along with his wife, he had received unprecedented marks of royal favour—not even Elizabeth or James I had bestowed so much largesse on their chosen cronies. After Blenheim, the Queen had even wanted to bestow his annual dole of £5,000 on his heirs in perpetuity, but the Tories voted this down in parliament. Once, around this time, elderly John Evelyn came across 'the Victorious Duke of Marlborow' at Whitehall, wearing 'a most rich George [Garter badge] in a Sardonix, set with Diamonds of an inestimable Value'. 'For the rest', Evelyn adds with seeming surprise, 'very plaine' (*ED* v. 584).

THE PALACE

On 17 February 1705 that the Queen announced to parliament her plans concerning the 'castle' she was giving to the Churchills. Within a month the necessary Act (3 & 4 Anne, c. 4) had been passed. The measure conferred on the Duke, in recognition of his services during the war, the title to some 1,800 acres of Oxfordshire, the site of a medieval palace and a royal hunting ground. It comprised 'all that piece or parcel of ground commonly called . . . Woodstock Park'.[9]

From the moment that the foundation-stone was laid in the following June, Blenheim served as a shrine not just to the battle but to its victor: the stone itself was 8 feet square and inlaid in pewter with an inscription, ending with the name of the benefactor—Anna Regina. Actually the Queen never set eyes on the house. In time the palace of the Churchills would be lined with paintings and tapestries lauding the Duke's feats, as well as trophies of the war. 'For ten years the shuttles flew . . . weaving the bright wools back and forth, transforming the carnage of war into great art, and canny Jack Churchill into a great British hero.'[10] Sarah herself could not help complaining that the tapestry showing the great battle on the wall of the Bow Window Room was on too large a scale—it measured 25 feet by 14 feet. Then there were the drums and standards of his defeated opponents, and even, on the south front, a marble bust of Louis XIV, weighing 30 tons, which had been filched from the siege

---

[8] As has been pointed out, an obvious association of the reference to 'the Fights of *Lu*' would be William III's palace, Het Loo (see Erskine-Hill 1984: 190; 1996: 80–1). The king had restored an old castle near Apeldoorn in Gelderland at great expense between 1685 and 1694: Tory critics complained that Windsor had been gutted to 'aggrandise' Loo in sumptuous style.

[9] Green (1997: 67).   [10] Fowler (1991: 40).

of Tournai.[68] Gifts from the crowned heads of Europe were squeezed in among the gilded Italian furniture and the serried rows of old masters. A giant silver centre-piece portrayed the Duke on horseback, writing back to his wife news of his victory on the Danube (see p. 144). Vast *trompe-l'œil* murals in the Saloon by Louis Laguerre depicted Marlborough's triumphs, and rivalled anything Verrio could do for the Stuarts at Windsor. On the ceiling of the Great Hall, James Thornhill painted *The Glorification of the Duke of Marlborough* at a height of almost 70 feet from the ground: Britannia offers a wreath to the Mars-like warrior, with Plenty pouring out a cornucopia of fruits. (Pope reserves these mythological properties for the destiny of the nation itself: *WF*, 42, 91–2). Further up still on the rooftop, among the para-pets and finials, huge pinnacles carved by Grinling Gibbons depicted the Duke's coronet crushing the fleur-de-lis beneath it. The colonnades were stuffed with the trophies of battle.

The ancient manor of Woodstock had just about survived, perched in romantic neglect above the rivulet of the Glyme trickling towards the Thames. Locals found it amusing that the architect should have designed a bridge worthy of a Roman con-queror to span the valley formed by this piddling little river, and an epigram on the Duke was coined: 'The lofty arch his high ambition shows, | The stream an emblem of his bounty flows.'[11] With Henry II's manor, there were at least some genuine his-torical associations to link the place with royalty: Elizabeth I had been imprisoned in the gatehouse during the reign of her sister. In the Civil War the house had served as a royalist garrison until the parliamentary forces launched a successful siege in 1646: it was acquired by a private citizen who sold off many of its materials. Van-brugh liked the ruins none the less, and took up residence there for a time. He even sent to Sarah some reasons to 'preserve the small Remains of ancient Woodstock Manour'.[12] But the practically minded Duchess was enraged that he had failed to demolish the antiquated structure, and finally got rid both of the architect and what she called his 'folly'. When Pope visited the site, he was favourably impressed by Rosamond's Well and the nearby 'hill where remains only a piece of a wall of the old Palace of *Henry* the Second' (*Corr.* i. 432). This single portion of Blenheim immune from the poet's criticism was the very thing Sarah had determined to pull down. It was levelled in 1723. By that time the Duchess had finally broken off relations with Vanbrugh, and banned him from visiting Blenheim at all.

The park and gardens had been laid out by Henry Wise, who was famous in his time for turning a wilderness into Eden. Pope does not mention them, but he prob-ably cared little for the huge 'military' plantations and sanded paths, the forests of full-grown trees imported, the alleys of plaited limes, the rigid parterres near the house and the straight avenues.[13] 'Grove nods at grove, each alley has a brother.' Van-brugh himself had drawn up the original plan for the formal gardens, with a poly-gonal space filled by a parterre around which curled a fortified walkway, a small bastion at each corner. The adjoining trees were shaped into an almost military hexagon. It was all showy ornament, and no use. Nothing could compare with the

---

[11] Fowler (1991: 63).   [12] Downes (1987: 347).   [13] Green (1967: 107–8).

sacred groves of Windsor, which Pope was able to regard with some indulgence as a
microcosm of the nation and a site of modest private life.

Just occasionally, during the Duke's lifetime, the palace was used for amateur the-
atricals, as when *All for Love* was performed by a cast including the Churchill grand-
daughters in 1719. But all along it had served as a kind of a giant stage-set.[14] What
makes the building so evocative today, and so appropriate to the heritage industry,
is partly this feeling it gives off, of histrionic splendour invading a domestic space.
To Pope it was a gift, a symbol in the making of everything *Windsor-Forest* opposes.
It is apt that Sarah's former page, who played Mark Antony in the Blenheim production, should have worn a diamond-hilted sword which had been given to John
Churchill by the Emperor himself. Even the costumes were made from Italian silks
that had been intended to drape the walls of the house. Everything, in this place,
turned into conspicuous display; and almost everything derived, in one way or another, from the spoils of war. The palace spoke of private grandeur and military
glory. Unlike the castle at Windsor, with its noble and sometimes tragic past,
Blenheim was a storehouse of 'inglorious Triumphs', preserved in the Brobdigna-
gian mounds of loot amassed by its overreaching master and mistress.

It was quite impossible then for anyone to move around the house without
bumping into some heroic image of its owner:

Then all the mighty Dukes of Marlborough joined in: the white marble Duke above the Hall
doorway, the blue-togaed Duke on the Hall ceiling, the chariot-driving Duke above the
Saloon's marble wastes. And in the many great gilded mirrors . . . was the real Duke . . . [as]
he took a long look at Kneller's portrait of handsome John Churchill in his prime, life-size in
armour, the Garter on his knee, a crimson and ermine mantle on his left arm.[15]

One day in 1720 a sculpture of Minerva, in her guise as martial goddess, 'clutching
her javelin in one hand and her shield in the other, toppled from her perch atop the
great north-front portico, and crashed on the roof'. It was never properly repaired.[16]
Soon afterwards the Duke tumbled from his own perch, and all the megalomaniac
display could not save him from the common fate of humanity.

The palace was not yet ready for occupation when *Windsor-Forest* appeared, but its
progress had long been monitored by Marlborough's friends. As early as 1705 a
group of leading Kit-Cat luminaries, accompanied by Vanbrugh and Jacob Tonson,
had made a special visit to check progress on the building work, when they were received by Nicholas Hawksmoor, then assistant surveyor. Along with them went
none other than George Granville.[17] It is well attested that Pope regarded Blenheim
as showy and lacking in that delicate balance of scale and propriety he sought in
architecture. The best evidence comes in a letter to an unnamed correspondent,
possibly Martha Blount, which the editor dates around September 1717:

I will not describe *Bl*—in particular . . . only take a short account, which I will hazard my

---

[14] For theatrical models in the design, see McCormick (1991: 89–95.)
[15] Fowler (1991: 69).   [16] Fowler (1991: 70).   [17] Lynch (1971: 59).

little credit is not an unjust one. I never saw so great a thing with so much littleness in it: I think the Architect built it entirely in compliance to the taste of its Owners: for it is the most inhospitable thing imaginable, and the most selfish: it has, like their own hearts, no room for strangers, and no reception for any person of superior quality to themselves.

The physical appearance of the house reflected this lack of propriety and judgement:

When you look upon the Outside, you'd think it large enough for a Prince; when you see the Inside, it is too little for a Subject; and has not conveniency to lodge a common family. It is a house of Entries and Passages; among which are three Vista's through the whole, very use-lessly handsome . . . And as if it were fatal [fated?] that some trifling littleness should every where destroy the grandeur, there are in the chief front two semicircles of a lower structure than the rest, that cut off the angles, and look as if they were purposely design'd to hide a loftier and nobler piece of building, the top of which appears above them. In a word, the whole is a most expensive absurdity; and the Duke of Shrewsbury gave a true character of it, when he said, it was a great *Quarry of Stones above ground*. (*Corr*. i. 431–2)[18]

The entire passage calls to mind the satire of bad architectural taste in the *Epistle to Burlington*, especially the reference there to 'huge heaps of littleness around' (109). The allusion to the painted ceilings of the chapel in that *Epistle*, where we see 'sprawl the Saints of Verrio or Laguerre', lends credence to the theory that Pope used Blenheim as one of his models for Timon's villa.[19]

A year after the last letter, Pope wrote to Martha Blount from his temporary base near Oxford, in the wake of heavy thunder. He observes, 'I must acquaint you that here in our neighbourhood, Blenheim, the most proud & extravagant heap of Tow-ers in the nation, stands untouchd' (*Corr*. i. 480). This makes a direct contrast with the fitting majesty of 'Windsor-Domes' (352). It matters little that the jocular epitaph on Vanbrugh, 'Lie heavy on him, Earth, for he | Laid many a heavy load on thee', may not be by Pope at all. There are many signs that Pope from early on regarded Blenheim as all too apt a residence for its grasping owners.[20]

Late in life the poet projected two odes on moral subjects. One was concerned with the folly of ambition, and told of a massive heap of stones found by a traveller lying in a desert landscape. The clue to this enigmatic sight is provided by a shep-herd: 'From the rubble of history and legend that he supplies, the traveler eventually makes out that these are the remains of Blenheim, all that is apparently now left of the Marlborough name and of the once spirited and cultivated people who built that palace for "the Deliverer of Europe".'[21] This fable makes perfect sense in rela-tion to *Windsor-Forest*—and *of* the poem. Marlborough will be consigned to the

---

[18] Similar ideas are expressed in an epigram 'Upon the Duke of Marlborough's House at Woodstock', which has generally been attributed to Pope: see *TE* vi. 412.

[19] See Brownell (1978: 309–17); *Prose*, ii. 420.

[20] Sarah herself had admitted by this time that the work at Blenheim had become 'a chaos which only God Almighty could finish' (quoted by Green 1997: 78).

[21] Quoted in *Life*, 771. Benjamin Hoadly's prologue for the performance of *All for Love* likewise sees the palace as built from 'a heap of stones', but asserts that, although these stones would eventually crum-ble, the Duke's great name would stand through the ages (see Fowler 1991: 32).

rubble of history, like his grandiose mansion. Deliverance, if it comes, will be the work of Anne, aided by the public-spirited virtue of her ministers.

The story has a curious and little-known epilogue, as far as Pope is concerned. As soon as the Duke died, his widow chose to set up further memorials. Their palace became the private version of an imperial war museum. Here arose a triumphal arch with proud inscriptions in Latin; and here was planted a bust for the gallery. There a Doric column of victory was launched 130 feet into the sky, citing the Acts of Parliament by which Blenheim was endowed on the Churchills in perpetuity. On its top was placed a lead statue of the hero in classical costume which rose 25 feet from the top of the pillar. Sarah was most anxious that the fourth side of the obelisk, facing the main house, should carry a suitable panegyric to the Duke. After his death his widow asked her elderly suitor, the Duke of Somerset, to approach Pope, as a possible author for this encomium—even though the Churchills had long recognized that the poet's 'inclinations [were] so different from ours as to Liberty'. According to Somerset, Pope expressed himself willing to undertake the commission, although he had never done anything of the sort before. His one condition was that he should remain anonymous. In the event the Duchess decided not to go ahead, believing that she might end up in the Tower if the column were to proclaim the truth of what had gone on under Anne: her *bête noire* Walpole now ruled affairs. So Pope's unlikely panegyric to the Duke never came into existence. It was replaced by an inscription composed by Bolingbroke, who had always held Marlborough in high personal esteem despite their often antithetical politics. Sarah claimed she had come to feel a certain fondness for 'useful knaves', and approved the draft of a terse, almost Tacitean account of that heroic victory near the Danube. So the marble slab finally bore a tribute by one who had done so much to bring an end to 'the Marlborough wars' and to cut down the general in his pride.[22]

Apart from the column of victory, the main shrine in the Churchills' palace was the chapel, where Sarah had set up an elaborate baroque tomb. It was executed by Rysbrack to a design by William Kent. Vaingloriously, the tomb showed on its base the French surrender at Blenheim, rather than the Duke's surrender of his soul to the Almighty. The dragon of Envy was crushed underfoot; Fame brandished her trumpet, and the whole edifice was surmounted by Churchill's arms, themselves capped by the ducal coronet which Oxford and Bolingbroke had never attained. All this was redolent of the flourish and swagger of the Roman purple. Sarah even had the effrontery to put up a life-size statue of Queen Anne in her Garter badge—reclaiming the dignities she had lost during the Queen's lifetime. If the Churchills' home could be literally described as palatial, then their furnishings and fittings were imperial. In the eyes of the Tories, it rankled too that the Duke and Duchess had been granted the royal manor at Woodstock—a historic demesne which inspired almost as much monarchical and poetic legend as Windsor itself. Tickell had boasted

---

[22] Green (1967: 247–50). Other memorials to the Duke were projected: Hawksmoor designed a second great arch, 36 feet high, to seal off the end of the Grand Avenue (a double row of 686 elm trees, laid out on a castellated design). But this and further schemes were never carried out.

of the removal of 'Britannia's hero' to the 'fairest spot of fair Britannia's isle', and fancied that the 'weary'd champion' might be glimpsed by 'Rosamonda fleeting o'er the green' (Chalmers, iii. 378). Commoners by birth, both of them, the couple had appropriated the legacy of centuries.

Perhaps the Duke and Duchess acted like royalty, but so in a sense they were. After Blenheim, had not the Holy Roman Emperor created Marlborough the prince of Mindelheim? The offer was first made by Leopold I, as one of the last acts in his own reign, and renewed by his son and successor, Joseph I. The honour cost the Duke some £4,500. Thus it came about that in November 1706 he was formally invested with the Bavarian fiefdom, though the elaborate ceremonial went on in his absence (Coxe, i. 380). The Queen was happy enough to countenance the deed. (As a result of the full peace treaty in 1714, the Duke lost this dignity when Bavaria was returned to its former Elector.) So the new prince could festoon his palace, not just with his armour and his ceremonial sword, but also with his coat of arms, which now bore the Habsburg double-eagle 'displayed'. Heraldically speaking, this was a supporter, but it seemed almost to crush the insignia of the Garter in its embrace. Out of the ducal coronet sprang the eagle's two heads, and above them in Laguerre's painting for the saloon at Blenheim was a further coronet, surmounted by a ball and cross, the insignia of a prince—or of the Queen herself. 'King John II', his opponents had labelled him (Churchill, iv. 158).

In his shrewd way Defoe perceived the fact that this was a 'national Building', displaying the 'Bounty' of the state, for it was a palace 'too big for any British Subject to fill, if he lives at his own expence'. Nothing else in his opinion could justify 'the vast Design', with a grand bridge without a river 'like the *Escurial* in *Spain*', offices big enough for a family of three hundred, and outhouses 'fit for the Lodgings of a Regiment of Guards.' Further:

The Extent of the Fabric, the Avenues, the Salons, Galleries, and Royal Apartments; nothing below Royalty and a Prince, can support such an Equipage suitable to the living in such a House: And one may without a Spirit of Prophecy say, it seems to intimate, that some time or other *Blenheim* may and will return to be as the *Old Woodstock* once was, *the Palace of a King*. (*Tour*, ii. 427–8)

A bad prophecy, read in a literal-minded way, but one that expresses the common view—manifestly shared by Pope—that the Churchills had fallen victim to a monstrous *folie de grandeur*. They had privatized a national asset, and defrauded the country which had sacrificed so much during those long years of war. At the same time they had built a grand town house in St James's, set on the line of the Mall with the palace, and looking out on the Queen's own garden. Wren began the designs in 1709, and it was ready in two years. Once again Laguerre was employed to burnish the walls with frescos of military glory.

The classical status which had been accorded to Marlborough reached its apogee just one year before *Windsor-Forest* with the appearance of Jacob Tonson's edition of *C. Julii Caesaris Quae Extant*, edited by Samuel Clarke, the liberal divine—some were to say Arian heretic. The frontispiece to this resplendent folio spreads across two pages, with a bust of Caesar attended by a muse blowing a trumpet, against a backdrop of palatial Roman buildings. The dedication to Marlborough flanks Kneller's portrait. Full-page plates are garnished with the coat of arms of subscribers. In the text elaborate illustrations depict landscapes featured in the *Commentaries*, with mountains, rivers, and walled towns:

The foreground provides side-framing trees with luxuriant foliage, shading resting warriors. Everywhere there is precise and exquisite detail: in every leaf of the trees, every curl of a horse's mane, in the foreground; and in the clustered houses of the towns, the ships at sea, and the tiny figures of individual horsemen in the middle ground.[23]

The whole spectacular project, which has been described as 'the most sumptuous classical work which this country has produced', was stage-managed by Tonson, publisher to the great and the good. It constituted a kind of Whig vindication of the war—no accident that the engravings were based on the work of Dutch topographic artists such as Cornelis Huyberts. Right at the heart of the project is the dedication to Marlborough, the modern Caesar. Nor was it by chance that this came about: in 1709 the Duke of Marlborough had been 'admitted extraordinary' to the Kit-Cat Club, and Jacob Tonson was 'order'd to dedicate Caesar's Commentaries to him, and not to the Duke of Ormond as he had promised'.[24] Six members of the club were deputed to compose the dedicatory epistle. Plainly, *Windsor-Forest* had much to undo in order to reinstate the Queen at the centre of Pope's Arcadian landscape.

THE CAPTAIN DEPARTS

When Marlborough died at Windsor Lodge in 1722, the send-off he received was truly worthy of his rank, 'a scene of solemn splendour and martial pomp'. The funeral was delayed for almost eight weeks, until 9 August. In the meanwhile the press had been full of comments for and against the departed hero. Ponderous elegies proclaimed his greatness, while Mist's *Journal* launched an attack which resulted in the arrest of its printers. The rival *Journal* of John Applebee carried a sounding threnody, probably from the hand of Daniel Defoe, which meditated on the end of mortal life: 'Not all his immense Wealth, the Spoils and Trophies of his Enemies, the Bounty of his grateful Mistress, and the Treasures amass'd in War and Peace; not all the mighty bulk of Gold . . . could either give him Life, or continue it one Moment, but He is Dead.' Twenty-four of the nation's leading families went into mourning. The Whigs planned 'a national funeral on so magnificent a scale that the Tories might see once and for all how great was the man they had tried to dishonour'. Sarah Churchill for her part wished to make George I across the yard from her in St James's realize 'the almost royal greatness of the dead hero'.[25]

No expense, then, would be spared in preparing to solemnize the Duke's obsequies. One thing made it even worse to the jaundiced gaze of a Stuart supporter: the

---

[23] Lynch (1971: 122).   [24] Lynch (1971: 47).   [25] Sutherland (1939: 204–12).

general had amassed so much money that his widow could pay for the whole occasion. Five state-rooms at Marlborough House were draped in black, with heraldic devices and badges of the Garter covering the walls. More black baize lined the route, with 200 yards of it spread around the chapel in the Abbey where the Duke would be buried. At half past twelve the procession began, winding slowly through the Park, round Piccadilly into St James's, and down into Westminster:

> The nobility, the army, and the College of Heralds followed the funeral carriage as it wended its solemn way past huge crowds to Westminster Abbey. There were eight Dukes, Knights of the Garter, following the Duke of Montagu, who was chief mourner, as well as a number of generals headed by the new commander in chief, Cadogan, who had shared in Marlborough's days of glory and misfortune. (Churchill, iv. 540)

It took two sheets of paper to list the members of this retinue. An officer led with a silken rein 'the Horse of Honour, richly caparisoned,' like a heraldic beast. There were four pursuivants and five heralds, not including Garter King of Arms, who served as master of ceremonies. Indeed, as one historian describes it, the funeral took on the air of a national pageant: 'Amidst the long files of heralds, officers-at-arms, mourners, and assistants, the eye was caught by the banners and guidons emblazoned with his armorial achievements, among which was displayed, on a lance, the standard of Woodstock, exhibiting the arms of France on the cross of St. George' (Coxe, iii. 423).[26] At the heart of the cavalcade, the Duke's coffin was borne on an open chariot, under a gorgeous canopy, adorned with 'plumes, military trophies and heraldic achievements'.[27] On either side, shields were fixed, 'exhibiting emblematic representations of the battles he had gained, and the towns he had conquered'. Most striking of all, the chariot was flanked by outriders, 'five captains in military mourning, bearing aloft a series of bannerols, charged with the different quarterings of the Churchill and Jennings families'.

At the end of the ceremony, Garter King of Arms advanced to the graveside, and recited 'the various titles and honours of the deceased' (Coxe, iii. 424). Throughout these rites the guns at the Tower had continued to sound off at intervals of a minute. At six o'clock the body was lowered into the tomb, and the Duke's principal functionaries broke their staffs of office, so that Garter could throw them on to the coffin. A signal was given, and artillery rounds let off in the Park.[28] Nothing could have been a greater contrast to the quiet and private funeral of Anne, the mistress of the Duke who (according to Applebee's story) had dispensed her grateful 'bounty' upon him. It is a nice irony that Garter, like the Dean who performed the service—Atterbury—should have been an unregenerate Jacobite. Not long before John Anstis had bested Vanbrugh in his struggle for heraldic supremacy (see Chapter 5, above). In addition, by this date Vanbrugh found himself lodged in a bitter contest with Sarah

---

[26] The Duke's own arms were carried by Colonel Hopkey, whom we have encountered as a technical wizard behind the celebrations for the Peace in 1713 (see Ch. 3).

[27] Sarah was charged for 48 yards of cloth to line the mourning coach, which she thought was 'enough to cover my garden' (Green 1967: 229).

[28] Sutherland (1939: 221–2).

Churchill, who had taken her complaints to the House of Lords: prudently Vanbrugh seems to have absented himself from the funeral.[29]

In fact Atterbury viewed the ceremony with distaste, describing it to Pope as the
Duke's 'last scene of pompous vanity' (*Corr.* ii. 129). By a bitter reversal of the
bishop's intent, this was to be his own last act as a churchman: two weeks later he was
bundled off to the Tower in connection with the planned Jacobite rising. A few days
before, Pope had written to his friend, suggesting that he himself would attend the
ceremony: he planned 'to lye at the Deanery, and moralize one evening with you on
the vanity of human glory'.[30] All that *Windsor-Forest* denied the Captain-General
and reserved for the Queen, the funeral put back once more into the blazonry of
Marlborough. In death he achieved the regal eminence which, his opponents used
to say, he had always sought in life.[31]

Pope did not forget the events of 1722. A passage in the fourth epistle of the *Essay
on Man* seems to have the Duke in mind, with its references to plundered provinces,
laurels stained with blood and ill-fated wealth. The likelihood grows greater when
we come to this:

> Some greedy minion, or imperious wife,
> The trophy'd arches, story'd halls invade,
> And haunt their slumbers in the pompous shade.
>
> (iv. 302–4)

But the match is closer still when we turn to an expansion of this passage, left in
manuscript until recent years:

> Dead, by regardless Vet'rans born on high
> Dry pomps and Obsequies without a sigh.
>
> (*TE* vi. 358)[32]

Dry pomps were the reverse of the ceremonials played out within the text of
Windsor-Forest.

At the height of their power and glory, a decade earlier, the Churchills had been subjected to a barrage of hostile criticism in the press. An orchestrated campaign on behalf of the Harley administration portrayed the Duke as avaricious, self-seeking,
and ready to prolong the war at all costs: here Swift dealt some of the sharpest blows.
Harley himself alleged that Marlborough and Godolphin had depleted the wealth of
the country, especially the landed gentry, to feather their own family nest, and had
interposed between the monarch and the people.[33] There were scathing words

---

[29] Downes (1987: 401–3).

[30] See *Corr.* ii. 127. This may well be a joke, and there is no evidence that Pope actually went to the funeral service. However, he did describe the behaviour of Lord Cadogan in terms which suggest he either
attended or had a first-hand account of the proceedings (*Anecdotes*, i. 165).

[31] See also Sutherland (1939: 204–24). Thomas Hearne, who never tired of reviling 'that compleat Vil-
lain', the Duke, for his disloyalty to James II, noted that the funeral was conducted 'with the greatest Pomp
and Splendour ever any Prince was buried there' (Hearne, 248).

[32] See also *Anecdotes*, i. 161–7.   [33] Downie (1979: 105).

about the Marlboroughs' apparent nepotism, involving two daughters who served as ladies of the bedchamber, while their husbands also held court positions. A third daughter was the wife of the Master of the Horse to Prince George, and the fourth was married to the Master of the Great Wardrobe. Paranoid fears arose among the Tories regarding the malign influence which the Duchess held over the Queen. In fact the extent to which Sarah was able to control matters such as patronage was severely exaggerated by her adversaries; but it is true that after her dismissal from court she set up a kind of Whig anti-court and even planned an opposition ball on the evening of the Queen's birthday in 1712, during the visit of the Duke's wartime ally and friend Eugène of Savoy (Bucholz, 227).

It was in the course of this visit that the divide became most obvious. Eugène sailed to London in January 1712 in spite of strong opposition from the government, with Strafford making unavailing attempts to detain him at the Hague. He was greeted with a good deal of popular enthusiasm, and the Oxford administration was forced to accord him due respect. Eugène had several audiences with the Queen, who presented him with a jewelled sword at a full-dress ceremony on her birthday: however, she declined to enter into further negotiations concerning the peace process. But if the Prince was unable to change the course of diplomatic activity, he shared with Marlborough a major coup in public relations. At a grand reception and ball given by the Whig leadership, the two war heroes were fented until five in the morning. To the accompaniment of trumpets and drums, a banquet of more than royal proportions was held to honour the Alliance—the one which Oxford and his colleagues were in the process of dismantling—and the potentates who had helped to create it.

Perhaps the most damaging caricature of both Churchills had come from Delarivier Manley in her scandalous 'secret history', *The Court of Atalantis* (1709), a work to which Pope makes scathing reference in *The Rape of the Lock*. According to this source, Count Fortunatus (the Duke) was on the lookout for a throne to buy with his ill-gotten wealth: 'Suppose him a candidate for the crown of Poland, if among the many pretenders . . . he have the deepest purse, 'tis more than probable his success will be the highest.'[34] One aim of the Tory campaign was to accuse the Whigs of disloyalty in supporting a Pretender of their own, in the shape of the Duke. Marlborough himself was widely thought to have maintained a lifeline to the claimant, although it is now believed that he did no more than engage in some 'dabbling in Jacobitism for reinsurance purposes'.[35]

In this context the famous comparative 'bills' of Roman and British gratitude, published in *Examiner*, no. 17 (23 November 1710), need to be recalled. Swift had set out the items on either side of a balance sheet, with the imperial outlay on the left: 'A Bull for Sacrifice', 'A Crown of Lawrel', 'A Statue', 'A Trophy', 'A thousand Copper Medals', 'A Triumphal Arch', and 'Casual Charges at the Triumph' among them. The total outlay was computed at £994.11s. 10d. By contrast Marlborough's acquisitions, including Woodstock, Blenheim, the Post Office grant, the Mildenheim patent (overcharged at £30,000), pictures, jewels, and 'Employments' are costed at

---

[34] Manley (1991: 7).   [35] Szechi (1994: 61).

£540,000 (Swift, *Prose*, iii. 27). Imperial largesse could go no further. The Tory propagandists continued to accuse the Duke of corruptly using public funds: see, for instance, *A Fable of the Widow and her Cat* (1712), which has been attributed to both
Swift and Prior. In the event, the Commission of Accounts was never able to make
good its allegations of peculation, even when the government forced a hostile
motion through the Commons in January 1712. We may well regard almost all of
these charges as grossly exaggerated, even where they were not simply trumped up
to fit the political needs of the moment. But by 1713 they had done their work.

From the vantage point of royalist ideology, the main task was to reclaim the imperial thunder which had been stolen by Marlborough. Addison's *Campaign* (1704)
had indeed given Blenheim the status of a modern Philippi, which would settle the
destiny of nations, but also would act like a cosmic wind passing across the face of
Europe (see Chapter 8, below). British achievement is reidentified in *Windsor-Forest* with national, rather than personal, glory: only the Queen and, in a limited
scribal way, Lansdowne are granted individual recognition. There is no general
showering of honours, as in much Whig panegyric poetry; the implication is that
the Duke has been given enough medals by the Dutch, and a new era of *public*
spending will be devoted to enhancing British prestige. The cult of personality
which had grown up around Marlborough will fade with the war which had promoted it. Further, the poem reinscribes as a national emblem the cross which Marlborough was allowed to wear as the principal charge on his own coat of arms (387).

FOREIGN FIELDS

Beyond doubt, contemporary readers would have noticed this erasure of the
Churchills much more quickly than we do. When they read of British blood spilt on
foreign fields (367–8), they would recall the Tory campaign after Malplaquet in 1709,
to represent the general as a 'butcher', indifferent to the cries of widows and orphans
as he pursued his private ambitions. Other readers might have thought of Marlborough's devastation of Bavaria, a masterpiece of scorched-earth warfare, when they
came to the lines about the Norman tyrants who laid waste cities, stormed dens and
caves, and bestrode the land as 'The lonely Lords of empty Wilds and Woods' (see
43–52). They may even have seen Nimrod as an antetype not just of William III, but
also of the great Duke, who levelled towns and crushed the local populace. It is true
that Marlborough was not himself a 'great hunter', but symbolically he could be cast
as a violent destroyer of human beings—especially as his own army suffered heavy
casualties, partly as a result of his aggressive tactics. It happens that the only official
post Sarah was allowed to keep was that of ranger of Windsor Park, and she retained
her residence at Windsor Lodge, later known as Cumberland Lodge, which stands
in the Great Park over towards Egham. It was here that the Duke died in 1722, and
here that Pope visited his elderly widow in 1742, when their strange friendship flow-
ered late in the poet's life. But in 1713 Sarah was the Whig termagant who had dared
to challenge her royal mistress. As for depredations on the Forest, readers might

soon be able to cite the case of Marlborough's righthand man, Lord Cadogan, who was to take up residence at Caversham Park near Reading, and then suffer as the first victim of the Berkshire Blacks in 1722.[36] The locals chose Cadogan, apparently, as a pushy incomer. On another raid, the Blacks claimed they would have taken wine with the Duchess of Marlborough, if she had been at home.

Another, possibly fanciful interpretation might be offered of the lines which immediately follow the Nimrod episode. Here 'the excitements of the chase are here shown as providing man with a "moral substitute for war", and it is this fact which explains the many military metaphors with which these hunting scenes abound' (*TE* i. 139). Thus, in ll. 98–104, we have 'the simple pastime of netting partridges', and then in ll. 105–10 'a simile that recalls the siege and capture of some rich . . . city by British troops'. At this point Pope supplies a symmetrical passage to that of the partridge, describing the death of a pheasant (111–18). No military simile is afforded this time. But a contemporary might have been able to read behind the lines, as the whirring pheasant 'mounts exulting on triumphant wings'. This was just what the angel representing Marlborough did in the most famous simile of recent poetic history, that is the image in Addison's *Campaign*, which Steele in the *Tatler* called 'one of the noblest thoughts that ever entered into the heart of man', and which Johnson seventy years later still regarded as a *locus classicus*.[37] The Duke's direction of the battle of Blenheim is likened to the act of angel who 'Rides in the whirlwind and directs the storm'—a verse Pope would adopt in *The Dunciad* (iii. 264).

The lines in *Windsor-Forest* proceed, 'Short is his Joy! he feels the fiery Wound' (113), followed by a favourite anthology piece:

> Ah! what avail his glossie, varying Dyes,
> His purple Crest, and Scarlet-circled Eyes,
> The vivid Green his shining Plumes unfold;
> His painted Wings, and Breast that flames with Gold?
>
> (115–18)

In the manuscript, there is an interlineated verse at l. 114, to form a triplet: 'Stretch'd out in all his plumy Pride he lies!' (Schmitz, 26). (This was probably removed to avoid the close repetition of 'plume'.) We recall that thirty lines before, William Rufus had similarly lain 'Stretch'd on the Lawn' (81). It does not seem a very different exercise to compare the death of the pheasant with the fate of Marlborough, as we have just compared the capture of the partridge with the raising of a siege. The Duke had been forced to resign just a year before Pope wrote, and had been accused by a House of Committee of misusing funds. Some had expected him to be impeached. But by now he was in voluntary exile, and regarded by the Tories as a spent force. How were the mighty fallen! What, the poem seems to be asking, do all his honours and trophies now avail him? His 'plumy Pride', expressed in his quest for yet more decorations and baubles, means nothing. Like the destructive kings of the Norman forest, the great modern destroyer has been prostrated. For all his heraldic

---

[36] For fuller details, see *SDW*, ch. 5.   [37] Johnson (1905, ii. 129).

glitter, he is now a mere bundle of tawdry feathers waiting to be scraped off the ground.[38]

This identification with Nimrod and with the pheasant is, confessedly, speculative. There is no doubt, however, that many knowing readers would have regarded the 'Inglorious Triumphs, and dishonest Scars' (326) which littered recent history as the culmination of Marlborough's management of the war.[39] The reference to lances glittering on the Rhine (364) might have been intended to recall the inconclusive campaigns in the Palatinate of 1704–5—and by chance the Duke and Duchess were embarking on a tour of the Rhineland, from Aix-la-Chapelle to Frankfurt, when *Windsor-Forest* came out. Beyond this, one couplet was launched unmistakably against Marlborough's destructive progress over Europe:

> No more my sons shall dye with *British* Blood
> Red *Iber*'s Sands, or *Ister*'s foaming Flood . . .

> (367–8)

Here *Ister* is a poeticism for the Danube, and by synecdoche Blenheim. The verses point directly at the Duke's march down the Rhine into Bavaria, in the summer of 1704, followed by his systematic devastation of the countryside surrounding Blenheim. In the process, he lost approaching 40 per cent of his own men in some units. Opponents argued that the carnage had not sated his lust to see more blood 'foaming'. As editors have noted, in these lines 'Pope meant to furnish an argument for the Peace by intimating that the war was kept up, at the sacrifice of English life, for the benefit of other nations' (*EC* i. 363).

With a show of evenhandedness, Pope thrusts also at Stanhope, another Whig hero, when he writes of *Iber*, for the Ebro, to refer to the Peninsular campaign, and specifically the victory at Saragossa in 1710.[40] By the time Pope was writing, both generals had been ousted: the Duke, as we have seen, was dismissed as captain-general at the end of 1711. Meanwhile Stanhope, who had acted as a leading manager in the prosecution of Dr Sacheverell, was defeated and taken prisoner at Brihuega in December 1710. During a long debate in the House of Lords, Tories like Peterborough blamed him for the unsuccessful course which the war had taken in Spain, and the ministry at first made no effort to obtain his freedom. It was almost two years before he was released. After the death of the Queen, Stanhope gained his revenge as he rose to the top of the political ladder and conducted the impeachment of Ormonde. That, however, lay in the future when *Windsor-Forest* came out.

---

[38] The suggestion here of an equivalence of Marlborough with the pheasant was anticipated by Varney (1974). Though his general argument is not altogether convincing, Varney is surely right to see this particular connection.

[39] Erskine-Hill (1996: 69), plausibly argues that 'Inglorious Triumphs' is a hit directed at the 'Glorious Revolution'.

[40] A major feature of the battle of Saragossa was the passage of the Ebro by Stanhope, with 2,000 horses, to approach the enemy. The battle was fought on the dried bed of a torrent called the 'ravine of the dead' (Trevelyan, iii. 101–2), so Pope's diction is surprisingly apt. The army was also accused of desecrating images and shrines on its progress through Catalonia, something which would have outraged Pope.

As for the final list of evils which were to be 'Exil'd' by peace (413), some people doubtless thought it should start with Marlborough's own name, in view of his recent act in decamping to the Continent. Pride, ambition, vengeance, persecution, faction, and even rebellion (in his shift of loyalties from the king in 1688) had all been laid to the Duke's charge. Two *Examiner* papers early in 1712, for example, set forth an allegory of a Man of Gold who usurps the throne of Mater Patriae Augusta, just as the monarch is about to bestow peace of the nation. He is assisted by Rapine, Penury, Ambition, Avarice, and Poverty. Eventually Augusta reassumes her throne, a rod held by a Statesman (clearly representing Oxford) touches the Man of Gold, and he bursts apart, as the monster Faction rushes out of his heart.[41] This is a crude programmatic satire, and it certainly represents a vitriolic judgement on the Duke's conduct, especially as the lines in *Windsor-Forest* suggest that the promoter of discord should be not only exiled but imprisoned in brazen bonds. What may be hard for us to remember is that two years later Marlborough, by now reinstated as captain-general, held technical command over the operation to crush the Jacobite rising, which left many Stuart supporters dead or incarcerated. It is intellectually far from prudent to underestimate the degree of bitterness which was felt at this time.

There is one other subtle form of insult directed against the Duke. In downplaying victories on land, and emphasizing the power of the navy, Pope was doing more than reviving earlier efforts to boost Rooke in opposition to Marlborough (see Chapter 3, above). He was also refreshing the memory of John Churchill's younger brother George—a serving officer in the navy, who rose to the rank of admiral and managed naval affairs for the titular head of the admiralty, Prince George. The younger brother was a committed Tory, who was forced out of office in 1708 after a long campaign by the Whigs; he died two years later. Many thought that he had an unhealthy influence over the Queen's consort, but Anne herself defended him when he was accused of exercising a lax administration of the navy, which permitted French warships to attack the fleet with impunity. To side with George Churchill, as Pope implicitly does, was to rebuke John, who held a low opinion of his brother's stewardship.

Marlborough suffered at the hands of Swift in his own day, and at those of Macaulay a hundred years later. In this century he has commanded much more respect. G. M. Trevelyan, who disagreed with Winston Churchill on many issues, came to find himself 'in full agreement with Churchill's portrayal of the great Duke', in defiance of his own great-uncle's views.[42] Authorities in several areas of specialist knowledge have rehabilitated Marlborough, so that he stands high in the estimation of experts in political, diplomatic, and military history. Sarah Churchill, too, is now seen as a woman of extraordinary energy and character.[43] It is Addison and Tickell, followed by a swarm of anonymous hacks, who were closer to our modern judgement on the couple than the brilliant Tory satirists, with all their vitriol.

Yet Pope had no great personal animosity towards the Duke—less, certainly, than Swift, and even *he* could allow military prowess to Marlborough. It is rather that

---

[41] See Beattie (1967: 159–60).   [42] Cannadine (1993: 131).   [43] Harris (1991).

Stuart ideology had invested the Churchills with rapacity and treachery, and the rhetorical needs of the poem enjoined Pope to cast his opponents as betraying the cause of peace. So *Windsor-Forest* mortifies them by innuendo, and embodies one supreme insult—its massive silence with regard to the great hero of the reign.

THE FOUR INDIAN KINGS

Commentators on the poem have always been struck by an allusion to a famous episode which took place late in Anne's reign, almost at the time of the fall of the Godolphin ministry. This occurs near the end of the poem, where Pope enumerates the blessings of peace in promoting navigation and trade around the globe:

> Earth's distant Ends our Glory shall behold,
> And the new World launch forth to seek the Old.
> Then Ships of uncouth Form shall stem the Tyde,
> And Feather'd People crowd my wealthy Side,
> And naked Youths and painted Chiefs admire
> Our Speech, our Colour, and our strange Attire!
>
> (401–6)

The last line points unmistakably at the visit to London of the four so-called Iroquois kings in April 1710. In fact they were not really kings, and only one of them qualified as a sachem. One of them was not even an Iroquois. They were young, hand-picked representatives of the tribes most compliant with the British colonists, and they were in England for a purpose. This aim has been explored most thoroughly in an acute recent discussion by Eric Hinderaker, to whom we are indebted for many fresh insights.[44]

The visit was stage-managed to perform several overlapping functions. It was the colonial governors, backed by the Massachusetts government, who were behind the idea, in support of their request for royal aid in opposing the French in Acadia. The first aim was to atone for an unsuccessful expedition in the summer of 1709 to wrest control of French Canada. This had been led by Samuel Vetch (later governor of Nova Scotia) in conjunction with the experienced colonial official Francis Nicholson. Like the attempt to take Quebec, led by Colonel Jack Hill (brother of Abigail Masham) in 1711, the adventure of 1709 had achieved little, despite the support of the five Indian nations. The colonists waited in vain for assistance from the British fleet, on which they had been counting throughout their expedition.

A second aim was to boost the strategy for a naval campaign which the Tories had promoted since the early days of the war. The Godolphin ministry was steadily unraveling: it was on 6 April 1710 that the final showdown between the Queen and the Duchess of Marlborough took place (they would never meet again). The Earl of Kent was dismissed as Lord Chamberlain on 14 April, at the instigation primarily of

[44] See Hinderaker (1996: 487–526). The full-length study by R. P. Bond (1952), is still useful, though a little less instructive on the political undercurrents of the visit.

Robert Harley. Four days later Anne refused to sign a list of commissions prepared by the Duke of Marlborough, from which Jack Hill and Samuel Masham were pointed omissions. It seemed as if the great commander, who had dominated the campaigns on the mainland of Europe for eight years, was losing his hold as a policy-maker and grand planner. For the Tories, this was the chance to strike and implement their own vision of global strategy. At the same time, they were able to use the Indians' visit 'to dramatize their differences with the Whig leaders'.[45]

Moreover, a growing awareness of imperial opportunities underlay the invitation to the Indian chiefs. Their 'rude' monarchy set off the polished European court of Queen Anne, but it also suggested a valuable acquisition and a useful alliance for the nation. Unlike the 'Other' who needed to be naturalized when new colonies were set up, the Indian could be seen as benign, cooperative, 'stripped of menace'.[46] For Pope, the visit could be seen as the harbinger of 'countless future acts of pilgrimage, in which savages would be drawn to the seat of imperial civilization'. In fact Pope was not the first to reverse the usual direction of colonial gaze: Addison had already written a celebrated *Spectator* essay in April 1711 (inspired, Swift claimed, by a suggestion of his own), in which one of the Indian kings gives his own account of what he has seen in London. This is in the vein of Montesquieu and Goldsmith, presenting a seemingly innocent outsider's view. The paper ends with a trope of relativism: the misreadings of the outsider will be matched by our own narrow thinking, 'when we fancy the Customs, Dresses and Manners of other Countries are ridiculous, if they do not resemble those of our own'.[47] This prefigures the final couplet in the passage quoted from *Windsor-Forest* (405–6). However, Pope's brief reference provides a more radical switch in perspective: England is converted into a tourist site (the exact fate of Windsor Castle), while the colonized stare at the colonizers. Furthermore, there is a cultural oxymoron in the notion of a new world setting out in quest of the old.[48]

The entire visit, as Hinderaker demonstrates, was pervaded by a strong element of masquerade and histrionics. For example, the chiefs were taken to a theatrical dresser before they went to court on 19 April to be received by the Queen. When they arrived at St James's for their audience, the party was presented in form by the master of ceremonies, Sir Clement Cotterell. They were given scarlet mantles with gilt edges, almost a parody of court dress. In a speech delivered through an interpreter, the kings addressed 'our *Great Queen*', asserting that she would be 'acquainted with our long and tedious War, in Conjunction with her Children (meaning Subjects) against Her Enemies the French'. It would be hard for British listeners not to spot a parallel with the domestic situation. The declamation went on with an appeal for plans to reduce the French in Canada to be revived, since 'after the effecting thereof, We should have *Free Hunting* and a great Trade with Our *Great Queen*'s Children'.[49] If this sounds like the hopes expressed in the last section of *Windsor-Forest*, as it

[45] Hinderaker (1996: 490). [46] Hinderaker (1996: 504–5). [47] D. F. Bond (1965: i. 215).
[48] This idea is developed at greater length in *SDW*, ch. 7.
[49] This speech is reprinted from a contemporary half-sheet in R. P. Bond (1952: 94–5).

surely does, then we might recall that this speech was frequently reprinted in the months to come.

Meanwhile, for the entertainment of the Indians, the playhouses mounted gala performances of *Macbeth* and other stage favourites. It was intended to put on Congreve's *Old Bachelor* at the Haymarket, but Pope's old friend Betterton seems to have been indisposed. Instead, the actor Robert Wilks invited them on to the stage of the theatre, to receive applause from the audience: they had become the spectacle, rather than the spectators. At Powell's Punch theatre, a version of the battle of Malplaquet was performed by puppets. An extensive body of street literature commemorated the exotic strangers. They became indeed 'actors and symbols in a great array of contexts'.[50] On one level a kind of outré noble savage, the Indian could also be used to figure the political possibilities of an enlarged American empire. Each was painted by John Verelst, who was paid £100 by the Queen for his services.[51] They appear in the guise of a primitive wood-ranger; one of them has even acquired the buskins, belt, and quiver of a male Diana. A print of these likenesses showed the kings' totem arks, described as their 'Coat of Arms'.

During the visit, another spin to this publicity jaunt was given by the Church, which invited the four kings to meet a number of its leaders. The Bishop of London, Henry Compton, preached to them at St James's Chapel. The Archbishop of Canterbury, who was president of the Society for the Propagation of the Gospel, gave each of them a bible, and proposals were mooted for extensive missionary work among the Indian tribes. It was suggested that the Scriptures should be translated into Iroquois languages. Again, the visitors had been appropriated to lend prestige to what was both a predominantly Tory cause, and one that appealed to the Queen personally. A further visit, on 22 April, was to the Banqueting House at Whitehall: an event whose significance to the Stuart ideology of *Windsor-Forest* scarcely needs to be underlined. A final audience at court took place early in May, when the sachems presented an address to the Queen. On 3 May the group left London, visiting Hampton Court and Windsor on their way to Portsmouth, ready for departure five days later.

Most of these highly orchestrated events were arranged by the Tories. This is certainly true of their patronage by the Duke of Ormonde, who was quite soon to succeed Marlborough as commander-in-chief and whose Jacobite sympathies had never been fully disguised. The Duke gave them dinner on 20 April at his home in Richmond. Next day the group visited the centre of naval operations at Greenwich: everywhere they went the Indians would have come across, the stately edifices of Christopher Wren, the architect of Stuart reconstruction—as they would do when surveying the dome of St Paul's 'both above and below'. It was Ormonde again who paraded the Life Guards in Hyde Park for the benefit of the visitors. The sachems appeared before the Board of Trade and Plantations, while the Lord Commissioners of the Admiralty gave them a meal on board one of the royal yachts; and after this the Astronomer Royal, unsinkable old John Flamsteed, added his welcome. Before their

[50] Hinderaker (1996: 496).   [51] R. P. Bond (1952: 66–7).

final departure, the Indian kings were entertained at Spithead by the commander of the fleet on his flagship, the *Royal Sovereign*. It cannot be said that the Iroquois nations wielded much sea power, but a realistic strategy for the takeover of French Canada involved more effective use of naval forces. As it was to prove, the expedition mounted on Quebec in 1711 suffered from incompetent management, and the majority of the French possessions in Canada remained out of the grasp of the British negotiators at Utrecht, although Arcadia (now Nova Scotia) was successfully occupied in the autumn of 1710 and its possession confirmed in the peace treaty. The sheltered base of Port Royal, from which the French had attacked British shipping, was renamed Annapolis, a gesture much in the spirit of *Windsor-Forest*.

It may be no accident that Pope's vision of the spread of imperial power (*WF*, 387–92) suggests expansion in the east, north, and south—but not in the west. The entire Quebec enterprise was a disaster, and thus justified Marlborough's opposition to the plan to launch an expedition in Canada, which he had voiced at time of the sachems' visit to London. As chief sponsor of the scheme, Henry St John in particular emerged with a loss of prestige. Swift went to Hill's sister Mrs Masham to 'condole' with her when news of the debacle reached London, and noted, 'The secretary is much mortified about Hill; because this expedition was of his contrivance, and he counted much upon it' (*JTS* ii. 378). Hill himself managed to survive the reverse, despite criticism of his generalship, and was elected as one of the brothers in the 'Society' soon afterwards. As we have seen in Chapter 2, this was a nucleus of Tory intellectual and social power: its members generally favoured St John against Harley. The messages Pope received from his friends in the Society must have urged that nothing in the text of *Windsor-Forest* should point to the ministry's ill-starred attempts to take French Canada. Harley himself had stood out against the venture, and he is the hero of this concluding section.

Obviously, Pope was far from alone among poets in drawing attention to the visit. Most relevant are the pindaric verses which Elkanah Settle wrote in praise of the Society for the Propagation of the Gospel in Foreign Parts (1711). In his prefatory address to the Queen, Settle contrasts harsh treatment of native American peoples by 'the barbarous *Spaniard*' with the pacific rule of the British: 'Yes the Benign *BRITANNIA* to the Immortal Honour of her *Sovereign MISTRESS* sends no *Cortesian Tyrants*, no *Bloody Streamers* to hang out amongst them.' The poem itself describes the beneficent effects of the Society's missionary zeal, with 'Jesus dawning thro the *Indian* Skyes'. The envoys of 'the *English* Miter' will chase away vapours 'And the exterminated Shades supply | With the bright Aspect of the *British* Sky.' There follows a significant couplet:

> See there their *Indian* Majesties on Knees
> Waiting for Heav'ns, & Royal *Anne*'s Decrees . . .[52]

This points directly to the text of *Windsor-Forest* (e.g. 383–4) and more generally anticipates Anne's famous decree at ll. 327–8. Pope had read Settle's work from

---

[52] Settle's *Pindaric Poem*, quoted by R. P. Bond (1952: 73–4).

boyhood, and he would make the City Poet one of the major figures in *The Dunciad*. It is at least possible that he recalled these lines on 'the swarthy Monarchs' who had visited London, as he composed the prophetic section of *Windsor-Forest*.

When the chieftains left England and sailed back to the New World, they were presented with a large stock of goods, as well as a picture of the Queen together with her coat of arms. This was on top of an earlier gift from the monarch of 200 guineas apiece. The sachems figured among Indian leaders who met at Albany in August 1710 with the new governor of New York: this was Robert Hunter, a military veteran of Blenheim who claimed friendship with Swift and Addison.[53] Hunter handed over to the each of the Five Nations a medal inscribed with the royal effigy, as well as pictures of the Queen 'to be given to the chief warriors as a token of their readiness to fight under her banner against the common enemy [France and her Indian supporters].'[54] We can see the attempt to portray the kings as loyal subjects of Anne's reign, a hope which Pope also expresses (*WF*, 403–8).

In fact, the Five Nations were unrepresentative of the Indian peoples at large, and the 'kings' who came to England were in some ways unrepresentative of their communities. However, the tribes loyal to Britain stood in need of a gesture of support, just as the European residents felt they were entitled to military backing from the homeland. Obviously, the visit had been engineered by the colonial leadership for its own political ends, and in this respect some short-term goals were achieved. Unfortunately, little success attended the missionary effort, even though the Governor helped to set up Queen Anne's Chapel at a garrison on the south bank of the Mohawk river, to be known as Fort Hunter. The Queen sent some communion plate inscribed with the royal cipher and coat of arms, besides ninety-seven prints of the queen's effigy and arms to be distributed among the Indians. But the chaplain appointed to this remote cure struggled for six years to bring the word to the Mohawks, and he finally left defeated in his aims.[55] This was as direct an attempt as any to realize the optimistic prophecy which rounds off *Windsor-Forest*—yet the venture gained no spiritual ground and made little political headway.[56]

On strategic grounds Marlborough had resisted any involvement in colonial squabbles, thus leaving an opportunity for his enemies to capitalize on the popularity of the visitors and to shift the war in the direction which the Tories had always sought. It is altogether apt that a poem celebrating the settlement at Utrecht should invoke the long-term possibilities for imperial expansion in the Western hemisphere, even though the Quebec expedition needed to be kept in decent obscurity.[57]

[53] It was to Hunter as 'Captain-General and Governor' of New York and surrounding areas that the Queen had written in Feb. 1711, outlining the objectives of the expedition to Quebec. Revealingly this document proclaims that if the French could be driven out, 'the several Indian Nations will be under Our Subjection'. See B. C. Brown (1935: 322).

[54] R. P. Bond (1952: 45).   [55] R. P. Bond (1952: 57–63).

[56] A somewhat bizarre addition: Hunter was also involved in buying a mansion in New Jersey intended as the palace for a new colonial bishop. He wrote to Swift about this undertaking in 1712, and clearly hoped that his friend might himself take up this appointment (which Swift had once described to him as 'my Virginian Bishoprick'). See Swift, *Corr*. i. 120–1, 334–5.

[57] Tickell's poem *On the Prospect of Peace* had already mentioned the 'painted' Indian kings as they lay their scepters at the feet of the Queen: see *TE* i. 192.

As he recalled the visit, Pope was harking back to a significant moment in the Queen's reign, when polarized attitudes towards the wider world became sharply visible.

SOUTHERN SKIES

In the prophecy which resonates at the end of *Windsor-Forest*, one important component has been virtually ignored. Here Pope envisages the spread of the nation's trade as her ships navigate around the four corners of the earth. This section of the poem is explored more fully in *SDW*, chapter 6, but one short passage needs to be looked at here, as it has immediate relevance to events surrounding the peace:

> Tempt Icy Seas, where scarce the Waters roll,
> Where clearer Flames glow round the frozen pole;
> Or under Southern Skies exalt their Sails,
> Led by new Stars, and born by spicy Gales!
>
> (389–92)

The vision extends to a harmonious world of free trade, where seas 'but join the Region they divide' (400). These lines culminate in the declaration of a hope that Peace will stretch her reign 'Till Conquest cease, and Slav'ry be no more' (192). The Twickenham editors comment, 'One cannot help remembering that the Anglo-Spanish treaty signed at Utrecht "accorded to Great Britain and the British South Sea Company . . . the sole right of importing negroes into Spanish America" . . . and that Pope put some of his money into the company' (*TE* i. 192). Both factors are apposite, especially the first, but the matter goes deeper than this.

In fact, the entire declamation constitutes a tribute to the South Sea Company, and to its founding father, Oxford. The crucial fact is that in 1711–12 the company was widely seen as a symbol of a new commercial push, made possible by the concessions France and her allies would be forced to make as part of the peace negotiations. In the event, however, the Spanish were not forced to cede American territories as the preliminary treaty had envisaged. We think of the South Sea operation as a device in public financing, an expedient to fund the national debt, and an opportunity for unscrupulous City dealers to move in. It was seen differently at the outset:

The South Sea Company was not in 1711 the wild-cat scheme it had become by 1720. It represented the trade with South America that Britain would be privileged to drive, free of French and Dutch competition, as soon as the terms of peace designed by the Ministry were secured . . . The finances of the country were based in May 1711 on the assumption that the *Asiento*, or monopoly of the slave trade with Spanish America, would be wrested from France as an integral part of the terms of peace. (Trevelyan, iii. 143–4)

Thus any praise of trade to this region, offering too the promise of 'freed *Indians*' and restored kingdoms in Mexico and Peru (*WF*, 409–12), must constitute an endorsement of the negotiating strategy of the government over the previous two years.

The presumptuous grant to the company actually spoke of a monopoly, consisting of sole trade to the territories of Spanish America on both Atlantic and Pacific coasts. It covered places 'which are reputed to belong to the Crown of Spain', a nicely engineered dubiety, but also those 'which shall hereafter be found or discovered' (see also p. 233, below). Here is the optimistic rush of energy as the trees of Windsor carry Britain's 'Thunder' to the 'distant Ends' of the earth (*WF*, 387, 401). In reality, the South Sea project was a natural culmination of the war, with its aim of curbing the world power of Spain and France: within the poem, Pope's paean to liberty naturally follows on the verses which directly celebrate the achievement of the peace.

When Harley proclaimed the formation of the company to parliament at the start of May 1711, it proved to be one of his most triumphant moments in office, suitably capped by his earldom just six days later. There were bonfires and bells in London. For once, all factions of Harley's own party achieved a brief state of unity, and even Whig financiers like James Brydges (later Duke of Chandos) were won over. The plan was that short-term government creditors would exchange their notes for shares in the new corporation, with a guaranteed annual return from the Treasury of 6 per cent, allowing for a dividend to be paid to investors. This prospect was enough of an inducement to get credit moving again; the magnates of the City who had controlled and extended the war could now be outflanked; and the Whig and Williamite institutions which had governed the economy, like the Bank of England, would be forced to cede some of their power. As well as the dream of rich plunder in the new world, the scheme appeared to offer a special outlet for Tory money, that is a means of circulating the inherited funds of the landed class without recourse to stock-jobbers and moneylenders (who, in the xenophobic mind of the time, were likely to be Huguenots if not Jewish). There was something providential about such an outcome to the long and expensive war:

Whereas the Whig interest seemed to thrive on Continental war and the piling up of debt for destructive activities, the new Tory moneyed interest would be inextricably interwoven with peace, with a peace treaty, and with the native Tory policy of isolation from Europe and expansion overseas. (Churchill, iv. 336)

To backwoodsmen, it was almost as good as a cut in the land tax. To Tories engaged in commerce and finance (a much more numerous group than is often supposed), it was both economically and politically acceptable.

Oxford's parliamentary strength, it has been noted, rested 'on the proposition that for the past ten years the public purse had been scandalously mismanaged for the glory of the Duke of Marlborough and the benefit of the foreigners and the Bank of England'. The shortfall for the current year was put at £9,000,000. Added to this, the lure of fabulous wealth on the Spanish Main tempted government debtors to take up shares. Oxford himself converted £8,000 in securities so as to qualify for the governorship. From 1 August, the body would be entitled to carry on 'the sole trade and traffick . . . into unto and from the Kingdoms, Lands etc. of America, on the east side from the river Aranoca, the southernmost part of the Tierra del Fuego, on the west side thereof from the said southernmost part through the South Seas to the northernmost part of America, and into unto and from all countries in the same limits, reputed to belong to the crown of Spain, or which shall hereafter be discovered'. The company acquired a coat of arms, which bore the royal insignia on the shield together with a map of the western hemisphere, displaying the entire continent of America in its naked accessibility. There was also a vainglorious motto in Latin, translated as 'From Cadiz to the Dawn': this is directly paraphrased in the poem as a movement 'To the bright Regions of the rising Day' (*WF*, 388). The shield is more honest than the motto in designating those 'distant Ends' of the earth which the company actually intended to exploit.

It is this sweeping vision of the future which excited enthusiasm in the City, and which underlies Pope's verses. The ore ripening to gold serves to remind us of Spanish mines; when 'other *Mexico*'s be roofed in Gold' (412), the subliminal message is that British merchants will be sharing in the action. The Spanish Empire had been symbolized by its rich galleons, like those Rooke had plundered at Vigo Bay (see Chapter 3, above) or those Woodes Rogers had recently brought back in tow to London, as we shall see in a moment. Now some of this bullion would be making its way to England instead. At one swoop, the pamphleteers announced, a solution had been found to the rising national debt and the prospect opened up of lucrative commerce all over the western hemisphere. What was not revealed was 'the chimerical nature of the trade itself', which made the project from the outset a sham as a business proposition.[58]

The bill to incorporate the company passed on 12 June as 9 Anne, c.15. Swift, who like Arbuthnot was a shareholder, greeted its arrival in the *Examiner* as the brainchild of 'the same great person' who had recently promoted the 'pious and noble Work' of funding fifty new churches.[59] On 7 September 1711 the body was officially instituted as 'the Company of Merchants of Great Britain trading to the South Seas and the other Parts of America'. In the following summer the directors of the company (dominated by Oxford's allies) were allowed to purchase merchandise to be sent to the West Indies in two ships, in the expectation of concessions from Spain as part of the ongoing peace negotiations. We must realize that, although the acquisition of the *asiento* was a key part of the strategy, and one that the Dutch would bitterly resist, it initially represented only one element in the whole project. Moreover, the South Sea act 'effectually pledged government to make peace', and to renege upon agreements with the Dutch during earlier negotiations (Trevelyan, iii. 144).

When Oxford addressed the court of the South Sea Company as their governor for the first time in September 1711, he was bullish about the prospects for expansion. Throughout the summer, secret negotiations for a preliminary treaty with France had been going on: Matthew Prior was dispatched to Paris with a set of

[58] The last two paragraphs are based chiefly on Carswell (2001: esp. 50–7). Harley promised the Commons that the monopoly would 'yearly bring in vast Riches from Peru and Mexico into Great-Britain'.
[59] Ellis (1985: 468). For the churches, see Ch. 4, above. John Barber, a friend of Swift and later of Pope, was appointed official printer to the company. St John was among the directors.

demands, which relevantly included the handover of four fortified towns in Spanish America to guarantee British trading rights in this sector. The aim was to secure a foothold in New Spain for two-way commerce. Pope's friend and patron the Duke of Buckinghamshire had pressed particularly hard for this. As it turned out, the French knew that the Bourbon King of Spain would not accede to the proposal, and it was one of the demands ultimately dropped. However, the trading community grew ever more confident that substantial posts would be set up in what was still the Spanish empire—something Oxford's loyal servant Daniel Defoe had long been advocating.[60] When Jack Hill's ill-fated expedition left for Quebec around the same time (see above), many people assumed that its purpose was to attack targets in America with a view to establishing a presence for the company. For good military and political reasons, the ministry did not try to correct this impression. Swift was evidently deceived about the purposes of the mission, for he reported a conversation in July 1711 with 'a great Man who is deepest in the project of it', that is St John, and giving his own opinion that such ventures to the South Seas never worked (Swift, *Corr.* i. 238). Then the company itself projected an expedition to seize such bases by force: in January 1712 they actually told Oxford they would need four thousand troops, together with twenty men of war and forty transport ships.[61] In the light of subsequent events this looks totally absurd: but when Pope was writing the concluding passages of *Windsor-Forest*, it was the general scale of expectation. The company was all set to stretch the British reign, once peace was confirmed.

So Oxford drafted a speech for the Queen to deliver at the opening of parliament in February 1714, which exactly recapitulates the concluding sentiments of *Windsor-Forest*: 'It is with great pleasure I see my subjects delivered from a consuming war, and entering upon such a peace as nothing but their own *intestine broils* can hinder the effects of it in an universal increase of trade.' The speech went on to deplore the effect of faction in turning men's heads from the love of their country to pursue 'their private lucre'; and to restate the Tory view that 'it is this nation's interest to aggrandise itself by trade, and when a war is necessary it is their interest as well as safety to carry it on by sea'.[62] As usual, the Earl's prose is confused syntactically and inelegant: he must have been grateful for the eloquence with which Pope had set out his programme a year earlier.

In time, the high hopes which had been aroused would turn to ashes. The South Sea Company failed to become a genuine trading corporation, like the Royal African or the East India Companies. Though it acquired the *asiento* rights, it proved much less efficient than the African Company in exercising these and, as a matter of fact, it never made a profit on the operation. The directors lacked experience in interna-

---

[60] He sent Oxford three memoranda in July 1711, outlining the possibilities for establishing permanent trading posts in countries like Chile (Defoe 1955: 339–41, 343–9). He believed that the last-named country would yield 'incredible' quantities of gold.
[61] Hill (1988: 190).
[62] Oxford's draft in Harley papers, quoted by Holmes and Speck (1967: 96). Cf. 'Intestine Wars' (*WF*, 325).

tional commerce. Further delays in settling the treaty of commerce with Spain, eventually signed in July 1713 but not ratified until the following November, impaired progress. Traders who had bought goods in expectation of early profits were forced to sell out at a loss.[63] The monopoly of trade promised to investors amounted, in effect, to 100 per cent of almost nothing. It is true that the Company was granted some rights to set up unfortified trading posts at seven towns including Buenos Aires, Cartegena, and Porto Bello: but these never grew into anything commercially important.[64]

Scandal, too, soon began to dog the company. Allegations of corruption involving Bolingbroke, directly or indirectly, surfaced in 1714. Much worse, the Queen herself was not immune from the stink. It emerged that her allocation of almost a quarter of the company's shares had been assigned to nominees such as the Treasury official William Lowndes. The true beneficiaries were Lady Masham, Bolingbroke, and one of his cronies, Arthur Moore. Anne was forced to divest herself of her share in the company's trading profits, and at her last appearance before parliament, on 9 July, she faced a sceptical opposition. Prorogation was intended to stem the tide of criticism which had been launched against South Sea. Already, after a few months of (largely nominal) trading, the precipitous descent towards the lasting infamy of the Bubble had begun. Pope himself may have emerged from the collapse of the company relatively unscathed: but friends such as Gay were hit hard, and as we have seen the dedicatee Lansdowne lost almost £10,000 in South Sea investments.

If *Windsor-Forest* had appeared a year later, it is certain that Pope would have exercised more caution in his fulsome welcome to the new company. Lady Masham, Moore, and Lowndes all subscribed to the *Iliad*: much of the mud stuck to Bolingbroke, Pope's friend and mentor. The Queen's covert patronage of the venture had become an embarrassment. Above all, the poet would have been forced to recognize that this central prop of Oxford's policy had largely failed: the South Sea venture would not work without the wider peace process, and the terms extracted from France and Spain did not measure up to the prospectus implied in the company's charter.

Pope had no chance of foreseeing all this in 1712. Most likely he drafted the culminating vision of Father Thames around the autumn of that year, when the prospects for the company were at their most glowing. It is inconceivable that he could have written as he did, looking towards the opening up of the Spanish possessions in America, and heralding contact between the new world and the old, without intending to link the peace process with the formation of the company. As Erskine-Hill remarks (*Milieu*, 177), it would be surprising if Pope did not discuss matters with his new friend Swift, who would show him how Harley had managed to put an end to corruption in public finance, and to curb the excessive power of Whig magnates in the City of London: but this may not have occurred before *Windsor-Forest* went to the press. In this context, 'Southern Skies' would

---

[63] Roberts (1975: 95).
[64] For the facts cited here, see Carswell (2001: 55–64); Dickson (1967: 64–75).

automatically bring with it a precise resonance: nobody else, after all, was planning to carry British mercantile interests to the Pacific. The existing companies had no stake in South America and a limited amount in the West Indies. Significantly, all the textual detail in this prophetic section of *Windsor-Forest* is either neutral or specifically applicable to the Americas—not a single phrase points directly to Africa, for example. (Earlier in the poem there is reference to India at ll. 9–32.) Equally, Pope must have known that this speech would enshrine Oxford as the, literally, unsung hero of the conclusion. The technique is oblique enough not to affront Bolingbroke, but nothing could conceal the fact that a single name was associated with the project. When he first took the measure to parliament, Harley had been personally congratulated for 'opening such a vein of riches as may make this nation more than sufficient amends for the vast expenses of two successive tedious wars' (Green, 249).[65] *Windsor-Forest* lauds the very same thing, and it does so in terms that precisely mirror the hopes of the original subscribers to the Company.[66]

Closely connected to the South Sea project was another news story which came before the public in 1712. This related to the most famous privateering expedition ever undertaken, that mounted by Woodes Rogers between 1708 and 1711, described in his book *A Cruising Voyage Round the World*—the source of the immortal tale of Alexander Selkirk. In fact, the venture led by the commander-in-chief and his associates (who included William Dampier and Thomas Dover) owed its origins to harassment by Spanish and French ships of British overseas trade. The merchants had petitioned the Queen to redress the situation, and one outcome was the Prize Act of March 1708 by which the crown relinquished its claim to one-fifth of the proceeds of any privateering expedition. Later that year a group of Bristol traders fitted out two frigates, named aptly enough the *Duke* and the *Duchess*, to range the waters around South America in particular, in search of hostile vessels. As the letter of marque from Prince George put it, members of the expedition were 'to cruise . . . in the *South Seas*, against her Majesty's Enemies the *French* and the *Spanish*'. The ships sailed from Bristol on 2 August 1708. Just over three years later, they returned, landing on the Thames estuary at the start of October 1711. In the course of their travels they had sacked the Spanish port of Guayaquil in what is now Ecuador: they also captured a Manila galleon and brought it back as their main prize. The East India Company, largely a Whiggish institution, attempted to claim most of the booty from the expedition, but this attempt crumbled.

   In the following year two narratives of the voyage were issued—both, as it happens, by the publisher of *Windsor-Forest*, Bernard Lintot. First into the fray came Edward Cooke, originally second-in-command on the *Duchess*, who produced *A Voyage to the South Sea*, completed in a second volume later in the year. The other nar-

[65] Swift referred to the 'transcendent Genius for Publick Affairs' Harley had displayed in the measures he had brought forward as Chancellor of the Exchequer: see *Examiner*, 45 (7 June 1711), in Ellis (1985: 467).
[66] The hope expressed by Pope that 'London may be made a FREE PORT' (note to *WF*, 398) echoes a proposal of John Blunt, the financier whose ideas underlay Oxford's entire South Sea project. Cf. *Milieu*, 191.

rative, the *Cruising Voyage* by Rogers, has acquired much greater fame, as it contains the story of Selkirk, which was given extensive publicity by Steele in the *Guardian* during 1713. However, Cooke's account holds more relevance for our purposes. It is inscribed to the Earl of Oxford in terms fulsome even for an eighteenth-century dedicator. The Oxford ministry is identified with peace and prosperity, with its desire to bring relief to a nation 'groaning under a tedious and destructive War' (a Tory shibboleth) contrasted with the aims of those promoting 'factious Animosities at Home'. The Earl stands at the head of those who prefer 'the Blessings of Peace' to the prejudices of party.[67] It could all have been composed by Oxford's speech-writer.

To Cooke, it is self-evident that the interests of the nation are to be found in exploiting the vast resources of the Americas. In language close to that used by Defoe, when he promoted South Sea trade in the pages of the *Review*, Cooke urges the nation to pay special attention to 'the great and wealthy Countries lying along the *South* Sea, being the Object on which the Eyes and Thought of all Men are at present fix'd'.[68] It is a further proof of the close identification of South Sea trade and colonization with the current ministry and its peace policy.[69] In sober truth, the privateering expedition had been a form of war by other means; but Cooke is able to suggest that the end of hostilities will greatly increase the opportunities for lucrative trade in this richly endowed quarter of the world. The penultimate paragraph in *Windsor-Forest*, then, works on one level as a versification of the expansionist rhetoric Cooke had used in his address to Lord Oxford.

FREED INDIANS

The company gave up its *asiento* contract to Spain in 1751 and ceased trading. By that time its attempts to break the Spanish monopoly in South America had embroiled the nation in the War of Jenkins' Ear. In the short term, Pope's hopeful promises were all negated. To see them realized, we should have to adopt a longer time-span, and look to the decline of Spanish imperial power and the ultimate independence of its American colonies, along with the rise of the first British empire.

In her avowedly hostile reading of Pope, which has its own perverse attractiveness, Laura Brown writes as though *Windsor-Forest* were designed to celebrate the Peace of Paris in 1763. It was the gains made fifty years later in the Seven Years War which established the imperium described by Brown. As noted, the peroration to the poem makes no explicit reference to India, and since the East India Company was a private chartered company, funded by what has been called 'the cosmopolitan mercantile plutocracy of the City of London', this is no surprise.[70] It was the epitome

---

[67] Cooke (1712: i. A2^{v-r}).   [68] Cooke (1712: ii. 1).

[69] In the partially convincing allegorical reading he offered of his own poem in *A Key to the Lock*, Pope jokingly identified Ariel with Oxford: 'His sitting on the Mast of a Vessel shows his presiding over the S——th S–a Tr–de' (*Prose*, i. 190). Much later, the Duchess of Ormonde wrote to Swift, 'You remember & so do I, w^n the S: Sea was said to be my Lord Ox——d's brat, & must be starved at Nurse' (Swift, *Corr.* ii. 344).   [70] Dickson (1967: 263).

of Whig financial management from the point of view of Pope and his friends, while
its day-to-day operations caused few ripples on national politics at this date. One
can search through many volumes of the papers of Oxford and Bolingbroke without finding a single reference to Indian affairs, and whole sessions of Anne's parliament passed without the business of the Old or New Company (united in 1709)
making any impact on the party struggle. It is wholly anachronistic to read into
Pope's age the military, political, and legal battles in the second half of the century.
At this stage the British government had no responsibility, even de facto, for the detailed running of company affairs; and only by a reckless extension of the language
could India be viewed as a colony in 1713. Moreover, the peace treaty (Pope's ostensible subject) had virtually no bearing on anything in the eastern hemisphere.

Laura Brown writes of 'Pope's representation of "the great age" of English impe-
rialism'—but he would have had to possess extraordinary prescience to represent
this decades in advance of its existence. At the heart of Brown's argument lies her
statement that 'the displacement of the military and political into the pastoral
makes an evocation of imperial oppression possible even in this celebration of the
English nation'. To this we might retort, first that 'displacement' falsifies the poetic
method, since the pastoral element is not just the vehicle of a political metaphor, but
a mode of cognition in its own right; and second, that that 'imperial oppression' is
not effaced—it is directly brought up at ll. 408–12 (unmentioned by Brown),
although of course in respect of the legacy of the Spanish empire:

> Till Conquest cease, and Slav'ry be no more:
> Till the freed *Indians* in their native Groves
> Reap their own Fruits, and woo their sable Loves,
> *Peru* once more a race of Kings behold,
> And other *Mexico*'s be roof'd with Gold.

Pope's vision of the future, or 'fantasy' as Brown calls it, may or may not have been
realized in subsequent history: that depends on the view we take of the later *pax Britannica*. But this prophecy certainly involves the millennial dream of a world where
conquest and slavery will be no more. (Notice, too, how the pastoral language of
groves and fruits awards the native people the same blessings which Stuart rule had
guaranteed the British people, earlier in the poem.) Brown does not neglect to mention that Pope invested in the South Sea Company in 1720; she fails to observe that
the poem (boldly for its age) looks to a time when what proved to be the Company's
main activity would be redundant.[71] Howard Erskine-Hill has convincingly shown
that Pope connects the notion of slavery in the poem with the dispossessed (as at

[71] L. Brown (1985: 28–42). Pope actually contemplated investing in the Company as early as 1716, as he
told Martha Blount, and seems to have done so (*Corr.* i. 379, 395). He always kept an eye on the French
market, where his father had taken out an annuity on the life of his son in 1707—the rates on these had
fallen in 1713, one of the financial consequences of the costly war effort. So the debates over commercial
clauses in the peace treaty were not altogether academic to the Pope family. The dealings of Pope, Swift
and Gay are analysed in Nicholson (1994: 51–81). Swift had invested through his friend Francis Stratford
(whom Oxford appointed to the company board) and thought, wrongly, that he would lose his money
when Stratford failed in early 1712 (*JTS* ii. 462–3, 501–2).

l. 64), and that its concluding oration 'totally repudiates slavery'. Indeed, Erskine-Hill after extensive research could find 'no other English poem commenting on the Treaty or Peace which squarely confronts, let alone opposes, slavery in the New World'.[72]

This is the measure of Pope's independence. He was prepared to make a clear statement on an aspect of the peace which would command unquestioning Tory loyalty, especially after the Queen had singled out the *asiento* in her speech from the throne on 6 June 1712, as one of the points on which the government had insisted in recent negotiations.[73] Significantly, the Whig opposition, bent on destroying every last clause of the peace agreement, never objected on moral or even economic grounds to the acquisition of the contract. Brown seems almost to blame Pope for the existence of slavery: if more people had felt as he did, the whole institution might have come to an end a century earlier.

It took courage, too, for Pope to criticize the Spanish conquest of America, since this has been undertaken in the name of the Holy Church—Pope's own church. That the faults of the conquistadores might also be laid at the door of the English colonists in North America is suggested by comments in a letter to Caryll on 5 December 1712, which has already been cited on the subject of revisions to *Windsor-Forest* then under way. Pope compares his vulnerable situation in the face of calumnies to that of the native Americans: 'A plain man encounters them at a great disadvantage; as the poor Indians did our guns and fire arms.'[74] The poem envisages a world made free by peace and trade, with ancient empires like that of the Incas and Aztecs restored, and the blessings of humanity passed to all corners of the globe. This may have been an idealized dream, but it does not contradict any other sentiment in the poem, and it remains a noble concept of civilization.

[72] Erskine-Hill (1998: 35–9). For an important recent discussion of cognate matters, see Richardson (2001: 1–17, at 1), where the author's main concern is 'the question of what [Pope's] muted protest, together with others' comments on the peace, reveals about linguistic habits concerning slavery and about the mental attitudes informing those habits'.

[73] Quoted by Erskine-Hill (1998: 34).

[74] The relevance of this passage (*Corr.* i. 162) has been pointed out by Erskine-Hill (1998: 34).

7

Classical and Renaissance Literature

Far more than any other eighteenth-century writer, Pope belongs to the mainstream of English poetry as it had evolved across the centuries, and *Windsor-Forest* demonstrates this fact more comprehensively than any other of his works. Yet to see the poem as a decisive stage in Pope's development as a writer carries with it a wholesale reconfiguration of his career. We have generally thought of *The Rape of the Lock* as the culmination of his early career, and arguably it is the poet's greatest achievement in the first part of his life, or at least prior to the translations of Homer. However, the *Rape* has come to occupy this place because we exercise the wisdom of hindsight. In terms of the concerns which mark the poetry up to 1717, it is *Windsor-Forest* which most completely establishes Pope's literary ground. In addition, this work adumbrates the issues which would dominate Pope's private and political life in the wake of the Hanoverian accession, as it articulates the identity crisis which supporters of the Stuart cause felt as one Jacobite rising after another came and went.

Just as in the *Rape*, Pope enlists a variety of literary models in *Windsor-Forest*. The most important are georgic and epic strains derived from Virgil, together with a mythological vein based on Ovid. The epic model inscribes a narrative of empire and peaceful conquest: it is linked to forms of panegyric and prophecy, and points towards Dryden. Georgic leads the way towards Denham and Cowley amongst others. In visual art it is in tune with the paintings of Poussin: iconographically it calls up the world of court masque and the architecture of triumph. The Ovidian line defines a narrative of vulnerability, of conflict and surrender. It recalls the pastoral world of Spenser and Shakespeare, and it is restated in the work of Drayton and Evelyn. Iconographically it suggests the paintings by Rubens on subjects drawn from myth. Underlying both stories is a historical plot most usefully related by Camden.

The following sections are devoted to the main literary inheritance of *Windsor-Forest*. Initially we shall consider the legacy of classical writers and then those of the high Renaissance, culminating in Milton. Ben Jonson is reserved for treatment elsewhere: see *SDW*, chapter 1, where his use of masque and spectacle helps to define a mode of Stuart art which is central to Pope's purposes. No attempt is made to cover every possible borrowing which has been charted by the editors. Short passages of *Windsor-Forest* may be indebted to a large range of authors: there are touches of Lucan, Statius, Horace, Waller, Otway, and others. Here, the argument will fix on those modes and works which provide a sustained input into the poem.

VIRGIL AND THE ENGLISH GEORGIC

It was only with the appearance of Dryden's translation of *The Works of Virgil* in 1697 that the *Georgics* attained high prominence in English literature. Together with Addison's 'Essay' on the *Georgics*, which prefaced the verses, the new rendering created a new national sense of this branch of poetry. The translation remained standard for a century or more: its only serious rival, the version by Joseph Warton (1753), never achieved such a dominant position. True, sections of Virgil's work, usually a single *Georgic*, had several times been translated by previous authors, including Vaughan, Cowley, Sheffield (later Duke of Buckinghamshire), and Creech, as well as by Dryden and Addison themselves in editions of Tonson's *Miscellanies*.[1] Moreover, as Anthony Low has argued, a current of georgic sentiment can be discerned in works by many of the major seventeenth-century poets.[2] However, it was Dryden's version which enhanced the reputation of Virgil generally, of the *Georgics* especially, and of didactic verse as a mode of writing.

Many of Pope's models, as we are able to identify them in this book, had taken a particular interest in this area. As will be seen in Chapter 8, Cowley's friend John Evelyn made extensive reference to the poems in his masterpiece *Sylva*, and indeed throughout his career Evelyn displayed a particular fondness for Latin didactic verse: he translated the first book of Lucretius, whilst his son rendered the neo-georgic poem *Horti* by René Rapin. Equally, there is a Virgilian dimension to *Cooper's Hill*, notably when Denham activates the retirement topos (*CH*, 273–88). However, in Chalker's words, 'it is in the lines on the Thames (ll. 160 ff.) that the most significant, and the most interestingly developed, Georgic parallel occurs'. Denham picks up on Virgil's panegyric of Italy in his second book, but extends this by dilating upon the 'civilizing effects of exploration and colonization and the sense that the whole world is being brought into a new harmony by the expansion of trade'.[3] This was a crucial example for both Dryden and Pope. As for the former, while *Annus Mirabilis* is not commonly related to georgic, its vision of national expansion in the wake of a *pax Britannica* owes much to Virgil as mediated through Denham. In the preface to the poem, Dryden even makes the heretical claim that the 'Divinest part of all [Virgil's] writings' was to be found in the *Georgics* (Dryden, i. 54–5). The theme of a divinely ordained dispensation working through trade and empire was even more central to Pope's design, as he sought to give his conclusion a prophetic and cosmic ordering which would cement its political and imperial message.

In time, the currency thus acquired gave rise to 'an astonishing vogue for georgic poetry which lasted for most of the eighteenth century', and this development in taste has been linked to the rise of country house and a new concern for agriculture.[4] Unquestionably social forces played some part in the fashion, and we might add to

---

[1] Another contributor to the *Miscellanies* of 1693 was the youthful Henry Sacheverell, then a friend of Addison, with a portion of the first *Georgic*. John Ogilby had produced two complete versions of Virgil at the mid-century; unlike his Homer, these left no visible mark on Pope. For the background, see Durling (1935).

[2] Low (1985: esp. 221–95).   [3] Chalker (1969: 87).   [4] Wilkinson (1969: 299–300).

those named the passion for landscape gardening and the particular obsession with silviculture which Evelyn helped to engender. In the last analysis, however, this was a *literary* cult, one which depended on certain attitudes and qualities of mind which readers had now discovered in the four Virgilian poems. Where the Elizabethans had prized epic and idyll, and the Romantics would turn especially towards lyric, eighteenth-century writers and readers found a new resonance in didactic kinds. The *Eclogues* had previously received more attention, as befitting the established position of pastoral within the literary kinds. Only now did georgic poetry find its proper place in generic classification, and then with its increasing popularity begin to spill over into the better recognized kinds. In 1706 came what was generally perceived as the first truly English georgic (i.e. one not translated or imitated from earlier models), in the shape of *Cyder*, by John Philips. By 1710 Swift was burlesquing the form in his 'Description of a City Shadow', foreshadowing the more extensive redeployment of georgic motifs in John Gay's *Trivia* (1715). Meanwhile, in 1711, Addison's protégé Thomas Tickell was lecturing at Oxford on didactic epic, putting it second only to epic, and then contributing a georgic or hunting (cynegetic) to the *Guardian* in 1713, complete with a section on the founder of this activity, the biblical Nimrod. A better known series of lectures was delivered at Oxford by Joseph Trapp, the professor of poetry, and published between 1711 and 1719. One of the lectures, which came out in 1715, was entitled *De poemate didactico*, a branch of writing which Trapp regards as potentially among the most elevated of all kinds. Only Virgil has fully realized this potential, according to the lectures, in a manner which places the *Georgics* at the very peak of his achievement.[5]

It was Dryden and Addison who had begun this *renversement des alliances* in critical theory. True, Cowley and Evelyn had both looked on Virgil as 'the best of poets', supplanting the orthodox preference for Homer. But the later critics went further, disrupting the traditional hierarchy of kinds by finding in the *Georgics* 'that best poem of the best poet', and 'the most complete, elaborate, and finish'd piece of all antiquity'. It is admitted that the *Aeneid* is 'of a Nobler kind; but the *Georgic* is more perfect in its kind' (Dryden, v. 153). At other moments Addison's preface appears to suggest that this superiority is not something casual, but rooted in the form itself, since georgic has 'the most delightful part of Nature for its Province' (Addison, v. 146). Moreover, he indicates that digressions, whilst permissible, must be woven into 'the main design of the *Georgic*', a test which, if rigorously applied, many of the great epics might be said to pass only with difficulty. It is a lesson Pope was to keep in mind when he composed *Windsor-Forest*. In the most frequently quoted passage of his essay, Addison clinches a contrast with Hesiod by commending Virgil's verbal decorum: 'He delivers the meanest of his Precepts with a kind of Grandeur, he breaks the Clods and tosses the Dung about with an air of gracefulness' (Addison, v. 151). The preface constructs a more elevated and sublime piece of writing than modern criticism would recognize, and Dryden's translation sometimes performs a

---

[5] See Durling (1935: 21–2). Trapp, who later produced a translation of the *Aeneid* in blank verse, also wrote a poem on the Peace in 1713. By this date he was a firm admirer of Pope: see p. 60, above.

similar magnification at the verbal level, partly for mock-heroic purposes. But the *Georgics* undoubtedly contain an element of nobility and grandeur, and it is this side of the work which Pope drew on.

Although Samuel Johnson considered the preface a juvenile and superficial performance, it is easy to see why Addison clarified Augustan feelings with regard to georgic. His opening passage makes an effective distinction with pastoral and epic, forms where Theocritus and Homer were unrivalled, with georgic, where the Latin poet was able to able to excel his Greek predecessors in the middle style. There is a laborious feel to the next section, where Addison seeks to show that georgic should be exempt from the rules of pastoral, where it had previously been placed. But the criticism picks up again with an energetic defence of the aesthetic possibilities of the form: 'This kind of Poetry I am now speaking of, addresses it self wholly to the Imagination: It is altogether Conversant among the Fields and Woods . . . It raises in our Minds a pleasing variety of Scenes and Landskips, whilst it teaches us: and makes the dryest of its Precepts look like a Description' (Dryden, v. 146).[6] Equally telling is a passage in which Addison suggests the manner in which georgic permits a precept to enter the mind 'as it were through a By-way' (Addison, v. 148). This strategy of oblique commentary was to be vital to *Windsor-Forest*.

In tandem, Dryden's rendition and Addison's articulate defence of Virgil's achievement provided a favourable literary climate when Pope moved on from pastoral to a quasi-georgic genre, a move signalled in the last line of *Windsor-Forest*. The 'vogue' had already been instituted by *Cyder*. What is notable is that Pope devotes none of his attention to the homely details of beekeeping or any other rural craft. In one sense his poem scarcely belongs to the English georgic, with its delight in the practicalities of country living, as exemplified by John Philips or John Dyer. His courtly strain allows only a dignified reference to the intellectual pursuits of the retired statesman, together with a depiction of seasonal sports—the most overtly 'georgic' material in the entire work.

The element in Virgil which Pope does repeatedly draw on is what might be termed the eco-political. Both poems have a deep sense of the fragility of the landscape, as an index of the vulnerability of the state and of all human contrivances. In both cases, we observe a landscape ravaged by internal struggles. The Roman civil war, culminating for Virgil in the battle of Philippi (42 BC) and the Treaty of Brundisium (40 BC), had left its scars on the countryside. Worse, it meant that returning veterans were given grants of land, so that small yeomen were evicted from their properties. Pope writes directly about the displacement of 'industrious Swains' by brutal Norman kings (43–84). The entire logic of the poem, as this book should make clear, suggests that the poet has in mind the treatment of forest residents, first in the time of William III, but second and proleptically in the forthcoming reign of George I. Thus the threat to the very soil of Windsor is also a threat to the civic identity of those like the Pope family who belonged to a politically unacceptable order.

---

[6] Part of this passage is quoted by the Twickenham editors (*TE* i. 135), who correctly observe that this is 'an essay which Pope could not have failed to note'.

There is a direct link here with Virgil, which does not seem to have been mentioned in Pope scholarship. In the second book, the poet makes a passing reference to a recent episode in history:

Qualem in felix amisit Mantua campum.

(*Georgics*, ii. 198)

This alludes to a series of land-confiscations by Octavian's representative Varus in 40 BC, which in time extended to an area around Mantua, Virgil's birthplace. The ninth of his *Eclogues* deals more fully with this process. In that poem the poet trying to halt these evictions is named Menalcas, but he is generally believed to stand for Virgil, who may well have had his ancestral farm confiscated. (If so, it was possibly restored after an appeal; the facts are not clear.) The entire situation is strikingly similar to the one in which Pope would find himself as soon as the Hanoverians came to power, when his family estate had to be forfeited—as we saw in Chapter 1. Even if Virgil was not personally involved in the land transactions, which is not especially likely, he knew in considerable detail about what was going on. What have been called the 'green politics' of the *Eclogues* were based on an intimate sense of the after-effects of civil war.[7]

Now the *Eclogues* are politely stated to have been instigated by Virgil's first important patron, C. Asinius Pollio, one of the major sponsors of literature in the late Republic.[8] We need not believe this, but the famous fourth *Eclogue* is certainly inscribed to Pollio in the wake of the Brundisium accord, which he had helped to arrange. Pollio was consul in 40 BC, and a year later was to be awarded a triumph for a victory in Illyria. Only then did he seek retirement, abating his former support for Antony in a pose of studied neutrality. In this he resembles Pope's main patron, Trumbull (even though the latter had long retired into private life), for Trumbull had clearly disavowed his strong loyalty to the Whig cause by the time of *Windsor-Forest*. Moreover, Pollio had taken up the young Virgil, as Trumbull had taken up Pope; he had embarked on a history of the civil wars, as Trumbull had begun memoirs of his times; he founded a public library in Rome, and earned the commendations of Horace. If Lansdowne is required to play the role of Maecenas, then Trumbull in many ways comes closer to Pollio than to his acknowledged models, Scipio and Atticus (*WF*, 257–8). It was Pollio, in one version of the story, who assisted Virgil in his efforts to resist eviction from his farm.[9] Sadly for Pope, the parallel breaks down here. Trumbull could do nothing in 1715 and 1716; Pope hoped that he might do something to soften the malignancies of the neighbourhood, but it was all to no avail (see Chapter 1). The family was ejected from Binfield prior to Trumbull's death at the end of 1716.

Besides these glancing contacts Pope had a body of history supporting his case, to which he makes oblique allusion by calling up apposite mythology. Most obviously,

---

[7] Charles Martindale's use of the phrase is roguish, if not ironic, but his commentary illuminates Pope's use of 'green' vocabulary (see Martindale 1997: 109).

[8] See Gold (1987: 170).

[9] For the use of the *Eclogues* in prophetic verse, see *SDW*, ch. 6.

the English Civil War, which had threatened the Trumbull family timber, had left its marks all over the English landscape. For John Evelyn, it was the 'late prodigious Spoilers', the parliamentarian incomers, who had desecrated the 'goodly Woods' (see Chapter 8, below). An essential part of Stuart ideology lay in the belief that the 'usurpers' after their triumph in the war had sequestrated land from the loyal gentry, and torn down large tracts of woodland to make money and furnish their own estates. According to this version of history, the parliamentarians were the latest in the line of despoilers, going back to the Normans and to Henry VIII.

At the start of his first *Georgic*, after invoking Maecenas, Virgil turns to an array of harvest deities as protectors of the soil and patrons of its cultivation. Attention is usually focused on Octavian, who is introduced at the end of the list (i. 24–42) as one who will soon rival these in divinity. The twelve authentic deities include *alma Ceres*, as the patron of agriculture and the one who introduced the cultivation of corn to the human race. She is named along with Liber, identified by the Romans with Bacchus. There follow the Fauns, woodland deities who were the guardians of crops and herds, together with the Dryads, whose special care lay in the trees. Dryden translates, 'Ye Nymphs that haunt the Mountain and the Plain', and Pope's invocation picks up on this: 'Be present, Sylvan Maids!' (3). Just afterwards Pan himself (otherwise Faunus), who figures in *Windsor-Forest* (37) as the god of shepherds, prior to his appearance as the lascivious pursuer of a forest spirit. In that central episode, Pope refers to Lodona as 'a rural Nymph' (171), but her position as one of Diana's train establishes her as a nymph charged to protect the sacred groves. Her story thus recalls the myth of Callisto, as well as that of Erisichthon, both fables of violation expressed through the despoliation of the forest. Virgil's list also embraces Neptune (*WF*, 223), the god of rivers and fountains as well as the sea, but present chiefly as the creator of the horse; and Minerva, inventor of the olive, which is a symbol of peace Pope invokes at the end of his poem (429). The most important of these for Pope was Ceres (see Chapter 5, above), and it is apt that Virgil should have returned to the goddess later in the first book (*Georgics*, i. 338–50) for a description of the rites of her annual festival. Contemporary readers might also have recalled that Plutus, the god of wealth, was the daughter of Ceres, but was brought up by the goddess of peace Pax. (The common depiction of Pax was with Plutus in her lap, and a cornucopia in her hand.) All these mythological connections serve for both Virgil and Pope to establish a sense of rural prosperity and harmony after the ravages of war; the message of the *Georgics* might be stated as, 'Peace and Plenty tell, a CAESAR reigns.'

Another central passage in the first book deals with the loss of the Golden Age, an episode which translators had often chosen to attempt. The end of the primal era came with the invention of the plough, thanks to Ceres, and pastimes such as snaring and trapping the birds and beasts. This 'Jovian fall' had long been paralleled to the fall of man in Genesis, and Pope's Eden plainly includes elements both of the biblical Paradise and the classical Golden Age. Equally, the image of desecration in the section on the Norman yoke is drawn in part from Virgil's picture of a plague-ridden landscape in his third book (*Georgics*, iii. 478–566). In a more sustained way than any previous English poet, Pope takes over the Virgilian metaphor identifying the health of the landscape with the health of the state. The main difference is that Pope historicizes the material more overtly: there are distinct temporal phases which the forest has undergone, and there are culprits who can be named for its periods of distress. What in Virgil is attributed to the large impersonal forces of nature becomes in Pope the consequence of human rapacity and folly. On the other hand, he comes close to matching the deification of Octavian, by attributing the renewal of a Golden Age to a particular dynasty and, in the present, to a particular monarch—an almost deified Anne.

Several other direct allusions can be traced. The famous description of the beauties of Italy in Virgil's second book (*Georgics*, ii. 109–76) underlies Pope's evocation of an English Eden. More specifically, there is the technique of defining by negatives which Virgil uses (*Sed neque Mediorum silvae, ditessima terra | nec pulcher Ganges atque auro turbidus Hermus | laudibus Italiae certent, non Bactra neque Indi | totaque turiferis Panchaia pinguis harenis*, *Georgics*, ii. 136–9). Pope borrows this more than once, especially at ll. 29–36 and 223–34. It is true that there may be some mediation here through Addison's *Letter from Italy*, one of the author's best poems and certainly his most Virgilian. Towards the end, after extolling the physical beauties of Italy in his master's vein, Addison turns the stock motif, 'We not envy [foreign country x]', to a paean in favour of British liberty:

> We envy not the warmer clime, that lies
> In ten degrees of more indulgent skies,
> Nor at the coarseness of our heaven repine,
> Though o'er our heads the frozen Pleiads shine:
> 'Tis liberty that crowns Britannia's isle,
> And makes her barren rocks and her bleak mountains shine.
>
> (Addison, i. 36–7)[10]

Even if Addison had been there first, Pope has been able to find his own equivalent for the georgic formulas. Particularly successful is his adaptation of Virgil's comparisons in a later part of *Windsor-Forest*:

> Let *Volga*'s Banks with Iron Squadrons shine,
> And Groves of Lances glitter on the *Rhine*,
> Let barb'rous *Ganges* arm a servile Train;
> Be mine the Blessings of a peaceful Reign.
>
> (363–6)

Here the glamorous object of comparison really is not superior, which could be said only dubiously about the vaunting contrasts made earlier with Olympus or the Po.

An equally close parallel can be drawn in respect of the theme of retirement. In his passage beginning *O fortunatos nimium*, Virgil praises a life of calm self-sufficiency, involving study of the 'causes of things', a lack of ambition, and a care for

---

[10] Pope recommended Addison's passage on liberty to Jervas in August 1714 (*Corr.* i. 245).

the immediate environment (ii. 458–540). Cowley had translated this favourite excerpt in 1668 (see Chapter 8, below), and Pope may have felt that he had no need to present the material at length. His abbreviated passage (235–58) is a masterpiece of poetic distillation, packing in most of Virgil's significant detail. The structure is closely mimicked: Virgil's progression *felix qui potuit . . . fortunatus et ille* (ii. 490, 493) is matched by Pope's 'Happy the Man . . . Happy next him' (*WF*, 235, 237). Again there is one departure: Pope describes a hermit-like figure, with little obvious social contact. By contrast Virgil's retiree celebrates Bacchus, and engages in rural pursuits alongside the people in his neighbourhood. It is usually stated that Pope had other famous renditions of the theme in his head, most notably Horatian treatments of the *beatus ille* topos. This must be true, but the general organization of the passage owes more to the passage in the *Georgics* than any other source.

Other broad similarities have been pointed out by earlier commentators. In the most sustained discussion of the georgic properties of *Windsor-Forest*, Chalker accurately describes the nature of Pope's political attitudes: 'Civilisation, balance, order—these are states that are constantly assailed, and that must be constantly defended of they are to be maintained. The Peace of Utrecht . . . is to be welcomed, even rapturously . . . but [it] is placed in an historical context that makes facile optimism inappropriate.'[11] We could say much the same of Virgil: his faith in the young Octavian, standing on the brink of some forty-five years virtually unchallenged as emperor, is naturally stronger than anything Pope can command in respect of the ageing Queen. The big difference is that Augustus came at the start of an imperial line, whereas Anne was the last of hers (unless something very dramatic, which Pope feared to contemplate, should occur). There is consequently a note of strain in the English poet's evocation of a new Augustan age, which Virgil is able to avoid despite his Messianic tone. At the end of the first book, the poet describes evil portents which were observed after the murder of Julius Caesar, in language Pope recalled when he characterized the broken landscape under Norman oppression (compare *Georgics*, i. 466–88, with *WF*, 65–72). The bloody fields of Philippi and Pharsalia are living reminders of the scourge of civil war. Yet hope is hand: Virgil prays that Father Romulus and Mother Earth will join with Octavian to 'save the sinking Age' (as Dryden puts it), and that the blood already spilt should atone for past crimes. Pope offers up a similar prayer, but the Stuarts were not themselves the victors of the tumultuous struggles to which *Windsor-Forest* alludes. Each poet dramatizes the sorry past and the uncertain present, but Virgil is much more convincing in his vision of a Golden Age to come.

There is one more significant discrepancy in the respective methods of the two writers. Where Virgil uses agriculture as the vehicle of his main metaphoric plot, it is rather trade and commerce which will usher in the millennium. The point has been best expressed by David B. Morris: 'The idea of a "better" Golden Age underlies Pope's choice of commerce as a resolving image and reflects an attitude wholly, if not exclusively, Virgilian. It affirms the lesson of the *Georgics*: that the new Age of

[11] Chalker (1969: 86).

Gold will not be achieved through nostalgia and pastoral ease but through the noble discipline of art and labor'. This difference again has a political undertow. As the same critic observes, 'Both poets . . . associate a condition of general harmony with enlightened government. Although both discover in contemporary rulers grounds for hope in future peace and order, however, they do not encourage partisan or utopian claims, nor do they forget that their subject is the unideal state of fallen humanity'.[12] Yet Virgil could rationally suppose that imperial Rome might match or surpass republican Rome in virtue as well as in might. Pope must struggle to convince us (or himself) that the new Britain will come closer to a human paradise than the previous centuries had been able to achieve. The carnage of the Roman civil wars was recent, and their mere cessation a cause for relief. In Britain the great clash had taken place more than half a century before, and yet the wounds had still not healed. Charles II had been restored and with this many royalist dreams fulfilled; but the subsequent course of history had quite failed to trace the proper providential curve.[13]

Both poets have their patriotic, not to say nationalistic, aims. Virgil had in a sense to create an Italian nation, since the country still lacked a true identity despite its gradual expansion northwards. We tend to forget that 'at the time when Virgil began the *Georgics* his native region between the Po and the Alps had only just officially become part of Italy'. Pope might have seen a comparable problem in the recent accession of Scotland after the Union of parliaments, but he chooses to leave this issue aside. Again, the propaganda for Octavian was designed to portray him as the great unifier, a supporter of the provinces against the narrow and corrupt elite of the metropolis. 'Actium was, in one sense, a victory for a party largely recruited from Roman knights of the towns of Italy over the degenerate aristocracy of the capital, for the peoples whom Virgil extolled in the *Georgics*'.[14] It would have been possible for Pope to adapt this circumstance to Tory ideology, and represent Anne's most loyal supporters as rural squires confronting the power of the Whig city magnates who had bankrolled the war; but this might have made the poem too close to day-to-day jockeying for power—too embroiled in politics under its most trivial aspects.

A large number of detailed parallels remain. It is sometimes unclear whether Pope is remembering the original *Georgics* or whether he has Dryden's translation in his head. To take a simple example, his expression 'if small Things we may with great compare' (*WF*, 105) might come from Virgil, *si parva licet componere magnis* (*Georgics*, iv. 176). But Dryden had rendered this almost proverbial line, 'If little things with great we may compare' (Dryden, v. 247), suggesting that Pope may wish us to reach back to the Roman poet through his English follower, as the cadence is almost identical in Dryden and Pope. The Twickenham editors note eight verbal borrowings from the Dryden translation, but others may be detected. (The most

---

[12] Morris (1973: 246, 239–40).

[13] See also *TE* i. 137–8 on the Golden Age in Virgil and Pope.

[14] Wilkinson (1969: 154). This author has a chapter on the afterlife of the *Georgics*, including a section on 'the eighteenth-century vogue', but surprisingly does not mention *WF* at all.

striking parallels occur at ll. 129, 146, and 186: while Pope's line, 'When moist *Arcturus* clouds the Sky' (119) echoes the structure of Dryden's 'When cold *Arcturus* rises with the Sun,' more closely than the original at *Georgics*, i. 67–8).

If any doubts should remain that Dryden's translation would have been strongly present in Pope's mind, these can be settled by recalling one circumstance. As we have already seen in Chapter 1, the *Works of Virgil in English* (1697) were garnished with many splendid accoutrements. Not the least of these were the hundred illustrations, each bearing a dedication to a subscriber. We observed earlier that the list of subscribers includes most of the good and great in the land, as these things were then reckoned, beginning with the Lord Chancellor and Lord Privy Seal. The first two dedicatees for the *Aeneid* were Prince George of Denmark and his wife, Princess Anne, indicating that the hierarchy of kinds counted for more than merely priority in the sequence of works as printed. Others represented were 'Henry *St. Johns, Esq.*', Pope's early friend William Walsh, and Sir Godfrey Kneller. Most appropriately of all, a passage in the fourth *Georgic* is accompanied by a plate illustrating the flight of bees, and dedicated to Sir William Trumbull, 'Principall Secretary of State & one of his mai^ties Most Honble Privy Councill'. The family coat of arms is reproduced, along with the motto 'VIRTUTE ET INDUSTRIA'. It is a suitably georgic sentiment, and one that Pope must have confronted when he made his youthful visits to Sir William's library.

One other recent English poem affected the poet's use of georgic properties. This was John Philips's *Cyder* (1708), a popular didactic treatment of a branch of agriculture mainly practised in the west of England. Philips employs a consciously mockheroic style, with frequent Miltonisms, but his aims are not altogether flippant. Pope must already have known his Tory riposte to Addison's *Campaign*, that is *Bleinheim* (1705), written seemingly at the suggestion of Harley and St John. The Twickenham editors note five allusions in *Windsor-Forest* to *Cyder* (though only one to *Bleinheim*). Of these the most obvious are at l. 134, drawing on Philips's 'they [birds] leave their little lives'; ll. 240–2, recalling Philips on herbs and minerals; and l. 321, following Philips, who refers to the killing of Charles I as 'O Fact | Unparalleled!' We may add the passage on Edward III (303–6), which harks back to the second canto of Philips's poem; and the lines on the British cross (387–8), resembling the closing section of *Cyder*. The most direct debt has not been previously noted: it also relates to the last verse paragraph of *Cyder* (ll. 657–9), immediately following the verses on the cross. Philips writes as follows:

> Meanwhile the swains
> Shall unmolested reap what plenty strows
> From well stor'd horn, rich grain, and timely fruits.

> (Chalmers, ii. 118)

This is taken up in the oration by Father Thames, with the concluding noun in Philips' first line used as a rhyme word:

> Safe on my Shore each unmolested Swain
> Shall tend the Flocks, or reap the bearded Grain.

> (*WF*, 369–70)

More generally, Philips anticipated Pope in redirecting Virgil's political ideology towards British history, when he wrote bitterly of the 'Apostate, Atheist rebels' who defied the king, and celebrated the reign of Anne as 'restraining' the rage of monarchs abroad.[15]

We could summarize Pope's relation to the *Georgics* in this way. *Windsor-Forest* is a georgic stripped of its element of didaxis, especially the practical advice on cultivation and husbandry. Apart from glancing references to this material, mostly in the section on rural sports, the poem extracts those parts of the source in Virgil which deal with myth and prophetic history and uses these for their political import. The *Georgics* are filtered through earlier English translations and adaptations, crucially those of Denham and Dryden, whilst the poem owes a little in style and ideological structure to *Cyder*. The central theme of Pope's British 'georgic' is the threat to the nation posed by the imminent dissolution of the Stuart line, an eventuality which will bring an end to the monarch's stewardship of the national demesne, and will potentially lead to the reimposition of chaos in the state and desolation for the landscape.

The georgic element does not exhaust the Virgilian contribution to *Windsor-Forest*. A number of allusions to the *Aeneid* and the *Eclogues* have been discovered. The Twickenham notes list about a dozen parallels with the *Aeneid*: most of these are glancing verbal similarities, and several are examples of stock epic diction taken from Dryden's translation. For instance, l. 173, 'Lodona's Fate, in long Oblivion cast,' echoes both *Aeneid*, vi. 715 and Dryden, vi. 968; while 'purple Deaths' in *WF*, 323 harks back to Dryden, xii. 1090. On this level the debt may be said to represent a general immersion of Pope's language in the idiom of heroic poetry.

It is only in recent times that more pervasive influences have been detected. Maynard Mack was the first to show that reminiscences of the fourth *Eclogue*, addressed to the consul Pollio (see above, p. 244), jostle with allusions to the Book of Isaiah to create a prophetic context for Pope's ending. In Mack's terms, 'As an essay in the georgic vein, glimmering from its first lines with quiet allusions to the great Roman original that educated contemporaries sometimes knew by heart, *Windsor-Forest* carried in its very makeup the apocalyptic dream' (*Life*, 201). Equally, the fund of references to other parts of the Virgilian canon supports the poem's milleniary conclusion. Naturally Pope had to hand the version of the fourth *Eclogue* in Dryden's translation of 1697 (an earlier rendition had appeared on the *Miscellanies* in 1684). It is hard to believe that ll. 88–9 are not to meant to call up Virgil (*Eclogues*, iv. 28–30), perhaps through Dryden: 'Unlabour'd Harvests shall the Fields adorn, | And cluster'd Grapes shall blush on every Thorn' (*Dryden*, iv. 33–4). The entire passage beginning, 'The Merchant still shall plough the deep for gain' (*Dryden*, iv. 38 ff.)

[15] In his useful discussion of *Cyder*, Chalker (1969: 45), rightly observes that *WF*, like Gay's *Trivia*, is not 'a straightforward imitation' of Virgil in the manner of Philips's poem. It is noteworthy that Philips describes a particular locality within England (mostly Herefordshire, rather than Shropshire, as Chalker would have it) and in this sense helps to prolong the loco-descriptive line of local patriotism. Pope's Windsor is very definitely a national shrine, and not one of the beauties of Berkshire.

underlies Pope's climactic prophecy (355–412); indeed, the lines in *Windsor-Forest* might be seen as a wonderful amplification of the source, adopting almost every idea present in Virgil or Dryden, and relating them to the immediate situation ushered in by the Peace. This is all the more remarkable since Pope had no boy-prince to stand in for Octavian: to allot this role openly to the Pretender would have been insulting to the Queen, and political dynamite. In fact James Francis Edward was 24 when *Windsor-Forest* came out, a year or two younger than Octavian when the *Eclogues* appeared.

We can be sure that Pope also had in his mind the sixth *Eclogue,* since the epigraph to *Windsor-Forest* is drawn from this source. At the start of his poem, Virgil asserts that he is unwilling to rehearse the military successes of his dedicatee, Alfenus Varus, and states his intention to confine himself to the province of the rustic muse:

> *Non iniussa cano: Te nostre,* Vare, *Myricae*
> *Te Nemus omne canet; nec Phebo gratior ulla est*
> *Quam sibi quae* Vari *praescripsit Pagina nomen.*
>
> (*Eclogue,* vi. 9–12)[16]

(I do not sing unordered. All our woods, every tamarisk bush will sing of you, Varus; no page is more agreeable to Apollo than one inscribed with the name of Varus at its head.)

This rejection of epic ambition was a rhetorical commonplace in lesser genres such as pastoral. Pope had no military exploits on which he could congratulate Lansdowne, but in any case he seems to be enlisting the passage to emphasize his commitment to the sylvan world around Windsor, with its overtones of retirement, peace, and humility.

A more sustained current of allusion in the poem makes a link with the *Aeneid.* The most obvious common factor lies in the exploitation of a personified river, Tiber and then Thames, to enunciate the destiny of the respective chosen race, a topic discussed at length in *SDW,* chapter 4. In addition, both Mack and Morris point to the recollection of Jove's prophecy in the first book of the *Aeneid* (see esp. i. 257–96), and show how Pope adapts Virgil's prophecy of a new Troy to fit the British context. To cite Mack again, the peace is seen as 'an achievement within history reminiscent of the Pax Romana of Augustus' (*Life,* 202), and the literary work which had most fully enshrined this view of Roman history was of course the *Aeneid.* There is a further recollection in Pope's train of personified vices who will be exiled by peace (413–22), as they bring to mind the entrance to the underworld, when the Sybil conducts Aeneas to meet the ghost of his father. Dryden translates:

> Just in the Gate, and in the Jaws of Hell,
> Revengeful Cares, and sullen Sorrows dwell;
> And pale Diseases, and repining Age;
> Want, Fear, and Famine's unresisted rage.
> Here Toils, and Death, and Death's half-brother, Sleep,
> Forms terrible to view, their Centry keep:

---

[16] Pope omits one line, 'if anyone possessed by love should read my verses'.

> With anxious Pleasures of a guilty Mind,
> Deep Frauds before, and open Force behind:
> The Furies Iron Beds, and Strife that shakes
> Her hissing Tresses, and unfolds her Snakes.
>
> (*Dryden*, vi. 384–93)

Pope was to revisit this scene in the *Dunciad*, but already in *Windsor-Forest* he contrived to find in the stock allegorical figures a particularized meaning to suit the immediate context. Pride and ambition cannot fail to remind us of Marlborough, as the poem has been proceeding; vengeance and persecution suggest the likelihood that the incoming Hanoverians would seek to punish the Tories who had opposed their accession; and faction and rebellion call up the clashes which were just over the horizon in 1713. By the middle of the century, a dispossessed Jacobite might well think that the reigns of George I and George II had acted out this nightmare destiny all too accurately, once the task of 'exiling' devolved upon these monarchs. The official message supplied by the conclusion is that Albion's golden days will come again, as Virgil had foreseen the return of the Golden Age under Augustus. But *Windsor-Forest* seems to intuit the prospect of a different turn of events, one that would usher in a world closer to the infernal regions of *Aeneid* VI. According to the orthodox teleology inscribed in classical history, Virgil's prophecy had largely come true. Perhaps the malignant possibilities suggested by Pope's allegorical train would equally be realized.

OVID'S GOLD AND SILVER

Like other manifestoes of a defeated party, *Windsor-Forest* celebrates the Golden Age Restored. Indeed, much of its language alludes directly to the notion of *aetas aurea*, one as old as Hesiod but given its classical expression by Ovid (*Metamorphoses*, i. 89). This was the phase reigned over by Saturn, himself a king later to be banished. At this period, too, Astraea lived on earth, dispensing justice; in later times she fled to the skies, despairing of the wickedness of men, and became the constellation Virgo. In Pope, the 'chaste' Queen (162) certainly identifies Anne principally with Diana, but since she is ruler of the land which is to become 'the World's great Oracle in Times to come' (382), the expression suggests an Astraean role as fount of justice. All this relates *Windsor-Forest* to the traditional chronology of the ages of humanity.[17]

However, Pope's poetic masters in this work are Virgil and Ovid, both of them prime figures in what was early known as the Golden Age in Latin literature. Among the ideals which came to the fore when Augustus rose to power were the imperial

---

[17] Plowden (1983, 44–55), rather unconvincingly tries to show that Ovid's myth of Creation, as set out in the opening passage of the *Metamorphoses*, underlies the entire poem, along with the *Astronomica* of Marcus Manilius. There may be glancing references, but neither 'source' appears to be as pervasive as Plowden suggests.

mission of Rome and the restoration of a golden age. There is thus an implied compliment and a boast in Pope's alignment of his own undertaking with the works of his ancient predecessors. All who follow him, we may deduce, can aspire to the rank of no more than silver poets.

Furthermore, the poem trades on other associations of the Latin word *aureus*. As a noun it referred to the standard gold coin of Rome, and as we have seen *Windsor-Forest* recreates in several places the effects of numismatic design. As an adjective, apart from its literal sense, the word could mean 'gilded,' in a narrow or extended application; from this comes a sense of 'glittering,' so that both Virgil and Ovid use it to qualify the sun (see, for example, *Georgics*, i. 431). Further along its metaphoric line, *aureus* meant 'beautiful or splendid,' in respect of either physical or mental excellences, as Lewis and Short rather primly phrase it. Thus we have the golden mean in Horace's *Odes*, ii. 10 (*auream quisquis mediocratatem | Diligit*). At the end of the same author's sixteenth *Epode*, we hear of the islands of the blessed, in the western ocean, where Jupiter preserves a little bit of the golden era—*tempus aureum*—in an age of iron (63–6).[18]

One specific usage in Latin literature was the so-called golden line, a verse built on a highly stylized pattern of adjective + noun + verb + adjective + noun. Like other concepts involving gold, it had its silver equivalent: adjective + noun + verb + noun + adjective. Virgil uses the golden line sparingly, and in the *Georgics* it is almost always employed to round off a sentence emphatically, as at i. 468.[19] In an uninflected language such as English, it is virtually impossible to have a series of words without small articles or prepositions intervening. Moreover, Pope's essential unit is the couplet, whereas his Roman predecessors generally wrote extended discursive poetry in metrical forms based on a single line (the one exception is the elegiac couplet, not employed in the main poems influencing Pope). However, what we find in *Windsor-Forest* is a number of syntactical devices to achieve a comparable balance—and these too are most often found in passages of conclusive force or other special emphasis. The pattern adjective + noun + adjective + noun + verb occurs at 1. 17, in relation to the 'checquer'd Scene'. An alternative is proper noun + common noun + common noun + proper noun + verb is found at 1. 37: here, as sometimes in Latin, phonetic parallels underpin the symmetry. However, an exact 'golden' pattern (ANVAN) is used at 1. 92, even though we really need the end of the previous line for the full semantic effect:

> Fair *Liberty, Britannia*'s Goddess, rears
> Her chearful Head, and leads the golden Years.

It *may* be a coincidence that this climactic statement of a theme central to the entire poem has recourse to a golden line. But since the sentiment is expressly Stuart, enacting the message of restoration so vital to the cause, then it is not stretching the evidence to suggest it may be far from a coincidence.

---

[18] In hermetic lore the *aurea hora* signifies the end of the night of unknowing, and the dawn of enlightenment, ushered in by Aurora. Pope's golden years, ushered in by Anne, represent the end of Cromwellian and Williamite night.   [19] Wilkinson (1983: 35).

There are variants of this basic structure at other significant moments in the poem. Another verse concluding a paragraph is l. 290, on Granville's claim to the Garter (this runs VANAN). The catalogue of rivers ends with a variant employing a participle form, that is AN[V]AN (348). Sometimes the verb comes first, but this requires a copulative which weakens the tautness of the form: 'Paints the green Forests and the flow'ry Plains' (428). An exact replica of the golden line is not frequent, but it does occur, for instance at l. 404, 'And Feather'd People crowd my wealthy Side'. Among the variants are patterns usually described in rhetorical terms as chiasmus or antimetabole; but they can also be viewed syntactically, as English equivalents of the favourite word-patterns of Golden Latin verse.[20]

Even this does not exhaust the mythic potential of gold. The poem celebrates the productive harvests of Windsor, connoting peace and prosperity in the nation at large. These are figuratively expressed as '*Ceres*'s Gifts' (39). Ceres was the daughter of Saturn (or, in Greek terms, Demeter was the daughter of Kronos). She is thus mythologically linked with the Golden Age; and emblematically she is *dea flava*, the goddess with yellow or golden hair. Finally it is relevant that she also 'performed the duties of a legislator, and the Sicilians experienced the advantage of her salutary laws'.[21]

The phrase *dea flava* comes from Ovid, but not from the *Metamorphoses*. It occurs near the start of a long passage in the *Fasti*, where the poet relates the story of Proserpina, who was of course the daughter of Ceres and Jupiter. This is one of the most resonant among the myths of the Western world, with a memorable passage by Milton as a *locus classicus* (see *PL* iv. 268–72). Yet it is important to notice that it follows a pattern common to the *Metamorphoses* and to *Windsor-Forest*: that is, the narrative of a virgin torn from the care of a tutelary female figure, and ultimately transformed from her mortal guise. The allegory of Proserpina places her mother Ceres in a role immediately comparable to that of Diana in the Lodona episode; more directly still, it relates the appearance of the goddess here to her participation in the myth of Erisichthon (see below, pp. 270–1).

It was in Virgil that Sir James Frazer found his golden bough, or at least the best-known literary treatment of a motif associated with the cult of Diana. Fittingly, Frazer went on to edit and translate the *Fasti*. From his translation of Book IV we may extract some key lines on the festival commemorating the abduction of Proserpina, which was celebrated in April (the feast of Ceres herself occurred in the autumn). Ceres is lauded as the first to introduce tillage to humankind, and as the instigator of a new order: *pace Ceres laeta est* ('Ceres delights in peace; and you, ye husbandmen, pray for perpetual peace and for a pacific prince').[22] The games of Ceres were actually held on 12 April, one of the *Fasti* which Ovid's poem dignifies;

[20] Rhetorically conceived, there is a chiasmic structure in l. 71, 'the Fox obscene to gaping Tombs retires', but the placing of the verb outside the symmetrical reversal precludes what might be called a golden effect.

[21] Lemprière (1994: 156). Yellow and golden are interchangable in English poetic diction, just as in heraldic description, during Pope's lifetime: note that 'milder Autumn' (97) was originally 'yellow Autumn' in the manuscript (Schmitz, 24).

[22] Frazer (1929: i. 107).

and by a happy chance this chimed with the modern calendar—it was just one day after the formal ratification of the peace which Pope's work sets out to commemorate. Ovid then tells the story of the abduction of Proserpina by Pluto, and her mother's desperate search for the girl. Eventually Jupiter permits Proserpina to return to her mother for six months in the year. During her absence the earth had lain barren and all cultivation had come to a stop. With her restoration came a rich harvest and a reassumption of the land by laughing Ceres: in Frazer's rendering, 'Then at last Ceres recovered her looks and her spirits, and set wreaths of corn ears ion her hair; and the laggard fields yielded a plenteous harvest, and the threshing-floor could hardly hold the high-piled sheaves'.[23]

Thus we see how the mythical presence of Ceres helps Pope to link several crucial elements in his design: the threat of rape and abduction, the union of peace and plenty, the return of the seasons, the transformation of the countryside under beneficent female rule. Pope's readers would have known the *Fasti* a little less intimately than the *Metamorphoses*, but they were assuredly familiar with the story of Proserpina from literary and iconographical sources. It is uncertain how many of the echoes of the story would have resonated in the mind of the first readers of *Windsor-Forest*, but it is prudent to state that this foundation myth for agriculture would have been a commonplace to most people who came on the 'yellow Harvests' and '*Ceres*' Gifts' in the poem.[24]

Nothing shows the place of Ovid in the early Augustan imagination more clearly than Tonson's edition of the *Metamorphoses* (1717). This lavishly mounted translation appeared after the arrival of the Hanoverians and it was dedicated to the Princess of Wales, whose portrait by Kneller served as frontispiece. (Each individual book carries its own dedication to a notable woman of the time, with coats of arms attached to all their names.) However, most of the translations used were in existence, in fact already in print, years earlier. Dryden contributed long sections, including the whole of the first book. Addison contributed the second and third books; Samuel Garth, the editor, chose Book XIV for his own translation. The last book, like a number of others, was rendered by several hands. Among the poets represented were Rowe, Croxall, Maynwaring, Eusden, Tate, and John Gay, who was responsible for much of Book IX. And Pope himself appeared in the list, with the episode of Dryope in this same book.[25]

Naturally the most relevant segment of the edition, for Pope's long-term purposes, is the translation of Book I, by Dryden, with its treatment of the myth of creation and the ages of mankind. Pope would have known this version from a time not very long after its appearance in 1693. Likewise Pope could become familiar with Addison's renderings of Books II and III when they came out in the fifth

---

[23] Frazer (1929: i. 221).

[24] The translator of Book VIII in the Tonson *Metamorphoses*, the obscure Thomas Vernon, has Ceres bowing her consent to suppliants who came to her grove: 'The beauteous Goddess with a graceful air, | Bow'd in consent, and nodded to their pray'r. | The awful motion shook the fruitful ground, | And wav'd the fields with golden harvests crown'd.'

[25] This was a very early work, written in the poet's teens. See *TE* i. 338–9.

Miscellanies of 1703. The episode of Hermaphroditus from Book IV had been published by Tonson in the fifth *Miscellany* a few years earlier. Pope's own contribution
shows him honing his Ovidian manner, and a few phrases were actually transplanted direct into *Windsor-Forest*. All the same, the portions he felt closest to, when
he revised *Windsor-Forest*, may have included those translated by his friends, Gay,
Rowe, Congreve, and Garth himself—most of these seem to have been more recent
undertakings (some may even have postdated 1713). Of course, another friend,
Swift, had produced what is virtually a travesty of the Baucis and Philemon episode
in 1709, in the sixth *Miscellanies*, and had elicited Addison's help in doing this; but
there was never much sign that Pope wanted to follow Swift into this vein of poetry.

Obviously, it is the story of Lodona which provides Pope with the chance to introduce the most pervasive Ovidian colouring into his poem. An excellent analysis of
this passage by David R. Hauser shows how it served multiple purposes: among
these functions are to supply a transition from the Forest to the world at large, to
represent war and peace allegorically, and to anticipate parts of the concluding
prophecy. Hauser argues that Pope may have been familiar with the moral glosses
on the *Metamorphoses* provided by numerous mythographers, and demonstrates
how the interpretation of Diana in these sources would aid Pope's design 'to view
Arcadia-England under divine guidance'. The Ovidian tales instanced by Hauser
include those of Arethusa, Syrinx, Daphne, and Callisto. To these we should add
Erisichthon (see pp. 270–1 below), and perhaps briefly Acis and Galatea. Finally,
Hauser produces additional evidence to support the presence of an Astraean myth
underlying Pope's references to the golden years in prospect—a possibility already
raised in Chapter 4.[26]

   The episode of Lodona is segued into the description of the hunt by means of two
brief passages, each of which establishes the relevance of Diana as goddess of the
forest. First comes a sentence of three balanced couplets, placing Anne at the centre
of the mythic design:

> Let old *Arcadia* boast her ample Plain,
> Th' immortal Huntress, and her Virgin Train;
> Nor envy *Windsor*! since thy Shades have seen
> As bright a Goddess, and as chast a Queen;
> Whose Care, like hers, protects the Sylvan Reign,
> The Earth's fair Light, and Empress of the Main.

(159–64)

Here the standard associations of Artemis/Diana are all to the immediate purpose.
'She was a goddess of wild life, a virgin huntress, attended by a train of nymphs . . .
She was also identified with the moon . . . She was especially worshipped by
women . . . her most famous cult, as *Diana Nemorensis* ("of the grove") was at

---

[26] Hauser (1966: 465–82): one of the most important and most unaccountably neglected essays ever
devoted to *WF*. A further linked suggestion is that Father Thames occupies the role of Saturn, the father
of Astraea (Hauser 1966: 481–2).

Aricia in the Alban hills where her shrine stood in a grove'.[27] Anne's 'Sylvan reign' is yoked by the rhyme with her empire 'of the Main,' another reminder that the trees of the forest will form the basis of Britain's naval strength in war and peace.

The poem proceeds with a symmetrically constructed sentence, again occupying six lines:

> Here too, 'tis sung, of old *Diana* stray'd,
> And *Cynthus'* Top forsook for *Windsor* Shade;
> Here was she seen o'er Airy wastes to rove,
> Seek the clear Spring, or haunt the pathless Grove;
> Here arm'd with Silver Bows, in early Dawn,
> Her buskin'd Virgins trac'd the Dewy Lawn.
>
> (165–70)

The transference of classical Arcadia to the environs of Windsor is cemented by the device of imagining Diana to have left her native mountain of Cynthus (the root of the appellation Cynthia, as at l. 200) to 'haunt' the royal forest. Compared with the legends of Brut or Joseph of Arimethea visiting Albion, there is a grace and propriety about this fancy. The theme of virginity is invoked, and, as we shall see, it is precisely the violation of innocence which extends from the mythical Lodona to the political England.[28]

Pope's reference to the 'Silver Bows' of Diana's train sets up a pattern of reference to the attributes of Diana as moon-deity. When Lodona enters the text, we are told that she was a daughter of the Thames, a 'rural Nymph' who resembled her mistress so closely that she and the goddess could be distinguished 'But by the Crescent and the golden Zone' (176). Otherwise Lodona is accoutred like others in Diana's train: 'She scorn'd the Praise of Beauty, and the Care; | A Belt her Waste, a Fillet binds her Hair, | A painted Quiver on her Shoulder sounds, | And with her Dart the flying Deer she wounds' (177–80). There are of course innumerable sources for this picture of Diana and her followers, but Pope probably has in mind the episode of Callisto and Jupiter in the second book of the *Metamorphoses*. This is how Addison translated the relevant verses in the Tonson edition:

> The nymph nor spun, nor dress'd with artful pride,
> Her vest was gather'd up, her hair was try'd;
> Now in her hand a splender spear she bore,
> Now a light quiver on her shoulders wore;
> To chaste *Diana* from her youth inclin'd,
> The sprightly warriors of the wood she joyn'd.[29]

Callisto, we recall, emerged from her encounter with Jupiter deflowered and disgraced. Lodona too succumbs to her predator and feels shame like Callisto. Having

---

[27] Harvey (1937: 52, 143–4).
[28] Note also that the final verse quoted takes the form ANVAN—a perfect golden line, if we allow for the necessary English particles, 'her' and 'the'.
[29] Ovid (1961: 51).

'stray'd' beyond the forest's 'verdant Limits' (182), she undergoes a kind of fall, of the sort which England may undergo if its protective timber 'walls' are weakened.

Ovid is undeniably the main literary source here. Yet other texts may intervene, including perhaps the Mutability Cantos of the *Faerie Queene*, where it is Faunus, often identified with Pan, who spies on the naked Diana (see p. 272, below). But the material belongs at a fundamental level to what has been called 'the Ovidian nexus'. It is more than the fact that the mythical personages appear in the *Metamorphoses*, behaving in analogous ways. Rather, we find in the Lodona episode an appropriation of Ovid's moral and psychological properties, and especially the identification of Arcadia with a place of secrecy invaded by a tyrannical male.[30]

One more echo may be mentioned. As mentioned in Chapter 3, Pope interested himself around 1717–18 in the translation of Geoffrey of Monmouth prepared by Revd Aaron Thompson. The larger impact of this work relates to Pope's projected *Brutiad*, a plan which like Milton's *Arthuriad* remained unfulfilled. One task which he did accomplish was to translate for Thompson the Latin verses addressed by Brutus to Diana, in eight lines beginning, 'Goddess of Woods, tremendous in the chace' (*TE* vi. 192). The passage as a whole shows that it is Diana who suggests Britain as a home for the new Trojan realm, in response to the question by Brutus, 'In what new nation shall we fix our Seat?' By a natural transference we can read the monarch's seat (*WF*, 2) as the destined home of a new imperial civilization, chosen as a fit setting by the goddess who ruled over 'Mountain-wolves and all the savage race', and who merited the praise of 'Quires of Virgins' at 'hallow'd Altars'. Pagan and Christian themes come together here: Anne has triumphed over the barbarism and savagery of the previous century, in the role of the tremendous hunter-queen Diana, and now she incites national thanksgiving in a collective act of worship at the end of the war.

The presence of Ovid, naturally, does not preclude the coexistence of the wider mythical and iconographic pattern we have been tracing. Lodona's transformation is couched in what must be significantly charged language, given the special emphasis of repetition:

> She said, and melting as in Tears she lay,
> In a soft, silver Stream dissolv'd away.
> The silver Stream her Virgin Coldness keeps,
> For ever murmurs, and for ever weeps;
> Still bears the Name the hapless Virgin bore,
> And bathes the Forest where she rang's before.
> In her chast Current of the Goddess laves,
> And with Celestial Tears augments the Waves.
>
>   (203–10)

---

[30] We might also note that Ovid refers to the Arcadian landscape as surviving 'heav'n's destructive fire': in terms close to those of *WF*, he adds, 'The fields and woods revive, and Nature smiles again' (Ovid 1961: 51). So the forest symbolizes England's regeneration after the ravages of the 17th century.

So intense a use of iteration is not just a rhetorical trick in the poet's fingers; it is employed to set up a kind of barcarolle, with the waves gently lapping as the goddess of inviolate spaces laments the ravished woodland virgin who strayed beyond her protection. Everything is *argenteus*, silver, silvery, or silvered. We recall that, heraldically, argent is depicted (sometimes by the use of lead, more often in stylized graphic terms) as white, the colour of purity and modesty: some writers have even tried to show that a field argent itself represents chastity.[31] That may not be historically accurate; but allegorically silver does have a long association with innocence.

As we saw in the Introduction, the colour silver was involved in a network of elaborate connections which together composed an entire lunar symbolism. The alchemists had always linked Diana with the process of whitening or purification in the distillation of the celestial dew or 'philosopher's vitriol'. On occasions Luna was even identified with the Virgin of Christian lore, as 'mary, the female stone of loveliness'; on the other hand, the naked Diana could be viewed as nature unclothed—hence Giordano Bruno regarded Actaeon as a kind of explorer-hero, searching fearlessly for truth. Thus there are many ways in which the silver goddess Diana/Luna/moon/female complements the golden Ceres.

Diana is most often associated with the element of water, as against the linkage of Ceres with earth. The 'watry Landskip' of the Lodona section goes with the cold-moist, liquid attributes of winter in the traditional schema, as Lodona transformed into a river will retain for all time her 'Virgin Coldness' (205). Alchemists and Rosicrucians likewise identified silver with the female principle, with moist and cold characteristics, and with the moon—as in the chemical symbol ☽. It is apt to recall a statement by John Evelyn, in a passage he devotes to the correct time of year to fell timber:

Then for the Age of the Moon, it has religiously been observ'd; and that Dianas presidency in Sylvis was not so much celebrated to credit the fictions of the Poets; as for the dominion of the moist Planet, and her influence over Timber: For my part, I am not so much inclin'd to these Criticisms, that I should altogether govern a Felling at the pleasure of this mutable Lady; however there is doubtless some regard to be had, *Nec frusta signorum obitus speculamur & ornus.* (Evelyn, 299)

The quotation comes from the first of the *Georgics*: 'not in vain do we watch the rise and setting of the signs'. For Evelyn, there is still a half-belief that the moist and changeable goddess of the moon rules over his woodlands. Alchemy, too, was described as 'celestial agriculture', whereby gold and silver acted as a fermenting agent if combined at the right season.

In fact, much of the material we have just examined could be reconstructed in terms of a narrative of alchemy. The chemical wedding, as is well known, symbolized the reconciliation of opposites, whereby contrary matters were united to form a new and purer essence. The so-called *coniunctio* was effected in the retort by means of a 'marriage' between Sol and Luna, figuring respectively the active and

---

[31] It is noteworthy that Claudian is able to refer to the goddess as 'Diana candida', that is brilliant but also white.

passive, hot/dry and cold/moist, male and female, sun and moon. It was common to express this union as 'an incestuous copulation between brother and sister'.[32] Repeatedly, we have seen, Pope identifies the Queen with Diana, the mythological embodiment of the alchemic Luna. In the central act of creating the philosopher's stone, it was necessary for Luna to join with the masculine principle, Sol, otherwise known as the King. The only contemporary figure to whom Anne could decently be united in symbolic matrimony was her half-brother, James.

Such a concord is perhaps adumbrated in the famous verses describing *concors discordia* (*WF*, 11–16). The paragraph ends in an equally familiar series of lines:

> See *Pan* with Flocks, with Fruits *Pomona* crown'd,
> Here blushing *Flora* paints th'enamel'd Ground,
> Here *Ceres'* Gifts in waving Prospect stand,
> And nodding tempt the joyful Reaper's Hand,
> Rich Industry sits smiling on the Plains,
> And Peace and Plenty tell, a STUART reigns.
>
> (37–42)

It adds to the richness of the design we have been exploring in this chapter if we remember that the production of the stone, generated by sun and moon, was termed 'the gathering of the golden harvest'. 'Fruit' was a term used of 'the precious raw gold before it [was] dissolved into the philosopher's stone' or 'the seed of gold from which gold was thought to have grown'.[33] In a later passage *Windsor-Forest* refers to the belief underlying this usage, when Pope writes of how Phoebus will 'warm the ripening Ore to Gold' (396). *TE* i. 190 glosses this by reference to a 'belief' that gold was ripened into maturity by the sun; but this is more than an arcane geological theory, it is a central ingredient of alchemical lore. In the same way, flowers symbolized the stone, with the brilliant colours which appear in the alembic at the climax of the process described as blossoms. Thus Pope's lines make *perfect* sense in terms of alchemy: the restorative magic of the chemical fusion serves as a metaphor for the recovery of the nation from its leaden years under William. The 'yellow Harvests' which foretell the golden years of liberty under Anne make the same connection, for the alchemic opus was 'often compared to the "art" of agriculture, especially the cultivation, harvesting and winnowing of grain'.[34] Once again we discover that Virgil and Ovid become more strongly visible, singly and collectively, if we trace within the poem the hermetic ideas which Stuart apologists had called to the aid of the royalist cause.

Pope is most unlikely to have held any fully fledged beliefs when it comes to alchemy: *An Essay on Man* speaks dismissively of 'The starving chemist in his golden views | Supremely blest' (*TE* iii/1. 87). But as we have seen in Chapter 3, he knew something of the subject, employing technical terms such as the 'exaltation' practised by the hermit of the forest; and in this respect he drew ever closer to the idiom

---

[32] Abraham (1998: 36). This work provides a concise guide to many of the leading notions of alchemy, as utilized in the discussion here.
[33] Abraham (1998: 152).   [34] Abraham (1998: 95).

of Stuart eulogists. It was hard to write in praise of the dynasty, in any sophisticated figural way, without straying into such symbolic language.

LODONA

The transformation scene in *Windsor-Forest* carries echoes of another great moment in Ovid, that is the climax of the story of Acis and Galatea. Dryden had translated this section of Book XIII and it was his version which appeared in the Garth translation. The youth Acis is pursued, just as maidens like Syrinx had been: he too calls unavailingly for help. Destroyed by a rock hurled by the giant Polyphemus, he too is turned into a river:

> And *Acis* chang'd into a stream he was;
> But mine no more; he rowls along the plains,
> With rapid motion, and his name retains.

So Pope tells us that Lodona, now become a silver stream, 'Still bears the Name the hapless Virgin bore' (207).[35]

Ovid has been renewed by later poets in myriad ways.[36] The particular strategy of *Windsor-Forest* is to take a characteristic narrative of transformation, and to imbue it with a historical and political level of meaning. Pope does this partly by a process of symbolic reification. Metaphoric Golden Age poetry is rewritten in poetry of a new golden age. But, above all, the poet seizes on Ovid's favourite theme of rural sanctity profaned by an imperious outsider. The groves of Diana and Ceres are invaded by Jupiter, Pluto, Erisichthon, and Faunus in the *Urtext* of Ovid (followed by Spenser, Milton, and others); virginity is assailed by brute power. Pope follows this model in his story of Lodona and Pan. However, in the design of *Windsor-Forest*, this myth translates into the rape of the nation by foreign tyrants like William III, or alien spirits like Cromwell and the new Whig landlords. Stuart rule will restore this fallen world, and the golden days will return: or so the poet would devoutly wish to believe.

The mythical narrative of the poem sustains this version of political history by a further Ovidian reminiscence. As we have seen in Chapter 3, Pope uses his section on the medieval forest to draw a parallel between the Norman kings and William III. The episode concludes with a picture of William II, 'At once the Chaser and at once the Prey' (82), a fate the nymph-huntress Lodona will share. Pope describes William Rufus as he 'Bleeds in the Forest, like a wounded Hart' (84). No sophisticated reader of Pope's age could have read these lines without instantly recalling the story of Actaeon in Book III of the *Metamorphoses*. The young huntsman came on Diana with her nymphs in her secret haunt in a wooded vale, as the goddess bathed in a pool surrounded by grassy banks. Transformed into a stag to punish this violation

---

[35] It is possible, but not proved, that Pope contributed to the libretto for Handel's *Acis and Galatea* (*c*.1717), mainly written by Gay.

[36] See Martindale (1988).

of a sacred space, Actaeon was torn to pieces by his own hounds. Like Lodona, he had attempted to flee over the ground where once he pursued his own quarry. But the inner meaning of the episode for Pope is related to the violation of the consecrated groves of England by a brutal invader. Instead of the Ovid *moralisé* of the Renaissance, which interpreted the tale as an emblem of sensual passion, the Augustan Ovid serves to dramatize a fable of national survival.[37] The chastity of Diana stands for the moral and political purity of England.

One specific issue remains. The description just cited of Lodona, as she melts into the form of a river, has one obvious analogue in Ovid. This comes in the story of Arethusa in the fifth book of the *Metamorphoses*, where the nymph of Elis is transformed into a spring by Diana. She had been pursued to Sicily by the river god Alpheus, who eventually mingles his waters with hers. Here we encounter a topographic myth, unlike most of the fables in Ovid, but very like some of the legends in *Poly-Olbion*. The underlying narrative is supplied by Lemprière: 'Diana opened a secret passage under the earth and under the sea, through which the waters of Arethusa disappeared, and rose in the island of Ortygia, in Sicily. The river Alpheus followed her also under the sea, and rose likewise in Ortygia; so that, as mythologists relate, whatever is thrown into the Alpheus in Elis, rises again . . . in the fountain Arethusa, near Syracuse.'[38] The story thus could be used to explain a geographical phenomenon. The Alpheus had strong literary overtones, as it rose in Arcadia, and flowed past Olympia to the sea. Its god was regarded, like other rivers, as a son of Oceanus and Tethys.[39]

Pope takes up several details of the story. Lodona, like Arethusa, is a nymph in the train of Diana. She calls out to the goddess for help, as does Arethusa in the source-myth. In describing the pursuit of the nymph, both poets mention the way in which she feels her pursuer's breath fan her hair (*Metamorphoses*, v. 617; *WF*, 195–6). Of course the poet does not suggest an exact equivalence; he wishes rather to fill out the Arcadian association recently invoked (l. 159), and he does this with an easygoing recognition that the Loddon no more resembled a Greek mountain stream than the gentle slopes of Berkshire resembled Olympus. In sober reality, the little Loddon ran on a curving line north-eastwards from its source near Basingstoke, to join the Thames above Henley. It passed within about 5 miles of Binfield, traversing the western edge of the forest. So the mythical episode in a manner 'explains' the course of the river through the hinterland of Windsor, gradually acquiring a larger flow as it is joined by the Blackwater and then debouches into the Thames.

There was another contemporary translation of the episode in Ovid, too. This

---

[37] See Bate (1993: 146), for the tradition in Shakespeare and other Elizabethan writers. It is worth noting that as *WF* came to its completion, in Nov. and Dec. 1712, Handel was staging his Arcadian opera *Il pastor fido* at Vanbrugh's theatre in the Haymarket. The opera, whose cast-list is replete with Diana and her train, did poor business.

[38] Lemprière (1994: 77).

[39] Arethusa also appears in *Georgics*, iv. 344, at the start of the long episode involving the story of Orpheus and Eurydice. She is found among a group of nereids surrounding Cyrene, as a swift huntress with her arrows laid aside, and she raises her head above the water, much as Thames will surface in *WF*.

was an item called 'The Story of Arethusa', which appeared in Lintot's *Miscellany* in May 1712, along with the original two-canto *Rape of the Locke* and six other poems by Pope. The suggestion has been made that Pope himself was also responsible for the translation of the Arethusa episode (Ault, 28–48). It is at least certain that Pope must have been familiar with the poem, given the manner in which it appeared.

The episode in Ovid is related by the muse Calliope, and it immediately follows another story of assault and would-be abduction, in this case successful, that of the rape of Proserpina. Ceres listens to the narration with mounting concern, and learns from Arethusa that on her flight beneath the sea the nymph had caught a glimpse of Proserpina in the underworld. At the end of Calliope's story Ceres is relieved to find her daughter is restored to her, and she turns to Arethusa to learn more of the latter's history. The *Miscellany* rendering is faithful to the Latin, if not literal, and so it is hard to be sure whether Pope might have drawn on it, as well as the original text. (This is to disregard other possible versions intervening, notably the famous Carolinian translation by George Sandys.) A close comparison of the Lodona episode with the *Miscellany* poem can yield only an inconclusive verdict: it is very possible, but not certain, that Pope used the lines which Lintot had printed.

To take a particular instance: Pope's verse, 'She scorn'd the Praise of Beauty, and the Care' (177), corresponds to Ovid's description of Arethusa (*Metamorphoses*, v. 580–2). Closer to the original is the *Miscellany*:

> And tho' no Toys, nor Dress I made my Care,
> Tho' bold; yet I was still reputed Fair.
> Our Female Arts I scorn'd, preventing Praise . . .
>
> (11–13)[40]

The Praise/Care antithesis in *Windsor-Forest* is present in the other poem, distributed to the rhyme-words in successive couplets. Again, the passage describing Arethusa's flight in Ovid (ll. 605–6) turns into the following in Lintot's text:

> As the Dove trembling from the Faulcron flies,
> As his fleet Wings th'approaching Falcon plies:
> So hasten'd I, so he pursued his prize.
>
> (39–41)

This, the only triplet in the *Miscellany* version, is matched in its rhetorical patterning by the lines in *Windsor-Forest*:

> Not half so swift the trembling Doves can fly,
> When the fierce Eagle cleaves the liquid Sky;
> Not half so swiftly the fierce Eagle moves,
> When thro' the Clouds he drives the trembling Doves.
>
> (185–8)

Even if Pope was not actually borrowing from himself, there are signs that he may

---

[40] The *Miscellany* translation is quoted from Ault, 39–41.

have found the Lintot translation helpful at this point—Ovid's compressed opposition (*ut fugere accipitrem penna trepidnate columbae,* | *ut solet accipter trepidas urgere columbas*) is expanded on both occasions into symmetrical English pairs. A few lines later, the *Miscellany* poet has 'fann'd my Tresses' where Pope writes, 'fans her parting Hair' (196).

While this comparison may not definitively settle the question of authorship, or even establish beyond doubt Pope's dependence on the earlier translation, it does serve to show up his greater verbal finesse in *Windsor-Forest*.[41] The language stock from which both English poets draw is a conventional one, and since they are both following more or less closely the Latin account of Arethusa some overlap in diction is inevitable.[42] Consequently, we should not place too much weight on the coincidence of words like *dissolv'd*, which turns up in each location, as does the expression *his sounding Steps* (Alpheus at l. 50; Pan at l. 192). It is impossible to doubt, however, that Pope had the Arethusa passage firmly in his mind all the time he was composing his fable of Lodona, and English versions such as that of the *Miscellany* may well have intervened. They would serve to underpin the main purposes of the episode: and they would remind us that Ceres was herself lamenting the abduction of a daughter, an emblem of the fragility of the landscape, and that violent acts had taken place within the seemingly peaceful Arcadian scenery of the forest.

CAMDEN AND DRAYTON

The form in which Pope knew *Britannia* was almost certainly that of the magnificent version, translated and updated, which was prepared by Edmund Gibson and his team of expert scholars in 1695.[43] However, we need to recall the original Latin text of 1586 and the later editions published in Camden's lifetime; and to remind ourselves that Camden also wrote accounts of the reigns of Elizabeth and James I. *Britannia* is the work of an antiquarian, a herald, and (on its first appearance) an Elizabethan: it lends itself to embellishment, and by 1695 it contains elaborate prefatory sections on topics ranging from British, Roman, and Saxon coins to the 'degrees' of the nation. It may be apposite that the cult of Britannia seems to flourish most when a female monarch occupies the throne, and it is no accident that Pope's work merges nation and ruler in its symbolic design in a manner strongly reminiscent of *The Faerie Queene*. Camden gave Pope a good deal of information, but his book also supplied the poet with a ready-made template on which to construct his own mythic account of a British Tempe. In other words, Pope got much of his usable past not from a dry chronicler, but from a kind of nationalist mythmaker, who clothed events in the symbolic vestures of monarchical propaganda.

[41] A possibility never considered is that Pope wrote the Lodona episode first, and then later put together the Arethusa translation with some remembrance of his draft for *WF*; but this seems unlikely.
[42] We can ignore parallels which relate purely to a shared used of stock diction: Pope's 'burning with Desire' (183) may go back to Dryden's *Aeneid* (see *EC* i. 351), though it is also reminiscent of the *Miscellany*'s expression, 'with raging Passion burn' (36).   [43] See Parry (1995: 331–57).

It would be a mistake, as a matter of fact, to think that the influence of *Britannia* was limited to particular raids by Pope on its topographic information. Kevin Sharpe has emphasized that Camden was increasingly absorbed by recent history. Thanks in part to the guidance of his disciple Sir Robert Cotton, who made a large contribution to later editions, the master-work gradually extended its coverage up to the reign of James I. Both Camden and Cotton were involved in a significant English antiquarian movement which affected the course of historiography and other branches of writing. We recall that 'Ben Jonson borrowed medieval and classical manuscripts, and Inigo Jones researched into volumes of sixteenth-century triumphs and celebrations for the court masques.' More widely, Camden witnessed to a sense of Britain as a great nation which had formed a significant part of the Roman empire.[44] Pope's own purposes required him to invoke a Roman grandeur as the backdrop to Britain's imperial destiny, and *Britannia* afforded his most comprehensive historical model for such a task.

In his prefatory material, Camden states as his aim the desire inspired by the geographer Abraham Ortelius *ut Britanniae antiquatem, et suae antiquitati Britanniam restituerem*—to restore antiquity to Britain, and to Britain to her antiquity (*Britannia*, sig. 2ᵛ). His impact on his pupil Ben Jonson is considered in *SDW*, chapter 6; here it is enough to note a sense that the Roman past lay 'directly underfoot', as Richard Peterson nicely puts it, which was transmitted to many other writers later in the century.[45] Inevitably, the idea of 'restoring' the nation to its past could be used by conservative thinkers in a more overtly political sense than Camden probably intended. To put it briefly: by the time of Pope's birth, there were two prime overtones of the word 'restoration'. One referred to the return of the monarchy in 1660: the other to the rebuilding of London after the devastations of the Great Fire. However, it was a common strategy in royalist polemic to link any form of restitution with the recovery of a golden age, which generally meant getting back to the ways thing were under the early Stuarts.

When the narrative arrives at Windsor as part of the coverage of Berkshire, Camden devotes a long section to the Forest. After mentioning a charter of Edward the Confessor, granting the district to the monks of Westminster Abbey, the author goes on to describe how William I brought the forest back under royal control, granting the monastery in return some land in Essex, and adducing as his reasons the fact that the place 'seems commodious by the nearness of the forest, the forest fit for hunting, and many other particulars therein convenient for Kings; being likewise a place for the King's entertainment' (see also the version in Ashmole, 128). Next, Camden evokes the 'pleasant situation' and 'admirable prospect' enjoyed by the Castle, which 'in front overlooks a long and wide valley, chequer'd with cornfields and green meadows, clothed on each side with groves, and water'd with the calm

[44] For the facts in this paragraph, see Sharpe (1979: at 76). Among those who benefitted from the example of Camden and Cotton were John Selden and Sir William Dugdale, two of the antiquarian scholars whom Pope may well have consulted in preparing the intellectual ground for *WF*.

[45] See Peterson (1981: 56–9), where it is pointed out that Thomas Fuller asserted in 1642 that Camden 'restored Britain to herself.'

and gentle Thames'. Beside it are the hills, 'neither craggy, nor over-high, adorn'd
with woods, and as it were consecrated by nature itself to *Hunting*'.[46] We might
almost suppose that Pope wrote his opening description of Eden (*WF*, 7–42) without leaving his library, so close are these two accounts. In reality, Pope had self-
evidently an intimate first-hand knowledge of the locality. At the end of Chapter 5,
it was argued that the poet saw in this scene the opportunity for a heraldic display of
linguistic virtuosity; but then the 'source' in Camden is the Anglicized version
of a piece of ceremonial Latin, written by a man who was soon to be appointed
Clarenceux king of arms. In it we find the hills and vales, the woodland and the
plain, the earth and water, the waving groves, and, of course, the 'checquer'd Scene'.
It is hard to believe that at some level Pope was not replaying Camden's vision of this
'consecrated' ground. He may also have recalled a passage slightly later in the text,
where Camden turns to the portion of the county which includes Binfield: 'The rest
of *Barkshire*, that is southward from *Windsor*, and is shadow'd with woods and
groves, is commonly call'd *Windsor-Forest*' (*Britannia*, 148).

Britannia had been the direct source for another poet hymning the Thames, long
before Pope. This was Drayton, who describes the progress of the river in Song XV
of *Poly-Olbion*. The key passage has 'this Emperiall Stream' making his way past
Henley, and then reaching 'His Wood nymph *Windsors* seate, her lovely site to view'.
The river and the forest join in a loving embrace:

> Whose most delightful face when once the River sees,
> Which shewes her selfe attir'd in tall and stately trees,
> He in such earnest love with amorous gestures wooes,
> That looking still at her, his way was like to loose;
> And wandring in and out so wildly seems to goe,
> As headlong he himself into her lap would throw.
> Him with the like desire the Forrest does imbrace,
> And with her presence strives her *Tames* as much to grace.
> No Forrest, of them all, so fit as she does stand.
> When Princes, for their sports, her pleasure will command,
> No Wood-nymph as her selfe such troupes have ever seene,
> Nor can such Quarries boast as have in *Windsor* beene.

(*PO* xv. 299–310)

Pope transfers these languishing gestures to the nymph Lodona, who dissolves in to
the 'soft, silver Stream' (204), and he shifts the claim in the penultimate lines to the
Queen herself with reference to the boasts of Arcadia (159–62). He also may have
remembered Drayton's epithet 'headlong' at l. 304 when he described the image of
the 'floating Forests' reflected in the water after Lodona's transformation, with 'the
headlong Mountains and the downward Skies' (212).

Another direct debt to *Britannia* may be suspected in Pope's poem (305), where
he refers to the 'Monarchs chain'd'. This alludes to the captivity of David II of
Scotland and Jean le Bon of France—a familiar topic, versified by Otway and

---

[46] *Britannia*, 145; see also Ashmole, 130. For a fuller citation of this passage, see *SDW*, ch. 4.

Denham (see *TE* i. 178), but more explicitly spelt out in Camden's narrative (*Britannia*, 145). The account moves directly on to the foundation of the Order of the Garter, explaining how Edward III instituted this 'most noble society of Knights' with the aim of 'adorning [military virtue] with honours, reward and glory'. So Lansdowne is enjoined to 'sing those Honours you deserve to wear, | And add new Lustre to her Silver *Star*' (289–90). The Garter itself is described, with an observation that the knights fasten the insignia 'with a buckle of gold, as a token of Concord'. This is the very attribute hymned in the concluding section of *Windsor-Forest*, when discord is exiled (414 ff.).

Drayton is brief on St George's Chapel and the Order, but even so he does enough to have given a possible nudge to Pope's memory, if one was needed:

> Then, hand in hand, her *Tames* the Forrest softly brings,
> To that supreamest place of the great English Kings,
> The *Garters* Royall seate, from him who did advance
> That Princely Order first, our first that conquered *France*;
> The Temple of *Saint George*, whereas his honored Knights,
> Upon his hallowed day, observe their ancient rites.
>
> (*PO* xv. 313–22)

This is Windsor as 'At once the Monarch's and the Muse's Seat', just as in Pope (*WF*, 2). It is notable again that Drayton goes on to refers to the adjacent Eton College—unlike Pope, who may have associated the school with Whiggery, especially under the provostship (1695–1707) of Henry Godolphin, brother of Lord Treasurer Godolphin, as a contrast to that nursery of Tory striplings, Westminster School.

Equally worthy of attention is the fact that Camden makes conspicuous reference to Hampton Court, and it is even more striking that his reviser in 1695 added a note drawing attention to the improvements which William and Mary had carried out to the palace.[47] By contrast Pope is totally silent on this topic. We have seen in Chapter 3 that he elided the reign of Henry VIII in his chronicle of English kings. But the palace was now especially associated with William III, who had employed Verrio amongst others to create an alternative Windsor, by plastering the walls with allegorical triumphs of the Glorious Revolution. The omission is the more striking, in that Pope was soon to place a crucial scene in *The Rape of the Lock* at this very location. We can fairly conclude that the progress downriver is intended to parallel the course of history, in this as in other respects. Hampton Court represents two stages of tyrannical monarchy, to be bypassed as the nation, like the poem, reaches its joyful consummation in Anne's reborn capital.[48]

The Twickenham editors were right to identify as Pope's unnamed 'monkish writer'

---

[47] Drayton has two passing allusions to Hampton Court as one of the splendid 'Kingly houses' along the banks of the river (*PO* xvii. 85).

[48] Similarly there is no mention of the splendours of Greenwich, where Jones and Wren had created some of the noblest buildings of the Stuart era. One reason might be that James Thornhill had recently borrowed the idiom of Rubens's ceiling at Whitehall to hymn peace and liberty in the Painted Hall—regrettably, from Pope's point of view, using the uncongenial allegorical personae of William and Mary.

the author of verses on the New Forest, Bishop John White, who is quoted by Camden (*Britannia*, 115). Camden's own paraphrase is just as relevant: 'William the Conqueror destroy'd all the towns, villages, and churches; and turning out the poor inhabitants made a forest for wild beasts' (*Britannia*, 115; cf. *WF*, 75).[49] The king is described as 'more merciful to beasts than to mankind', which may have given a hint for Pope: 'But while the Subject starv'd, the Beast was fed' (*WF*, 60). Camden suggests that one reason for this course of action on William's part was 'to make a more easie access for his Normans into England . . . in case there should be a new insurrection in this Island after his suppos'd Conquest of it' (*Britannia*, 152). This is historically dubious, but it fits the rather paranoid thinking behind the dread of the Norman Yoke, and of course it could be used to suggest the drain of Dutch courtiers into England during the 1690s in order to strengthen the hold of a later 'invader', who needed to bolster his occupying forces. Finally it is worth noting that Camden quotes a definition of the term *forest* from the Black Book of the Exchequer: 'a safe harbour for beasts'—but only for *wild* beasts (149). This bears on the entire passage in *Windsor-Forest* and illuminates the note on forest law in *TE* i. 153.[50]

However, as we have just seen, there is another important mediating presence between Camden and Pope, in this case pervasively rather than incidentally present. This is *Poly-Olbion*, whose images and cadences seem to have echoed in Pope's mind far more than has been appreciated. For example, the diligent Twickenham editors list only five possible allusions in the text of *Windsor-Forest*, outside a dense cluster in the catalogue of rivers.[51] For our immediate purposes, the most important of these is a note at ll. 79–84, citing Song XVII of *Poly-Olbion*: 'the deaths of Richard and William Rufus "have been thought as divine revenges on *William* the first, who destroy'd in *Hantshire* xxxvi. parish Churches to make dens for wild beasts" ' (*TE* i. 157). Actually this passage comes from Selden's note (Drayton, iv. 343), and a clear reminiscence in Drayton's own text is overlooked. Where Pope has '*Rufus*, tugging at the deadly Dart' (83), Drayton had 'His second *Rufus* next usurpt the wronged raigne: | And by a fatall dart, in his *New Forrest* slaine' (*PO* xvii. 119–20). Admittedly, Camden is the main source for *Poly-Olbion* here; but there are several emphases in Drayton which have no immediate derivation from *Britannia*.

The last passage quoted comes at the beginning of a catalogue of the English monarchs, proclaimed by the Thames as the poem reaches the capital. Drayton is less selective and squeamish than Pope, and he has no difficulty in mentioning the dissolution of the monasteries (*PO* xvii. 321–4) or, naturally, in celebrating Elizabeth

---

[49] Later historians have not been able to confirm the allegations of the medieval chroniclers with regard to the alleged destruction of villages: the most amusing refutation is that of Cobbett in *Rural Rides*. Modern research has confirmed that the New Forest was sparsely populated in the twelfth century, and may have suffered some drop in its population; but the settlements were sparse even at the time of Domesday. See Darby and Campbell (1962: 324–38).

[50] We have noted that Pope's conception of Nimrod as the archetypal tyrant derives from sources other than Camden, notably the Archangel Michael's discourse with Adam in *PL* xii. 24–78: see p. 275 below.

[51] Among other echoes not previously noted may be remarked verses on the Earl of Surrey: 'That famous Hëroe fit both for the Speare and Pen' (*PO* xviii. 590). Compare *WF*, 293, 'Matchless his Pen, victorious was his Lance'.

by name (*PO* xvii. 341–52). But it is not only in the section on the monarchs that Drayton confronts 'Bastard William' who 'brought the *Norman* Rule upon the English name' (*PO* xvii. 111–12), together with his sons. There are two even more significant episodes much earlier in the poem, which occur in the second song. The first concerns the area around Cranborne Chase:

> How then the bloodie *Dane* subdu'd the *Saxon* race;
> And, next, the *Norman* took possession of the place:
> Those ages, once expir'd, the Fates to bring about,
> The *British* Line restor'd; the *Norman* lineage out.
> Then, those prodigious signes to ponder shee began,
> Which afterward againe the *Britans* wrack fore-ran;
> How here the Owle at noone in publique streets was seene,
> As though the peopled Townes had way-less Deserts been.
> And while the loathly Toad out of his hole does crall,
> And makes his fulsome stoole amid the Princes hall,
> The crystall fountaine turn'd into a gory wound,
> And bloody issues brake (like ulcers) from the ground.
>
> (*PO* ii. 157–68)

The language here grows increasingly Virgilian, but there is no mistaking how close the opening lines are to Pope's description of the ravaged countryside under Norman rule. The first line quoted answers directly to Pope's 'Whom ev'n the *Saxon* spar'd, and bloody *Dane*' (77); while Drayton's verses on the prodigies of disaster several times recall Pope's picture of the 'levell'd Towns', and most specifically his vision of animal infestation: 'The Fox obscene to gaping Tombs retires, | And savage Howlings fill the sacred Quires' (71–2), an image famously developed by Thomas Gray.[52]

Within two verse paragraphs, *Poly-Olbion* has reached the New Forest, and it is here that Drayton recalls the history, mythical or otherwise, of Norman England. He alludes to the rivers Avon and Stour, which

> at *New-forrests* foote into the Sea doe fall,
> Which every day bewaile that deed so full of dred
> Whereby shee (now so proud) became first Forrested;
> Shee now who for her site even blundless seem'd to lie,
> Her beeing that receiv'd by *Williams* tyrannie;
> Providing Lawes to keep those Beasts heere planted then;
> Whose lawless will from hence had driven men;
> That where the harth was warm'd with Winters feasting fiers,
> The melancholie Hare is form'd in brakes and briers:
> The aged ranpick trunk where Plow-men cast their seed,
> And Churches over-whelm'd with nettles, ferne and weed,
> By Conquering *William* first cut off from every trade,
> That heere the *Norman* still might enter to invade . . .
>
> (*PO* ii. 196–208)

---

[52] On obscene foxes and shrieking owls, see Sherbo (1994).

While Pope does not pick up the idea that the Normans afforested land as a device to ensure ease of immigration, as Camden had suggested, he does borrow attitudes from Drayton which have no root in *Britannia*. The poetic evocation of churches overrun by weeds goes straight into *Windsor-Forest* (66–9); while the *laws/lawless* opposition is taken over (45, 51). Just as significantly, the gloss Selden wrote to this passage quotes verses from the chronicle of Robert of Gloucester, describing William I's depredations and the death of his sons.[53]

Insistently, *Poly-Olbion* regrets the destruction of forests to meet the needs of growing towns, especially for use in iron-smelting.[54] For John Evelyn, this process was especially dangerous because it threatened England's capacity to renew her 'wooden walls', the navy (see pp. 298–9, below). In Drayton's case, there seems to be a more general lament for the old rural habitations, as they were jeopardized by urban development. One such passage occurs in relation to the Forest of Wyre in Song VII, where the poet declaims against those who 'of whole Forrests . . . in these impious times have been the vile decay'. He ends his fulmination: 'How manie grieved soules in future time shall starve, | For that which they have rapt their beast-lie lust to serve!' (*PO* vii. 285–6, 289–90). Discreetly Pope allocates this corrupt exploitation of a needy people to a safely distant period, more than six centuries earlier; but the rhetoric of the entire poem suggests that incomers are taking over the forest, much as Dutch incomers to the court are stripping the nation bare as they prolong the war for their own interests.

In *Poly-Olbion* the point is enforced by a reference to the ill consequences that followed when an oak in Thessaly belonging to a nymph of Ceres was cut down. This alludes to the eighth book of the *Metamorphoses*, where Ovid tells the story of Erisichthon's offence and his punishment by Ceres. Erisichthon violated a sacred grove by felling an ancient oak of massive proportions, despite a warning from the nymph who inhabited the tree. He destroyed the oak with heavy blows from his axe, so that blood flowed from wounds in its trunk, and as it toppled it brought down a great part of the grove. The dryads complained to Ceres, and asked for the wrong-doer to be punished. Ceres assented with a nod of her head, and as she bowed her head the grain in the fields, ready to be harvested, bowed too. This is a key poetic source for *Windsor-Forest*:

> Here *Ceres'* Gifts in waving Prospect stand,
> And nodding tempt the joyful Reaper's Hand.

> (39–40)

In this way Pope links the idea of rape of an innocent landscape with the preservative role of Ceres, something which is made possible by his use of Ovid's story. Erisichthon's fate was decreed by the goddess; he would suffer from the pangs of an unquenchable appetite, and famine would constantly ravage him. What would have been enough for an entire city or a nation, was not sufficient to appease his hunger. The political import seems clear: the warmongers and contractors abet Marlbor-

---

[53] See Drayton, iv. 46.   [54] See *SDW*, ch. 4.

ough in his endless desire for ever more victories, ever more conquests, ever more blood.

Pope's own Ovidian myth follows a different trajectory, but it is of imagination compact with Drayton's tale of a grove desecrated by an impious and brutal male. In terms of the inner logic of *Windsor-Forest*, the sacred oak-groves of England are protected by Ceres = Anne. Condign punishment should be visited upon Pan (or Erisichthon) = Norman/Williamite rapists. Similarly, earlier in the same song, Drayton narrates the rape of Sabrina's nymphs by satyrs in the Forest of Dean. Sabrina appeals for aid to 'her Sire', Neptune, much as Lodona appeals to Father Thames, a river god with Neptunian attributes, in Pope's myth (*PO* vii. 33–52). As Selden and the modern editors explain, Drayton here 'poeticizes the robberies for which the Dean forest was notorious [mentioned by Camden] into rapes by the satyrs' (Drayton, v. 234). It is all too plausible that Pope's ravisher might have a modern equivalent, too.

Many critics have noted that violence and violation play a central role in the poem. Recently Christa Knellwolf has explored this theme in terms of sexual and imperial politics, finding that Pope's text contains 'a depressing message', and suggesting that 'we refuse to accept Lodona's transformation into an object of art with a clearly defined meaning'. Instead, Knellwolf recommends that we substitute for Pope's 'unsatisfactory solution' our own project, that is 'to search for ways of coping with violence that reduce its force'.[55] One key element that this account overlooks is the *dynastic* and national import of violation, rather than its implications for gender narrowly conceived. The Stuart line had always been coded female since the time of Mary Queen of Scots, while its opponents such as Cromwell and William III, we have seen, were figured as brutal and oppressive males. Pope extends this myth by emphasizing the vulnerability of the royal demesne around Windsor. The rape of Diana's nymph, like the ravishment of Sabrina's, connotes something more than a sexual attack on an isolated girl.

SPENSER, SHAKESPEARE, AND MILTON

From boyhood on, Pope numbered Spenser among his favourite poets. He attempted a heroic poem in his youth, never to be completed, in which he tried to assemble 'all the beauties of the great epic writers into one piece': 'There was Milton's style in one part and Cowley's in another, here the style of Spenser imitated, and there Statius, here Homer and Virgil, and there Ovid and Claudian' (*Anecdotes*, i. 18). One of his earliest surviving works is the imitation of Spenser, entitled 'The Alley', which he probably composed in his teens. From the same period come the *Pastorals*, which avowedly took *The Shepheardes Calendar* as one of its prime models. Much later in life he was still under the thrall of his great predecessor: a planned epigraph for *The Dunciad*, later rejected, was taken from the very first canto of *The*

---

[55] Knellwolf (1998: 82–3). See also Introduction, p. 3, above.

Faerie Queene, where the Red Cross Knight swats away the loathsome bugs infesting Error's noisome body (*Life*, 475). In any case, an attentive reading of Pope's oeuvre will discover several major works coloured by Spenser's epic: *The Rape of the Lock*, above all, together with *The Dunciad*.

The situation with regard to *Windsor-Forest* is more complicated. Spenser was active in many genres, and some of these are at least vestigially present in Pope's text. For example, the lines which lament the dead poets who had lived near the Thames (267–76) offer a highly patterned version of pastoral elegy, and inevitably call up memories of Spenser's tribute to Philip Sidney, *Astrophel*. Equally, the pendant verses A *Pastorall Aeglogue* summon the Thames, the Humber, and the Severn to witness the 'sad pomp funerall' of the corpse passing through Neptune's kingdom, much as the Muses in *Windsor-Forest* lead the poet to observe 'the sad Pomp' of Cowley's water-borne funeral cortège (274). To move to a different vein: a stanza near the end of Ruines of Rome (407–14) may have contributed something to Pope's image of the 'yellow Harvests' rising where the land had lain waste. It is also possible that *The Ruines of Time* supplied images of destruction, particularly in a stanza (127–33) which contrasts the tall towers of old Verulam with the present 'heap of lyme and sand', which serves only for the 'Schriche-owle to build her balefull bowre' (see *WF*, 66–72).

It is, however, *The Faerie Queene* which offers the most extensive and concrete parallels. The Mutability cantos supply an Ovidian myth in the story of the nymph Molanna, one of the followers of Diana on Arlo hill.[56] Faunus attempts to seduce the maiden, in order to gain access to her mistress as Cynthia, that is Diana, bathes naked. After he is caught, Faunus is subjected to a number of punishments: Actaeon-like, he is covered in a deerskin and hunted down by Diana's hounds, as he flies through woods and dales. Resilience is a prime characteristic of the god Pan, and he survives. Molanna herself is stoned as a punishment for her disloyalty, marries her lover Fanchin, and finds them both transformed into a river. Diana abandons the forests of Arlo and leaves its formerly Arcadian glades to the mercies of wolves and robbers. It is a myth of rural degradation which fits snugly into the ideology of *Poly-Olbion*, and supplies more than a hint to Pope in turn.

The most explicit source-material in Spenser for *Windsor-Forest* concerns passages of river poetry, notably the bejewelled description of the marriage of Thames and Medway in Book IV of *The Faerie Queene*, along with the sinuous 'spousall verse' of *Prothalamion*. Detailed description of these passages is given in *SDW*, chapter 4, where they are placed in the context of Renaissance river poems more generally. Pope would come to such passages with a strong sense of Spenser as a moral and even a political poet: it is not as if he simply lit down on these excerpts from the oeuvre which concerned the Thames and which bore on his own theme. We need to remember that Spenser had remained a live classic of English poetry: in

---

[56] The first commentator to have seen a link between the story of Molanna and *WF* was Williams (1974), in a pioneering and still valuable study. The additional contextual material supplied in this book should more fully document the connections suggested by Williams, and may further justify her recognition of 'how deeply Pope seems to have understood Spenser's intention' (1974: 600).

1715, for example, John Hughes brought out an edition of the works, long popular with readers.[57]

Shakespeare is the most elusive literary presence in *Windsor-Forest*. Plainly, a decade before Pope embarked on his edition of the plays, the poet had already absorbed a great deal of the work which was now recognized as the greatest treasure of English literature. In 1709 Jacob Tonson brought out the first fully edited version of Shakespeare, compiled by Nicholas Rowe.[58] Two years later Pope wrote to Caryll that he kept pictures of Dryden, Milton, and Shakespeare in his chamber, 'round about me, that the constant remembrance of 'em may keep me always humble' (*Corr.* i. 120), a somewhat unctuous formulation which must none the less reflect the young man's genuine aspirations. Late in life Pope was presented by the Prince of Wales with busts attributed to Peter Scheemakers depicting Spenser, Shakespeare, Milton, and Dryden, which were kept in the library at Pope's villa. It is no coincidence that Scheemakers is best known for executing the monument to Shakespeare in Westminster Abbey, designed by William Kent, for Pope was one of the prime movers in setting up this famous image of the dramatist.[59]

Shakespeare's comedies, especially *A Midsummer Night's Dream*, left an unmistakable impress on a nearly contemporary poem, *The Rape of the Lock*. The influence is subtler in *Windsor-Forest*; but faint echoes of *As You Like It* run through the poem, as when the exiled Duke comes to Arden with his courtiers, arrayed like foresters:

> Now, my comates and brothers in exile,
> Hath not old custom made this life more sweet
> Than that of painted pomp? Are not these woods
> More free from peril than the envious Court?
>
> (II. i. 1–4)

These words immediately suggest the superannuated courtier Trumbull, 'exiled' to the forest after losing his position in the palace revolutions of William's reign. Trumbull, as the blessed figure of retirement (*WF*, 235–58) studies his surroundings just as Duke senior in *As You Like It*:

[57] In Apr. 1713, a month after *WF* appeared, Pope wrote his first surviving letter to Hughes, who was one of the Button's set over which Addison presided (*Corr.* i. 218). On 7 Oct. 1715 Pope wrote to Hughes from Binfield, praising the essays attached to the edition, and avowing that 'Spenser has ever been a favourite poet to me' (*Corr.* i. 316). The two men were on good terms until Hughes's death in 1720.

[58] Pope knew Rowe by the time *WF* appeared: he wrote an epilogue, not used, for the first performance of *Jane Shore* on 2 Feb. 1713 (see Ault, 133–8, and *TE* vi. 115). By the late summer of the year they were exchanging friendly letters, and Rowe came down to Binfield to spend a week with Pope in September, when he impressed his host with his vivacity (*Corr.* i. 190). The prologue was meant to be spoken by Anne Oldfield, who played Jane Shore; she was soon to portray Cato's daughter, and of course was a well-known Shakespearian actress as well. Pope continued to mention Rowe in his correspondence with Sir William Trumbull especially, passing on a copy of *Jane Shore* to his mentor, and stating that Rowe had Trumbull's books for his 'memorandums' when translating Lucan (New Letts. 402–3).

[59] *Life*, 733–4: see also *TE* vi. 395–6. Dobson (1992: 139–40), suggests that the Shakespeare monument became 'a locus for Jacobite idealizations of the lost days of Stuart rule'. The busts from Pope's library were bequeathed to Lord Lyttelton, and survive today at Hagley (*Garden and City*, 251).

> And this our life exempt from public haunt
> Finds tongues in trees, books in the running brooks,
> Sermons in stones, and good in everything.
>
> (II. i. 15–17)

Amiens responds, 'Happy is your Grace, |That can translate the stubbornness of fortune |Into so quiet and so sweet a style' (II. i. 18–20). Equally, Pope's philosopher-hermit of the woods finds the humbler joys of 'home-felt Quiet please' (239). More pervasively, the world of Arden with its deer-hunts, rural sports, and sylvan philosophy is translated to Windsor.

The comedy ends with an incursion of courtly modes into the forest, with the rites of Hymen. Pope, of course, had no marriage to celebrate; but he did take over some of the motifs of court masque, and here the echoes recall the visions called up by Prospero in *The Tempest*:

> Ceres, most bounteous lady, thy rich leas
> Of wheat, rye, barley, vetches, oats and pease;
> Thy turfy mountains, where live nibbling sheep,
> And flat meads thatched with stover, them to keep;
> Thy banks with pioned and twilled brims,
> Which spongy April at thy hest betrims
> To makes cold nymphs chaste crowns; and thy broom groves
> Whose shadow the dismissed bachelor loves . . .
>
> (IV. i. 60–7)

Ceres herself refers in an almost Augustan cadence to 'My bosky acres and my unshrubbed down' (81), which the rainbow will 'crown'. She gives a final blessing, celebrating 'Earth's increase, foison plenty| . . . Vines with clustering branches growing, |Plants with goodly burden bowing', so that 'Scarcity and want shall shun you' (110–16). We should not be misled by the more racy and demotic cast of Shakespeare's language, which prefers 'nibbling sheep' to Pope's formulaic 'flocks'. The literary and mythological context is almost identical in the two sources: and even on the verbal level there are direct reminiscences—compare Pope's banks, groves, and especially the 'Blessings' of peace and plenty ushered in by Ceres and her fellows. This time the masque seems to have been introduced by Shakespeare as a compliment to Princess Elizabeth on her wedding in February 1613, for *The Tempest* was one of the plays specially performed at court (see *SDW*, chapter 1). Another play which almost certainly refers to the marriage is *Henry VIII*, one of the works which seem most to have inspired political readings in Pope's day.[60]

The great example of Milton dominated Pope's imagination throughout his career. We have only to think of his greatest poems, *The Rape of the Lock* and *The Dunciad*, to see how deep was the impact of *Paradise Lost* in particular. This influence is

---

[60] Colley Cibber describes in his autobiography how he would make lines in a speech by Wolsey apt to the politics of George I, and would note the king's reaction when he performed the role at Hampton Court (as in 1717). Cited by Wikander (1993: 15–16).

present in *Windsor-Forest* in, so to speak, lower solution. The description of the 'happy rural seat of various view' (*PL* iv. 247) is certainly recalled in Pope's evocation of his Eden at the start of *Windsor-Forest*. It is an echo so open and unmissable that no contemporary could have failed to make the connection. Just as obvious is a verbal echo drawn from the same book: Milton compares the assembled squadron of angels to an agrarian landscape: 'as when a field| Of Ceres ripe for harvest waving bends | Her bearded grove of ears' (*PL* iv. 980–2), and Pope plainly had this in his ears—'Here *Ceres'* Gifts in waving Prospect stand, | And nodding tempt the joyful Reaper's Hand' (*WF*, 39–40). Beyond this, however, only one passage in Milton's epic is crucial to the strategies of the poem, but it proves to be relevant to much of the first portion of Pope's work.

Wasserman was the first to indicate the significance of the passage (*PL* xii. 13–113). Strangely the Twickenham editors did not follow up on this insight, and so it will bear further elucidation here. At the opening of the last book of his epic, Milton continues the narrative by the Archangel Michael to Adam of the course of history, moving on from the Flood to the postdiluvian state of Israel. From the Book of Genesis comes the basis for the story of Nimrod, a tyrant 'of proud ambitious heart' who drove concord and the law of nature from the face of the earth. The hunter derives his name from rebellion, and sets up confusion when he erects the tower of Babel. This episode is glossed in a dialogue between Michael and Adam, where it is revealed that Nimrod's actions caused the loss of 'Rational liberty' in Mankind. It is not surprising that the passage was often invoked in political discourse, especially in the seventeenth century.[61] All these features recall Pope's train of personifications at the end of *Windsor-Forest*, where ambition, rebellion, discord, and persecution are cast out by the benevolent providence associated with the Peace.

The most direct recollection of Milton occurs earlier, when Pope explicitly identifies Nimrod with the rapacious Norman kings:

> Proud *Nimrod* first the bloody Chace began,
> A *mighty* Hunter, and his Prey was Man.
> Our haughty *Norman* boasts that barb'rous Name,
> And makes his *trembling* Slaves the Royal Game.
>
> (*WF*, 61–4)

Wasserman observes that 'the name Nimrod is "barb'rous" in the sense that it bespeaks his cruelty and savagery'; but equally 'a barbarous name is also a "foreign" one; and the name the Conqueror publicly boasted was "William", an importation from France—and also, as it conveniently happened, the name the foreign invader from Orange' (Wasserman, 118).[62] Pope's identification of the first two Williams

---

[61] The figure of Nimrod was used both by Whigs and republicans drawing on Milton's example (for whom he symbolized the fall of patriarchal government to usurping monarchs) and by royalists who enlisted Nimrod as a destructive tyrant in the mould of Cromwell. See Miller (1979: 180–1).

[62] Brooks-Davies (1985: 71), aptly points out that the 'hideous gabble' Milton describes in Babel applies in Pope to 'the confusion of tongues' introduced by William III, as later to the early Hanoverian monarchs—who spoke with what their opponents regarded as a guttural dialect.

with the third is thus eased by his Miltonic allusion. More directly still, the phrase 'his Prey was Man', along with lines such as 'While the Subjects starv'd, the Beast was fed' (*WF*, 60), goes straight back to Milton, who had foreseen the role of Nimrod as hunter: 'And Men not Beasts shall be his game' (*PL* xii. 30).[63] The basis for this entire section, which sees the Normans as antetypes of William III in tyranny and devastation, lies not so much in the bare narrative of Genesis 10, or even in the scriptural exegetes of this text, as in the politicized version of the story found in Michael's narrative.

Milton's minor poems contributed less to *Windsor-Forest*, but the 'checquer'd Scene' of *WF*, 17 recalls *L'Allegro*, 96, and Pope's reference to 'old *Belerium*' (316) perhaps owed something to *Lycidas*, 160. The philosophic hermit musing over the night-sky has one of his origins in the melancholy astronomical watcher in *Il Penseroso*, 85–92 (a link not previously made). As for *Arcades*, l. 84 ('O'er the smooth enameled green') points towards *WF*, 38, another fresh suggestion; and the 'goddess bright' of l. 18 looks to *WF*, 162. More widely the pastoral diction used by the Genius of the Wood may have sounded faintly in Pope's ear as he composed his own description of Arcadia: e.g. 'Fair silver-buskined nymphs as great and good', l. 33, as a basis for *WF*, 169–70.

It should occasion little surprise that that the poem thrust so many tendrils into the poetry of the previous century. Milton and Marvell died in the decade before Pope was born, and thus they were no more remote to the poet as he formed his identity as an author than T. S. Eliot would be to a young writer in his or her thirties today. Pope's own father (a Catholic convert) was born in 1646, his mother in 1643; even his nurse, the other key member of the household during his upbringing, came into the world as early as 1648. The poet's most important mentor, Sir William Trumbull, was old enough to retain boyhood memories of the Civil War, since he first saw light in 1639. Close friends among the local gentry included Anthony Englefield, about two years senior to Trumbull.[64] Young Alexander's early development and reading were supervised by men of this generation: among his other mentors at this stage were William Wycherley, born about 1640, and Thomas Betterton, born about 1635. The sponsors of his *Pastorals* included another dramatist, Thomas Southerne (b. 1659); the Marquess of Dorchester (b. *c*.1665); Lord Wharton (b. 1648); Sir Samuel Garth (b. 1661); Sir Henry Sheeres (b. *ante* 1650); and the Duke of Buckinghamshire (b. 1648). All members of this group were at least fifteen years senior to Pope. His new literary friends around 1712–13 included Swift (b. 1667), Arbuthnot (b. 1667), and Prior (b. 1664). The dedicatee of *Windsor-Forest* was Granville (also b. 1667), himself a seventeenth-century poet. Most, though not all, of this group came from

[63]   The verbal link was indicated by Wasserman, 119–20.

[64]   A 'Learned and Politique Gentleman', Englefield, who died in 1712, was described in Pope's personal necrology as a great wit and wag, but his more serious interests included mathematics and astronomy, extending to the building of sundials (*Life*, 88–9).

a royalist background: it is just as significant that they belonged to a cohort who had lived through the contentious aftermath of the political and religious struggles of the mid-seventeenth century. Such men provided the intellectual and literary coordinates within which Pope came to maturity.

8

Later Literary Contexts

Pope's unquestioned affinity with John Dryden has led us to underrate the influence of other 'modern' writers on his work. These include a number of authors who were active in the post-Civil War period, some of them known personally to the young Pope's mentors. Dryden himself has been reserved for separate attention: his main contribution to *Windsor-Forest* is explored in *SDW*, chapter 6, as this relates to the prophetic goals of the poem. Here we consider in turn Denham and Cowley, who were still close to the *dernier cri* when Pope began writing, along with John Evelyn, whose significance as a source of themes and attitudes for *Windsor-Forest* awaits full analysis. Evelyn's friend and colleague, Christopher Wren, is another unspoken presence in the poem. After this come immediately contemporary models and controls which enable us to gauge Pope's achievement more precisely: the most relevant figure here is Addison.

THE LEGACY OF *COOPER'S HILL*

Pope never attempted to conceal what he owed to Sir John Denham's famous poem, and indeed he signalized his relation to his predecessor within the text of *Windsor-Forest*. When he invokes the muses who have celebrated the Thames valley, it is Denham who heads the list, in front of Cowley, Surrey, and even Granville:

> To *Thames's* Banks which fragrant Breezes fill,
> Or where ye Muses sport on *Cooper's* Hill.
> (On *Cooper's* Hill eternal Wreaths shall grow,
> While lasts the Mountain, or while *Thames* shall flow.)
>
> (263–6)

The 'Wreaths' suggest not just poetic laurels, but also funerary tributes such as the martyr-kings of Windsor will receive. The region is made venerable by 'God-like Poets', and before all stands the man who had given it a mythic identity: 'Here his first Lays majestic *Denham* sung' (271). It soon became the fashion to place Denham at the start of a new literary genre, the loco-descriptive poem, with Pope as his most important successor. It is a role which Pope himself chose not to repudiate, even though we may today see the category as too narrow to define the scope of *Windsor-Forest*.

There is evidence elsewhere that Pope continued to admire Denham's achievement. In a note to Book XVI of his *Iliad* translation, which first appeared in 1718, he made this clear:

> I must do a noble *English* Poet the justice to observe, that it is this particular Art that is the very distinguishing excellence of *Cooper's-Hill*: throughout which, the Descriptions of Places, and Images rais'd by the Poet, are still tending to some Hint, or leading into some Reflection, upon some moral Life or political Institution: Much as the real Sight of such Scenes and Prospects is apt to give the Mind a compos'd Turn, and incline it to Thoughts and Contemplations that have a Relation to the Object. (*TE* viii. 261)

Pope's own 'Scenes and Prospects' have a similar end in view. They are meant to prompt moral and political reflections; and they follow their models in *Cooper's Hill* in bodying forth a complex set of interrelated ideas, connected in some cases only loosely or associatively with the precise locations named in the text. This was part of the 'failure' of *Windsor-Forest* for the post-Romantic sensibility, for any purely 'descriptive' function is sacrificed in favour of a technique using moral emblems and ideological codes, and the landscape in itself counts for little. The attempt in modern criticism to restore this element of Pope's design gains cogency if we pay heed to Pope's own words, notably his careful statement of the particular qualities he valued in Denham.[1]

The superficial similarities between the two works had always been apparent. In both of its main versions (1642 and 1655), *Cooper's Hill* offered Pope much of the underlying programme for his poem.[2] Denham uses a Thames-side locale and three elevated points along the course of the river: Ludgate Hill, on which St Paul's Cathedral stands; St Ann's Hill, near Chertsey; and Windsor Hill, site of the castle. Wasserman is right to see in the 1642 text a reference to the efforts by Charles I and his minister Archbishop Laud to put right the decaying condition of old St Paul's, as an allegory of the restoration of the Church and of the City of London, beset by popular uprisings (Wasserman, 51).[3] In fact, worse was to come, during the Civil War:

> In 1643 all the Materials, *&c.* assign'd for the Repairs were seiz'd, the Scaffolds pull'd down; and the Body of the Church converted to a Horse-quarter for Soldiers; the beautiful Pillars of *Inigo Jones's Portico* were shamefully hew'd and defac'd for support of the Timber-work of Shops, for Seamstresses and other Trades; for which sordid Uses, that stately *Colonade* was wholly taken up.[4]

---

[1] The earliest drafts date from 1641, the last main draft from 1653–4; but Denham was tinkering with the poem even after it appeared in his collected *Poems and Translations* in 1668, a year before his death. Denham also translated portions of the *Aeneid*, but there is no sign that Pope made any use of this.

[2] It is likely that Pope, along with most of his contemporaries, was most familiar with the later text.

[3] The restoration of St Paul's, originally projected by James I, was seen as a conscious gesture of royal support for the Church, as well as a way of dignifying the capital. Inigo Jones recast parts of the cathedral in a classical guise, with a large Corinthian portico at the west end, paid for by the king. The undertaking provoked a eulogy in verse by Waller. 'As Solomon had built the Temple in Jerusalem, so the British Solomon was intent on re-edifying the Temple in his new Jerusalem' (Parry, 248). For the links between architecture, Stuart ideology, and church politics, see Parry, 247–52.

[4] From Dugdale's *History* of St Paul's (1716), quoted by Wren, 273.

These events constitute an allegory of the destructive effects of the Great Rebellion, as seen from a royalist perspective.

Pope, too, was to use the re-edification of London as an emblem of the restoration of the Established Church. However, by 1668 many readers, if not Denham himself, must also have been thinking of the destruction of the old cathedral in the Great Fire, when they came to the lines on the preservation of the building by 'the best of Kings' (*CH*, 24)—this would now be the son, Charles II. Wren, after all, was beginning to demolish the former structure and embark on its replacement in this very year, 1668. A further consideration is that Denham had served as surveyor-general from 1660 to 1668, which is a dimension of the authorial stance Wasserman neglects. As for St Ann's Hill, the crucial feature here is certainly 'the adjoining Abby' of Chertsey, demolished by Henry VIII; and again it is right to see this as a critique of monarchical tyranny (Wasserman, 52). We recall Pope's depiction of the Norman depredations, in which the kings wrested their 'Fanes' from gods (*WF*, 66). The third eminence, that of Windsor itself, needs no special attention. It is enough to note the stress laid on Edward III, the Black Prince, and the Order of the Garter. St George is described as 'Souldier and Martyr' (*CH*, 102), prompting a comparison with Charles I as 'himself the Souldier and the saint' (*CH*, 110). Though this section is more diffuse than Pope's treatment of identical themes, the underlying concerns are all of a piece (see Chapter 5, above).

Deliberately, Pope makes no use of St Paul's or Chertsey, though he mentions the temples of the city and the palace of Whitehall. He could easily have introduced the abbey, since the remains of Henry VI were originally laid there (l. 312), and Abraham Cowley had roamed on St Ann's Hill during his residence at Chertsey (l. 272). Likewise Pope alludes only in passing to Cooper's Hill itself (*WF*, 262–4): this was a relatively small elevation between Chertsey and Windsor, close to the town of Egham. The crucial feature of the hill was its proximity to Runnymede, where Magna Carta had been signed (see *CH*, 329 ff.). Once more Wasserman is helpful in seeing the link between the rapacious hunter King John, as against the benevolent Charles, and the rapacious 'Nimrod', as against the benevolent goddess of the hunt, Anne. For Pope the original charter is supplemented by the equally important Charter of the Forest, also granted by John: indeed, Wasserman argues convincingly that in *Windsor-Forest* 'the Forest Charter, whose principles were violated by the chase, is a surrogate for all of Magna Carta' (124). It thus forms part of the symbolic design whereby Pope uses the tyranny of the Norman monarchs, and implicitly that of Henry VIII, to foreshadow the brutal treatment of poor and defenceless people, most notably Catholics, by William III—even, in a figure of prolepsis, by George I.

The other obvious point of comparison lies in the extensive use of the hunt by both poets. There can be no doubt that the stag-hunt in *Cooper's Hill* allegorizes recent political history. The slain stag almost certainly represents Charles's fallen minister Strafford, as most fully argued by Wassermann. The same commentator adds that 'it is quite possibly significant' that Strafford was admitted to the Garter. He notes that 'in September 1640, in an extraordinary and memorably impressive ceremony, Charles entered Strafford into the Order', so that 'ultimately, like St George,

Strafford also became both "Souldier and Martyr" ' (Wasserman, 76). We can go further, in the light of evidence already assembled in this book. The earl was beheaded on Tower Hill just eight months later, on 11 May 1641, after a crudely mounted show trial amid something resembling paranoia on the part of his supporters and detractors alike. The Civil War began in earnest the following year, when Charles raised his standard at Nottingham.

Pope could reasonably have feared that his allies might suffer a similar fate to that of Strafford, once the Hanoverians took over. As it was, Lansdowne found himself in the Tower within little more than two years from the appearance of *Windsor-Forest*, as did Oxford and Prior, while Bolingbroke underwent attainder and exile. The current Earl of Strafford, a great-nephew of the minister to Charles I, was faced with arraignment for high crimes and misdemeanours. Then a bitter civil war broke out in September 1715, as the Jacobites raised *their* standard. Beyond this there may even be a sense that Anne herself has become a royal martyr, driven towards death in an exacting war fomented by greedy Whig financiers and the insatiable Marlborough. If Lansdowne were to receive his silver star, as the poem recommends, might not he go the way of the earlier recipient Strafford?

These links all operate on a more or less literal level, though there is an undertow of symbolic congruence. It was the major achievement of Wasserman, in what remains the most searching account of the moral and political ideology of *Windsor-Forest*, to detect a deeper level of contact between Denham and Pope. In both poems he discovered a prevailing theme, that of *concordia discors*, and he was able to show that *Windsor-Forest* in particular offers a running dialectic of balanced contrarieties—these work mostly around notions such as discord and concord themselves, as well as activity/contemplation, engagement/retirement, war/peace, and aggression/benevolence, but they extend to other concepts including description/allegory, history/myth, conquest/trade, and much more. Some have felt that Wasserman places too much weight on one master-theme; but it is striking that his central notion fits not just the ideological drift of the poem ('Order in Variety'), but also its generic architecture and its local effects in terms of grammar, rhythm, and versification. After all, Pope's model Denham attained his greatest fame as the author of a single couplet in *Cooper's Hill* (191–2) built around metrically and syntactically balanced antitheses.

However, Wasserman's argument did something more. For the first time, it gave the Lodona episode the thematic centrality which its positioning within the poem obviously requires. The reading unites the mythical and political purposes of *Windsor-Forest*, by showing that 'the Ovidian fable, as reconstituted by Pope, is a tightly coherent and thoroughly congruent mythic representation of the subject of the poem, the War and Peace of Utrecht as seen from a Tory perspective, just as the historical account of William the Conqueror served to sketch the Whig background and origin of the War' (Wasserman, 135). It is indeed the aim of this book to bring more evidence to bear on both the historic and the mythic aspects of the book, to demonstrate that Wasserman's claim can be even more strongly stated. His assertion that the hunting episodes allegorize 'the entire course of the war' becomes more cogent as we assemble more contextual data, both on the events of Anne's reign and on the mythological matrix which Pope employed (see Chapters 4 and 7, above). Wasserman also shed considerable light on the passage celebrating Trumbull's retirement (*WF*, 235–58), as for example in his observation that the hermit philosopher's studies are 'carefully arranged in a hierarchy leading progressively to the purely spiritual: medicine, chemistry, astronomy, geography, history, ethics, and religion' (Wasserman, 148). He made better sense than any other critic, before or since, of Pope's history of England (see Chapter 3, above), insisting that by assenting to the peace 'Anne has become the fulfilment of English history. England's sin against the sacred order—the slaying of Charles—has been expiated' (Wasserman, 161). As is shown elsewhere in this book, this providential pattern can be seen in many parts of the work, including portions to which Wasserman gives little or no attention.

Above all, Wasserman's reading of the poem in terms of Renaissance cosmic and moral thought gave it not just intellectual coherence but also poetic integrity. It is based on his sense that 'neoclassic art is not the art of creating, but of inventing, or finding—the art of pursuing with perfect and unstrained consistency a system of similitudes inherent in the given materials' (Wasserman, 123). This is an unfashionably Aristotelian and 'Augustan' version of eighteenth-century poetic practice, but it may well provide a fuller basis for understanding the poem than any other schema which has been put forward.

Today, we feel a need to supplement any reading of Pope based on orthodox philosophic tradition with some consideration of what came to be seen as less respectable bodies of thought. We should, for example, pay attention to the concealed languages of occult learning, to the coded messages of Jacobitism, and to the ritualized vocabulary of ceremonial events and staged spectacles—issues which are examined in other chapters of this book. Further, we have to recognize some overt political themes and some literary legacies (mirrored respectively by such things as Evelyn's views on deafforestation and by the georgic tradition), omitted from the 'straight' reading. But these will refine an account based on the thematics of *concordia discors*, rather than supplant this version of the poem.[5]

In any case, *Cooper's Hill* and *Windsor-Forest* share more than a loco-descriptive framework or a Thames-side setting. Each sets up a series of correspondences between natural and human phenomena, between the landscape and the polity, and between realms of experience (e.g. war and hunting). As we have seen in Chapter 7, both poems enlist a current of georgic feeling in the service of a wider political purpose. Each is organized around a succession of tableaux, portraying different times or places as segments of a developing plot. Each uses traditional myth and creates a new mythology of its own. Like its great exemplar, *Cooper's Hill*, Pope's poem attempts to narrate recent history by providing events with a systematic context derived from earlier chronicles, from mythic episodes, from literary tradition and parallels, and from social or topographic reality. It is very much what we so often

---

[5] For the most cogent statement of reservations concerning Wasserman's case, see Cummings (1987: 63–77).

find in Pope. The more he dug into Denham's work, the more clearly he was able to realize his own ambitions and the more original his own vision of national destiny became. He only properly saw how things were going in 1713 when he contemplated 1642, as *Cooper's Hill* mediated that juncture; and the similarities he discovered were, in many instances, not such as to comfort him.

COWLEY

Denham and Cowley are united in a short passage (267–82). This serves to couple these loyal adherents of the crown who have made the banks of the river, as it flowed downstream from Windsor, into a hallowed region, 'By God-like Poets Venerable made'. Both men were unreconstructed royalists, even if Cowley may have wavered a little in the late 1650s, and both had close associations with the district. Each had suffered for the faith: Denham had been deprived of his estates, and like Cowley had been forced to flee to the Continent. There is a simple consideration which effectively proves that the pairing was based largely on political grounds. This is the fact, which must have been perfectly familiar to Pope, that John Milton had lived at Horton from 1632 to 1637, and produced much of his early poetry there. His mother died in the village in 1637 and was buried in the parish church. Horton lay as close to the Thames as did Chertsey, and much closer to Windsor than Cooper's Hill: across the river the young poet could easily glimpse that famous skyline: 'Towers and battlements it sees | Bosomed high in tufted trees' (*L'Allegro*). It would not have been hard to draw Milton's pastoral writing into a purely topographic account of the region. We can only conclude that Pope had other criteria than literary achievements or local connections.

In fact Cowley, like Denham, was useful to Pope's purposes over a broad range of issues. It takes only a few lines to integrate him into the poem's design, beginning with a neat antithetical construction:

> Here his first Lays Majestick *Denham* sung;
> There the last Numbers flow'd from *Cowley's* Tongue.
> O early lost! What Tears the River shed
> When the sad Pomp along his Banks was led?
> His drooping Swans on ev'ry Note expire,
> And on his Willows hung each Muse's Lyre.

(271–6)

Some of the allusions are straightforward. Thus the last line clearly echoes a famous verse from Psalm 137, 'We hanged our harps upon the willows in the midst thereof.' The psalmist is remembering Zion as he sits by the rivers of Babylon; so the exiled Stuarts chose to see themselves as banished from their homeland. There is also an allusion to a line by Cowley himself, 'Begin the *Song*, and strike the *Living Lyre*' (see *TE* i. 174). The swans and willows derive from conventional motifs in pastoral, expressive of death and sorrow. However, we are naturally reminded of the Swan of

Mantua and the Swan of Avon among Pope's great predecessors, of the white swans in Spenser's *Prothalamion,* and of the royal swans which lived on the Thames.[6] As elsewhere, elegiac and loyalist sentiments are blended. Some readers might recall, too, that the swan is also 'a very favourite charge' in heraldry, or that it is 'essentially a bird of chivalry, of queens, and knight-errantry'—for example, it was used on the banners of Lancastrian knights at tournaments in the Plantagenet age (Fox-Davies, 245; Rothery, 52). But the emblem is apt in calling up ideas of elegiac poetry, of the river, and of solemn ceremonial.

As for the 'sad Pomp': we know that Evelyn attended the elaborate funeral of his friend Cowley at Westminster Abbey in 1667, after the body had been floated down on a barge from Chertsey. In their gloss to these lines, the Twickenham editors aptly cite Cowley's epitaph in the Abbey, with its reference to the *honorifica pompa* with which he was carried out to burial from the house of Buckingham (see *TE* l. 174). The root sense of *pompa* is a ceremonial procession, and this is yet one more place where the poetic idiom draws us towards ritual and public display. The epitaph became extremely well known, after it had been translated by Sprat and appeared in Cowley's collected works.

If the forest is to recover from its sorrowful mood, someone must replace Denham and Cowley in the setting where the poet 'strung | His living Harp'. On cue, Lansdowne arrives:

> But hark! The Groves rejoice, the Forest rings!
> Are these reviv'd? or is it *Granville* sings?
>
> (281–2)

In alchemy, it was necessary for the swan, as a symbol of the white elixir (the lunar tincture), to revive: then, an eighteenth-century 'mythohermetic' dictionary explained, 'life has vanquished death, then the king is resurrected'.[7] Few will easily be convinced that Pope had an intimate knowledge of such hermetic lore, yet it is undeniable that the traditional emblems of restoration pervade the text of *Windsor-Forest.*

Cowley was one of Pope's early masters: it could not have been otherwise, in view of the poet's immense currency both in lyric and quasi-epic forms. What is probably the first surviving work by Pope, the 'Ode on Solitude', plainly derives from Cowley's *Essays, in Verse and Prose* (*TE* i. 4). From the same period come the 'Verses in Imitation of Cowley, by a Youth of Thirteen'. When Pope projected his teenage epic *Alcander,* as described in Chapter 7, one of the English models he chose for its style was Cowley, along with Spenser and Milton. Among the best known of the poems written in Pope's adolescence are the imitations of English poets, including 'The Garden', in emulation of Cowley. There is an immediate foretaste of the vocabulary which would be drawn on in *Windsor-Forest*:

---

[6] In the annual ceremony of swan-upping on the Thames, the royal swans were marked with five nicks. Lansdowne's brother, Sir Bevil Granville, held the unlikely office of Master Swanherd of all the Royalties belonging to the Crown on the Thames and other waters (Handasyde 1933: 32).

[7] Quoted by Roob (1997: 201).

Here *Orange*-trees with blooms and pendants shine,
And vernal honours to their autumn join;
Exceed their promise in the ripen'd store,
Yet in the rising blossom promise more.
There in bright drops the crystal Fountains play,
By *Laurels* shielded from the piercing Day:
Where *Daphne*, now a tree as once a maid,
Still from *Apollo* vindicates her shade,
Still turns her beauties from th'invading beam,
Nor seeks in vain from succour to the Stream.
The stream at once preserves her virgin leaves,
At once a shelter from her boughs receives,
Where *Summer*'s beauty midst of *Winter*'s stays,
And *Winter*'s Coldness spite of *Summer*'s rays.

(17–30)

To take only a selection of the parallels which are possible: the *here/there* construction is taken over in *WF*, 17–21, 23–4; Daphne seeks protection in her 'shade', as does Lodona (*WF*, 201–2); while l. 27 of 'The Garden' is echoed in thought and syntax by *WF*, 205, 'The silver Stream her Virgin Coldness keeps'.[8] All in all, 'The Garden' is the most obvious precursor of *Windsor-Forest*, along with the *Pastorals*, in Pope's juvenile output, and it serves to confirm the unrecognized debt to Cowley in the later poem.

Nor did Pope's interest in his predecessor end with his boyhood. Late in life he talked extensively with Spencer about Cowley, repeating an unreliable story about the poet's death at Chertsey (*Anecdotes* i. 192–3). It is important to remember that Cowley had been widely considered the greatest poet of his day—not excluding Milton—and two other aspects of his career would have made him especially attractive to Pope. The first was his pronounced concern with horticulture and silviculture, objects of obsession he shared with his friend John Evelyn, the subject of our next section. The second was his residence alongside the Thames at Chertsey, a town easily visible 2 miles downriver as Pope reached Staines on journeys between London and Binfield. Pope's note to *WF*, 272 accurately states that 'Mr. *Cowley* died at *Chertsey*, on the Borders of the Forest.' On his doorstep the poet had an excellent spot to refresh his mind and body, that is up on the slopes of St Ann's Hill, by the side of the demolished Abbey: both, of course, are features mentioned by Denham at the beginning of *Cooper's Hill*. A brook which rose on the hill came flowing past the old timber house with its pointed gables. According to William Stukeley, who visited the town to inspect the ruins of the abbey in 1752, Cowley had constructed some 'very good' fishponds.[9]

Moreover, the earlier poet had chosen this site, on land formerly belonging to his longtime patron Queen Henrietta Maria, for an exercise in self-conscious Horatian

---

[8] The earlier portion of 'The Garden' has Narcissus, transformed, gazing on himself (cf. the end of the Lodona episode), and uses the diction epithet *painted*.

[9] Quoted by Nethercot (1967: 253).

retirement. Here he attempted to live a philosophic country existence on something that could be vaguely construed as a Sabine farm. For the last two years of his life, Cowley studied nature, religion, and morality. Earlier he had devoted himself to medicine and had been awarded the degree of doctor of physic by Oxford University in 1657. It is not entirely clear how far this indicates any technical skill in diagnostics and treatment. However, we do know that Cowley studied anatomy under his friend Dr Charles Scarborough, later physician to Charles II; that he proceeded to 'the consideration of simples', and then retired to 'a fruitful part of Kent', where 'every field and wood might show him the real figures of those plants of which he read'.[10] In this respect he serves as an obvious model for the blessed retiree of *Windsor-Forest*, 'whom Nature charms, and whom the Muse inspires' (238), gathering herbs in the forest and medicinal plants in the fields.

Just how well established this version of Cowley's life had become is illustrated by a passage in Defoe's *Tour of Great Britain*, published a decade after *Windsor-Forest*. It is after a reference to the Forest, indeed, that Defoe proceeds downriver to Staines, where he cites the famous couplet from *Cooper's Hill*, and then to Chertsey. 'This Town was made famous, by being the Burial Place of *Henry* VI. till his Bones were after removed to *Windsor* by *Henry* VII.', the entry begins. But the town has another claim to reputation: 'Also by being the Retreat of the Incomparable *Cowley*, where he liv'd withdrawn from the Hurries of Court and Town, and where he dy'd so much a recluse, as to be almost wholly taken up in Country business, Farming, and Husbandry, for his Diversion, not for *Bread*, according to the publick flight of his own Fancy' (*Tour* i. 144). The disdainful note of this final clause notwithstanding, it is evident that Defoe has inherited the legend of Cowley as an icon of retirement. Pope's treatment of Cowley is much subtler, insofar as it implicitly looks back to the portrait of the noble scholar-hermit; but it does bear some relation to the orthodox impression people had of Cowley.

The concerns just described find expression in many items in Cowley's *oeuvre*, particularly those which appeared posthumously in his collected works—volumes which continued to appear at regular intervals in Pope's lifetime, some issued by Jacob Tonson. Most relevantly, the 1668 folio collection, which included a life of the poet by Thomas Sprat, also featured 'Several Discourses, by way of Essays, in Verse and Prose'. Several of the essays here express hostility to urbanism and luxury, and celebrate the virtues of simple living in a rural society. 'Of Solitude', for example, begins by quoting 'the excellent *Scipio*' as author of a proverbial saying, *Numquam minus solus, quam cum solus*; Cowley actually terms Scipio 'the most Wise, most Worthy, most Happy, and Greatest of all Mankind'.[11] The virtues endorsed are those for which 'great *Scipio*' is held up for admiration in *Windsor-Forest* (257). The next essay, 'Of Obscurity', develops these themes: the description of a

---

[10] Nethercot (1967: 169). This is a slightly revised reprint of the biography first published in 1931. A new life is needed, but Nethercot remains the fullest and generally the most reliable source at present.

[11] Grosart (1967: ii. 316).

peaceful and stealthy death after a healthy life was taken over directly in the ending of Pope's 'Ode on Solitude'.

Following this, 'Of Agriculture' praises the husbandman, starting with Virgil, and makes the political message explicit when the writer observes that all other trades contributed to the 'twenty Years Ruin of [the] Country' during 'our late and miserable Civil Wars', whereas no husbandman was involved—or at least none according to Cowley.[12] The underlying myth of *Windsor-Forest* implies in just the same way that the parliamentarians and their successors, like William III, were destroyers, and their royalist opponents were guardians of the land. The link becomes even more plain when Cowley finishes his essay with a translation of the *beatus ille* passage in the second *Georgic*. As we saw earlier in this chapter, Pope's adaptation distils the essence of Virgil, and we might not need to look any further for a model: conceivably a verse in Cowley, 'All sorts of Fruit crown the rich Autumn's Pride', lingered in Pope's mind when he wrote his own line, 'See *Pan* with Flocks, with Fruits *Pomona* crown'd' (*WF*, 37), although *Georgics*, ii. 516–17 lies behind both passages. This is still not the end of the story, however: another appendage to the essay is an English translation of part of Cowley's Latin poem, *Sex libri plantarum*, Book IV, rendering the same ideas. Like Virgil and Pope, Cowley sets out the names of noble exemplars of virtuous retirement; they are drawn from antiquity. It was an innovatory act on Pope's part to introduce a modern, Trumbull.

Probably the best known of the essays, 'The Garden', had originally been written as a letter to Evelyn on 16 August 1666, a few days before the outbreak of the Great Fire set people thinking in a different direction. It culminates in a Pindaric ode addressed to Evelyn, which its grateful recipient reclaimed to use in front of the text of *Sylva* (3rd edn., 1679). The essay left its mark on later writers such as Shaftesbury, but it does not seem to have been used in *Windsor-Forest*. Nevertheless, the mindset of these essays pervades Pope's whole attitude to horticulture and allied studies.

The poem *De plantarum* gradually expanded from two books to six. It begins with a kind of symposium, or court of flowers, over which Flora presides. The flowers of each season present themselves in turn. In the third book, Cowley describes the Maytime gathering as taking place at an auspicious date: *Annus erat longe ante alios pulcherrimus annos* . . . Nahum Tate's faithful translation underlines the debt to the idiom of panegyric and prophetic verse:

> It was the Year, (thrice blest that beauteous Year,),
> When mighty CHARLES's sacred Name did bear,
> A Golden Year the Heavens brought about
> In high Procession with a joyful Shout.[13]

Pope similarly tries to link natural phenomena with the celebrations for the peace, although the pomp in 1713 was less than such gilded language requires. Book V turns to the subject of trees, and indeed in his title *Sylva* Cowley looks back to Statius and across to the almost exactly contemporaneous work by his friend Evelyn. The book

---

[12] Grosart (1967: ii. 320). For another direct borrowing from this essay at *WF*, 122, see *TE* i. 162.
[13] Grosart (1967: ii. 172, 268).

contains a catalogue of sylvan species, as does Evelyn's work, but this time contending for supremacy at a banquet of Pomona. At the end Apollo prophesies a noble future for America, now held in thrall by Spanish lust for gold; already savage customs like cannibalism have been expunged, and in time civilization will spread to the New World, as Europe will concurrently fall. It is a vision of an apocalyptic future brought about by trade, peace, and domestic virtue, in the course of 'long rowling Years'.[14] Much of this went into Pope's concluding vision of a new world order where slavery has been banished, the Indians freed, and both Peru and Mexico restored to greatness.

Book VI, which was also entitled 'Sylva' and translated by Aphra Behn, represents the most significant portion of the work for our purposes. Cowley describes a Golden Age under Charles I disrupted by carnage, preceded by natural prodigies including comets which were witnessed by Cowley as a boy. The signs were ignored and England thrown into disorder. Under Cromwell sturdy oaks which had been growing for a thousand years were uprooted; the forest groves robbed of form, rigour, and scent. Monsters invaded the scene, and other portents which only the dryads fully understood. At this point the poem is given a precise location, defined in a note by Cowley as 'Nobilissima Sylva (the Forest of Dean)', set between the Wye and the Severn, and termed by Giraldus Cambrensis the forest of the Danes. However, Camden has warranted the derivation of the name from Arden, and it is this which is used in the text of the poem: *Ardennae quondam praenobile nomen* | *Nunc Denae datur.* Both these etymologies are false. However, Camden's is the more interesting on its own terms, and much more suggestive for our present purposes. It is deeply instructive that a poet bent on celebrating the English woodland should attempt to transfer Arden to another site: that is what Pope himself does.[15] Still more significant is the appeal to Camden, as the repository of a central core of the matter of Britain, to settle such a dispute. All that is lacking, as respects the argument of this book, is an application to Drayton, who had already given both Arden and Dean a mythological potential ready for Pope to use.

The sylvan goddesses are called to assemble in this location, enabling Cowley to run through the main British species of tree, deciduous and coniferous. They encircle their monarch, the 'Sceptre-bearing *Dryas*', that is the oak. There follows an account of the ages of mankind, ultimately derived perhaps from Hesiod, describing a primitive simplicity undone by a quest for luxury. The oak provides salvation, as it permits the revival of the great republic of the world through trade and exploration (here a paean to Francis Drake). There follows a familiar passage of comparative nationalism, translated by Behn in this way:

> Oh, how has Nature blest the *British* Land,
> Who both the valued *Indies* can command!
> What tho' thy Banks the Cedars do not grace
> Those lofty Beauties of fam'd *Libanus*:
> The Pine, or Palm of *Idumean* Plains;

---

[14] Grosart (1967: ii. 214, 278–9).   [15] See *SDW*, ch. 5.

> *Arab*'s rich Woods, or its sweet-swelling Greens,
> Or lovely Plantan, whose large leafy Boughs
> A pleasant and a noble Shade allows.
> She has thy warlike Groves and Mountains blest
> With sturdy Oaks, o'er all the World the best;
> And for the happy Island's sure Defence,
> Has wall'd it with a Mote of Seas immense;
> While to declare her Safety and thy Pride,
> With Oaken Ships that Sea is fortify'd.[16]

This is exactly the rhetorical trope Pope uses (29–35), and of course the notion of forest oaks maintaining naval power turns up repeatedly in *Windsor-Forest*.

The queen goes on to speak of her own descent, and then to read the auguries out of British history, from Aeneas and his grandson Brutus onward. The evil omens presage recent disasters: the intervention of the Scots, the death of Strafford, the first skirmish near the Severn, that is presumably Powick Bridge, and all the griefs provoked by 'our first Intestine Wars' (Behn's phrase at l. 904: compare Pope's 'Series of Intestine Wars', *WF*, 325). The narrative moves on to Edgehill, Newbury, and Naseby. This was as far as Cowley had been able to take the story in *The Civil War*, but after the Restoration he was able to write with more resolve and candour. In particular, he could now confront the death of the king in some of the most fanciful and baroque writing—the fatal deed is committed in a half-line breaking the regular series of hexameters:

> *Carnificisque manu.*

After this the oak is cleft by a thousand sighs which break through her bark in tears—an image worthy of Cowley's friend Crashaw. Britain is imaged as a deformed trunk, out of which spring the pullulating vermin of the anti-royalist party. The accumulated treasures of the nation are destroyed. Heedless of the call of religion to avoid the profanation of the woodlands, the barbarous conquerors move into these hallowed regions, and tear up trees from their roots. After the defeat of the king's son at Worcester, he flies to safety in the royal oak:

> Even his blue Garter now he wil discharge,
> Nor keep the warlike figure of St *George*,
> That holy Champion now is vanquish'd quite,
> Alas! The Dragon has subdu'd the Knight.[17]

The remainder of the poem describes the eventual defeat of the 'usurpers' and the joyous return of the king to his country, as bonfires light up the nation and gild the surface of the Thames. The first royal act is to recolonize the stripped forests with trees, and purge the long neglected gardens of their weeds, as an emblem of restoring national honour. *De plantarum* is certainly an uneven poem, often garrulous and linguistically ornate: it is not surprising that it has been largely forgotten, quite

---

[16] Grosart (1967: ii. 249). For the idea of Britain as preserved inviolate in its insular state, see *SDW*, ch. 6.
[17] Grosart (1967: ii. 254). See Ch. 5, above for a similar incident involving the Duke of Monmouth.

apart from the fact that it is, so to speak, encrypted in what has now become almost a dead language.

Twenty years earlier, as the author of *The Civil War*, Cowley had already confronted the large political issues which continued to divide men and women of Pope's day: the work has recently been seen as 'the unfinished or unfinishable epic forged from the conflicts of the seventeenth century'.[18] Only the first book of *The Civil War* had been published in Pope's day: it appeared in 1670, in 1709, and again in Tonson's *Miscellanies* (1716; 1727). Cowley had actually carried the narrative forward in three books as far as the battle of Naseby, but discouraged by the course of the war he had desisted: he never sought to print the poem in his lifetime. Whilst there is no proof that Pope knew the work, it would be rash to suppose that he did not. *The Civil War* enlists poets whom we are certain Pope admired: Statius, Lucan, Claudian. Even more directly than the last book of *De plantarum*, it offered a royalist view of the Caroline age and its violent termination.

The poem begins with a review of English greatness under earlier monarchs. One who gains a warm mention is Richard I as valiant crusader: ''Gainst the proud *Moon*, Hee th' *English Crosse* displaid' (i. 23). This might even be a source for Pope, but it is assuredly a close analogue: 'Bear *Britain*'s Thunder, and her Cross display' (*WF*, 387). The next in sequence is Edward III, as the poet deplores the modern lack of that national spirit which was in evidence at Crécy and Poitiers. 'Two Kings at once we brought sad Captives home' (i. 47)—an allusion to the 'Monarchs chain'd' in *WF*, 305, that is David II of Scotland and Jean II of France. After a passage on Henry V, Cowley moves on to the country's glorious history under Elizabeth: 'To her great *Neptune* homag'd all his Streames, | And all the wide strecht *Ocean* was her *Thames*' (i. 63–4): compare *WF*, 223–4. Such heroes have no parallel in the present age: 'We' are not their *offspring*, sure our *Heralds* ly' (i. 69).[19] Then comes a celebration of the happy sixteen years at the start of Charles I's reign, a time for the poet of peace and justice, interrupted by the onset of the Bishops' War: here the historical narrative is close to that of *De plantarum* two decades later. The story leads up ineluctably to the moment when the king raised his standard at Nottingham in 1642.[20]

At this point Cowley constructs a masque-like scene depicting the battle of Edgehill, which was still quite recent news when he was writing, as it was fought on 23 October 1642. In this '*Fiends*' like schism, sedition, oppression, rapine, and murder combat their adversaries, religion, loyalty, learning, murder, and justice. It is an exercise very close in its mode and methods to the allegorical sequence at the end of *Windsor-Forest*. There are parallels in phrasing and iconographic detail: thus, Cowley writes,

[18] MacLean (1990: 181). Trotter (1979: 5–21), suggests that the poem had already become an untenable project by the time Cowley was forced to relinquish the task.

[19] The quoted passage follows the punctuation of the first edition of 1668, as recorded by the editor, Allan Pritchard, in Cowley (1989: i. 115). This is the edition cited throughout.

[20] As in his later Latin poem, Cowley refers to an opening skirmish near Worcester, which can be identified as the battle of Powick Bridge on 23 Sept. 1642.

Sedition there her crimson *Banner* spreads,
Shakes all her Hands, and roars with all her Heads.
Her knotty haires were with dire *Serpents* twist,
And all her *Serpents* at each other hist.

(i. 221–4)

This is another version of what we see in *WF*, 417–19: compare also Cowley's 'Here *Loyalty* an humble *Crosse* displaid' with *WF*, 387. As might be expected, *The Civil War* gives a decidedly royalist view of this inconclusive encounter, citing the implausible claim that ten fell on the parliamentary side for every man lost by the king's forces under Prince Rupert.

The gradual decline of royalist fortunes is charted in the remainder of the poem. Pope, as noted, could only have seen the first book: this would have allowed him to read Cowley's disparaging account of John Hampden (i. 377–92), and a description of the campaign in the South-West. This leads up to an impassioned tribute to Sir Bevil Granville, killed at the battle of Lansdowne in July 1643, and a leading figure in royalist martyrology. We have already seen in Chapter 2 that Sir Bevil was the grandson of Pope's dedicatee, who had signalized his family piety and political attachment when he took the name of Lord Lansdowne, a year before *Windsor-Forest* appeared. In the remainder of Book I Cowley describes the 'white *day*' of the battle of Roundway Down, which took place a week after Lansdowne. Again the parliamentary forces are characterized in terms of furies and serpent-coiled harpies. Even though Pope's treatment of the Civil War is discreetly brief, the matrix of ideas on which he drew to bolster Stuart credentials in *Windsor-Forest* is very closely allied to that which is apparent in Cowley's poem.

It is not altogether easy to summarize Cowley's presence in the complex of themes, ideas, literary practices, and moods which inform *Windsor-Forest*. Virgil and Denham gave Pope a generic base; Ovid and Camden gave him a plot, either mythological or historical. By comparison Cowley left a more dispersed impact on the poem, deriving from a number of different works. In a few places Pope recalls actual phrases of his mentor; more often, he inherits attitudes and states of mind. Cowley is most evident as a writer who had connected husbandry with the large political issues of the seventeenth century. A recurrent suggestion is that the Civil War had disrupted the natural order, and had resulted from urbanizing tendencies which needed to be resisted. Thus tree-planting has become a moral imperative as well as a social programme. This was a theme to be enunciated in accents that were even more loud and clear by Cowley's close friend, Evelyn.

EVELYN AND WREN

A tutelary presence behind *Windsor-Forest* is provided by John Evelyn's great work of national restoration, *Sylva*. More than any other book, this had established the role of trees, oaks in particular, as guardians of the realm. Pope's apostrophe to the trees of 'fair *Windsor*' (385–92) appeals to a set of commonplaces which Evelyn had expressed most memorably and cogently.

In many ways Evelyn was admirably fitted to perform the role of one of the ancestral voices blending in the rich choral arrangement of Pope's poem. Since the publication of his diary in 1818, Evelyn's other literary works have been thrown into the shade, but he was a writer of considerable virtuosity with some of the qualities of Burton and Browne in his language. A royalist who had suffered exile and discomfort if not martyrdom for his beliefs, he was enough of a cosmopolitan to see the limitations of Britain, in spite of an almost unquestioning patriotism. Like Pope, he despised the lax and affected manners of the court of Charles II. His central interests overlapped with those of Pope: *virtù*, collecting, gardening, architecture, antiquarianism, language, classical literature, bibliophilia. He was enough of a herald to be able to submit drafts for the arms and motto of the Royal Society on its foundation (*ED* iii. 332).

Most revealingly, several of these pursuits were *directly* to the purposes of *Windsor-Forest*. For instance, Evelyn applied his architectural interests to the reconstruction of London after the Fire, in his plan for a redesigned and regenerated capital, *London Redivivum* (written in 1666). In general Evelyn disliked the narrowness and squalour of the old city, most of it designated 'rubbish'. Earlier he had deplored the lack of 'publique and honourable works' such as Paris possessed, as well as the 'uniform and conspicuous Structures' of Italy. By contrast the surroundings of old St Paul's were 'lothsome', 'a Golgotha' (Evelyn, 79).[21] Among the few buildings he exempted was the Banqueting House at Whitehall. He envisaged recreating London with noble Burlingtonian public buildings: 'The Gates and Entries of the city, which are to be rebuilt, might be the subjects of handsome architecture, in form of triumphal arches, adorned with Statues, Relievos, and apposite Inscriptions' (Evelyn, 343). This is a vision close to that of *Windsor-Forest* (375–80) and of the *Epistle to Burlington*.[22] Evelyn also furnished additions to the account of Surrey in the 1695 version of *Britannia*, one of Pope's prime sources.[23] Just as relevant to our purposes, he wrote a formal *Panegyric* on Charles II (1661), which gives a pointer to one dimension of Pope's undertaking.

One of Evelyn's close friends was Sir Christopher Wren, to whom he dedicated his treatise on *Architects and Architecture* (1706).[24] Together the two men represent a strain of seventeenth-century humanism which survived into Pope's day. Among all their diverse concerns, they were virtuosi, scholars, antiquarians, architectural propagandists, and of course prominent Fellows of the Royal Society. Local factors, too, linked Wren with the world of Pope's poem: his father and uncle had both acted as registrar of the Garter while serving as dean of Windsor, whilst he himself would be

---

[21] Wren and Evelyn inspected the site of the old cathedral in Aug. 1666, days before its destruction in the Fire (*ED* iii. 449). For Wren's suggested repairs (agreed to by Evelyn) see Wren, 274–7; Soo (1998: 48–55).

[22] Another friend was Hugh May, who remodelled Windsor Castle for Charles II.

[23] Wheatley and Bray (1879: iii. 475–6).

[24] Wren possessed a copy of Evelyn's translation of Fréart's *Parallèle de l'architecture antique et de la moderne* (1664): Soo (1998: 6).

MP for Old Windsor (as would his son at the end of Anne's reign). A loyal adherent of the Stuart court, Sir Christopher was turfed out of his office as surveyor—which he had held for fifty years, since the death of Denham in 1668—soon after the Hanoverians came to the throne. Pope later recalled this event (see p. 138, below). Even though Wren's Frenchified baroque had come to seem old-fashioned to fastidious Palladians by the time he died in 1723, he was universally recognized as the greatest English architect since Inigo Jones, and notable above all for his part in the reconstruction of London after its destruction in 1666. Here his role in rebuilding the City churches was almost as famous as his design of St Paul's; and in addition he was appointed a commissioner for the new 'Queen Anne' churches, planned in the Act of 1708, to which Pope refers in *Windsor-Forest*.[25] Conservative Anglicans would also recall his impressive college and university buildings at Oxford and Cambridge, together with his public architecture at Greenwich and elsewhere. But his main claim on posterity lay in the fact that, more than anyone else, he had been responsible for the physical restoration of London, with its 'glitt'ring Spires', and the 'Temples' which furnished 'the beauteous Works of Peace' (*WF*, 377–8)—in fact he had even restored Temple Bar and parts of the Temple. So Evelyn contends that Wren 'needs no *Panegyrick*, or other *History*' to eternize his achievements 'than the *greatest City of the Universe*, which he hath *rebuilt* and *beautified*'. If the whole art of building were lost, the argument continues, it could be recovered from the works which the architect will leave behind him (Wren, 343).

In *Nusmismata* (1697), Evelyn pays a warm tribute to his friend's work on the Monument, regretting only that the memorial was not sited where the Great Fire ended, rather than where it began, since the column was designed 'as a grateful *Monument* and *Recognition to Almighty God* for its Extinction'. More apt at the scene of the outbreak of the fire would be 'a plain *lugubrous Marble* with some apposite Inscription'. Pope naturally resented the crude anti-papist message added to the column (see Chapter 4, above). Wren had envisaged a much more measured inscription in Latin, lamenting the extensive destruction and lauding the recreation of the City from its ashes—no blame is attached to anyone.[26] What Evelyn says about the need for the Monument sums up orthodox Stuart ideology:

Our late Discoveries of new Worlds, and Conflicts at Sea; the *sanglant* Battles that have been fought on Land; the Fortitude and Sufferings of an excellent Prince; the Restoration of his Successor; the Conflagration, and re-edifying of the greatest City in the World in less than Twenty Years . . . call aloud for their *Medals* apart.[27]

It does not take much effort to locate here some of the key themes and images in *Windsor-Forest*. Nor is it surprising to find that the sculpture by Caius Gabriel Cibber on the west side of the Monument showed Peace and Plenty seated in a

[25] See Ch. 4, above. For Wren's letter to a friend on the policy which should be adopted in constructing the fifty new churches, in terms of land-use and the like, see Wren, 318–21.

[26] Wren, 323. In the text, Wren's son adapts the remark of Suetonius about Augustus, that he found Rome brick and left it marble.

[27] Cited in Wren, 322. As we have seen in Ch. 5, Wren was the designated architect of a mausoleum at Windsor to the memory of Charles I, never executed for reasons that are unclear.

cloud, while allegorical figures including Liberty and Architecture flanked the King as he trampled down Envy.

The entire career of Christopher Wren as a court architect traces the same trajectory as Pope's ideological history of the nation. After he had played a major role in 'restoring' the nation under the Stuarts, his salary for the work on St Paul's was suspended under William in 1697, pending completion of the cathedral. In 1710 his son laid the highest stone on the lantern (just below the cross), but Wren still had to petition parliament in the following January to get the remaining half of his salary paid. Just at the time that *Windsor-Forest* appeared, in 1712–13, his supervision of the work came into question with an anonymous pamphlet called *Frauds and Abuses at St. Paul's*, which elicited further comments pro and con. When the Hanoverian regime took over, the Office of Works was placed in commission and efforts made to ease the architect into retirement. His plans for exterior detailing on the cathedral were overruled. Eventually, as we have already noted, Wren was ousted in 1718 by the Whig amateur William Benson. Sir Christopher spent most of his last days at a Thames-side villa near Hampton Court, which had been leased to him by Queen Anne. Pope would note his replacement by Benson in *The Dunciad*, with the plaintive addition, 'While Wren with sorrow to the grave descends' (*TE* v. 189). Originally, the plaque over the architect's tomb in the crypt of his greatest building was very plain, but later his son added the famous inscription, *Si monumentum requiris, circumspice.* So Pope had wished to inscribe a commemorative message on the bare tomb of Charles I in *Windsor-Forest*.

Like Evelyn, Christopher Wren remains as a shadowy presence throughout the poem. This can be seen most clearly when Pope turns to the rebuilding of London and the projected reconstruction of Whitehall:

> Behold! *Augusta*'s glitt'ring Spires increase,
> And Temples rise, the beauteous Works of Peace.
> I see, I see where two fair Cities bend
> Their ample Bow, a new *White-Hall* ascend!

> (377–80)

The speaker is the god of the Thames, and it was on the banks of the river that many of Wren's most splendid royal buildings had been erected. As surveyor-general he had supervised the public 'Works' (known by this name) for decades. He had designed projects for constructions or reconstructions at Windsor, Hampton Court, Westminster Abbey, and Whitehall Palace, as we have seen. In an earlier Stuart reign he had created the Royal Hospital at Chelsea. Then, at the instigation of Anne's sister Mary, he had embarked on the Hospital for Seamen at Greenwich. His scheme comprised four blocks affording a view from the Thames towards the Queen's House, built by his great predecessor Inigo Jones—much, indeed, as Jones had created perspectival vistas for court masques. Begun in the mid-1690s, the first blocks were adorned with two sumptuous domes early in the new reign: as a later writer expressed it, the project 'rose to perfection' under Anne. The impressive Painted Hall in King William's Block was ready in 1708 to be decorated by James Thornhill. By

May 1714, the artist had completed his famous allegory of Peace and Prosperity, which showed William and Mary presenting Liberty to Europe, while trampling on vices. On a nearby pediment Anne's cipher was displayed with the emblem of the Garter. After her death the Queen would be depicted by Thornhill on the ceiling of the Upper Hall as *Anna Optima Regina*, at the centre of an elaborate allegorical design. Meanwhile work had begun on Queen Anne's Block, although it was not finished until 1727. The Queen had taken a personal interest in this charitable undertaking, and she even allocated £5,000 from the booty of the condemned pirate William Kidd to the revenues of the hospital. Wren's charitable intent was made plain by his refusal to accept any fee for his work.

Anne herself, Wren, Evelyn as treasurer of the commissioners—all were involved in this conspicuous outlay of royal bounty, in a project which benefited the Navy, and indeed the very men who would carry the British cross to the corners of the world (a motif found, as it happens, in Thornhill's mural designs), the theme of *WF*, 385–92. Moreover, the Greenwich scheme was the fulfilment of a dream going back to James I, and kept alive under Charles I, Charles II, and William and Mary, before it achieved realization under Anne—except for the Dutch king, an unbroken line of Stuarts. Finally, the hospital was itself a benevolent institution, of a kind which became 'the locus in which Painting proved its civic value'.[29] All this reflects Pope's architectural ideal: that is, noble classical buildings erected for a public purpose, enhancing the Thames-side skyline as the poem moves on towards the sea, and dignifying the monarch who sponsored their construction. Along with St Paul's and the City churches, Greenwich best represents the 'beauteous Works of Peace' which were coming into being, even as Pope wrote.[30]

Late in life Evelyn had published his study of medals, *Numismata*, with about a hundred engravings. This was an area of enquiry which Pope also entered, as his poem to Addison shows (see Chapter 2, above), and as the iconography of *Windsor-Forest* confirms.[31] We know that Pope was acquainted with Evelyn's book at first hand: he wrote a satiric quatrain in a copy belonging to William Kent, which he probably saw at Chiswick when the artist was given rooms there by Lord Burlington.[32] The work treats coins as 'Vocal monuments of Antiquity', and suggests that British history could be illuminated by their study, as well as the orthodox use to which they were put in the understanding of antiquity.[33] This was something that any alert reader of *Britannia* could discern, in the light of its extensive coverage of British, Roman, and

---

[28] Wren, 23 (second pagination).　　　　　　　　　　　　　[29] Murdoch (1989: 264).

[30] Adjoining the Royal Hospital (later, equally aptly, the Royal Naval College) stood another building designed by Wren, the Royal Observatory—the site from which astronomers would mark 'the Course of rolling Orbs on high' (*WF*, 245).

[31] Wren's son, Christopher, the author of *Parentalia*, himself published a study of ancient coinage, *Numismatum antiquorum sylloge* (1708). Wren senior owned a collection of Greek medals.

[32] See *TE* vi. 340–1. The subject of the quarrel which is alleged to have provoked the poem was an inscription on the monument to Pope's father, where the epithet *pio* was supposedly used; while the wit of the quatrain lies in a pun on the word 'coin'.

[33] The best discussion of *Numismata* in its historical context is that of Levine (1991: 338–42).

Saxon coins. There is no doubt that Evelyn did much to spark the growth of interest in numismatics, which was given its literary spin first by Addison and then by Pope (see also *SDW*, chapter 2).

Evelyn earned his chief renown by his devotion to horticulture and planting. His *Kalendarium Hortense*, first issued as an appendix to *Sylva* but later frequently reprinted on its own, stands out as one of the earliest detailed guides to the gardening year. It was dedicated to Abraham Cowley, already distinguished as a key figure in Pope's mental formation, and a resident of the Thames-side region commemorated in the poem. As we have seen, the third edition of *Sylva* (1679) included in its preliminaries Cowley's essay *The Garden*. We have also observed that Evelyn attended the funeral of Cowley, held at Westminster Abbey in 1666: this event lurks behind the text of *Windsor-Forest* at ll. 273–6.[34]

Like his friends Cowley and Wren, Evelyn was a foundation fellow of the Royal Society, and it was he who gave the new body its name in 1661. Two years earlier, he had proposed to Robert Boyle a society of his own: for this purpose, an estate should be purchased no more than 25 miles from London (Windsor lies some 24 miles west of the centre of the city). Evelyn suggested that there should be six cells for each member of the group, with living facilities and a private garden attached to each. There would be a laboratory for specimens, an aviary, a dovecote, an herb garden, a vegetable garden, an orchard, a conservatory, and a stable. Visitors would be admitted only at appointed times. Members might leave the estate for a month every year, to visit London or the universities. The aim of the society was to be 'the promotion of natural knowledge'.[35] It sounds like the academy in *Love's Labour's Lost*, a little toned down; in any case Boyle seems to have shown no interest. This domesticated version of hermetic life would have certainly have appealed to one individual: Pope's rural philosopher, as he practised herbalism, physic, chemistry, botany, astronomy, and antiquarian study, following nature in 'the silent Wood' (249).

Furthermore, Evelyn was a careful student of portents, prodigies of nature, and other 'signs', with a marked interest in astrology. Quite late in life, he attended the trial of a peer, Viscount Stafford, who was accused of taking part in a Catholic plot in 1681. This event reminded Evelyn of another trial held in Westminster Hall back in 1641, and he convinced himself that a comet he saw at this time resembled one he had witnessed during the progress of the earlier trial. The first occasion had been the arraignment of Charles I's minister, the Earl of Strafford. (Both peers ended up on the scaffold.) Misled by the similarity in their names, Evelyn had conflated events. In fact the first comet he had seen occurred in 1643.[36] Almost forty years on, it is evident that Evelyn had not forgotten the fall of Strafford. On 12 May 1641 he had actually attended the beheading on Tower Hill, which seemed to presage the execution of King Charles himself.[37] So the omens clung on in the memory of Stuart supporters, long after the Civil War and the Restoration: this was a legacy on which Pope was to draw heavily.

---

[34] Wheatley and Bray (1879: ii. 222).   [35] Stimson (1968: 20–1).   [36] Geneva (1995: 94–5).
[37] The diarist had been unable to attend the execution of the king, appalled by what he regarded as a villainous murder: he kept the day as a time of fast (*ED* ii. 547).

At the same time, Evelyn was a keen observer of public events, and gives us some of our fullest accounts of ceremonial occasions such as the coronation of Charles II. He survived long enough to witness Anne crowned in 1702, 'with all possible magnificence and Pomp', and to attend the great celebration for the victory at Blenheim, held at St Paul's in September 1704. In fact he had a family interest in the battle, since news of its successful outcome was brought to the Queen by Daniel Parke, whose mother was his own first cousin (see Chapter 4, above). When 'my Co: Parke' reached London, the diarist reported, there was 'nothing but triumphs & demonstrations of Joy in the City'.[38]

Although Evelyn died in 1706, one member of the family was active at the date of *Windsor-Forest*: this was his grandson and heir Sir John Evelyn (1682–1763), who was responsible for bringing out later editions of some of his grandfather's works. The baronetcy dates from the same year as the poem: it was created in 1713 to reward the younger Evelyn's services as an MP and in minor government office under Anne. The younger man inherited the architectural tastes of his grandfather, and was elected to the Royal Society. Soon after leaving Oxford, he helped the aged patriarch repair damage to the timber on the family estate at Wotton. Immediately to the purpose, he subscribed to the *Iliad* and the *Odyssey*, just as he did to Prior's *Poems*. Once John Caryll suggested that Pope might have stayed at Wotton, on the way to Ladyholt (*Corr.* ii. 78, 112). In fact the two men became acquainted through the agency of the Harcourt family: Sir John Evelyn's sister Elizabeth had married Simon Harcourt, secretary of the October Club and a particular favourite of Pope (*EC*, vi. 278).

John Evelyn the writer and virtuoso died, full of years and honours, in 1706, and was buried at Wotton. An inscription on his tomb proclaimed that his fame would be perpetuated 'by far more lasting Monuments than those of Stone, or Brass' (*ED*, v. 623). The blend of classical and Christian in this valedictory statement had run through Evelyn's entire life. His legacy was to extend over generations to come, but it was nowhere more marked than in *Windsor-Forest*—a poem already in gestation by 1706.

SYLVA

The full title of Evelyn's greatest book is *Sylva: Or a Discourse of Forest-Trees, and the Propagation of Timber in His Majesties Dominion &c.* It followed on an urgent inquiry from the Commissioners of the Navy to the newly formed Royal Society. This in turn proceeded from anxiety felt at the speed with which the stock of the nation's timber, so vital for shipbuilding, was being depleted. 'Unfortunately during the Interregnum the destruction of landed estates, royal forests, and other woodland in search of quick profits had created a potential crisis for the restored monarchy. With intense commercial rivalry on the high seas from the Dutch it was essential to

---

[38] *ED* v. 498, 574–5. Evelyn was a frequent visitor to Windsor, where he lamented over the tomb of the 'blessed *Martyr*' Charles; admired the 'incomparable Prospect' from the Crace of the castle; and lingered over Verrio's pictures of St George and the Black Prince in St George's Hall (see Ch. 5, above).

rebuild timber stocks' (Evelyn, 173). As one of a committee of three to whom the matter was referred, Evelyn reported to the Society on 15 October 1662, and an order was made for the report to be printed. The dedication to Charles II is dated 29 May 1663, but the volume did not appear until February 1664. Nobody has ever doubted that the book proceeded almost entirely from Evelyn's own pen: it is hard to imagine anything less like the usual committee findings than this learned, allusive, and highly personal essay.

The dedication begins by recalling the king's role as founder of the Royal Society, and his providential escape from capture at the Boscobel Oak: 'You are our Θος λιχος, *Nemorensis Rex*, as having once your Temple, and Court too under that Holy-Oak which you consecrated with your Presence, and We celebrate with just Acknowledgement to God for your Preservation' (Evelyn, 183). The King, too, has outdone all his predecessors in his zeal for new plantations, and in 'cultivating our decaying Woods' has contributed to the wealth and safety of nation. He is thus 'furnish'd to send forth those Argos, and Trojan Horses, about this your Island' (Evelyn, 183–4). There follows an address to the reader, in which Evelyn places the blame for the current crisis squarely on the felling policy which prevailed under the Commonwealth:

But what shall I then say of our late prodigious Spoilers, whose furious devastation of so many goodly Woods and Forests have left an infamy on their Names and Memories not quickly to be forgotten! I mean our unhappy Usurpers, and injurious Sequestrators; Not here to mention the deplorable necessities of a Gallant and Loyal Gentry, who for their Compositions were (many of them) compell'd to add yet to this Waste, by an inhumane and unparallel'd Tyranny over them, to preserve the poor remainder of their Fortunes, and to find them Bread. (Evelyn, 187)

If Pope read these words, as he assuredly did—perhaps in the fourth edition of 1706—he must have been aware of the experience of individuals still alive, including Trumbull, whose own family estate had been depleted at this time, and had possibly lost timber also (see Chapter 1, above). The 'Tyranny' of the parliamentary incomers was replicated for the poet by the invasions of the Williamite grandees, as metaphorically expressed in the Nimrod section. While the anti-puritan strain in Evelyn may lead to some exaggeration, since oaks took almost a century to mature and earlier planting policy must come into question (not to mention the depredations which had been permitted in the Forest of Dean under Charles I), it is clear that the timber crisis was perceived at the time to have been intensified by what happened in the Commonwealth era.[39]

There had actually been a shortage of timber since the time of Henry VIII, and anxiety continued into the time of Pope and beyond. Defoe, no lover of the Stuarts, was heretical in claiming that England need not fear the loss of sufficient timber to build future navies, since she contained in just three southern counties 'one inexhaustible Store-House of Timber' (*Tour*, i. 126). Major planting had first been undertaken by the government at Windsor Park in the reign of Elizabeth: larger

---

[39] See also Albion (1926).

initiatives followed in the Forest of Dean, under Charles II, and in the New Forest, under William II.[40] Evelyn was certainly the prime inspiration for the 1668 scheme, and *Sylva* also encouraged private landowners to embark on commercial forestry, especially where the land was unsuitable for agricultural use.

A brief introduction by Evelyn provides a gloss on Virgil's arboricultural advice in the second book of the *Georgics*. After this, the bulk of *Sylva* is devoted to a review of about thirty species of tree, followed by chapters on practical management—pruning, felling, seasoning of timber, and the like. Inevitably the survey begins with the oak, on the grounds of the esteem which the Romans ('these wise, and glorious people') had for this tree. Evelyn recommends planting the oak, especially the *Quernus Sylvestris*, in royal forests and chases, where the widely spaced trees would create a pleasant scene 'benignly visited with the distant Landskips appearing through the glades, and frequent Vallies' (Evelyn, 205).

The author reaches his 'Paraenesis, and Conclusion' with a proposal that the king should enclose areas such as Sherwood and the Forest of Dean, but with a care for the inhabitants, 'Foresters and Bordurers', whose independent spirit has led them to resist authority. He recommends that the outlying land should be 'well Tenanted, by long Terms, and easie Rents', while the interior of the forest should be reserved for the monarch (Evelyn, 322–3). Noting that iron mills had been introduced into New England, he suggests that with their 'surfeit of the Woods which we want', the colonists should supply iron to the mother country, and allow Britain to leave its forests unfelled. This would leave the king as 'the great Sovereign of the Ocean, free Commerce, *Nemorum Vindex & Instaurator Magnus*' (Evelyn, 325). Thus Evelyn connects the plantation of timber with the manifest destiny of the nation, with Charles as ruler of the sea and promoter of international trade. This was a monarchical role which Pope transfers to a later Stuart. In his final paragraph Evelyn re-emphasizes the necessity for planting and improving woods, which he terms 'a right noble and royal undertakings', with the significant addition, 'as that of the Forest of Dean &c. in particular (where it is bravely manag'd) an Imperial design; and I do pronounce it more worthy of a Prince who truly consults his glory in the highest Interest of his Subjects, then that of gaining Battels, or subduing a Province' (Evelyn, 331). If Pope needed a text for his sermon on the peace, this might serve.[41]

Evelyn's was not a lone voice. It is noteworthy that Camden's editors in 1695 had revived an old legend, to the effect that the forces of the Spanish Armada had been instructed to destroy the timber of the Forest of Dean, after landing in England. 'What a foreign power could not effect', we are told, 'our own Civil dissentions did; for it went miserably to waste in the *Civil wars*' (*Britannia*, 245). This line of thinking, from an unimpeachable antiquarian source, bolsters Pope's insistence on the role of the oaks in preserving Britain as a naval and trading power. Gibson and his co-workers were not an overtly Tory group, but their natural bent towards an ideology of continuity would incline them to view the Civil War as a disruptive process.

---

[40] Thomas (1984: 199).
[41] The efforts of Charles II in the Forest of Dean, as well as those of William III in the New Forest, had largely fizzled out within a few years. See Albion (1926).

Those with an open commitment to the Stuart cause were able to harness such arguments as 'objective' evidence of the harm which had been done to the nation during the Commonwealth.

In editions subsequent to the 1664 printing, Evelyn added to the text in other ways. A section entitled 'Dendrologia' in 1706 included a chapter which had been gradually evolving since the second edition, entitled 'An Historical Account of the Sacrednesse and Use of Standing Groves'; it was in effect a rationale for the new gardening styles of the later seventeenth century. It charted what has been well described as 'the shift from the contained traditional garden (often identified as Dutch) to large open estates in the French manner whose chief effects were dependent on trees'.[42] There is now broad recognition, as Chambers observes, that Evelyn's literary and practical example in afforestation and horticulture provided the basis on which William Kent's 'revolution' in garden design was built. Apart from this, Evelyn was among the first to associate native English woodland with a quasi-spiritual quality instinct in the mythologized landscape; or as he once put it when writing to Pepys of his own estate at Wotton in Surrey, 'Here is a wood and water, meadows and mountains, the Dryads and Hamadryads.' In 'Dendrologia' he assimilated the deities of the ancient world to the Cambro-British mythology of inspired seers: 'Here then is the true *Parnassus, Castalia,* and the *Muses,* and at every call in a *Grove* of Venerable *Oaks,* methinks I hear the Answer of an hundred old *Druids,* and the *Bards* of our Inspired Ancestors.' Pope deliberately refused to follow the Druidic line, but *Windsor-Forest* is pervaded by a sense that Parnassus has come to Berkshire, and a feeling for the vatic wisdom reserved to 'him who to these Shades retires', and 'whom the Muse inspires' (237–8). The 'Groves of *Eden*' are a transplanted paradise at Windsor, exactly corresponding to John Evelyn's '*Grove* of Venerable Oaks'.[43]

At the beginning of the poem as it was published, Pope invokes an undifferentiated group of 'Sylvan Maids' (3). However, in the manuscript he had set out the identity of these presiding spirits more fully, as a note added in 1736 would confirm. The manuscript reads as follows:

> Chast Goddess of the Woods,
> Nymphs of the Vales, and Naiads of the Floods,
> Lead me, oh lead me thro' the Bow'rs and Glades,
> Unlock your Springs, and open all your Shades.
>
> (Schmitz, 16)

It is not wholly clear why Pope amended this passage. Later on Diana is identified with the Queen, and it would aid rather than damage the design if Anne were to be enlisted as a guardian spirit or *genius loci* in this oblique and delicate manner. Moreover, the verses call up the nymphs and naiads of forest and river so as to prepare the way for the Ovidian episode in mid-poem. Finally, the nouns of location (bowers, glades, springs, shades) all serve to draw the landscape of Windsor into a world of

---

[42] Chambers (1993: 34).

[43] This paragraph draws heavily on the brilliant discussion by Douglas Chambers in *The Planters of the English Landscape Garden*: see Chambers (1993: 33–49).

Arcadian associations. If the passage had been left to stand in its original form, the link with Evelyn's vision of a woodland peopled by mythological deities would have been more apparent.

There are two other revelatory facts. First, the inclusion of an appendix called *Pomona*, on cider cultivation, in early editions of *Sylva*. This was a favourite Georgic subject, most obviously in John Philips's *Cyder* (1708), a text *Windsor-Forest* echoes more than once (see Chapter 7, above). The goddess Pomona of course makes a brief appearance by name in Pope's poem (37), while a year earlier he had published in Lintot's miscellany a translation of the episode of Vertumnus and Pomona, from Book XIV of the *Metamorphoses*, as noted in Chapter 7. We recall that in *Paradise Lost* Eve in the garden is related to Pomona as well as to Diana, Ceres, and Persephone (*PL* ix. 386–96). Moreover, in the iconography of the seasons, Pomona represented spring, just as Ceres represented autumn. The goddesses were in some ways complementary, and Pope juxtaposes them deliberately in order to suggest the different attributes of the forest and the contrasting seasonal vocations of its inhabitants. Second, Evelyn planned a major work on gardening which he was never to complete; it is likely that portions of *Sylva* and *Kalendarium Hortense* indicate the nature of its contents. The title of this missing work was *Elysium Britannicum*—a notion which Pope aimed to actualize in his own gardening practice, and to which he gave lasting expression in his lines on the 'Groves of Eden' (7–42).

Near the end of his life, Evelyn witnessed the Great Storm which struck southern England on 26 November 1703. He was appalled by the sight of thousands of trees which the gale had suddenly torn from the ground, in the New Forest and Forest of Dean especially. Even in the capital, at St James's, Queen Anne grew alarmed as the storm rampaged through the park, and the ancient oaks planted by Cardinal Wolsey were felled (Green, 121). The diarist recorded his own losses, more than two thousand trees, in setting out the 'dismall Effects of the Hurecan', and then in a passage added to the fourth edition of *Sylva*, Evelyn set out a characteristic lament for what had been lost: 'I still feel the dismal Groans . . . of our *Forests*; that late dreadful *Hurrican* having subverted so many thousand of goodly Oaks prostrating the trees laying them in ghastly Postures like whole *Regiments* fallen in Battle, by the sword of the *Conqueror* crushing all that grew beneath them.'[44] As indicated, Pope could have read the fourth edition, brought out by Evelyn's grandson in 1706. If he did, he would have found a congenial sense in *Sylva* of the vulnerability both of the landscape and of the people 'Till Conquest cease' (408).

In his *Pastorals*, Pope had described the blast of winter: 'Sharp *Boreas* blows, and Nature feels Decay, | Time conquers All, and We must Time obey' (87–8). Perhaps the solemn commonplace has behind it a recollection of the recent storm, since the poem was supposed to have been written in 1704. Equally, the ravages of the Norman era, when an 'Oppressor' like William I could sway 'ev'n the Elements', carry into *Windsor-Forest* a sense of natural devastation, with the creation of 'a gloomy

---

[44] *ED* v. 550, citing the 4th edn. of *Sylva*. Schama (1995: 163), quotes the passage, and makes good sense of the 'dirges' for the oaks of old England.

Desart and a gloomy Waste' (44). That is much how Evelyn felt about the overthrow of woodlands at the hands of a meteorological 'Conqueror'.

Midway through his poem, Pope addresses the Thames in a manner which would scarcely have been possible without the example of Sylva:

> Thou too, great Father of the British Floods!
> With joyful Pride survey'st our lofty Woods,
> Where tow'ring Oaks their growing Honours rear,
> And future Navies on thy Shores appear.

> (219–22)

However, Evelyn's book offered Pope more than a political programme designed to furnish the navy with timber. When the second edition of Sylva came out, Margaret Cavendish, Duchess of Newcastle, wrote to congratulate the author on having 'planted a forest full of delight and profit, and though it is large through number and variety, yet you have enclosed it with elegancy and eloquence' (Evelyn, 175). The qualities which were identified by the Duchess reflect Pope's own literary aims, and they also correspond with the attributes of the Edenic forest. Evelyn is praised for having set out a diversified textual landscape, where the various species are dispersed agreeably in an eloquent intellectual pattern; Pope equally seeks to create a poem rich in events and reflections, ordered so that they make up a progressive series of interspersed scenes. As with Sylva, the trees of Windsor further the material greatness of Britain, but equally they constitute a symbolic space for the national imagination. The woodland is a site of profit and delight.

A deeper congruence exists. With some self-deception perhaps, Pope came to regard the forest as his natural domain, albeit one which was threatened by the incursion of a foreign master. Evelyn could go further, and see himself as literally a native of the woodland. In describing the evil effects of the Commonwealth period ('those Improvident Wretches, who . . . did (with the Royal Patrimony) swallow likewise Gods own Inheritance'), he alludes to the same Ovidian myth which Drayton used to evoke the sanctity of the ancient forests:

while I leave the Guilty to their proper Scorpions, and to their Erisichthnian fate, . . . the vengeance of the Dryads, and to their Tutelar better Genius, if any yet remain, who love the solid Honour and Ornament of their Country: For what could I say less, Ὑλεγγνης and Wood-born as I am, in behalf of those sacred Shades, which both grace our Dwellings, and protect our Nation? (Evelyn, 190)[45]

Here we see the curious intermixture of pagan and folkloric elements which underlies Shakespeare and Drayton among other English writers, and which survives into works such as The Rape of the Lock. The Lodona episode in Windsor-Forest functions to reanimate this sense, drawn from the Metamorphoses, of a secret glade of 'feminine' innocence, which is imperilled by the destructive 'masculine' urges of Pan. Wood-born Pope was not: yet his 'green Retreats' at the start, and his 'silent Shade'

---

[45] Compare Evelyn's letter to Lady Sunderland in 1690, where he refers to his work on Sylva as 'suitable to my rural genius, born as I was at Wotton, among the woods' (cited by Chambers 1993: 33).

at the end, both recall the 'sacred Shades' where Evelyn located his own myth of national identity.[46]

THE LORE OF THE SEASONS

In many ways Pope's description of the country pursuits (93–164) is amongst the most conventional sections of his poem, for it uses a series of traditional topoi associated with the seasons. Quite apart from its exploitation of standard activities linked to particular times of the year, this section brings in stock language and familiar iconographic details. Moreover, there is more reference to astrological and meteorological lore than in any other part of *Windsor-Forest*. As in *The Rape of the Lock*, a set of correspondences based on the four elements can been detected: in this case autumn/earth, winter/air, spring/water, summer/fire.[47] Such conventionality would once have been thought to weaken the poem. It does not seem unduly complacent to say that we are now better placed to understand the aesthetic value which may accrue from this method of writing, insofar as it knits together symbolic threads to produce a sense of a coherent cosmic order. In other words, Pope writes like the Renaissance man he was, at least at this phase of his career.

The first in the sequence, autumn, exhibits almost all the features just described. In the published text, Pope begins this section with a relatively bland expression, 'When milder Autumn Summer's heat succeeds' (97)—which could be construed as a near-golden line built around the chiasmic pattern of mildness/autumn/summer/heat. In the earlier draft the lines had run:

> When yellow Autumn Summer's Heat succeeds,
> And into Wine the purple Harvest bleeds.

A marginal note read, 'quaere if allowable to describe the season by a circumstance not proper to our climate, the vintage?' (Schmitz, 25). What Pope gained in the chiasmus he lost in terms of symbolic language—'yellow' reminds us of the role of Ceres in the poem (cf. l. 88), and 'purple' looks back to the 'Purple Dies' staining the heathlands of Windsor (l. 25). Moreover, these words belong to the vocabulary of stylized coloration which pervades the work (see *SDW*, chapter 3). Perhaps it would have been better to strain the truth about vine-growing in order to maintain this particular decorum.[48]

Winter is introduced with a calendrical reference: 'when moist *Arcturus* clouds

---

[46] Another of Evelyn's references to Ovid comes in his section on the black poplar: 'Divers stately ones of these I remember about the banks of the Po in Italy, which river being the old *Eridanus* so celebrated in which the temerarious Phaëton is said to have been precipitated, doubtless gave argument to that fiction of his sad Sisters Metamorphosis into these Trees' (Evelyn, 236–7, alluding to *Metamorphoses*, II, where Eridanus is transformed also into a constellation). See *SDW*, chs. 4 and 6.

[47] See Plowden (1983: 49–50). There is some apparent wrenching of the evidence here, and Plowden does not mention that this reverses the conventional associations of winter and spring.

[48] As Pope had done in his *Pastorals*: see 'Autumn', 72–5. In any case, as pointed out in *TE* i. 85, Pope was to plant a vineyard in his garden at Twickenham.

the sky' (119). Pope is remembering two references to the star in the first *Georgic*, as
he had done already in 'Autumn' (72). The ancient belief, mentioned by *EC* i. 289,
was that the morning rising of Arcturus in September ushered in a period of great
tempests coincident with the wine-harvest and the return of cattle from upland
passages. The mythical origin of the star lay in the story of Callisto and her son
Arcas, king of the Arcadians (see *SDW*, chapter 1): in this way the Ovidian background of the poem is further enhanced. But it is a little awkward to find that this
heavenly phenomenon took place in ancient times around 12 September (it now
occurs in October), since within a few lines we are amid the 'leafless Trees' of midwinter. Pope seems to have had trouble with these transitions, and again there is an
early manuscript version which was rejected:

> When hoary Winter cloaths the Year in White,
> The Woods and Fields to pleasing Toils invite.
>
> (Schmitz, 27)

As well as losing the attractive piece of antithetical diction in 'pleasing Toils', the
revision once more meant that Pope had to sacrifice a stock seasonal image, 'hoary'
winter, and an item of stylized colouring. White was indeed the conventional
marker of winter in the elaborate system of correspondences which underlay traditional lore of the seasons.

Yet another revision was made at the beginning of the next section. The printed
text has, 'In genial Spring, beneath the quiv'ring Shade | When cooling Vapours
breathe along the Mead . . .' (135–6). Pope had originally written, 'At Spring's
Return . . .' (Schmitz, 27). This is a more pointed rewriting, as the word 'genial' belongs to the specialized vocabulary apt to this season: in James Thomson's *Spring*,
a decade later, the key terms include *genial* along with *balmy, tender, lenient,
infusive, full, ripe, generous,* and *benevolent*. Of course, English poetic diction is
here following older models, especially classical Latin. Pope's own use of 'genial'
carries with it memories of a whole congeries of Latin words related to birth, generation, genius, descent, and origin. The direct etymological connection is with
genialis, meaning connected with marriage, merry or festive. There are overtones
of words like fostering, mild, creative. In the system of correspondences spring
was attached to the sanguine humour, as a relatively cool temperature becomes an
emblem of a calm and cheerful 'temperament'—both climate and personality-type
are temperate, indeed.

The most noteworthy revision occurs at the start of the remaining season. Summer opens in the published text with a direct reference to the zodiac, something
which might also be implied at l. 246: ' Now *Cancer* glows with *Phœbus'* fiery Car'
(147). The manuscript version reads, 'But when bright Phœbus from the Twins in-
vites | Our active Genius to more free Delights'.[49] As the editors note, 'The sun
(Phoebus's car) is in the constellation of the Twins (the zodiacal sign of Gemini)

---

[49] Schmitz, 28. There was an even earlier, rather inert draft: 'But when the Summer's fav'ring Reign
invites . . .'

from about May 21 to June 22. It enters the constellation of the Crab (the zodiacal sign of Cancer) at the summer solstice, June 22' (*TE* i. 163–4). Like all his contemporaries Pope, born on the cusp of Taurus and Gemini, was familiar with the materials of judicial astrology; even though the claims of the once potent occult had been considerably scaled down, the flow of almanacs had scarcely abated. The decision to switch from the outgoing sign to the incoming brought with it many consequences: not least, the replacement of a sign governed by Mercury to one governed by the moon—the only one in the zodiac so governed, in fact. The passage here, of course, involves the description of a hunt, culminating with a reference to Diana as 'Th' Immortal Huntress, and her Virgin Train', and the chaste Queen Anne. It *could* be an accident that the single house over which the moon had domination, out of twelve throughout the annual cycle, was the one which Pope selected for this purpose; but that is an implausible bet on an outsider.

As it turns out, Pope elects to mute the greater part of these astrological implications, which could easily have spread beyond control: first because of the wide polysemous range of this symbolism, and second because of the complicated political associations which were now wrapped up in the language of star signs. As an example of the former difficulty, we might consider that summer might be associated with noon, youth, the sun, Apollo, fire, density, yellow bile, choler, gold, and very much more. Each of the planets had its own similar (but not identical) associations in various realms of knowledge—astrology, alchemy, Masonry, and so on. Thus Mars might stand for war, iron, fire, masculinity, redness, Tuesday, and much else, while Venus could represent love, copper, water, femininity, greenness, Friday, and so on.[50] It is understandable that Pope did not wish to open up Pandora's box in this way. He chose rather to give a brief hint of the underlying symbolism which underlay traditional descriptions of the seasons: a quick reference to Cancer would place it accurately enough for his readers.

Pope was aware of a long-sustained literary chorus hymning the seasons. He found hints in Hesiod's *Works and Days*, in Ovid's *Fasti*, and in the *Georgics* themselves. In English literature he could have consulted *The Shepheardes Calendar* and many later bucolic or georgic works, not least his own *Pastorals*. In fact he made less effort to characterize the various seasons than he had in his earlier sequence of poems, where atmosphere and climate are carefully distinguished. See for example 'Spring', esp. 17–34, with many references to the dawn, to early youth, to the air, to mildness and other traditional attributes of spring. In this pastoral, too, we have a kind of ecphrasis, with the four seasons carved in relief on a bowl depicting 'The various Seasons of the rowling Year' (38), immediately followed by a reference to the 'twelve fair Signs' which lie 'in beauteous Order' (40). It is apparent that Pope was perfectly familiar with these literary conventions, and it was a deliberate act to curtail their presence in his later poem. Most likely he put little faith in judicial astrology, as his scornful reference to John Partridge in *The Rape of the Lock* would

---

[50] Geneva (1995: 271), gives a list of symbolic meanings for Mars, to illustrate the 'multiple denotations' of astrological symbology; but her list is by no means complete. See also pp. 5–6 above.

indicate; but the same poem shows that he knew all about days of ill omen, a super-stition with some basis in astrology.[51]

Just as significant, *Windsor-Forest* makes no direct use of the most famous device of visual art on this subject. Pope avoids any personification of the seasons, al-though he had abundant models at hand, whether from masters such as Botticelli or from iconographic manuals such as Ripa. By now it may be labouring the obvious to remark that the seasons were quite commonly used as characters in masques and pageants.[52] Nor does Pope allude to the biblical schema used by Poussin. Instead, Pope confines himself to seasonal activities, with a few terms which help to specify the time of year: the 'furrow'd Grounds' in autumn (100), the 'naked Groves' of win-ter (126), the 'cooling Vapours' of spring (136), and the sun's 'fiery Car' in summer (147). The effect is to remove us from any immediate passage of time, and to suggest a repetitive annual cycle of events, set in a not very firmly anchored present tense—until we reach the Queen herself, that is.

Overall the seasons are used as a discrete episode to impart variety—vigorous ac-tivity, rural customs, a sense of the animal as well as vegetable constituents of the forest, a holiday mood to contrast with the courtly spectacle elsewhere. Only one element can be regarded as providing an orthodox literary allusion, and this is the description of the hunt in the verse paragraph devoted to summer. As has been pre-viously recognized, the scene recalls both Virgil and Denham. The royal hunt and storm in the fourth book of the *Aeneid* is not far away here: in Dryden's translation (iv. 190–3), the 'lofty Courser' of Queen Dido 'paws the Ground' in his anxiety to be off, while Pope's 'impatient Courser' is described as 'pawing' as he 'seems to beat the distant Plain' (152). Behind Denham, however, there is an unnoticed presence: that of the stag hunt in Drayton's account of Arden in Song XIII of *Poly-Olbion*.[53] Most important of all, the episode provides a neat transition to the fable of Lodona. Pope evokes first Diana, then her modern equivalent Queen Anne, and then an Ovidian assembly of woodland nymphs, to prepare the way for the story of Diana's hand-maiden. It would be easy to allegorize the fable in terms of this introductory pas-sage: the nymph clearly represents the forest under threat, earlier from William III and now from the Hanoverians to come—that much is pretty well on the surface. We remember, too, that Anne's principal 'Care' (163) was the Church of England, and the myth could be read as enciphering the assault of Whigs, freethinkers, and Dissenters on the purity of the Anglican faith. In any event, the significance to this narrative of Lodona of the preceding account of the seasons, especially summer, stands out clearly.

One other source, much closer in time, can be identified for the treatment of the seasons in *Windsor-Forest*. This is the account of Sir Roger de Coverley as a hunter,

---

[51]　Thomas (1973: 735–45), has little to say about the astrological side, but is helpful on other issues. He quotes a writer in 1714 to show that belief in unlucky days was now on the wane, but Pope's reference (*ROL* iv. 161–6) makes it plain that the notion was still alive and available for satiric treatment.

[52]　See e.g. Spring in Jonson's *Chloridia* (1631), attended by the naiads, 'who are the Nymph's, *Foun-tayunes*, and Seruants of the Season' (Jonson, vii. 752).

[53]　The evidence is set out in *SDW*, ch. 5.

which appears in *Spectator*, no. 116, dated 13 July 1711—a paper written by Eustace Budgell. Sir Roger has given up fox hunting, but still pursues the 'circling' hare (cf. *WF*, 122). Most obviously relevant, however, is the *Spectator*'s depiction of the 'cheerfulness' of the scene, as the baying of the hounds, the horns, and the 'hallowing' of the sportsmen echo across the neighbouring hills, and lift the narrator's 'Spirits' into 'a most lively Pleasure'.[54] This was a famous and recent evocation of the joys of 'rural Diversions' as practised by an archetypal countryman, and it is as certain that Pope knew the passage as that he knew the catechism. Such recollections provide ample evidence that the first three hundred lines were heavily rewritten, at least, as late as 1711 or 1712 (see also Chapter 1, above).

ADDISON

The completion and publication of *Windsor-Forest* coincide with the beginnings of a rift between Pope and Joseph Addison. Pope would long have been aware of the older writer, notably on account of his influential preface to Dryden's *Georgics* and his *Letter from Italy* (see Chapters 2 and 7, above). However, the two men had known each other personally for quite a short time: their acquaintance probably started about the same time that the *Spectator*, the great literary triumph of this era, began publication in 1711. (It is likely that Pope met Steele at Will's coffee-house in the spring of that year.) Initially the relationship was altogether friendly. The *Spectator* carried a warm commendation of the *Essay on Criticism* on 20 December, and Pope—guessing wrongly that Steele was the author—wrote a thank-you letter ten days letter (*Corr.* i. 139–40). Addison seemed anxious to take the young poet under his wing; possibly, as Sherburn suggested, this friendliness was 'in part due to a desire to control his pen for the Whigs' (*Career*, 64). At some stage Addison also gave Pope his first encouragement to embark on the translation of Homer. But it was not long before the first cracks started to show, and the steady decline in cordiality between the two men had scarcely been arrested by the time of Addison's death in 1719. 'The curse of party', which led Swift to cut all ties with Steele and Addison, assuredly had something to do with the process.[55] Unsurprisingly, the quarrel between Pope and Addison hardened after the accession of George I, when the older man held a serious of important offices in government.

None of this means that overt hostilities immediately took over. In early 1713 Pope was contributing to the *Guardian*, which Steele had set up as a follow-up to the *Spectator*. He had also been asked to write the prologue for Addison's triumphantly successful tragedy *Cato*, and he is likely to have attended the first night on 14 April, when 'the fullest audience that ever was known' took noisy sides. According to George Berkeley, some parts of the prologue, 'which were written by Mr. Pope, a Tory and even a Papist, were hissed, being thought to savour of whiggism'. As Mack observes, this may have been occasioned by Pope's reference to 'the World's great

---

[54] Bond (1965: i. 478).   [55] See Goldgar (1961: esp. 109–51).

Victor 'who passed 'unheeded by' at the triumph of Julius Caesar (*Life*, 221). According to this reading, for which Pope must have made at least some allowance in his effort to please both sides, such a rejection of Caesar by the crowd in favour of Cato could be seen as a reference to the dismissal of Marlborough. But the prologue as a whole does not suggest that the Roman crowd were wrong to ignore Caesar. On the contrary, it contrasts the austere and stoical patriot Cato with the arrogant general:

> Ev'n when proud *Caesar*'midst triumphal cars,
> The spoils of nations, and the pomp of wars,
> Ignobly vain and impotently great,
> Show'd *Rome* her *Cato*'s figure drawn in state . . .

> (*TE* vi. 96–7)

All the sympathy is with the ally of Pompey, and the man who had delivered his famous denunciation of Caesar as tribune in 63 BC. Only those with strongly Whig-tinted spectacles in the audience can have supposed that the passage expressed genuine regret for the fall of the great Duke. It is easy to understand why Pope should have written to John Caryll on 30 April in mock surprise that 'the prologue-writer . . . was clapped into a stanch Whig sore against his will, at almost very two lines' (*Corr.* i. 175). If the very obvious message of the prologue could be wrenched out of its surface meaning, what chance for an unprejudiced reading of that much more complicated text, *Windsor-Forest*, which had appeared a month earlier?

The growing distance between Pope and Addison in years to come has been well charted by scholars. As we have seen, two days after Tickell's poem *On the Prospect of Peace* had appeared in October 1712, Addison wrote a warm commendation on its behalf in the *Spectator*, and warned poets like Pope to shun the props of classical mythology in their commendations of the upcoming treaty (see Chapter 1, above). Earlier critics sometimes found it puzzling that Addison should have issued such a warning to his young friend, and that he should have been 'inexpressibly chagrined' by the conclusion of *Windsor-Forest*. But Robert Cummings is surely right to see the published poem as reflecting basically different values, political and moral, from those of Addison's work, especially his famous poem *The Campaign* (1705).

In his subtly argued essay Cummings draws out a number of ways in which Pope might have identified the weaknesses, in literary terms, of Addison's poem; and he makes a telling contrast between the attitudes of the two writers, with radically opposed notions of military glory and of action in general.[57] Pointing the comparison less favourably for Pope, Cummings further suggests that Addison might reasonably have resented Pope's 'dereliction' of poetic duty, caused by a 'falsification of his genre'—a view which rests in part on Cummings's belief that Pope lost the *raison d'être* for his georgic when he revised the poem in the light of the peace process (see Chapter 1, above). But there are more specific confrontations than previous com-

---

[56] See Ault, 101–27 for the fullest study of Addison's relations with Pope.
[57] See Cummings (1988: 143–58).

mentators have recognized.[58] For example, Addison has 'Britannia's colours in the zephyrs fly' (48), where Pope has 'high in air *Britannia's* standard flies' (110). Addison may well have sensed—especially if he had seen an advance copy of *Windsor-Forest*, as has been speculated—that Pope's new work would do more than offer a Tory reply to the Whig panegyric: it could also undermine the whole ideological and literary support-system which had brought *The Campaign* to such a pitch of popularity.

The most obvious way in which Pope set himself against Addison becomes apparent when we examine the closing lines of *The Campaign*. The poet expresses his desire to rehearse the story of 'Britannia's wars', if possible without the adventitious aid of poetic embellishment:

> When actions, unadorn'd, are faint and weak,
> Cities and countries must be taught to speak;
> Gods may descend in factions from the skies,
> And rivers form their oozy beds arise;
> Fiction may deck the truth with spurious rays.
> And round the hero cast a borrow'd blaze.
>
> (Addison, i. 54)

By contrast Marlborough's deeds stand up without any false burnishing, proudly shining 'in their own native light'. This was a repudiation of the entire basis of mythological poetry, and an onslaught on the conventions of Stuart panegyric. In the event, Pope did more than ignore this 'well-meant' advice. He utilized the pagan machinery to its utmost, he engaged in bold allegorical flights, and he depicted the god of the Thames rising 'from his Oozy Bed' at a climactic moment (*WF*, 330). This was to dismiss the Whig attempt to legislate on the aesthetics of praise. By couching *Windsor-Forest* in the form he did, Pope sought to reclaim the historic idiom of royalist eulogies. One implication might be that, if Marlborough was not worth all these epic attributes, then Queen Anne certainly was. In this sense *Windsor-Forest* is a studied riposte to the naturalistic ideology which lies behind the conclusion of *The Campaign*—an outlook also made apparent in Addison's *Spectator* paper.

Significantly, one of the epigraphs to *The Campaign* cites verses by Claudian on the conquest of the Rhine and the Ister (Danube), as Pope may have remembered in (*WF*, 364, 368). The force of the passage in *Windsor-Forest*, we have observed, is to degrade Marlborough's military triumphs, which Addison had lauded. More generally, it seems that Addison directed Pope's attention towards the panegyrics of Claudian.[59]

As a follow-up to *The Campaign*, Addison brought out his opera *Rosamond* in 1707, with music by Thomas Clayton. The text was dedicated to the Duchess of Marlborough, and the entire work is designed to extol the Churchills as proper inheritors of the royal domain at Woodstock. In the third act, an angel pays tribute to

---

[58] Cummings rightly notes that Pope picked up Addison's expression 'tainted gales' (l. 122: cf. *WF*, 101).
[59] See *SDW*, ch. 6.

'the glorious pile now ascending'. The scene shifts to a view of the new palace, with the vision of 'Columns swelling, arches bending, | Domes in awful pomp arising' (Addison, i. 75). Pope may well have remembered this in the *Epistle to Burlington*: 'To rear the Column, or the Arch to bend' (*TE* iii/2. 141): but at the time of *Windsor-Forest* he would see the lines as one more assertion of hubristic pride, as they suggest that Blenheim might rival the site downriver 'Where *Windsor*-Domes and pompous Turrets rise' (352). By his assiduous cultivation of Marlborough's interest, Addison had already begun to lay the foundations for the later breach with Pope.

Conclusion: Death in Arcady

The expression 'Queen Anne is dead', meaning that news is stale, seems to have quickly gained currency after the shattering events on 1 August 1714. A story is told that the President of St John's College, Oxford, replied to the statement that her death had not yet been confirmed, 'Dead! She is a dead as Julius Caesar' (Trevelyan, iii. 331).[1] To see how Pope had prepared the ground for this abrupt cessation of Stuart hopes, we should make one final survey of the text, recalling where necessary our earlier findings.

Windsor-Forest is much possessed by death. It is indeed hard to think of a poem not expressly concerned with mortality—as Young's *Night Thoughts* are, for example—which invokes the theme so insistently. Not until we reach a book such as *Bleak House*, well over a century later, do we find major literary works with the same degree of obsessive concern. Of course, there are passages in Pope which are filled with images of life and exaltation. All the same, it is a matter for surprise that no reading of the poem draws much attention to this aspect of its artistic operations.

The passage on the Norman Yoke begins by emphasizing the effects of royal savagery on inhabitants of the forest. While nature blossomed, mankind dwindled away:

> In vain kind Seasons swell'd the teeming Grain,
> Soft Show'rs distill'd, and Suns grew warm in vain;
> The Swain with Tears his frustrate Labour yields.
> And famish'd dies amidst his ripen'd Fields.
>
> (53–6)

This disharmony contrasts abruptly with the ecological balance seen under Stuart rule, and figured towards the close by images of benign coexistence ('Safe on my Shore each unmolested Swain | Shall tend the Flocks, or reap the bearded Grain', 369–70). However, the focus quickly shifts from the victims of the Norman rulers to the kings themselves. William the Conqueror is 'himself deny'd a Grave' (80); his son William Rufus undergoes a still more exemplary end:

> Stretch'd on the Lawn his second Hope survey,
> At once the Chaser and at once the Prey.
> Lo *Rufus*, tugging at the deadly Dart,
> Bleeds in the Forest, like a wounded Hart.
>
> (81–4)

---

[1] For the later history of the expression, see Apperson (1993: 518). In *Polite Conversation* Swift would use a variant, 'Queen Elizabeth is dead.'

The language here directly anticipates the following sections, which describe the hunt in the evocation of summer (147–64), and set up a dramatic situation in readiness for the myth of Lodona. As for the Norman episode, this concludes with a vision of the forest under its current Stuart management, with Liberty rearing her 'chearful' head to introduce the 'golden Years' (92)—an affirmation of England restored after Cromwellian and Williamite interventions, but also a magically transmuted environment, gold instead of lead, life instead of death.

The rural sports convey a sense of youth and vitality, yet the poem never disguises the fact that these activities end with a death in the morning. In autumn, sportsmen scheme to net the unsuspecting partridge (referred to as 'the Prey' at l. 102). Pope's extended simile compares this to feats of the nation at war, when 'some thoughtless Town' is taken (107). Pope knew that the sieges which Marlborough had undertaken in Flanders had rarely found an enemy objective unprepared for the struggle. Most recently, the siege of Bouchain in August 1711 had been opened against a well-defended fortress, crammed with the opponent's best troops, and stuffed with heavy artillery. These sieges were seldom conducted without considerable loss of life. For instance, the assault on the citadel of Tournai in 1709 lasted from June to September, 'a grim affair where the besiegers were up to their thighs in mud and water, and where a peculiarly horrific struggle took place in the close darkness of galleries dug to plant mines and counter-mines . . . The length and bloodshed of the siege had its effect on the morale of the allied troops. The more thinking of them began to wonder if they were not dying unnecessarily because allied statesmen had bungled the peace.'[2] Marlborough himself, rather than Prince Eugène as on previous occasions, oversaw the siege. It seems likely Pope was using the netting of the partridge to insinuate a comment on the war under the cover of this innocent-looking analogy.

There ensues the famous description of the pheasant as a shot brings it to earth: 'He feels the fiery Wound, | Flutters in Blood, and panting beats the Ground' (113–14). As we have seen, this was one of the few passages in the poem which appealed to Victorian taste. Its blend of pathos with vivid denotation of the bird's plumage obviously hit a nineteenth-century chord, even though the vocabulary is not so much sensuous in the Keatsian way as emblematic. What is clear is that the passage captures sudden dissolution in the midst of a bright and seemingly joyous existence.

In winter the object of pursuit changes to that of hare-coursing. Even nature appears to be without life, with 'naked Groves' and 'leafless Trees' (126–7). Paradoxically 'unweary'd', the fowler roves 'with slaught'ring Guns' in his quest:

> He lifts the Tube, and levels with his Eye;
> Strait a short Thunder breaks the frozen Sky.
>
> (129–30)

The outcome is stated with clinical accuracy:

> Oft, as in Airy Rings they skim the Heath,
> The clam'rous Lapwings feel the leaden Death:

[2] Barnett (1974: 232–3).

> Oft as the mounting Larks their Notes prepare,
> They fall, and leave their little Lives in Air.
>
> (131–4)

There has been debate as to how far Pope shared later humanitarian ideals. Whatever view we take on this issue, it is undeniable that his verse regularly fixed on the moment at which life is snuffed out in a sudden access of violence. The short paragraph on angling makes no explicit reference to death, but the contrast is palpable between 'genial Spring' and the cool operations of 'the patient Fisher' as he plans to entrap the various species of fish, ending with pike, 'the Tyrants of the watry Plains' (135–46).

Finally we reach summer, and the full ritualized pomp of the stag-hunt. Again the stress is on the hunter and his horse, rather than the object, which is described simply as 'the fleet Hart'. But even if we are not to feel any pity for the beast—and that is an open question—we cannot be unaware of the end-result of the pursuit. This passage moves seamlessly into the story of Lodona, the child of the Thames and nymph of Diana. Pursued by Pan, she flees until, as exhausted as the hind, she endures his embrace. 'Faint, breathless', she appeals to Diana one last time: no longer for rescue, but for a return to her 'native shades':

> She said, and melting as in tears she lay,
> In a soft, silver Stream dissolv'd away.
>
> (203–4)

Metamorphosed into the 'silver stream' of the Loddon, she retains her 'Virgin Coldness', now flowing as a 'chast Current' for ever merging its water with that of the Thames. Pope has brilliantly reanimated the Ovidian transformation with a graphic pun on the word 'dissolv'd': Lodona is liquified into an eternal movement of tearlike waves, but her dissolution is also the mortal end of the nymph, killed by her forced act of unchastity.

The theme is resumed when the poem moves down river to the haunts of the poets: 'I seem thro' consecrated Walks to rove, | I hear soft Musick dye along the Grove' (267–8). Most plangent of all is the scene of Cowley's death at Chertsey:

> Here his first Lays Majestick *Denham* sung;
> There the last Numbers flow'd from *Cowley's* Tongue.
> O early lost! what Tears the River shed
> When the sad Pomp along his Banks was led?
> His drooping Swans on ev'ry Note expire,
> And on his Willows hung each Muse's Lyre.
>
> (271–6)

This is the section of the poem most completely absorbed into the idiom of pastoral elegy in its classic form—that is perhaps why Elwin objected to it so strongly.[3] Pope's note supplies a more businesslike air: 'Mr. *Cowley* died at *Chertsey*, on the Borders of the Forest, and was from thence convey'd to *Westminster*.' However, the very

---

[3] See above, pp. 283–4.

mode of Cowley's funeral cortège takes on the feeling of a solemn procession on
water, recalling the ceremonies of the ancient world, or myths recounting the obsequies of heroes and heroines. It needed Pope to see that this real event, which had
taken place as recently as 1667, could be adapted to this elegiac purpose. The link is
then made to the present:

> Since Fate relentless stop'd their Heav'nly Voice,
> No more the Forest ring, or Groves rejoice;
> Who now shall charm the Shades where *Cowley* strung
> His living Harp, and lofty *Denham* sung?
> But hark! the Groves rejoice, the Forest rings!
> Are these reviv'd? or is it *Granville* sings?
>
> (277–82)

This is perhaps closer to the laments of Theocritus and Bion than anything in Pope's
own *Pastorals*. It is a miniature lyric in the middle of the poem, organized around
the contrasts of death and life (ll. 278, 281). Lansdowne's role in the poem is to 'revive' poetry here as Anne has restored Windsor to its former glory. Restoration implies an earlier decay, and the poem constantly moves between these notions.

Then comes one of the most crucial stages in the elegiac narrative of *Windsor-
Forest*. The poem reaches the castle and fixes on St George's Chapel as the symbolic
heart of the nation's past. Lansdowne is enjoined to celebrate Windsor, by raising
with his verse 'old Warriors whose ador'd Remains | In weeping Vaults her hallow'd
Earth contains!' (301–2). After the triumphs of its founder, Edward III, the history
which is recorded in the Chapel tells sad stories of the death of kings:

> Let softer Strains Ill-fated *Henry* mourn,
> And Palms Eternal flourish round his Urn.
> Here o'er the Martyr-King the Marble weeps,
> And fast beside him, once-fear'd *Edward* sleeps:
> Whom not th'extended *Albion* could contain,
> From old *Belerium* to the *Northern* Main,
> The Grave unites; where ev'n the Great find Rest,
> And blended lie th'Oppressor and th'Opprest!
>
> (311–18)

It is perhaps only the symmetrical verbal architecture of this passage which has
stopped us recognizing that Pope is working in a clear-cut Renaissance convention
here. There are echoes of Milton, hints of Marvell, a mood akin to Ben Jonson in his
elegiac vein. The verses constitute an inscription fit for a baroque funeral monument, as was argued in Chapter 5, above.

Immediately after this occurs a passage inspired by the then unmarked grave of
Charles I. We have looked at this before as an element in Pope's Stuart martyrology,
but the entire paragraph is relevant to our present concerns:

> Make sacred *Charles*'s Tomb for ever known,
> (Obscure the Place, and uninscrib'd the Stone)

Oh Fact accurst! What Tears has *Albion* shed,
Heav'ns! what new Wounds, and how her old have bled?
She saw her Sons with purple Deaths expire,
Her sacred Domes involv'd in rolling Fire,
A dreadful Series of Intestine Wars,
Inglorious Triumphs, and dishonest Scars.

(319–26)

The 'new Wounds' of the seventeenth century (the Civil War, the Plague, and the Fire) have opened up the 'old', as Charles's martyrdom recalls that of Christ. More recently the contests over the Monmouth rising and the Revolution of 1688, almost bloodless as that was, have spread more 'Discord' (327) to be dispersed by 'great *ANNA*'—and it is hard to think that the 'inglorious Triumphs' do not include the victories of Marlborough as the war dragged on, against the wishes of the Queen.

Once Anne has given her God-like decree, the note changes, as Father Thames apostrophizes peace and its blessings. The pacific tone is accompanied by a series of allusions to Isaiah, which relate to the supersession of the arts of war. 'No more my Sons shall dye with *British* Blood | Red *Iber*'s Sands, or *Ister*'s foaming Flood' (367–8)—the syntax of the first line here leads us to expect a construction with 'dye' as an intransitive verb. And just after this:

The shady Empire shall retain no Trace
Of War or Blood, but in the Sylvan Chace,
The Trumpets sleep, while chearful Horns are blown,
And Arms employ'd on Birds and Beasts alone.

(371–4)

Earlier the death of the beasts had been metaphorically identified with the bloodshed of war; now the realms are separated, as hunting is reinscribed in the plot as the antonym of war, rather than a transference of warlike energies. From this point on, the poem devotes itself to images of life, couched in terms of expansion, opening, and transcendence. Peace will in a sense undo history: the civilizations of Peru and Mexico will be rebuilt, almost as though their slain victims could be brought back to life. The agencies of death are themselves destroyed, as peace conquers vengeance, rebellion and 'gaping Furies' who 'thirst for Blood in vain' (422). The implicit message is close to that of 'Death, thou shalt die.'

Through the entire poem, we have juxtaposed forces working for and against life: these are sometimes imaged as succeeding temporal phases, sometimes personified as hostile powers such as liberty or discord. 'Oh stretch thy Reign, fair *Peace*! From Shore to Shore, | Till Conquest Cease, and Slav'ry be no more' (407–8). It is all the more evocative because of our clear sense that Pope knew full well just how fragile his hopes must be. It took only two years for death to claim the Queen, for the rising of 1715 to witness slaughter on the battlefield and judicial victims condemned to re-enact the destiny of earlier Stuarts on Tower Hill.

The relevance of this last issue to the theme of mortality in *Windsor-Forest* can be underlined if we consider Daniel Szechi's remarkable essay on 'The Jacobite Theatre of Death'. This describes the behaviour of Jacobites on the scaffold, showing that condemned men used their place of execution as a platform for seditious speeches and anti-Hanoverian proclamations. Instead of taking 'the traditional path of contrition and submission' which earlier state criminals had followed, they justified their conduct, appealed to the public to take up their cause, and professed their enduring loyalty to the Stuart line. Whether Catholic or (more often) Protestant, they used their religious faith to vindicate their opposition to the government: 'What moved these men to plot, fight and use their last minutes as macabre drama in support of the Stuart cause was a deep sense of spiritual mission.'[4]

All these dying statements characteristically view martyrdom as a necessary part of the fulfilment of God's planned destiny for Britain. 'By 1746 this vision of self-sacrifice had matured into a mystical interpretation of the significance of the Jacobites and their deaths in terms of martyrdom and witness.' Behind this, Szechi argues, lay the much quoted text from Matthew 5: 10: 'Blessed are they which are persecuted for Righteousness sake: for theirs is the kingdom of heaven.' Many of the condemned went to the gibbet convinced that they were acting nobly, and indeed dying 'like a saint and hero'. Among the most interesting of Szechi's observations is that the faithful drew strength from the example of Charles I, who had 'adroitly manipulated the proceedings [of his trial] to highlight his own interpretation of events, and hence his own rectitude'. Moreover, the king had 'turned his own execution into a devastating piece of anti-Parliamentary propaganda'.[5] Most royalists would have seen the events of 1649 in this light, however near or far they stood to the Jacobite cause in later years. Certainly Pope's allusion to the regicides and the royal martyr supports this reading of history, as we saw in Chapter 5 especially.

It is just because death hovers so obviously around the corner, in this poem of 1713, that *Windsor-Forest* attains so much plangency. Every Jacobite 'martyr' put to death in the next five or ten years, was already active in the cause, in one way or another, when the poem appeared. The impenitent believers who went to the scaffold used a rhetoric that had been evolving since the time of Sir John Fenwick and the other conspirators against William III in the 1690s. Commonly those who were about to die in the aftermath of the 1715 rising expressed anti-Revolutionary language (Szechi quotes William Paul: 'You see what miseries and calamities have befallen these kingdoms by the Revolution'). The exiled Pretender was described as a prince of 'Justice, Virtue and honour'. Until he is restored, Paul told the listening gallery, 'the nation can never be happy'.[6] There is evidence that some of the crowd, at least, attending the executions felt sympathy with these utterances. The audience did not, we may be sure, include Alexander Pope. Nevertheless his poem had offered a script for part of these dying speeches. It had associated liberty, life, and the pursuit of national happiness with the beleaguered Stuarts.

---

[4] Szechi (1988: 69).   [5] Szechi (1988: 59, 69).   [6] Szechi (1988: 64, 68).

Among the most heartfelt letters Pope ever wrote are those he sent to John Caryll and Edward Blount in the first half of 1716. They were composed when the poet was being forcibly transported from his home at Binfield, when Catholics were subject to ever greater pressures by the authorities, and when the condemned Jacobites were facing execution—matters documented in Chapter 1. *Windsor-Forest* had looked forward, more in hope than expectation, to a continuance of the golden years under Stuart rule. Events had quickly dispelled this dream. By the summer of 1720, the fool's gold of the South Sea scheme had replaced the alchemically charged noble metal with its own base coinage. Robert Digby addressed his friend Pope with what seems like bitter irony:

I congratulate you, dear sir, on the return of the golden age, for sure this must be such, in which money is showered down in such abundance upon us. I hope this overflowing will produce great and good fruits, and bring back the figurative moral golden age to us. (*Corr.* ii. 51)

Pope's later poetry would explore this new magic economy, more dependent on paper than on hard cash. The 'moral' meaning of Pope's metaphor had been lost, at least for a Stuart supporter, with the disintegration of the Old Pretender's cause. It was no longer possible to sustain the myth of an Astraean future.

The saddest part of it all is that Pope had foreseen what was coming. *Windsor-Forest* is pervaded by a profound sense of an impending doom.[7] As Douglas Brooks-Davies has perceived, 'Pope knows that vatic utterance has to contend with the hard political reality of the Act of Settlement. The "Golden Days" will blacken under Hanover.'[8] This is a text which identifies merit with suffering, oppression, and martyrdom: only in the fullness of time is there any hope for the long-expected days of peace and justice. Before these golden years could come, Pope sensed, the righteous would endure their own sacrifice, and the faithful would see their homes wrested from them, as the Conqueror had ravaged the hearths of forest-dwellers so many centuries earlier. A new foreign monarch stands poised to bring the Stuart castle at Windsor metaphorically tumbling down, and to exile people like Pope from their forest retreat. In this light, the poem's insistence on death and destruction has an ominous topicality.

[7] In 1716 Pope would tell Swift that he judged the Church of Rome 'to be in a declining condition' (*Corr.* i. 342); his poem three years before had intuited the fatal fall of the house of Stuart.

[8] Brooks-Davies (1985: 17). This account, resting on the sense of *WF* as 'a prophetic georgic . . . founded on uncertainty', supports the reading of the poem offered in this book, and could be extended in the light of findings in previous chapters.

Sources

References to the most frequently cited sources are incorporated into the text and are listed in the Abbreviations above. These sources are not repeated here.

In order to make this list less cumbersome, sources are listed in alphabetical order for each chapter separately.

INTRODUCTION

Brooks-Davies, Douglas (1988), '"Thoughts of Gods": Messianic Alchemy in *Windsor-Forest*', *Yearbook of English Studies*, 18: 125–42.

Erskine-Hill, Howard (1996), *Poetry of Opposition and Revolution: Dryden to Wordsworth* (Oxford: Clarendon Press).

Hammond, Brean S. (1997), *Professional Imaginative Writing in England, 1670–1740: 'Hackney for Bread'* (Oxford: Clarendon Press).

Knellwolf, Christa (1998), *A Contradiction Still: Representations of Women in the Poetry of Alexander Pope* (Manchester: Manchester University Press).

CHAPTER 1

Bond, Donald F. (ed.) (1965), *The Spectator*, 5 vols. (Oxford: Clarendon Press).

Brownell, Morris (1978), *Alexander Pope and the Arts of Georgian England* (Oxford: Clarendon Press).

Cummings, Robert (1987), '*Windsor-Forest* as a Sylvan Poem', *ELH*, 54: 63–77.

—— (1988), 'Addison's "Inexpressible Chagrin" and Pope's Poem on the Peace', *Yearbook of English Studies*, 18: 143–58.

Dickinson, H. T. (1970), *Bolingbroke* (London, Constable).

Erskine-Hill, Howard (1973), 'A New Pope Letter', *Notes & Queries*, 218: 207–9.

Gabriner, Paul (1990), 'The Papist's House, The Papist's Horse: Alexander Pope and the Removal from Binfield', in C. C. Barfoot and T. D'Haen (eds.), *Centennial Hauntings: Pope, Byron and Eliot* (Amsterdam), 13–64.

Garrett, Jane (1980), *The Triumphs of Providence: The Assassination Plot, 1696* (Cambridge: Cambridge University Press).

Gerrard, Christine (2001), 'Political Passions,' in J. Sitter (ed.), *The Cambridge Companion to Eighteenth-Century Poetry* (Cambridge: Cambridge University Press), 37–62.

Hatton, Ragnhild (1977), *George I: Elector and King* (London: Thames and Hudson).

Lynch, Kathleen M. (1971), *Jacob Tonson: Kit-Cat Publisher* (Knoxville, Tenno: University of Tennessee Press).

Miller, Peggy (1965), *A Wife for the Pretender* (New York: Harcourt, Brace and World).

Parnell, Thomas (1989), *Collected Poems*, ed. C. Rawson and F. P. Lock (Newark, Del.: University of Delaware Press).

Rawson, C. J. (1959), 'Some Unpublished Letters of Pope and Gay', *Review of English Studies*, 10: 371–87.

Rumbold, Valerie (1989), *Women's Place in Pope's World* (Cambridge: Cambridge University Press).

Somerville, Dorothy (1962), *The King of Hearts: Charles Talbot, Duke of Shrewsbury* (London: Allen & Unwin).

CHAPTER 2

Aitken, G. A. (1968), *The Life and Works of John Arbuthnot* (New York: Russell & Russell; first pub. 1892).

Beattie, Lester M. (1967), *John Arbuthnot: Mathematician and Satirist* (New York: Russell & Russell; first pub. 1935).

Burrows, Donald (1994), *Handel* (New York: Schirmer).

Clements, Frances M. (1972), 'Lansdowne, Pope, and the Unity of *Windsor-Forest*', *Modern Language Quarterly*, 33: 44–53.

Cook, Alan (1998), *Edmond Halley: Charting the Heavens and the Seas* (Oxford: Clarendon Press).

Cruickshanks, Eveline, and Black, Jeremy (1988) (eds.), *The Jacobite Challenge* (Edinburgh: John Donald).

Cummings, Robert (1988), 'Addison's "Inexpressible Chagrin" and Pope's Poem on the Peace', *Yearbook of English Studies*, 18: 143–58.

Dickinson, H. T. (1970), *Bolingbroke* (London: Constable).

Ehrenpreis, Irvin (1962–83), *Swift: The Man, his Works and the Age*, 3 vols. (London: Methuen).

Erskine-Hill, Howard (1965), 'The Medal against Time: A Study of Pope's *Epistle to Mr Addison*', *Journal of the Warburg and Courtauld Institutes*, 28: 274–98.

Forsythe, Robert Stanley (1928), *A Noble Rake: The Life of Charles, Fourth Lord Mohun* (Cambridge, Mass.: Harvard University Press).

Foster, Joseph (1902), *Some Feudal Coats of Arms* (London: James Parker).

Fowler, Alastair (1988), 'The Paradoxical Machinery of *The Rape of the Lock*', in C. Nicholson (ed.), *Alexander Pope: Essays for the Tercentenary* (Aberdeen: Aberdeen University Press), 151–70.

Gay, John (1974), *Poetry and Prose*, ed. V. A. Dearing and C. E. Beckwith, 2 vols. (Oxford: Clarendon).

Hamilton, Elizabeth (1969), *The Backstairs Dragon: A Life of Robert Harley, Earl of Oxford* (London: Hamish Hamilton).

Hammond, Brean S. (1984), *Pope and Bolingbroke: A Study of Friendship and Influence* (Columbia, Mo.: University of Missouri Press).

Handasyde, Elizabeth (1933), *Granville the Polite: The Life of George Granville, Lord Lansdowne 1666–1734* (London: Oxford University Press).

Holmes, Geoffrey (1987), *British Politics in the Age of Queen Anne* (London: Hambledon Press; first pub. 1967).

Kerby-Miller, Charles (1950) (ed.), *Memoirs of the Extraordinary Life, Works and Discoveries of Martinus Scriblerus* (New Haven: Yale University Press).

Manley, Delarivier (1991), *New Atalantis*, ed. R. Ballaster (Harmondsworth: Penguin).

Nokes, David (1995), *John Gay: A Profession of Friendship* (Oxford: Oxford University Press).

Parnell, Thomas (1989), *Collected Poems*, ed. C. Rawson and F. P. Lock (Newark, Del.: University of Delaware Press).

Scott-Giles, C. W. (1965), *The Romance of Heraldry* (London: Dent).

Speck, W. A. (1970), *Tory and Whig: The Struggle in the Constituencies* (London: Macmillan).

Stater, Victor (1999), *Duke Hamilton is Dead! A Story of Aristocratic Life and Death in Stuart Britain* (New York: Hill and Wang).

Thompson, Paul V. and Dorothy J. (1984) (eds.), *The Account Books of Jonathan Swift* (Newark, Del.: University of Delaware Press).

Weinbrot, Howard D. (1993), *Britannia's Issue: The Rise of British Literature from Dryden to Osian* (Cambridge: Cambridge University Press).

Wood, Nigel (1988), 'Gay and the Ironies of Rustic Simplicity', in P. Lewis and N. Wood (eds.), *John Gay and the Scriblerians* (London: Vision Press), 94–121.

CHAPTER 3

Aden, John M. (1978), *Pope's Once and Future Kings: Satire and Politics in the Early Career* (Knoxville: University of Tennessee Press).

Backscheider, Paula (1989), *Daniel Defoe: His Life* (Baltimore: Johns Hopkins University Press).

Bossewell, John (1572), *Workes of Armorie* (London).

Brooks-Davies, Douglas (1985), *Pope's Dunciad and the Queen of the Night: A Study of Emotional Jacobitism* (Manchester: Manchester University Press).

Brown, Laura (1985), *Alexander Pope* (Oxford: Blackwell).

Burrows, Donald (1994), *Handel* (New York: Schirmer).

Carretta, Vincent (1981), 'Anne and Elizabeth: The Poet as Historian', *Studies in English Literature 1500–1900*, 21: 425–38.

Chambers, Douglas (1996), *The Reinvention of the World: English Writing 1650–1750* (London: Arnold).

Clark, Jane (1995), ' "Lord Burlington is Here" ', in T. Barnard and J. Clark (eds.), *Burlington: Architecture, Art and Life* (London: Hambledon Press), 251–310.

Corp, Edward (1998) (ed.), *Lord Burlington—the Man and his Politics: Questions of Loyalty* (Lampeter: Edward Mellen).

Cruickshanks, Eveline, and Black, Jeremy (1988) (eds.), *The Jacobite Challenge* (Edinburgh: John Donald).

Dean, Winton (1959), *Handel's Dramatic Oratorios and Masques* (Oxford: Oxford University Press).

Dickinson, H. T. (1970), *Bolingbroke* (London: Constable).

Downie, J. A. (1979), *Robert Harley and the Press: Propaganda and Public Opinion in the Age of Swift and Defoe* (Cambridge: Cambridge University Press).

Erskine-Hill, Howard (1982*a*), 'Literature and the Jacobite Cause: Was there a Rhetoric of Jacobitism?', in E. Cruickshanks (ed.), *Ideology and Conspiracy: Aspects of Jacobitism 1689–1759* (Edinburgh: John Donald), 48–69.

——(1982*b*), 'Under which Caesar? Pope in the Journal of Mrs Charles Caesar, 1724–1741', *Review of English Studies*, 33 (1982), 436–44.

——(1982*c*), 'Alexander Pope: The Political Poet in His Time', *Eighteenth-Century Studies*, 15: 123–6.

Erskine-Hill, Howard (1995), 'The Third Earl of Burlington and Alexander Pope', in T. Barnard and J. Clark (eds.), *Burlington: Architecture, Art and Life* (London: Hambledon), 217–29.

——— (1996), *Poetry of Opposition and Revolution: Dryden to Wordsworth* (Oxford: Clarendon Press).

Holmes, Geoffrey (1987), *British Politics in the Age of Queen Anne* (London: Hambledon Press; first pub. 1967).

Jacob, Margaret C. (1991), *Living the Enlightenment: Freemasonry and Politics in Eighteenth-Century Europe* (New York: Oxford University Press).

Jones, George Hilton (1954), *The Main Stream of Jacobitism* (Cambridge, Mass.: Harvard University Press).

Lenman, Bruce (1980), *The Jacobite Risings in Britain 1689–1746* (London: Eyre Methuen).

Lobel, Richard et al. (1997), *Coincraft's Standard Catalogue of English and UK 1066 to Date* (London: Coincraft).

London Stage, The, 1660–1800 (1960–8), ed. G. W. Stone et al., 5 vols. (Carbondale, Ill.: Southern Illinois University Press).

MacLachlan, A. D. (1969), 'The Road to Peace, 1710–1713', in G. Holmes (ed.), *Britain after the Glorious Revolution 1689–1713* (London: Macmillan), 197–215.

McLynn, Frank (1991), *Bonnie Prince Charlie: A Tragedy in Many Acts* (Oxford: Oxford University Press; first pub. 1988).

Moore, John Robert (1951), '*Windsor-Forest* and William III', *Modern Language Notes*, 66: 451–4.

Rivington, Charles A. (1989), '*Tyrant*': *The Story of John Barber 1675 to 1741* (York: William Sessions).

Roberts, Philip (1975) (ed.), *The Diary of Sir David Hamilton 1709–1714* (Oxford: Clarendon Press).

Rogers, Nicholas (1998), *Crowds, Culture and Politics in Georgian Britain* (Oxford: Clarendon Press).

Rumbold, Valerie (1989), *Women's Place in Pope's World* (Cambridge: Cambridge University Press).

——— (1992), 'The Jacobite Vision of Mary Caesar', in I. Grundy and S. Wiseman (eds.), *Women, Writing, History 1640–1740* (Athens, Ga.: University of Georgia Press), 178–98.

Seaby, Peter (1990), *The Story of British Coinage* (London: Seaby).

Select Documents for Queen Anne's Reign (1929), ed. G. M. Trevelyan (Cambridge: Cambridge University Press).

Sharp, Richard (1996), *The Engraved Record of the Jacobite Movement* (Aldershot: Scolar Press).

Sinclair-Stevenson, Christopher (1973), *Inglorious Rebellion: The Jacobite Risings of 1708, 1715 and 1719* (London: Panther).

Stephens, John Calhoun (1982) (ed.), *The Guardian* (Lexington, Ky.: University of Kentucky Press).

Szechi, Daniel (1984), *Jacobitism and Tory Politics 1710–1714* (Edinburgh: John Donald).

Torchiana, Donald T. (1962), 'Brutus: Pope's Last Hero', *Journal of English and Germanic Philology*, 61: 853–67.

Underdown, David (1992), *Fire from Heaven: Life in an English Town in the Seventeenth Century* (New Haven: Yale University Press).

Weinbrot, Howard D. (1993), *Britannia's Issue: The Rise of British Literature from Dryden to Ossian* (Cambridge: Cambridge University Press).

CHAPTER 4

Ashton, John (1883), *Social Life in the Reign of Queen Anne* (London: Chatto & Windus).

Barash, Carol (1996), *English Women's Poetry, 1649–1714: Politics, Community, and Linguistic Authority* (Oxford: Clarendon Press).

Bossewell, John (1572), *Workes of Armorie* (London).

Brooks-Davies, Douglas (1985), *Pope's* Dunciad *and the Queen of the Night: A Study of Emotional Jacobitism* (Manchester: Manchester University Press).

Burke, Peter (1992), *The Fabrication of Louis XIV* (New Haven: Yale University Press).

Burrows, Donald (1994), *Handel* (New York: Schirmer).

Carpenter, Edward (1936), *Thomas Sherlock 1678–1761* (London: SPCK).

Cressy, David (1989), *Bonfires and Bells: National Memory and the Protestant Calendar in Elizabethan and Stuart England* (Berkeley and Los Angeles: University of California Press).

Ellis, Frank H. (1985) (ed.), *Swift vs. Mainwaring:* The Examiner *and* The Medley (Oxford: Clarendon Press).

Erskine-Hill, Howard (1984), 'The Satirical Game at Cards in Pope and Wordsworth,' *YES* 14: 182–95.

——(1996), *Poetry of Opposition and Revolution: Dryden to Wordsworth* (Oxford: Clarendon Press).

Friar, Peter, (1997), *Heraldry for the Local Historian and Genealogist* (London: Grange Books).

Hawkins, Edward (1978), *Medallic Illustrations of the History of Great Britain and Ireland to the Death of George II*, ed. A. W. Franks and H. A. Grueber, 2 vols. (London: Spink & Son; first pub. 1885).

Hill, B. J. W. (1957), *Windsor and Eton* (London: Batsford).

Holmes, Geoffrey, and Speck, W. A. (1967) (eds.), *The Divided Society: Parries and Politics in England, 1694–1716* (London: Arnold).

Hotson, Leslie (1977), *Shakespeare's Hilliard* (Berkeley and Los Angeles: University of California Press).

Hutton, Ronald (1996), *The Stations of the Sun: A History of the Ritual Year in Britain* (Oxford: Oxford University Press).

Little, Bryan (1955), *The Life and Works of James Gibbs 1682–1754* (London: Batsford).

Luttrell, Narcissus (1857), *A Brief Historical Relation of State Affairs*, 6 vols.

McLynn, Frank (1991), *Bonnie Prince Charlie: A Tragedy in Many Acts* (Oxford: Oxford University Press; first pub. 1988).

Marshall, W. Gerald (1979), 'Pope's *Windsor-Forest* as Providential History', *Tennessee Studies in Literature*, 24: 82–93.

Michael, Wolfgang (1970), *England under George I*, 2 vols. (London: Macmillan) (first pub. 1936).

Richards, James O. (1972), *Party Propaganda under Queen Anne* (Athens, Ga.: University of Georgia Press).

Roberts, Philip (ed.) (1975), *The Diary of Sir David Hamilton 1709–1714* (Oxford: Clarendon Press).

Seaby, Peter (1990), *The Story of British Coinage* (London: Seaby).

Soo, Lynda M. (1998), *Wren's 'Treatises' on Architecture and Other Writings* (Cambridge: Cambridge University Press).

Stephens, John Calhoun (1982) (ed.), *The Guardian* (Lexington, Ky.: University of Kentucky Press).

Strickland, Agnes (1885), *Lives of the Queens of England*, 8 vols. (London).

Thomas, Keith (1973), *Religion and the Decline of Magic* (Harmondsworth: Penguin; first pub. 1971).

Weinbrot, Howard D. (1997), 'Fine Ladies, Saints in Heaven, and Pope's *Rape of the Lock*: Genealogy, Catholicism, and the Irenic Muse', in *Augustan Subjects: Essays in Honor of Martin C. Battestin* (Newark, Del.: University of Delaware Press), 150–75.

Willis, Debrorah (1992), 'The Monarch and the Sacred: Shakespeare and the Ceremony for the Healing of the King's Evil', in L. Woodbridge and E. Berry (eds.), *True Rites and Maimed Rites: Ritual and Anti-Ritual in Shakespeare and his Age* (Urbana, Ill.: University of Illinois Press), 147–68.

Young, Bruce W. (1992), 'Ritual as an Instrument of Grace: Parental Blessings in *Richard III*, *All's Well that Ends Well*, and *The Winter's Tale*', in L. Woodbridge and E. Berry (eds.), *True Rites and Maimed Rites: Ritual and Anti-Ritual in Shakespeare and his Age* (Urbana, Ill.: University of Illinois Press), 169–200.

CHAPTER 5

Aitken, G. A. (1968), *The Life and Works of John Arbuthnot* (New York: Russell & Russell; first pub. 1892).

Ashton, John (1883), *Social Life in the Reign of Queen Anne* (London: Chatto & Windus).

Beard, Geoffrey (1986), *Craftsmen and Interior Decoration in England 1660–1820* (London: Bloomsbury).

Beattie, Lester M. (1967), *John Arbuthnot: Mathematic and Satirist* (New York: Russell & Russell; first pub. 1935).

Bossewell, John (1572), *Workes of Armorie* (London).

Brockhampton Press (1997), *Dictionary of Heraldry* (London: Brockhampton Press).

Brooks-Davies, Douglas (1988), ' "Thoughts of Gods": Messianic Alchemy in *Windsor-Forest*', *Yearbook of English Studies*, 18: 125–42.

Collingwood, R. G., and Wright, R. P. (1965), *The Roman Inscriptions of Britain*, 2 vols. (Oxford: Clarendon Press).

Cressy, David (1989), *Bonfires and Bells: National Memory and the Protestant Calendar in Elizabethan and Stuart England* (Berkeley and Los Angeles: University of California Press).

Dickinson, H. T. (1970), *Bolingbroke* (London: Constable).

Downes, Kerry (1987), *Sir John Vanbrugh: A Biography* (New York: St Martin's Press).

Ellis, Frank H. (1985) (ed.), *Swift vs. Mainwaring:* The Examiner *and* The Medley (Oxford: Clarendon Press).

Erskine-Hill, Howard (1988), 'Life into Letters, Death into Art: Pope's Epitaph on Francis Atterbury', *Yearbook of English Studies*, 18: 200–20.

Ferguson, Arthur (1986), *The Chivalric Tradition in Elizabethan England* (Cranbury, NJ: Associated University Presses).

French, Peter (1989), *John Dee: The World of an Elizabethan Magus* (New York: Dorset Press; first pub. 1972).

Friar, Peter (1997), *Heraldry for the Local Historian and Genealogist* (London: Grange Books).

Hamilton, Elizabeth (1972), *William's Mary: A Biography of Mary II* (New York: Taplinger).

Handasyde, Elizabeth (1933), *Granville the Polite: The Life of George Granville, Lord Lansdowne 1666–1734* (London: Oxford University Press).

Harrison, William (1994), *The Description of England*, ed. G. Edelen (Washington, DC: Folger Library).

Holme, Randle (1688), *An Academie of Armory: or, the Store House of Armory and Blazon* (Chester) (made up of parts, separately paginated).

Howatson, M. C., and Chilvers, Ian (1993) (eds.), *The Concise Oxford Companion to Classical Literature* (Oxford: Oxford University Press).

Hutton, Ronald (1994), *The Rise and Fall of Merry England: The Ritual Year 1400–1700* (Oxford: Oxford University Press).

—— (1996), *The Stations of the Sun: A History of the Ritual Year in Britain* (Oxford: Oxford University Press).

Kerby-Miller, Charles (1950) (ed.), *Memoirs of the Extraordinary Life, Works and Discoveries of Martinus Scriblerus* (New Haven: Yale University Press).

Laroque, François (1991), *Shakespeare's Festive World: Elizabethan Seasonal Entertainment and the Professional Stage*, tr. J. Lloyd (Cambridge: Cambridge University Press).

Levine, Joseph M. (1977), *Dr Woodward's Shield: History, Science, and Satire in Augustan England* (Berkeley and Los Angeles: University of California Press).

—— (1991), *The Battle of the Books: History and Literature in the Augustan Age* (Ithaca, NY: Cornell University Press).

Llewellyn, Nigel (1990), 'Claims to Status through Visual Codes: Heraldry on Post-Reformation Funeral Monuments', in S. Anglo (ed.), *Chivalry in the Renaissance* (Woodbridge, Suffolk: Boydell, 1990), 145–60.

McWhir, Anne (1981), 'Alternate Tides: Structure in Pope's "Windsor-Forest"', *English Studies in Canada*, 7: 296–311.

Mackworth-Young, Robin (1982), *The History and Treasures of Windsor Castle* (New York: Vendome Press).

Manley, Delarivier (1991), *New Atlantis*, ed. R. Ballaster (Harmondsworth: Penguin).

Miller, Rachel A. (1979), 'Regal Hunting: Dryden's Influence on *Windsor Forest*', *ELH* 13: 169–88.

Neubecker, Ottfried (1997), *Heraldry: Sources, Symbols and Meaning* (London: Tiger Books International).

Perry, Ruth (1986), *The Celebrated Mary Astell: An Early English Feminist* (Chicago: University of Chicago Press).

Rogers, Nicholas (1998), *Crowds, Culture and Politics in Georgian Britain* (Oxford: Clarendon Press).

Rumbold, Valerie (1989), *Women's Place in Pope's World* (Cambridge: Cambridge University Press).

Scodel, Joshua (1991), *The English Poetic Epitaph: Commemoration and Conflict from Jonson to Wordsworth* (Ithaca, NY: Cornell University Press).

Scott-Giles, C. W. (1965), *The Romance of Heraldry* (London: Dent).

Seaby, Peter (1990), *The Story of British Coinage* (London: Searby).

Soo, Lynda M. (1998) (ed.), *Wren's 'Treatises' on Architecture and Other Writings* (Cambridge: Cambridge University Press).

Sparrow, John (1969), *Visible Words: A Study of Inscriptions in and as Works of Art* (Cambridge).

Starkey, David (1999), 'The Real Image of Regal Power', *Times Literary Supplement*, 12 Mar., pp. 18–19.

Stone, Lawrence (1967), *The Crisis of the Aristocracy 1558–1641* (Oxford: Clarendon Press).

Sutherland, James (1939), 'The Funeral of the Duke of Marlborough', in *Background for Queen Anne* (London: Methuen), 204–24.

Swift, Jonathan (1958), *Poems*, ed. H. Williams, 3 vols. (Oxford: Clarendon).

Thomas, Keith (1973), *Religion and the Decline of Magic* (Harmondsworth, Penguin; first pub. 1971).

Wagner, Anthony (1960), *English Genealogy* (Oxford: Clarendon Press).

—— (1967), *Heralds of England: A History of the Office and College of Arms* (London: HMSO).

—— and **Rowse, A. L.** (1992), *John Anstis: Garter King of Arms* (London: HMSO).

Weever, John (1631), *Ancient Funerall Monuments* (London).

CHAPTER 6

Barnett, Correlli (1974), *The First Churchill: Marlborough Soldier and Statesman* (New York: Putnam).

Beattie, Lester M. (1967), *John Arbuthnot: Mathematician and Satirist* (New York: Russell & Russell; first pub. 1935).

Berkeley, George (1948–57), *Works*, ed. A. A. Luce and T. E. Jessop, 9 vols. (London: Nelson).

Bond, Donald F. (1965) (ed.), *The Spectator*, 5 vols. (Oxford: Clarendon Press).

Bond, Richmond P. (1952), *Queen Anne's American Kings* (Oxford: Clarendon Press).

Brown, Beatrice Curtis (1935) (ed.), *The Letters and Diplomatic Instructions of Queen Anne* (London: Cassell).

Brown, Laura (1985), *Alexander Pope* (Oxford: Blackwell).

Brownell, Morris (1978), *Alexander Pope and the Arts of Georgian England* (Oxford: Clarendon Press).

Cannadine, David (1993), *G. M. Trevelyan: A Life in History* (New York: Norton).

Carswell, John (2001), *The South Sea Bubble* (Stroud: Sutton).

Cooke, Edward (1712), *A Voyage to the South Sea, and round the World* (London: Lintot).

Defoe, Daniel (1955), *Letters*, ed. G. H. Healey (Oxford: Clarendon Press).

Dickson, P. G. M. (1967), *The Financial Revolution: A Study in the Development of Public Credit, 1688–1756* (London: Macmillan).

Downes, Kerry (1987), *Sir John Vanbrugh: A Biography* (New York: St Martin's Press).

Downie, J. A. (1979), *Robert Harley and the Press: Propaganda and Public Opinion in the Age of Swift and Defoe* (Cambridge: Cambridge University Press).

Ellis, Frank H. (ed.) (1985), *Swift vs. Mainwaring:* The Examiner *and* The Medley (Oxford: Clarendon Press).

Erskine-Hill, Howard (1984), 'The Satirical Game at Cards in Pope and Wordsworth,' *Yearbook of English Studies*, 14 (1984), 182–95.

—— (1996), *Poetry of Opposition and Revolution: Dryden to Wordsworth* (Oxford: Clarendon Press).

—— (1998), 'Pope and Slavery', in *Alexander Pope: World and Word* (Oxford: Oxford University Press), 27–53.

Fowler, Marian (1991), *Blenheim: Biography of a Palace* (Harmondsworth: Penguin).

Green, David (1967), *Sarah Duchess of Marlborough* (London: Collins).

—— (1997), 'Blenheim: The Palace and Gardens under Vanbrugh, Hawksmoor and Wise', in J. Bond and K. Tiller (eds.), *Blenheim: Landscape for a Palace* (Stroud: Alan Sutton, 2nd edn.), 67–79.

Handasyde, Elizabeth (1933), *Granville the Polite: The Life of George Granville, Lord Lansdowne 1666–1734* (London: Oxford University Press).

Harris, Frances (1991), *A Passion for Government: The Life of Sarah, Duchess of Marlborough* (Oxford: Clarendon Press).

Hill, Brian W. (1988), *Robert Harley: Speaker, Secretary of State, Premier Minister* (New Haven: Yale University Press).

Hinderaker, Eric (1996), 'The "Four Indian Kings" and the Imaginative Construction of the First British Empire', *William & Mary Quarterly*, 33: 487–526.

Holmes, Geoffrey, and Speck, W. A. (1967) (eds.), *The Divided Society: Parties and Politics in England, 1694–1716* (London: Arnold).

Johnson, Samuel (1905), *The Lives of the Poets*, ed. G. B. Hill, 3 vols. (Oxford: Clarendon Press).

Lynch, Kathleen M. (1971), *Jacob Tonson: Kit-Cat Publisher* (Knoxville, Tenn.: University of Tennessee Press).

McCormick, Frank (1991), *Sir John Vanbrugh: The Playwright as Architect* (University Park, Pa.: Pennsylvania State University Press).

Manley, Delarivier (1991), *New Atalantis*, ed. R. Ballaster (Harmondsworth: Penguin).

Nicholson, Colin (1994), *Writing and the Rise of Commerce: Capital Satires of the Early Eighteenth Century* (Cambridge: Cambridge University Press).

Richards, James O. (1972), *Party Propaganda under Queen Anne* (Athens, Ga.: University of Georgia Press).

Richardson, John (2001), 'Alexander Pope's *Windsor Forest*: Its Context and Attitudes toward Slavery', *Eighteenth-Century Studies*, 35: 1–17.

Roberts, Philip (1975) (ed.), *The Diary of Sir David Hamilton 1709–1714* (Oxford: Clarendon Press).

Speck, W. A. (1970), *Tory and Whig: The Struggle in the Constituencies 1701–1715* (London: Macmillan).

Sutherland, James (1939), 'The Funeral of the Duke of Marlborough', *Background for Queen Anne* (London: Methuen), 204–24.

Szechi, Daniel (1994), *The Jacobites: Britain and Europe 1688–1788* (Manchester: Manchester University Press).

Varney, Andrew (1974), 'The Composition of *Windsor-Forest*', *Durham University Journal*, 36: 57–67.

CHAPTER 7

Abraham, Lindy (1998), *A Dictionary of Alchemical Imagery* (Cambridge: Cambridge University Press).

Bate, Jonathan (1993), *Shakespeare and Ovid* (Oxford: Clarendon Press).

Brooks-Davies, Douglas (1985), *Pope's Dunciad and the Queen of the Night: A Study of Emotional Jacobitism* (Manchester: Manchester University Press).

Chalker, John (1969), *The English Georgic* (London: Routledge).

Darby, H. C. and Campbell, E. M. J. (1962), *Domesday Geography of South-East England* (Cambridge: Cambridge University Press).

Dobson, Michael (1992), *The Making of the National Poet: Shakespeare, Adaptation, and Authorship, 1660–1769* (Oxford: Clarendon Press).

Durling, Dwight L. (1935), *Georgic Tradition in English Poetry* (New York: Columbia University Press).

Frazer, J. G. (ed.) (1929), *Publii Ovidii Nasonis Fastorum libri sex*, 5 vols. (London: Macmillan).

Gold, Barbara K. (1987), *Literary Patronage in Greece and Rome* (Chapel Hill, NC: University of North Carolina Press).

Harvey, Sir Paul (1937), *The Oxford Companion to Classical Literature* (Oxford: Clarendon Press).

Hauser, David R. (1966), 'Pope's Lodona and the Uses of Mythology', *Studies in English Literature 1500–1900*, 6: 465–82.

Knellwolf, Christa (1998), *A Contradiction Still: Representations of Women in the Poetry of Alexander Pope* (Manchester: Manchester University Press).

Lemprière, John (1994), *Classical Dictionary* (London: Bracken Books).

Low, Anthony (1985), *The Georgic Revolution* (Princeton: Princeton University Press).

Martindale, Charles (ed.) (1988), *Ovid Renewed: Ovidian Influence on Literature and Art from the Middle Ages to the Twentieth Century* (Cambridge: Cambridge University Press).

—— (1997), 'Green Politics: The *Eclogues*', in C. Martindale (ed.), *The Cambridge Companion to Virgil* (Cambridge: Cambridge University Press), 107–24.

Miller, Rachel A. (1979), 'Regal Hunting: Dryden's Influence on *Windsor Forest*', *ELH*, 13: 169–88.

Morris, David B. (1973), 'Virgilian Attitudes in Pope's *Windsor-Forest*', *Texas Studies in Literature and Language*, 15: 231–50.

Ovid (1961), *Metamorphoses in Fifteen Books*, tr. J. Dryden et al. (New York: Heritage Books).

Parry, Graham (1995), *The Trophies of Time: English Antiquarians of the Seventeenth Century* (Oxford: Oxford University Press).

Peterson, Richard F. (1981), *Imitation and Praise in the Poems of Ben Jonson* (New Haven: Yale University Press).

Plowden, G. F. C. (1983), *Pope on Classic Ground* (Athens, Ga.: University of Georgia Press).

Sharpe, Kevin (1979), *Sir Robert Cotton 1586–1631: History and Politics in Early Modern England* (Oxford: Oxford University Press).

Sherbo, Arthur (1994), 'Pope's "Fox Obscene"', *Notes & Queries*, 239: 187–8.

Wikander, Matthew H. (1993), *Princes to Act: Royal Audience and Royal Performance 1578–1792* (Baltimore: Johns Hopkins University Press).

Wilkinson, L. P. (1969), *The Georgics of Virgil: A Critical Survey* (Cambridge: Cambridge University Press).

—— (1983), 'The *Georgics*', in E. J. Kenney and W. V. Clausen (eds.), *The Cambridge History of Classical Literature: The Age of Augustus* (Cambridge: Cambridge University Press), 24–36.

Williams, Kathleen (1974), 'The Moralized Song: Some Renaissance Themes in Pope', *ELH*, 41: 578–601.

CHAPTER 8

Albion, Robert Greenhalgh (1926), *Forests and Sea Power* (Cambridge, Mass.: Harvard University Press).

Bond, Donald F. (ed.) (1965), *The Spectator*, 5 vols. (Oxford: Clarendon Press).

Chambers, Douglas D. C. (1993), *The Planters of the English Landscape Garden: Botany, Trees, and the Georgics* (New Haven: Yale University Press).

Cowley, Abraham (1989), *The Collected Works*, ed. T. O. Calhoun, L. Heyworth, and A. Pritchard (Newark, Del.: University of Delaware Press), 1 vol. published, in progress.

Cummings, Robert (1987), '*Windsor-Forest* as a Sylvan Poem', *ELH* 54: 63–77.

—— (1988), 'Addison's "Inexpressible Chagrin" and Pope's Poem on the Peace', *Yearbook of English Studies*, 18: 143–58.

Geneva, Ann (1995), *Astrology and the Seventeenth-Century Mind: William Lilly and the Language of the Stars* (Manchester: Manchester University Press).

Goldgar, Bertrand (1961), *The Curse of Party: Swift's Relations with Addison and Steele* (Lincoln, Nebr.: University of Nebraska Press).

Grosart, A. B. (1967) (ed.), *The Complete Works of Abraham Cowley*, 2 vols., (New York: AMS Press; first pub. 1881).

Handasyde, Elizabeth (1933), *Granville the Polite: The Life of George Granville, Lord Lansdowne 1666–1734* (London: Oxford University Press).

Knellwolf, Christa (1998), *A Contradiction Still: Representations of Women in the Poetry of Alexander Pope* (Manchester: Manchester University Press).

Levine, Joseph M. (1991), *The Battle of the Books: History and Literature in the Augustan Age* (Ithaca, NY: Cornell University Press).

MacLean, Gerald (1990), *Time's Witness: Historical Representation in English Poetry, 1603–1660* (Madison: University of Wisconsin Press).

Murdoch, John (1989), 'Painting: From Astraea to Augustus', in *The Cambridge Guide to the Arts in Britain*, iv. *The Seventeenth Century*, ed. B. Ford (Cambridge: Cambridge University Press), 235–75.

Nethercot, A. H. (1967), *Abraham Cowley: The Muse's Hannibal* (New York: Russell & Russell; first pub. 1931).

Plowden, G. F. C. (1983), *Pope on Classic Ground* (Athens, Ga.: University of Georgia Press).

Roob, Alexander (1997), *The Hermetic Museum: Alchemy & Mysticism*, tr. S. Whiteside (Cologne: Taschen).

Schama, Simon (1995), *Landscape and Memory* (London: HarperCollins).

Soo, Lynda M. (ed.) (1998), *Wren's 'Treatises' on Architecture and Other Writings* (Cambridge: Cambridge University Press).

Stimson, Dorothy (1968), *Scientists and Amateurs: A History of the Royal Society* (New York: Greenwood Press; first pub. 1948).

Thomas, Keith (1984), *Man and the Natural World: Changing Attitudes in England 1500–1800* (Harmondsworth: Penguin).

—— (1973), *Religion and the Decline of Magic* (Harmondsworth: Penguin).

Trotter, David (1979), *The Poetry of Abraham Cowley* (Totawa, NJ: Rowman and Littlefield).

Wheatley, H. B. and Bray, William (1879) (eds.), *Diary of John Evelyn*, 4 vols. (London: Bickers & Son).

CONCLUSION

Apperson, G. L. (1993), *The Wordsworth Dictionary of Proverbs* (Ware, Hertfordshire: Wordsworth).

Barnett, Correlli (1974), *The First Churchill: Marlborough Soldier and Statesman* (New York: Putnam).

Brooks-Davies, Douglas (1985), *Pope's Dunciad and the Queen of the Night: A Study of Emotional Jacobitism* (Manchester: Manchester University Press).

Szechi, Daniel (1988), 'The Jacobite Theatre of Death', in Eveline Cruickshanks and Jeremy Black (eds.), *The Jacobite Challenge* (Edinburgh: John Donald), 57–73.

Index

Main entries are printed in bold type. AP = Alexander Pope; *WF* = *Windsor-Forest*.

Index of Passages in Pope's Poetry

Entries relate to those passages in Pope's early poetry which are cited or to which explicit reference is made in the text of this book. The first figure indicates the line number in the poem.